ENCYCLOPEDIA OF TARIFFS AND TRADE IN U.S. HISTORY

Volume I. The Encyclopedia

ENCYCLOPEDIA OF TARIFFS AND TRADE IN U.S. HISTORY

Volume I. The Encyclopedia

Edited by Cynthia Clark Northrup and
Elaine C. Prange Turney

GREENWOOD PRESS
Westport, Connecticut • London

Library of Congress Cataloging-in-Publication Data

Encyclopedia of tariffs and trade in U.S. history / edited by Cynthia Clark Northrup
and Elaine C. Prange Turney.
    p. cm.
    Includes bibliographical references and index.
    ISBN 0–313–32789–0 (set : alk. paper)—ISBN 0–313–31943–X (v. 1 : alk. paper)—ISBN 0–313–31944–8
(v. 2 : alk. paper)—ISBN 0–313–31945–6 (v. 3 : alk. paper)
    1. Tariff—United States—History—Encyclopedias. 2. Taxation—United
States—History—Encyclopedias. 3. United States—Commercial
policy—History—Encyclopedias. 4. Free trade—United States—History—Encyclopedias.
5. Protectionism—United States—History—Encyclopedias. 6. United States—History—
Encyclopedias. I. Title: Encyclopedia of tariffs and trade in US history. II. Northrup,
Cynthia Clark, 1959– III. Turney, Elaine C. Prange, 1957–
HF1705.T37   2003
382'.7'097303—dc21   2002019506

British Library Cataloguing in Publication Data is available.

Library of Congress Catalog Card Number: 2002019506
ISBN: 0–313–32789–0 (set)
     0–313–31943–X (Vol. I)
     0–313–31944–8 (Vol. II)
     0–313–31945–6 (Vol. III)

First published in 2003

Greenwood Press, 88 Post Road West, Westport, CT 06881
An imprint of Greenwood Publishing Group, Inc.
www.greenwood.com

Printed in the United States of America

The paper used in this book complies with the
Permanent Paper Standard issued by the National
Information Standards Organization (Z39.48–1984).

10 9 8 7 6 5 4 3 2 1

Contents

Contents

Contents

Contents

Contents

Contents

Contents

Contents

Contents

Contents

A Note on Using the Encyclopedia

The development of the tariff and its relationship to trade in U.S. history from the 1600s to 2003 is a complicated and often overlooked topic. Designed as a reference tool for anyone wishing to learn more about this neglected subject, the *Encyclopedia*'s three volumes include numerous entries dealing with specific issues as well as selected primary documents and a complete collection of the tariffs through 1930. Volume I contains more than 500 biographical and topical entries arranged alphabetically. The biographical essays provide brief but significant details about key individuals while concentrating on the specific role each played in relation to the tariff. Topical entries include relevant dates and names of individuals involved as well as a description of the item and its impact on the tariff. Throughout U.S. history, Congress did not refer to tariff acts by easily identifiable titles or dates; as a result this work lists many of the tariffs by the year of their passage (e.g., you will find the Tariff of 1816 under the

Ts). Some tariffs, particularly after 1860, became more widely known by the names of the congressmen who sponsored them, such as the Payne-Aldrich Tariff Act of 1909. Readers should look for those items under the accepted formal title in alphabetical order.

Entries in volume I contain a brief Selected Bibliography that leads to more thorough studies of the individual topic as well as a "see also" section designed to direct the reader to other related topics included in the reference work. A comprehensive bibliography with full citations is also included at the end of volume I. Detailed indexes can be found at the end of volumes I and III. Because the tariff has played a decisive role in U.S. history, selected primary sources have been included in volume II. These documents represent the various debates surrounding the issue of the tariff and illustrate the arguments for and against free trade and protectionism. Volume III contains all of the tariff acts Congress passed from

1790 to 1930. After World War I the detailed categorization of items by weight, volume, size, or value resulted in a need for expanded administration provisions. Due to spatial limitations, the tedious administrative sections of the last two tariffs have been omitted. The inquiring reader can find this information in the Public Statutes at Large. Volume III ends at 1930, when Congress allowed the executive branch to negotiate reciprocal trade agreements too numerous to include in this work. After World War II, the trend toward free trade resulted in the negotiation of multilateral agreements such as the General Agreement on Tariffs and Trade (GATT), the North American Free Trade Agreement (NAFTA), and the World Trade Organization (WTO). Once again the executive branch assumed responsibility for orchestrating trade policy, thereby diminishing the legislative role of Congress.

The three-volume *Encyclopedia of Tariffs and Trade in U.S. History* contains material that provides detailed information on each tariff and the individuals and debates involved in the events that shaped the formation of economic policies in the United States from its infancy to the present day. Although the materials are extensive, space prohibits the comprehensive inclusion of every person or action connected to the process because such an effort would require numerous volumes. This three-volume set addresses the most prominent matters and presents a thorough, yet easy to understand, account of an issue that continues to dictate both the domestic and foreign economic policies of the United States.

Acknowledgments

We would like to thank Dr. Peter Levy who recommended us to Greenwood Press for his *Shapers of the Great Debate* series and as editors for *Encyclopedia of Tariffs and Trade in U.S. History*. Numerous people have provided invaluable advice, assistance, and encouragement for which we are grateful. We want to offer a special thanks to Ben Procter, Mark Gilderhus, Steven Boyd, and Spencer Tucker for their various roles in motivating us not only to focus on the tariff and examine its impact on U.S. domestic and foreign policy, but also for their constant encouragement to strive for the highest goals. A special thanks to Alfred E. Eckes Jr. who corrected some misguided assumptions and also provided encouragement to see this work through to its completion.

Throughout the entire project we have had the support of the Departments of History at the University of Texas at Arlington and the University of Dallas and we appreciate the opportunity to teach at these institutions. We would be remiss if we did not thank the reference librarians (the unsung heroes of many scholars) at Texas Christian University, the Dallas Public Library, and especially at the University of Texas at Arlington where we took advantage of an extensive library collection to verify the multitude of details in this volume.

Without the support and impressive effort of our contributors this work would not have been possible. Many of the authors diverted their time and energy from other projects to ensure the success of this encyclopedia. A special thanks to those individuals who assisted during the final stages of compiling the work by writing the last few entries on relatively short notice and for doing so with such welcomed enthusiasm. For their assistance in typing many of the tariffs in volume three, our deepest appreciation goes to Vonnie Peach and Dorothy Prange.

To our families we owe a debt of gratitude. Through months of telephone calls, correspondence, writing, and editing they continued to provide support and encouragement.

Introduction

Encyclopedia of Tariffs and Trade in U.S. History provides detailed information on the formation of tariff policy throughout American history and reveals the continued importance of the subject in an era of free trade. Historically, issues involving trade and protectionism have played a prominent role in U.S. policymaking. The tariff has influenced decisions leading up to or after major wars—such as the passage of the Tariff of 1816 to help collect revenue after military costs from the War of 1812 drained the U.S. Treasury. Domestically such topics have antagonized sectional differences and led to economic and social trends that have affected the lives of all Americans. The tariff issue, for example, proved instrumental in further separating the nineteenth-century North and South ideologically as witnessed in South Carolina's protest of the Tariff of 1828, which led to the documents that validated secession from the Union, the South Carolina Exposition and Protest. High protectionism in the post–Civil War period gave birth to the Era of Big Business, the creation of which spurred the labor movements of the late nineteenth and twentieth centuries. During modern times a shift toward free trade has raised new questions concerning environmental and human rights issues. Affecting both consumers and producers, custom duties impact all aspects of life yet, traditionally, the subject remains one of the most elusive and misunderstand.

Historically, governments have instituted tariffs (also known as duties and taxes) on imported goods to protect industry within their own borders. Great Britain's Trade and Navigation Acts of the seventeenth and eighteenth centuries remain the best early examples of this practice. Governments traditionally levied such tariffs in one of two ways, with an *ad valorem* duty determining the tax as a percentage of the item's value or a specific duty establishing a set amount of import tax based on the item itself or a measurement such as pounds or barrels. Initially, the U.S. federal government established tariffs to provide revenue for the fledgling national treasury.

In the United States during the early republic, tariffs also helped to protect infant industries and restrict the amount of goods imported by raising the price of a foreign product and providing domestic producers with a cost advantage that essentially encouraged Americans to buy items made in the United States. While this aided both Northern manufacturers and consumers, it proved costly to southern consumers who frequently imported items from Europe because of the ease of oceanic transport compared to that of overland transportation. This situation only exacerbated already heated sectional differences throughout the antebellum period.

Post–Civil War America witnessed a rise in big business. The age of American imperialism ushered in a foreign policy designed to push U.S. surpluses on a competitive world market, which helped create modern and mature businesses. In theory, once industries reached such a developed stage the need for protection diminished. If the government then failed to reduce the tariff on given items, manufacturers had the opportunity to raise prices to that of their foreign competition and thereby increase their profits. The failure of Congress to reduce tariffs during the Gilded Age increased the capital accumulation of the captains of industry in just this manner.

Often periods of overproduction led foreign governments to resort to dumping goods at below-cost prices on the U.S. market, at which time the federal government could implement tariffs to prevent and punish such activities,

subsequently protecting domestic companies from unfair business practices. Congress could also authorize the collection of countervailing duties to offset any advantage realized by manufacturers of imported goods produced with the assistance of government subsidies.

The complex history of the U.S. tariff has its roots in the philosophic and economic thinking of the European Enlightenment. After the ratification of the U.S. Constitution, the issue of the tariff falls into three distinct periods. Between 1789 and 1860 the tariff provided the federal government with revenue and protected infant industries but emphasized sectional disparity. During the second period, from 1861 to 1933, the Republican-dominated Congress passed high protective tariffs during a period of immense industrial growth. The last period, from 1934 to 2003, realized a shift in trade policies from an emphasis on protection to one of free trade designed to reduce international tensions and promote globalization.

EARLY EUROPEAN ECONOMIC THEORISTS

A shift from an agricultural to an industrial economy in northern European countries during the late seventeenth and early eighteenth centuries raised new questions concerning economic relationships. The publication of Adam Smith's *An Inquiry into the Nature and Causes of the Wealth of Nations* in 1776 attacked the mercantilist system that employed a variety of trade barriers for the benefit of Great Britain. Advocating free trade in all instances, except for national defense or if a similar tax existed on domestically produced items, Smith influenced leaders in the American colonies, including Benjamin Franklin and Alexander Hamilton. In 1798, Thomas Malthus published his work *Essays on the Principle of Population and Its Affects on the Future Improvement of Society*. Malthus, like Smith, supported free trade on the basis that a reduction of taxes or duties would not benefit the poor but would only result in decreased production. In 1803, the French economist Jean-Baptiste Say argued for free trade in *A Treatise on Political Economy*. After the end of the Napoleonic Wars, other economists continued to support free trade and the principle of laissez-faire economics. Proponents included David Ricardo and John Stuart Mill, who pointed out that customs duties and restrictions like the English Corn Law only benefited the landed gentry. Americans read the works of these European economists as they struggled to define a trade policy for the fledgling nation. Many American statesmen supported the concept of free trade, but reluctantly compromised and modified their position as Great Britain, France, and the Netherlands erected trade barriers against the United States.

COLONIAL TIMES TO 1789

Originally part of the British Empire, the colonies fought for independence from the mother country over issues of taxation. In the seventeenth century, colonial politics and commerce developed independently during a period of "salutary neglect" as a result of political turmoil in England. The signing of the Peace of Utrecht in 1713 ushered in an era of peace in Europe and burgeoning commercial trade between the colonies and England. With increased contact between American colonists and their English brethren, an awareness of English rights and liberties developed. At the end of the Seven Years' War (known to the colonists as the French and Indian War) in 1763, imperial policy shifted. Mounting war debts caused the British crown to reassess North American contributions to the empire. Through Parliament and local governments the crown strengthened its control over colonial affairs in an effort to collect more significant financial and economic contributions from its New World Empire. Colonists resisted British interference in the political and economic autonomy that had developed up until 1763. The passage of a series of acts designed to raise revenue for the British government at the direct expense of the colonies resulted in protests, petitions, and finally a decision to declare independence on July 4, 1776. The central theme of the prerevolutionary period revolved around the slogan "taxation without representation is tyranny."

After the signing of the Declaration of Independence the colonies formed a loose confederation of independent states and assigned the right to levy taxes to individual state legislatures. The central government then relied on the confederate governments to comply with the requisition of funds for national needs. The failure of this system led to the adoption of the U.S. Constitution with broad authority to tax under Article I, Section 10. Dealing with the issue of taxation based on representation, delegates at the Constitutional Convention agreed to a compromise that restricted the power to initiate money and tax bills to the House of Representatives because population determined representation in the lower chamber of Congress. Debates over taxation included a compromise between northern and southern states over how to count slaves. The inclusion of the ⅗ Clause and an agreement not to place a direct tax on slaves imported into the country placated southern leaders who feared an attack on the institution of slavery through the process of taxation. An additional concern over the taxation of exports and the potential power of the federal government to oppress the states through this type of legislation resulted in an agreement not to tax exports. The U.S. government relied on tariff duties and excise taxes as its primary source of funding.

CONSTITUTION TO CIVIL WAR PERIOD, 1789–1860

The first tariff, passed in 1789, defined the purpose of import duties for the first three decades under the Constitution. James Madison's original bill authorized a 5 percent *ad valorem* duty on imports with an additional list of enumerated goods taxable on a specific amount instead of a percentage of value. Designed to raise revenue, tariff rates remained at a level high enough to offer some protection from the influx of inexpensive European goods but not high enough to ignite a trade war with Great Britain. Dissatisfied with the tariff-for-revenue-only plan, Alexander Hamilton issued his *Report on Manufactures* in 1791 advocating the creation of a protectionist tariff designed to stimulate fledgling American industries. Congress rejected Hamilton's proposal,

but did increase the tariff rates twenty-four times over the next twenty-five years.

At the turn of the century, the French Revolution and Napoleonic Wars stimulated U.S. trade and commerce and the additional revenues from imports allowed the government to reduce the national debt by $33 million and purchase the Louisiana Territory from France for $11 million in cash. By 1808, both France and Great Britain had threatened the autonomy of the United States by seizing neutral American ships conducting commerce with both of the belligerent nations. Britain added additional injury to the nation's pride by impressing American sailors into the Royal Navy. In retaliation to the efforts of both Britain and France to curb American free trade, Thomas Jefferson authorized an embargo against both countries in 1803. The measure not only failed to impress the great European powers but also came at great expense to the American public as well as the treasury. Shortly before James Madison became president in 1809, Congress lifted the embargo while implementing another series of failed diplomatic and commercial initiatives. Anticipating a rise in hostilities between the United States and Britain, legislators passed a tariff that doubled the previous rates on imports. Hostilities did materialize with an American declaration of war in 1812 and customs revenues decreased by 50 percent, forcing Congress to levy direct internal taxes on carriages, distilled spirits, and refined sugar. As the United States entered the War of 1812, these war revenue measures provided additional funds for the government while the people remained secure in the knowledge that the taxes would be abolished one year after the war ended. In 1815, Secretary of the Treasury Alexander Dallas proposed an income tax to raise additional revenue, but the measure never passed because the conflict ended before Congress could debate the issue.

After the War of 1812, congressional leaders transformed the system of taxation. Although the tariff traditionally had been established for the purpose of generating revenue, the effect of the war on the American economy and the subsequent dumping of English goods in the United States forced legislators to reconsider the purpose of taxation. The Tariff of 1816, although protectionist in nature, passed the House by a vote of eighty-four to fifty-four votes and the Senate by fifty-four to forty-eight despite opposition from some influential southern statesmen. The Panic of 1819 continued to foster a strong desire for protective tariffs that would assist America's infant industries and allow them to grow at the expense of foreign competitors. In 1820, Congress proposed a 5 percent increase on the entire tariff schedule with even higher rates on such items as cotton, wool cloth, finished clothes, and iron. Although the measure failed, the trend toward protection continued.

In 1828, Henry Clay and other protectionists in the House of Representatives sponsored a bill that raised the rate on iron, wool, cotton, and hemp to 35 percent. This measure would enable New England textile manufacturers to compete with English firms whose technology surpassed that of the United States. The issue of protectionism entered the presidential race for the first time in 1828 with Andrew Jackson and his supporters calling for a 50 percent duty on hemp, fur, wool, liquor, and textiles. The Tariff of 1828, referred to by southerners as the Tariff of Abominations, protected New England manufacturers, but hurt southern agricultural producers by reducing the amount of cotton purchased by Great Britain. Southern leaders, led by John C. Calhoun of South Carolina, argued that Congress could only pass legislation for the benefit of all the states. A constitutional crisis threatened the fiber of the American government as states' rights advocates argued that states had the power to nullify federal law. Jackson responded by persuading Congress to pass the Force Bill, which authorized the president to use the military to uphold federal law. The efforts of Henry Clay averted a dangerous confrontation as he introduced a compromise that gradually reduced the tariff rates over a ten-year period.

During the remainder of the 1830s, large land sales and a prosperous economy created a surplus in the U.S. Treasury. Henry Clay proposed that the federal government disperse such excess funds to the states for internal improvements. Designed to lower the surplus while leaving the protectionist tariff rates intact, Congress approved the measure, but an unanticipated shortfall in the U.S. budget in the early 1840s prevented the transfer of funds to the states.

By 1846, the treasury again held a surplus. During the administration of James K. Polk, Secretary of the Treasury Robert Walker proposed the downward revision of tariff rates and Congress responded positively. Another reduction, in 1857, moved the United States closer to a system of free trade just as Great Britain's repeal of the Corn Laws pushed it in a similar direction.

PROTECTIONISM AND BIG BUSINESS, 1861–1933

From the Civil War to 1934, the Republican-dominated Congress passed a series of protectionist measures. Each revised schedule increased the rate on imports while the U.S. Treasury enjoyed a surplus. The Morrill Tariff of 1861, passed after southern states seceded, reverted to a system of specific duties, particularly on wool and iron. Designed to offset revenue deficits after the Panic of 1857, the high rates helped finance the war. After the end of hostilities, Congress, failing to heed the advice of David A. Wells, special commissioner of the revenue from 1866 until 1870, decreased the rates on revenue items but not on protected items. In 1872, a slight decrease of 10 percent on protective items remained in effect for one year until the Panic of 1873 forced Congress to once again raise the rates. From the mid-1870s to the early 1880s, the United States enjoyed a surplus. Henry Clay proposed the use of the funds for internal improvements such as the railroad instead of reducing the rates. The higher duties provided an important benefit by stimulating westward expansion since the government could sell land cheaper during periods of surplus. As Americans pushed west for affordable land, the manufacturing sector moved from New England to the Midwest.

President Grover Cleveland, the first Democratic president elected since the Civil War, sought to lower the tariff for the benefit of American farmers, middle-class consumers, and business owners. After devoting his entire State of the Union address to the topic, he campaigned for a reduction, but in 1888 voters elected the Republican candidate Benjamin Harrison instead. During Harrison's administration the United States initiated a policy of tariff reciprocity to gain access to foreign markets, particularly in Latin America. In addition, legislators reduced the duty on sugar from two cents per pound to one-half cent per pound, but sugar producers received a bounty. When Congress placed sugar on the duty-free list in 1891 American planters in Hawaii attempted to overthrow the monarchy of Queen Liliuokalani. Cleveland refused to annex the island nation, but a few years later President William McKinley signed such an act following the Spanish-American War. In 1892, Cleveland won the presidency for a second, nonconsecutive, term. Perceived as a mandate for tariff reform, Cleveland advocated the reduction of tariff rates. Although Congress passed the Wilson-Gorman Tariff in 1894, reducing rates overall, the net effect after concessions to special interests remained much the same as before. In combination with the Wilson-Gorman Tariff, Congress provided for a 2 percent tax on incomes over $4,000, an act that the Supreme Court later declared unconstitutional. Throughout his second administration Cleveland faced economic and social difficulties that resulted in removing sugar from the free list, this time sparking a revolution in Cuba where planters depended on exports to the United States. The depression of the early

1890s caused a shift from a government surplus to a deficit, which forced Congress to pass the Dingley Tariff, raising rates to a record high. During the Spanish-American War Congress levied an inheritance tax of 15 percent on estates valued at over $1 million. The $22.5 million in inheritance revenue collected during the war paid for the military expenditures without any additional taxes being levied.

The entrance of the United States into world politics after 1900 fused the relationship between issues of trade and foreign policy. Secretary of State John Hay called on European powers to recognize the territorial integrity of nations such as China in the "Open Door Notes." Closer to home, the government pursued favorable tariff rates with Latin and South America through the use of reciprocity agreements. Still the primary source of taxation in the United States, the tariff continued to generate a surplus throughout the first decade of the twentieth century. Theodore Roosevelt ignored the advice of Secretary of State John Hay, choosing instead to sidestep the politically explosive issue. He warned his successor, William Howard Taft, of the dangers of such action, but Taft called Congress into special session to revise the tariff schedule. The resulting Payne-Aldrich Tariff produced mixed results, with a decrease in rates for steel, pig iron, and other manufacturing items while increasing the rates for agricultural goods. The debate over the tariff divided the Republican Party and during the election of 1912 many of the Insurgents, led by Robert M. LaFollette, abandoned Taft.

When Woodrow Wilson became president in 1913, he pushed for a reduction in the general rates. As a tactic to defeat the revisions, Republicans supported a constitutional amendment that allowed for a personal income tax. The Underwood-Simmons Tariff Act decreased duties from 40 to 25 percent and attacked trusts while decreasing the cost of living. Interruptions in international trade as a result of World War I led Congress to once again increase trade barriers through the 1920s. Passing the Emergency Tariff Act of 1921 and the Fordney-McCumber Tariff of 1922, Congress addressed the growing agricultural crisis affecting American farmers. While most Americans prospered between 1922 and 1929, farmers struggled as crop prices continued to drop. Herbert Hoover requested that Congress provide relief for the agricultural community by raising specific rates. In 1930, legislators responded to the president's initiative by passing the Hawley-Smoot Tariff, the second highest in American history next to the Morrill Tariff, just months after the stock market crashed and the Federal Reserve Board tightened the money supply. Instead of just increasing import taxes on agricultural items, Congress also raised rates on manufacturing goods as well. Many historians argue that the Hawley-Smoot Tariff created a worldwide depression, even though evidence suggests that the international economic crisis started before the passage of the bill. Foreign countries did erect retaliatory barriers against the United States starting in 1932 with the establishment of the Ottawa preferences between Canada and Great Britain.

ERA OF FREE TRADE, 1934–2003

Beginning in 1934 and continuing into the twenty-first century, the United States concluded a series of agreements that have promoted free trade. Under President Franklin D. Roosevelt, Congress passed the Reciprocal Trade Agreements Act, authorizing the executive branch to negotiate trade agreements with foreign countries and reducing the 1930 rates by up to 50 percent. Although the term of the act expired after three years, successive renewals have provided the president with continued foreign policy leverage. The Trade Agreements Extension Act, passed in 1945, allowed the president to reduce rates by up to 50 percent of the 1945 rates. Between 1934 and 1947, the executive branch concluded twenty-nine treaties involving the reduction of trade barriers. In 1947, the United States joined other signatories in signing the General Agreement on Tariffs and Trade (GATT), a voluntary agreement that promoted free trade worldwide. GATT included a "general escape clause" that allowed countries to impose restrictions if the amount of imports substantially injured domestic producers. After 1947, the United States adopted the general escape clause for all trade agreements. Since the United States joined GATT in 1947, the average rate of import duties has been reduced from 15 to less than 5 percent. Although GATT has allowed foreign companies easier access to the American market, the United States has not enjoyed a reciprocal relationship with all of its trading partners.

After the Republicans recaptured the White House in 1952, Dwight D. Eisenhower continued the move toward free trade while facing the challenge of dealing with the emerging European Community. The formation of free trade zones and customs unions resulted in discriminatory barriers against the United States. In an effort to defend itself against such barriers, the United States conducted a series of negotiations known as Rounds. Operating under the auspices of GATT, these efforts attempted to promote free trade on a worldwide basis. The Rounds also witnessed the passing of domestic legislation such as the Trade Expansion Act of 1962 and 1974, both authorizing the president to eliminate duties of less than 5 percent and reduce rates above 5 percent by up to 60 percent. By 1976, the United States had eliminated import duties on over 2,700 categories from the Third World.

The growing strength of regional free trade zones and a burgeoning trade deficit in the United States, caused by discrimination abroad and freer access to American markets, prompted the United States to establish the North American Free Trade Agreement (NAFTA). Negotiated under the administration of George Herbert Walker Bush and ratified during the first term of William Jefferson Clinton's administration, NAFTA lowered barriers between the United States, Canada, and Mexico. Opponents argued that the agreement would produce a negative impact on the environment and raise human rights issues. The success of NAFTA encouraged officials to expand the free trade area to encompass the entire Western Hemisphere, blocking Cuba's participation because of that nation's disregard for democratic principles.

On a worldwide basis, the signers of the General Agreement on Tariffs and Trade transformed the voluntary arrangement into a formalized institution with the creation of the World Trade Organization (WTO). The beginning of the twenty-first century has signaled a continuing era of free trade.

Guide to Selected Topics

Banking

Federal Reserve Bank

Broad Issues

American farmers
Cartels
Colonial currencies
Consumerism
Economy
Environmental issues
Foreign policy
Free trade
Human rights
Imperialism
Infant industries
Labor
Lobbying
Navigation and Trade Acts
Pirates
Protests

Religion
Sectionalism
Slavery
Smuggling
Tariff reform
Veto power of the president
Wages
Women

Business and Businessmen

Aldrich, Winthrop
Atkinson, Edward
Automobile industry
Baruch, Bernard Mannes
Carnegie, Andrew
Dow, Herbert H.
East India Company
Ford, Henry
Iacocca, Lido Anthony (Lee)
International Harvester
Lowell, Francis Cabot

Guide to Selected Topics

McCormick, Cyrus
Mellon, Andrew W.
Metcalf, Edwin D.
Peek, George N.
Robber barons
Schwab, Charles M.
Trusts
U.S. Steel Corp.
Wharton, Joseph

Commodities

Coal
Coffee
Copper
Cotton
Fish
Fur trade
Hides and skins
Iron
Linen
Molasses
Oil
Rum
Silver
Steel
Sugar
Tea
Technology
Textiles
Tin ore
Tobacco
Wool and woolens

Conferences and Committees

Bretton Woods Conference
Capehart Committee

Commission on Foreign Economic
Policy (CFEP)
Committee for Reciprocity Information
Economic Commission for Latin
America (ECLA)
Executive Committee on Commercial
Policy (ECCP)
Federal Trade Commission (FTC)
General Committee of One Hundred
Harrisburg Convention of 1827
London World Economic Conference
National Conference for the Expansion of Foreign Trade
Tariff Commission

Definitions

Ad valorem vs. specific duties
Balance of trade
Countervailing duties
Dollar Gap
Drawbacks
Dumping
Escape clause
Excise
Exports
Gross National Product (GNP)
Maximum-Minimum Tariff
Most Favored Nation (MFN)
Trade deficits

Economic Philosophy

Economic Darwinism

Economic Systems

Capitalism
Communism

Mercantilism

Protectionism

Socialism

Economists

Adams, Henry Carter

Bastiat, Claude-Frèdèric

Comte, Auguste (Isidore-Auguste-
    Marie-François Xavier Comte)

Ely, Richard T.

Hume, David

Keynes, John Maynard

List, Friedrich

Malthus, Thomas

Mill, John Stuart

Montesquieu, Charles-Louis de Secon-
    dant, Baron de La Brède et de

Patten, Simon

Prebisch, Raul

Raymond, Daniel

Ricardo, David

Say, Jean-Baptiste

Sayre, Francis B.

Smith, Adam

Events

American Revolution

Boxer Rebellion

Civil War (American)

Cold War

Crisis of 1837

Crisis of 1857

Faneuil Hall

Great Depression

Industrial Revolution

North–South Conflict

Nullification

Panama Canal

Reconstruction

War of 1812

World War I

World War II

Foreign Countries, Regions, and Leaders

Bolivia

Canada

Chile

Cuba

France

Germany

Great Britain

Japan

Latin America

Liliuokalani, Lydia Paki Kamekeha

Mexico

Mulroney, Brian

People's Republic of China

Salinas de Gortari, Carlos

Third World

Venezuela

Government

American System

Articles of Confederation

Colonial administration

Confederate Constitution

Congress

Constitutionality

American Protective Tariff League (APTL)

American Reciprocal Tariff League (ARTL)

Boston Home Market Club

Center for Strategic and International Studies

Conseil Intergovernemental des Pays Exportateurs de Cuivre (CIPEC)

Economic Policy Institute (EPI)

European Community (EC)

International Chamber of Commerce (ICC)

International Free Trade Alliance

International Monetary Fund (IMF)

International Trade Commission (ITC)

International Trade Organization (ITO)

Merchants Association of New York (MANY)

National Association of Manufacturers (NAM)

National Civic Federation

National Council of Commerce

National Foreign Trade Council (NFTC)

National Reciprocity League (NRL)

National Tariff Commission Association (NTCA)

Organization of American States (OAS)

Organization of Petroleum Exporting Countries (OPEC)

Sierra Club

Trade Associations

U.S.–NAFTA Coalition

United Nations

World Trade Organization (WTO)

World Wildlife Fund

Political Movements

Greenback Movement

Insurgents

Isolationism

Jacksoniansim

Jeffersonianism

Non-consumption movement

Progressives

Tariff Reform

Tariff Reform Movement

Political Parties and Groups

Anti-Federalists

Democratic Party

Federalists

Know-Nothing Party

Origins of political parties

Populists

Presidential campaigns

Republican Party

Union Labor Party

Whig Party

Politicians

Adams, Charles Francis

Adams, John

Adams, John Quincy

Aldrich, Nelson W.

Ames, Fisher

Arthur, Chester Alan

Bailey, Joseph Weldon

Baldwin, Henry

Barbour, Philip Pendleton

Benton, Thomas H.

Beveridge, Albert Jeremiah

Blaine, James Gillespie

Borah, William Edgar

Breckinridge, Clifton R.

Breckinridge, William C.P.

Bryan, William Jennings

Bryant, William Cullen

Buchanan, Patrick J.

Bush, George Herbert Walker

Calhoun, John Caldwell

Cambreleng, Churchill Caldom

Cannon, Joseph Gurney

Capehart, Homer Earl

Carlisle, John Griffin

Clark, James Beauchamp (Champ)

Clay, Henry

Cleveland, Stephen Grover

Clinton, William Jefferson (Bill)

Coolidge, John Calvin

Crawford, William H.

Crisp, Charles Frederick

Cummins, Albert Baird

Dallas, Alexander

Dallas, George Mifflin

Davis, Jefferson

Dingley, Nelson, Jr.

Dolliver, Jonathan P.

Eisenhower, Dwight D. (Ike)

Fillmore, Millard

Fitzsimons, Thomas

Fordney, Joseph Warren

Franklin, Benjamin

Gallatin, Abraham Alfonse Albert

Garfield, James A.

Gephardt, Richard

Gore, Albert Arnold, Jr.

Gorman, Arthur Pue

Greeley, Horace

Hamilton, James

Hancock, John

Hancock, Winfield S.

Harrison, Benjamin

Hawley, Willis C.

Hayne, Robert Y.

Hoover, Herbert

Hull, Cordell

Jackson, Andrew

Jefferson, Thomas

Kennedy, John F.

Knox, Philander Chase

LaFollette, Robert Marion

Lincoln, Abraham

Lodge, Henry Cabot

Longworth, Nicholas

Lowndes, William Jones

Maclay, William

Madison, James

McCleary, James Thompson

McDuffie, George

McDuffie, John

McKenna, Joseph E.

McKinley, William

McMillin, Benton

Mills, Roger Q.

Monroe, James

Morrill, Justin S.

Payne, Sereno E.

Perot, Henry Ross

Pinckney, Charles Cotesworth

Pierce, Franklin

Polk, James K.

Guide to Selected Topics

Tariff of 1832

Tariff of 1833 (Compromise Tariff)

Tariff of 1842

Tariff of 1846 (Walker's Tariff)

Tariff of 1857

Tariff of 1862

Tariff of 1864

Tariff of 1865

Tariff of 1866

Tariff of 1867

Tariff of 1870

Tariff of 1872

Tariff of 1883 (Mongrel Tariff)

Tariff of 1891

Tariff of 1895

Tariff of 1896

Underwood-Simmons Tariff (Tariff of 1913)

Wilson-Gorman Tariff (Tariff of 1894)

Tariff Opponents

Beecher, Henry Ward

Bellamy, Edward

Emerson, Ralph Waldo

Friends of the Earth

Garrison, William Lloyd

Grady, Henry W.

Hayes, John L.

Higginson, Thomas Wentworth

Lease, Mary Elizabeth Clyens

Lee, Henry

Miles, Herbert Edwin

Mobilization on Development, Trade, Labor and the Environment (MODTLE)

Nader, Ralph

Smith, Gerrit

Tugwell, Rexford G.

Twain, Mark

Whitman, Walt

Trade Policies

Alliance for Progress

Free Trade Area of the Americas (FTAA)

Good Neighbor Policy

Open Door Notes

Unions

Amalgamated Association of Iron and Steel Workers

American Federation of Labor (AFL)

American Federation of Labor–Congress of Industrial Organizations (AFL-CIO)

Congress of Industrial Organizations (CIO)

A

AD VALOREM vs. SPECIFIC DUTIES

During the nineteenth century, debate over the use of *ad valorem* or specific duties spurred controversy between manufacturers and importers of finished products.

Traditionally, Congress based tariff rates on an *ad valorem* basis, meaning that the import tax equaled a percentage of the value of the asset. During the election of 1828, the tariff issue became politicized when woolen manufacturers petitioned Congress asking that the *ad valorem* rate remain constant, but that an additional specific duty be placed on yards of cloth. A specific duty based the tax on the weight or quantity of the item instead of the value. Churchill C. Cambreleng of New York objected to the inclusion of the specific duties unless Congress authorized a similar tax on bar iron. Cambreleng, a lifelong opponent of protectionism, offered the proposal as a means of defeating the measure indirectly because at the time he re-mained allied with Martin Van Buren in a political maneuver to defeat President John Quincy Adams in his re-election bid by raising the prospect of a higher tariff. Congress subsequently approved specific duties, but Secretary of the Treasury Robert Walker raised the issue again in 1846. Walker argued that specific duties discriminated against cheaper articles and would harm the poor consumer more than the rich consumer. For instance, under specific duties the tax on all salt remained equal regardless of whether the product was coarse or fine. Walker prevailed by eliminating all specific duties. The debate continued under the administrations of Millard Fillmore, Abraham Lincoln, and Grover Cleveland, with Democrats preferring specific duties while Republicans favored *ad valorem* taxes.

See also: Adams, John Quincy; Cambreleng, Churchill Caldom; Cleveland, Stephen Grover; Fillmore, Millard; Lincoln, Abraham; Maximum-Minimum

Tariff; Van Buren, Martin; Walker, Robert John; Walker's Report. **Vol. II**: Walker's Report. **Vol. III**: Tariff of 1795; Tariff of 1842; Tariff of 1846 (Walker's Tariff).

Selected Bibliography:

Edward Stanwood, *American Tariff Controversies in the Nineteenth Century*, 1967.

Cynthia Clark Northrup

ADAMS, CHARLES FRANCIS (August 18, 1807–November 21, 1886)

U.S. congressman and minister to Great Britain during the Civil War.

The son and grandson of presidents, at the age of two years he accompanied his father on a diplomatic mission to Russia. Adams received his early education in England, and graduated from Harvard in 1825. He entered Massachusetts politics and became the vice-presidential nominee of the antislavery Free-Soil Party in 1848. Elected to the Thirty-sixth Congress as a Republican in 1858, he participated in the highly contentious and divided House of Representatives that took two months just to elect a Speaker and would continue in session until the summer of 1860. Abraham Lincoln appointed him as the minister to Great Britain and Adams served in that capacity from 1861 until 1868, unquestionably one of the thorniest periods in Anglo-American relations since independence. He faced widespread sympathy for the southern cause among the British ruling aristocracy, an attitude only exacerbated by the Union naval blockade that kept raw cotton from English textile mills. He became deeply embroiled in the controversy created by the seizure of the Confederate commissioners, James Mason and John Slidell, aboard the British mail steamer *Trent* late in 1861. Adams, who realized that the United States had violated international law, succeeded in defusing the situation, largely due to the intervention of Prince Albert. Mason and Slidell regained their freedom, resolving the major diplomatic crisis that could have had serious consequences between the countries. Thereafter Adams served in a watchdog role, seeking violations of British neutrality, particularly regarding shipbuilding and arms shipments for the Confederacy. He attempted to prove that the Confederacy had commissioned a ship under construction at the Birkenhead dry dock of Jonathan Laird. The dilatory tactics of British government officials resulted in the *Alabama*'s sailing from England despite the vigorous protestations of Adams and set the backdrop for the postwar *Alabama* claims talks in Geneva, Switzerland. Largely due to Adams's skill as head of the American delegation to these talks, the United States won reparations for the wartime ravaging of its commerce by British-built ships. At one point later in the war, Adams even threatened hostilities to keep Britain from delivering armored rams to the South. Following his retirement as the minister to the Court of St. James, he edited the papers of his father and grandfather.

Adams emerged into public life again only briefly in 1872, when the Liberal Republican Party met in Ohio to nominate its presidential candidate. Unhappy with the trends in the conservative Republican Party, the Liberal Republicans supported extreme tariff reduction and opposed the reelection of Ulysses S. Grant. A strong free trader faction, largely from the East, pushed vigorously for the nomination of Adams because of his support for lower tariffs. Ultimately, the party nomination went to Horace Greeley, whose position on reform proved lukewarm.

The reelection of Grant in 1872 and the Panic of 1873 led to a shift in political priorities. Throughout the Gilded Age, the tariff issue would only emerge as a diversionary tactic. So the tariff and the short-lived political career of Adams disappeared from the political scene. Yet for his Civil War service to the country, many historians consider Adams as valuable as any Union general in the field.

See also: Adams, John; Adams, John Quincy; Lincoln, Abraham.

Selected Bibliography:

Martin B. Duberman, *Charles Francis Adams, 1807–1886*, 1968; Edward Stanwood, *American Tariff Controversies in the Nineteenth Century*, 1967.

David E. Long and Elaine C. Prange Turney

ADAMS, HENRY CARTER (December 31, 1851–August 11, 1921)

American economist and statistician who opposed the protective tariff and criticized laissez faire economics in the United States.

Born in Davenport, Iowa, Adams could not attend school because of his poor health, so his father tutored him. He earned a Bachelor of Arts degree from Iowa College (now Grinnell College) in 1874. His father wanted him to become a minister and he spent one year at Andover Academy before realizing that he did not share his father's dream. Adams then attended a new school, Johns Hopkins University in Baltimore, on a fellowship. In 1878, he received the school's first Ph.D. in political science. To build on his education, he traveled and studied in Europe.

On returning to the United States, he received an appointment as an economics lecturer at Cornell University and later he held a similar appointment at the University of Michigan. He alternated between the two schools until Cornell University fired him for advocating "radical" notions in favor of the practice of collective bargaining. He spent the remainder of his academic career at Michigan.

Known for his early thinking on the relationship of government and the economy, Adams published his first criticism of laissez-faire economics, "The Relation of the State to Industrial Action," in 1887. He then published *Public Debt* in 1887 and *The Science of Finance* in 1898. He also worked as a statistician for the Interstate Commerce Commission and the Bureau of the Census.

He opposed the protective tariff, arguing that Congress should not compel the consumer to purchase from the home producer. In his view, the tariff should only be used to raise revenue and then only gradually. He argued that the first step in removing the tariff should be to put raw materials on the free list.

Adams died in Ann Arbor, Michigan, on August 11, 1921.

See also: Free trade.

Selected Bibliography:

Joseph Dorfman, ed., *Two Essays by Henry Carter Adams*, 1969.

John David Rausch Jr.

ADAMS, JOHN (October 30, 1735–July 4, 1826)

Second president of the United States; supported Alexander Hamilton's fiscal plan, including continuing the use of a high protective tariff.

John and Susanna Boyleston Adams welcomed their son John, the great-great-grandson of pilgrims John and Priscilla Alden, into the world on October 30, 1735, in Braintree (now Quincy), Massachusetts. Adams's family ties also included a great-uncle, Dr. Zabdiel Boyleston, who introduced the practice of inoculation to America during a flu epidemic in 1761, and the famed patriot and fellow signer of the Declaration of Independence, Samuel Adams, a second cousin. Adams's father wanted his oldest of three sons to attend Harvard College and become a preacher and stressed a good education to that end, teaching young John to read at an early age. Adams did enter Harvard College in 1751 and developed a strong interest in math and philosophy. On his graduation in 1755, he decided to study law under James Putnam and gained admission to the Massachusetts bar in November 1758.

On October 25, 1764, Adams married his third cousin, a woman nine years his junior, named Abigail Smith. Together they had four children, Abigail "Nabby," John Quincy, Charles, and Thomas. In addition to raising a family, he built a strong legal career and held various local political offices, including selectman and surveyor of highways. In 1770, he made the unpopular decision to defend the British soldiers charged with instigating the Boston Massacre. Although the decision nearly cost him his career, he proved himself a strong litigator, winning an acquittal for six men and getting the charge reduced to manslaughter for two others. In time he won back the respect of his colleagues, and from 1770 until 1774 he held a seat as the Boston representative to the General Court of Massachusetts.

In 1774, Adams became an elected delegate to the Continental Congress where he worked to include the southern colonies in the rebellion, nominated George Washington as commander of the Continental Army, and signed the Declaration of Independence. When the American Revolution ended, Adams served on the diplomatic team that negotiated the 1783 Treaty of Paris. He also drafted the Massachusetts state constitution in 1789 after showing ardent support for the passage of the federal Constitution.

Like many of the founding generation, Adams's early writings show a propensity for free trade. Inspired by Enlightenment philosophers and early modern economists, men of the Revolutionary generation envisioned a world thriving in an atmosphere free of protective barriers. But only a few years after declaring independence from Great Britain, many of these men began to see that free trade could not combat the protectionist spirit of Europe. Adams began to believe that the fledgling nation had to fight European protectionism with some trade barriers of its own. As the first U.S. minister to Great Britain, Adams had the difficult responsibility of negotiating commercial arrangements with the former mother country. Britain refused to remove its restrictive trade policies, causing Adams to counter with the threat of prohibitive measures from the United States. Under the Articles of Confederation, Britain and other European nations knew that the U.S. Congress had no power to enforce such laws and felt no threat from Adams's words. Frustrated with such impasses, Adams recalled himself as minister in February 1788.

From 1789 to 1797, Adams served as the first American vice president under George Washington and quickly allied himself with Alexander Hamilton in support of the latter's fiscal plan that included the collection of import duties to increase revenue and promote American manufacturing. In 1796, when Washington decided to step down after two terms as president, Adams became the de facto Federalist presidential candidate. Without being nominated, he ran against and defeated Thomas Jefferson, in part because he had the endorsement of the still much-revered Washington. Adams campaigned on the success of Federalism, the need for a strong central government, and the condemnation of the bloody French Revolution. Neither his inaugural address nor any of his annual messages actually promoted the tariff for the purpose of protecting American manufacturing. He supported the tariff more as a way of raising revenue, an issue so important to him that, as president, he also approved the first legislation for federal taxes on property. Adams knew the necessity of revenue in the new nation; when he was the U.S. minister to Great Britain the United States could not even raise the interest on its debt.

In 1800, Adams again ran against Jefferson and in one of the closest elections in U.S. history failed to gain a second term in office. Jefferson claimed his victory as revolutionary and promised to dismantle the Federalist system, including protective tariffs. As history played out, the Jeffersonian Republicans instituted the first truly protective tariff in 1816.

By 1817, manufacturers began courting the former president to gain his support for protectionism through high tariffs. Adams, along with Jefferson, Madison, and Monroe, all endorsed a New York society dedicated to the protection of American industry through high tariffs and a nineteenth-century campaign encouraging Americans to buy products made only in the United States. Like most of the founding generation, Adams turned from the enlightened ideals of free trade to the protectionist notions of a new nation struggling with old ways.

Adams fell ill just before the celebration of the fiftieth anniversary of the Declaration of Independence. At about noon on July 4, 1826, he awoke from a labored sleep to comment that "Jefferson still survives," a phrase that has evoked much historical interpretation down through the years. He then fell back into unconsciousness and died at about six o'clock in the evening in his beloved home in Quincy, Massachusetts. At nearly ninety-one years of age, he proved the longest lived president in U.S. history prior to Ronald Reagan.

See also: Adams, John Quincy; American Revolution; Federalists; Franklin,

Benjamin; Hamilton, Alexander; Jefferson, Thomas.

Selected Bibliography:

David McCullough, *John Adams*, 2001; Edward Stanwood, *American Tariff Controversies in the Nineteenth Century*, 1967.

Elaine C. Prange Turney

ADAMS, JOHN QUINCY July 11, 1767– February 23, 1848)

Sixth president of the United States; advocated active national policies to stimulate U.S. economic development, including enacting high tariffs to protect domestic industries.

Born to John and Abigail Adams in Braintree, Massachusetts, Adams came of age during the American Revolution and in the early American republic. After his graduation from Harvard College in 1787, he studied law and won admittance to the bar in 1791. Adams began his public life in U.S. diplomacy and excelled as a primary architect of American foreign policy during the nation's first half-century. From 1794 until 1817, except for his tenure in the U.S. Senate from 1803 until 1808, Adams served as U.S. minister to the Netherlands, Prussia, Russia, and Great Britain. He supported the Louisiana Purchase and the embargo policy of President Thomas Jefferson during the Franco-British hostilities that occurred between 1803 and 1809. Adams headed the American mission that negotiated the Treaty of Ghent in December 1814, the accord that officially ended the War of 1812 between Great Britain and the United States. As secretary of state under James Monroe, Adams pursued expansionist foreign policies as expressed by the Anglo-American Convention of 1818 and the Transcontinental Treaty with Spain. He helped develop the principles of the Monroe Doctrine, which crystallized the foundations of American foreign policy for the nineteenth century.

Tainted by the inconclusive election of 1824 and weakened by his political ineptitude, Adams's presidency constituted an unpopular administration. As chief executive, he followed Hamiltonian governmental philosophies and argued for strong national authority to foster economic development. He endorsed the Bank of the United States as part of his national fiscal authority, supported a broad national program of internal improvements, the national administration of public lands, and national direction in education, and proposed aid to encourage the development of science and technology. He supported high protective tariffs to diversify American manufacturing interests. Aided by his congressional allies, Adams shaped a new tariff bill in 1827 that increased custom duties on both primary industries and raw materials. Passed by Congress prior to the election of 1828, this legislation, sometimes called the Tariff of Abominations, remained controversial and provided ammunition for Andrew Jackson to defeat Adams. From 1831 to 1848, Adams served in Congress and played a major role in opposing the extension of slavery, the "gag rule," and the War with Mexico. He died on February 23, 1848, in the Capitol Building, Washington, D.C.

See also: Adams, John; American Revolution; American System; Clay, Henry; Great Britain; Hamilton,

Alexander; Jacksonianism; Jefferson, Thomas; Monroe, James; War of 1812.

Selected Bibliography:

Mary Hargreaves, *The Presidency of John Quincy Adams*, 1985; Greg Russell, *John Quincy Adams and the Public Virtues of Diplomacy*, 1995.

Guoqiang Zheng

AGRICULTURAL ADJUSTMENT ACT (AAA)

An early New Deal act passed by Congress in May 1933 to promote agricultural recovery from the Depression of the 1930s.

The act provided American farmers with immediate relief equivalent to the tariff protection and special subsidies that the federal government extended to manufacturers. The law had at its heart a voluntary domestic allotment plan that subsidized farmers who agreed to production controls in order to raise the prices of seven basic farm commodities, including wheat, corn, cotton, hogs, tobacco, rice, and dairy products. Legislators believed that this policy would help restore the purchasing power of the individual farmer to the parity level that harkened back to the prosperous period of 1909 to 1914. The funds to finance the program would come from custom duties on certain enumerated items, particularly from new taxes imposed on the processing of farm produce, which would be automatically passed on to consumers in higher prices.

The legislation helped improve agricultural conditions. Farm prices rose from 52 percent of parity in 1932 to 88 percent in 1935, and gross farm income climbed by 50 percent the same year. But landowning farmers and larger commercial growers benefited most by using AAA payments, as they mechanized production and thereby reduced their need for farm labor. Meanwhile, tenant farmers and sharecroppers often faced eviction and dislocation due to the production restrictions. In January 1936, the U.S. Supreme Court declared the Agricultural Adjustment Act unconstitutional in *United States v. Butler*. Congress passed another Agricultural Adjustment Act in 1938, thereby maintaining the federal role in agricultural planning and price setting for decades to come.

See also: American farmers; Great Depression; Roosevelt, Franklin D.

Selected Bibliography:

William Leuchtenberg, *The FDR Years: On Roosevelt and His Legacy*, 1995.

Guoqiang Zheng

ALDRICH, NELSON W. (November 6, 1841–April 16, 1915)

Member of the U.S. House of Representatives and U.S. Senate from Rhode Island who helped in the passage of the Payne-Aldrich Tariff of 1909.

Born in Foster, Rhode Island, and educated at the East Greenwich Academy, by age seventeen Aldrich had worked as a clerk and bookkeeper for Waldron, Wightman & Co., a large grocery wholesaler in Providence. During the Civil War, he served with the Tenth Rhode Island Volunteers garrisoning in Washington, D.C. After returning home to Providence, he became a junior partner at Waldron, Wightman.

Aldrich entered politics in 1869 when the people of Providence elected him to the city council. In 1875, he won a seat in the Rhode Island General Assembly, serving as Speaker from 1876 to 1877. Aldrich served in the U.S. House of Representatives as a Republican from 1878 to 1880 and was a member of the District of Columbia Committee. In 1881, the Rhode Island legislature elected Aldrich to the U.S. Senate to replace Ambrose Burnside. He served in the Senate from 1886 to 1910.

As a U.S. senator, Aldrich worked to develop the United States as an industrial nation by finding ways that government could best serve business. He opposed much government regulation and voted against the Interstate Commerce Act of 1887. As chairman of the Senate Finance Committee, Aldrich used the protective tariff to serve the interests of eastern manufacturers. He helped draft the Mongrel Tariff of 1883. Aldrich also presented an alternative to the Democratic Mills Bill of 1888. He played a key role in the passage of the McKinley Tariff of 1890. To prevent deep cuts in the rates, he regularly bargained with senators from the Democratic Party when that party controlled the chamber. Although a protectionist, Aldrich did not always seek the highest tariff rates. He worked to reduce import duties on raw sugar to benefit eastern sugar processors. Some accused Aldrich of accepting a bribe for this action when they discovered that a sugar magnate advanced Aldrich money that allowed him to buy and improve the electric streetcar system in Providence.

As a leader in the Republican-dominated Senate, Aldrich aided his party in opposing free silver and helped pass the Gold Standard Act of 1900. In an effort to increase markets, Aldrich also worked to ratify the treaty by which the United States acquired the Philippines and Puerto Rico. As a Senate leader, he frequently opposed progressive president Theodore Roosevelt.

In 1909, President William Howard Taft sought to enact tariff reform. The legislation, guided by Representative Sereno Payne, passed the House. Aldrich amended the House measure by raising the tariffs on most goods. A conference committee approved the amended bill and President Taft signed it into law. During the debate over the bill, Aldrich offered a constitutional amendment authorizing a federal income tax as a way of appeasing progressive Republicans. The senator did not seek reelection in 1910. He died on April 16, 1915, in New York City.

See also: Democratic Party; Dingley Tariff (Tariff of 1897); McKinley Tariff (Tariff of 1890); Mills Bill; Payne, Sereno; Payne-Aldrich Tariff (Tariff of 1909); Senate Finance Committee; Silver; Sugar; Taft, William Howard. **Vol. II**: Inaugural Address of William Howard Taft; William Howard Taft's Winona Speech; William Howard Taft's 1912 Acceptance Speech. **Vol. III**: Tariff of 1890 (McKinley Tariff); Tariff of 1897 (Dingley Tariff); Tariff of 1909 (Payne-Aldrich Tariff).

Selected Bibliography:

Nathaniel W. Stephenson, *Nelson W. Aldrich: A Leader in American Politics*, 1971; Paul Wolman, *Most Favored Nation: The Re-

publican Revisionists and U.S. Tariff Policy, 1897–1912, 1992.

John David Rausch Jr.

ALDRICH, WINTHROP (November 2, 1885–February 15, 1974)

Chairman of the Board of Chase National Bank of New York and head of the International Chamber of Commerce; advocated the reduction of high tariffs.

Born in Providence, Rhode Island, Aldrich ranked eighth of nine children born to Nelson W. Aldrich and his wife. Nelson Aldrich, Republican senator from Rhode Island and chairman of the Senate Finance Committee, played an important role in raising tariff rates in the Payne-Aldrich Tariff of 1909. Unlike his father, Winthrop Aldrich advocated the reduction of tariff rates.

Aldrich, a lawyer who specialized in finance, practiced law from 1919 to 1929. In 1930, he accepted the position as president of Chase National Bank of New York and three years later, at the height of the Great Depression, the Board of Directors appointed him Chairman of the Board. While chairman, Aldrich also served as a director of the International Chamber of Commerce. At the end of World War II, Aldrich, renouncing the tariff policies held by his father, supported the 1945 Tariff Reciprocity measure that authorized the president to reduce tariff rates by up to 50 percent and promoted the use of trade instead of aid as the most cost-efficient method of rebuilding war-torn Europe. Appointed by President Dwight D. Eisenhower, he served as the U.S. ambassador to Great Brit-

ain. Although Aldrich sought a reduction in tariff rates as a means of preventing future wars, he stopped short of advocating free trade. Aldrich died in New York City at the age of eighty-eight.

See also: Aldrich, Nelson W.; Eisenhower, Dwight D. (Ike); Great Britain; Great Depression; International Chamber of Commerce (ICC).

Selected Bibliography:

Alfred E. Eckes, *Opening America's Market: U.S. Foreign Trade Policy Since 1776,* 1995; Arthur Menzies Johnson, *Winthrop W. Aldrich: Lawyer, Banker, Diplomat,* 1968.

Cynthia Clark Northrup

ALLIANCE FOR PROGRESS

Created by John F. Kennedy as an inter-American social and economic program to combat social unrest in Latin America.

Announced in Kennedy's inaugural address and launched at the Punta del Este meeting of the Organization of American States in August 1961, the Alliance for Progress promised $20 billion in assistance from the United States and international organizations to Latin America over ten years. Motivated by the fear of social revolution in Latin America, Kennedy proposed the plan at the height of the Cold War. United States policymakers believed that a proactive policy promoting economic development and social reform could ease the plight of the masses and avoid another Cuban-style revolution.

The heart of the alliance centered on U.S. support of long-range economic planning, economic integration, and commodity stabilization. It also provided for technical and educational assistance, cultural exchanges, and social works programs. Its more ambitious elements called for a modest redistribution of wealth in Latin America through tax and land reform. The Alliance for Progress received a warm reception in Latin America, where leaders had long called for a Marshall Plan for the region. For its part, the United States committed almost $2 billion in assistance in the first two years of the program.

The Alliance for Progress did not achieve its initial promise for a number of reasons. Within Latin America, local elites resisted changes, a shortage of skilled personnel hampered planning efforts, nationalists resented U.S. guidance, and self-serving bureaucracies squandered assistance dollars. In the United States, bureaucratic infighting in the State Department, hesitant private investors, and Cold War pragmatism hampered attempts to reduce the disparities that fueled revolution in the developing world.

By 1967, when President Lyndon B. Johnson flew south for a presidential summit with Latin American counterparts in Uruguay, the alliance had noticeably shifted its emphasis from social and economic reform to economic integration through private investment and the elimination of trade barriers. Begun as early as 1963, this shift returned U.S. policy to its traditional base by tying Latin American development to American business. When President Richard Nixon took office in 1969, the Alliance for Progress died, except in name.

See also: Cold War; Kennedy, John F.; Latin America; Organization of American States (OAS). **Vol. II**: Alliance for Progress.

Selected Bibliography:

Jerome Levinson and Juan de Onís, *The Alliance That Lost Its Way: A Critical Report on the Alliance for Progress*, 1970; Stephen G. Rabe, *The Most Dangerous Area in the World: John F. Kennedy Confronts Communist Revolution in Latin America*, 1998.

John D. Coats

AMALGAMATED ASSOCIATION OF IRON AND STEEL WORKERS

Union that strongly supported tariffs in the late nineteenth century.

Founded in 1876, members of the Amalgamated Association of Iron and Steel Workers played a central role in the industrialization of America. Membership in the Amalgamated, limited to skilled workers in the rolling mills and puddling furnaces, reached upwards of 25,000 at its height, making it one of the most powerful unions in America. The combination of a crushing defeat at Homestead, Pennsylvania, in 1892 and the formation of the U.S. Steel Corporation in 1901 resulted in steel becoming not only one of the most monopolized but also one of the most anti-union industries in the nation.

The Amalgamated developed into one of the most pro-tariff unions in the Gilded Age. Production of steel in the United States, monopolized by Andrew Carnegie before he sold out to U.S. Steel, faced fierce competition from Great Britain. Steel companies actively lobbied and benefited dramatically from tariff protection. The Amalgamated supported this policy too. In 1880, Pittsburgh represented the center of American steel production and there the spring gathering of the union drew an enormous crowd of 20,000, which essentially turned into a demonstration for higher tariffs. The Amalgamated refused to join the American Federation of Labor because of the latter's opposition to tariffs.

See also: American Federation of Labor (AFL); Carnegie, Andrew; Great Britain; U.S. Steel Corp.

Selected Bibliography:

Philip S. Foner, "From the Founding of the American Federation of Labor to the Emergence of American Capitalism," *History of the Labor Movement in the United States,* 1975.

Peter Cole

AMERASIA

A highly controversial publication printed from 1937 to 1947 that dealt with U.S.-Asian trade relations.

Amerasia first appeared in March 1937, thanks to backing from the Institute of Pacific Relations, which itself received financial support from the Rockefeller Foundation and the Carnegie Corporation. Edited by Philip Jaffe, *Amerasia* proved popular in various government circles during the presidency of Franklin Delano Roosevelt. Early concerns about the purported pro-communist slant of the journal produced criticism and resulted in the resignations of various board members. In mid-1945, a furor

unfolded with the arrest of six individuals, including Jaffe, charged with engaging in espionage at the behest of Chinese communists. Eventually, the courts convicted Jaffe and a State Department official of illegally possessing classified government documents.

Notwithstanding its increased difficulty with government operatives, *Amerasia* continued articulating a position on trade policy that undoubtedly piqued the ire of top figures in the new Truman administration. In a series of articles, the journal called into question the Philippine Trade Act devised by the U.S. Congress. The measure mandated passage of an amendment to the Philippine constitution that placed American businesses on the same footing as Filipino enterprises. The Trade Act enabled American manufacturers to ship U.S.-made products into the Philippines "free of duty, quotas, and price ceilings"; at the same time, it established a quota on products shipped into the United States from the islands. Additionally, the act required the shipment of leading Filipino products, including copra and lumber, directly to the United States. *Amerasia* charged that the Filipinos who favored the Trade Act opposed independence. It termed the legislation "the triumph of the monopoly interests," which sought to ensure that the Philippines remained "an economic colony of the United States." Moreover, *Amerasia* asserted, the Trade Act belied the United States' purported support for free trade, resulting in "the charge of sham and hypocrisy."

See also: Roosevelt, Franklin D.

Selected Bibliography:

Amerasia, 1945–1947; Harvey Klehr and Ronald Radosh, *The Amerasia Spy Case: Prelude to McCarthyism*, 1996.

                                      Robert C. Cottrell

AMERICAN FARMERS

Segment of American producers most often affected by high tariff policies.

The bountiful farmland of the United States provided farmers with the opportunity to produce surpluses that required an overseas market. From the first protective tariff of 1816, farmers experienced difficulty in selling their produce and raw materials abroad, while at the same time paying high duties on goods imported from foreign countries. The pressure from this dichotomy made farmers one of the most vocal participants in the tariff debate throughout U.S. history.

During the early republic, southern and western farmers lacked access to markets and struggled to move beyond mere subsistence. Self-interest made them support early protective tariffs and later Henry Clay's American System. They agreed that protection would hold wages high and make their domestic markets more lucrative. They also understood that internal improvements proved critical for moving surpluses to both their domestic and overseas markets. Farmers bought into the protectionist argument throughout much of the nineteenth century. When agricultural prices fell in the 1880s and 1890s, farmers felt the sting from high tariffs as their spending power diminished. The desire for price stabilization led many to support the Populist Party. At the same time, the McKinley Tariff of 1890 set higher tariff rates for agricultural as well as nonagricultural products, causing farmers to lean toward support for the Republican Party. As the sponsor of the bill, McKinley also established the principle of agricultural subsidies and reciprocity, which theoretically would help farmers penetrate foreign markets with their ever-growing surpluses. By 1900, the depression had ended, many of the Populist platform planks had been co-opted by Congress, weather conditions had improved, and the plight of the American farmer appeared to advance temporarily. Yet foreign markets remained elusive until the onset of World War I.

Meanwhile, in 1913 the Underwood-Simmons Tariff became the first tariff since before the American Civil War to put many agricultural items on the free list while lowering others; unfortunately, this benefited the consumer, not the producer. Moreover, the lower tariff rates failed to provide farmers with access to foreign markets. World War I did bring prosperity, but postwar recovery brought sustained agricultural depression as evidenced by farm values that had increased every year between 1850 and 1920, but fell by more than 50 percent between 1920 and 1935.

Limited relief for the farmer came with the 1922 passage of the Fordney-McCumber Tariff, which increased rates on wheat, sugar, wool, butter, milk, lemons, and flaxseed. Agricultural implements, binder twine, potash and hides, leather, boots, and shoes remained on the free list. Nothing provided enough relief as farmers produced surplus, year after year. By 1926, agriculture reached a full depression;

the country and the world soon followed.

In 1929, President Herbert Hoover called a special session for farm relief and tariff adjustment. Agricultural leaders wanted control of the home market and called for lower industrial tariffs to equalize manufacturing and farming prices. Industry, fearing competition, wanted more protection. The farmers got the Agricultural Marketing Act for internal help, but tariff reform remained slow in coming. The Hawley-Smoot Tariff Act of 1930 proved extremely protective to industry and damaging to agriculture. Farmers gained only marginal or no utility from some of the increases. Hides, leather, shoes, timber, cement, long-staple cotton, and brick dropped from the free list. Other nations, to protect their own economies, established high tariff walls against American products, including agricultural stuffs. Between 1929 and 1932, national income fell by half and exports dropped from $5.4 billion to $1.6 billion.

In 1934, tariff barriers gave way to reciprocity, with protection for farmers. The Agricultural Adjustment Acts of 1933 and 1938 established parity and between 1934 and the onset of World War II farmers got $4.4 billion in subsidies. Import quotas and import fees protected many agricultural products. Export subsidies in 1944 reached $118 million for wheat, cotton, corn, tobacco, fruits, nuts, dairy, and meat products. Franklin D. Roosevelt's lend-lease program boosted exports by over $5 billion. Agricultural income doubled from prewar levels. Postwar subsidies continued in the Agricultural Act of 1948 and the 1951 Trade Extension Act.

Between 1934 and 1947, the United States negotiated one-on-one agreements with twenty-nine countries. In 1939 alone, agreements reduced duties on over $700 million worth of imports. The Trade Expansion Act of 1962 and Trade Act of 1974 helped farmers and others by providing federal assistance to those adversely affected by imports. Since 1934, the U.S. government has pursued a policy that minimized tariffs, maximized free trade, and protected American farmers through government subsidies and punishment of unfair practices.

See also: Agricultural Adjustment Act (AAA); American System; Fordney-McCumber Tariff (Tariff of 1922); Hawley-Smoot Tariff (Tariff of 1930); McKinley Tariff (Tariff of 1890); Trade Expansion Act of 1962; Trade Act of 1974; Underwood-Simmons Tariff (Tariff of 1913).

Selected Bibliography:

John M. Dobson, *Two Centuries of Tariffs: The Background and Emergence of the U.S. International Trade Commission*, 1976; Judith Goldstein, *Ideas, Interests, and American Trade Policy*, 1993; Sidney Ratner, *The Tariff in American History*, 1972.

John Herschel Barnhill

AMERICAN FEDERATION OF LABOR (AFL)

Powerful union that eventually supported tariffs.

The American Federation of Labor (AFL) formed in 1886 out of a confederation of craft unions that organized workers who shared the same skills, such as carpenters, coal miners, or longshoremen. Craft unions differ from an industrial union that joins together many types of workers who labor in the same industry. Generally, unions existed only in trades of highly skilled, native-born, white male workers. By organizing only skilled, hard-to-replace workers, craft unions affiliated with the AFL often had significant leverage to affect issues that included wages, hours, work conditions, and work rules. The AFL's membership fluctuated widely from 300,000 in 1886 to more than four million in the late 1930s. The AFL merged with the Congress of Industrial Organizations (CIO) in 1955 to form the present-day AFL-CIO.

The AFL's policy on tariffs changed dramatically from its inception. At first, the AFL supported a protective tariff, but soon it totally reversed itself and opposed tariffs on the basis that they would raise the cost of all goods produced and consumed. Some member unions petitioned the AFL to support tariffs with no success. In the early twentieth century, the AFL moved increasingly closer to the Democratic Party since the Republican Party, from the Morrill Tariff of 1861 through Hawley-Smoot in 1930, supported higher tariffs. Thus, the AFL stood with other Democrats in the period prior to World War II in promoting lower tariffs. Since 1945, organized labor has become quite fearful of foreign competition that could undersell American production. Foreign competition often possesses lower labor costs due to nonunion workforces. Consequently, in the decade following World War II, the AFL often promoted higher tariffs to protect American workers and jobs.

See also: Congress of Industrial Organizations (CIO); Democratic Party; Hawley-Smoot Tariff (Tariff of 1930); Morrill Tariff (Tariff of 1861); Republican Party.

Selected Bibliography:

Mollie Ray Carroll, *Labor and Politics: The Attitude of the American Federation of Labor Toward Legislation and Politics*, 1969.

Peter Cole

AMERICAN FEDERATION OF LABOR–CONGRESS OF INDUSTRIAL ORGANIZATIONS (AFL-CIO)

Created in 1955 out of a merger of the American Federation of Labor and the Congress of Industrial Organizations, the AFL-CIO became a major critic of American trade policy by the 1970s.

The new organization called for "growth of international trade and—even if necessarily slow—decrease of trade barriers." It endorsed expanded trade, yet warned that trade policy should take into account the impact on workers. During the 1960s, the AFL-CIO consistently supported lowering tariffs, while expressing some concern over balance of trade issues and loss of jobs. By the late 1960s, with international competition threatening American jobs, the AFL-CIO shifted to a more critical perspective, insisting on the incorporation of "international labor standards" in trade agreements. The AFL-CIO advocated the revision of trade laws and criticized the growth of international business conglomerations. In 1971, for instance, it demanded a revision of the 1921 anti-dumping laws and the passage of new tax measures that would stop the export of U.S. jobs. The AFL-CIO put some hope in the Burke-Hartke Bill, designed to use public funds to ease worker displacement resulting from international competition, but little support materialized for such measures. Concerns about the role of international trade grew during the 1980s. The AFL-CIO heaped invectives on the "studied indifference" of the Reagan administration. In the 1990s, even the Democratic Party, with whom labor had enjoyed a close relationship, embraced calls for free trade. The labor organization labeled the passage of the North American Free Trade Agreement (NAFTA), under a Democratic administration in 1993, "a bitter disappointment." The AFL-CIO remains the largest, most powerful organization dedicated to halting trends toward free trade in favor of protection for American manufacturing, the environment—and, most important, jobs.

See also: American Federation of Labor (AFL); Congress of Industrial Organizations (CIO); North American Free Trade Agreement (NAFTA).

Selected Bibliography:

John J. Sweeney and David Kusnet, *America Needs a Raise: Fighting for Economic Security and Social Justice*, 2000; Robert Zieger, *American Workers, American Unions, 1920–1985*, 1994.

Edmund F. Wehrle

AMERICAN FREE TRADE LEAGUE (AFTL)

Concerned with tariff reform, the American Free Trade League (AFTL) began in 1865 and grew steadily through the post–Civil War years.

Spreading its message nationally through books, clubs, conventions, and public speeches, the AFTL kept tariff reform alive. The primary issue concerned the amount of governmental control over the economy. The league felt that protective tariffs hindered the economy as well as the ability of artisans to prosper. It further argued that protective tariffs infringed on individual rights and favored large capitalists over smaller merchants and artisans.

The AFTL stated that every man should be allowed to sell his goods wherever he could get the best price and to make his living in his own way; anything less it considered slavery. The AFTL saw itself as the defender of the right to enjoy the benefits of one's own labor. The free traders believed that the government should remove all obstacles to home industry and allow the free exchange of goods.

One particular contention concerned the surplus of money. Under high protective tariffs, the government acquired a hefty cache of funds. The AFTL fully supported taxes, duties, and tariffs, which met the needs of the government, but strongly denounced the collection of any funds that served an individual group or went to surplus. It also supported the Mills Bill, which sought to prevent the accumulation of revenue by reducing the current rates. The tariff issue created many bitter and heated debates.

The AFTL favored a more laissez-faire approach to the economy, calling the protective system "ignorant national selfishness." High tariffs protected capitalists and kept ordinary farmers and artisans from breaking out of their class. Further, because tariffs promoted the accumulation of wealth they encouraged corruption.

The first AFTL supporters in 1865 included abolitionists such as William Lloyd Garrison and Ralph Waldo Emerson and other advocates of freedom over privilege. Dying with the Republican nomination of Horace Greeley in 1872, the Free Trade Alliance replaced the AFTL and later became the Council for Tariff Reform. In 1882, a second American Free Trade League formed and remained the backbone of the reform movement until 1932. It coordinated the numerous free trade groups that sprang up all over the country. Its leaders worked to promote free trade over high protective tariffs.

The reform movement reached its peak around 1914. The American Free Trade League continued to send information to political leaders, but failed to bring new blood into their ranks. Eventually their numbers dwindled and the organization ceased to exist.

See also: Emerson, Ralph Waldo; Greeley, Horace; Mills Bill; Tariff Reform Movement.

Selected Bibliography:

Joanne Reitano, *The Tariff Question in the Gilded Age: The Great Debate of 1888*, 1994.

Lisa A. Ennis

AMERICAN IRON AND STEEL INSTITUTE (AISI)

A membership-based organization responsible for more than two-thirds of raw steel production in the United States, Canada, and Mexico.

The American Iron and Steel Institute, headquartered in Washington, D.C., and organized in 1908, absorbed the American Iron and Steel Association (AISA) in 1912. AISA had roots dating back to 1855 with the founding of the American Iron and Associates, which became AISA in 1864. Fifty North American steel producers compose its membership. These producer-members operate steel mills, blast furnaces, finishing mills, and iron ore mines.

The mission of the institute centers on the promotion of competitiveness within the North American steel industry and its member corporations. AISI conducts extensive research programs on manufacturing technology, basic materials, environmental quality control, and energy and fuel consumption.

Since the 1970s, massive government subsidies, closed markets, pervasive dumping, and anticompetitive (cartel) practices have characterized the world steel industry. By the early 1980s, this led to overcapacity in steelmaking, huge financial losses for U.S. steel companies, and lost jobs. Due to this steel trade distortion, President Ronald Reagan initiated and President George H.W. Bush extended the U.S. program of steel Voluntary Restraint Arrangements (VRAs). The Bush administration also initiated negotiations for a Multilateral Steel Agreement (MSA) to replace the VRAs, which expired in 1992. By 2000, the Asian dumping of 120 million tons of steel out of a total of 160 million tons produced had glutted the market.

AISI's primary concern includes the protection of the United States against unfair trade, especially the anti-dumping and countervailing duty laws. Its membership believes that a properly trained customs service must strictly enforce these trade laws. AISI also supports the North American Free Trade Agreement and the General Agreement on Tariffs and Trade.

The Institute publishes *American Iron and Steel Institute* and *Annual Statistical Report* and holds an annual conference.

See also: Bush, George Herbert Walker; Countervailing duties; Dumping; General Agreement on Tariffs and Trade (GATT); North American Free Trade Agreement (NAFTA).

Selected Bibliography:

Website: http://www.steel.org; Joanne Reitano, *The Tariff Question in the Gilded Age: The Great Debate of 1888*, 1994.

Russell M. Magnaghi

AMERICAN PROTECTIVE TARIFF LEAGUE (APTL)

A group that strongly supported protectionism.

In 1885, organizers founded the American Protective Tariff League; its headquarters are in New York City. The founders cited both "political and patriotic" reasons for the creation of the league, including the protection of American agricultural, manufacturing, and commercial laborers against the low-priced labor of foreign countries, through necessary duties on imported foreign goods. The league believed in the need for a "judicious protective tariff" so that intelligent, skillful, and ambitious American laborers could compete successfully with the "cheap and unintelligent labor" everywhere.

Protection had enabled the country to keep the cost of production low and the standard of living high. As the cost of production fell so did the price of manufactured items, thereby enabling many Americans to enjoy them.

The election of 1884 provided the impetus for the formation of the organization. Democrat Grover Cleveland became president and proposed revising the duties to bring down government surpluses. His annual message in 1887, devoted solely to the tariff question, caused "widespread anxiety" in protectionist circles. The American Protective Tariff League organized to counter the "wrecker's hand."

The APTL represented glass, dye, railway, machine tool, cutlery, and cotton manufacturers. The league's early leaders and organizers included Le Grand B. Cannon, Edward H. Ammindown, Smith M. Weld, Alfred R. Whitney, Morris M. Budlong, and Edward M. Knox. Most of the members and leaders came from the North, especially New York, and the Midwest. Nevertheless, the league had organizations in every state and territory of the union. At the state level, a vice president and a state secretary headed the league. It consistently opposed tariff revision, and saw organizations and lobby groups working for revision as "tariff wreckers."

The APTL made its views on the tariff known to the public and government officials. It participated in discussions, debates, and congressional hearings. The organization published and distributed pamphlets like "The Farmer and the Tariff," "Workingman and the Tariff," "Some Views on the Tariff by an Old Businessman," and

"The Advantages of the Protective Tariff to the Labor Industries of the United States." The league also published articles in newspapers and conducted essay competitions on economic subjects among college students, corresponded with key people, and sponsored public meetings and addresses. The APTL sent out millions of pamphlets on tariff issues in its monthly publication, the *Tariff Bulletin*. It mailed letters to the press, to important people all over the country, and to its members. In addition, the League published a weekly, the *American Economist*. The magazine lent a powerful voice in opposing the calls for a downward revision in the tariff and the creation of a tariff commission. The tariff remained a dominant national issue for several years in large part because of the effectiveness of the APTL's tactics.

The league inspired the formation of other organizations committed to keeping the tariff high. The American Protective Tariff Leagues of California and Missouri and the Home Market Clubs of Boston and Chicago drew inspiration from the APTL. The league continued its work well into the 1920s.

See also: Boston Home Market Club; Cleveland, Stephen Grover.

Selected Bibliography:

American Protective Tariff League, *The American Protective Tariff League, Organized May 1885, Principles, Constitution and By-Laws, List of Officers and Members with the President's Annual Address, List of Documents, Etc.*, 1889; Paul Wolman, *Most Favored Nation: The Republican Revisionists and U.S. Tariff Policy, 1897–1912*, 1992.

George Thadathil

AMERICAN RECIPROCAL TARIFF LEAGUE (ARTL)

League dedicated to international fair trade that organized largely around the agricultural industry.

In August 1909, the Chicago Reciprocity Conference convened to develop a platform against unfair protectionism. Delegates approved the creation of a lobby group to work toward tariff reduction, a notable achievement of the conference. Alan H. Sanders, the editor of the *Breeder's Gazette*, spearheaded the group of midwestern organizers who dominated the League and elected Sanders as its chairman. The board of directors included members of the National Livestock Association like Gustav H. Schwab, A.B. Farquhaar, and Eugene N. Foss. It also included northeastern tariff revisionists, as well as representatives of the stock-growing industry, including Murdo Mackenzie of Colorado and Samuel H. Cowan of Texas. Sanders also attempted to recruit President Theodore Roosevelt as the group's godfather, but failed.

The ARTL began actively promoting the idea of a maximum-minimum tariff and a tariff commission. The group suggested that the Dingley Tariff of 1897 already incorporated the idea. Moreover, it advocated that the nation would benefit from an effective downward revision of the tariff because of European competition and retaliation against American exports.

The league offered no new ideas, but did call attention to important international trade issues. Between 1905 and 1907, growing concern about the proposed German tariff laws and their impact on American export-import trade resulted in the eruption of a trade war between the two countries. The protectionists in the Congress refused to reduce the tariff to appease the Germans. Roosevelt, in agreement with Congress, appointed a three-member commission to negotiate more equitable tariff rates with Germany. One of its members, Nahum I. Stone, also served as an informal advisor to ARTL. The group lobbied unsuccessfully for the inclusion of an agricultural expert on the commission, but did manage to inundate the state department with advice on concessions that the group endorsed as a result of the commission's work.

Germany restricted the importation of American meat by implementing stringent sanitary inspections. The ARTL wanted the commission to address this issue during its upcoming meeting in Germany. The commission successfully secured this key ARTL demand by convincing the Germans to lift their inspections on packaged U.S. meat.

The agreement with Germany signaled a departure for U.S. tariff policy. The ARTL united all interested revisionist groups under its banner and thereby exerted pressure on the government to complete the German agreement. Unhappy with the slow pace of tariff changes, the revisionists sought to establish a tariff commission approved by Congress and consisting of presidential appointees. The idea ran into opposition both inside and outside of revisionist ranks. The ARTL played a key role in building a coalition group supporting the commission movement.

Sanders worked hard to iron out differences between agricultural and industrial interests in the movement. Close cooperation between ARTL and the National Association of Manufacturers existed. They encouraged Senator Albert I. Beveridge of Indiana to introduce a bill for a tariff commission. They also organized a delegation to the capitol in support of the Beveridge bill.

Although the commission idea itself did not sit well with the Congress, the lobbying groups exerted considerable pressure on the national tariff policy-making process. Yet Speaker of the House Joseph G. Cannon remained unimpressed by the reductionism efforts. Nevertheless, ARTL received credit for causing a shift in Republican attitude toward the tariff. The ARTL aided in passing the Payne-Aldrich Tariff of 1909. Moreover, the changes effected during the Republican administrations between 1905 and 1912 paved the way for more revisions under the succeeding Democratic presidency of Woodrow Wilson.

See also: Beveridge, Albert Jeremiah; Cannon, Joseph Gurney; Dingley Tariff (Tariff of 1897); Germany; Kasson Treaties; Lodge, Henry Cabot; Maximum-Minimum Tariff; Roosevelt, Theodore; Tariff Commission.

Selected Bibliography:

Paul Wolman, *Most Favored Nation: The Republican Revisionists and U.S. Tariff Policy, 1897–1912*, 1992.

George Thadathil

AMERICAN REVOLUTION

Conflict that transpired between the Anglo-American colonies and the British government as a result of colonial interpretation of British policy from 1763 until 1776.

The American Revolution had its roots in imperial economic policies aimed at maintaining British authority in relation to its empire. At the beginning of the eighteenth century, England initiated a major consolidation of its power that transformed the nation from an agrarian-sea power to an industrial-sea power, capable of exerting influence in European politics as well as expanding the English state around the globe. In 1707, the Act of Union between England and Scotland created Great Britain, which included Ireland and Wales. For the first time, a United Kingdom spoke in one voice for the peoples of the British Isles. This political consolidation created hostility on the European continent, particularly from the French and Spanish, who feared that a newly empowered and largely Protestant Britain would challenge the Bourbon powers for hegemony in Europe. To gird itself for war, Britain adopted a radically new economic approach to statecraft in the 1720s when it created a stock market, a national bank, and an enlarged military force. The fiscal-military revolution subverted the traditional agricultural economy of England to the new industrial economy of Britain.

Britain, with a significantly smaller population than its continental competitors, managed to fight four successive world wars that culminated in 1763 with a magnificent victory in the Seven Years' War (French and Indian War). That conflict left Great Britain in command of much of North America as the British forced the French to cede Canada to the British crown. But the victory created a huge financial debt

and forced the mother country to look to its colonies to share the cost of empire. Britain had taxed its colonies before. Since the 1650s, Parliament had levied a series of navigation laws, which essentially served as a tariff to protect English goods entering the colonies. In the imperial system known as mercantilism, these laws made perfect sense. British colonies existed to promote the interests of the mother country, providing raw materials and resources shipped to England where craftsmen produced fine finished products that could be sold in England or transported back across the Atlantic to colonial consumers. The British aimed the first navigation laws at Dutch dominance over the major lines of English trade. England ordered that English ships or ships made in the British Empire must carry imports bought within its borders. It also placed various duties, or tariffs, on Dutch commodities. These taxes made it difficult for the Dutch to sell their wares in the British Empire. As the years passed the crown extended the navigation acts to include other nations and to codify production and trade in British North America. Initially, Americans acquiesced to the regulation of their trade because they accrued certain benefits in the bargain. The British Royal Navy protected American exports on the seas, allowing the colonists to trade within the empire and ensuring the Americans access to markets closed to other nations.

But, by the early 1760s, Americans began to chafe under the imperial system of trade regulation. A growing awareness of the potential size and strength of the Anglo-American people developed in North America. Americans rejected arguments that the taxes and trade restrictions helped pay for colonial rule on the North American continent. Colonists argued that Britain intended to keep the agricultural economies of the colonies in the New World from industrializing and reaching a stage of economic power that would rival, if not exceed, that of the mother country. British actions seemed to validate American claims. In the name of economy, the king and Parliament carried through a series of acts in the 1760s that, while based on the principle of the old navigation laws, fundamentally reoriented the way in which Britain taxed its colonies. The older system tariffs brought in revenue indirectly, promoting and protecting American industries as well as British. The new form of taxation, which began in 1764 with the Sugar Act, sought to procure revenue directly in order to enhance the British military and legal presence in the colonies. In other words, the colonists paid for British courts and soldiers to reorient the Anglo-American economy in a way more advantageous for Great Britain. Parliament codified this policy through a series of acts, including the Currency Acts of 1764, the Stamp and Declaratory Acts of 1765, and the Townshend Duties of 1767 that sought to enumerate the subservient position of the colonies into imperial law. The acts produced the opposite effect as the colonists, primarily in Boston, Philadelphia, and the Chesapeake Bay area, recognized the damage British tax and tariff policies would have on their future economic opportunities. The colonists declared independence in 1776, partly as a response to the British challenge to an American economy just beginning to compete with rather than

complement that of the mother country.

At a deeper level, the revolutionaries in America believed that continued attachment with Britain would endanger several existing economic institutions in the colonies. The British Empire phased out slavery, and colonists in the South feared that continued allegiance to the Empire might force them to follow a general imperial policy of emancipation. Shopkeepers in New England believed the Parliamentary Acts of the 1760s provided unfair advantage to British goods while making it difficult for the infant American manufacturing market to grow and mature. At the conclusion of the war, these two powerful economic blocs worked diligently to protect their interests. The new American nation sanctioned both slavery and market capitalism. Ultimately, these two contradictory forms of economic agency would divide the country, leading to civil war, another legacy of the Revolution.

See also: *Cato's Letters*; Colonial administration; Great Britain; Mercantilism; Navigation and Trade Acts.

Selected Bibliography:

Bernard Bailyn, *The Ideological Origins of the American Revolution*, 1967; Don Cook, *The Long Fuse: How England Lost the American Colonies, 1760–1785*, 1995; Edward Countryman, *The American Revolution*, 1985.

David S. Brown

AMERICAN SYSTEM

Henry Clay's program of economic nationalism.

In January 1824, Congressman John

Tod of Pennsylvania proposed an increase in tariff rates. As chairman of the House Committee on Manufactures, Tod argued that higher tariffs would help American manufacturers of woolens, iron, cotton bagging, glass, and spirits. Although many congressmen objected to Tod's proposals, Speaker of the House Henry Clay defended the tariff increase. He used the debate over the new rates to set forth a program of economic nationalism that he called the American System.

Clay argued that the new system would save the country from financial ruin. With foreign trade declining, farm prices continued their downward spiral. Bankruptcies and unemployment continued to rise. Clay believed that peace in Europe following Napoleon's defeat coupled with foreign restrictions on American trade had brought the business of the nation to a standstill. Only direct government intervention could reinvigorate the struggling economy.

As part of his American System, Clay proposed that the United States develop a home market for its manufactured and agricultural goods. Manufacturers in the East and farmers in the West had to work together to promote the prosperity of all. He further suggested that Congress should pass laws in three areas to integrate and strengthen the overall economy. First, imported manufactured goods and raw materials that competed with similar American products should carry a high protective tariff. These measures would benefit manufacturers and farmers alike. Congress should also fund internal improvements such as roads and canals. These projects would allow for

the shipment of manufactured goods from east to west, and the movement of raw materials from west to east. Finally, the Bank of the United States must continue to operate and provide a stable currency and necessary credit for the developing nation.

Clay defended his American System against those who attacked it on political, sectional, and constitutional grounds. He argued that Washington, Hamilton, and Jefferson had supported similar measures in the first days of the republic. He believed that encouraging manufacturing in the North would help every section including the South by making cheaper goods available to all. Finally, since Article I gave Congress full power over foreign and interstate commerce, he argued the constitutionality of protective tariffs and internal improvements.

Throughout his long political career, Clay supported specific measures to implement his American System. He proved instrumental in choosing Wheeling in western Virginia as the site where the National Road crossed the Ohio River. He also won congressional approval for canal construction in several western states. But in the area of protective tariffs he proved less successful. Clay continued to push relentlessly for higher rates until the Tariffs of 1828 and 1832 set off the Nullification Crisis. Although a southerner himself, Clay never accepted the argument put forth by John C. Calhoun of South Carolina that the American System benefited the North and West at the expense of the South. Calhoun believed that tariff rates averaging 33 percent made imported goods too expensive for the South to buy and also threatened British retaliation against cotton imported from the United States.

Clay worked with his political rival President Andrew Jackson to hold the union together when South Carolina threatened to secede over the Tariff of 1832. Jackson proposed the Force Bill to raise an army and restore order to South Carolina, while Clay worked out a compromise tariff that gradually lowered rates over a ten-year period. He hoped the new tariff would help the nation as a whole by giving the North another decade to develop manufacturing while assuring the South that high tariffs would eventually end.

Despite their work to end the Nullification Crisis, Clay and Jackson soon disagreed on another part of the American System. Jackson vetoed the new charter of the Second Bank of the United States. Over the strenuous objections of Clay, Jackson removed all national deposits from the Bank of the United States and placed them in state and local banks. Clay's political setbacks continued even after Jackson left the White House. Although personally popular throughout much of the nation, he never won the presidency, the one office that might have assured the success of his American System.

Ironically, his ideas won the support of younger politicians in the last years of his life and even after his death. Senator Stephen Douglas of Illinois called for land grants and loans to develop western railroads. During the Civil War, President Abraham Lincoln implemented much of the American System, including higher tariffs, government support for the construction of the transcontinental railroad, and a national banking system.

See also: Calhoun, John Caldwell; Clay, Henry; Jackson, Andrew; Lincoln, Abraham; Nullification; Tariff of 1828 (Tariff of Abominations); Tariff of 1833 (Compromise Tariff).

Selected Bibliography:

Maurice G. Baxter, *Henry Clay and the American System*, 1995.

Mary Stockwell

AMES, FISHER (April 9, 1758–July 4, 1808)

Federalist politician of the 1790s and a proponent of Secretary of the Treasury Alexander Hamilton's financial proposals.

Having graduated from Harvard College in 1774, Ames taught school and studied law before he defeated Samuel Adams for a seat in the first session of the U.S. House of Representatives in 1788. During the initial debate over revenue measures, Ames played a key role in persuading Congress that a high duty would create ill will with the people. He particularly argued against a higher rate on nails that could be produced cheaply in the United States as well as on rum, a staple item in American homes. Congress reduced some of the proposed tariff rates and allowed a three-cent-a-gallon drawback on rum exported out of the country. Ames, reelected in 1790, 1792, and 1794, retired from public service in 1796. After returning to Dedham, Massachusetts, he persuaded New England Federalists to oppose the French revolutionaries, even proposing that the United States should declare war against the Jacobites. His actions resulted in the development

of a distinct New England consciousness.

See also: Hamilton, Alexander.

Selected Bibliography:

Winfield E.A. Bernard, *Fisher Ames, Federalist and Statesman, 1758–1808*, 1965.

Cynthia Clark Northrup

ANTI-FEDERALISTS

Resisted the ratification of the Constitution, in part because they opposed
the establishment of a federal government that could pass high tariff bills
and otherwise control trade.

Anti-Federalists feared that a strong
central government would restore the
high taxes and tyrannical rule of the
British system. Individual state government, they believed, could best protect
their interests. Many Anti-Federalists
lived in the South or on the western
frontier where the economy revolved
around agriculture. They raised cash
crops to export and depended on imports for their nonagricultural needs.
High import and export duties,
therefore, would have a negative impact on their economy. They believed
that the power of a strong central government would undermine the independence for which they had fought.
After all, the customs duties that Britain had imposed in the 1760s had led
the colonies to revolution.

George Mason of Virginia, a delegate
to the Constitutional Convention, refused to sign the newly created document, arguing that it subverted every
principle by which they had been
governed and threatened to annihilate
individual rights. Another Anti-

Federalist, Patrick Henry, called attention to the immense taxing power
given to the national government. To
secure funds for operation, Henry
prophesied, the government would tax
as it pleased and suspend the laws and
rights of the individual state as it
willed.

The predominantly Federalist northern mercantilists hoped for high tariffs
to protect burgeoning American manufacturing. They eagerly called for federal assistance in the way of navigation
acts that would favor American over
foreign ships in coastal and overseas
trade. Southern Anti-Federalists, exporters but not shipowners, wanted the
admittance of foreign ships without
discriminating tariffs so that they could
benefit from greater competition. The
arguments concerning this issue delayed acceptance of the Constitution
until delegates reached a compromise.
Southern Anti-Federalists traded their
desire for a ban on navigation acts for
a free hand concerning slavery.

After the implementation of the Constitution, factions formed in response
to Alexander Hamilton's financial plan
for the Union. Secretary of the Treasury Hamilton planned several measures to strengthen central government
through the power of the purse. His
plans for assumption of state debts, redemption of Confederation bonds at
face value, federal assistance for the
rapid rise of industry, and the congressional establishment of a Bank of the
United States split the national legislature into irreconcilable factions.
Hamilton's supporters took for themselves the name "Federalist"; Thomas
Jefferson and James Madison became
leaders of the opposing faction. As Virginia agrarians, they believed Hamil-

ton's proposals gave the central government the power of the purse that had previously rested with local assemblies. Jefferson, more visible to the public than Madison, symbolized the principle of republicanism. Followers of those principles identified themselves as "Jeffersonians." Most Anti-Federalists claimed complete loyalty to the republican ideal.

See also: Articles of Confederation; Hamilton, Alexander; Jeffersonianism.

Selected Bibliography:

Forest McDonald, *Novus Orrdo Seclorum: The Intellectual Origins of the Constitution*, 1985; Gordon S. Wood, *The Creation of the American Republic, 1776–1787*, 1969.

Carol Terry

ARTHUR, CHESTER ALAN (October 5, 1829–November 18, 1886)

Twenty-first president of the United States; recommended a significant reduction in tariff duties but demonstrated little inclination to push his program through Congress.

Born in Fairfield, Vermont, Arthur graduated from Union College in Schenectady, New York, in 1848. During the Civil War, he served as both a brigadier general and a quartermaster general. As an ally of New York Senator Roscoe Conkling, Arthur served as the collector of the New York customhouse from 1871 to 1878. In 1880, the Republican national convention nominated Arthur as James A. Garfield's vice-presidential running mate to balance the ticket geographically and placate the Stalwart faction of the party. When Garfield died as the result of an assas-

sin's bullet on September 19, 1881, Arthur became the new president.

The high tariff enacted during the Civil War had created a large treasury surplus by 1882. The Democratic Party, generally opposed to a high protective tariff, strongly criticized the existence of this surplus. In 1882, Congress created a commission to recommend a reduction in tariff revenue without eliminating the basic use of the tariff. But before the issuance of the report, the success of the Democratic Party in the congressional elections created political pressure for an even more dramatic reduction in the tariff rate. Indeed, the 1882 elections resulted in substantial Democratic gains in congressional, gubernatorial, and local races. This major setback for the Republicans led Chester Arthur to pass various pieces of reform legislation, including a significant reduction in tariff duties. But Arthur showed little interest in driving his program through Congress, and the protected interests limited the reductions included in the Tariff of 1883. The tariff issue remained a major national topic.

The Republican Party did not nominate Arthur to run for reelection in 1884. His health quickly declined after he left the presidency, and he died of a massive cerebral hemorrhage in New York City on November 18, 1886.

See also: Democratic Party; Garfield, James A.; Republican Party; Tariff of 1883 (Mongrel Tariff). **Vol. III**: Tariff of 1883 (Mongrel Tariff).

Selected Bibliography:

Justus Doenecke, *The Presidencies of James A. Garfield and Chester A. Arthur*, 1981.

Steven E. Siry

ARTICLES OF CONFEDERATION

Preceded the U.S. Constitution as the law of the land from 1781 to 1789.

The authors of the Articles of Confederation, fearing centralized authority, gave Congress full authority over coinage and borrowing money, but no power to levy taxes. First proposed by Richard Henry Lee in 1776, John Dickerson wrote the draft, "Articles of Confederation and Perpetual Union," and Congress adopted it in 1777. Twelve of the original states promptly ratified the articles. Maryland held out because of land issues, but ultimately ratified the document, making it effective in March 1781.

The document gave Congress a great deal of responsibility yet very little power. For instance, Congress could enter into a treaty, but had no authority to enforce the rules of the treaty. Further, acts dealing with treaties as well as war, privateering, coinage, finances, army, and navy required a majority of nine states to gain approval. The articles required unanimous approval to issue a tariff or an amendment. Consequently, taxation and tariff control remained in the power of the states. Congress had no regulatory power over interstate or foreign commerce either. States paid taxes based on the value of their land and provided troops based on the population of white residents.

The articles did not provide for an executive or a court system. Congressional authority rested with the will of the individual states, but the articles did call for three national officials. Robert Livingston served as secretary of foreign affairs, General Benjamin Lincoln as secretary of war, and Robert Morris as superintendent of finance. Eventually, the shortcomings of the articles would end the Confederation Congress. Each year Congress's debt grew while its currency lost value. In 1787, delegates met to draft a new document, giving more power to a central government.

See also: Continental Congress.

Selected Bibliography:

Congressional Quarterly's Guide to Congress, 1991; Merrill Jensen, *The Articles of Confederation*, 1940.

Lisa A. Ennis

ATKINSON, EDWARD (February 10, 1827–December 11, 1905)

A well-known businessman and spokesman for laissez-faire political causes including free trade, hard money, and anti-imperialism.

Atkinson served as a financial agent for a number of important textile mills from 1850 to 1878, and received recognition as an authority on the production and manufacture of cotton, as well as on governmental policy toward the cotton industry. From 1878 to his death in 1905, he served as president of the Boston Manufacturers' Mutual Fire Insurance Company. He also invented automatic sprinklers. Best known to his fellow Americans for his prolific writing on political and economic issues, he counted as friends and correspondents a great many members of Congress, as well as Andrew Carnegie, Ulysses Grant, James Garfield, and Grover Cleveland.

He shared the conviction, fundamental to the nineteenth-century classical liberalism that he articulately espoused, that the economy operated in a self-regulating fashion and state interference with the free flow of goods only disrupted the natural tendency toward efficiency and equilibrium that bore the traces of a benign Providence. More specifically, Atkinson argued that the practice of worldwide free trade ensured that each area of the globe concentrated on producing those goods that uniquely suited the peculiarities of its climate, terrain, and proximity to natural resources. Tariffs, on the other hand, encouraged the wasteful and inefficient manufacture of goods in locations that, for whatever reason, remained less suited to their production, thereby diverting scarce resources into wasteful projects and lowering the overall standard of living of everyone involved.

Throughout his career, Atkinson had insisted that tariff reform, although urgent, ought to be done gradually, to prevent undue dislocation to people and firms. For this reason, Atkinson found himself opposed from time to time by less patient partisans of laissez-faire.

His influence remained significant, and indeed in 1893, when the issue of tariff reform resurfaced as a national issue, people spoke of the drafting of "the Atkinson bill" in Congress. In its original form, the legislation called for a variety of free raw materials, including coal, iron ore, lumber, and wool, as well as moderate reductions on nearly all manufactured goods. By the following year, Atkinson had grown so anxious for at least some positive action on the tariff that he indicated his willingness to compromise and counseled his friends in Congress accordingly. Apart

from the survival of free wool from the legislation of the previous year, the tariff bill of 1894 bore little of the Atkinson imprint so conspicuous in the original bill. Most free traders considered the measure disappointing, even though Atkinson suggested that its positive features constituted at least a first step in a lengthy process. By 1894, the question of hard versus soft money had reemerged, and in defending the integrity of the gold standard, Atkinson found himself devoting his time to what he considered a more pressing issue, confident that tariff reform "will go fast enough on its own merits."

See also: Carnegie, Andrew; Cleveland, Stephen Grover; Garfield, James A.; Wool and woolens.

Selected Bibliography:

Harold Francis Williamson, *Edward Atkinson: The Biography of an American Liberal, 1827–1905,* 1972.

Thomas E. Woods Jr.

AUTOMOBILE INDUSTRY

One of the largest industries in the United States; initially encouraged the lowering of tariffs until the 1970s when imports soared.

As the first country to mass-produce automobiles, the United States enjoyed a distinct advantage in the auto industry. Auto manufacturers during the early twentieth century encouraged lawmakers to lower tariff rates as an incentive for foreign countries to reduce trade barriers on American cars. The tariff rate established by the Hawley-Smoot Tariff Act of 1930 called for a 10 percent duty on imported vehicles. The increase in taxes, combined with the onset of a worldwide depression, led other countries to discriminate against the United States based on their own domestic economic interests and to protect their markets for national security reasons as Europe marched closer to war. The U.S. automakers circumvented the tariff duties by establishing manufacturing plants overseas. By 1938, Great Britain raised the rate on American auto imports to 33.3 percent while the United States retained the 10 percent rate. The success of the auto industry during the war resulted in a recommendation by the Public Advisory Board for Mutual Security under President Harry S Truman for the elimination of all tariffs on automobiles since the well-established industry needed no further protection. Two years later, trade representatives met with Japanese officials and attempted to persuade them that the United States already dominated the auto industry and that Japan would want to focus on trading other types of products. The Japanese government did not agree. As the United States moved to lower the rate down to 8.5 percent in 1956, then to 6.5 percent after the Dillon Round, and finally to 3 percent *ad valorem* after the Kennedy Round, the Japanese invested heavily in automobile manufacturing facilities. Between 1968 and 1969, imports of foreign cars doubled and by 1974 foreign companies controlled over 15 percent of the U.S. market. As imports continued to rise, domestic producers petitioned the federal government to enforce the escape clause, citing injury to the industry. President Jimmy Carter asked the International Trade Commission to issue a ruling on the petition as quickly as possible, hoping to receive a decision before the November election. The final recommendation, issued by the ITC one week after the election, denied any injury to domestic manufacturers and stated that customer preferences for more fuel-efficient cars and general recession conditions accounted for the decline of domestic sales. In 1981, carmakers worked with Congress to arrange a voluntary reduction of imports from Japan.

See also: Escape clause; Great Britain; Great Depression; Hawley-Smoot Tariff (Tariff of 1930); Japan; Kennedy Round; Truman, Harry S.

Selected Bibliography:

Alfred E. Eckes, *Opening America's Market: U.S. Foreign Trade Policy Since 1776*, 1995.

Cynthia Clark Northrup

B

BAILEY, JOSEPH WELDON (October 6, 1863–April 13, 1929)

U.S. congressman and senator from Texas who supported the tariff for revenue only policy of the Democratic Party while striving to provide protective rates for manufacturers in his home state.

Born in Crystal Springs, Mississippi, and educated at the Universities of Mississippi and Virginia, Vanderbilt, and the Cumberland University (Tennessee) law school, Bailey practiced law in Hazelhurst, Mississippi, until the violent death of a prominent Republican during a political confrontation necessitated his resettlement to Gainesville, Texas, in 1885. Elected to Congress in 1890 on a platform of the free coinage of silver, tariff reduction, and the creation of a state railroad commission, he quickly gained a reputation as a master parliamentarian and powerful orator who utilized those skills to kill numerous private bills introduced by congressmen from both parties. Although breaking with President Grover Cleveland by advocating free silver and a federal income tax, Bailey nevertheless led the anti–William Jennings Bryan delegation from Texas to the Democratic National Convention in 1896.

Elected minority leader of the House in 1897, he led the fight against the extremely protectionist Dingley Tariff, and opposed the annexation of Hawaii, the Philippines, and Puerto Rico. Despite charges of using his influence to obtain a license for a Standard Oil–connected company convicted of antitrust violations in exchange for a loan, the Texas legislature elected Bailey to the U.S. Senate, at least partly because he branded the incumbent a high protectionist. During his first term, he concentrated on railroad regulation, helping to enact the Hepburn Rate Act in 1906. Even while developing a personal friendship with President William Howard Taft in 1909, he joined Democratic-Insurgent Republican opposition to the highly protectionist Payne-Aldrich Tariff and introduced a measure providing for a federal income tax that helped force Taft to propose the enactment of a corporation excise tax and the submission of what eventually became the Sixteenth Amendment. He broke with progressives of both parties in opposing the addition of raw materials, especially Texas-produced lumber, sugar, cotton, wool, and beef, to the free list. Styling himself as the "Last Democrat," and professing Jeffersonian principles of limited government, states' rights, and strict construction of the Constitution, Bailey became increasingly alienated from the reformist Democratic surge that elected Woodrow Wilson president in 1912. Upset with the Democratic endorsement of the recall provision in the proposed constitution of Arizona, Bailey declined to run for reelection in 1912, opened a private law practice in Washington, and lobbied Congress against Wilson's foreign policy, women's suffrage, and prohibition. After an unsuccessful try for the governorship of Texas in 1920, he opened a law practice in Dallas and distinguished himself as a vigorous opponent of the Ku Klux Klan, even though Bailey himself remained the state's most notorious race-baiter and fervid opponent of miscegenation. Dying "with his boots on," Bailey collapsed while making an argument during a trial in a Sherman, Texas, courtroom.

See also: Bryan, William Jennings; Cleveland, Stephen Grover; Dingley Tariff (Tariff of 1897); Insurgents; Personal income tax (Sixteenth Constitutional Amendment); Progressives; Taft, William Howard; Wilson, Thomas Woodrow.

Selected Bibliography:

Sam Hanna Acheson, *Joe Bailey: The Last Democrat*, 1932; Lewis L. Gould, *Progressives and Prohibitionists: Texas Democrats in the Wilson Era*, 1973.

John D. Buenker

BALANCE OF TRADE

Concern over the balance of trade originated with the mercantilist doctrine in the sixteenth and seventeenth centuries.

Although traditionally associated with English essayists and pamphleteers, early-modern mercantilism actually began with Spanish regulation of colonial trade in the Americas and Far East. Spain maintained its balance of trade through royal licenses and monopoly contracts for trade (*asientos*) and the organization of merchant guilds (*consulados*) that funneled luxury goods through a limited number of ports across the Spanish Empire (Seville and later Cadiz, Vera Cruz, and Acapulco in Mexico, Portobello in Panama, Lima in Peru, Manila in the Philippines, and Havana in Cuba). Such restrictions afforded an important degree of state oversight of international trade and collection of taxes and duties (tariffs) channeled by the state for purposes of war in Europe and defense of overseas possessions.

Lacking direct access to the silver-producing colonies of New Spain (Mexico) and Peru, English theorists such as Thomas Mun and William Petty adapted Spanish policy to English economic realities such as comparative poverty and backwardness. Their primary goal concerned the increased influx of precious metals and the reduction of their outflow, otherwise known as bullionism. To accomplish their task, English mercantilists advocated state intervention to control the flow of bullion and encourage international trade. Although the seventeenth-century civil wars limited state action, early legislation took some steps toward the control of bullion exports while later parliamentary action focused on trade itself by limiting or seeking to regulate the flow of goods on English ships and increasing the oversight of this flow for the purpose of taxation through the navigation acts.

By the end of the seventeenth century, the French, under the absolutist state of Louis XIV and his chief advisor, Jean Batiste Colbert, best articulated the mercantilist doctrine. Put simply, mercantilism promoted a trade in manufactured goods such as silk and cotton textiles produced by the mother country in exchange for raw materials such as sugar or indigo produced in colonies abroad. In this way, states were better able to monitor bullion flows by creating limited, tightly controlled spheres of exchange.

The next phase of the battle to control the balance of trade came in England with the advent of political economists from Bernard Mandeville through Adam Smith during the eighteenth century. They challenged the underpinnings of bullionist and mercantilist doctrine, favoring instead an emphasis on domestic productivity and development, even to the extent of using tariffs to protect nascent manufacturing sectors. To paraphrase Smith,

a country with a silver mine, such as Spain with Mexico and Peru, need not concern itself with local economic development while a country without access to such natural endowments had but one recourse: the industrious development of manufacturing and its domestic economy.

Although there is little to suggest that early political economy saw an answer to the problem of a negative balance of trade in such proposals, it is clear that the long-term implications of their advocacy remained decidedly positive. By eschewing bullionism and mercantilism, Smith and others refocused the policy debates surrounding trade. This in turn led to a shift to concerns about domestic prosperity through manufacture that created in England an example for industrialization and supremacy in production, emphasizing lower costs per unit produced. These notions carried the day in theoretical and political terms well into the nineteenth century. Competition for markets, determined by cost and quality, ultimately led to a reversal in the outflow of bullion as it did in England, for example, after the 1810s, and a positive balance of trade for its imitators.

In the United States the government experienced a negative balance of trade until the post–Civil War period. The age of high protectionism ushered in an era of trade surpluses that continued until the United States unilaterally cut tariff rates under the General Agreement on Tariffs and Trade (GATT). After the Kennedy Round, the surplus disappeared and the country has continued to operate under a trade deficit while encouraging other nations to reduce their trade barriers.

See also: General Agreement on Tariffs and Trade (GATT); Kennedy Round; Mercantilism; Navigation and Trade Acts; Smith, Adam.

Selected Bibliography:

Mark Blaug, *Economic Theory in Retrospect*, 1985; Charles Wilson, *England's Apprenticeship, 1603–1763*, 1965.

David J. Weiland III

BALDWIN, HENRY (January 14, 1780–April 21, 1844)

American legislator and jurist from western Pennsylvania who supported high tariffs, corporate interests, and unimpeded interstate commerce.

Born in New Haven, Connecticut, Baldwin graduated from Yale College in 1797 before moving to Philadelphia, where he studied law and joined the bar. In the rapidly emerging town of Pittsburgh he established a prominent law practice, jointly owned a newspaper, and co-owned a number of iron, textile, and woolen mills. Although Baldwin grew up a Federalist, he soon joined a faction of the Republican Party and engaged in local politics. The removal of double duties in the tariff schedule during the War of 1812 upset western Pennsylvania business interests. Not satisfied with the increased protection of the Tariff Act of 1816, leading businessmen sent Baldwin to Congress to argue for even higher tariffs.

Elected in 1816, Baldwin spent three terms in the House, and served as Chairman of the House Committee on Domestic Manufactures where his protectionist views met critical opposition from rural Jeffersonian interests. De-spite his support for southern congressmen on slavery issues, Baldwin failed to gain their backing for his protective tariff bill of 1820, which the Senate postponed by two votes. In 1822, poor health forced his resignation from Congress, but he later recovered and resumed an active role in local politics.

Baldwin became a strong supporter of Andrew Jackson, who rewarded him in 1830 with a nomination for treasury secretary. Jackson's vice president, John C. Calhoun, blocked the nomination because of Baldwin's strong protectionist views on trade policy. When Jackson nominated Baldwin to the U.S. Supreme Court, Calhoun and his supporters could only delay the nomination, but Baldwin finally received confirmation. He served fourteen years on the bench as a judicial moderate. While he sought to preserve states' rights and regarded slaves as private property, he also voted to uphold the constitutionality of unobstructed interstate commerce. Toward the end of his life he became mentally unstable and heavily in debt. He died of paralysis on April 21, 1844, at the age of sixty-four.

See also: Barbour, Philip Pendleton; Calhoun, John Caldwell; Clay, Henry; Jackson, Andrew; Protectionism; Tariff of 1818; Textiles; Tyler, John; Wool and woolens.

Selected Bibliography:

Henry Baldwin, *A General View of the Origin and Nature of the Constitution and Government of the United States*, 1837; Malcolm Rogers Eiselen, *The Rise of Pennsylvania Protectionism*, 1974; Frank Otto Gatell, "Henry Baldwin," *The Justices of the United States Supreme Court 1789–1969: Their Lives and Major Opinions*, 1969; Flavia M. Taylor,

"The Political and Civic Career of Henry Baldwin, 1799–1830," *Western Pennsylvania Historical Magazine*, 1941.

Artemus Ward

BARBOUR, PHILIP PENDLETON (May 25, 1783–February 25, 1841)

American legislator and jurist who argued for the principle of states' rights, state sovereignty, and free trade in the face of a growing national government and economy shielded by protective tariffs.

Born in Orange County, Virginia, to a politically active and well-connected plantation family, Barbour studied law in his home state at the College of William and Mary before beginning his legal career. He won election to the Virginia House of Delegates in 1812 and the U.S. House of Representatives in 1814. Through 1830, Barbour showed strong leadership among the Jeffersonian Republicans and later the Jacksonian Democrats in Congress arguing against such national policies as the protective tariff and the Bank of the United States. In 1820, his speech against legislative protectionism offered by western Pennsylvania protectionist Henry Baldwin pitted him against House Speaker Henry Clay. Barbour not only helped the bill go down to defeat by two votes in the Senate, he took over as Speaker of the House for two years from 1821 until 1823 before Henry Clay reclaimed the post. Barbour clashed with Clay over tariffs again in 1824 when he strenuously urged Congress to reject protectionist principles and challenged Clay to defend them. Clay responded with a speech that lasted over two days, es-pousing the merits of economic nationalism and "a genuine American System." Although Daniel Webster, Barbour, and others argued against it, in the end Clay marshaled enough support to win passage of the Tariff Act of 1824.

Jackson appointed Barbour to the U.S. Circuit Court in 1830. During the nullification crisis, Barbour assured the Jackson administration that Virginia would not follow South Carolina's lead in repudiating the president's unionist policies. Southerners touted Barbour as a possible vice-presidential candidate on Jackson's 1832 ticket, but Barbour stepped aside in favor of Martin Van Buren and Jackson rewarded him with a seat on the U.S. Supreme Court in 1836. Barbour helped shape a new constitutional era as John Marshall and other old-order nationalist judges finally relinquished control of the federal judiciary. On the bench, Justice Barbour continued his philosophy of state sovereignty, siding with the new chief justice Roger Taney and the majority in cases like *Charles River Bridge v. Warren Bridge* in 1837. After only five years on the Court, he died of a heart attack on February 25, 1841, at the age of fifty-seven.

See also: American System; Baldwin, Henry; Clay, Henry; Nullification; Tariff of 1824; Van Buren, Martin; Webster, Daniel.

Selected Bibliography:

P.P. Cynn, "Philip Pendleton Barbour," *John P. Branch Historical Papers of Randolph-Macon College*, 1913; Frank Otto Gatell, "Philip P. Barbour," *The Justices of the United States Supreme Court 1789–1969: Their Lives and Major Opinions*, 1969;

Charles D. Lowery, *James Barbour: A Jeffersonian Republican*, 1984.

Artemus Ward

BARUCH, BERNARD MANNES
(August 19, 1870–June 23, 1965)

American investor and presidential counselor.

As a conservative stockbroker, Baruch invested adventurously with his own money—buying stocks on 10 percent margin. In 1897, he invested in American Sugar Refining Company, an enterprise that became prosperous because a tariff barred foreign sugar. Baruch reasoned that a Senate bill to lower the duty would not pass. When Congress defeated the measure, Baruch realized a profit of $60,000 on an investment of $300.

Baruch made millions on Wall Street, although he occasionally suffered huge losses. By 1913, he served as a "progressive" New York Stock Exchange governor. Although against regulation, he did not strenuously oppose the incorporation of the exchange even after some had suggested that the change would dilute the discipline of the governors and bring regulation by the state of New York.

In 1910, after Baruch supported William Gaynor's mayoral candidacy, Gaynor made him a trustee of College of the City of New York. Although a Republican, Baruch went to the 1912 Democratic convention in support of Gaynor's presidential aspirations. During the ensuing campaign, Baruch met Woodrow Wilson, a low-tariff reform candidate. He sympathized with reform, and enthusiastically supported Wilson even though he held stock in the American Beet Sugar Company, an organization dependent on the high tariff. After Wilson's election, the company's stock price plummeted and some accused Baruch of stock manipulation, but he faced no charges.

Wilson made Baruch a member and then chairman of the War Industries Board. Baruch also served on the postwar Reparations Commission. While favoring wartime controls, he believed the postwar economy should encourage a free market and stated that "a just and continuing peace should include a just and equal access to the raw materials and manufacturing facilities of the world, thus eliminating preferential tariffs. No nation, including neutrals, should be permitted to enter into economic alliance, to the detriment of any other nations." Baruch thought that the U.S. government should lend to foreign governments sparingly, and only on the condition that they establish free trade.

Although ambivalent about the McNary-Haugen Bill of the 1920s, Baruch did help write the Democratic platform plank, calling for the "establishment of an export marketing corporation or commission in order that the exportable surplus may not establish the price of the whole crop." Manufacturers sold in a tariff-protected market, but farmers had to take an unprotected price for crops. The McNary-Haugen solution would broaden the tariff. Government would sell farm surpluses abroad, and farmers would finance the program by an equalization tax. Baruch endorsed higher commodity prices and the equalization tax, but opposed protectionism. Republican president Calvin Coolidge twice vetoed McNary-Haugen legislation.

Baruch suggested that he had abandoned the stock market when he entered public service, but he actively traded. He claimed that he foresaw the 1929 crash and sold his stocks. This presumed wisdom advanced his reputation as an insightful investor. Financial records indicate that he did not sell in time. After the crash, having the means to hang on, he waited.

Although Baruch preferred a more conservative candidate, he supported the election of Franklin D. Roosevelt, who later kept Baruch out of the cabinet and consulted him only sparingly. Still, Baruch gained a reputation of being "requisitioned by successive presidents." He privately opposed many New Deal reforms, but maintained White House access. During World War II, he served as chairman of the Rubber Committee that investigated alternative production processes and confronted gasoline rationing. Before the Baruch Report appeared, only 49 percent of the public supported gasoline rationing to conserve tires. After the report, support rose to 73 percent.

Baruch served as American delegate to the United Nations Atomic Energy Commission. His White House access lasted through the administration of President John F. Kennedy.

See also: Roosevelt, Franklin D.; Sugar; Wilson, Thomas Woodrow.

Selected Bibliography:

James Grant, *Bernard Baruch: The Adventures of a Wall Street Legend*, 1983.

Theo Edwin Maloy

BASTIAT, CLAUDE-FRÈDÈRIC (June 29, 1801–December 24, 1850)

A popular essayist in nineteenth-century France who wrote on behalf of economic freedom and free trade.

Born near Bayonne in 1801, Bastiat became a liberal through studying Adam Smith and Jean-Baptiste Say as a young man. After years of little or no interest in his work, he established himself as a serious economic writer and thinker with an 1844 article in the prestigious *Journal des economistes* on the effects of tariffs in England and France. As a result of this article, Bastiat also struck up a correspondence with Richard Cobden of Britain's Anti-Corn Law League that continued until his death. In 1846, he established the Association for Free Trade, promoting his antiprotectionist views in the association's journal, *Le Libre-Èchange*. He went on to spearhead a national free trade league of his own in France, and served as deputy to the Constituent and Legislative Assemblies of 1848. Since he died in Rome on December 24, 1850, his reputation as a writer rests on only six years of work.

Bastiat often noted the negative economic repercussions suffered by ordinary people because of a regime of high tariffs, but ultimately he focused on an argument of morality: free trade remained a supremely moral policy and the only one liable to promote peace and freedom.

He took delight in refuting what he considered the fallacies of protectionist thinking. In his satirical piece in the form of an open letter to the Chamber of Deputies, he complained of the "ruinous competition of a foreign rival"—the sun's gratuitous light. He asked that in retaliation the French government order citizens to close all windows, drapes, and shutters. What industry would not be stimulated by this protection of the domestic lighting industry? The need for more candles means more livestock; more whale oil means a better shipping industry. In short, he wrote in a commentary on his own absurd example, when a product can be produced abroad more cheaply than at home, the difference is a "gratuitous gift" showered upon France, and it makes no more sense to reject this gift than it would to reject the sun.

Bastiat's influence in the United States reached considerable heights. Businessman and popular economic writer Edward Atkinson, according to his biographer, converted to the principle of free trade through the study of Bastiat and Adam Smith. Perhaps greater still, Bastiat influenced Henry Hazlitt, a free-market economist and *New York Times* editorial writer of the 1940s. Hazlitt explained in the introduction to his book *Economics in One Lesson* published in 1946, a libertarian classic still in print, that he took his inspiration from Bastiat's fundamental insights to assert his arguments for free trade and free markets. The libertarian Foundation for Economic Education in Irvington-on-Hudson, New York, founded in 1946, continues to publish and distribute Bastiat's work as an outstanding overview of classical liberal thought.

See also: Atkinson, Edward; Free trade; Say, Jean-Baptiste; Smith, Adam.

Selected Bibliography:

George Charles Roche III, *Frederic Bastiat: A Man Alone*, 1971.

Thomas E. Woods, Jr.

BEECHER, HENRY WARD (June 24, 1813–March 8, 1887)

Liberal Congregational minister known for his exceptional oratorical skills.

One of thirteen children of the prominent Protestant clergyman Lyman Beecher, Henry Ward Beecher became as well known and highly regarded as his prominent sister Harriet Beecher Stowe. A stern Christian moralist gifted with a silver tongue and a flair for the dramatic, in the 1850s he developed into the most renowned and influential clergyman in the country. As the minister of the Plymouth Congregationalist Church in Brooklyn, New York, he preached to the largest congregation in the country. At the time of Beecher's arrival there, Brooklyn had just begun a tremendous population explosion that would, in less than two decades, swell from 30,000 to 295,000 inhabitants, making it the third largest city in the country. The dynamism of Henry Ward Beecher flourished in Brooklyn. In 1848, to dramatize the evils of slavery, Beecher turned his pulpit into a mock slave market. Affecting the appearance and voice of a southern slave auctioneer, he demonstrated, in caricature, the inhumanity and callousness of a process that treated human beings exactly as a farm animal would be treated on the auction block. The effect proved electric. People shouted and cried and opened their pocketbooks in support of his causes. His ability to arouse the middle-class morality of his large congregation led to the raising of large sums of money that Beecher used for purchasing the freedom of slaves. But perhaps his best known act as an antislavery leader came in the aftermath of the Kansas-Nebraska Act. Beecher led an effort in his own church to purchase Sharp's rifles for the free-soil settlers in Kansas, referring to the guns as a "truly moral agency" with more power than a hundred Bibles. For this well-publicized effort, Sharp's rifles became known in the North as "Beecher's Bibles" and Plymouth Church as "the Church of the Holy Rifles."

During the Civil War, Beecher traveled to England and spoke to crowds that had displayed hostility toward him at first. The British reacted initially to his much-publicized remarks during the *Trent* crisis in 1861, when Union naval forces had seized Confederate commissioners from a British mail ship transporting them to England. Beecher had said, "the best blood of England must be shed to atone for the *Trent* affair." But despite the hostile reception, Beecher demonstrated much pluck and aplomb, tossing aside the pages of his prepared speech and spending the next several hours addressing the individual shouts and taunts from the crowd, and in the process winning them over. Minister to Britain Charles Francis Adams and others credited Beecher for having done much to weaken British support for the Confederacy. After the Civil War he continued as pastor of the Plymouth Church, advocated political reform, fought for women's suffrage, and supported free trade. Beecher spoke out against protectionism, arguing that high tariffs violated the principles of liberty, making it anti-

Christian and immoral. Accusations of adultery committed with the wives of several important members of his congregation, one of them prominent antislavery leader Theodore Tilton, clouded the last years of his life. The charges resulted in a hearing before church authorities and a hung jury in a civil trial. The star that had shone so brightly for most of his life, now tainted by suspicion and doubt, died in 1887.

See also: Adams, Charles Francis; Civil War (American); Slavery.

Selected Bibliography:

Lyman Abbott, *Henry Ward Beecher*, 1980.

David E. Long

BELLAMY, EDWARD (March 26, 1850– May 22, 1898)

Journalist, novelist, and utopian socialist of the late nineteenth century whose most famous work, *Looking Backward 2000–1887*, imagined a society in which a national syndicate controlled all the means of production and enforced absolute economic equality; he served as a source of inspiration for several generations of reformers.

Born in Chicopee Falls, Massachusetts, he attended Union College, studied law, and, in 1880, he both founded the *Springfield* (Massachusetts) *Daily News* and wrote his first novel, *Dr. Heidenhoff's Process*. Increasingly agitated by the adverse effects of rapid, massive industrialization, Bellamy believed that nothing short of collective ownership and absolute economic equality would eliminate poverty, social injustice, and industrial strife. In *Looking Backward*,

Bellamy's protagonist, Julian West, falls asleep in 1887 and awakens in the year 2000 to find all of the nation's economic resources under the control of a single national syndicate, which manages the four "armies" of industrial workers, professionals, women, and invalids, all of whom share equally in the economy's benefits. With the economy thus run according to scientific, rational, and humanitarian principles, and people freed from the fear of want, everyone works for the honor derived from service to the community. This remarkable transformation has occurred through a "triumph of common sense," a peaceful evolution from capitalism to socialism.

Translated into several languages, *Looking Backward* became an instant best-seller, fostered the proliferation of Bellamy Nationalist Clubs, and spawned a monthly journal, *The Nationalist*, and a weekly magazine, *New Nation*, all of which advocated nationalization of industry and redistribution of wealth. Although the Nationalist Movement ended quickly, such otherwise diverse social critics as the People's Party, Charles Beard, John Dewey, Thorstein Veblen, William Allen White, Mark Twain, Norman Thomas, and Adolph A. Berle Jr. all paid homage to Bellamy's profound influence.

Since he envisioned a world of self-sufficient industrial democracies, each producing only what its own population needed, he believed that international trade would virtually disappear, with each country importing only those few essential products unavailable internally. The perennial acrimonious argument between free traders and tariff protectionists would become obsolete, the use of foreign markets as "dumping grounds" for surplus production would cease, and people all over the world would enjoy a uniformly high standard of living. What little trade existed among nations that survived would be carefully regulated by an International Council, which would inspect all goods exchanged, establish policies toward "backward" countries, make sure that no product sold abroad for more than its domestic price, and supervise the settling of accounts among nations.

See also: Twain, Mark.

Selected Bibliography:

Sylvia E. Bowman, *The Year 2000: A Critical Biography of Edward Bellamy*, 1958; Arthur E. Morgan, *Edward Bellamy*, 1944; John L. Thomas, *Alternative America: Henry George, Edward Bellamy, Henry Demarest Lloyd and the Adversary Tradition*, 1983.

John D. Buenker

BENTON, THOMAS HART (March 14, 1782–April 10, 1858)

American writer, U.S. representative, and senator from Missouri who advocated a strong protectionist position.

Born near Hillsborough, North Carolina, in 1782, Benton attended Chapel Hill College before receiving his law degree from William and Mary College. Admitted to the bar in Nashville, Tennessee, in 1806, Benton practiced law until 1811, when he became aide-de-camp to General Andrew Jackson. After the War of 1812 ended, Benton moved to Missouri, practiced law, and edited the *Missouri Inquirer* until elected to the U.S. Senate in 1821, when Missouri became a state. He served in the Senate until 1850. During the debate over the tariff of 1828, Benton argued for a total restriction on the importation of wool. Although Benton consistently maintained a strong protectionist stance on the tariff issue, he proposed an amendment prohibiting the use of foreign wool designed to make the tariff legislation detestable and thereby ensuring its defeat. The political ploy of using the tariff against President John Quincy Adams, and to advance the presidential ambitions of Jackson, resulted in the passage of the Tariff of Abominations. Senator Benton also authored an unsuccessful resolution to expunge the Senate resolution censuring Andrew Jackson.

After losing his Senate reelection bid in 1850, Benton returned to Missouri and voters elected him to the U.S. House of Representatives, where he served from March 4, 1853, to March 3, 1855. In 1856, he unsuccessfully ran for governor of Missouri before returning to the nation's capital where he pursued his literary interests. Benton died in Washington, D.C., on April 10, 1858, with interment in Bellefontaine Cemetery in St. Louis, Missouri.

See also: Jackson, Andrew; Jacksonianism; Tariff of 1828 (Tariff of Abominations); Wool and woolens.

Selected Bibliography:

Edward Stanwood, *American Tariff Controversies in the Nineteenth Century*, 1967.

Cynthia Clark Northrup

BEVERIDGE, ALBERT JEREMIAH (October 6, 1862–April 27, 1927)

American senator known as one of the strongest advocates of militant impe-

rial expansion during the pre–World War I era.

Born in Highland County, Ohio, Beveridge graduated from DePauw University in 1885. After gaining admission to the bar in 1887, he became involved in Republican Party politics in Indiana. Depicting the Spanish-American-Cuban-Filipino War as a divinely bestowed opportunity to spread American commercial supremacy, he won election to the U.S. Senate in 1898.

In the Senate, he championed U.S. acquisition of Cuba and the Philippines. He also advocated total U.S. dominance of the Caribbean. He justified American supremacy and expansion with three arguments. The first focused on racial theories. In his famous speech, "America's Destiny" in 1900, he proposed that God chose the American nation to "lead in the regeneration of the world." Second, he believed that the United States should expand for the purpose of disposing its surplus domestic production, and, finally, he believed in the need for expansion as a matter of national defense. Although not interested in the spread of U.S. democratic ideals, he promoted the opening of new American markets, or what he termed "commercial extensions of the Republic." Adhering to a Darwinian view of international relations, he argued that since the European market remained well supplied, the United States must turn to the Far East, primarily China, to market its goods. His work, *The Russian Advance*, published in 1903, reveals his focus on economic imperialism. In it he accepts and even admires Russian autocracy as a legitimate way of providing stability. But to ensure U.S. stability, he encouraged the development of a strong navy that would serve not as a conqueror, but as a protector of overseas markets and commerce.

Because of a rift with the administration of William Howard Taft, Beveridge lost his Senate seat in 1911. Despite joining Theodore Roosevelt and other Progressives and, later, returning to the Republican fold, he would never again win election to public office. When World War I broke out, he argued in favor of U.S. neutrality on the grounds that the United States should not entangle itself in conflicts that do not serve its own interests. During the war, he visited the belligerent countries in Europe where a romantic sense of battle captivated him. In the manner of nineteenth-century nationalists, he wrote, "Peace is a Heavenly thing, but the brain grows fat and the soul small in the midst of its comfortable and selfish routine." At the end of the war his nationalism and Anglophobia emerged as he vehemently opposed U.S. entry into the League of Nations.

After the war he continued to write primarily historical and biographical works, including *What Is the Back of War*, *The State of the Nation*, and biographies of John Marshall and Abraham Lincoln. Beveridge died of heart disease on April 27, 1927, in Indianapolis.

See also: Cuba; Progressives; Roosevelt, Theodore; Taft, William Howard.

Selected Bibliography:

John Braeman, *Albert J. Beveridge: American Nationalist*, 1971; John A. Thompson, "An Imperialist and the First World War: The Case of Albert J. Beveridge," *Journal of American Studies*, 1971.

Christopher Ohan

BLAINE, JAMES GILLESPIE (January 31, 1830–January 27, 1893)

Republican politician from Maine known for his ardent support of protective tariffs and trade expansion, for his rise as Speaker of the House of Representatives, and as secretary of the State Department.

Born and raised in West Brownsville, Pennsylvania, Blaine graduated from Washington (and Jefferson) College at the age of seventeen. He began his adult life as a teacher at a small military school in Kentucky, but after marrying Harriet Stanwood in 1850, he relocated to Philadelphia to teach at an institute for the blind. Four years later he moved to Augusta, Maine, where he left teaching for journalism. He became coeditor and part owner of the *Kennebec Journal* and through this association became increasingly interested and active in politics.

A devotee of Henry Clay, Blaine supported the Whig Party. He backed fully Clay's designs for an American System that promoted federal aid for railroad development and other internal improvements as well as governmental protection of commerce through high tariffs. His fervent opposition to the western expansion of slavery led him to participate in the founding of a new political organization, the Republican Party. In 1856, he served as a Maine delegate to the first Republican National Convention, and soon after became an admirer of Abraham Lincoln. Blaine took up the political cause full time in 1858 when he won election to the State House of Representatives in Maine under the Republican banner. Reelected three times, he served as Speaker from 1861 to 1862.

In the midst of the Civil War, the charismatic Blaine, only thirty-two, won election to the U.S. House of Representatives. He labored there for a dozen years, steadily accumulating power and wielding influence. During the war, he remained a Lincoln loyalist, supporting the circulation of greenbacks, the subsidization of the transcontinental railroad, and the administration of taxes on exports to pay war debts. Throughout Reconstruction, he proved a moderate politician, although siding with radical Republicans on the abolition of slavery, the enfranchisement of blacks, and the impeachment of Andrew Johnson. Blaine advocated protectionism for the benefit of U.S. industries and actively promoted the cultivation of foreign markets for surplus American products. In 1869, his fellow congressmen elected him Speaker of the House, a position he managed successfully until the Democrats reclaimed the majority six years later.

Maine's governor plucked Blaine from the lower chamber in July 1876 and appointed him to the state's open U.S. Senate seat. A few months later, the state legislature granted him a full, six-year term. As Maine's junior senator, he concentrated on nationalist economic policies such as enlarging the merchant marine, excluding Chinese labor, returning to hard currency, and maintaining high tariffs. When the Republican Party divided into duel factions—the Stalwarts, who supported the political resurrection of former president Ulysses S. Grant, and the opposing "Half Breeds," Blaine emerged as the leader and presumptive presidential nominee of the anti-Grant forces. Unable to carry the nomination

at the 1880 Republican convention, he threw his support to Ohio's James A. Garfield, who managed a narrow victory in the November election.

Garfield selected his close friend from Maine to serve as secretary of the state. Together, the men pursued an aggressive foreign policy to expand U.S. political and economic influence in Latin America and the Pacific. But Garfield's assassination in July 1881 led to the resignation of Blaine, who, after more than two decades of public service, retired to write his multi-volume memoir, *Twenty Years of Congress: From Lincoln to Garfield*. Blaine returned to the political stage during the 1884 Republican convention where he won the presidential nomination over the unpopular incumbent Chester A. Arthur. But allegations of political corruption, the defection of reform-minded "mugwump" Republicans, and the Democratic candidacy of Grover Cleveland combined to halt his comeback bid. Consequently, he returned to private life, spending considerable time in Europe. Politics beckoned once more in 1887 when President Cleveland called for a drastic reduction in American tariffs. Blaine responded immediately from Paris by publishing in U.S. newspapers a vigorous defense of protectionism, arguing that high duties benefited farmers, laborers, and businessmen alike. Sensing a winning issue for the Republican Party, he successfully pushed for the presidential nomination of his friend, Benjamin Harrison of Indiana.

Blaine returned to America to campaign for Harrison, who captured the White House and reappointed his Maine benefactor as secretary of state. The two Republicans chartered an ambitious foreign policy course to expand U.S. power in the Pacific, the Caribbean, and Central and South America. In late 1889, Blaine organized and presided over the First International Conference of the American States, the forerunner to the Organization of American States. The next year, he supported passage of the McKinley Tariff, which greatly increased import duties. He and the president had insisted that the tariff act include a commercial reciprocity amendment that permitted them to negotiate separate bilateral trade pacts. In the end, the administration concluded a series of reciprocity treaties with Latin American nations, including Cuba, Puerto Rico, Brazil, Honduras, and Nicaragua.

With his health in serious decline and his relationship with Harrison deteriorating, Blaine abruptly resigned in June 1892. He died in Washington, D.C., less than a year later. Probably the most popular and influential Republican of the Gilded Age, Blaine's most enduring legacy remains his vision for an informal American empire, especially the displacement of Great Britain as the dominant power in the Western Hemisphere. His plans for American greatness depended in large part on the economic policy of protectionism and the selective application of trade reciprocity.

See also: American System; Civil War (American); Clay, Henry; Cuba; Garfield, James A.; Latin America; Lincoln, Abraham; McKinley Tariff (Tariff of 1890); Organization of American States (OAS); Protectionism; Reconstruction; Republican Party; Slavery; Whig Party.

Selected Bibliography:

Edward P. Crapol, *James G. Blaine: Architect of Empire*, 2000; H. Wayne Morgan, *From Hayes to McKinley: National Party Politics, 1877–1896*, 1969; David S. Muzzey, *James G. Blaine: A Political Idol of Other Days*, 1934; Tom E. Terrill, *The Tariff, Politics, and American Foreign Policy, 1874–1901*, 1973.

Jeffrey J. Matthews

BOARD OF GENERAL APPRAISERS

Established on June 10, 1890, the Board of General Appraisers exercised authority over cases concerning U.S. tariff acts.

Prior to its creation, jurisdiction over import duties rested with the U.S. District and Circuit Courts. The Board of General Appraisers established the value of items entering the United States for taxation purposes. On May 28, 1926, the U.S. Customs Court replaced the Board of General Appraisers. On October 10, 1980, Congress changed the name again to the U.S. Court of International Trade and, like its predecessors, it hears and decides cases involving civil lawsuits relating to tariff issues and exercises final authority over eligibility for adjustment assistance under the Trade Act of 1974. It also oversees the recovery of custom duties or bonds by petitioning companies.

See also: Trade Act of 1974.

Selected Bibliography:

Alfred E. Eckes, *Opening America's Market: U.S. Foreign Trade Policy Since 1776*, 1995.

Cynthia Clark Northrup

BOLIVIA

The site of the largest concentration of silver exploited in human history.

Potosi in Bolivia, known as Spanish colonial Upper Peru, produced between three and ten times the volume of silver to that of Mexico between 1150 and 1650. As a result, Potosi and Bolivia served as the foundations of Spanish imperial finance and European trade with Asia for nearly a century.

Tightly controlled within the emerging Spanish mercantile system, colonial Bolivia provided an important source of revenue in a crucial era. The enormous wealth of the area created an opportunity for corruption and fraud. By the early seventeenth century, Upper Peru had become synonymous with all the ills of Spanish colonialism in the Americas. Contemporaries noted that the viceroy in Lima, the colonial capital of all Peru, who did not enrich himself while in office proved a fool. They argued that he must be too honest, too stupid, or a bit of both. Such administrative difficulties did not prevent "the mountain of silver" from becoming the envy of the Western world.

The enormous and rapid influx of Bolivian silver onto the international stage during the late sixteenth century compelled the writings of the "bullionists" and "mercantilists" of England and France, Spain's competitors for western European hegemony, to consider alternative paths to power. Although unaware that Bolivian silver production had already begun to decline, perhaps as early as the 1610s, the writings of Thomas Mun and William Petty influenced their generation. The challenge of the silver-backed preeminence of Spain had already initiated a series of debates that led Spain's rivals down very different paths to prosperity. These alternative notions shaped the acquisition and development of other colonies and resources that eventually sparked the Industrial Revolution.

During modern times, Bolivia has exported a large amount of lead and zinc. In 1954, U.S. tariff commissioners investigated charges that foreign imports of the metals from Bolivia, Mexico, Peru, and Canada seriously harmed American producers. The State Department persuaded the Eisenhower administration to reject the recommendation to ensure regional solidarity and prevent the spread of Communism into these countries in the Western Hemisphere.

See also: Industrial Revolution; Silver; Tin ore.

Selected Bibliography:

Peter John Bakewell, *Miners of the Red Mountain: Indian Labor in Potosí, 1545–1650*, 1984; Enrique Tandeter, *Coercion and Market: Silver Mining in Colonial Potosí, 1692–1826*, 1993.

David J. Weiland III

BORAH, WILLIAM EDGAR (June 29, 1865–January 19, 1940)

U.S. senator from Idaho known for heading the Senate Foreign Relations Committee and for opposing reciprocal trade because he thought that it sacrificed the interests of farmers to those of the manufacturers.

Born in Fairfield, Illinois, Borah attended the University of Kansas, but left without a degree because he contracted tuberculosis. After reading law in the office of his brother-in-law, he practiced in Lyons, Kansas, before settling in Boise, Idaho, in 1890. He gained some success as a trial lawyer, but his work became primarily that of attorney for some of the largest corporations in Idaho. At the time of his election to the Senate, he probably had the most lucrative law practice in the state, but gave it up due to the demands of public service.

A Republican with Populist leanings, Borah entered the Senate in 1906. His first significant political contribution came when he opposed the reciprocal trade agreements with Canada proposed by the Taft administration. Borah accused business interests of favoring reciprocity in order to fatten their own profits while subjecting farmers to the competition of cheap imported produce. He argued, as he would again against the Reciprocal Trade Agreements Bill of 1934, that reciprocity unconstitutionally delegated congressional powers to the chief executive. Outspoken and independent, Borah became increasingly involved with foreign affairs and, in 1913, gained a place on the Committee on Foreign Relations. Firmly committed to neutrality, Borah fought the League of Nations, opposed interference in Latin America, and advocated having as little as possible to do politically with Europe. He persistently stressed the importance of foreign markets, but not to the point of American military involvement. In December 1923, Borah proposed an international economic conference that would deal with the means of restoring international trade and sound financial conditions in the post–World War I world, but the idea never got off the ground.

For sixteen years, he campaigned for the recognition of Soviet Russia, arguing that the United States would benefit economically from a resumption of commercial relations. His belated victory came under Franklin Roosevelt in 1933, by which time Borah's golden age had drawn to a close. During the 1936 and 1937 debates over the "cash and carry" attempt to circumvent the danger of wartime trade by having belligerents take immediate control of the American goods they purchased, Borah's warnings of military retaliation by belligerents against traders went unheeded. When Roosevelt declined to invoke an impartial embargo against warring Japan and China in 1937 by refusing to find a state of war, Borah supported him because the president had acted in the interests of peace. In October 1939, he lost the fight with Roosevelt over the removal of an embargo on arms. A few months later, on January 19, 1940, Borah succumbed to a cerebral hemorrhage in Washington, D.C. Throughout his years in office, Borah's reputation rested on his ability to obstruct the policies of others. More of a debater than a leader, Borah professed his yearning for international cooperation, yet opposed every serious effort to bring it about.

See also: Latin America; Reciprocal Trade Agreements Act (RTAA); Roosevelt, Franklin D.

Selected Bibliography:

Claudius O. Johnson, *Borah of Idaho*, 1936; Robert James Maddox, *William E. Borah and American Foreign Policy*, 1969.

Caryn E. Neumann

BOSTON HOME MARKET CLUB

Founded in April 1887 as a protectionist lobbying group that opposed the reduction of the tariff proposed by President Grover Cleveland.

During the debate over the lowering of tariff rates in the late 1880s, the Democratic platform advocated a general reduction. Lobbying groups such as the American Protective Tariff League and the American Iron and Steel Association formed to oppose Cleveland and his economic proposals. The Boston Home Market Club, founded by George F. Draper, a Massachusetts textile manufacturer, focused its efforts on educating the public through the distribution of pamphlets and cartoons. The organization's motto proclaimed the benefits of "American wages . . . American markets . . . and American homes." Members decried the position of free traders by arguing that their philosophy opened up American markets and destroyed American jobs. The club experienced some success in getting its message to the public.

See also: American Iron and Steel Institute (AISI); American Protective Tariff League (APTL).

Selected Bibliography:

Joanne Reitano, *The Tariff Question in the Gilded Age: The Great Debate of 1888*, 1994.

Cynthia Clark Northrup

BOWKER, RICHARD ROGERS
(September 4, 1848–November 12, 1933)

American editor and publisher who served as the head of the tariff reform organizations in New York from 1883 through the first decade of the twentieth century.

Born in Salem, Massachusetts, Bowker graduated from City College in New York City before pursuing a literary career. He worked for both the *New York Evening Mail* and the *New York Tribune*. He published several bibliographic works, including the *Library Journal*, the *Annual Library Index*, the *American Catalog*, and *Publishers Weekly*. He also authored several books on copyright history, law, and literature. Bowker actively participated in the politics of the day, helping to form the Independent Republican Party, also called the mugwumps, in 1879 in opposition to the Republican nomination of James Blaine for president.

When President Grover Cleveland proposed the reduction of the tariff, Bowker joined many others in creating reform organizations. The various groups, centered primarily in the Northeast, advocated a modified form of free trade. Acknowledging the need for limited government involvement, Bowker wrote four books for the American public that discussed the desirability of other forms of taxation such as land, inheritance, corporate, and personal income taxes. Bowker and his associates attempted to pave a middle course during the tariff debate of the 1880s. Instead of an extremely high or low tariff rate, the reformers sought a moderate duty with government revenue augmented by funds derived from other forms of taxation. After a long and important career, Bowker died on November 12, 1933, in Stockbridge, Massachusetts.

See also: Cleveland, Stephen Grover; Newspapers and media; Taxation.

Selected Bibliography:

Joanne Reitano, *The Tariff Question in the Gilded Age: The Great Debate of 1888*, 1994.

Cynthia Clark Northrup

BOXER REBELLION

A Chinese movement that sought to expel all foreigners from China.

The defeat of China by Japan in 1894 led to Emperor Kuang-hsu's 1898 attempt to reform China along Western lines. The Hundred Days Reform attempted to bring provincial governments under control while creating a Western educational system and utilizing Western industrial techniques. But the emperor lacked the support of the military commanders who resisted the attempt at reform. The Boxer Rebellion, part of this reaction to reform, began through the actions of a group, the Righteous and Harmonious Fists, who practiced an ancient boxing art. The band, which believed its fighting style protected them from harm, challenged Chinese converts to Christianity and foreign missionaries. It soon developed into a movement to destroy all things foreign. By 1900, the Boxers had killed numerous Chinese converts and foreigners in North China and worked to rid China of all foreigners. The Chinese market proved too important to various European nations as well as the United States, so they sent in naval detachments that caused the Boxers to declare war. The Boxers laid siege to Peking, but on August 14, 1900, the foreign armies started to flow in and quickly put down the rebellion. China received unfavorable terms in the peace negotiations, including more trade concessions and indemnity payments. Because of the 1899 announcement by the United States of its Open Door Policy that sought to open markets dominated by foreign imperial powers within China, the country avoided division by the imperial powers. The issue of free trade, and the elimination of trade barriers imposed on China by the Western Powers, ensured the continuation of China's sovereignty.

See also: Imperialism; Open Door Notes.

Selected Bibliography:

Diane Preston, *The Boxer Rebellion: The Dramatic Story of China's War on Foreigners That Shook the World in the Summer of 1900*, 2000.

Ty M. Reese

BRECKINRIDGE, CLIFTON R. (November 22, 1846–December 3, 1932)

U.S. congressman from Arkansas who served during the great tariff debate of 1888 and sought to destroy the trusts that benefited from high protective trade measures.

Born near Lexington, Kentucky, in 1846, Breckinridge served in the Confederate Navy during the Civil War before attending Washington College (now Washington and Lee University). After his graduation, he settled down in Arkansas and, for the next thirteen years, farmed cotton. In 1882, the people of Arkansas elected him to Congress, where he remained until 1894.

An opponent of big business and trusts, Breckinridge introduced six antitrust bills into Congress during the 1888 presidential campaign. During this election the candidates, Democrat Grover Cleveland and Republican James G. Blaine, focused on the tariff as a major issue. Cleveland vowed to lower the tariff because it hurt the farmer and average American while lining the pockets of giant corporations. Blaine argued that the federal government could not regulate trusts because they remained under the authority of the states, making them private affairs. In response to this position Breckinridge introduced his bills. The debate of 1888 polarized Congress and cost Cleveland the election. The Republicans regained control of the White House.

After retiring from Congress in 1894, Cleveland appointed Breckinridge minister to Russia and he remained there until 1897 when he returned to Arkansas. Between 1900 and 1905, he served as a member of the Dawes Commission and then participated in the banking industry until he moved back to Kentucky where he died on December 3, 1932, with interment in Lexington Cemetery.

See also: Blaine, James Gillespie; Cleveland, Stephen Grover; Trusts.

Selected Bibliography:

Joanne Reitano, *The Tariff Question in the Gilded Age: The Great Debate of 1888*, 1994.

Cynthia Clark Northrup

BRECKINRIDGE, WILLIAM CHARLES PRESTON (August 28, 1837–November 19, 1904)

Five-term Kentucky Democrat in the U.S. House of Representatives, he served as a spokesman for free trade, particularly advocating lowering the tariffs on agriculture-related items.

Born in Baltimore, Maryland, Breckinridge received a B.A. degree from Centre College in Danville, Kentucky, and graduated from the law department of the University of Louisville in 1857. A passionate believer in the idea that all Americans enjoyed equal opportunities, he argued that government favoritism gave the wealthiest and "most powerful combinations in the land" an advantage that prevented the exercise of equal access. In his mind, the protective tariff represented the ultimate evil that would strangle economic growth, and he fought the McKinley and Wilson Tariffs, arguing that they would have a particularly deleterious effect on the American worker. His most memorable speeches attacked the protectionism imposed by these two taxes and centered on the argument that manufacturers defined the tariff schedules. He maintained that the resulting economic system punished the poor by establishing rates of 78 percent on items that they consumed every day, whereas luxury items, used by the wealthy, often bore rates as low as 5 percent.

Shortly before his reelection bid in 1894, Breckinridge became a party to a breach-of-contract marriage suit by Madeline Pollard, which helped make his campaign the most widely reported congressional race in the late nineteenth century. Breckinridge narrowly lost to Will Owen, ending the political career of the silver-tongued orator, one of the most articulate Democratic members in the House, and one of the most ardent opponents of protective tariff.

He died in Lexington, Kentucky, and was interred in Lexington Cemetery.

See also: McKinley Tariff (Tariff of 1890); Protectionism; Wilson-Gorman Tariff (Tariff of 1894).

Selected Bibliography:

James C. Klotter, *The Breckinridges of Kentucky, 1760–1981*, 1986.

Glynn Ingram

BRETTON WOODS CONFERENCE

Conference held in Bretton Woods, New Hampshire, in July 1944 to determine postwar economic arrangements.

Convening during World War II and attended by representatives from forty-four countries, the primary objectives of the attendees included the establishment of the International Bank for Reconstruction and Development, known as the World Bank, and the International Monetary Fund (IMF). The World Bank, created to provide access to long-term financing for countries in urgent need of funds for capital expenditures, and the IMF, designed to facilitate short-term loans due to trade imbalances, formed the core of the postwar world economic system. Although nations attending the conference recognized that tariff and trade barriers would continue to exist during the postwar period, the participants

agreed that the discriminatory practices must end to ensure a stable international financial situation that could help prevent future wars. The World Bank, formed in 1945, and the IMF, founded in 1946, continue to work together to alleviate both short- and long-term financial difficulties for nations around the world.

See also: Free trade; General Agreement on Tariffs and Trade (GATT); World War II.

Selected Bibliography:

Georg Schild, *Bretton Woods and Dumbarton Oaks: American Economic and Political Postwar Planning in the Summer of 1944*, 1995.

Cynthia Clark Northrup

BRYAN, WILLIAM JENNINGS (March 19, 1860–July 26, 1925)

Democratic Party leader at the turn of the twentieth century who vigorously opposed protective tariffs.

Born in Salem, Illinois, in 1860, Bryan made a name for himself as a young congressman from Nebraska. Elected to the House of Representatives in 1890, Bryan shared the concerns and prejudices of his region. He opposed the tariff because it raised rates on goods and materials purchased by the citizens of the West. A devout Christian, Bryan saw the tariff issue in stark moral terms: it remained a sinful curse against the agricultural state, protecting a wealthy manufacturing elite at the expense of the poor and the farming class. The year 1890 proved auspicious for the issue of protection because the McKinley Tariff passed by Congress raised duties on manufactured goods to an average of nearly 50 percent. Bryan recognized that to become a serious figure in the Democratic Party he must educate himself on the tariff question. He spent so much time studying the history of the tariff in America that he tried to entice the New York publisher G.P. Putnam and Sons to publish a book he considered writing on tariff reform.

In 1896, Bryan won his party's nomination for the presidency and opposed Ohio senator William McKinley for the office. Bryan, whose nickname "The Commoner" denoted his humble background, campaigned on two major issues: a downward revision of the tariff and the promotion of free silver (bimetallism) in contrast to the gold standard favored by bankers, industrialists, and the Republican Party. Bryan and his supporters linked both issues, believing that by enlarging the money supply with the coining of silver and lowering tariff rates the nation's producers, farmers and factory workers, would escape the grip of a deflationary financial system that appeared designed to keep them in debt. Aside from these issues, Bryan also supported the abolition of monopolies, the right of Congress to prohibit land ownership by nonresidents (absentee landlords), the popular elections of senators, and the Australian (secret) ballot. Industrialists believed Bryan's populist appeal to the people endangered the economic system that the major trusts had created in the wake of the Civil War and they joined with the Republican Party to ensure his defeat through lavish spending on McKinley's campaign. Bryan's defeat in the election, along with defeats against McKinley in 1900 and William Howard

Taft in 1908, made him the second American to lose three presidential bids, with Henry Clay also holding that distinction.

Despite his failure in national politics, Bryan remained a regional power and in 1912 helped Woodrow Wilson win the White House by supporting Wilson in the West. For his efforts Wilson rewarded him by nominating him as secretary of state. Bryan, a pacifist and isolationist, advocated a policy of collective arbitration to ensure the prevention of wars through the mediation of international disputes. He successfully lobbied thirty-one nations to agree that a one-year "cooling-off" period between rival nations would allow time for an international commission to investigate and settle disputed questions. Bryan's efforts ended with the onset of World War I. When President Wilson sent a stiff note to Germany in protest of the sinking of the British passenger liner *Lusitania* with Americans aboard, Bryan resigned. The former secretary believed Wilson's actions failed to keep America neutral, but rather favored the British over the Germans. Further, Bryan's base of support in Nebraska remained heavily isolationist and consisted of many Americans of German dissent. Bryan viewed the British nation as he had the tariff and the gold standard—all had served as instruments of international finance meant to benefit an industrial master class at the expense of the majority who produced the actual wealth that the world enjoyed.

At the conclusion of the war, Bryan settled into the position of elder statesman for the fading western branch of the Democratic Party. He often supported unpopular positions and lost some of his luster in later years. Bryan's support, for example, of the Ku Klux Klan, prohibition, and Christian fundamentalism put him at odds with a party and a nation moving rapidly in a more urban, ethnic, and "modern" direction. Though many loved and revered him until his death, the Democratic Party of Bryan's generation, with its concern over free silver, the tariff, and the dignity of the farmer gave way to the modern Democratic Party epitomized by Franklin D. Roosevelt and the New Deal.

See also: Congress (United States); Democratic Party; McKinley Tariff (Tariff of 1890); Taft, William Howard; Wilson, Thomas Woodrow; World War I.

Selected Bibliography:

Lawrence Goodwyn, *Democratic Promise: The Populist Moment in America*, 1976; Louis W. Koenig, *Bryan: A Political Biography of William Jennings Bryan*, 1971.

David S. Brown

BRYANT, WILLIAM CULLEN (November 3, 1794–June 12, 1878)

Trained as an attorney, Bryant became one of the leading poets and editors in the United States.

Born in Cummington, Massachusetts, on November 3, 1794, Bryant hoped to attend Yale but a lack of money forced him to decide to study law under the direction of a local attorney. Bryant authored the acclaimed "Thanatopsis," in which he examined the meaning of death, before becoming editor of the *New York Review*, *Atheneum Magazine*, and the *New York Evening Post*. Initially a staunch supporter of the Democratic Party, he championed labor rights, free speech, free trade, and the eradication of slavery; he also supported the carving out of Central Park in New York City and the establishment of the Metropolitan Museum of Art.

Bryant's antislavery stance led him to champion a Free-Soil position regarding new territories and eventually to join the Republican Party in the 1850s. He backed the presidential candidacy of Abraham Lincoln and supported Union forces during the Civil War.

In his columns, Bryant articulated the position of the *Evening Post* regarding the tariff, one of the most contentious political issues in the United States during the nineteenth century. Agitating for free trade, Bryant condemned a proposed bill in 1827 to strengthen tariff barriers. In a blistering editorial, he charged, "The provisions . . . should call forth a general cry of indignation from Maine to Florida. Their effect will be a legal robbery of that part of the community whose interests are most entitled to protection." Consumers of inexpensive woolen products, on the other hand, would pay the price. This failed to trouble "noisy and hungry manufacturers," Bryant charged, who "feel nothing of the distresses of the poor" and "will set themselves to work without remorse of conscience to double the burdens of the poor." Given Andrew Jackson's opposition to the tariff and internal improvements, Bryant readily supported his presidential candidacy in 1828. Throughout Jackson's tenure in the White House, Bryant and the *Evening Post* continued to support reductions in tariff rates, criticizing opponents who prevented discussion of the issue in the House of Representatives. When Congress finally presented proposals regarding tariff revisions, Bryant remained unimpressed. Protection prevailed, Bryant charged, resulting in southern threats to nullify federal law or to secede. With the establishment of equitable rates Bryant prophesied, "We should hear no more of nullification." Bryant viewed favorably the compromise tariff of 1833, claiming that a confrontation between the federal government and angry southerners had thereby been averted. He also claimed that it discarded protectionism, but remained "altogether a clumsy piece of legislation." He believed that his own newspaper's support of free trade helped produce the compromise.

See also: Free trade; Newspapers and media.

Selected Bibliography:

Charles H. Brown, *William Cullen Bryant: A Biography*, 1971.

Robert C. Cottrell

BUCHANAN, PATRICK J. (November 2, 1938–)

Opponent of free trade who ran against President George Herbert Walker Bush for the Republican nomination in 1992.

Born in Washington, D.C., in 1938, Buchanan earned an A.B. in English from Georgetown University in 1961 and a M.S. degree from the School of Journalism at Columbia University in New York City the following year. For the next four years he worked as a journalist for the *St. Louis Globe-Democrat* before landing a position as an assistant speechwriter for Richard M. Nixon during his 1972 reelection campaign. After Nixon's resignation, Buchanan turned to a career as a radio and television personality, commenting on political events. In 1985, he became the communications director for President Ronald Reagan. When Bush won the election of 1988, Buchanan returned to his career in the private sector, but reemerged in 1992 to oppose Bush during the Republican primary.

Campaigning on a ticket of anti-immigration and anti–free trade, Buchanan opposed the proposed North American Free Trade Agreement (NAFTA) that the Bush administration had initiated. Warning that free trade threatened American jobs and U.S. workers, Buchanan argued for a higher tariff and a temporary ban on immigration. Although he failed to secure the party's nomination in 1992 and again in 1996, Republicans and Democrats increasingly viewed Buchanan as an isolationist. He turned his back on both parties in 1999, seeking instead the nomination of a third political group known as the Reform Party. The author of several books, in 1998 Buchanan wrote *The Great Betrayal*, describing the negative impact on American society created by the free trade measures ushered in under NAFTA.

See also: Bush, George Herbert Walker; North American Free Trade Agreement (NAFTA).

Selected Bibliography:

George Grant, *Buchanan: Caught in the Crossfire*, 1996.

Cynthia Clark Northrup

BUREAU OF FOREIGN AND DOMESTIC COMMERCE (BFDC)

On August 23, 1912, the Department of Commerce created the Bureau of Foreign and Domestic Commerce (BFDC) by consolidating the Bureau of Statistics and the Bureau of Manufactures.

The reorganization created a single unit dedicated to promoting U.S. commerce and industry by compiling and distributing information on domestic and foreign trade, manufacturing, material resources, and market opportunities. This departmental concern reflected the federal government's cognizance of the increasing importance of foreign commerce to the growth and stability of the U.S. economy.

Since its inception during the Republican administration of William Howard Taft, when Congress charged the bureau with carrying out business surveys and economic research, reporting on foreign trade opportunities, and publishing its findings, the BFDC has undergone several evolutions. In 1923, the Bureau of Customs Statistics of the Treasury Department transferred to the Department of Commerce and became part of BFDC. The consolidation enhanced BFDC's ability to provide American businesses with information useful in cultivating overseas resources and markets. The bureau played a particularly active role during Herbert Hoover's tenure as secretary of commerce. He regarded the BFDC as the fulcrum of the department's services to the American business community. It also became a location in which the commercial and foreign policies of the U.S. government intersected. In close collaboration with BFDC Director Julius Klein, Hoover actively involved the bureau's information and analysis services in working through such important foreign policy areas as European World War I debts, U.S. banking overseas, and a China loan consortium. The next major restructuring occurred in 1945, when Congress created five major offices (international trade, small business, domestic commerce, business economics, and field service) within the Bureau. In 1952, a departmental reorganization made the heads of BFDC offices assistant secretaries. BFDC's current administrative units include the Puerto Rico Office, the Specialty Division, the Motion Picture Division, the Division of Metals and Minerals, the Division of Transportation, the Division of Economic Research, and the Publications Committee. The Bureau also oversees the National Committee on wood utilization, the Timber Conservation Board, the Interdepartmental Committee on Shipping Policy, and Ocean Mail Contracts. Although BFDC programs advance private-sector business interests, their functions remain distinct from the types of planning-oriented industrial policy pursued by other advanced industrial nations, such as Japan and France.

See also: Hoover, Herbert; Taft, William Howard.

Selected Bibliography:

Michael J. Hogan, *Informal Entente*, 1991; Joan Hoff Wilson, *American Business and Foreign Policy, 1922–1933*, 1971.

Sayuri Shimizu

BUREAU OF TRADE RELATIONS (BTR)

Bureau within the U.S. Department of State that formulated trade policy during the Taft administration.

In 1903, the Bureau of Foreign Commerce (BTR), established in 1898, became the Bureau of Trade Relations (BTR) under the State Department. Its duties included the compilation of information from officers within the diplomatic corps and then the processing of that information for the State Department and the president. During the administration of William Howard Taft, the BTR assumed the primary role for trade negotiations even prior to the passage of the Payne-Aldrich Tariff. Focusing on the minimum-maximum tariff rates, the bureau sought to entice foreign countries to extend preferential tariff rates to the United States. The BTR concentrated its efforts on Canada, where an imperial rate and a Most Favored Nation rate coexisted. The United States, through the BTR, attempted to negotiate a reduction that would provide American business with the same duty that the French paid under the second schedule of tariff rates. Charles M. Pepper of the BTR, a political appointee of Taft, argued that, by lowering the U.S. rates for Canadian products, a reciprocal relationship could be developed that would allow U.S. products to enter Canada at the lower Most Favored Nation rate. The close proximity and cheaper transportation costs would then make American goods less expensive than European products. Although the BTR worked with the newly created U.S. Tariff Board, the State Department rep-resentatives dominated the negotiating process, molding tariff policy to advance U.S. foreign policy objectives. In 1911, the Bureau of Trade Relations became the Office of the Foreign Trade Adviser, the forerunner of the Bureau of Economic and Business Affairs.

See also: Payne-Aldrich Tariff (Tariff of 1909); Taft, William Howard.

Selected Bibliography:

Paul Wolman, *Most Favored Nation: The Republican Revisionists and U.S. Tariff Policy, 1897–1912*, 1992.

Cynthia Clark Northrup

BUSH, GEORGE HERBERT WALKER (June 12, 1924–   )

Forty-first president of the United States and proponent of free trade who launched the Enterprise for the Americas Initiative and completed negotiations on the North American Free Trade Agreement (NAFTA).

Bush, the son of Senator Prescott Bush of Connecticut and his wife Dorothy Walker Bush, was born on June 12, 1924, in Milton, Massachusetts. On his eighteenth birthday he joined the U.S. Navy as a Seaman 2nd Class and within a year received a commission, making him the youngest pilot in the navy during 1943. Stationed in the Pacific from 1942 until 1945, Bush flew bombing missions off the U.S.S. *San Jacinto*. Decorated with the Distinguished Flying Cross and three other medals for his bravery, Bush returned to the United States and married Barbara Pierce on January 6, 1945.

After the Japanese surrender, Bush attended Yale University, where he majored in economics and played baseball. In 1948, George and Barbara Bush moved to Texas, where he worked first for Dresser Industries before co-founding the Bush-Overby Oil Development Company in 1951, followed by the Zapata Petroleum Corporation and the Zapata Off-Shore Company in 1954. In 1964, Bush decided to follow his father into public service. He ran for the Senate, but lost. In 1966, he won a seat in the U.S. House of Representatives and held that seat until 1970 when he ran a second time for the Senate and lost again.

By 1970, President Richard M. Nixon realized that Bush possessed leadership qualities and appointed him to a series of high-level positions. Bush served as the U.S. Ambassador to the United Nations from 1971 to 1973, when he accepted the position of chairman of the Republican National Committee. The following year he traveled to China as the chief of the U.S. Liaison Office in Peking just as the United States and the People's Republic of China renewed relations. In 1976, President Gerald Ford appointed Bush director of the Central Intelligence Agency.

During the campaign of 1980, Bush ran against Ronald Reagan for the Republican presidential nomination. Reagan won the candidacy, choosing Bush as his running mate. For the next eight years Bush served as vice president, focusing his efforts on the international war on drugs and terrorism. In 1988, he defeated Democrat governor Michael Dukakis of Massachusetts and became the forty-first president of the United States.

Foreign policy issues dominated Bush's term in office. Events in Europe transpired quickly, with the fall of the Berlin Wall, Germany's reunification, and the collapse of the Soviet Union occurring in rapid succession. A new era of open diplomatic relations with Russia resulted in the signing of the Strategic Arms Reduction Talks (START) I and II disarmament treaties. Bush faced another challenge when Iraqi president Saddam Hussein ordered troops to invade neighboring Kuwait. He organized an international coalition under the auspices of the United Nations to restore the Kuwaiti government. After driving the Iraqi forces back across the border, the United States imposed severe restrictions on Iraq. American pilots continue to patrol the "no-fly zone" between the two countries.

Although much of his administration dealt with military or Cold War issues, Bush's primary objective in the Western Hemisphere remained the reduction of trade and tariff barriers and the formation of a free trade zone. On June 27, 1990, Bush announced the Enterprise for the Americas Initiative, calling for new economic policies governing trade, investment, and debt repayment in the Western Hemisphere. Hoping to eliminate all trade barriers between countries in North, South, and Central America, Bush instructed U.S. Trade Representative Carla Hill to propose deeper tariff reductions for products of interest to those countries participating in the ongoing Uruguay Round negotiations. Attempting to attract capital into the less developed countries, Bush announced the creation of a new investment fund that would provide $300 million a year in grants, $100 million of which would come from the United States. The Inter-American Development Bank, the International Monetary Fund, and the World Bank Debt would oversee debt reduction on a case-by-case basis. That same month discussions between Bush and Mexican President Carlos Salinas de Gortari resulted in an agreement to pursue a U.S.–Mexico free trade agreement. Trade representatives from both countries met to negotiate the terms of the treaty. Canada joined the talks in February 1991 and the negotiations resulted in the North American Free Trade Agreement (NAFTA). The signing ceremony occurred on December 17, 1992, but Congress ratified the treaty after William Jefferson Clinton became president in 1993. Designed as a free trade zone, NAFTA created the largest free market in the world, with over 360 million people and $6 trillion in annual output.

After leaving office, Bush and his wife retired to Houston, Texas. In 2000, their son George Walker Bush became the forty-third president of the United States, the second time in American history when the son of a president also won the presidency.

See also: Clinton, William Jefferson (Bill); Cold War; North American Free Trade Agreement (NAFTA); Salinas de Gortari, Carlos; Uruguay Round. **Vol. II**: The Enterprise for the Americas Initiative; Presidential Debate over the North American Free Trade Agreement; Gore-Perot Debate over the Ratification of the North American Free Trade Agreement.

Selected Bibliography:

George Bush, *All the Best, George Bush: My Life in Letters and Other Writings*, 1999; John Robert Greene, *The Presidency of George Bush*, 2000; Steven Hurst, *The Foreign Policy of the Bush Administration: In Search of a New World Order*, 1999.

Cynthia Clark Northrup

C

CALHOUN, JOHN CALDWELL (March 18, 1782–March 31, 1850)

South Carolinian dedicated to the elimination of the protectionist tariff and chief proponent of nullification, a doctrine that advocated state sovereignty over federal law.

Born near Calhoun Mills, South Carolina, on March 18, 1782, Calhoun served in the South Carolina House of Representatives from 1808 until 1809. In 1811, he won a seat in the U.S. House of Representatives and remained there until November 3, 1817, when he resigned to become secretary of war under President James Monroe. While in Congress he supported a low tariff designed to raise money for both the army and a national communications system. He held his cabinet position under Monroe until 1824 and then became the vice president under John Quincy Adams between 1824 and 1828.

While Calhoun served as vice president, Congress pushed through a bill outlining a high protectionist tariff. The Tariff of 1828, also known as the Tariff of Abominations, placed duties as high as 50 percent on some imports. Like other southerners, Calhoun believed that high tariffs had led to the recent decrease in the price of cotton. Nevertheless, he went along with the tariff, believing it would fail before becoming law. Adams signed the tariff into law in May 1828, surprising even its proponents.

Late in 1828, a member of the South Carolina legislature asked Calhoun to write a justification for a state's right to nullify federal laws deemed injurious to the state, such as the Tariff of 1828. Over the course of two weeks in November 1828, he drafted the South Carolina *Exposition*. In this document, he stated that the tariff represented the tyranny of the unchecked power of the majority over the few. He added that individual states had the right to decide for themselves the value of various contested issues. He also asserted that state conventions could decide the unconstitutionality of a law. The *Exposition* went before the South Carolina Special Committee on December 19. Although his name did not appear on the document, the public knew Calhoun had authored it. His tie to the *Exposition* provided the first hint of tension between the vice president and the new president, Andrew Jackson. Calhoun had been elected to a second term as vice president, putting him in close proximity to Jackson, whom many believed had a more protectionist stance toward the tariff. Not until 1831 did their relationship deteriorate appreciably over the tariff.

In 1831, South Carolina continued to rail against the Tariff of Abominations, claiming discrimination against the South. The vice president served as his home state's tacit leader of discontent. In June, he gave his *Fort Hill Address*, in which he posited in full detail the principles of nullification. If a state felt that Congress passed an unconstitutional law, he argued that state had the right to veto it, declaring the law null and void within its borders. The *Pendleton Messenger* published the *Fort Hill Address* on July 26.

Congress passed a nominally lower tariff in 1832, leaving South Carolina unsatisfied. The state quickly passed a nullification ordinance, which declared that unless Congress lowered duties the state would consider the tariff null and void after February 1, 1833, and would not collect it. Calhoun gave his approval to this ordinance and as a result bore some of the antipathy President Jackson felt toward his home state. The vice president finally tendered his resignation on December 28, 1832, to take on a senatorial position

and orchestrate nullification efforts from there.

Calhoun's confrontations with Jackson continued to fester. On January 16, 1833, the president arranged for the introduction of a Force Bill in Congress. This bill made it easier for the president to enforce the tariff in South Carolina. To back up the legislation, Jackson positioned ships in Charleston Harbor, ready to intervene if necessary. Calhoun strongly criticized the bill, calling it the "Bloody Act." Nevertheless, the bill passed and became the Force Act.

While Congress deliberated over the Force Bill, they also considered compromise tariffs that might ease the crisis. Henry Clay, senator from Kentucky, put forward one such tariff in January 1833. Calhoun had informed his colleague that South Carolina would approve a reasonable compromise, and Clay's suggested bill gave up enough protection to gain acceptance. On February 2, Calhoun endorsed the tariff in the Senate to great applause. Clay's Compromise passed the House and Senate by March 1 and Jackson signed it into law.

Despite this step in the right direction, Calhoun remained unsatisfied by later tariff adjustments throughout the rest of his career. Reelected to the Senate in 1834 and 1840, Calhoun served until March 3, 1843, when he accepted the cabinet position of secretary of state in John Tyler's administration in 1844. He criticized the Polk administration for not scaling down the levels of the Tariff of 1842. In July 1846, Polk signed the Walker Tariff into law. This tariff played at free trade, but proved mildly protectionist, with duties at 30 percent *ad valorem*. As Calhoun had wanted a general reduction in rates, he expressed his acceptance with aspects of the Walker Tariff, but overall hoped for more scaling down of duties.

Calhoun returned to the Senate on November 26, 1845, and served until his death on March 31, 1850, in Washington, D.C.

See also: Clay, Henry; Clay's Compromise; Force Act; Jackson, Andrew; South Carolina *Exposition* and *Protest*; Tariff of 1828 (Tariff of Abominations).

Selected Bibliography:

Irving H. Bartlett, *John C. Calhoun: A Biography*, 1993; John Niven, *John C. Calhoun and the Price of Union: A Biography*, 1988; Merrill D. Peterson, *The Great Triumvirate: Webster, Clay, and Calhoun*, 1987.

Adrienne Caughfield

CAMBRELENG, CHURCHILL CALDOM
(October 24, 1786–April 30, 1862)

New York City congressman best known for his vigorous opposition to protective tariffs.

Born in Washington, Beaufort County, North Carolina, Cambreleng attended school in nearby New Bern before moving to New York City in 1802. After a three-year stint as a clerk in Providence, Rhode Island, he returned to Manhattan in 1809 to found at least two commercial houses and to work for John Jacob Astor, for whom he traveled widely in Europe.

In 1821, the same year he published a tract opposing the 1820 tariff, Cambreleng began his career in Congress. He allied with the emerging Jacksonian Democratic Party and demonstrated his free trade views by opposing the 1824 and 1828 tariffs. A loyal Democrat, he supported Andrew Jackson's hard money position as well as the president's veto of the bill to recharter the Second Bank of the United States. He successively chaired three key committees: Commerce, Foreign Affairs, and Ways and Means. Defeated for reelection in 1838, Cambreleng accepted an appointment from President Martin Van Buren as minister to Russia, a position he held from May 1840 to July 1841.

Although he never again held elective office, Cambreleng remained active in politics. A delegate to the 1846 New York state constitutional convention, he also presided over the 1847 convention of New York Democrats, known as "Barnburners," who opposed the extension of slavery into new federal territories and broke with their party over the issue. In 1848, Cambreleng attended the Barnburners' Utica convention that nominated Martin Van Buren for president; a few months later, the new Free-Soil Party ratified that choice.

Cambreleng died on April 30, 1862, at his home near Huntingdon, Suffolk County, New York.

See also: Jackson, Andrew; Tariff of 1828 (Tariff of Abominations); Van Buren, Martin.

Selected Bibliography:

Rodney P. Carlisle, "Cambreleng, Churchill Caldom," *American National Biography*, 1999.

Adrienne Caughfield

CANADA

In Canada, the Finance Department sets taxing laws, including the tariff, while Customs and Excise administers them.

The colonial French raised money by having an export duty on furs and later collected import duties. The British used customs for revenue and enforcement of the navigation acts. In the 1840s, the British turned toward free trade and customs and excise became a revenue producer. The colonies taxed manufactured goods from each other and foreign nations. In 1867, with confederation, tariffs became the domain of the federal government. Canada's Customs Act, adopted in 1866, set the average tariff at 15 percent two years later. In 1879, Prime Minister Sir John A. Macdonald introduced a higher tariff that protected developing Canadian industries, especially from the United States. Until World War I the tariff generated about 75 percent of Canada's federal revenue.

The struggle between protectionists and free traders has remained strong and lively in Canada. In 1854, Canada and the United States signed a reciprocity treaty, which allowed fish, lumber, coal, and grain to enter the lucrative American market. This brought prosperity, but made Canadians more dependent on U.S. trade policies. The United States abrogated the treaty in 1866. Not until 1935 did the two nations extend Most Favored Nation treatment to each other.

The General Agreement on Tariffs and Trade (GATT) breached high tariff walls in 1947. By 1985, nearly 80 percent of Canadian exports went to the United States. The ongoing struggle between protection and free trade continued. The Free Trade Agreement (FTA), signed by Prime Minister Brian Mulroney in 1987, removed tariffs and import duties between the two nations and gained support from the Canadian people. In January 1994, Prime Minister Jean Chrétien signed the North American Free Trade Agreement (NAFTA) that greatly expanded Mulroney's original FTA and included Mexico. Since then, the two economies have integrated.

See also: Free trade; Free Trade Area of the Americas (FTAA); Navigation and Trade Acts; North American Free Trade Agreement (NAFTA).

Selected Bibliography:

Duncan Cameron and Mel Watkins, eds., *Canada Under Free Trade*, 1993; Michael Hart, *Fifty Years of Canadian Tradecraft: Canada at the GATT 1947–1997*, 1998.

Russell M. Magnaghi

CANNON, JOSEPH GURNEY (May 7, 1836–November 12, 1926)

Speaker of the U.S. House of Representatives who strongly opposed tariff reform.

Born at New Garden, North Carolina, Cannon did not attend college but studied law for six months at the Cincinnati Law School and joined the bar in 1858. From 1861 to 1868, Cannon, a Republican, served as the attorney for the twenty-seventh judicial district in Illinois. In 1872, he won a seat in the U.S. House of Representatives and would serve, except for two terms, until 1923.

In December 1887, President Grover Cleveland devoted his entire annual message to the subject of tariff revision. The president argued that the tariff proved unfair to American consumers and that the government surplus could soon hurt the business community. Cannon, an ardent protectionist, attacked the Cleveland administration's Mills Bill for tariff reduction. Cannon ridiculed the Democratic argument that tariff reduction provided the best way to combat the trusts in the United States. He contended that a protective tariff remained the "quickening principle" underlying American prosperity and progress by providing a lucrative domestic market for nine-tenths of the items produced in the United States. The Republican victory in the 1888 election prevented the passage of the Mills Bill.

Two years later, the McKinley Tariff gave Cannon a chance to demonstrate his protectionist stance. He especially favored the maintenance of works of art on the dutiable list since they were luxuries that cheap labor in foreign countries often produced. Cannon's amendment failed to pass, but he continued his support of the tariff bill that President Benjamin Harrison signed into law just in time to make it the primary campaign issue in the congressional elections of 1890. Because the cost of living had increased, the tariff became a major problem for the protectionist Republicans, including Cannon, who lost his bid for reelection.

Nevertheless, by 1892, he had mended his political fences and won election to Congress. Known as "Uncle Joe," Cannon led the Old Guard, a group that unshakably defended the status quo. As Speaker of the House of Representatives from 1903 to 1911, Cannon appointed only like-minded individuals to chairmanships of important House committees. In addition, as chairman of the Rules Committee, he controlled which major bills reached the floor. As a result, many issues received little attention under his control. Hostile to the progressive wing of the Republican Party, he opposed efforts to lower the tariff. When President Theodore Roosevelt suggested tariff revision early in 1905, despite the country's general prosperity, Cannon vigorously disapproved and Roosevelt dropped the issue rather than jeopardize the rest of his legislative agenda by alienating the Speaker of the House. Cannon then clinched the matter by assigning only avowed opponents of tariff revision to the House Ways and Means Committee.

The widespread belief that large business combinations used the protective tariff to fix prices and rake in high profits led the Republican Party, in 1908, to pledge a reduction of tariff duties. Cannon subsequently played an instrumental role in the passage of the Payne-Aldrich Tariff of 1909. Many viewed it as an unsatisfactory compromise that overall reduced duties, but raised rates on major items like coal and iron. The act therefore helped to split the Democratic majority in the House of Representatives. In 1910, Democrats and progressive Republicans worked together to limit Cannon's power, and the Speaker's authority finally declined. He retired in 1923 after serving nearly fifty years in the House of Representatives. Three years later Cannon died at the age of ninety.

See also: Cleveland, Stephen Grover; Harrison, Benjamin; House Ways and Means Committee; McKinley Tariff (Tariff of 1890); Mills Bill; Payne-Aldrich Tariff (Tariff of 1909).

Selected Bibliography:

William Rea Gwinn, *Uncle Joe Cannon, Archfoe of Insurgency; A History of the Rise and Fall of Cannonism*, 1957.

Steven E. Siry

CAPEHART, HOMER EARL (June 6, 1897–September 3, 1979)

U.S. senator from Indiana who personified midwestern conservatism during the mid-twentieth century.

Capehart, a staunch Republican conservative during the Truman, Eisenhower, and Kennedy administrations, was born in Algiers, Indiana, in 1897 into a family of wealthy farmers. He joined the army in 1917 and served at various posts on the West Coast. On his discharge in 1919, Capehart went into business and found success first as a farm equipment salesman, then in the popcorn industry, and finally as an early advocate and manufacturer of various electric components, such as the jukebox, radio, phonograph, and television. In response to perceived failures of the New Deal in his home state, Capehart turned his eye toward politics.

After a successful election bid to the Senate in 1944, Capehart worked for the advancement and protection of American industry at home and abroad. He felt strongly that the federal government should abstain from interference in matters of the economy and instead only provide the arena for busi-

ness expansion and growth. Capehart began his career as a strict isolationist and briefly aligned with Senator Joseph R. McCarthy in an effort to combat the alleged communist threat in the United States. With the election of President Dwight D. Eisenhower, Capehart moved away from the anticommunist fringe to more moderate policies and ideologies. He also retreated from his isolationist philosophy and became a strong supporter of foreign trade, especially in Latin America, leading several envoys to the region.

Finding himself a product of another generation politically, Capehart lost his bid for reelection in 1962. He lived in Indiana and continued his business ventures until his death in 1979.

See also: Capehart Committee; Eisenhower, Dwight D. (Ike).

Selected Bibliography:

William B. Pickett, *Homer E. Capehart: A Senator's Life, 1897–1979*, 1990.

Jonathan V. Parrent

CAPEHART COMMITTEE

A collection of businesspeople, politicians, and citizens who advocated the development of business and trade relations between Latin America and the United States.

In the early 1950s, Republican Senator Homer E. Capehart of Indiana grew interested in the expansion of cultural and economic trade with Latin America. After introducing a successful resolution in the Senate to establish a study for the development of trade expansion, Capehart organized a group of bankers, businessmen, farmers, citizens, and labor leaders to discuss the possibilities. Prominent figures such as John L. Lewis, president of the United Mine Workers; Henry P. Bristol, chairman of the board of Bristol-Meyers; Paul G. Hoffman, chairman of the board of the Studebaker Corporation; and George Meany, president of the American Federation of Labor attended these meetings.

Senator Capehart assembled a team for a Latin America tour that would view firsthand the problems and difficulties in developing trade. The group, thirty members strong, traveled to over fifteen countries between October and December 1953 and met with dozens of international leaders. Once Capehart returned, he became one of the leading authorities on Latin American issues. The committee's report, released in 1954, found that low per-capita income, a shortage of investment capital, unstable prices, and poor infrastructure blocked development. The report went on to suggest the United States should continue adjusting tariff rates, assist in improving the socioeconomic conditions of the region, and allow for more purchases of Latin American products. The committee gave Senator Homer E. Capehart a high profile and elevated him to a position of hemispheric importance.

See also: American Federation of Labor (AFL); Latin America.

Selected Bibliography:

William B. Pickett, *Homer E. Capehart: A Senator's Life, 1897–1979*, 1990.

Jonathan V. Parrent

CAPITALISM

Most frequently associated with the economic system described in Karl Marx's *Das Kapital*, the word derives from the early seventeenth-century term *capital*, referring to the accumulated wealth of an individual.

The sense of an "environment of capitalism" predates Marx by some years, paralleling his study of the uses of capital for new economic structures and goals. By the mid-nineteenth century, capitalism referred to an economic system that contributed to the development of wealth in new ways and acted as an ethos or driving force behind such innovations in policy, practice, and production that made capital accumulation both possible and desirable within the framework of this new system.

Karl Marx, Friedrich Engels, and Émile Durkheim thoroughly enunciated the necessities, peculiarities, characteristics, and shortcomings of capitalism, although many Western observers already recognized the existence and possibilities. The combined writings of Marx and Engels, in particular, served as a baseline for interpretation, comparative analysis, and debate over the qualities and evils of capitalism for more than a century.

The essential formulation of capitalism lies in Marxian terminology. For Marx, capitalism involved the allocation of basic inputs—land, labor, and capital (money)—in new ways and for new purposes. Marx argued that a number of circumstances preceded the rise of capitalism, including the decline of feudalism, the rise of towns, and a rise in population. Perhaps the most important element in the rise of capitalism proved the pursuit of profit through forms of "primitive accumulation." This amassing of capital steadily evolved from the exploitation of political advantage or more simple plunder into a more concerted, concrete concern for expanding export markets. The doctrine of mercantilism and its successors from among the eighteenth-century political economists and the formulation of various notions of economic growth, both domestic and international, typified the idea of accumulation.

The rise of the bourgeoisie and their emerging self-awareness as a socioeconomic and political class with political power proved of great significance for Marx. The growing pursuit of self-interest, both economically and politically, paved the way for a transition from petty to capitalist accumulation. In driving this transformation, Marx argues, not only did the technical processes of production change, but the social process as well. For in their rising economic power and political influence, the bourgeoisie set themselves apart from the mass of society, the pool of citizenry that became the working class.

The importance of population growth, a seeming by-product of protocapitalist improvements in agriculture during the late seventeenth and throughout the eighteenth centuries, resulted in the creation of a "surplus pool of labor." Migration from rural areas to towns and cities by workers in pursuit of opportunities no longer available in the countryside, traditionally explained in England as a result of the "Enclosure Movement" but less easily explainable

as a phenomenon elsewhere, led to the formation of a separate class. This development concerned Marx, who feared that this new class might develop its own self-identity—economically, socially, and, most important, politically. Driven by his firsthand observance of the uprisings in Paris in 1848, he became convinced that such popular challenges had initiated a process that would develop and endure. As the result of the changing economic arena of western Europe, Marx envisioned the development of a working-class "consciousness" akin to that of the bourgeoisie. In his formulation, this consciousness preceded the development of a fully self-articulated working class, or proletariat, whose own united pursuit of self-interest would bring about revolutionary change. As a consequence, capitalism would give way to socialism and ultimately a utopian worker's state, or communism, would emerge.

To date, this egalitarian vision has yet to materialize. Although concerted worker action and the rise of unions between 1880 and 1920 led to a series of governmental reforms betokening the rise of socialism, the closing decades of the twentieth century brought numerous reversals, including a new anti-union, anti-worker, conservative economic reorganization. In particular, the advent of free trade zones in Europe, North America, Latin America, and Southeast Asia have undermined the position of the traditional working class in First World industrial manufacturing as jobs have moved beyond state borders to Second and Third World regions, where wages remain far lower. The assembly line now works as well in Mexico, Central America, India, or South Korea as it once did in Detroit. The high cost of union labor in the industrialized West could not compete with an equally willing and no less competent foreign industrial manufacturing process whose workers receive an eighth, a tenth, or less in wages. In this, the so-called "New Right" has answered the challenge of proletarianization, Marx's vision seemingly fell with the Berlin Wall, and the "New Left" can only lament what might have occurred except for the steady decline of protectionism.

See also: Communism; Free trade; Industrial Revolution; Labor; Socialism; Third World.

Selected Bibliography:

Maurice Herbert Dobb, *Studies in the Development of Capitalism*, 1963; David S. Landes, *The Wealth and Poverty of Nations: Why Some Are So Rich and Some So Poor*, 1998.

David J. Weiland III

CAREY, HENRY CHARLES (December 15, 1793–October 13, 1879)

Publisher, social scientist, and prolific author of books on economic theory.

Born in Philadelphia, Carey possessed no formal education but received training from his father, an Irish patriot and political exile. Self-taught in political economy, Carey published his *Essay on the Rate of Wages* in 1835, a work advocating laissez-faire and the principle of free trade. He expanded his economic theory in the three-volume *Principles of Political Economy*, published between 1837 and 1840,

again as a champion of free trade. In 1842, when Congress passed a protective tariff, Carey condemned the bill and predicted dire economic circumstances for the United States. For reasons that biographers disagree about, in 1844 he became a convert to protectionism and remained an advocate until his death. Among his more notable efforts in later years, he helped finance *The Plough, the Loom, and the Anvil*, a protectionist journal of the 1850s, and he elaborated on his protectionist principles in *Harmony of Interests: Agricultural, Manufacturing, and Commercial*, published in 1851. In *Principles of Social Science*, a three-volume work published in 1859, he emphasized the important link between politics and economy, arguing that government action could actually shape economic patterns, particularly with tariff laws.

Although it is unclear to what extent the writings of Carey shaped the political economic beliefs of members of Congress, members who supported protection frequently discussed his works. He died in Philadelphia.

See also: Free trade; Protectionism.

Selected Bibliography:

Rodney J. Morrison, *Henry Charles Carey and American Economic Development*, 1986.

Glynn Ingram

CARLISLE, JOHN GRIFFIN (September 5, 1835–July 31, 1910)

Member of the U.S. House of Representatives from 1877 to 1890, the U.S. Senate from 1890 to 1893, and secretary of the treasury from 1893 to 1897.

Born on September 5, 1835, in Key West, Campbell County, Kentucky, Carlisle left his parents and ten siblings and, at the age of sixteen, began teaching in Covington, Kentucky. He started studying law in 1856 and joined the law firm of William Kinkead in 1858. During his career in Kentucky, he served as a member of the Kentucky State House of Representatives and the Kentucky State Senate, and as lieutenant governor under Governor Preston H. Leslie.

Carlisle's Kentucky constituents elected him to the U.S. House of Representatives in 1877. He served in this capacity until 1890, when he filled a vacancy in the U.S. Senate. In 1893, President Grover Cleveland appointed him secretary of the treasury.

As secretary of the treasury, Carlisle opposed stringent trade tariffs and advocated a gold monetary standard. These two issues led to a wane in Carlisle's popularity, and he retired from public life in 1897. Carlisle returned to law and died in New York City on July 31, 1910.

See also: Cleveland, Stephen Grover; Free trade; Protectionism.

Selected Bibliography:

Jim Reis, "John Griffin Carlisle," *The Kentucky Encyclopedia*, 1992.

Carrie Dowdy

CARNEGIE, ANDREW (November 25, 1835–August 11, 1919)

One of the great industrial barons, philanthropists, and opinion leaders of the late nineteenth century.

Born in Dunfermline, Scotland, Carnegie immigrated to the United States at age thirteen and soon began working in the telegraph and railroad industries, where he had the good fortune of securing a mentor in the person of Thomas A. Scott, a railroad executive. Carnegie worked his way up the corporate ladder in the Pennsylvania Railroad before turning his attention to finance and ultimately the iron and steel industry. He changed manufacturing in the United States by embracing cost accounting, research and development, and vertical integration. Through his company, Carnegie Steel, he dominated an industry until his decision in 1900 to sell his interest to financier J.P. Morgan for $480 million.

A staunch Republican, Carnegie, for most of his adult life, supported protectionism. He demonstrated the flexibility to make concessions on some tariff issues, guarded duties on iron and steel, and attacked those who viewed the tariff only as means to raise revenue. He worked with the American Iron and Steel Association to lobby Congress, and the protectionist provisions of the McKinley and Wilson Tariffs demonstrate their success in representing the industry.

Carnegie's position on the tariff shifted after he left the steel industry. In 1901, Carnegie publicly stated that he believed the tariff had lost much of its usefulness as both a protective measure and a source of revenue. By 1908, he went further, writing an article for *The Century Magazine* in which he called for an end to protective tariffs, while at the same time arguing that he had never varied his position on the issue. Following the lead of economist John Stuart Mill, Carnegie argued that tariffs only temporarily protected new industries. American industry, he contended, had passed from infancy to maturity and could compete without government intervention.

Published as debate began on revision of the Dingley Tariff of 1897, his remarks, along with his testimony before the House Ways and Means Committee, caused a furor in both the protectionist and free trade communities. Despite Carnegie's intervention, the United States continued its protectionist policies in the Payne-Aldrich Tariff. When President Woodrow Wilson pushed the reformist Underwood-Simmons Tariff Act through Congress in 1913, Carnegie applauded the action.

His move from the protectionist to free trade camps paralleled his move from being a captain of industry to philanthropist. Believing that "the man who dies rich dies disgraced," Carnegie donated $350 million of his fortune to philanthropic endeavors. He also took an active role in supporting the League of Nations and other efforts to bring peace to the world. He died in 1919 in Lenox, Massachusetts.

See also: American Iron and Steel Institute (AISI); Dingley Tariff (Tariff of 1897); McKinley Tariff (Tariff of 1890); Mill, John Stuart; Payne-Aldrich Tariff (Tariff of 1909); Underwood-Simmons Tariff (Tariff of 1913); Wilson, Thomas Woodrow; Wilson-Gorman Tariff (Tariff of 1894).

Selected Bibliography:

John Frazier Wall, *Andrew Carnegie*, 1970.

John D. Coats

CARTELS

Organizations of firms producing similar commodities that attempt, by regulating the quantities their members produce and allocating markets, to maintain high prices and stable demand for the commodities; they act much like tariffs with respect to the market conditions they seek to achieve.

In the late nineteenth century, when modern cartels first appeared in Germany and then in other European countries, they remained national in scope and sought tariff protection as one form of state support to achieve their aims. Cartels have never flourished within the United States mainly because the Sherman Antitrust Act of 1890 classified them as trusts, making them illegal. Yet American corporations and the U.S. government have had to deal with cartels throughout the twentieth century, and at times issues concerning tariffs have arisen in such dealings. In the 1920s, for example, U.S. chemical companies, especially DuPont, called for tariff increases on imports from Germany as a means of strengthening their hand in negotiations with the German chemical cartel IG Farben, which possessed a near-monopoly on chemical patents. One of the aims of U.S. policy toward Germany during the post–1945 occupation sought the breakup of Germany's cartels, a policy that did not entirely succeed.

The term "cartel" in recent years refers to associations made up of the governments of countries that produce particular primary commodities sold on the world market. The best known of these is the Organization of Petroleum Exporting Countries (OPEC).

See also: Germany; Organization of Petroleum Exporting Countries (OPEC); Trusts.

Selected Bibliography:

George W. Stocking and Myron W. Watkins, *Cartels in Action: Case Studies in International Business Diplomacy*, 1946.

Woodruff D. Smith

CATO'S LETTERS

One of the most influential works on political and economic thought in eighteenth- and nineteenth-century America.

Written by John Trenchard and Thomas Gordon under the pseudonym Cato, and published between 1720 and 1723 in England, these letters appeared in collected editions and as excerpts in newspapers and pamphlets to the American colonies, where their basic ideas circulated widely. Preoccupied with the abuse of power, *Cato's Letters* attacked trade regulation of all kinds. The promotion of economic efficiency, along the lines later charted by Adam Smith, concerned "Cato" less than the concept of preventing the accumulation of too much wealth, and therefore too much political power in the hands of a few ambitious men. According to "Cato," those who benefited from monopolies over trade granted by Parliament would use their wealth to corrupt legislators in order to defend or increase their economic privileges. The letters directed their attack against the large corporations chartered at the end of the eighteenth century, such as the Bank of England and the South Sea Company. After the Revolution, many Americans continued to hold the same suspicions as those expressed in *Cato's Letters* against legally sanctioned economic privileges. These ideas became particularly influential in Andrew Jackson's Democratic Party, and some of the popular reaction against the Bank of the United States and against tariff protection, as late as the 1830s, developed from the influence of these eighteenth-century authors.

See also: American Revolution; Democratic Party; Jackson, Andrew; Smith, Adam.

Selected Bibliography:

Caroline Robbins, *The Eighteenth-Century Commonwealthman: Studies in the Transmission, Development, and Circumstance of English Liberal Thought*, 1961.

John P. Barrington

CENTER FOR STRATEGIC AND INTERNATIONAL STUDIES

Privately funded organization founded in 1962 for the purpose of providing expert advice and analysis on government economic policies and their impact.

Contributions from more than 300 corporations, foundations, and private citizens finance 85 percent of the center's $17 million budget. Qualified resident scholars discuss problems and solutions for all geographical areas and such key issues as energy and international finance. They also analyze legislation and the possible consequences, with specialists testifying before Congress on a wide array of topics. The center releases information through a variety of sources, including conferences, media appearances and articles, and the publication of books and periodicals including *The Washington Quarterly* and *The Washington Papers*. Former U.S. Senator Sam Nunn currently heads the Board of Trustees, which is composed of business leaders, academic scholars, and public policy experts. During the negotiations concerning the North American Free Trade Agreement (NAFTA), the Center for Strategic and International Studies advocated the passage of the treaty. Several of the organization's members, including Sidney Weintraub, Georges Fauniol, and Delal Baer, joined other academic leaders in signing a letter supporting a free trade area with Mexico.

See also: North American Free Trade Agreement (NAFTA).

Selected Bibliography:

Hermann von Bertrab, *Negotiating NAFTA: A Mexican Envoy's Account*, 1997.

Cynthia Clark Northrup

CHILE

Key copper exporting country lying on a north–south axis along the Pacific; Southern Cone of South America.

The largest, lower-cost producer of copper, Chile took the lead in founding Conseil Inter gouvernemental des Pays Exportateurs de Cuivre (CIPEC). In 1972, the elected government of Salvador Allende Gossens nationalized the country's large, foreign-owned copper mines. The government refused compensation in a dispute over valuation of assets and claims of underpayments of past taxes. The United States imposed economic sanctions by blocking multilateral loans and releasing copper stockpiles to lower the price of copper. Kennecott Corporation sought to forestall nationalization by using future copper production from its Chilean mines as collateral for loans from international banks, which induced the banks to cooperate with a U.S. policy of isolation.

The Nixon administration conducted a covert campaign against Chile intended, according to Secretary of State Henry Kissinger, "to make the economy scream." In September 1973, a coup ousted Allende and brought General Augusto Pinochet to power. A team of economists, known as the "Chicago Boys" because of their enthusiastic embrace of laissez-faire and comparative advantage, designed Pinochet's economic policies that included increasing production from the state company and attracting foreign investors to open new mines. In response, domestic U.S. producers tried unsuccessfully to convince the Reagan administration to implement antidumping sanctions. In 1989, Chileans protested restraint of trade restrictions on its fruit exports after the U.S. Food and Drug Administration found traces of cyanide in a single grape. The United States lifted restrictions the following year.

In 1990, a civilian, elected president replaced Pinochet, but overall Chilean trade and development policies remained the most consistently neoliberal in the hemisphere. In 1995, President William Jefferson Clinton negotiated a bilateral treaty intended to prepare the way for incorporating Chile into NAFTA and advance toward the Free Trade Area of the Americas. The U.S. Congress never ratified the agreement because of combined opposition from Republicans and Democrats concerned about human rights, labor, and environmental issues.

See also: Clinton, William Jefferson (Bill); Conseil Intergouvernemental des Pays Exportateurs de Cuivre (CIPEC); Copper; Dumping; Free Trade Area of the Americas (FTAA); North American Free Trade Agreement (NAFTA).

Selected Bibliography:

Rudiger Dornbusch and Raúl Labán, *The Chilean Economy: Policy Lessons and Challenges*, 1994; Theodore H. Moran, *Multinational Corporations and the Politics of Dependence*, 1974.

Daniel C. Hellinger

CIVIL WAR (AMERICAN)

A four-year war between the northern and southern United States fought over the issues of slavery, states' rights, and trade and tariffs.

During the period between the War of 1812 and the Civil War, the nation struggled to resolve divisive problems with different factions threatening to secede several times, but compromises prevented a breach until 1860. On each occasion the position of the states divided along regional lines. The first potential threat to the country's unity arose just prior to the War of 1812. President Thomas Jefferson initiated an embargo that affected northern merchants and manufacturers more than their southern counterparts. After James Madison became president, New England representatives insisted on the elimination of all trade restrictions, claiming that the United States had resorted to mercantilist practices. A group of northern Federalists from Connecticut, Rhode Island, Massachusetts, New Hampshire, and Vermont held a meeting in Hartford, Connecticut, from December 14, 1814, through January 5, 1815, and passed a series of resolutions against the commercial regulations, asserting a strong states' rights position. The Hartford Convention delegates threatened to secede from the Union if the federal government refused to lift the trade barriers and adopt other changes proposed by the group, but their demands reached Washington after the signing of the Treaty of Ghent and the end of the war. Although the Federalist Party suffered as a result of the failed political maneuver, the seed of secession had been sown.

Trade and tariff questions entered national politics as a major issue again in the years after the War of 1812 as Congress adopted the first protectionist measures. Having relied on the tariff primarily as a source of revenue until 1816, the legislature examined the need for developing infant industries as a means of securing national independence from foreign countries, especially Great Britain. Both the North and South acquiesced to the shift in economic policy until southerners realized that the legislation benefited their northern counterparts at their expense. The issue reached crisis proportions after the passage of the Tariff of 1828. Known as the Tariff of Abominations, the act adversely affected the cotton-producing South while protecting the new industrial growth of New England. The politicization of the act during the 1828 election between John Quincy Adams and Andrew Jackson continued after Jackson took office, eventually resulting in the resignation of Vice President John C. Calhoun. Although Jackson and Calhoun disagreed on other issues, the rift between them widened once Calhoun wrote the South Carolina *Exposition* arguing for a state's right to nullify federal law. When South Carolina threatened to secede, Jackson asked for, and received, authority from Congress to resort to the use of force if necessary to ensure the collection of tariff duties within the state. Although Henry Clay negotiated a compromise that prevented the use of federal troops, the issue of states' rights gained national prominence once again. This time the parties threatening action remained active in politics helping pave the way for a final threat in 1860.

In the years between 1833 and 1860, the controversy over the extension of slavery increased tensions between the northern and southern states. Meanwhile, the Democrats and Republicans refined their position on the tariff, with the Democrats seeking a reduction of rates during periods when the treasury experienced surpluses. Republicans cautioned that the federal government required additional reserves to ensure adequate resources during periods of financial stress.

The election of Abraham Lincoln in 1860 divided the nation. After the election, but prior to the Republicans assuming office, southern states seceded from the Union. During the war, Congress increased the tariff duties in an effort to finance military expenditures. The Morrill Tariff increased rates to the highest level in American history to that time. After the war, the Republican-dominated Congress continued to pass increases in tariff rates throughout the rest of the nineteenth century, using the funds to finance internal improvements like the trans-continental railroad. Grover Cleveland, the only Democratic president elected between the Civil War and the opening of the twentieth century, attempted to lower the tariff, but Republicans defeated the measure. The tariff issue, which helped fuel the onset of the Civil War, continued to define the position of the major political parties throughout the remainder of the century.

See also: Calhoun, John Caldwell; Clay, Henry; Cleveland, Stephen Grover; Democratic Party; Federalists; Jackson, Andrew; Jefferson, Thomas; Madison, James; Morrill, Justin S.; Morrill Tariff (Tariff of 1861); Nullification; Republican Party; Slavery; Tariff of 1816; Tariff of 1828 (Tariff of Abominations); War of 1812.

Selected Bibliography:

Heather Cox Richardson, *The Greatest Nation of the Earth: Republican Economic Policies During the Civil War*, 1997; Edward Stanwood, *American Tariff Controversies in the Nineteenth Century*, 1967.

Cynthia Clark Northrup

CLARK, JAMES BEAUCHAMP (CHAMP) (March 7, 1850–March 2, 1921)

Missouri Democrat who served in the U.S. House of Representatives from 1893 until 1895 and again from 1897 until 1921; he proved a staunch advocate of low tariffs and of the federal income tax as a revenue supplement.

Born in Lawrenceburg, Kentucky, Clark attended Transylvania University and Bethany College before obtaining his degree from the Cincinnati Law School in 1875. He moved to Louisiana, Missouri, where he taught school, practiced law, became a Democratic presidential elector in 1880, and served as the prosecuting attorney of Pike County for four years before winning a seat in the state legislature in 1888. There he wrote Missouri's Australian ballot law and its first antitrust legislation, laying the groundwork for his election to the U.S. House of Representatives in 1892. Along the way, he gained such a reputation as a stirring orator that colleagues nicknamed him the "Ring-Tailed Roarer" and he became a longtime fixture on the Chautauqua circuit. During his first term in Congress, Clark was one of the Democratic delegation's most outspoken champions of downward tariff revision and the income tax, the free coinage of silver, and the direct election of senators. Defeated for reelection during the nationwide Republican landslide of 1894, he regained his seat two years later and continued to represent Missouri's ninth district until his death.

As minority leader in 1909, Clark helped forge a volatile Democrat–Insurgent Republican coalition that opposed the excesses of the Payne-Aldrich Tariff, forced President William Howard Taft to propose a corporation excise tax and the submission to the states of what eventually became the Sixteenth Amendment, and curbed the powers of authoritarian Republican Speaker Joseph G. Cannon. When his party gained control of the House in 1911, Clark, as Speaker, generally proved himself an effective leader, but sabotaged what might have become his greatest achievement—a general reciprocity treaty with Canada—by boasting that the agreement would enable the United States to annex "every foot of the British North American possessions, no matter how far north they may extend." A serious contender for the Democratic presidential nomination in 1912, Clark lost out to Woodrow Wilson on the forty-sixth ballot after losing the support of William Jennings Bryan and several key party "bosses." During Wilson's first term, Clark skillfully managed the Democratic caucus on behalf of such notable progressive measures as the Underwood-Simmons Tariff Act, a federal income tax, the Clayton Anti-Trust Act, the Federal Trade Commission, and the Federal Reserve Act. He did break with Wilson over Panama Canal tolls and military preparedness, and led the band of agrarian Democrats who opposed the president's war policies. He lost the Speakership as a result of the Republican resurgence of 1918, and his congressional seat during the G.O.P. landslide two years later. Before his death the following year, Clark completed writing his memoirs, a quirky volume with occasional gems of inside politics hidden among piles of pretentious prose.

See also: Cannon, Joseph Gurney; Federal Reserve Bank; Federal Trade Commission (FTC); Insurgents; Payne-Aldrich Tariff (Tariff of 1909); Personal income tax (Sixteenth Constitutional Amendment); Taft, William Howard; Wilson-Gorman Tariff (Tariff of 1894).

Selected Bibliography:

Champ Clark, *My Quarter Century of American Politics*, 1920; Lewis L. Gould, *Reform and Regulation: American Politics from Roosevelt to Wilson*, 1986; David Sarasohn, *The Party of Reform: Democrats in the Progressive Era*, 1989.

John D. Buenker

CLAY, HENRY (April 12, 1777–June 29, 1852)

The "Great Compromiser"; champion of the tariff by means of his American System and agent of compromise between factions during the Nullification Crisis.

Born in Hanover County, Virginia, on April 12, 1777, after a stint in the Senate between 1807 and 1811, Clay became Speaker of the House in 1811, representing Kentucky. A virulent war hawk during the War of 1812, Clay worried about British trade at the end of the war. He feared that British goods would overwhelm inferior American goods and eventually destroy young businesses across the nation. As a result, he became keenly protectionist, endorsing high duties on imported wares to raise their price and give American products a competitive edge. The protectionist tariff became one prong in Clay's pro-business American System.

In 1824, Clay pushed for a raise in *ad valorem* rates for both raw and manufactured goods. His tariff passed the House on April 16 by a vote of 107 to 102. The next month it passed the Senate and became law on May 25. Instituting a rate of 35 percent *ad valorem*, Clay's tariff achieved a truly protectionist level.

Clay continued to endorse a high tariff while acting as John Quincy Adams's secretary of state from 1825 to 1828. During the Adams administration, Congress passed the Tariff of 1828, which set prohibitive rates on numerous products. This tariff faced the ire of numerous Americans adversely affected by it, particularly southerners, earning it the name Tariff of Abomi-

nations. Congress began to work to revise it. Back in the Senate by 1832, Clay remained a protectionist struggling to save his American System. At the same time, he understood the political implications of the tariff. As the presidential nominee of the National Republicans, he decided to recommend adjustments. Citing a potential surplus due to the last tariff, Clay put forward a resolution in January 1832 to abolish duties on all noncompetitive imports except wine and silk, which would retain only slight duties. Aside from these, he wanted to keep prohibitive duties on competitive imports. Nevertheless, his willingness to compromise won him friends in his presidential race, although he lost soundly to Andrew Jackson.

Despite the lower rates of the Tariff of 1832, southerners remained unsatisfied. South Carolina, encouraged by favorite son John C. Calhoun, passed the Nullification Ordinance, which would declare the tariff null and void in that state after February 1, 1833. This led Jackson to threaten the state with what became known as the Force Bill.

Meanwhile, Clay's 1832 defeat made him consider retiring from public life. Still he knew that many Americans saw him as the only possible savior of the Union during the crisis. At the same time, Jackson had begun to endorse the Verplanck Bill, which would drop tariffs far below the level Clay deemed comfortable. Realizing that whoever championed the tariff that won out would be held in high esteem, he set to work on his own compromise. He first introduced his compromise tariff in December 1832. He then reintroduced the plan to the Senate on February 12, 1833. Clay's Compromise, also known as the Compromise of 1833, satisfied the South Carolinians. While debate over his compromise bill continued, Clay abstained from the vote on the Force Bill in order to retain his ties to the South. Clay's endeavors resulted in a peaceful end to the Nullification Crisis.

Clay remained a strong proponent of the tariff for the rest of his life. For this reason, the tariff continued to define his career. With his compromise tariff due to expire at the end of June 1842, Clay knew duties would either remain at 20 percent *ad valorem* or disappear altogether. To prevent a loss of protection, in February he called for increased rates along with the repeal of a distribution law requiring the suspension of allocation of funds if duties went above 20 percent. His resolution resulted in the "Little Tariff," designed to postpone the expiration of the Treaty of 1833 by one month while Congress deliberated. The tariff that eventually passed reinstated the rates of 1833. Clay watched from a distance, since he had resigned from the Senate earlier that year.

Clay ran for president in 1844, losing to James K. Polk, and sought nomination again in 1848, but failed to gain the nomination. All the while, the tariff remained central to his thinking and his campaigns. Clay died of tuberculosis in a Washington, D.C., hotel room on June 29, 1852.

See also: Calhoun, John Caldwell; Clay's Compromise; Jackson, Andrew; Nullification; Tariff of 1828 (Tariff of Abominations); Tariff of 1832. **Vol. II**: Daniel Webster's Speech Defending His Support of the Tariff of 1828; Robert Young Hayne's 1832 Speech in Support of Free Trade; Proclamation to the People of South Carolina; Andrew Jackson's Message to Congress on the Nullification Crisis; Force Act. **Vol. III**: Tariff of 1828 (Tariff of Abominations); Tariff of 1832; Tariff of 1833 (Compromise Tariff).

Selected Bibliography:

Maurice G. Baxter, *Henry Clay and the American System*, 1995; Merrill D. Peterson, *The Great Triumvirate: Webster, Clay, and Calhoun*, 1987; Robert V. Remini, *Henry Clay: Statesman for the Union*, 1991.

Adrienne Caughfield

CLAY'S COMPROMISE

A compromise tariff designed in 1833 to ease sectional tensions during the Nullification Crisis when South Carolinians lashed out against federal government restrictions by declaring the Tariff of 1828, also known as the Tariff of Abominations, and the Tariff of 1832 null and void.

Under the leadership of Vice President John C. Calhoun, South Carolinians said they would no longer collect duties in their state after February 1, 1833. In response, President Andrew Jackson called for a Force Bill designed to foment military duress in the state if it refused to acquiesce.

Fresh from his defeat in the presidential election of 1832, Henry Clay considered retirement. Nevertheless, he recognized his appointed role as the "Great Compromiser" and chose instead to remain in public life and work toward a compromise. In December 1832, he proposed that the United States maintain current tariff rates until March 3, 1840. After this, the government would lower rates until they reached the level of 20 percent *ad valorem*.

Unfortunately, as Clay worked out the details of his plan, Jackson began to push his Force Bill through the Senate and into the House of Representatives. Angered by the president's actions, South Carolina threatened to secede. The process of nullification soon went into effect, and South Carolina showed no sign of backing down.

On February 12, 1833, Clay presented his compromise tariff to the Senate. It called for a gradual reduction in the tariff. Every two years through 1839, the duties would be lowered slightly in uneven increments. In 1841, half of what remained over 20 percent would be cut, and the other half would be eliminated in 1842. By 1842, the tariff would rest at 20 percent *ad valorem*, with more raw materials placed on the duty-free list. In addition, Clay's compromise allowed for the cash payment of customs instead of the traditional credit system, bringing more immediate revenue into the United States.

Clay then hashed out the plan with fellow protectionists, including Daniel Webster. Webster wanted a more selective compromise so that it would remain protectionist. Delaware senator John M. Clayton recommended a home valuation amendment to Clay's bill. This would add five to ten points to duties, which would compensate for the loss of protection. Clay introduced the amendment in the Senate as his own. It passed by a vote of 26 to 16. Calhoun reluctantly accepted the compromise.

The House of Representatives adopted Clay's Compromise Bill on February 25 with a vote of 119 to 85. The Senate approved it on March 1 and passed it along with the newly approved Force Bill to President Jackson for signature. Jackson, although still angry at South Carolina and his wayward vice president, accepted the compromise and signed it into law the next day.

After Jackson's approval, Calhoun took the Compromise Act to Columbia, South Carolina, for the approval of the state convention. The convention accepted it and repealed its earlier Nullification Ordinance. The state declared its favorite son the savior of the Union. Nullification, they proclaimed, had overthrown protectionism at last.

See also: Calhoun, John Caldwell; Clay, Henry; Jackson, Andrew; Nullification; Tariff of 1828 (Tariff of Abominations); Tariff of 1832.

Selected Bibliography:

Richard E. Ellis, *The Union at Risk: Jacksonian Democracy, States' Rights, and the Nullification Crisis*, 1987; Merrill D. Peterson, *The Great Triumvirate: Webster, Clay, and Calhoun*, 1987.

Adrienne Caughfield

CLEVELAND, STEPHEN GROVER (March 18, 1837–June 24, 1908)

American president who served two nonconsecutive terms and whose career hinged on tariff and fiscal policies.

Born in Caldwell, New Jersey, Cleveland ranked as the fifth child of his father Richard, a poor minister. After his father's death in 1853, Cleveland studied law in Buffalo, New York, and earned a reputation as an honest lawyer, which helped him win a series of elected positions as the supervisor of the Second Ward in 1862 and as sheriff of Erie County in 1871. He won the election for mayor of Buffalo in 1881 and governor of New York two years later. Cleveland proved himself an enemy of the Tammany Hall political machine in New York by promoting civil service reform. When he ran for president in 1884, his opponents criticized his character because he had hired a substitute to fight for him in the Civil War and had fathered an illegitimate child. Still, he narrowly defeated the staunch protectionist, James G. Blaine. Cleveland benefited from a split in the Republican ranks among political idealists, called mugwups, and the staunch conservatives. The nomination of Blaine drove many reform-minded Republicans into the Cleveland camp.

Although the passage of several significant legislative bills filled Cleveland's first term, limiting federal expenditures and promoting financial responsibility were the most important themes in his agenda. For this reason, he refused to give federal funds to relieve Texas farmers during a drought. Faced with a budget surplus of $94 million in 1887, Cleveland called for a tariff reduction to prevent Congress from squandering funds. While he and John G. Carlisle made plans for tariff reduction, Blaine convinced many that Cleveland supported outright free trade. Republican Benjamin Harrison won the presidency in 1888 largely because people feared that abandoning tariffs would mean higher taxes, lower wages, and greater unemployment.

Ironically, financial matters reopened the door for Cleveland's political career when the "Billion Dollar Congress" passed the unpopular McKinley Tariff, driving tariffs to their highest point. Cleveland quickly became one of the most outspoken opponents of this tariff. Yet he also criticized financial extremists at the other end of the spectrum, the Populists pushing for inflated currency. Democrats successfully took control of Congress in the 1890 elections. Cleveland won the presidency in 1892 running on a platform of tariff reform and the gold standard.

In Cleveland's second presidential term he faced many domestic problems stemming from an economic depression that began in 1893. The resulting poverty, illustrated by the desperate march of Jacob Coxey's Army, labor unrest, the 1894 Pullman strike, and J.P. Morgan's substantial loan to the federal government, perceived by many to be unjustly tying the government to the notorious financier, darkened Cleveland's second term. Moreover, the tariff bill proposed by Congress in 1894 disappointed him. Introduced by William L. Wilson, the bill initially meant to ease tariff rates moderately, but the addition of over 600 amendments, many of which placed duties on everyday items, resulted in the Wilson-Gorman Tariff, which hardly satisfied Cleveland's desire to lower tariffs. The bill passed without Cleveland's signature. Given the choice between the protectionist stance of William McKinley and the free-silver stance of William Jennings Bryan, Cleveland supported McKinley in 1896. The former president died in Princeton, New Jersey, on June 24, 1908.

See also: Blaine, James Gillespie; Bryan, William Jennings; Carlisle, John Griffin; Harrison, Benjamin; McKinley, William; McKinley Tariff (Tariff of

1890); Populists; Wilson, William L.; Wilson-Gorman Tariff (Tariff of 1894). **Vol. II**: Grover Cleveland's 1887 State of the Union Address; Benjamin Harrison's 1889 State of the Union Address. **Vol. III**: Tariff of 1883 (Mongrel Tariff); Tariff of 1894 (Wilson-Gorman Tariff).

Selected Bibliography:

Paul H. Jeffers, *An Honest President: The Life and Presidencies of Grover Cleveland*, 2000; Richard E. Welch Jr., *The Presidencies of Grover Cleveland*, 1988.

Matt McCook

CLINTON, WILLIAM JEFFERSON (BILL) (August 19, 1946–   )

Inaugurated forty-second president of the United States in 1993 and re-elected to a second term in 1996.

Born William Jefferson Blythe IV in Hope, Arkansas, Clinton took his stepfather's last name in high school. A graduate of Georgetown University and Yale Law School, he won a Rhodes scholarship to Oxford University in 1968. In 1974, he married Yale Law School graduate Hillary Rodham. Clinton won the governorship of Arkansas in 1978, lost a bid for a second consecutive term, and then regained the office four years later and held that position until he won the presidency in 1992, defeating incumbent George H.W. Bush. After serving a second term as president, Clinton retired to New York, where Hillary became the first former first lady to win a seat in the U.S. Senate in the year 2000.

Clinton's administration gained congressional approval of several important pieces of free trade legislation despite significant opposition within his own Democratic Party. He secured ratification of the North American Free Trade Agreement (NAFTA) in 1993 after George H.W. Bush had obtained the signatures of member nations just prior to the 1992 presidential election. In late 1994, he also pioneered a sweeping tariff-cutting pact, boosting the World Trade Organization (WTO), and in 2000 he instituted the normalization of economic relations with and extension of Most Favored Nation status to China. His administration lowered trade barriers with Africa and induced Japan to lower import restrictions.

In the 1992 presidential campaign, Clinton had criticized President George H.W. Bush for placing business interests ahead of human rights, labor, and environmental safeguards in Mexico and China. Later Clinton's critics raised similar objections to his own policies. Unions feared NAFTA would cost U.S. jobs, a theme seconded by H. Ross Perot, a maverick businessman and influential Third Party candidate for president in 1992.

Clinton advanced his trade agenda in Congress over significant opposition in his own party, including that of Richard Gephardt, Democratic leader in the House of Representatives. The president strengthened his hand by first getting Gephardt and Congress to agree to vote on NAFTA as fast-track legislation. He negotiated and submitted separate "side agreements" dealing with labor rights and the environment, and accepted revisions providing relief to industries such as citrus and textiles in key legislative districts. He encouraged business leaders to mount a media campaign to promote the agreement, and sent Vice President Albert Gore to debate Perot on national television. Only a minority of Democrats voted for NAFTA, but overwhelming Republican Party support secured its passage. A similar coalition passed the WTO accord. As the congressional majority after 1994, Republicans eased the approval of Clinton's China initiative.

Clinton's trade agenda also suffered setbacks. Seeking Democratic support for eventually admitting Chile to NAFTA, he proposed including provisions similar to the side agreements for NAFTA in the body of a bilateral agreement for Chile. The Republican majority in Congress rejected this approach, setting back Clinton's goal of creating the Free Trade Area of the Americas. In November 1999, labor and environmental groups disrupted a Seattle conference called to expand the WTO into a Mutual Agreement on Investment (MAI). Clinton responded to the demonstrations with a call for "rule-based trade," which many Third World nations feared meant protectionism, restricted access to the U.S. market, and a compromise of their sovereignty. The conference ended in discord and significantly set back negotiations on the MAI.

See also: Bush, George Herbert Walker; Democratic Party; Fast-track legislation; Free Trade Area of the Americas (FTAA); Gephardt, Richard; Gore, Albert Arnold, Jr.; Human rights; Mexico; Most Favored Nation (MFN); North American Free Trade Agreement (NAFTA); Perot, Henry Ross; Presidential campaigns; World Trade Organization (WTO). **Vol. II**: Presidential Debate over the North American Free Trade Agreement.

Selected Bibliography:

John R. MacArthur, *The Selling of Free Trade: NAFTA, Washington, and the Subversion of American Democracy*, 2000; William A. Orme, *Understanding NAFTA: Mexico, Free Trade and the New North America*, 1996.

Daniel C. Hellinger

COAL

A material used for both manufacturing and domestic purposes.

Coal, unimportant as a raw material in colonial times, became increasingly vital in the early republic, especially in the northeastern states. Although plentiful supplies of coal existed in the Appalachian Mountains between Pennsylvania and Virginia, lack of transportation made it uneconomical to exploit these resources so the coal that Americans consumed came largely from Great Britain. The War of 1812 cut off the British supply and, following the war, the introduction of tariffs encouraged the development of domestic coal sources. The canal boom of the years after the War of 1812 helped cheapen the transportation of bulky products, and coal became one of the most important commodities transported by this method. The Delaware and Hudson Canal, completed in 1828, linked the Hudson River, Erie Canal, and Great Lakes with the Pennsylvania coalfields, while the Union Canal, finished in 1825, transported coal to the Susquehanna Valley and Chesapeake Bay. By the late nineteenth century, U.S. population and industry had spread westward to the Pacific, allowing Canada and Australia to compete for western markets with the northeastern coalfields. A battle over tariffs raged during the nineteenth century between manufacturers, who depended on coal, and the mine owners. Congress raised tariffs on coal during the Civil War for revenue purposes, then lowered them in 1894, raised them again in 1897, then lowered them once more in 1909, and finally abolished them in 1913.

See also: Canada; Civil War (American); Great Britain; War of 1812.

Selected Bibliography:

Ronald E. Shaw, *Canals for a Nation: The Canal Era in the United States, 1790–1860*, 1990.

John P. Barrington

COFFEE

A popular tropical product exported by many Latin American countries to the United States.

Originating in sixth-century Ethiopia, coffee production later spread to Asia and Latin America. A minor luxury import into the English colonies, coffee became popular after the Boston Tea Party (1773), as North Americans substituted coffee for tea. Early imports to the United States came principally from Cuba, Haiti, and other Caribbean islands. In the nineteenth century, Central America and Colombia replaced the Caribbean as the principal source of coffee, but eventually Brazil became the largest exporter. Because of the many subvarieties and qualities of the two types of coffee, *arabica* and *robusta*, prices vary considerably, even today. Finer grades came from Central America and Colombia, while Brazil provided the bulk of the product.

Annual per capita consumption of coffee in the United States grew from three pounds in 1830 to more than twelve pounds by the beginning of the twentieth century, at which time the United States consumed nearly half of the world's coffee. Twentieth-century consumption in the United States remained around twelve pounds per capita during the first half of the century, but dropped off in the latter part, as most U.S. customers came to prefer weaker coffee. Specialty marketing brought a slight increase again by the end of the century.

Climatic conditions and other factors caused coffee production and prices to fluctuate considerably, contributing to market speculation. The United States ended import tariffs on coffee in 1873. Coffee-producing states, in collaboration with international financiers, meanwhile, sought ways to stabilize the market. An International Coffee Conference in 1902 had little success, but Brazil began a program of "valorization" in 1906 to limit supplies in order to stabilize or raise prices, a process opposed by the United States, which threatened to restore a duty on Brazilian coffee.

The large volume of coffee imports into the United States played an important role in expanding U.S.–Latin American trade in the twentieth century. World War II increased U.S. domination of the Latin American coffee trade by cutting off the important German market. The Third Pan American Coffee Conference in New York in June 1940, attended by delegates of fourteen producing countries, laid the groundwork for a quota system that guaranteed each producing state a portion of the U.S. market. The system helped both to stabilize prices and to save the Latin American coffee producers. African producing nations later joined the system as falling prices led to the International Coffee Agreement (ICA) in 1962, not fully implemented until 1965, establishing new quotas. Subsequent ICA agreements in 1968, 1976, and 1983 readjusted the quotas, but in the 1980s the fragile alliance of coffee producers broke down in the face of increased competition. Failure to reach agreement on renewal in 1989 led to a sharp fall in coffee prices, with the end of quotas driving smaller producers out of production. A new Association of Coffee Producing Countries (ACPC) tried to restore higher prices, but in the 1990s the United States favored a free-market approach, which kept prices low.

See also: Latin America.

Selected Bibliography:

Mark Pendergrast, *Uncommon Grounds: The History of Coffee and How It Transformed Our World*, 1999.

Ralph Lee Woodward Jr.

COLD WAR

The titanic struggle between the United States and the Soviet Union in the last half of the twentieth century for worldwide economic and political dominance.

After the end of World War II, the United States and the Soviet Union emerged as the world's leading superpowers, but the two countries had ideologically opposed systems of government. The Soviets adhered to revolutionary communism and prophesied that one day the working classes would rise up against the bourgeois elite. On the other hand, the United States practiced democratic liberalism and supported the very type of capitalist economy that the Soviets denounced. The amount of power each nation held in the postwar world fueled this ideological conflict, and the superpowers stood at odds on almost every conceivable issue. The magnitude of the Cold War affected nearly every aspect of life in the United States, but America's trade relationships occupied a place of special importance.

One of the crucial concerns for the United States during the Cold War focused on the loyalty of the so-called Third World. America's wars in Korea and Vietnam, along with the Soviet Union's struggle in Afghanistan demonstrate the importance of the Third World to the superpowers during the Cold War. American leaders believed in a bipolar postwar world in which the United States and the Soviet Union led two competing camps, and the other nations in the world favored one side or the other. Following this line of reasoning, the uncommitted nations of the world would eventually have to choose. The U.S. State Department viewed trade relationships as one of the best ways of increasing the number of America's friends and allies. Trade concessions to nations already favorable to the United States could ensure their continued loyalty and support, and favorable tariffs and aid programs could persuade the undecided nations of the Third World that the United

States best represented their interests. By building up economic relationships, American planners believed they could contain the Soviet Union and keep international communism from spreading.

Harry S Truman, the first president to confront the Cold War, set the precedent on the role trade would play in the conflict. Truman placed foreign policy issues over concerns with domestic industry. The rebuilding of Western Europe through the use of the Marshall Plan served as the first step for the Truman administration. By rebuilding these Western nations, the government hoped to create self-sufficient allies that could eventually trade in American markets. Then a push for more open trade followed, and the administration called for lower tariffs and reciprocity rather than complete free trade. The Truman administration failed to realize the goal of reciprocity. The United States lowered its tariffs and provided aid to weaker foreign nations, but other nations did not open their doors for America. Essentially, the United States discriminated against itself in order to help its allies recover. Military alliances, such as the North Atlantic Treaty Organization (NATO), and the fear of communism convinced the American people and Congress to support these trade policies. Although not necessarily the best course for the growth of domestic industry, the administration's course proved relatively painless since the American economy remained by far the strongest in the world after World War II.

Truman envisioned the International Trade Organization (ITO) as the principle forum for creating a more open international economy and bolstering America's allies, but protectionist Republicans controlled Congress and rejected American membership in the organization. To assure the ability to negotiate multilateral tariff agreements, the Truman administration then pushed for the adoption of the General Agreement on Tariffs and Trade (GATT). Designed as a temporary replacement for the ITO, GATT actually became the main forum for tariff negotiations during the Cold War. The pursuit of multilateral trade negotiations represented a significant shift from the prewar policy of individual bilateral agreements. Rather than linking individual nations only to the United States, Truman and his advisors sought to create an integrated system designed to bind anticommunist allies together in economic strength.

In 1949, Mao Zedong and his followers created the communist People's Republic of China, and the United States sent troops to Korea in 1950 when the North Korean military moved south. As the Cold War turned hot in Asia, American trade policies began to shift. When Dwight D. Eisenhower came into office in 1953 at the end of the Korean War, Eisenhower and Secretary of State John Foster Dulles finalized the change and focused their trade policies on East Asia rather than on Europe. Citing the spread of communism through Asia, the Eisenhower administration put forth what has become known as the Domino Theory. Essentially, this idea held that if another Asian nation turned to communism, then the rest of the nations in the region would fall like dominoes, possibly even spreading to Australia or the Middle East. To keep this from happening, the government created the Southeast Asian Treaty Organization (SEATO) to coordinate military affairs, but also placed a heavy reliance on economic policy in the region. Recognizing the regional economic importance of Japan, Eisenhower sought to rebuild the Japanese economy while pulling it closer to the anticommunist nations. Following this policy, the Eisenhower administration gave Japan more favorable concessions than Britain, especially in the textile industry, and they also secured Japanese membership in GATT despite British protests.

Eisenhower's military background left him unfamiliar with economic issues and domestic concerns. It was simpler to view such things in terms of Cold War strategy. As a result, when formulating a policy to bolster Asian anticommunism, Eisenhower rejected protectionism. Although most Republicans, notably Herbert Hoover, had opposed Truman's push for lower tariffs, Eisenhower believed that unequal trade relationships placed other nations at odds with the United States, and the country must avoid such problems at all costs during the Cold War. Eisenhower perceived free trade as simply another method of fighting communism. Trade bolstered international relationships that the United States needed, and so, like Truman, Eisenhower placed foreign policy interests above the concerns of domestic industry. However, in the 1950s, Europe and Japan had rebuilt a great deal of their industrial infrastructure, and they began renewed competition with American industry. The New England textile industry suffered first. Textile exports declined throughout the 1950s as they faced British and Japanese competition. The textile industry lobbied heavily against Eisenhower's tariff policies, and Congress ultimately placed restraints on the executive office's ability to control tariffs.

John F. Kennedy made protection of the textile industry one of the issues of his campaign in the 1960 presidential election. Yet, when he won, he pushed a free trade agenda akin to those of the earlier Cold War presidents. He did provide a measure of protectionism for the textile industry, and Congress increased the executive's authority to negotiate tariffs once again in the 1962 Trade Expansion Act. Kennedy also shifted the focus of American trade policy away from Asia. The rise of Fidel Castro in Cuba led Kennedy to pay more attention to Latin America than his predecessors, and the Alliance for Progress promised economic aid to Latin America. Despite increased interest in Latin America, Kennedy's biggest concern remained Europe. The creation of the European Economic Community (EEC) in 1957 turned Western Europe into a single major competitor for the United States. Domestic industries feared European competition, but Kennedy favored the EEC as a method of strengthening the western anticommunist nations. Kennedy accepted injury to some domestic industries and argued that international competition would refresh the American economy. After Kennedy's assassination, Lyndon B. Johnson continued to reject protectionism and followed much the same course.

American presidents favored free trade and rejected protectionism in the early Cold War, but the Vietnam conflict disrupted American trade policies as much as so many other aspects of

American life. After Richard Nixon won the presidential election in 1968, tariff policies began to change. Nixon rejected the false reciprocal trade policies of the earlier Cold War administrations. Instead, he promoted true reciprocity. The United States would continue to support free trade in the world, but would no longer do so to its own detriment. By the 1970s, tariffs no longer constituted the only barrier to free trade, and Nixon initiated the Tokyo Round of GATT that placed more attention on nontariff barriers. As a result, tariff negotiations ceased to occupy as much attention in America's trade policy for the remainder of the Cold War.

When the Soviet Union broke apart in 1991, the Cold War ended. It seemed that the United States had won a victory, and the decline of the Soviet economy accounts for much of the American triumph. When considered in this light, it becomes clear that America's tariff and trade policies occupy a place of importance in the history of the Cold War.

See also: Eisenhower, Dwight D. (Ike); General Agreement on Tariffs and Trade (GATT); Hoover, Herbert; International Trade Organization (ITO); Kennedy, John F.; Third World; Truman, Harry S.

Selected Bibliography:

Susan Ariel Aaronson, *Trade and the American Dream: A Social History of Postwar Trade Policy*, 1996; Alfred E. Eckes, *Opening America's Market: U.S. Foreign Trade Policy Since 1776*, 1995.

John K. Franklin

COLLIER ACT OF 1932

Tariff legislation designed to force President Herbert Hoover to negotiate reciprocal trade agreements during the Great Depression.

After the passage of the Hawley-Smoot Tariff Act, voters elected a new Congress in 1930. Republicans maintained a one-vote majority in the Senate, but many of them voted with Democrats, securing passage of the Collier Act of 1932. This legislation required the president to negotiate treaties with foreign countries based on mutual trade concessions. Hoover vetoed the bill since it included a clause allowing congressional approval of the agreements instead of leaving the authority with the U.S. Trade Commission. Designed to provide a political issue to use against Hoover in the campaign of 1932, Democrats designed the measure as a political ploy instead of a serious attempt to modify tariff policies.

See also: Hawley-Smoot Tariff (Tariff of 1930); Hoover, Herbert.

Selected Bibliography:

Alfred E. Eckes, *Opening America's Market: U.S. Foreign Trade Policy Since 1776*, 1995.

Cynthia Clark Northrup

COLONIAL ADMINISTRATION

British system created for governing the colonies and enforcing trade regulations.

Although primarily concerned with the tariff and the development of the United States, an understanding of the era of English colonial rule of the thirteen colonies requires a wider, comparative perspective. Just as the British borrowed manufacturing techniques, machinery, and production skills, England also borrowed ideas of administration from abroad. But the initial colonial endeavors in North America produced outcomes decidedly different from the experiences of those from which they borrowed.

As English mercantilists voiced concerns over the comparative advantage of Spain and its American silver mines, English pirates from the 1560s to the early seventeenth century returned not only with plunder from the Caribbean but also important documents concerning Spanish and other political and economic policies. Haklyut even published a collection of these documents. The absence of silver mines from the Carolinas to New Brunswick led to paths of development along those lines described by Adam Smith.

Spain, seen as the weak, rigid state whose first-tier status depended wholly on its Atlantic lifeline of American silver, contrasted with England, perceived as the strong, adaptive state that fostered innovation and surpassed the colonial accomplishments of the Spanish. Although sixteenth- and seventeenth-century England remained somewhat weak, it also proved capable of maintaining its independence, evidenced by Elizabeth's refusal to marry Philip II and the defeat of the Spanish Armada. But England under the Tudors and the Stuarts lacked the domestic stability necessary to extend its domination abroad in the same fashion as Spain.

While royal charters opened the way for private, company-centered colonization, the turbulence of the Thirty Years War, the English Civil War, the era of Cromwell, and the rise of Parliament during the seventeenth century set the colonies politically adrift, opening the way for the emergence of a semiautonomous local and regional reality of self-government, which greatly limited the ability of Hanoverian absolutism to assert itself during the eighteenth century. For example, the Spanish collected 10 and 20 percent taxes on silver and gold production, additional tariffs on the export of bullion and other raw materials, and both capitation and sales taxes as early as the 1560s. During the next two centuries, the number of taxes collected in the Spanish colonies increased fivefold, the rates fourfold, and tax farming ended, all with little popular, let alone concerted or widespread, resistance. In contrast, the Townshend Acts and other measures aimed at lowering the debt incurred during the War of the Austrian Succession and the Seven Years' War stirred up heavy colonial opposition, leading to outright insurrection and revolution. These controversial measures included a tax on foreign molasses that could not be collected, the sale of stamped (taxed) paper, and taxes on tea and other commodities imported into the colonies. By the time the American Revolution broke out, Spain had been collecting taxes on liquor and its inputs, on paper, and all measure of consumer goods for more than 200 years.

To further illustrate the point, weak Spain in 1775 collected from Mexico alone a figure in silver pesos roughly equal to 30 percent of England's annual debt service. While both England and France struggled against ever-imminent financial ruin between 1760 and 1790, Spain successfully paid off its debts from the Seven Years' War by the early 1770s and from the American revolt by 1792. Certainly, Spain realized substantial benefits for its backwardness.

In the end, while both England and Spain lost the bulk of their American colonial possessions over questions of sovereignty, the causes differed. England's inability to enforce its tax laws cost it the territories that would become the United States. In contrast, while England struggled to recover from the financial woes inflicted between 1775 and 1783, Spain built a navy with Mexican silver and Cuban oak that came within half a dozen ships-of-the-line of equaling England's vaunted fleets that "ruled the Seven Seas." Moreover, Spain's loss of its colonies occurred as the result of the Napoleonic invasion, an irresistible force in continental Europe. Only the Russian winter and the English Channel prevented further conquest.

Thus, in assessing the comparative strengths and weaknesses of English colonial administration, the question remains whether the English government and Hanoverian absolutism became superior to Habsburg and Bourbon colonial rule. For by the end of the eighteenth century, England successfully ruled India, China, and Africa through conquest, and imposed local indigenous self-government, direct colonial tax and trade regulation, and mercantilist protectionism.

See also: American Revolution; Smith, Adam.

Selected Bibliography:

Miguel Artola, *La hacienda del Antiguo Régimen*, 1982; John Brewer, *The Sinews of Power: War, Money, and the English State, 1688–1783*, 1989; John Holland Rose, ed., *The Cambridge History of the British Empire*, 1929.

David J. Weiland III

COLONIAL CURRENCIES

An unintended and informal form of protectionism in the pre-revolutionary period.

Starting with Massachusetts in 1690, most of Britain's mainland American colonies issued their own currencies, in order to remedy shortages in the supply of gold and silver coin and also to help colonial governments meet revenue shortfalls, especially in wartime. The issuing governments originally intended that their currencies would convert to sterling at par or at least at a fixed and stable rate of exchange. In most cases, the overissue of paper currencies, along with insufficient guarantees for the redemption of the notes in coin in the near future, meant that the currencies depreciated against sterling. British merchants who sold manufactured goods on credit in the colonies frequently complained that the loss of value in the colonial currency against sterling between the time they sold the goods and the time they received payment for them eroded their profits. These merchants therefore raised the price they charged for their goods, in order to anticipate losses arising from currency depreciation. Thus, colonial currencies acted in some senses, though not in others, as a tariff: they did raise the prices of imports, but did not consciously act as a means of fostering domestic manufactures. The extent to which these "tariffs" affected the development of colonial economies remains immeasurable, but the possibility exists that the higher prices charged by British merchants helped to fuel inflation in certain colonies. The British government certainly believed that colonial currencies hindered British trade with America. In 1750, Parliament prohibited the issue of further paper money in New England, and ordered the speedy redemption of all notes currently circulating in those colonies. The Currency Act of 1764 then forbade any colonial government from issuing its own paper money.

See also: Great Britain; Massachusetts.

Selected Bibliography:

John J. McCusker and Russell R. Menard, *The Economy of British America, 1607–1789*, 1985.

John P. Barrington

COMMISSION ON FOREIGN ECONOMIC POLICY (CFEP)

In his special message to Congress on April 7, 1953, President Dwight D. Eisenhower requested that the Reciprocal Trade Agreements Act, originally passed in 1934, receive an extension of one year and called for the establishment of a commission to conduct a comprehensive review of U.S. foreign economic policy.

Public Law 215 entitled "Trade Agreements Extension of 1953" established the Commission on Foreign Economic Policy (CFEP) on August 7, 1953. Section 301 of this act provided for a seventeen-member bipartisan commission charged with examining and reporting on international trade.

They also reviewed foreign economic policy and the trade aspects of national security, as well as foreign policy. They recommended appropriate policies, measures, and practices to Congress. The president appointed seven members, the vice president appointed five from the Senate, and the Speaker of the House of Representatives chose five from the House. Eisenhower selected Clarence B. Randall, chairman of the Board of Inland Steel Company and a former steel consultant to the Marshall Plan, as chairman, expecting him to neutralize protectionist members of the commission because of his reputation as an ardent free trader.

The commission conducted closed-door hearings of government officials and business leaders in Washington and Paris in October and November 1953. At public hearings held in Washington late in October, representatives of national trade associations, labor unions, and other organizations concerned with foreign trade presented their views. The commission received over 300 written statements.

The CFEP presented its final report to Congress on January 23, 1954. Divided into twelve sections, the report included topics such as the dollar problem, foreign aid and technical assistance, U.S. foreign investment, tariffs and trade policy, East–West trade, labor standards in international competition, and agriculture and raw materials. Although its main thrust focused on trade liberalization through the reciprocal trade program, the report also included protectionist and fiscally conservative recommendations. This juxtaposition reflected the contested deliberations within the commission and a resilient strain of economic nationalism in postwar U.S. foreign economic policy. Thus, the specific proposals of the commission included recommendations for the termination of post–World War II emergency aid programs, an early end to foreign aid given on a grant basis, revisions in the Revenue Code to encourage private investment abroad and in the Buy American Act to improve the chances of successful bids by foreign countries on U.S. government procurement contracts.

Three members of the commission, Representative Richard Simpson (R-PA), Representative Daniel Reed (R-NY), and Senator Eugene Millikin (R-CO) dissented from the commission's conclusions. Reed and Simpson presented a separate minority report. The CFEP dissolved on April 23, 1954.

See also: Eisenhower, Dwight D. (Ike); Reciprocal Trade Agreements Act (RTAA).

Selected Bibliography:

Burton I. Kaufman, *Trade and Aid*, 1982.

Sayuri Shimizu

COMMITTEE FOR RECIPROCITY INFORMATION

The enactment of the Reciprocal Trade Agreements Act (RTAA) in 1934 led to the establishment of a number of federal agencies and interdepartmental committees charged with fulfilling the procedural requirements of the legislation.

The RTAA, as amended and extended, included detailed provisions to ensure against serious injury to domestic industry. The president issued public notification of intent to conduct tariff negotiations, published a list of prospective concessions, and held public hearings before entering negotiations.

The interdepartmental Committee for Reciprocity Information (CRI) conducted public hearings on proposed modifications of tariff rates and compiled the information provided by concerned domestic parties. Like the peril point investigations of the U.S. Tariff Commission, also required under the RTAA, hearings held by CRI allowed individuals and groups to supply relevant data and notify the executive branch of their views. The Interdepartmental Committee on Trade Agreements studied the material obtained from these hearings as the basis for recommendations to the president on what modifications the United States should actually offer and request in the course of negotiations.

The federal agencies and executive offices represented on CRI varied through its existence from 1934 to 1963, but the core group included the Departments of State, Commerce, Defense, the Treasury, Justice, Agriculture, and Labor. The president had created one of the key members of CRI, the Special Adviser to the President on Foreign Trade, by an executive order on March 23, 1934, under authority of the National Industrial Recovery Act (NIRA). This office coordinated information concerning U.S. foreign trade and negotiated specific trade transactions with any individual or group desiring federal assistance in financing or bartering. In cooperation with other federal agencies concerned with foreign trade, the special adviser's office also studied the trade resources of foreign countries and the amount of blocked American funds abroad.

The establishment of the Office of the Special Representative for Trade Negotiations (STR) by executive order on January 13, 1963, effectively terminated CRI. The Kennedy administration created the new office as part of its effort to streamline the formulation of foreign commercial policy and speed the Kennedy Round of the General Agreement on Tariffs and Trade (GATT) negotiations held between 1964 and 1967. The special representative later became a cabinet position, and its holder was given the title of ambassador.

See also: Reciprocal Trade Agreements Act (RTAA); Tariff Commission.

Selected Bibliography:

Thomas Zeiler, *American Trade and Power in the 1960s*, 1992.

Sayuri Shimizu

COMMUNISM

Political theory or economic system in which a classless society owns everything in common.

Nineteenth-century German immigrants to France, England, Switzerland, and Belgium laid the foundation of Marxist socialism by forming secret societies and organizing clubs to discuss social problems. Karl Marx and Friedrich Engels drafted the *Communist Manifesto* for the Communist Club in 1848. As early as 1830, Germans brought socialist ideas to the United States. After the American Civil War, the Marxist International influenced the labor movement and American socialists, but American Communism's relevance extended from the founding

of the Communist Party of the United States in 1919 until it reached obscurity in the 1960s. In 1917, Vladimir Lenin's Bolshevik Party seized the Russian government. In a revolutionary fervor, two American Communist parties formed in 1919. Charles Ruthenberg's Communist Party of America had 24,000 members. John Reed and Benjamin Gitlow's Communist Labor Party had 10,000 members, most of whom migrated from Russia. By 1930, a majority of American Communists had grown up in America and spoke English. Overthrowing the American government became the directive of both parties.

To establish control of revolutionary movements, Lenin created the Communist International in 1919. The Soviet Party dominated the Comintern, ostensibly a worldwide brotherhood of revolutionaries. When Joseph Stalin took power in the 1920s, the Soviet Union solidified its control.

In 1921, the Comintern forced the American parties to merge. Ruthenberg, who died in 1927, led a divided party. The Comintern decided all disagreements. In 1929, Stalin ordered leaders Jay Lovestone and Gitlow expelled after they refused to relinquish power to rivals. Earl Browder emerged as leader, a position he held until 1945.

Marxist and socialist political parties, including the Communist Party, have had little impact on election outcomes, on the major parties, or on American public policy. In Communist economics, tariffs exist, but remain unimportant. Profit belongs to the state. In a Soviet-type economy, importers' profits would be skimmed to make good the losses of exporters. The American Communist Party, unconcerned with tariff and trade, concentrated on support for and instructions from the Soviet leadership.

The Great Depression revived revolutionary fervor, and the party led strikes and demonstrations against unemployment and social injustices. Many idealistic Americans joined the Communist Party, but Franklin Roosevelt's New Deal reforms attracted even more Americans to a program within democratic traditions. In the 1920s, the Communist Party had created the Trade Union Unity League (TUUL) in opposition to the American Federation of Labor. As part of its Communist-liberal Popular Front strategy against fascism, the Communists dissolved the TUUL and sent its members into mainstream labor organizations. By the late 1930s, Communists led a quarter of the Congress of Industrial Organization's (CIO) members. Writers, artists, and intellectuals joined Communist-dominated groups. Communists led the American Youth Congress, a federation of the largest youth organizations. The Popular Front operated as a political force.

The growth of Communist influence coincided with Stalin's purges of millions of ordinary Russians and hundreds of thousands of Communists. The Soviet Union dictated the pronouncements of American Communists who did not believe or simply rationalized information that reached the West. Liberal disillusionment dissolved the Popular Front after the Nazi-Soviet Pact of 1939. When Germany attacked the Soviet Union, the Communist Party dropped its peace policies and demanded American entry into the war and aid for the Soviet Union.

After World War II, Browder, convinced of the permanent alliance between the Soviet Union, the United States, and Great Britain, reformed the Communist Party as the Communist Political Association and the Soviet Union ordered him ousted. The reborn party supported Soviet foreign policy goals and opposed President Truman's anti-Soviet containment policy. Communists supported Henry Wallace in his unsuccessful Progressive Party presidential campaign. Anti-Communists dominated American liberalism and the Democratic Party. CIO leaders evicted Communists and Communist-dominated unions.

By the late 1940s, most Americans saw the Communist Party as the puppet of the Soviet Union, America's most dangerous enemy. The party began its irreversible decline. Spy cases, including those of Alger Hiss and Julius and Ethel Rosenberg, intensified the Cold War. When the Korean War began in 1950, the Communist Party lost virtually all allies. Nikita Khrushchev's admittance of Stalin's crimes confirmed anti-Communist beliefs, leaving American Communists devastated. After World War II, party membership dropped to 70,000. By 1958, issues such as Khrushchev's speech, the Hungarian Revolution, and Soviet anti-Semitism had reduced party membership to 3,000. Sustained by secret Soviet subsidies, the American Communist Party remained the most pro-Soviet party in the world. When party leader Gus Hall criticized Mikhail Gorbachev's reform policies, Soviet subsidies ended. When Hall continued to back Communist hard-liners, half of the party members quit. By 2002, the

American Communist Party had less than 1,000 members.

See also: American Federation of Labor (AFL); Great Depression; Roosevelt, Franklin D.; Truman, Harry S.

Selected Bibliography:

Fred E. Haynes, *Social Politics in the United States*, 1970; Harvey Klehr, John Earl Haynes, and Fridrikh Igorevich Firsov, *The Secret World of American Communism*, 1995; Steven J. Rosenstone, Roy L. Behr, and Edward H. Lazarus, *Third Parties in America: Citizen Response to Major Party Failure*, 1984; P.J.D. Wiles, *Communist International Economics*, 1968.

Theo Edwin Maloy

COMTE, AUGUSTE (ISIDORE-AUGUSTE-MARIE-FRANÇOIS-XAVIER COMTE) (January 19, 1798–September 5, 1857)

French materialist philosopher, founder of positivism, and father of modern sociology.

Arguments for the scientific study of society and for policies based on such study formed the basis of Comte's *Cours de philosophie positive* (Course of Positive Philosophy), later supplemented by his work *Système de politique positiv* (System of Positivist Policy), in which he elaborated on his concepts of sociology and the organization of society. Claude-Henri de Rouvroy, Count of Saint-Simon, seriously influenced Comte's early works, although he rejected some of St. Simon's more socialist views of societal organization. Although Comte's emphasis on scientific knowledge caused him to reject metaphysical philosophy and promote materialist values, he also advocated strong moral values in his "religion of humanity." During his own lifetime Comte developed an enthusiastic following among French philosophy students and also in England, where John Stuart Mill reflected his ideas. Eventually, Comte's positivism had a powerful influence in Latin America, modifying nineteenth-century liberalism and supporting more active participation of strong governments in ordering social, political, and economic policy. Especially through the interpretations of Herbert Spencer (1820–1903), Comte also influenced the United States and its economic policy. Although his positive philosophy strongly supported the rise of industry and capitalism, he differed from classical liberals in his support of some government regulation and direction of the economy in order to advance the best interests of the population.

See also: Mill, John Stuart.

Selected Bibliography:

Mary Pickering, *Auguste Comte: An Intellectual Biography*, 1993.

Ralph Lee Woodward Jr.

CONFEDERATE CONSTITUTION

Government document establishing the Confederate States of America in February 1861.

Delegates from the seceding states met in Mobile, Alabama, on February 4, 1861, and drafted a new constitution based closely on the U.S. Constitution. The southern states adopted the new constitution on March 11, 1861.

The document addressed the tariff, long a point of contention between the North and the South, in Article 1, Section 8:

[Congress shall have power] to lay and collect taxes, duties, imposts, and excises for revenue, necessary to pay the debts, provide for the common defense, and carry on the Government of the Confederate States; but no bounties shall be granted from the Treasury; nor shall any duties or taxes on importations from foreign nations be laid to promote or foster any branch of industry; and all duties, imposts, and excises shall be uniform throughout the Confederate States.

Southerners had seen the tariff as a means used by the U.S. government to promote northern industry at the expense of southern consumers. Therefore, the Confederate Constitution allowed the Congress to issue a tariff, but not for the purpose of developing any particular industry. The issue of the tariff as addressed in the Confederate Constitution illustrates the South's displeasure with U.S. tariff policies in the past and its efforts to ensure that tariffs in the Confederate States of America would benefit all sections equally.

See also: Civil War (American).

Selected Bibliography:

James McPherson, *Ordeal by Fire: The Civil War and Reconstruction*, 2000.

Carrie Dowdy

CONGRESS (UNITED STATES)

A representative bicameral legislature (a House of Representatives and a Senate), which is key in establishing U.S. governmental policy and legislation.

Article I, Section 7 of the U.S. Constitution vests in the House of Representatives the responsibility for raising revenue, while the Senate "may propose or concur with Amendments." Further, Article I, Section 8 gives Congress the power to "lay and collect taxes, duties, imposts and excises." Thus, the burden of crafting national tax legislation resides in the U.S. Congress. This system for raising revenue represents a compromise. The Articles of Confederation had conferred all taxing authority to the individual states, where citizens enjoyed direct representation. The inadequacy of this tax structure became apparent during the American Revolution when the states resisted providing the funds needed to feed, clothe, and arm General George Washington's army. At the Philadelphia Constitutional Convention held in 1787, the Federalists urged the delegates to grant the national government the power of the purse. Although Anti-Federalists predicted such powers would lead to the demise of the states' authority and the resurgence of a distant, tyrannical government, the convention codified the authority to levy taxes as a function of the national government.

The document authorized members of the House of Representatives, who served the shortest terms and therefore answered most directly to the public, to create tax policy. Senators, elected through state legislatures, answered to the needs of their home states. Consequently, those elected officials most responsive to state and local interests levied taxes for the national budget. Resolving fiscal problems that emerged throughout the nineteenth century often proved a cumbersome task because of this unique federal system of finance in which the different branches of government ruled supreme within their sphere of authority. The executive branch guided the overall economic policy of the federal government, yet funding these national priorities fell to Congress.

Throughout the nineteenth century, except for the four years during the Civil War era, the government financed its operations primarily through the revenue generated by tariffs. This dependence on customs belies the fact that tariff financing remained an unpredictable source of government income. During the years of duress caused by war or economic downturns, the decrease in imports created deficits and exacerbated the nation's financial problems. Therefore, Congress created tariffs by balancing the demands of the executive branch with the needs and appeals of congressional constituents. The actions of Pennsylvania's congressmen throughout the nineteenth century illustrate this point.

During the colonial era, Great Britain imported iron. As part of their system of mercantilism, they encouraged iron production in the North American colonies. By the signing of the Declaration of Independence, the colonies produced one-seventh of the world's total iron output. While most of the thirteen colonies contributed to iron production, Pennsylvania had the most developed facilities. When the first U.S. Congress convened in 1789 and drafted the new nation's first tariff, a Pennsylvania representative, Thomas Fitzsimons, emerged as the primary spokesman for protection of the Keystone state's "young industry." Many Pennsylvania politicians, regardless of party affiliation, followed his lead throughout the century. James Buchanan, William Bigler, Thaddeus Stevens, and William D. "Pig Iron" Kelley all voted for the protection of iron and iron products during the course of their congressional careers.

Protection of the iron, cotton manufacturers, wool, hemp, and other domestic industries remained a recurrent theme in congressional tariff bills throughout the century. The American System, promoted by Kentucky representative and senator Henry Clay synthesized these regional concerns as voiced in Congress. "The American System was not so much a philosophy seeking embodiment in public policy as it was a set of policies, with distinct interests behind them, seeking the dignity of a philosophy," observed Merrill D. Peterson in *The Great Triumvirate*. Congress guarded these regional interests, in part, through tariff legislation.

The intensity of the congressional debates between the advocates of protection and free trade has often obscured the fact that the demand for revenue, not the prima facie development of domestic industries, directed tariff policy. The needs of the executive branch had to balance with local priorities. Noteworthy antebellum protectionist tariffs, such as those of 1816, 1842, and the Morrill Tariff of 1861, provided the means to raise more funds for the depleted treasury, but also reflected the desire to foster segments of the economy. The resulting compromises governed this federal system of finance.

The government's reliance on import duties for its fiscal health becomes apparent when one examines tariffs as general revenue measures, rather than products of a particular political persuasion. Similarly, the desire to reduce federal surpluses spawned the antebellum era of free trade initiated by the passage of the Tariff Act of 1846. The Walker Tariff of 1846, and, more dramatically, the Tariff Act of 1857, and the efforts to reduce import duties in 1888 resulted from a concern over growing waste and fraud in the government following the accumulation of large federal surpluses.

The Tariff Act of 1816 received broad support from representatives of both northern and southern states. This tariff, adopted to counter the effects of the War of 1812 and provide additional income to support defense spending, increased federal revenue from $7.3 million in 1815 to $26.3 million in 1817. Southerners, most notably John C. Calhoun, supported the tariff and its protection for textile manufacturers, sugar, and domestic production of leather, manufactured wood, paper, and other consumer goods. The new revenue from this tariff generated enough funds to invest in internal improvements, particularly roads deemed necessary for a strong national defense and domestic commercial development. The desire to generate additional revenue to build a defensive infrastructure inspired the passage of this bill.

Passage of the Tariff Act of 1833, known as the Compromise Tariff, also resulted from the merging of congressional and executive interests. Senators Henry Clay and John C. Calhoun, congressional leaders of the protectionists and the free traders, respectively, forged the compromise. Clay introduced the bill as a response to the Nullification Crisis, in which South Carolina, Senator Calhoun's home state, attempted to nullify the Tariff Acts of 1828 and 1832 and refused to collect duties. The bill aimed to lower tariff rates to 20 percent, the amount considered necessary to fund an efficient government and, more directly, to end the crisis that threatened to divide the nation.

The Tariff Act of 1842 also illustrates the relationship between the executive and legislative branches in tariff financing. Enacted to counter the economic depression that began in 1837 and reverse the deficits accumulated each year from 1837 to 1843, this tariff overturned the precipitous drop in tariff rates that took effect in 1842 through the Compromise Tariff by raising rates to an average of 33 percent. Levi Woodbury, President Martin Van Buren's secretary of the treasury, initially promoted this tariff. He warned Congress that the financial problems of the country would exacerbate if import duties did not increase. Although described generally as a protectionist tariff inspired by Whigs, the Tariff Act of 1842 reflects the Federalist nature of American finances. Customs revenue increased from $13.4 million in 1840 to $26.1 million in 1844 under the provisions of this bill. Thus, the executive branch and the U.S. Congress balanced their respective needs in crafting this tariff.

This balance tipped decisively toward Congress during and after the Civil War. Salmon P. Chase, the first Republican secretary of the treasury, developed a cautious plan for financing the Union's effort, but congressional leaders, including Justin S. Morrill and Thaddeus Stevens, instead prepared a more aggressive plan, featuring both internal taxation and higher tariff rates. Manufacturers and licenses provided most of the revenue, seconded by a comprehensive, albeit haphazard, series of excise taxes and the nation's first income tax. To shield businesses from the burden of these taxes, and in explicit support for protectionism, Congress raised import duties; the average custom duties reached as high as 42 percent in 1868. These Civil War tariffs formed the basis of the U.S. tariff system throughout the remainder of the nineteenth century. When the executive branch, under the direction of Secretary of the Treasury Hugh McCulloch and his friend and colleague Special Revenue Commissioner David A. Wells, encouraged Congress to lower rates in 1867, their appeals failed in the legislature. Protectionists ruled on Capitol Hill throughout the postbellum period.

Yet the tariff controversy of 1888 renewed the Federalist tie that bound the Congress to the executive branch. President Grover Cleveland urged Congress to reduce duties, particularly on raw materials, and made tariff revision one of the key issues in his reelection campaign. President Cleveland lost the election, but the tariff issue had now become a prominent feature of national politics. The Republicans believed their victory in the polls meant the public had given them a mandate for a continuation of the policy of protection. Thus, Congress enacted the Tariff Act of 1890, otherwise known as the McKinley Tariff. The McKinley Tariff presented the American people with a "radical extension of the protective system," according to historian Frank W. Taussig. Congress moved boldly to protect both manufactured goods and raw materials. As a salve to the voters, Congress removed all duties from imported sugar. The treasury had accumulated surpluses, negating the need to raise tariff rates and the justification for imposing these taxes. Immediately, the public voiced objection. The McKinley Tariff became law in October 1890; one month later in congressional elections, Republicans suffered a decisive loss in seats in the House of Representatives. The public responded to a tax increase deemed unnecessary just as the framers of the Constitution had anticipated.

Yet the Democratic Party failed to turn this mandate into effective legislation. Congress addressed two more tariff revisions before the dawn of the twentieth century. While Congress debated the Tariff Act of 1894, the country suffered an economic collapse, resulting in lackluster support for tariff reform. Overall tariff rates dropped to approximately 40 percent, but other economic concerns, most notably the controversy over the monetization of silver, rose to the foreground. William McKinley, the force behind the Tariff Act of 1890, won the presidency in 1896, and moved aggressively, once again, to raise tariff rates. The treasury had accumulated a deficit each year since the onset of the depression of 1893, and the president wanted to arrest the trend. McKinley called a special session of Congress for the sole purpose of revising the tariff. The Tariff Act of 1897 resulted from this effort. Average tariff rates rose again to near or above 50 percent under the provisions of this bill, which became the standard for import duties for the next twelve years.

The unique federal system of American public finance, in which the executive branch drafted the government's economic policy but Congress retained the authority to levy taxes, influenced U.S. tariff policy throughout the nineteenth century. The U.S. Congress held the power of the purse. Both the requests that came from the executive branch and the needs and interests of representatives' and senators' constituency guided the tariffs created by these elected officials. Throughout the antebellum era, the executive and legislative branches maintained a balance as they enacted tariffs in response, primarily, to the revenue needs of the government. Yet, in the period after the Civil War, protectionist sentiment in the Congress took precedence, and tariff policy became divorced more than ever from the fluctuations in government income. Members of Congress took the lead in creating tariffs more in response to the interests in their states and districts, than in the national revenue needs.

See also: American System; Anti-Federalists; Articles of Confederation; Calhoun, John Caldwell; Civil War (American); Clay, Henry; Cleveland, Stephen Grover; Democratic Party; Federalists; Fitzsimons, Thomas; Free trade; General Agreement on Tariffs and Trade (GATT); Iron; Jackson, Andrew; McKinley, William; Mercantilism; Morrill, Justin S.; North American Free Trade Agreement (NAFTA); Nullification; Protectionism; Republican Party; Stevens, Thaddeus; War of 1812; Webster, Daniel; Wells, David Ames.

Selected Bibliography:

Merrill D. Peterson, *The Great Triumvirate: Webster, Clay, and Calhoun*, 1987; Edward Stanwood, *American Tariff Controversies in the Nineteenth Century*, 1967; Frank W. Taussig, *The Tariff History of the United States*, 1967.

Jane Flaherty

CONGRESS OF INDUSTRIAL ORGANIZATIONS (CIO)

A proponent of industrial unionism that represented the largest worker organization in American history and politicized organized labor.

The Congress of Industrial Organizations started over a fistfight at an American Federation of Labor (AFL) conference. Angry at the lack of appeals by the AFL to industrial workers, John L. Lewis of the United Mine Workers (UMW) punched William L. Hutcheson of the Carpenters' Union. Lewis received immediate respect as a warrior for the rights of workers. A few weeks later, he invited a few dissident AFL union leaders to meet at UMW headquarters to form the Committee for Industrial Organization (CIO) with John Brophy as its head. In November 1939, the CIO separated entirely from the AFL. Veteran unionists, all former heads of AFL affiliates, provided leadership for the CIO. While all of these organizers criticized the AFL policies, none of the leaders repudiated the AFL's agenda of collective bargaining, centralized and authoritative union leadership, and fundamental support for basic American institutions. The CIO acted as a collection of labor unions, counting the United Automobile Workers, the United Packinghouse Workers, and the United Steelworkers among its many member groups. With a peak membership of five million, the CIO succeeded in triggering an explosion of unionism in the industrial core of the economy that transformed American politics. It contributed mightily to the labor movement by channeling working-class activism into politically effective focus, creating permanent labor unions for the first time in mass-production industry. The CIO's picket-line confrontations, its militarylike logistical innovations, its centralized organizing campaigns, and its enormous public demonstrations often made it seem like an irresistible juggernaut. The AFL proved less than enthusiastic about enlisting African American and lower-class workers. The CIO leaders targeted these male workers as recruits, but exhibited traditional views toward women. The vast majority of women workers remained concentrated in low-wage occupations, the CIO's primary fields of operation, but the union embraced the family wage concept because the employment of married women meant a defeat for the working-class household. While some CIO leaders advocated Communism, a majority believed that the Soviet Union represented a real danger to the workers and the union expelled its Communist-leaning affiliates in 1949 and 1950. After strongly supporting the war effort with a no strike pledge, in the years following World War II, the CIO supported the Marshall Plan as long as workers could participate in it,

and opposed business-supported deflationary plans for economic expansion. With collective bargaining, the CIO set standards of material success, personal dignity, and workplace comfort. Additionally, in an effort to better promote the interests of the workers, the CIO created and maintained organized labor's first modern political action committee. Not surprising, along with other labor organizations, the CIO opposed the Taft-Hartley Act of 1947 that aimed to curb the political and economic activities of unions. By the 1950s, the glory days of unionism had passed. In an attempt to revive the labor movement, the CIO merged with the AFL in December 1955. In recent years, the CIO branch of the AFL-CIO opposed fast track legislation for the North American Free Trade Agreement (NAFTA) and favored agreements on human rights, child labor, and environmental issues.

See also: American Federation of Labor (AFL).

Selected Bibliography:

Robert H. Zieger, *The CIO, 1935–1955*, 1995.

Caryn E. Neumann

CONSEIL INTERGOUVERNEMENTAL DES PAYS EXPORTATEURS DE CUIVRE (CIPEC)

Association of copper exporting countries founded in 1967 by the joint initiative of Chile and Zambia, along with Peru and Zaire, to coordinate export policies and support the management of nationalized mining industries.

The Organization of Petroleum Exporting Countries (OPEC) proved the inspiration for the formation of CIPEC (Intergovernmental Council of Copper Exporting Countries). During the oil price hikes of the mid-1970s, the organization enjoyed modest success coordinating cutbacks in production in the face of declining consumption, although these reductions did not stem from the general decline of copper prices in this period. In the late 1970s, Indonesia joined as a full member and Australia, Papua New Guinea, and Yugoslavia as associate members. Around 1980, the Philippines, Mexico, Poland, and Iran became members.

CIPEC accounted for more than half of world copper exports, but never achieved the success of OPEC. CIPEC supported a New International Economic Order under the auspices of the United Nations Conference on Trade and Development (UNCTAD). The failure of the G-7 nations to reach accords on a common fund to manage buffer stocks inhibited CIPEC's ability to control prices and supplies. Chile, the largest and lowest-cost producing nation, shifted its copper policy away from coordinating supplies and stabilization of prices to rapid expansion of production and exports after the overthrow of the Socialist president Salvador Allende Gossen in 1973. This policy, large new mining operations in several countries, and technological innovations that made older mines profitable all undermined CIPEC's effectiveness as a cartel. In 1992, its members abandoned coordinating supply and refounded the organization as the International Copper Study Group (ICSG), with the more modest purpose of exchanging technology and promoting increased demand.

See also: Chile; Copper; North–South Conflict; Organization of Petroleum Exporting Countries (OPEC).

Selected Bibliography:

Amer Salih Araim, *Intergovernmental Commodity Organizations and the New International Economic Order*, 1991.

Daniel C. Hellinger

CONSTITUTIONALITY

The authority to impose a tariff is allocated to Congress by Article 1 of the U.S. Constitution.

Specifically, Section 8 of Article 1 delineates the duties of revenue collection in clauses stating:

> The Congress shall have power to lay and collect Taxes, Duties Imposts and Excises, to pay the Debts and provide for the common Defense and general Welfare of the United States; but all Duties, Imposts and Excises shall be uniform throughout the United States. . . .
>
> To regulate Commerce with foreign Nations, and among the several States, and with the Indian Tribes . . .

Congress imposed tariffs and excises to raise revenue or to further protectionism, decreasing the debilitating effect imports have on the domestic economy. In the early nineteenth century, Secretary of the Treasury Robert Walker, a major proponent of free trade, perceived protectionism as both harmful and unjust, although the open borders he suggested would allow foreign merchandise to undercut American industry and act as a disincentive to begin new businesses. His weakly constructed argument failed to garner much popular support because he based it on the inclusive reading of the Article 1, Section 8 phrase "lay and collect." To Walker, this meant that the implementation of the former power required the ability and willingness to execute the latter. Opponents argued that the interpretation of the entire clause in a similar fashion would require Congress to simultaneously impose "imposts and excises." In reality, Walker's concern proved unwarranted, as Congress never laid duties they could not collect. Merchants, on selecting merchandise to import, had to pay the congressionally predetermined duty for the given product.

Mercantilism called for the imposition and execution of tariffs or elevating the export level above the import level to gain power from profit. Although nations imposed tariffs primarily for revenue purposes, the importance of mercantilism gradually lessened as other forms of financing gained popularity. The general level of charges continued to rise globally until the Hawley-Smoot Tariff Act of 1930, which constituted the peak of U.S. duties. Following the Great Depression, the international community acknowledged that competitively increasing imposts and excises would not necessarily expand world trade, and the passage of the Trade Agreements Act of 1934 reduced or modified tariffs.

See also: Congress (United States); Free trade; Great Depression; Hawley-Smoot Tariff (Tariff of 1930); Mercantilism; Protectionism; Walker, Robert John.

Selected Bibliography:

Percy Ashley, *Modern Tariff History*, 1970; Harry G. Johnson, *Aspects of the Theory of Tariffs*, 1972; Eugene T. Rossides, *U.S. Import Trade Regulation*, 1986; Edward Stanwood, *American Tariff Controversies in the Nineteenth Century*, 1967.

Carolyn E. Ginno and Artemus Ward

CONSUMERISM

Concern for the protection of the rights and interests of the consumer in reference to price, quality, and safety of products.

Traditionally, the argument for free trade included the supposition that consumers would benefit from lower prices. For example, an item arriving in the United States with a value of $3.00 would cost the consumer $5.33 after the importer and the retailer added their typical 33 ⅓ percent markup. If Congress authorized a 50 percent *ad valorem* duty on the same item, the cost before markups would equal $4.50 and the added profits for the importer and the merchant would increase the consumer's cost of the product to $8.00. The higher cost would discourage consumers from purchasing foreign goods and would stimulate domestic production. This, in turn, would benefit American labor. Opponents argue that American workers benefit more when their industries receive protection through high tariffs. Proponents of this line of reasoning suggest that only a small percentage of labor, primarily professionals and high-technology employees, would realize an increase in purchasing power while free trade would reduce the real income of 80 percent of all workers. Americans must weigh the price charged to consumers against the effect on wages since workers also purchase products.

See also: Free trade; Labor; Protectionism.

Selected Bibliography:

Ravi Batra, *The Myth of Free Trade: A Plan for America's Economic Revival*, 1993; Oswald Garrison Villard, *Free Trade—Free World*, 1947.

Cynthia Clark Northrup

CONTINENTAL CONGRESS

The legislative body that governed the thirteen colonies and later the United States from 1774 to 1789.

The Congress, consisting of delegates from each state, met in Philadelphia and operated under the Articles of Confederation. During its tenure, the Congress faced two major issues: funding and fighting the war of independence, and defining the legal relationship between the new federal and state governments. Tariff issues played an important role in both of these areas.

Unlike later tariffs designed to protect domestic industry from outside competition, members of the Continental Congress viewed tariffs almost exclusively as a way to raise revenue. The structure of government at the time, however, did not permit Congress to impose taxes on the states. The Articles of Confederation gave Congress only the right to request that each state contribute to the federal treasury, but Congress had no means to enforce this provision. In addition, it vested only the states with the power to tax. The need to raise funds and the lack of authority to do so forced Congress to raise the tariff issue from time to time.

In 1778 and again in 1780, special congressional committees proposed tariff legislation as a way to offset the growing cost of war. In both cases these recommendations failed to gain the support of Congress. Financial problems intensified as operating costs increased and states failed to meet their financial obligations. In 1781, Congress estimated that the country needed approximately $9 million to cover expenses for the year. It hoped to secure $4 million in loans and collect the rest from the states. By the end of the year, the states had contributed only $422,000 to the nation's treasury. The fact that states began imposing duties on each other and attempted to regulate interstate trade only compounded the problem. This created further divisions and weakened the bonds that held the new nation together.

In 1781, a congressional committee proposed another tariff plan to help stabilize the economy. As in the past, the plan faced serious opposition. Many believed that Congress had no right to ask the states for such power, but this time legislative members approved the proposal. This marks the first clear effort by Congress to expand its power over the states. The resolution asked that states grant Congress the power to levy a duty of 5 percent *ad valorem* on all imports and prize goods collected from captured ships to help pay off public debt.

To become law the measure needed the endorsement of all thirteen states. Rhode Island refused to support this bill, thus temporarily defeating the tariff issue. Delegates from Rhode Island argued that a tariff imposed by Congress would threaten the liberties of the country. Moreover, they suggested that, if this bill passed, it would lead to further legislation, all eroding the power of the states, and the newly independent republic would again be locked into the "yoke of tyranny."

In 1783, Congress again asked states for the power to impose taxes on imported goods. This new act, more detailed than previous legislation, itemized imports, proposed a schedule of taxes for each item, and established terms for securing customs house officials. Congress passed this bill, but the states failed to ratify it unanimously. This time, New York dissented.

Congress discussed the tariff issue again in 1786, but attention turned instead to the idea of a more thorough revision of the Articles of Confederation. A committee headed by Charles Pinckney of South Carolina suggested several amendments that would give Congress more authority, among them a measure granting Congress exclusive power to regulate commerce and the right to impose duties on imports and exports. This plan failed in part because of talk of a more formal meeting in Annapolis to review and possibly revise the articles. Although that meeting did not produce a more workable plan, a later gathering, the Constitutional Convention, replaced the articles with the current U.S. Constitution.

The passage of any of the tariff bills would have lessened the urgency for amending the articles, as Congress would have had both a source of revenue and the authority to collect it. Tariff issues exemplify the challenges facing the Continental Congress in the Revolutionary era.

See also: Articles of Confederation.

Selected Bibliography:

H. James Henderson, *Party Politics in the Continental Congress*, 1987; Calvin Jillson and Rick K. Wilson, *Congressional Dynamics: Structure, Coordination, and Choice in the First American Congress, 1774–1789*, 1994.

Virginia Jelatis

COOLIDGE, JOHN CALVIN (July 4, 1872–January 5, 1933)

Thirtieth president of the United States; a stalwart Republican who championed conservative policies, including high protective tariffs.

Born in Plymouth Notch, Vermont, Coolidge attended school at nearby Black River Academy before graduating from Amherst College in 1895. He practiced law for several years in Northampton, Massachusetts, and launched his political career there in 1899 when elected to the city council. Over the next two decades he won election to many local and state offices, including county clerk, mayor, state representative and senator, lieutenant governor, and governor. During this time he became a major force in the Massachusetts Republican Party. He compiled a moderate progressive record that promoted children's and women's labor laws, workmen's compensation, women's suffrage, the direct election of U.S. senators, and general fiscal responsibility.

Coolidge garnered national prominence and considerable praise in 1919, when as governor he opposed the

Boston police strike and intervened militarily to quell the crime wave that had ensued. The following year he emerged as the Republican Party's vice-presidential nominee. Calling for a return to "normalcy" after the catastrophe of World War I and the controversial debate over the League of Nations, the Warren G. Harding–Coolidge ticket won a landslide victory over Democrats James Cox and Franklin D. Roosevelt. As vice president, Coolidge attended cabinet meetings, presided over the Senate, and supported the administration's conservative economic agenda of reducing federal spending, debts, and taxes. Moreover, he endorsed the GOP policy of raising tariffs intended to spur commercial activity and protect industry, agriculture, and labor from foreign competition. In 1921, the government passed an emergency tariff increase that the Fordney-McCumber Tariff Act fortified the following year.

Because Coolidge lacked influence or even personal ties with national Republican leaders, many speculated that he would not appear on the presidential ticket in 1924. In August 1923, when Harding died suddenly, "Silent Cal" became president of the United States. Coolidge endorsed the conservative economic agenda of his predecessor by paying down the national debt and pushing a new tax reduction law through Congress. The cabinet he inherited included several capable men, including Andrew Mellon at the Treasury Department, Herbert Hoover at Commerce, and Charles E. Hughes at State. But the president also had to deal with the Teapot Dome and Elk Hills oil scandals that involved Harding's Interior Department and the attorney general's office. The new president deftly distanced himself from these controversies and skillfully maneuvered to secure his party's presidential nomination.

On November 4, 1924, Coolidge became president in his own right, easily defeating Democrat John W. Davis and Third Party candidate Robert M. La-Follette. The booming economy goes far toward explaining his victory, and Coolidge remained understandably reluctant to depart from the administration's pro-business economic policies. To solidify support for trade protectionism, a cornerstone of 1920s Republicanism, he gradually rid the Tariff Commission of all members advocating the reduction of duty rates. Although Section 315 of the Fordney-McCumber law authorized him to adjust rates downward and upward by 50 percent, Coolidge almost always preferred raising rates to lowering them.

Coolidge's trade strategy rankled many Mexican farmers who complained about buying supplies and equipment at artificially high prices in the United States and selling crop surpluses at low open-market prices abroad. Much to Coolidge's dismay, there emerged a powerful bipartisan bloc in Congress demanding comprehensive federal programs to deal with the farm problem. While willing to grant the agrarians tariff protection from low-priced imports, and to back farmer cooperatives, Coolidge refused to support the creation of a complex government system to set domestic prices and sell surpluses abroad. As a result, he exercised his veto power on several occasions to defeat the major farm-support initiatives in Congress that became known as McNary-Haugenism.

Although still quite popular, Coolidge decided not to run for reelection in 1928. He retired to Massachusetts, dying just four years later. Historians have recognized Coolidge's political skill and personal integrity, but they criticized his ultraconservative economic policies and general complacency as a leader. His staunch commitment to high tariffs, for example, has come under heavy attack because of its negative effect on Europe's postwar World War I economic recovery. On the other hand, Coolidge has recently become a popular figure among conservative Republicans for his unswerving faith in tax cuts, balanced budgets, and limited government as prescriptions for economic growth.

See also: American farmers; Congress (United States); Fordney-McCumber Tariff (Tariff of 1922); Hoover, Herbert; LaFollette, Robert Marion; Mellon, Andrew W.; Protectionism; Republican Party; Roosevelt, Franklin D.; Tariff Commission; Veto power of the president; World War I.

Selected Bibliography:

Robert Ferrell, *The Presidency of Calvin Coolidge*, 1998; Donald R. McCoy, *Calvin Coolidge: The Quiet President*, 1967; Robert Sobel, *Coolidge: An American Enigma*, 1998.

Jeffrey J. Matthews

COPPER

Copper mining and protective tariffs go back to the colonial origins of the nation.

As early as 1709, British colonists mined copper in Simsbury, Connecticut, and in the 1730s the French attempted to develop Lake Superior resources. Michigan's Upper Peninsula yielded America's first major copper deposits in the 1840s. In the years that followed, the great Calumet & Hecla Mining Company dominated the scene. Beginning in 1866, miners discovered copper deposits in Butte, Montana, and within twenty years these mines became the chief copper suppliers in the United States. Miners also located other copper deposits in Arizona in the Clifton-Morenci District, at Tombstone, and Jerome, with copper mines also developed in Utah, Nevada, Alaska, and to a lesser degree in California.

Federal tariff policies after 1790 included copper and brass manufactures, but not mining or smelting, as the tariffs of 1794, 1816, and 1818 attested. Ingot and scrap copper remained duty free until 1846 and copper sheathing had no duties until the Civil War.

A tariff bill in 1864 placed duties on raw and manufactured copper. Five years later a strong tariff bill protected Michigan copper, but had a devastating effect on East Coast smelting industries. Until 1890, an effective tariff protected domestic copper. The McKinley Tariff of 1890 realized lower duties on copper and the Wilson-Gorman Tariff of 1894 eliminated them completely. Copper companies made no serious effort to keep a protective tariff in place. Copper items remained on the duty-free list until 1932, when the government reintroduced protection.

The Defense Production Act of 1950 offered potential producers a variety of incentives to expand output, but guaranteed no protectionist tariff. In the years after 1963, most copper used in the United States came from foreign sources that, between 1960 and 1986, doubled production capacities. Since 1966, the Copper and Brass Fabricators Council has participated in federal regulatory matters.

See also: McKinley Tariff (Tariff of 1890); Wilson-Gorman Tariff (Tariff of 1894).

Selected Bibliography:

Joseph Gunter and Konrad J. Kundig, eds., *Copper: Its Trade, Manufacture, Use and Environmental Status*, 1998; Charles Hyde, *Copper for America: The United States Copper Industry from Colonial Times to the 1990s*, 1998.

Russell M. Magnaghi

COTTON

When cotton was king, the South, as a single-crop region, depended on other areas for finished goods, and on strong export markets for income.

Cotton growers disliked tariffs because protection would allow American manufacturers to keep prices artificially high, shielding them from foreign competition. As consumers, cotton growers pay higher prices for foreign and domestic goods and receive none of the benefits of protection.

Early on even some southerners supported the tariff. In 1816, William Lowndes of South Carolina sponsored a protective tariff supported by John C. Calhoun. Postwar nationalism extended to the southern states. Significant sentiment against the British dumping that followed the war's end led to a realization that independence would require economic self-sufficiency. Pragmatically, the South assumed it could readily develop its own textile industry as a market for its cotton, which had become more valuable than ever after Eli Whitney introduced the cotton gin in 1793. Southerners voted against the Tariff of 1816 by a vote of 39 to 25.

Still, cotton resided in a cash-strapped, dependent agricultural sector whether people called it king or not, and faired better with a low tariff that produced only revenue. Although the fully developed English textile industry relied on U.S. cotton with India as the only alternative, the industrialization of northeastern American industry had an adverse effect on southern cotton growers. Prices rose, as did fear of retaliation by the British in the form of reduced purchases of cotton.

By 1820, southerners declared protection detrimental to their self-interest, and started to vote consistently against protective tariffs. The most blatant example of southern frustration with the tariff occurred after the passage of the Tariff of 1828, known as the Tariff of Abominations, but other tariffs of the antebellum era also maintained high protection, causing southern cotton growers to decry that the federal government had rendered them financially disabled.

With abundant fertile land, reasonable access to shipping, and only a limited internal market, cotton growers looked naturally to export. In antebellum years, cotton developed as the major source of revenue in the United States. In 1830, the Atlantic cotton region produced more than the Gulf region. By 1835, the situation reversed, and from 1835 on the Gulf area and Arkansas produced three-fourths of the U.S. cotton crop.

Cotton production peaked at 4.54 million bales in 1859. Three-fourths of it went to Europe, and it brought roughly 60 percent of American export value in the prewar years. Prices fluctuated wildly. In 1800, cotton sold for 36 cents per pound, by the next year it increased to 44 cents and by 1811 it dropped to 8.9 cents. From 1839 to 1849, prices fell below cost, but in the boom of the 1850s cotton experienced high profitability despite prices of only 11 or 12 cents per pound. Panics in 1819 and 1837 created sustained depressions, with the latter lasting into the mid-1840s. By the late antebellum years, cotton appeared panic-proof. The 1857 panic had no adverse impact and market demand remained so strong that southern banks from 1858 to 1860 had a greater share of the country's supply of specie than ever before.

After the Civil War, even with Republican tariff rates highly protective, the economy boomed. Tariff rates became embarrassingly high, but cotton reestablished its prewar levels by 1880. The postwar cotton revival came about as American population numbers, except in the South, exploded from both a massive immigration and a substantial internal migration. The United States exported 298 million pounds in 1830, 2.5 billion pounds valued at $251 million in 1890.

Adverse effects from tariff policy no longer concerned cotton growers. The McKinley Tariff of 1890 established reciprocity, which, after ups and downs, became firm policy in the 1930s. Even though internal markets reduced the tariff as a factor, cotton growers had problems with other internal costs. Through the Gilded Age, tariffs remained high, but the king had died and reluctantly the South began to develop other products even as a significant southern textile industry that used much of the cotton crop. The South's economy slowly diversified and cotton production shifted to Western agribusinesses. Textile manufacturing shifted to Third World countries. In 1983, the crop yielded roughly 12 million bales; of that, 5.4 million bales went for domestic use, 5 million for export, and 1.6 million to government-subsidized storage as surplus.

See also: Calhoun, John Caldwell; Lowndes, William Jones; McKinley Tariff (Tariff of 1890); Tariff of 1816; Tariff of 1832. **Vol. II**: John Sherman's 1865 Speech in Favor of Increased Tariffs. **Vol. III**: Tariff of 1816; Tariff of 1828 (Tariff of Abominations); Tariff of 1832; Tariff of 1890 (McKinley Tariff).

Selected Bibliography:

Anthony Burton, *The Rise and Fall of King Cotton*, 1984; John M. Dobson, *Two Centuries of Tariffs: The Background and Emergence of the U.S. International Trade Commission*, 1976; Judith Goldstein, *Ideas, Interests, and American Trade Policy*, 1993; Nancy Kane, *Textiles in Transition: Technology, Wages, and Industry Relocation in the U.S. Textile Industry, 1880–1930*, 1972; Sidney Ratner, *The Tariff in American History*, 1972.

John Herschel Barnhill

COUNTERVAILING DUTIES

Additional duties assessed to offset the effects of subsidies provided by the country of origin for exported merchandise.

Countervailing duties (CVs) equalize prices and maintain fair competition among trading nations. In the United States, the Department of Commerce, the International Trade Commission, and the U.S. Customs Service enforce countervailing duty laws and investigate any allegations to determine whether American industries suffer from injury due to imports. Verification of unfair trade practices results in the issuance of a report sent to the president and Congress. If Congress orders a countervailing duty, the customs service must collect the tax, accepting only cash payments at the time the products enter the country.

See also: Dumping.

Selected Bibliography:

Alfred E. Eckes, *Opening America's Market: U.S. Foreign Trade Policy Since 1776*, 1995.

Cynthia Clark Northrup

CRAWFORD, WILLIAM H. (February 24, 1772–September 15, 1834)

An independent-minded southern Republican nationalist who served in several different posts in the federal government and who favored tariffs that provided benefits for all sections of the country.

Born in Nelson County, Virginia, to a wealthy planter family, Crawford attended school in Georgia after his family moved there. Crawford then taught school, studied law at the Richmond Academy, and opened a law practice in Lexington, Georgia, in 1799. His first experience as a public servant occurred in the Georgia legislature between 1803 and 1807. He represented Georgia in the U.S. Senate until 1813, proving his independent character by arguing for

the recharter of the Bank of the United States and supporting tariffs, unpopular positions among southern Republicans. In 1812, he voted with the majority in favor of declaring war on Britain. He served as minister to France between 1813 and 1815, before accepting a position in James Madison's cabinet as secretary of war, an office vacated by James Monroe. In that position Crawford proved an able administrator. He was also secretary of treasury from 1816 to 1825.

As treasurer, the precarious balancing act of minimizing surplus revenue while paying off the national debt challenged Crawford. Government income fluctuated erratically since it relied almost wholly on tariffs, a sum that varied based on annual imports. When the government had surplus revenue, Crawford favored cutting internal taxes, which Congress abolished in 1817. When deficits occurred, Crawford favored raising tariffs rather than reducing military expenditures as Monroe did in 1821. Although he saw tariffs primarily as a means of revenue, as an economic nationalist he did not object to tariffs meant to protect American industries. Like many Americans shaped by the war experience, Crawford saw the need for a strong military, an improved system of transportation, and increased industrialization.

In the 1824 presidential election, Crawford finished third behind Andrew Jackson and John Quincy Adams. When the House chose Adams as president, Crawford refused to serve as secretary of treasury. He retired from national politics and lived out his remaining years as a northern circuit judge in Georgia. In these years he opposed internal improvements and protective tariffs, believing that these measures benefited the North at the expense of the South. Although he pushed for a national convention to write a new Constitution, he did not favor secession and tariff nullification as John C. Calhoun did. His death in Elberton, Georgia, in 1834 preceded even greater sectional rivalry.

See also: Adams, John Quincy; Calhoun, John Caldwell; Jackson, Andrew; Madison, James; Monroe, James.

Selected Bibliography:

Chase C. Mooney, *William H. Crawford, 1772–1834*, 1974.

Matt McCook

CRISIS OF 1837

One of the worst economic disasters in nineteenth-century America.

The Crisis of 1837 grew from a confluence of events. In 1836, the Bank of England raised interest rates and limited credit, fearing a drain on specie reserves. English merchants responded by curtailing credit, demanding payment on outstanding debts, and reducing investments in American manufacturing and transportation. At the same time, an already unfavorable balance of trade increased as cotton prices plummeted. Likewise, an increase in the sale of public lands from $4.5 million to $39 million over the next two years resulted in unproductive, speculative investment. Finally, a disastrous fire in New York City in 1835 and poor grain harvests, requiring Americans to import grain from Europe, further drained resources.

By the summer of 1837, many fac-

tors, merchants, brokers, and mercantile houses had gone bankrupt. As a result, banks, reliant on these potential assets, could not cover their own liabilities. These institutions adopted a defensive posture by suspending specie payments to prevent a run on their reserves. While temporarily stabilizing banks, people responded by not accepting bank notes or checks as payment, further lowering the amount of currency from $276 billion in 1836 to only $158 billion in 1842. Although unpopular with many Americans, staunch Jacksonian Democrats, including Martin Van Buren, heralded the change as a fulfillment of their promise of a vigorous attack on banks and paper money. Opponents of the Van Buren administration maintained, however, that interference by the central government in business affairs, the destruction of the Bank of the United States, and Democrat hard money policies had brought about and exacerbated the panic.

In an effort to resolve the crisis, Van Buren made two critical decisions. The administration allowed merchants to defer their tariff payments. Van Buren also instituted an independent treasury for the deposit of surplus funds; control of federal finances would thereby come from the government rather than the banks.

The Crisis of 1837 proved a turning point in the Jacksonian period. First, the crisis caused severe unemployment and low agricultural prices. Second, eighty-two of eighty-eight deposit banks defaulted. Third, tariff collections declined dramatically with the reduction of imports. Sluggish sales in public lands combined to make the government move from disposing of a surplus to operating at a deficit. Next, Van Buren defined the tariff policy of the Democratic Party for the remainder of the nineteenth century. Democrats would pursue a low tariff and avoid governmental aid to business. The panic also demonstrated Van Buren's failings as president. He sought a political solution to the problem that involved personal gain over economic stability. The severity of the crisis fractured the Democratic Party for the remainder of the nineteenth century and galvanized Whig efforts.

See also: Jacksonianism; Van Buren, Martin.

Selected Bibliography:

Michael Holt, *The Rise and Fall of the Whig Party: Jacksonian Politics and the Onset of the Civil War*, 1999.

Dallas Cothrum

CRISIS OF 1857 (PANIC OF 1857)

Economic depression that began in the summer of 1857.

The failure of the largest bank in Ohio, the Ohio Life Insurance and Trust Company, sparked the Crisis of 1857. A wave of bank failures, business bankruptcies, unemployment, and declining commodity prices followed. Contemporaries blamed the economic troubles on various causes, primarily the recent Tariff of 1857, which had stuck to the principle of *ad valorem* rates and had lowered duties across the board. Because of economic crisis, tariff policy again became a political issue.

The Democratic Party had strongly favored low tariffs because they argued that tariffs should be designed only to earn revenue for the federal government, not to give advantages to business. According to Democrats, the Tariff of 1857 did not cause the crisis; reckless banking practices had unleashed a wave of bankruptcies. Most Democrats, particularly southern politicians such as Treasury Secretary Howell Cobb, favored retaining the low tariffs set earlier in 1857 even when the government began to lose revenue from declining imports. Rather than raise the tariff, they preferred additional borrowing or the auction of western lands on which settlers could not make payments.

The Crisis of 1857 affected the Republican Party quite differently. As a new party of former Democrats, Whigs, Free-Soilers, and independents, Republicans lacked a clear tariff philosophy. Many Republicans, favoring free trade, had voted for the Tariff of 1857. When depression hit, Republicans began to favor protectionism. Protectionists quickly blamed economic problems on the low tariff and the resulting loss of hard currency to Europe. Arguing that protection of American industry helped labor more than capitalists, advocates such as Henry C. Carey responded to labor unrest with calls for a higher tariff. As southern Democrats in Congress disparaged protectionism, Republicans began to rally around the concept as a key part of their antislavery, free labor ideology, and as a winning political strategy. In the key northern swing states of New Jersey and Pennsylvania, Republicans hammered home protectionist arguments during the 1858 midterm elections. In a stunning turnaround, they won converts to the party and elected a firm majority of both states' congressional delegation, cementing the importance of the issue for the presidential campaign of 1860. The Crisis of 1857 helped make the tariff a sectional issue.

See also: Carey, Henry Charles; Democratic Party; Labor; Presidential campaigns; Protectionism; Republican Party; Tariff of 1857.

Selected Bibliography:

James L. Huston, *The Panic of 1857 and the Coming of the Civil War*, 1987; Kenneth M. Stampp, *America in 1857: A Nation on the Brink*, 1990.

Christopher M. Paine

CRISP, CHARLES FREDERICK (January 29, 1845–October 23, 1896)

U.S. representative and House Speaker in the Fifty-second and Fifty-third Congresses who championed reduced tariffs and free silver during his congressional career.

Born in Sheffield, England, Crisp and his family moved to Savannah, Georgia, seven months later. He received his only formal education in the public schools. He passed the Georgia bar in 1866 and practiced law until he entered local politics in 1872.

His outspoken advocacy of free trade began while a member of the House Commerce and Manufactures committee. When Grover Cleveland converted to free trade in 1887, Crisp led the House attack against Speaker Thomas B. Reed, the leading defender of high protective tariffs and a proponent of the strongly protectionist McKinley Tariff of 1890. As newly elected Speaker in the Fifty-second Congress, when debate resurfaced on the McKin-

ley Tariff, Crisp delivered a stinging attack against Reed and protectionism, declaring that tariffs did nothing more than take from one class and give to another.

Later in 1892, when he failed to get a Democrat-backed tariff reduction through Congress, Crisp came under attack from members of his party, who argued that the Speaker appeared too consumed with supporting the silver issue and campaigning for the reelection of Grover Cleveland to give proper attention to the party agenda. In the Fifty-third Congress, the House did pass the Wilson Tariff, creating a significant tax reduction, only to see the bill emasculated in the Senate and eventually passed as the drastically altered Wilson-Gorman Tariff. Although Crisp never won the tariff reduction for which he so strongly fought, he continued his free trade crusade until his death in Atlanta, Georgia, on October 23, 1896.

See also: Cleveland, Stephen Grover; McKinley Tariff (Tariff of 1890); Reed, Thomas Brackett; Wilson-Gorman Tariff (Tariff of 1894).

Selected Bibliography:

Preston St. Clair, *The Political Career of Charles Frederick Crisp*, 1962.

Glynn Ingram

CUBA

A Spanish dominion from 1492 to 1898, when it gained nominal independence, but remained a U.S. protectorate until 1934.

Subsistence agriculture characterized Cuba's early economic history. Havana grew in importance to service the fleets of Seville and Cádiz that monopolized Spain's trade with America. Spain prohibited trade with foreigners or other Spanish colonies, but smuggling thrived as Cubans exchanged hides and tobacco for manufactured goods. In the eighteenth century, production of sugar cane, coffee, and tobacco, utilizing slave labor, grew rapidly. The Spanish Free Trade Act of 1765 and other reforms opened Cuban trade to most Spanish ports and encouraged agroexport production. Both legal (*registro*) and illegal trade with the United States grew thereafter and in the 1790s soared. The U.S. Tariff of 1789, which favored goods carried in U.S. ships, and the position of the United States as the leading neutral nation during the European wars of that decade aided in Cuba's increased trade. In 1818, Spain opened Cuba to international trade and U.S. imports of Cuban sugar rose steadily. Although sugar continued to enjoy a low U.S. tariff rate, Spanish wheat farmers pressured their government to limit imports of U.S. flour into Cuba and both nations raised tariffs in the 1820s and 1830s. Higher U.S. tariffs on Cuban coffee and other Cuban exports by 1834 led to a dramatic shift toward sugar production.

The Ten Years' War, fought from 1868 to 1878, devastated Cuba, the world's leading sugar producer by the mid-nineteenth century. The war resulted in some autonomy for Cuba without independence and began a gradual end of slavery, completed in 1886. Substantial modernization of production and refining after the war overcame recent gains made by European beet sugar in the U.S. market. A

commercial treaty with Spain in 1883, replacing the older "differential right of flags" schedule based on the national flag under which a ship sailed, favored Cuba and Puerto Rico. The McKinley Tariff of 1890 provided tax-free sugar imports to the United States in exchange for a reciprocal trade agreement, which the United States and Spain signed in 1891. The Wilson-Gorman Tariff of 1894 abrogated this agreement, causing a serious economic crisis in Cuba that led to a new war for independence in 1895. U.S. intervention in this conflict in 1898 resulted in Cuban independence, but imposed a U.S. military occupation until 1902, followed by a protectorate. The Cuban Reciprocity Treaty of 1902 lowered tariffs substantially and gave Cuban sugar a preferential position within the U.S. market. Several U.S. military interventions preceded the dictatorship of General Gerardo Machado in 1924.

The Great Depression hit Cuba hard and resulted in a labor uprising that overturned Machado in 1933. The government of Franklin D. Roosevelt refused to intervene, although Sumner Welles played an active role in diplomatic efforts to bring peace. Fulgencio Batista led a revolt of noncommissioned army officers in the same year and dominated the country for much of the next twenty-five years, enjoying substantial U.S. support until his overthrow by Fidel Castro in 1959. A new Reciprocal Trade Act with Cuba in 1934 further reduced tariffs and established quotas for Cuban sugar and tobacco within the U.S. market, making Cuba especially dependent on the United States. Sugar Acts of 1946 and 1956 increased the quotas for Cuban sugar, in return for increased Cuban imports of U.S. rice.

Castro's leftist tendencies brought Cold War consideration to U.S. policy. The United States imposed a trade embargo on Cuba in 1960 and broke diplomatic relations in January 1961, followed by the ill-fated U.S.-supported Bay of Pigs Invasion in April. The U.S. trade embargo continues to the present, although some other nations have refused to collaborate with the United States in isolating Cuba. Since 1962, Cuba has generally been excluded from Inter-American programs, including the Free Trade of the Americas plan at the beginning of the twenty-first century.

See also: Coffee; Cold War; Free Trade Area of the Americas (FTAA); Great Depression; Hides and skins; McKinley Tariff (Tariff of 1890); Roosevelt, Franklin D.; Slavery; Sugar; Tobacco; Wilson-Gorman Tariff (Tariff of 1894).

Selected Bibliography:

Morris H. Morley, *Imperial State and Revolution: The United States and Cuba, 1952–1987*, 1987; Louis A. Pérez Jr., *Cuba: Between Reform and Revolution*, 1995.

Ralph Lee Woodward Jr.

CUMMINS, ALBERT BAIRD (February 15, 1850–July 30, 1926)

Republican governor of Iowa and senator who opposed high protectionist tariffs.

Born near Carmichaels, Pennsylvania, Cummins attended schools in the East before moving to Iowa in 1869. Over the next nine years he worked as a carpenter, deputy county surveyor, and railroad employee before passing the bar exam and returning to Iowa to practice law. After serving in the Iowa state legislature from 1888 to 1890, he unsuccessfully ran for the Senate before being elected governor in 1902. In 1908, he resigned after voters elected him to the U.S. Senate. As a senator he joined other midwestern progressives such as Robert LaFollette in opposing protectionist tariffs primarily because they benefited trusts. He argued for the reduction of the tariff as a means of controlling the large conglomerate corporations. Unlike the Populists, Cummins focused on the needs of midwestern manufacturers instead of farmers. He proposed the "Iowa idea" in 1901, calling for reciprocity treaties and the elimination of all tariff protection on goods manufactured by monopolies. As part of the Insurgents, Cummins continued to push for the formation of a trade commission with the same authority as the Federal Trade Commission and with the power to adjust rates. Although the conservative elements within the Republican Party prevailed, Cummins, LaFollette, and other progressives continued to advocate the reduction of tariffs for the benefit of manufacturers and as a means of controlling big business. Cummins died in Des Moines, Iowa, on July 30, 1926.

See also: Insurgents; LaFollette, Robert Marion; Tariff Commission.

Selected Bibliography:

Paul Wolman, *Most Favored Nation: The Republican Revisionists and U.S. Tariff Policy, 1897–1912*, 1992.

Cynthia Clark Northrup

D

DALLAS, ALEXANDER (June 21, 1759– January 16, 1817)

Sixth secretary of the treasury; served under James Madison.

Born in Jamaica and educated in Great Britain, Alexander James Dallas immigrated to the United States in 1783. He settled in Philadelphia and quickly won fame as a writer, lawyer, and politician. He served as the secretary of the Commonwealth of Pennsylvania during the Whiskey Rebellion and also worked as the U.S. attorney for the eastern part of the state for many years. Although born into the British upper class, Dallas embraced the political ideals of Thomas Jefferson and James Madison. A master political organizer, he played an instrumental role in establishing the Democratic-Republican Party as the dominant power in Pennsylvania.

During Jefferson's second term as president, Dallas grew disenchanted with his party, mainly as a result of what he perceived as Jefferson's mis-handling of the economy. The alleged mismanagement continued under the presidency of James Madison. The nation remained on the verge of bankruptcy during much of the War of 1812. Dallas convinced wealthy merchants like Stephen Girard and John Jacob Astor to loan money to the United States. A grateful President Madison appointed Dallas secretary of the treasury in October 1814.

Dallas proposed two methods for stabilizing the American economy. First, he urged Congress to charter the Second Bank of the United States. Second, he recommended the division of tariffs into three categories. Goods produced in sufficient quantities to meet demand, such as paper and leather, received more protection with high tariffs. Items such as iron, pewter, tin, and brass produced in insufficient quantities to meet demand warranted moderate tariffs. Finally, goods produced exclusively overseas entered the country under a revenue-only tax. After much debate, Congress chartered the second national bank and incorporated the new impost system into the Tariff of 1816. When Dallas left office in October 1816, the nation operated as a solvent entity once again.

See also: Jefferson, Thomas; Madison, James; Tariff of 1816; War of 1812.

Selected Bibliography:

Raymond Walters Jr., *Alexander James Dallas: Lawyer, Politician, Financier 1759–1817,* 1969.

Mary Stockwell

DALLAS, GEORGE MIFFLIN (July 10, 1792–December 31, 1864)

Vice president under James K. Polk and son of Secretary of the Treasury Alexander J. Dallas.

Born in Philadelphia in 1792, Dallas graduated from Princeton in 1810 and began practicing law. In 1813, he served as secretary to Albert Gallatin on a mission to Russia during the War of 1812. After a term as mayor of Philadelphia and as U.S. district attorney for eastern Pennsylvania, Dallas became a U.S. senator in 1831. During the Nullification Crisis he supported President Andrew Jackson's position against South Carolina and assisted in the passage of the Force Act. After leaving the Senate in 1833, he served as attorney general of Pennsylvania before receiving an appointment as minister to Russia in 1837. In 1844, Dallas became vice president with the election of his running mate James K. Polk. Although Polk and Dallas ran on a pro-protectionist platform, in 1846 Polk's secretary of treasury, Robert Walker,

issued a report that the president forwarded to Congress, asking for a reduction of the tariff. After a lengthy debate, the House vote split evenly, forcing Vice President Dallas to cast the deciding vote. Opposing the position of his home state of Pennsylvania, he voted for the reduction of the tariff. The Tariff of 1846 resulted in an increase of foreign imports. Although opponents had argued that this would produce a negative impact on the U.S. economy, during the tariff's eleven-year duration, the United States experienced prosperity. After leaving the vice presidency, Dallas served as minister to Great Britain from 1856 to 1861 during which time he obtained an agreement from Parliament disavowing the right of British ships to search vessels of other nations. Dallas died in Philadelphia on December 31, 1864.

See also: Polk, James K.; Tariff of 1846 (Walker's Tariff); Walker, Robert John; Walker's Report.

Selected Bibliography:

John M. Belohlavek, *George Mifflin Dallas,* 1977; Edward Stanwood, *American Tariff Controversies in the Nineteenth Century,* 1967.

Cynthia Clark Northrup

DAVIS, JEFFERSON (June 3, 1808–December 5, 1889)

U.S. representative, senator, secretary of war, and president of the Confederate States of America.

Born in Christian (now Todd) County, Kentucky, in 1808, Davis graduated from West Point at the age of twenty. He then married the daughter of Zachary Taylor, but she died shortly after their wedding. In 1845, he married Varina Howell, the daughter of a wealthy plantation owner in Mississippi. Elected as a U.S. representative in 1846, he resigned from office to join his former father-in-law in Texas just prior to the Mexican-American War. During the conflict Davis prevented Taylor's defeat by holding his position at Buena Vista. After returning to Mississippi he served as secretary of war under Franklin Pierce before being elected to the Senate in 1857. During debates on a proposed tariff reduction, Davis argued for a return to the rates of the Tariff of 1846, duties that he deemed more democratic than the 1857 tariff that favored manufacturers. A final vote on the tariff measure occurred in April 1861 after southern states seceded from the union. During his term as president of the Confederate States of America, Davis discarded the use of the tariff as a revenue-generating option, choosing instead to issue paper money, a move that created high inflation in the South. After the war, Davis spent two years in prison charged with treason, but was never indicted. Returning to private life, he devoted much of his time to writing and conducting business transactions. He died at the age of eighty-one in New Orleans, Louisiana.

See also: Civil War (American); Tariff of 1846 (Walker Tariff); Tariff of 1857; Taylor, Zachary.

Selected Bibliography:

William J. Cooper, *Jefferson Davis, American*, 2000.

Cynthia Clark Northrup

DEMOCRATIC PARTY

Political party historically opposed to high protective tariffs.

The Democratic Party had its ideological origins in the early 1790s when Jeffersonians wanted to combat the growth of government power as pursued by the Federalists. Traditionally, Democrats resisted a loose interpretation of the Constitution, which granted powers to the federal government not explicitly enumerated, including the ability to create a national tariff. Tariffs damaged southern interests since they enhanced the economic opportunities of the industrial North by allowing New England commercial interests to sell their goods in a protected market. Southern agricultural products received no such protection and thus both large- and small-scale farmers below the Mason-Dixon Line had to purchase northern industrial commodities at high prices while selling their own crops in an unprotected and highly competitive international market. The commercial history of early nineteenth-century America reveals Democratic presidents promoting downward revisions of the tariff while Whig Party presidents (the ideological heirs to the Federalists) sought to maintain high duties. This economic argument between the sections concerning constitutionality helped provoke the American Civil War.

From the period of Reconstruction in the 1890s, the Democratic Party maintained its commitment to local rather than national power. Harsh economic conditions for many Americans in the South and West demonstrated to the Democrats that in the age of major trusts and monopolies, only a large central government could adequately look after the interests of the people. In the second decade of the twentieth century, Woodrow Wilson emerged as the first strong Democratic president since Andrew Jackson, nearly a century before. Wilson attempted to restore competition in the economy as a way to circumvent the power of the trusts. His program, the New Freedom, included support for the first major reduction of the tariff since the South had left the Union in 1861. The Underwood-Simmons Tariff Act signed by Wilson in 1913 replaced the Republican Payne-Aldrich Tariff of 1909. It brought the average *ad valorem* rate down from 40 percent to an average of 29 percent and placed dozens of products on the duty-free list.

The Democratic Party's emphasis on low tariffs ran into difficulty in the 1930s when the world depression persuaded many nations, including the United States, to secure their damaged economies by enacting protective tariffs. But the onset of World War II called this strategy into question. It seemed clear to Democratic president Franklin D. Roosevelt that the war had occurred in part over the division of the world's markets between established commercial powers like the United States and Great Britain and rising commercial powers like Germany and Japan. Roosevelt and his successor Harry S Truman worked diligently during and after the war to create institutions such as the International Monetary Fund (IMF) and the General Agreement on Tariffs and Trade (GATT) to serve as institutions capable of providing economic opportunities for the global community. More recently, the Democratic Party has found

itself in a difficult position on the domestic front concerning its support for free trade. The unions, which prefer protection for American industry, represent a major source of party strength. Support in the 1990s for the North American Free Trade Agreement (NAFTA) demonstrated both the Democratic Party's commitment to eradicating tariff barriers to global commerce as well as the dissension within the organization's ranks among pro- and anti-tariff supporters.

See also: Civil War (American); Federalists; General Agreement on Tariffs and Trade (GATT); Great Britain; Jackson, Andrew; Jefferson, Thomas; North American Free Trade Agreement (NAFTA); Payne-Aldrich Tariff (Tariff of 1909); Roosevelt, Franklin D.; Truman, Harry S; Underwood-Simmons Tariff (Tariff of 1913); Whig Party; Wilson, Thomas Woodrow; World War II.

Selected Bibliography:

David Burner, *The Politics of Provincialism: The Democratic Party in Transition, 1918–1932*, 1968; Richard Hofstadter, *The American Political Tradition and the Men Who Made It*, 1948.

David S. Brown

DINGLEY, NELSON, JR. (February 15, 1832–January 14, 1899)

U.S. congressman who, in 1897, sponsored the Dingley Tariff bill that created a record level of tariff duties.

Born in Durham, Maine, Dingley graduated from Dartmouth College in 1855. As the outspoken editor of the antislavery *Lexington Journal*, Dingley became a supporter of the Republican

Party and a close associate of Maine's James G. Blaine. After serving in the Maine legislature and as the governor of Maine, Dingley won a seat in the U.S. House of Representatives in 1881 and served there until his death.

As a member of the House, Dingley became an enthusiastic champion of the protective tariff. He helped William McKinley prepare what became known as the McKinley Tariff of 1890 that raised duties on manufactured goods to an average of about 49.5 percent, the highest to that time. In addition, during the second administration of Grover Cleveland, Dingley denounced the Wilson-Gorman Tariff of 1894, though it contained only modest reductions in duties.

When the Republican Party regained control of the House of Representatives after the 1894 elections, Dingley became the chairman of the House Ways and Means Committee. Declining the position of secretary of the treasury in the McKinley administration in 1897, Dingley developed a tariff bill that removed raw wool from the free list, but left hides and copper. It also placed high duties on linens, woolens, and silks, while leaving the main steel and iron schedules mostly untouched. The bill's most significant change involved doubling the duty on sugar, an important revenue-producing item, as a way to end the treasury deficits that had increased since the Depression of 1893. The Senate added 872 mostly insignificant amendments, but some altered the House's rates. In conference committee, the House won and the final bill closely resembled Dingley's original proposal. Signed into law by President McKinley on July 24, 1897, the Dingley Tariff raised average duties to

a record level of 52 percent, although the new sugar duty contributed significantly. Representing a final burst of nineteenth-century protectionism, the tariff remained in effect until the passage of the Payne-Aldrich Tariff Act in 1909. After developing pneumonia in December 1898, Dingley died in Washington, D.C.

See also: Cleveland, Stephen Grover; Dingley Tariff (Tariff of 1897); House Ways and Means Committee; McKinley, William; McKinley Tariff (Tariff of 1890); Payne-Aldrich Tariff (Tariff of 1909); Wilson-Gorman Tariff (Tariff of 1894). **Vol. II**: William McKinley's 1888 Speech on Tariff Benefits for Labor. **Vol. III**: Tariff of 1897 (Dingley Tariff).

Selected Bibliography:

Tom E. Terrill, *The Tariff, Politics, and American Foreign Policy: 1874–1901*, 1973.

Steven E. Siry

DINGLEY TARIFF (TARIFF OF 1897)

Passed in 1897 under President William McKinley, the Dingley Tariff raised rates to an average of 49 percent, up from the average duty rate of 40 percent under the Wilson-Gorman Tariff.

During the 1890s, the United States experienced a depression that drained government revenues. Although U.S. Customs collected $160 million in revenue in 1896, Congress authorized the levying of additional alcohol, tobacco, and stamp taxes to reduce the budget deficit. William McKinley, campaigning for president against William Jennings Bryan, informed voters that, if elected, he would seek an increase in the tariff rates and reduce the other forms of internal taxation, stimulate domestic industries and employment, and bring the financial crisis to an end. After winning the election, McKinley called a special session of Congress to revise the tariff. The resulting Dingley Tariff, sponsored by Representative Nelson Dingley Jr. from Maine, raised rates to the highest level in American history to that time. More important, the bill also provided the president with the power to negotiate tariff reductions of up to 20 percent or to remove items from the taxable list altogether in exchange for reciprocal reductions from other countries. In 1909, the Payne-Aldrich Tariff Act replaced the Dingley Tariff and lowered rates back down to an average of 42 percent.

See also: Bryan, William Jennings; Dingley, Nelson, Jr.; McKinley, William. **Vol. II**: William McKinley's 1888 Speech on Tariff Benefits for Labor. **Vol. III**: Tariff of 1897 (Dingley Tariff).

Selected Bibliography:

Paul Wolman, *Most Favored Nation: The Republican Revisionists and U.S. Tariff Policy, 1897–1912*, 1992.

Cynthia Clark Northrup

DOLLAR GAP

Economist Charles Kindleberger traced the first references to the term dollar gap (shortage) to a U.S. Department of Commerce study titled "The United States in the World Economy" and review articles that appeared in *The Economist* in 1943.

No firm consensus exists among the-

oreticians and practitioners regarding its definition, and the debate surrounding the concept is often loaded with political overtones. Most arguments note a permanent or chronic shortage of U.S. dollars or an unfavorable balance of payments. The phenomenon stems from the destruction suffered by a great number of countries during World War II. The war augmented American dominance in productive and financial capacities, making the United States the essential source of both needed goods and currency reserves.

Some participants in the debate alleged that only a massive transfusion of U.S. capital into the world economy could restore global economic equilibrium. As early as the 1930s, European observers blamed the United States for a good share of the dysfunction within the world economy. After World War II, they argued, the deficit countries were not, or were only slightly, responsible for the disequilibria in international payments, and could not correct the imbalance through the classical methods of disinflation or devaluation without excessive damage to domestic welfare. These theories provided intellectual and political justification for such large-scale transfers of U.S. capital as the Marshall Plan. The dollar gap also persuaded the United States to accept the discriminatory treatment of dollar goods and services by allies in the early Cold War period.

See also: Cold War; World War II.

Selected Bibliography:

Otto Hieronymi, *Economic Discrimination Against the United States in Western Europe,*

1945–1958, 1972; Charles P. Kindleberger, *The Dollar Shortage*, 1950.

Sayuri Shimizu

DOLLIVER, JONATHAN P. (February 6, 1858–October 15, 1910)

Virginia statesman best remembered as leader of the Progressive opposition to the Payne-Aldrich Tariff.

Born near Kingwood, Virginia, now West Virginia, Dolliver worked his way through college. Graduating at seventeen, he headed to Illinois and began his career, teaching during the winter and studying law during the summer. After attending the Republican convention of 1876, Dolliver discovered he had an interest in politics. At twenty, he moved to Iowa to launch his legal career. Dolliver's oratory and style caught the eye of Republicans and he received invitations to speak.

First elected congressman in 1888 and then reelected five times, he aligned himself along standard Republican lines. In 1895, he served on the House Ways and Means Committee. In 1900, he proved a serious vice-presidential candidate, but by 1903 his views changed and he found himself at odds with Senate leader Nelson W. Aldrich and in the favor of George Roberts. Dolliver's group supported limiting the power of the federal courts to suspend the actions of the Interstate Commerce Commission in railroad disputes. Dolliver further split with his party over the Payne-Aldrich Tariff. By 1909, partisan lines no longer clearly divided Democrats and Republicans.

The unforgiving Aldrich excluded Dolliver from important groups and committees, forcing him to become an Independent. Even in poor health, Dolliver continued to launch attacks against Aldrich's proposals. A week after doctors told him to retire he died.

See also: Aldrich, Nelson W.; Payne-Aldrich Tariff (Tariff of 1909).

Selected Bibliography:

Thomas Richard Ross, *Jonathan Prentiss Dolliver: A Study in Political Integrity and Independence*, 1958.

Lisa A. Ennis

DOW, HERBERT H. (February 26, 1866–October 15, 1930)

American chemist and industrialist who pioneered the chemical industry and founded Dow Chemical Company.

Born in Belleville, Ontario, Dow attended Case School of Applied Science (now Case Western Reserve University) in Cleveland and received his B.S. degree in 1888. While at Case, he became fascinated with extracting bromine from brine.

During the 1890s, Dow developed useful chemical processes and in May 1897 incorporated Dow Chemical Company, based in Midland, Michigan. At this time European producers held a chemical monopoly. The British United Alkali Company dominated the bleach market and the German Bromine Convention dominated the bromine market. By 1909, Dow Chemical's sales had surpassed both the British and the Germans, giving it nominal control of the market. During World War I, Dow further enhanced his company's market penetration by promoting chemical building blocks such as chlorine, bromine, and caustic soda. In

March 1917, Dow Chemical made the first synthetic indigo, and temporarily broke the German monopoly, which appeared largely untouched by the war.

Because of his single-handed struggle with the Europeans, congressmen often consulted Dow. These consultations resulted in the Fordney-McCumber Tariff Bill of 1922, which placed high duties on organic chemicals on a declining basis starting at 60 percent and declining to 45 percent in 1925. This allowed the American chemical industry to catch up with the Germans, whose chemical capacity continued uninterrupted during the war.

Because of the tariff and industrial efficiency, Dow Chemical boomed in the 1920s and continues today as a global giant. In 1930, just prior to his death in Rochester, Minnesota, Dow received the prestigious Perkin Medal.

See also: Fordney-McCumber Tariff (Tariff of 1922); World War I.

Selected Bibliography:

E.N. Brandt, *Growth Company: Dow Chemical's First Century*, 1997; Murray Campbell and Harrison Hatton, *Herbert E. Dow: Pioneer in Creative Chemistry*, 1951.

Russell M. Magnaghi

DRAWBACKS

A rebate or refund of tariff duties levied on imported products used to manufacture goods for export.

The United States has used drawbacks since 1797 when the duty for the importation of salt included a provision that allowed for a drawback on

salted provisions and pickled fish. During the late nineteenth and early twentieth centuries, the use of drawbacks increased as the government attempted to assist medium-size manufacturers in their efforts to import raw products used in their manufacturing process for the production of items that would subsequently be exported. The difficulties of implementing the necessary accounting and inventory management procedures to comply with the federal laws concerning drawbacks created a situation in which most companies could not take advantage of the provision on a cost-effective basis. The National Association of Manufacturers pushed for a revision of the law that would have allowed manufacturing interests to utilize a pound-equivalent export system to simplify the process, but Congress rejected the proposal. Larger companies such as U.S. Steel and Standard Oil did benefit from the use of drawbacks.

See also: National Association of Manufacturers (NAM); U.S. Steel Corp.

Selected Bibliography:

Paul Wolman, *Most Favored Nation: The Republican Revisionists and U.S. Tariff Policy, 1897–1912*, 1992.

Cynthia Clark Northrup

DUMPING

The placing of goods on the market in large quantities and at a low cost.

The practice of dumping in the United States dates back to the early 1800s. After the War of 1812, Congress passed a series of protectionist tariffs, prompting the British and French to dump goods on the U.S. market in an effort to eliminate fledging competitive industries. The practice continued sporadically throughout the remainder of the nineteenth century, but not on a large scale. Fearing an increase in dumping activities in the immediate post–World War I period, Congress passed the Fordney-McCumber Tariff, which returned the country to the prewar protectionist rates and provided for remedies. The U.S. Antidumping Act of 1921 remained in effect until the adoption of the international dumping code during the Kennedy Round, a provision included to ensure the acceptance of the negotiations and as a means of preventing foreign countries from using anti-dumping laws as tariff barriers against American manufacturers. In 1979, the secretary of the treasury received broad discretionary powers to investigate anti-dumping claims and determine fair value and injury. Although the majority of anti-dumping laws deal with products, modern trade practices also include social dumping of large labor-intensive surpluses produced overseas by Japan during the first part of the twentieth century and, more recently, by China.

See also: Fordney-McCumber Tariff (Tariff of 1922); Great Britain; Kennedy Round; War of 1812; World War I.

Selected Bibliography:

Alfred E. Eckes, *Opening America's Market: U.S. Foreign Policy Since 1776*, 1995.

Cynthia Clark Northrup

E

EAST INDIA COMPANY

A secular commercial venture, also called the English East India Company, that spearheaded mercantilism for Great Britain in Asia from the early seventeenth to the mid-nineteenth century.

Originally chartered by Queen Elizabeth I in December 1600 as "The Company of Merchants of London Trading into the East Indies," this enterprise had the primary objective of competing for the Dutch-dominated spice trade in Southeast Asia. When this goal failed due to the Dutch massacre of English traders at Amboina in 1623, the British withdrew to the shores of the Indian subcontinent and slowly built up trading posts at Madras, Bombay, and Calcutta. Granted the authority to coin money and exercise jurisdiction over British subjects in its posts and in relations with Asian states, the East India Company functioned as a sovereign power. From 1660 to 1700, the company monopolized the trade of Indian cotton, silks, indigo, spices, and saltpeter, and made substantial profits to pay its shareholders an annual average dividend of 25 percent.

When the rule of the Mughal Empire in India waned during the early eighteenth century, the company sought to consolidate its position in India and used arms to eradicate rivalry from other European powers, especially France. Robert Clive, an employee of the English East India Company in Madras, led the successful military endeavors in 1751 to defeat the French, subdued Bengal to a client state by winning the Battle of Plassey in 1757, and established de facto British rule in India. Excessive military expenses, corruption, and the plundering of Bengal brought the company to near collapse in the 1760s. To save it from bankruptcy, the English Parliament passed the Tea Act of 1773, granting the company a monopoly to sell low-priced yet dutiable tea to English North America; this act ignited civil unrest, leading in part to the American Revolution. The company increased its power in India and the fortunes of its officials mounted, but financial malpractice led to parliamentary inquiries and government intervention. The Regulating Act of 1773 put Bombay and Madras under the governor-general in Calcutta, an English government appointee. The Pitt India Act of 1784 further established political supervision over the company through a regulatory Board of Control responsible to Parliament, although the company could still control its commercial transactions. Lord Charles Cornwallis appointed governor-general of India from 1786 to 1793, began to transform this commercial venture into a managing agency for the British government in India.

Into the nineteenth century, the East India Company continued to advance English domination in India and Southeast Asia, as exemplified by the founding of Singapore in 1818 and the conquering of Burma in 1852. It also increased profits by funding the tea trade with illegal opium exports to China, an undertaking that eventually caused the first Anglo-Chinese War in 1839–1842. Meanwhile, the company gradually lost its trade monopoly and became a simple administrative entity by 1833. Its existence ended following the Indian Uprising of 1857, when the British monarch assumed direct rule of India.

See also: American Revolution; Mercantilism; Navigation and Trade Acts; Tea.

Selected Bibliography:

John Keay, *The Honourable Company*, 1993; Philip Lawson, *The East India Company: A History*, 1993.

Guoqiang Zheng

ECONOMIC COMMISSION FOR LATIN AMERICA (ECLA)

Established by United Nations Economic and Social Council Resolution 106 (VI) on February 25, 1948.

Headquartered in Santiago, Chile, the commission had three goals: (1) contribute to the economic development of Latin America; (2) coordinate regional actions aimed at this development; and (3) reinforce economic interaction among the countries of the region and with other nations of the world. Later on, social development joined the list as one of the commission's principal areas of concern. In 1984, the name of the organization expanded to Economic Commission for Latin America and the Caribbean (ECLAC), formally acknowledging the long-standing participation of this subregion.

During the 1950s and 1960s, under the directorship and influence of Raul Prebisch and the Dependency School (Structuralists), ECLA advocated a series of reforms targeting the neocolonial relationship between Latin America and the industrialized West, especially the United States. Focusing on the raw material export orientation of the Latin American economies and their resulting "dependency" on foreign First World manufactured goods, Prebisch and ECLA promoted a series of reforms favoring Latin American industrialization for domestic consumption in combination with protectionist tariffs encouraging the development of these nascent industries.

By the 1970s, the ECLA abandoned these reforms and policies for more right-wing, neoclassical doctrinaire policies supported by the IMF and

World Bank. In part the result of the emergence of numerous conservative or military dictatorships in the 1960s and 1970s, and in part the result of increasing pressure from the United States and international lending agencies, the earlier attempts at economic self-sufficiency, independence, and international economic equality gave way to large borrowing programs and ECLA promotion of development favoring "social homogeneity" and "exports."

The 1980s and 1990s saw ECLA take a hand in the emerging challenges of Latin America's "Debt Crisis," the result of overborrowing, as well as renewed efforts by the organization to change production patterns in favor of domestic "social equity."

See also: Latin America; Prebisch, Raul; Protectionism.

Selected Bibliography:

United Nations Economic Commission for Latin America, *The Economic Development of Latin America and Its Principal Problems*, 1950; http://www.eclac.org/.

David J. Weiland III

ECONOMIC DARWINISM

The application of Charles Darwin's biological principle of natural selection to the development of market capitalism.

In the late nineteenth century, officials used natural selection as a scientific justification for implementing laissez-faire economic policy. The resulting economic inequities and their attending social problems led governments in the twentieth century to increasingly experiment with collective management of economies. In the 1990s, in the wake of an international democratization movement, economists used the term to describe the increasingly competitive business climate that resulted from rapid liberalization, privatization, and deregulation of economies around the world.

Adam Smith established the foundations of liberal economics in *An Inquiry into the Nature and Causes of the Wealth of Nations* in 1776. Smith argued that natural law or the "invisible hand" of supply and demand should govern economics rather than government decree. By 1857, Herbert Spencer, building on the work of Smith, Jeremy Bentham, David Ricardo, and John Stuart Mill, expounded a theory of "survival of the fittest," suggesting that strong individuals and institutions would naturally drive weaker ones to extinction. Two years later, in *The Origin of Species*, Darwin not only popularized the idea of "survival of the fittest," but also gave it scientific justification by identifying the mechanism of natural selection through which it worked. According to Darwin, a healthy ecosystem required that strong organisms thrive while the weak die.

By the 1870s, the term "Darwinism" applied to social, economic, and imperial conditions. William Graham Sumner, the most prominent of many Social Darwinists, justified growing economic inequality by equating the accumulation of extravagant wealth with genetic dominance and, likewise, poverty with biological decline.

See also: Mill, John Stuart; Smith, Adam; Sumner, William Graham.

Selected Bibliography:

Robert Young, "Darwinism Is Social," *The Darwinian Heritage*, 1990.

John Grady Powell

ECONOMIC POLICY INSTITUTE (EPI)

Founded in 1986 by Jeff Faux, Barry Bluestone, Robert Kuttner, Ray Marshall, Robert Reich, and Lester Thurow, the Economic Policy Institute (EPI) provides economic analysis and issues reports with a special focus on issues concerning low- and middle-income workers.

EPI employs eleven Ph.D. economic experts who review government policies, including the North American Free Trade Agreement (NAFTA). During the debate over NAFTA, the organization participated in a movement known as "Mobilization on Development, Trade, Labor, and the Environment" composed of numerous groups that opposed the treaty but otherwise had no common agenda. At a conference held in Washington, D.C., the various organizations issued statements urging the inclusion of topics such as human rights, child labor, and the environment in an attempt to delay or prevent the passage of the treaty. EPI continued to oppose the agreement, claiming that a study by Raul Hinojosa, a California scholar, indicated that passage would lead to a decline in the living standard of American workers. Hinojosa objected to the EPI's interpretation of the study, arguing that his information illustrated only a slight temporary, not long-term, period of adjustment.

See also: Center for Strategic and International Studies; North American Free Trade Agreement (NAFTA).

Selected Bibliography:

Hermann von Bertrab, *Negotiating NAFTA: A Mexican Envoy's Account*, 1997.

Cynthia Clark Northrup

ECONOMY

The stability and growth of the U.S. economy has depended on the collection of revenue sufficient enough for the government to function and on the ability of manufacturers to produce goods and continually expand into new markets.

Tariffs constituted the largest share of federal revenue until the passage of the personal income tax amendment in 1913. Tariff legislation has also played an integral role in the development of industry in the United States, especially during the nineteenth century. As the economic strength of the United States surpassed all other competitors and the federal government replaced the tariff with internal taxation, government officials, led by the executive branch, moved toward a policy of free trade as the world economic situation shifted from colonization to globalization. Designed to stimulate the economy and prevent the formation of trade barriers in the post–World War II era, the concept of free trade has created resentment among the lesser developed countries of the world, who argue that the sale of raw materials in exchange for finished products in essence has created a disadvantage for these countries. Historical data indicate that the strong international trading position of the United States has in essence been adversely affected by the implementation of free trade since many foreign countries have taken advantage of the low duties on imported items while retaining high tariff rates on items exported into their country. Since the passage of the Kennedy Round, the economy of the United States has experienced an ever-widening trade deficit.

See also: General Agreement on Tariffs and Trade (GATT); Kennedy Round; Personal income tax (Sixteenth Constitutional Amendment); Protectionism; Third World; World Trade Organization (WTO); World War II.

Selected Bibliography:

Alfred E. Eckes, *Opening America's Market: U.S. Foreign Trade Policy Since 1776*, 1995.

Cynthia Clark Northrup

EISENHOWER, DWIGHT D. (IKE)
(October 14, 1890–March 28, 1968)

Supreme commander of the Allied Expeditionary Force in Europe during World War II and thirty-fourth president of the United States.

Born in Denison, Texas, Eisenhower and his parents moved to Abilene, Kansas, before he reached the age of two. Soon after finishing high school, Eisenhower entered the U.S. Military Academy at West Point, graduating in 1915. He did not see combat in World War I, and as a result moved slowly through the ranks after the war. Because of his record in training and maneuvers, Army Chief of Staff George C. Marshall quickly advanced Eisenhower once the United States became involved in World War II, and, in June 1942, Marshall promoted Eisenhower over scores of senior officers and named him commanding general of American forces in Europe. Ike planned American operations in North Africa and Italy. In December 1943, he became the supreme allied commander in Europe and led allied forces during the June 6, 1944, invasion of Normandy. After the war, Eisenhower replaced Marshall as chief of staff. In December 1950, he accepted an appointment as the first commander of the North Atlantic Treaty Organization's military forces.

While still in the military, both the Democratic and Republican parties courted Eisenhower as a possible presidential candidate, and the Republicans ultimately persuaded him to run in the 1952 election. He won handily and became the president in 1953. As president, Eisenhower oversaw the end of the Korean War, and he dealt with the anticommunism furor created by Senator Joseph R. McCarthy. Eisenhower witnessed the birth of the space age when the Soviet Union launched *Sputnik* in 1957. Civil Rights increasingly became an issue during the Eisenhower administration as the Warren Court ruled against school segregation in 1954. Eisenhower sent U.S. troops to Little Rock, Arkansas, in 1957 to force integration there. Another major achievement of the Eisenhower administration involved the creation of the interstate highway system.

Democrats feared that the first Republican in office since 1933 would dismantle the social programs of the New Deal as well as Franklin D. Roosevelt's tariff and trade policies. But Eisenhower practiced what he called Modern Republicanism. This policy consisted of streamlining the federal government while continuing most of the New Deal's social programs. In terms of trade, Eisenhower did not return to the protectionism of Herbert Hoover and the Hawley-Smoot Tariff Act. Instead, Ike viewed trade strategically. He believed the United States required freer trade in order to combat communism during the Cold War. The United States needed growing trade to bolster international relationships with its allies and neutral nations that the Soviet Union might pull into the communist world. In short, for the Eisenhower administration, foreign policy issues overruled concerns about domestic industry.

Eisenhower dealt with the European Economic Community (EEC) and he boosted trade with Canada with the building of the Saint Lawrence Seaway. Eisenhower and Secretary of State John Foster Dulles believed that a strong Japanese economy would prevent the country from falling to communism and provide stability in the region. But Japan had possessed a powerful textile industry before World War II and American and British textile interests, fearing competition from a revitalized Japan, encouraged the Eisenhower administration to create a protectionist tariff. Instead, Eisenhower sponsored Japanese membership in the General Agreement on Tariffs and Trade (GATT). Japan's economy strengthened dramatically as a result of the Eisenhower policies, and while Japan did become more closely tied to the West, the United States had a negative balance of trade with Japan by the end of the 1950s.

Eisenhower's emphasis on foreign policy objectives created domestic resentment for the control exercised by the executive branch over tariffs. A hostile Congress dominated by Democrats forced Eisenhower to create a commission, headed by Clarence Randall, to make recommendations on an overall trade policy. They also reduced the president's ability to make adjustments to the tariff. Eisenhower left office in 1961 after serving two full terms, and retired to his farm at Gettysburg. He died of heart failure in Washington, D.C.

See also: Cold War; General Agreement on Tariffs and Trade (GATT); Hawley-Smoot Tariff (Tariff of 1930); Hoover, Herbert; Roosevelt, Franklin D.; World War II.

Selected Bibliography:

Stephen E. Ambrose, *Eisenhower*, 1984; Robert A. Divine, *Eisenhower and the Cold War*, 1981; William B. Pickett, *Dwight D. Eisenhower and American Power*, 1995.

John K. Franklin

ELY, RICHARD T. (April 13, 1854–October 4, 1943)

Prominent economic philosopher, academic, and public servant known for his views on the "new economics" and who wrote prolifically on a variety of subjects from land to agricultural economics but who also sought to avoid taking a stand on subjects he considered too controversial, such as the tariff.

Born in Ripley, New York, Ely grew up in Fredonia. He received his education at a number of well-known academic institutions, including Dartmouth College, Columbia University, and Halle, Germany, where he met Simon Nelson Patten who became a close associate and friend. Like Patten, Ely studied under Professor Johannes Conrad, who encouraged his students to challenge the traditional economists of the classical school. He also studied under Professor Knies, who told Ely to use his creative talents as an economist. Completing his Ph.D. in agricultural economics, Ely received a fellowship and traveled throughout Europe, visiting Switzerland and Berlin. On returning to the United States, he joined the faculty of Johns Hopkins University in 1880.

A prolific writer, Ely examined a wide array of subjects, including land, rents, taxes, and agriculture. Typically, he emphasized common themes in all of his work and stressed the importance of Christian ethics in a person's outlook and upbringing. In studying economics he expected his students to apply Christian principles in their professional careers and studies. For himself, Ely concentrated, at least initially, on propounding the ideas of the "new economics" in which he proclaimed the abundance of society's natural resources, especially in the United States, the importance of inductive reasoning, and the rejection of the dismal and rigid classical theories of economics. To Ely, society functioned as a living and growing organism that could only be understood holistically, with each part interrelating to the others. He expected the government to play an active role in society and the economy by regulating business, restricting immigration, and promoting the general welfare.

Although an author and teacher, Ely also established professional organizations, including the American Economic Association, founded in 1885. He recruited students to work with him and develop other important organizations if the opportunity arose. In 1892, Ely moved on to the University of Wisconsin and began the "Wisconsin school." A social activist by nature, Ely gradually concluded that an Americanized form of socialism, whereby the federal government would control public utilities and transportation, might work. In fact, his "Wisconsin school" led in the Progressive Era reforms at the turn of the century.

In 1900, Ely entered public service when he supported Robert LaFollette for the governorship of Wisconsin. Ely remained a close advisor to LaFollette until 1917, when he broke openly with the progressive governor over the issue of American entry into World War I. While LaFollette supported isolationism, Ely favored American entry into the conflict. By the 1920s, Ely returned to academics at Northwestern University and began the *Journal of Land and Public Utilities*.

On the issue of the tariff, Ely proved ambivalent most of the time. He consistently advised his friends and students to avoid taking a stand on controversial issues like the tariff. His *Problems of To-Day: A Discussion of Protective Tariffs, Taxation, and Monopolies* remains the most significant work that he did on the tariff. In this study, Ely meticulously analyzed the argument used in favor of the tariff such as the "infant industries theory" and the "pauper labor theory." According to Ely, American industries had developed past the infant stage. In fact, business competition flourished and, when combined with America's abundant natural resources and the country's capable entrepreneurs, did not need a high tax on foreign goods. He also rejected the idea that tariffs protected the American worker from the low wages of Europe. He thought that the government could help labor by encouraging education. He disagreed with the argument that labor needed any subsidies. Nor did he agree that higher wages meant higher prices. Nevertheless, in concluding his analysis, Ely did not openly and directly come out against tariffs. Rather, he indicated his belief that free trade might prove more beneficial for American industry and American labor. Ely's ambivalent approach surprised those who knew of his forthrightness on issues about which he felt strongly. It seemed to him that the tariff generated so much controversy that the safest approach involved discussing the issue in a vague and indirect manner. In the end, Richard Ely left his mark on American academics and the discipline of economics.

See also: Labor; LaFollette, Robert Marion; Patten, Simon Nelson; Protectionism; World War I.

Selected Bibliography:

R.A. Gonce, "The Social Gospel, Ely and Commons' Initial Stage of Thought," *Journal of Economic Issues*, 1996; Don Leschohier, "Richard T. Ely in Retrospect," *Land Economics*, 1954; Benjamin Rader, *The Academic Mind and Reform: The Influence of Richard T. Ely in American Life*, 1966.

Michael V. Namorato

EMERSON, RALPH WALDO (May 25, 1803–April 27, 1882)

American author, poet, lecturer, philosopher, and minister whose transcendentalist writings inspired and supported the free trade movement.

Born in Boston, Massachusetts, Emerson attended Harvard University. Following his graduation at age eighteen, he taught for three years before returning to school to obtain ordination as a Unitarian minister. In 1829, he married Ellen Tucker, who died seventeen months later, and in 1832 he resigned from his church post and traveled to Europe. He returned in 1834 and moved to Concord, Massachusetts. That year he lectured and published *Nature*, his first book, which contains the essence of Transcendentalism, an idealist philosophy of the individual being free from artificial restraints. An inspiration to many, including Henry David Thoreau, Emerson lectured and wrote on the subject for such publications as *The Dial*, New England's journal of Transcendentalism. In 1842, he succeeded former editor Margaret Fuller until publication ceased in 1844. He traveled to Europe again for a time, and on returning to the United States became involved in national issues such as the abolition of slavery and free trade.

Emerson, along with several other abolitionists, founded the American Free Trade League in 1865. The group's ideology saw the rich getting richer at the expense of the labor force while the U.S. Congress passed multiple laws furthering protectionism, thus insulating American merchants against international competition. They witnessed an inexcusable irony in the protection agenda's imposition of considerable financial penalties on the workers themselves, since wealth remained impossible without workers. They also criticized protectionism's indirect incentive to hire foreign workers to re- duce expenditures. Free trade should extend beyond employment, they claimed, but they thought demanding congressional action in their favor more effective as a means of reparation than strikes, which they believed in practice often worked against workers.

See also: American Free Trade League (AFTL); Free trade; Protectionism.

Selected Bibliography:

Gay Wilson Allen, *Waldo Emerson: A Biography*, 1981; Moncure Daniel Conway, *Emerson: At Home and Abroad*, 1968.

Carolyn E. Ginno and Artemus Ward

ENVIRONMENTAL ISSUES

Interest in the lowering of trade barriers and protecting the environment have largely coincided.

Conservation had a long history in the United States when environmentalism burst onto the national scene in the early 1960s. Republican president Theodore Roosevelt signed the Antiquities Act of 1906 granting the authority to establish national monuments, thus affording added protection to public lands. Democratic president Franklin D. Roosevelt considered himself a tree farmer and fostered soil conservation.

Environmentalism and ecology in a fashion akin to international trade focus on the interrelationship of elements. Rachel Carson, a former employee of the U.S. Department of the Interior and best-selling author, published *Silent Spring* in 1962. The book highlighted the threat posed by pesticides, which she referred to as biocides,

to all living creatures. Most memorably, the book discussed how DDT, which had earlier garnered its inventor a Nobel Prize, weakened eagle shell eggs and so threatened the extinction of the living symbol of the United States of America. Secretary of the Interior Stewart L. Udall and President John F. Kennedy responded to her message even as representatives of the chemical industry disparaged her as a "hysterical woman." President Kennedy, that same year, signed legislation in which Congress delegated to the president powers to raise or lower tariffs on broad categories of goods. The following year the Kennedy Round opened a series of multilateral tariff negotiations that lasted from 1963 to 1967, a period when participating countries reduced tariffs by 50 percent on goods produced by noncommunist industrialized nations. Labor strongly supported these efforts.

As society started to perceive trade and ecological concerns as incompatible, divisions arose even among environmental groups. In an advertising campaign, groups like Rainforest Action Network, Public Citizen, the Sierra Club, Friends of the Earth, and Greenpeace launched an attack on the supporters of the North American Free Trade Agreement (NAFTA), including the National Wildlife Federation and the National Audubon Society. They asked, "Why are some 'green' groups so quick to sell off the North American environment? Maybe they are too cozy with corporate funders."

Environmental regulations can have an impact on the entry of foreign products into the marketplace. For example, controversy emerged when the United States excluded the importation of

Mexican tuna from the U.S. market because of regulations requiring that fishing procedures eliminate unnecessary risks to dolphins.

In promoting NAFTA, the Clinton administration employed a well-suited approach to the challenges posed by the juxtaposition of promoting trade, environmental safeguards, and labor standards. Democratic president Clinton secured passage of NAFTA, which had been negotiated by both Democratic and Republican administrations, by Congress with more support from Republicans than Democrats. Although Clinton wanted fast-track authority granted to the president to facilitate trade, he and Secretary of the Treasury Lloyd Bentsen also wanted side agreements negotiated that would serve to improve environmental and labor conditions throughout North America. Other American leaders have also demonstrated leadership in relating trade policy to a concern about nature.

In January 1974, the United States ratified the Convention on Trade in Endangered Species of Wild Fauna and Flora (CITES), the first nation to do so. The agreement provides for a series of trade permits. Most nations have signed CITES, with the notable exceptions of Mexico and South Korea, since it provides their endangered species with protection from illegal poachers. The African elephant, prized for its ivory, remains a controversial listing. A number of African nations held the view that they had managed their herds sufficiently, thus suggesting that the ivory trade could resume, but most nations, including the United States, where Congress held African ivory hearings, concluded otherwise.

The United States, notably during the administrations of George Herbert Walker Bush and George Walker Bush, has reluctantly supported environmental measures viewed as inhospitable to domestic economic growth. The United States refused to sign a convention on biodiversity developed at the Earth Summit held in Rio de Janeiro in June 1992, an agreement that 153 other nations did sign. In early spring of 2001, President George W. Bush announced that the United States would not follow the Kyoto Protocol, which had been designed to ameliorate global warming, because of the economic hardship it would impose on the U.S. economy; it was a position that provoked disapproval from Chancellor Gerhard Schroeder of Germany, other world leaders, and some groups within the United States. A few weeks earlier, the president had backed away from a pledge he had made on September 29, 2000, to mandate a reduction in carbon dioxide emissions from factories and industrial plants.

Trade issues touching on the environment can often cause both international and domestic cleavages. Some interests in the northwestern United States want tighter control over exports of timber to Pacific nations, most notably Japan, while other interests see profit in the trade. Considerable disagreements have certainly arisen in the United States about the nature of the relationship between promoting trade, protecting the environment, and shielding those individuals most frequently exposed to environmental hazards, namely the women and men of labor. These differences manifested themselves in December 1999, when environmentalists and labor union members vigorously protested the meeting of the World Trade Organization (WTO) in Seattle, Washington, even as President Clinton participated in it.

See also: Bush, George Herbert Walker; Clinton, William Jefferson (Bill); Fast-track legislation; Friends of the Earth; Kennedy, John F.; North American Free Trade Agreement (NAFTA); Roosevelt, Theodore; Sierra Club; World Trade Organization (WTO).

Selected Bibliography:

Rachel Carson, *Silent Spring*, 1994; Jacqueline Vaughn Switzer, *Environmental Politics: Domestic and Global Dimensions*, 1994.

Henry B. Sirgo

ESCAPE CLAUSE

A provision included in trade agreements designed to act as a safety mechanism for domestic producers.

In 1935, President Franklin D. Roosevelt and Secretary of State Cordell Hull included the first escape clause in an agreement with Belgium on cotton, steel, and building materials. Concern over a third country benefiting from steep concessions by dramatically increasing the amount of product sold in the American market motivated the administration to include a clause within the bilateral agreement. That clause allowed the United States to impose restrictions on third-party imports if the quantity increased so dramatically that domestic producers would suffer damage. Throughout the depression the administration failed to enforce the escape clause. After World War II, the international situation required a modification of the escape clause so that the United States could prevent surges of imports from any country, whether a third party or the original signatory of a bilateral agreement. President Harry S Truman insisted on the inclusion of the escape clause in trade agreements, including the General Agreement on Tariffs and Trade (GATT). Its use remained limited throughout the 1950s and 1960s. In 1974, Congress modified the clause to increase the protection of American manufacturers and workers. Under the Trade Act of 1974, Congress provided a five-year period for adjustments within specific industries experiencing difficulties due to a rise in imports. Throughout the Nixon, Carter, and Reagan administrations the enforcement of the escape clause occurred infrequently. By 1984, its use as a protectionist measure effectively ended. The doctrine of free trade prevailed over the protection of individual employees and American industries.

See also: General Agreement on Tariffs and Trade (GATT); Hull, Cordell; Roosevelt, Franklin D.; Trade Act of 1974; Truman, Harry S.

Selected Bibliography:

Alfred E. Eckes, *Opening America's Market: U.S. Foreign Trade Policy Since 1776*, 1995.

Cynthia Clark Northrup

EUROPEAN COMMUNITY (EC)

Association of European nations established to promote economic unity.

Founded on January 1, 1958, the European Community (EC), formerly the European Economic Community (EEC), initially served as a link to bind France and Germany financially.

France, the Republic of Germany, Italy, Luxembourg, and the Netherlands formed the group initially, with Denmark, Ireland, and the United Kingdom joining in January 1973; Greece joined in 1981; Portugal and Spain in 1986; and Austria, Finland, and Sweden rounded out the membership in 1995. Since 1973, the European Community has also promoted the political union of western European countries. The structure of the EC includes a Commission, the Council of Ministers, the Court of Justice, and the European Parliament. The primary goal of the organization included the elimination of tariff barriers and customs duties, an objective realized in July 1968 when the EC abolished all internal barriers. The taxation of imports into the region continues and quota systems remain in place, restricting access to the European Common Market. In 1962, the EC formed a common agricultural policy with guaranteed prices that discouraged the importation of foreign, especially American, agricultural products. Since the Dillon Round negotiations under the General Agreement on Tariffs and Trade (GATT), the EC has refused to negotiate the reduction of barriers on farm produce. During the Kennedy Round negotiators offered substantial cuts in American tariff rates in anticipation of access to the EC market. When it appeared that the talks would fail, the State Department persuaded administration officials that the sacrifice of American agriculture must occur for foreign policy reasons, primarily because the United States sought to prevent the spread of communism through the encouragement of the EC. Domestic criticism of the Kennedy Round proved founded since the U.S. trade surplus evaporated with the implementation of the agreement.

See also: General Agreement on Tariffs and Trade (GATT); Kennedy Round.

Selected Bibliography:

Dean C. Curry, *Global Transformation and Foreign Economic Policy: The Case of the United States–European Community Agricultural Relations, 1958–1979*, 1990; Nicholas V. Gianaris, *The European Community and the United States: Economic Relations*, 1991.

Cynthia Clark Northrup

EVARTS, WILLIAM (February 6, 1818– February 28, 1901)

Noted orator, Massachusetts lawyer, and statesman who served as the U.S. delegate to the International Monetary Conference in 1881.

At the International Monetary Conference, Evarts delivered a speech advocating bimetallism, the use of both gold and silver to create a standard in the international money system. Evarts argued that America stood in a unique position to benefit from the utilization of both metals because of the abundance of the metals found in North America. Evarts also supported a high protective tariff.

He attended Yale and helped found the *Yale Literary Magazine*. During his law career Evarts participated in many well-known and important cases, including the lead defense position in the impeachment trial of President Andrew Johnson. Evarts also served as secretary of state under Rutherford Hayes and in the Senate from 1885 to

1891, when his eyesight failed. He died at his home in New York City.

See also: International Monetary Fund (IMF); Protectionism.

Selected Bibliography:

Chester Barrows, *William M. Evarts: Lawyer, Diplomat, Statesman*, 1941.

Lisa A. Ennis

EXCISE

A tax imposed on items consumed rather than on goods imported.

The excise developed later than the tariff as an important source of revenue in America. British immigrants to America brought a deep suspicion of the excise with them: they hated this type of tax because it hit the poor especially hard and because it empowered tax collectors to conduct searches of homes and businesses without warrants. This hatred formed the basis for the colonists' violent protests against the Stamp Act of 1765, which, more than any other taxation measure, laid the foundation for the American Revolution. After independence, the federal government imposed an excise on whiskey in 1791, provoking the "Whiskey Rebellion" in western Pennsylvania in 1794, an uprising in which some 7,000 frontiersmen participated. The Federalist administrations of the 1790s also imposed excises on carriages, snuff, wine, and sugar, contributing to the electoral backlash against that party in 1800. Jefferson abolished all excises in 1802, in accordance with Democratic-Republican ideology. During the War of 1812, with foreign trade severely disrupted, the federal government temporarily reinstated the excise system, but abolished it once more in 1817. The excise became a permanent part of U.S. government revenues from the Civil War onward, for wartime excises on tobacco, liquor, and banknotes remained in place when the war ended. In the twentieth century, the high-revenue earners for the federal government included excise taxes on tobacco, liquor (except during the Prohibition years), and gasoline.

See also: American Revolution; Civil War (American); Jefferson, Thomas; War of 1812.

Selected Bibliography:

Thomas P. Slaughter, *The Whiskey Rebellion: Frontier Epilogue to the American Revolution*, 1986.

John P. Barrington

EXECUTIVE COMMITTEE ON COMMERCIAL POLICY (ECCP)

Executive branch interagency committee under the supervision of the U.S. Department of State.

In 1934, President Franklin Delano Roosevelt established the Executive Committee on Commercial Policy (ECCP). This advisory group, designed to coordinate and disseminate information during secret bilateral negotiations, worked with the Committee for Reciprocity Information and the Committee on Trade Agreements. After the formation of the committee, the U.S. Department of Treasury frequently relinquished responsibility for trade issues, allowing the State Department to formulate policy in the context of foreign affairs. On numerous occasions throughout the 1930s, the Treasury Department investigated charges of dumping and countervailing duties, but before imposing an order against the countries involved, the State Department interceded, resulting in the delay or suspension of the order. One example of such a practice occurred in 1935 when the Japanese continued to dump flycatchers on the U.S. market after the Executive Committee on Commercial Policy stated opposition to the imposition of any penalties; once fighting commenced during World War II, the State Department withdrew all objections and the Treasury Department issued an order to end the importation of Japanese flycatchers.

See also: Committee for Reciprocity Information; Roosevelt, Franklin D.

Selected Bibliography:

Alfred E. Eckes, *Opening America's Market: U.S. Foreign Trade Policy Since 1776*, 1995.

Cynthia Clark Northrup

EXPORTS

U.S. exports increased substantially from the Civil War period through the first part of the twentieth century, when a general decline occurred.

The first protective tariff, passed in 1816, failed to increase exports to a high level until after the Civil War. As the United States entered a period of big business, exports rose at an average annual growth rate of 10 percent between 1870 and 1880. The high tariff rates of the late nineteenth century promoted the exportation of products as opposed to the importation of foreign goods. By the end of the century, Congress attempted to enact a series of reciprocity agreements designed to lower the tariff. These efforts failed, but a compromise between the executive branch and Congress facilitated the passage of the Sixteenth Amendment, an act that allowed the government to legally levy taxes on personal incomes. During World War I, exports remained high, despite continual changes to the rate schedules. By 1930, Congress sought to increase the duty on imported agricultural products, but instead raised the tariff to a record high level on manufactured items as well. After the passage of the Hawley-Smoot Tariff Act and the onset of the Great Depression, exports dropped by 53 percent from 1929 to 1931 and by another 69 percent in the following year. While exports rose again during World War II and for a short time thereafter, by the 1960s the foreign and economic policies of the United States merged. In an effort to strengthen capitalistic societies fighting communism, the United States embarked on a policy of tariff reduction. The Kennedy Round lowered the rate on most items, including agricultural products. By the 1970s, Congress, having ignored unfair trade practices and the overall decline of exports, attempted to reduce the trade deficit. The concept of free trade managed to survive the congressional attack leading to the passage of the North American Free Trade Agreement (NAFTA) in 1993. In the period between 1950 and the passage of NAFTA, exports rose 9.8 percent while imports increased by 12 percent annually. Free trade has resulted in a trade deficit since other countries have failed to reduce their tariff barriers on a par with the United States.

See also: Civil War (American); Hawley-Smoot Tariff (Tariff of 1930); North American Free Trade Agreement (NAFTA); Trusts.

Selected Bibliography:

Alfred E. Eckes, *Opening America's Market: U.S. Foreign Trade Policy Since 1776*, 1995.

Cynthia Clark Northrup

F

FANEUIL HALL

Site of numerous rallies and speeches promoting liberty and the right to free trade.

Faneuil Hall, constructed in Boston in 1742, served as a meeting place for Bostonians throughout the early years of the United States. John Adams dubbed the hall "The Cradle of Liberty." The first colonial protest against the Sugar Act and the first public declaration of the doctrine of "no taxation without representation" took place in the Boston meeting hall. Rallies against the Stamp Act, the Townshend Act, and the landing of British troops also occurred there. In late 1773, Bostonians held a series of meetings at the hall to plan a protest demonstration against Britain's tax on tea. Colonists would carry out the plan they devised as the Boston Tea Party.

In 1820, Daniel Webster gave a speech to Boston businessmen gathered in Faneuil Hall, in which he attacked the idea of government assistance to industry through discriminating tariffs. Although he remained a product of New England Federalism, Webster objected to protective tariffs on constitutional grounds. He argued that unless tariff protection occurred as a purely unintentional result of duties levied for revenue purposes it was inadvisable, if not unconstitutional. Such policies could lead only to excessive reliance on government. Before the gathering of businessmen in the hall, Webster reasoned that protective tariffs would benefit only a few producers while consumers and taxpayers would suffer both higher costs for products and higher taxes to compensate for revenue lost on excluded imports.

Webster's speech echoed the republican theories of the virtuous, independent farmer. He reasoned that, by its nature, a manufacturing system tended to concentrate capital in the hands of a few and increased the number of poor and the level of their poverty. An agricultural society, he argued, demonstrated greater evidence of producing individual respectability and happiness, as well as ensuring the common good. Only with a society of independent agrarians could the future of the nation be secure. Factory laborers, owning no property and having no stake in society, have little incentive to exercise civic responsibility to state or society. The United States should remain a country predominantly of farmers, Webster told the group in Faneuil Hall, and leave the workshops in Europe.

See also: Adams, John; American farmers; American Revolution; Webster, Daniel.

Selected Bibliography:

Edward Stanwood, *American Tariff Controversies in the Nineteenth Century*, 1967.

Carol Terry

FAST-TRACK LEGISLATION

Grants the president the authority to conclude trade negotiations without Congress amending the treaties.

Congress designed the process of fast-track legislation to empower trade negotiators with the authority to agree to specific terms without having to receive congressional approval on each item and then having to renegotiate unacceptable clauses. With fast-track legislation Congress has the power to accept or reject, but not to amend, the treaty. Congress must receive an official request from the foreign government and the White House that outlines the objectives of the negotia-

tions before granting the president such authority. The House Ways and Means Committee and the Senate Finance Committee review the requests. The committees have sixty legislative days after receipt to reject or approve the process. President George H.W. Bush asked for and received fast-track authority to negotiate the North American Free Trade Agreement (NAFTA) with Mexico and Canada in May 1989 with a two-year time limit on the provision. Regular consultations between Congress and the president prevent the initiation of reverse fast-track legislation that would eliminate the authority immediately, thus preserving congressional oversight for trade negotiations. In 1991, with NAFTA negotiations still continuing, Bush asked for an extension and Congress agreed. The signing of NAFTA in December 1992 resulted in the treaty reaching the Senate for ratification without the option of amending the agreement. Passage, over the opposition of groups such as the AFL-CIO, illustrated the importance of the fast-track process. Congress has not always endorsed the use of fast-track legislation, but approval streamlines trade negotiations and eases the closure of such agreements.

See also: American Federation of Labor–Congress of Industrial Organizations (AFL-CIO); Bush, George Herbert Walker; North American Free Trade Agreement (NAFTA).

Selected Bibliography:

Hermann von Bertrab, *Negotiating NAFTA: A Mexican Envoy's Account*, 1997.

Cynthia Clark Northrup

FEDERAL RESERVE BANK

Established in 1913 with the passage of the Federal Reserve Act to provide elasticity of the money supply and act as a lender of last resort during periods of economic stringency.

Created as part of President Woodrow Wilson's progressive reforms, the Federal Reserve Bank (the Fed) consists of twelve district banks with equal standing located in Boston, New York, Philadelphia, Cleveland, Richmond, Atlanta, Chicago, St. Louis, Dallas, Minneapolis, Kansas City, and San Francisco. The Federal Reserve, supervised by a Board of Governors, issues national currency, conducts monetary policy, and supervises banks and bank holding companies. National commercial banks must purchase stock in the Federal Reserve Bank, but do not retain the right to trade that stock. If a bank leaves the system, the stock reverts back to the Fed. Responsible for controlling the money supply, the Federal Reserve has produced both positive and negative effects on the economy, but overall has provided stability to the national economy. Historians and economists disagree about the impact that the Fed has had on international trade, especially during the Great Depression. Some argue that the tightening of the money supply in 1930 following the passage of the protectionist Hawley-Smoot Tariff Act exacerbated the worldwide economic crisis and worsened the depression. Other scholars point out that the policy of the Federal Reserve Bank did not affect trade since the problem already existed prior to the change in monetary policy.

See also: Great Depression; Hawley-Smoot Tariff (Tariff of 1930); Wilson, Thomas Woodrow.

Selected Bibliography:

Alfred E. Eckes, *Opening America's Markets: U.S. Foreign Trade Policy Since 1776*, 1995.

Cynthia Clark Northrup

FEDERAL TRADE COMMISSION (FTC)

Federal regulatory agency, created by an act of Congress on September 26, 1914, to enforce legislation dealing with excessive concentration of control and practices "in restraint of trade" (such as price fixing and price discrimination), monitor unfair or deceptive commercial acts (such as false advertising, mislabeling, or sales misrepresentation), and conduct broad studies of business activities to determine the effectiveness of existing antitrust laws.

The establishment of the Federal Trade Commission (FTC) coincided with the development of several closely intertwined reformist trends of the Progressive Era—the antitrust movement, growing discontent over inflation, increasing pressures for significant downward revision of protective tariff duties, and the demand for a federal income tax based on the "ability to pay . . . from whatever source derived." The perception that all these measures aimed substantially at the same target, the giant industrial and financial corporations and their principal stockholders who had profited so immensely and inequitably from the rapid and massive industrialization of the recent past, linked them in the public's consciousness. The same mindset fueled the rise of the midwestern and western Insurgents and the fracturing of the Republican Party as well as the resultant triumph of the progressive wing of the Democratic Party in 1910 and 1912—a political upheaval that produced the Underwood-Simmons Tariff Act, a federal income tax, the Federal Reserve, Clayton Antitrust, and Federal Trade Commission acts during the first congressional session of Woodrow Wilson's administration.

Although Wilson's "New Freedom" rhetoric had pledged relief to small businessmen, farmers, workers, and consumers through a vigorous "trust-busting" campaign, the Clayton and FTC Acts, as finally adopted, much more closely resembled Theodore Roosevelt's "New Nationalism" approach of accepting the inevitability of big business and relying on the regulation of giant enterprise by the federal government. This acceptance of the new economic order also clearly rendered obsolete the central rationale of high tariff advocates: large and powerful enterprises that obviously had no need of the tariff protection afforded the nation's earlier "infant industries." The elimination, or serious reduction, of excessively protectionist rates would putatively enhance domestic competition, increase the leverage of small businessmen, farmers, and workers, decrease consumer prices, and curtail inflation. With that supposedly accomplished by the Underwood-Simmons Tariff Act, the Clayton Act then intended to remedy deficiencies in the Sherman Antitrust Act of 1890, which had clearly failed to prevent the "Great Merger Movement" of 1897 to 1905 and its con-

tinuous aftershocks. The original proponents of the measure succeeded in outlawing price fixing, price discrimination, interlocking directorates, and other forms of collusion, but only "where the effect may be to substantially lessen competition or tend to create a monopoly." To enforce the Sherman and Clayton Acts (as later amended by the Wheeler-Lea, Robinson-Patman, and Celler-Kefauver Acts), along with the Antitrust Division of the Department of Justice, Congress then replaced the existing Bureau of Corporations of the Department of Commerce with an independent, bipartisan trade commission, consisting of five members appointed by the president, with the consent of the Senate, for seven-year terms.

Congress empowered the new FTC with the authority to investigate complaints of illegal practices, issue "cease and desist orders," negotiate "consent decrees," and hold hearings before an administrative law judge. Although the court could review its rulings, most cases have never proceeded that far. The agency also issues advisory opinions and other guidance materials to promote voluntary compliance. With a jurisdiction exclusively domestic in nature, the FTC prevents oligopolistic practices. The maintenance of extremely high protectionist rates in any given industry has always provided an effective way of restricting price and product competition, both from foreign and domestic rivals. Moreover, those same protectionist rates can frequently have the effect of price fixing by keeping otherwise lower-priced foreign goods out of the domestic market altogether. Finally, the desire to circumvent tariff duties has sometimes acted as a driving force behind international mergers or foreign takeovers of American corporations.

See also: Federal Reserve Bank; Insurgents; Personal income tax (Sixteenth Constitutional Amendment); Progressives; Roosevelt, Theodore; Trusts; Underwood-Simmons Tariff (Tariff of 1913); Wilson, Thomas Woodrow.

Selected Bibliography:

Earl W. Kintner, *An Antitrust Primer: A Guide to Antitrust and Trade Regulation Laws for Businessmen*, 1973; Robert J. Larner and James W. Meehan Jr., eds., *Economics and Antitrust Policy*, 1989; Arthur S. Link, *Wilson: The New Freedom*, 1956.

John D. Buenker

THE FEDERALIST (FEDERALIST PAPERS)

A series of newspaper articles written by Alexander Hamilton, James Madison, and John Jay to promote and defend the ratification of the U.S. Constitution.

Once the delegates in Philadelphia formally adopted the Constitution in September 1787, the battle over ratification began in earnest. The nation divided between the Federalists, who supported the Constitution, and the Anti-Federalists, who opposed it. The greatest battleground between the two camps quickly developed in the states of New York, Virginia, Massachusetts, and Pennsylvania. New York represented some of the bitterest opposition to the Constitution. Like the other large states, New York had become a power in its own right under the Articles of Confederation. The state had grown rich by laying tariffs on goods imported from other states and nations.

Alexander Hamilton decided that a newspaper campaign might persuade his fellow New Yorkers to support the Constitution. He enlisted John Jay of New York and James Madison of Virginia to help him write a series of essays defending the Constitution. Jay wrote only a handful of the eighty-five articles, while Hamilton and Madison wrote the vast majority. These essays ran several times a week in four out of the five newspapers in New York throughout the spring of 1788. Collectively, they became known as *The Federalist*. Although the articles themselves had little direct effect on the ratification of the Constitution, they remain to this day the single greatest defense of the Constitution and the government it brought to life.

The essays attacked the feeble national government created under the Articles of Confederation. Hamilton and Madison reminded their readers that this weak government had led to the Constitutional Convention in Philadelphia. Congress, under the Articles of Confederation, had few powers, while the individual states retained full sovereignty in almost every important political matter. For the Federalists, the greatest flaw in the Articles of Confederation centered on the inability of Congress to lay taxes. This meant that the national government could not raise an army or navy, and thus could not provide for the common defense. Equally important, Congress had little control over domestic or foreign trade since each state could set its own policies. If this weak government continued, they argued, then the United States would remain vulnerable to foreign invasion, domestic unrest, and financial ruin. In support of the new Constitution, Hamilton and Madison emphasized the strengths of the proposed government. Both men stated that experienced and competent men had written the Constitution in a spirit of compromise. The government they had created would provide the nation with the best form of republicanism possible, while preventing the worst abuses of uncontrolled democracy. They lauded the separation of powers between the legislative, executive, and judicial branches. Hamilton especially emphasized the fact that the bicameral national legislature would provide the checks and balances necessary for a stable government. *The Federalist* had a profound effect on later interpreters of the Constitution, especially Chief Justice John Marshall.

See also: Anti-Federalists; Constitutionality; Federalists; Hamilton, Alexander; Madison, James. **Vol. II**: *The Federalist* (Federalist Papers); *Report on Manufactures*. **Vol. III**: Tariff of 1790; Tariff of 1792; Tariff of 1794; Tariff of 1816.

Selected Bibliography:

Alexander Hamilton, James Madison, and John Jay, *The Federalist Papers*, 1987.

Mary Stockwell

FEDERALISTS

Political faction that supported high tariffs to raise revenue for the federal treasury and protect the burgeoning manufacturing in America.

The Federalists developed as a political entity during the debates surrounding the ratification of the U.S. Constitution. They wanted a strong central government that would have the power and credibility to secure the U.S. place among the nations of the world. Alexander Hamilton, John Adams, John Jay, and James Madison (until after 1790) became the leading spokesmen for those who supported ratification and called themselves the Federalists. Those who opposed ratification, the Anti-Federalists, feared that a strong federal government would rob states of their rights. Hamilton, Jay, and Madison presented their arguments in support of the Constitution, in eighty-five essays published as *The Federalist*. They succeeded in gaining sufficient votes for ratification only after agreeing to add a bill of rights.

After the ratification of the Constitution in 1789, Federalists gained control of the executive branch through the unanimous election of George Washington, who both favored and helped entrench a strong central government. As the first president of the United States, Washington appointed Alexander Hamilton to the cabinet position of secretary of the treasury. In his economic plan for the new nation, Hamilton demonstrated the Federalists' position concerning government and the national economy. In his *Report on Manufactures*, he explained the weak position in which American trade floundered. He presented a coherent rationale for an American mercantilist system that would cut the costs of manufacturing and increase the quantity of production. Hamilton believed that through technological innovation and favorable public policy, America could, and should, increase production of manufactured goods to be sold on the world market. Through tariff protection or direct subsidies, Hamilton argued, American industry could soon compete with European producers.

Despite Washington's warnings against party factions in his infamous Farewell Address, those loyal to the Hamiltonian plan adopted the party title of Federalists and fought vigorously against the opposition who rallied under the leadership of Thomas Jefferson to form the (Jeffersonian) Republican Party. Republicans believed in a strict interpretation of the Constitution, argued in favor of states' rights, opposed a national bank, and favored an agrarian-based economy, arguing that tariffs hurt the farmer while unfairly protecting and bolstering northern industry. Unlike their opponents, Federalists had no problem allowing the central government to regulate trade. They believed that only through a strong central government could the nation profit from global trade. The Federalist Congress in 1789 imposed a tax of fifty cents a ton on foreign ships entering American ports and a duty of 5 to 15 percent on the value of imported goods. They did not intend to impose high protective tariffs on all products immediately; to do so would have hurt merchants and potential industrialists. They planned, rather, a gradual increase.

Jefferson's victory in the presidential election of 1800, a triumph that he dubbed a revolution, and subsequent Republican gains in congressional seats should have led the nation into an era of free trade. Yet Republicans began to rethink the idea of a tariff within the confines of an international economy dominated by protectionist-minded Europeans. In a twist of historical irony, and despite the constant rivalry between the Federalists and Republi-

cans over the tariff, a national bank, and other issues, the Hamiltonian ideal ultimately triumphed. In 1816, the once-Federalist-turned-ardent-Republican, James Madison, signed into law the first protective tariff in U.S. history. He also issued the first charter for a national bank. Between 1790 and 1820, customs revenue rose steadily and eventually provided about 90 percent of the national government's income, proving to all that the Federalist concept of a tariff had merit.

See also: *The Federalist* (Federalist Papers); Hamilton, Alexander; Jefferson, Thomas; Madison, James; *Report on Manufactures*; Tariff of 1816; Washington, George.

Selected Bibliography:

William Chambers, *Political Parties in a New Nation, 1776–1809*, 1963; Stanley Elkins and Eric McKitrick, *The Age of Federalism*, 1993; Edward Stanwood, *American Tariff Controversies in the Nineteenth Century*, 1967.

Carol Terry and Elaine C. Prange Turney

FILLMORE, MILLARD (January 7, 1800–March 8, 1874)

Thirteenth president of the United States; known best for the passage of the Compromise of 1850.

Born into dire poverty on a small farm in Buffalo, New York, on January 7, 1800, Fillmore had little formal education. He became an apprentice clothmaker at an early age. After fulfilling his obligation, Fillmore taught himself law and took the bar exam in 1823. His political career began first as a representative from the Anti-Masonic Party to the New York State Assembly and later he served as a member of the U.S. House of Representatives. During his tenure in Congress, he supported protective tariffs. He served as chairman of the House Ways and Means Committee and fought for the passage of the Tariff Act of 1842. This act raised duty levels to that of 1832 in response to the sagging economy and the crisis of 1837.

After serving as state comptroller of New York, the Whig Party selected Fillmore to run as the Whig vice-presidential candidate with General Zachary Taylor in 1848. The Whigs won the election, but in 1850 Taylor died unexpectedly, leaving Fillmore to preside over the increasing sectional crisis and the passage of the Compromise of 1850, as well as the Fugitive Slave Act. Fillmore sent Commodore Matthew C. Perry as the first U.S. trade emissary to Japan and worked on protective measures for Hawaii. He ran unsuccessfully for president in 1856 as a candidate from the Know-Nothing Party. After his defeat, Fillmore retired to Buffalo, where he resided until his death in 1874.

See also: House Ways and Means Committee; Tariff of 1842; Taylor, Zachary.

Selected Bibliography:

W.L. Barre, *The Life and Public Service of Millard Fillmore*, 1971; Robert J. Rayback, *Millard Fillmore: Biography of a President*, 1959.

Jonathan V. Parrent

FIRST REPORT ON PUBLIC CREDIT

Alexander Hamilton's first recommendation to Congress on the tariff.

In January 1790, Secretary of the Treasury Alexander Hamilton presented his First Report on Public Credit. Hamilton had prepared the report in response to a Congress that believed in the importance of the solid support of public credit for the "honor and prosperity" of the United States. Hamilton heartily agreed that the United States must place itself on a firm financial footing to win the respect of the world. He worked diligently for nearly four months to prepare his 20,000-word report.

The secretary calculated that the United States owed more than $11 million to foreign nations and over $40 million to its own citizens. He argued that the United States must pay its foreign debt according to the exact terms of the original loan agreements. He recommended the funding of the domestic debt at par. Calling in outstanding government securities and issuing new bonds of the same value in their place would accomplish this. The national government would also assume the remaining debts of the individual states and pay them off under similar terms. Finally, Congress needed to establish a sinking fund to guarantee payment of both the interest and principal of the national debt.

Hamilton recommended the repayment of the foreign debt by taking out new loans overseas. This would prevent a cash drain on the American economy. An increase in duties on imports and tonnage could fund the domestic debt. The government could raise more money by placing new duties on imported wines, distilled spirits, tea, and coffee. He suggested a tax of twenty cents to thirty-five cents per gallon on Madeira and other wines and twenty cents to forty cents per gallon on distilled spirits, depending on the proof. Duties on tea would range from twelve cents to forty cents per pound, with a duty of five cents per pound on coffee.

James Madison of Virginia led the congressional opposition to Hamilton's recommendations. Madison favored "discrimination," a policy that would pay all the original as well as current owners of government securities. He also opposed the assumption of state debts since Virginia and most of the other southern states had already paid off their debts. Hamilton convinced most representatives that discrimination would not work, but Congress remained deadlocked over assumption. In July 1790, Hamilton offered to move the national capital along the Potomac River in exchange for Madison's support. The compromise broke the deadlock and Congress approved Hamilton's plans.

See also: Hamilton, Alexander; Madison, James.

Selected Bibliography:

Alexander Hamilton, *The Papers of Alexander Hamilton*, 1963.

Mary Stockwell

FISH

One of the most important items of American trade since the colonial period.

Not enumerated in Great Britain's navigation acts, the British allowed the colonists to sell their catch directly to customers in Europe, especially to Catholic countries that bordered the Mediterranean. From this export trade in fish arose other trades, including the import of wine and salt from Spain and Portugal. Fishing helped to support important industries in New England, such as shipbuilding, as well as other economic activities, such as provisioning the fishing fleets. The freedom from regulation granted under the navigation laws thus enabled fishing to underpin considerable economic development in New England. In the negotiations at the end of the American Revolution, representatives of the United States such as Benjamin Franklin and John Jay fought successfully to retain fishing rights off the coasts of Nova Scotia and Newfoundland. After declaring independence, the U.S. government focused more on gaining trade concessions in foreign markets for American fishermen than on the protection of U.S. markets against imports of foreign fish. In the nineteenth century, New England whalers and fur traders began to frequent the Pacific Coast, soon opening up a new area for American fishing fleets. In the later part of the twentieth century, the free trade enjoyed by fishermen previously had given way to regulation, not in the form of tariffs but in the form of fishing quotas allocated to each nation that fishes in the Atlantic and Pacific Oceans.

See also: American Revolution; Franklin, Benjamin; Great Britain; Navigation and Trade Acts.

Selected Bibliography:

K.G. Davies, *The North Atlantic World in the Seventeenth Century*, 1974.

John P. Barrington

FITZSIMONS, THOMAS (Unknown month and date, 1741–August 26, 1811)

U.S. representative from Pennsylvania who supported Alexander Hamilton's nationalistic policies.

Born in Ireland in 1741, Fitzsimons immigrated to Philadelphia around 1760. After working with a local merchant, he married Catherine Meade, the daughter of a wealthy businessman who specialized in West India trade, and joined the family business of George Meade and Company. During the American Revolution he served in the militia and later attended the Continental Congress. Voted into office in 1789, Fitzsimons joined the newly formed U.S. House of Representatives and supported Hamilton and the Federalists who wanted a strong national government. During his three terms in office, he advocated the passage of a strong protective tariff and the retiring of the national debt. After leaving office in 1795, he devoted his energies to his business, the Bank of North America. Active in the Philadelphia Chamber of Commerce, Fitzsimons also founded and served as a director of the Insurance Company of North America. During Thomas Jefferson's second term, Fitzsimons suffered financially from the embargo, but in later years he recovered some of his losses. Throughout his entire life he continued to engage in philanthropic endeavors. He died in Philadelphia at the age of seventy.

See also: American Revolution; Continental Congress; Hamilton, Alexander; Jefferson, Thomas.

Selected Bibliography:

U.S. Army Center for Military History, *Thomas Fitzsimons*, 1986.

Cynthia Clark Northrup

FLEXIBLE CLAUSE

A provision of many national tariff commissions that allows for the undertaking of investigations, including public hearings, on petitions to increase, reduce, or even remove existing rates of duty, including any necessary change in tariff classification, for the purpose of protecting local industries or the economy as a whole.

Section 315 of the U.S. Tariff Act of 1922 provided for a flexible tariff. Congress authorized the Tariff Commission to investigate cost-of-production on imported items on the dutiable list and recommend changes designed to equalize the cost of domestic and foreign products to the president. The president could then increase or decrease the rates by up to 50 percent.

The United States, one of the last major nations to delegate tariff-negotiating authority to its executive, had industries reluctant to casually forego the protection afforded by tariffs and that favored retaining control of such negotiations by legislators whom they could more easily influence. In April 1973, the Nixon administration sought negotiating authority to participate in the Tokyo Round for both tariff and nontariff barriers. Congress would not empower the president to unilaterally change domestic law, but it did not want to undercut the negotiating authority of the executive branch. The Senate Finance Committee provided a solution that required Congress to act expeditiously to vote up or down on any agreement entered into by the executive branch. President Gerald R. Ford signed this approach into law on January 3, 1975, in the form of the Trade Act of 1974.

See also: Senate Finance Committee; Tariff Commission; Tokyo Round; Trade Act of 1974.

Selected Bibliography:

I.M. Destler, "Trade Consensus, SALT Stalemate: Congress and Foreign Policy in the 1970s," *The New Congress*, 1981.

Henry B. Sirgo

FORCE ACT

Legislation designed to punish South Carolina for its adherence to tariff nullification.

In 1832, Congress passed the Force Act at the request of President Andrew Jackson and in response to the passage of the Nullification Ordinance by South Carolina. This ordinance declared the tariffs of 1828, also known as the Tariff of Abominations, and 1832 null and void in that state as of February 1, 1833. Jackson's former vice president John C. Calhoun did not help matters when he placed himself firmly on the side of the Nullifiers. Because of this, the president faced opposition within his own administration.

Jackson called for assistance in January 1833. The Senate Judiciary Committee put forward the president's wishes in the form of the Force Bill on January 16. The bill garnered authority to facilitate customs collection and protect those who collected the tariff. It used U.S. warships as customs houses in towns such as Georgetown and Beaufort. It also made it possible to avoid state courts when trying violations of tariff collection. Most important, the bill called for a more effective use of the military in enforcing the tariff, allowing the president the right to use troops and call in the militia without a formal proclamation. Jackson indicated his support of the bill by creating a show of force in Charleston Harbor, where he stationed several naval vessels.

Massachusetts senator Daniel Webster, the best-known member of the Senate Judiciary Committee, spearheaded the bill in the Senate. He stood up against Calhoun, who saw the bill as a drive toward military despotism. Despite Calhoun's efforts, the Senate passed the Force Bill and sent it to the House of Representatives for consideration. In the House, congressmen tried to talk the bill out of existence by wearing down its proponents, but on the evening of March 1, the bill passed by a vote of 149 to 48.

While debate over the Force Bill raged, Henry Clay gained support for his compromise tariff. His conspicuous absence at the time of the vote on the Force Act helped win the support of southerners. Clay claimed he did not attend the session because he had difficulty staying in the House chamber after the chamber keeper lit the lights. Had he voted, he said, he would have voted for the bill. By his absence, the congressman maintained peace among his peers since New Englanders favored the Force Bill while rejecting Clay's Compromise and the South endorsed the proposed tariff, but loathed the Force Bill. Since his vote for the

Force Bill would anger southerners, he chose to abstain.

After approval by the House, the bill passed on to Jackson along with Clay's compromise tariff. He signed both into law, beginning with his beloved Force Act. On March 4, the same day that South Carolina repealed its nullification of the tariff, it nullified the Force Act. As a result, South Carolinians maintained their stand for states' rights, even while allowing the new compromise tariff. Jackson never implemented the Force Act.

See also: Calhoun, John Caldwell; Clay, Henry; Clay's Compromise; Force Act; Jackson, Andrew; Nullification; Tariff of 1828 (Tariff of Abominations). **Vol. II**: Daniel Webster's Speech Defending His Support of the Tariff of 1828; Henry Clay's 1832 Speech in Favor of the American System; South Carolina Ordinance of Nullification; Proclamation to the People of South Carolina; Andrew Jackson's Message to Congress on the Nullification Crisis; Force Act. **Vol. III**: Tariff of 1828 (Tariff of Abominations); Tariff of 1832; Tariff of 1833 (Compromise Tariff).

Selected Bibliography:

Richard E. Ellis, *The Union at Risk: Jacksonian Democracy, States' Rights, and the Nullification Crisis*, 1987; Merrill D. Peterson, *The Great Triumvirate: Webster, Clay, and Calhoun*, 1987.

Adrienne Caughfield

FORD, HENRY (July 30, 1863–April 7, 1947)

American inventor, international businessman, and automotive pioneer.

Born the first of six children to William and Mary Ford of Dearborn, Michigan, Ford demonstrated a mechanical ability at an early age. At sixteen he moved to Detroit, where he apprenticed for three years before returning to his parents' home. After marrying Clara Bryant in 1888, Ford ran a sawmill for three years and then accepted a position as an engineer with the Edison Illuminating Company in Detroit. After receiving a promotion to chief engineer, Ford devoted much of his time experimenting with combustion engines. He designed several vehicles, including the Quadricycle, a four-wheeled self-propelled vehicle. In 1903, he started Ford Motor Company and five years later he introduced the Model T. Ford revolutionized the transportation industry in 1913 when his engineers developed and implemented the moving assembly line. Using standardized interchangeable parts and a series of conveyor belts timed to provide employees with parts just as they needed them, Ford decreased the time and expense of manufacturing an automobile. By 1918, he controlled over half the American market. Paying his employees wages high enough so that they could afford the Model T, Ford created a strong middle class and other employers eventually recognized the genius of his strategy. As his business increased, so did his foreign sales. Unwilling to accept the tariff restrictions of other nations, Ford, and many other industrialists of his day, circumvented barriers by building plants in countries that discriminated against American goods. He opened his first overseas plant in Manchester, England, in 1911. The result of such actions created huge multinational corporations that remained relatively unaffected by tariff legislation while inhibiting the sale of goods produced by small and medium-sized companies. After establishing his company as the largest producer of automobiles in the world, Ford ran unsuccessfully for Congress. He died at his home on April 7, 1947, at the age of eighty-three.

See also: Automobile industry; International Harvester; Labor.

Selected Bibliography:

Allen Nivens, *Ford: The Times, The Man, The Company*, 1954; Oswald Garrison Villard, *Free Trade—Free World*, 1947.

Cynthia Clark Northrup

FORDNEY, JOSEPH WARREN
(November 5, 1853–January 8, 1932)

Representative from Michigan who co-sponsored the Fordney-McCumber Tariff.

Born in Indiana, Fordney and his family moved to Michigan, where he attended public schools and worked in the lumber industry before becoming an owner of a lumber enterprise. After working in business and serving in local government, Fordney successfully ran for congressional office as a representative from Michigan in 1899. He participated in several important committees before sponsoring the Fordney-McCumber Tariff of 1922. After the end of World War I, Congress raised tariff rates that had been lowered by the Underwood-Simmons Tariff. Much of the momentum for the new increases stemmed from the strong anti-foreign sentiment that developed after the war as well as the creation of several new nations out of the old European em-

pires that had disintegrated as a result of the war. The Fordney-McCumber Tariff remained in effect until the passage of the Hawley-Smoot Tariff, which raised duty rates even further. In 1922, Fordney withdrew his name from nomination for reelection and returned to the lumber business, where he remained until his death in 1932.

See also: Fordney-McCumber Tariff (Tariff of 1922).

Selected Bibliography:

John A. Russell, *Joseph Warren Fordney: An American Legislator*, 1928.

Cynthia Clark Northrup

FORDNEY-McCUMBER TARIFF (TARIFF OF 1922)

Passed at the end of World War I in an attempt to stop the flood of imports from Europe during the postwar recession.

Prior to World War I, President Woodrow Wilson persuaded Congress to pass the Underwood-Simmons Tariff Act, reducing duty rates from an average of 41 to 27 percent and placing over a hundred items on the free list. To offset the loss of revenue, Congress passed, and the states ratified, the Sixteenth Amendment, allowing for the collection of a personal income tax. Before the net effect of the tariff reductions could be realized, World War I disrupted the normal international trade patterns. At the end of the war, the U.S. economy underwent a period of recession. Congress responded by passing the Emergency Tariff Act of 1921 as well as the Fordney-McCumber Tariff of 1922. Under the Fordney-McCumber Tariff, custom rates increased to the highest level in American history, with duties jumping from 15.2 percent to 36.2 percent. In addition, the legislation provided the president with the authority to adjust tariffs to prevent unfair practices employed by foreign nations. The Fordney-McCumber Tariff failed to stem the flow of imports into the United States, but after 1923 the country entered a period of unprecedented prosperity and the tariff issue faded from the national spotlight until Herbert Hoover asked Congress to re-examine the issue to assist American farmers. After the stock market crash of October 1929, Congress revised the tariff schedule, raising rates an average of 20 percent with the passage of the Hawley-Smoot Tariff Act of 1930.

See also: Fordney, Joseph Warren; Hawley-Smoot Tariff (Tariff of 1930); Hoover, Herbert; Personal income tax (Sixteenth Constitutional Amendment); Wilson, Thomas Woodrow; World War I. **Vol. II**: Woodrow Wilson's Democratic Nomination Acceptance Speech; Joseph Ridgway Grundy's Speech in Favor of the Hawley-Smoot Tariff; Protest of American Economists over the Hawley-Smoot Tariff; Daniel Frederic Steck's Iowa Speech Against the Hawley-Smoot Tariff; Herbert Hoover's Statement of Intention to Approve the Hawley-Smoot Tariff Act; Andrew W. Mellon's Defense of the Hawley-Smoot Tariff for Economic Recovery; James Watson's Radio Address in Support of the Hawley-Smoot Tariff; Franklin D. Roosevelt's 1932 Campaign Radio Speech; Herbert Hoover's Response to Franklin D. Roosevelt. **Vol. III**: Tariff of 1922 (Fordney-McCumber Tariff); Tariff of 1930 (Hawley-Smoot Tariff).

Selected Bibliography:

Samuel Hopkins Adams, *Incredible Era: The Life and Times of Warren Gamaliel Harding*, 1979.

Cynthia Clark Northrup

FOREIGN POLICY

The formulation and implementation of foreign policy by the State Department often conflicted with congressional tariff legislation, leading the secretary of state to push for greater participation in the tariff decision process.

During the early years of the republic, the foreign policy of the United States involved trade questions, but Congress exercised greater authority over the tariff and, if diplomatic and economic issues conflicted, the will of Congress usually prevailed. After the Civil War, as the nation expanded its commercial influence around the world, foreign policy issues assumed a more important role. Under Abraham Lincoln and Andrew Johnson, Secretary of State William Seward negotiated bilateral tariff reduction agreements in an effort to achieve specific foreign policy objectives, but the U.S. Senate Finance Committee, dominated by Senator Justin Morrill, rejected the agreements, including one with the nation of Hawaii. Secretary of State Hamilton Fish achieved limited results under the administration of Ulysses S. Grant by persuading Congress to approve a reciprocal trade agreement with Hawaii that cost the government over $12.8 million in lost revenue from the importation tax on Hawaiian sugar after removing it from the free list. Congressional leaders opposed the involvement of the State Department in revenue matters, raising the issue of constitutionality. Hoping to continue the pattern established by Fish, Secretary of State Frederick T. Frelinghuysen, during the presidency of Chester Arthur, negotiated a free trade agreement with Mexico and Spain, but the Republican-controlled Senate refused to support these measures.

In 1889, when the Republican Party regained control of the White House, Secretary of State James G. Blaine proposed lowering tariff rates on products from Latin American countries to help open markets for American goods in the Western Hemisphere. Blaine argued that by raising the rates higher than Congress would have set them, the State Department could then reduce the duties in exchange for reciprocal considerations from countries in Latin America without substantially interfering with congressional authority. Congressional leaders refused to acquiesce, but Blaine gained the support of the American public, forcing Congress to devise a compromise plan. The State Department received authorization to impose duties on items on the free list such as sugar, molasses, coffee, tea, and hides if foreign countries refused to offer reciprocal agreements. In essence, the State Department could use the tariff as a punishment tool, but not as an enticement. As a result of this plan, Latin American countries reduced their rates, but resented American tactics. Congress repealed the State Department's authority under this measure in 1894. By this time the State Department realized the necessity of coordinating foreign policy with trade initiatives.

Reciprocal trade agreements negotiated with the input of the State Department continued through the first two decades of the twentieth century and assumed a renewed importance after the passage of the Hawley-Smoot Tariff Act in 1930. Secretary of State Cordell Hull and members of the State Department attempted to negotiate reciprocal agreements that would effectively reduce the high rates of Hawley-Smoot. The international crisis and worldwide depression added a sense of urgency and need that Hull used to push through several treaties. After World War II, the State Department continued to influence tariff-making decisions by insisting on a shift to free trade as a way of preventing future wars. Although the U.S. Constitution does not delegate authority over the tariff to the State Department, foreign policy has influenced much of the tariff legislation, especially since the Civil War.

See also: Blaine, James Gillespie; Constitutionality; Hawaii; Hawley-Smoot Tariff (Tariff of 1930); Hull, Cordell; Latin America; Lincoln, Abraham; Mexico; Morrill, Justin S.; Senate Finance Committee; Sugar; World War II.

Selected Bibliography:

Alfred E. Eckes, *Opening America's Market: U.S. Foreign Trade Policy Since 1776*, 1995.

Cynthia Clark Northrup

FRANCE

First country to sign a trade agreement with the United States on a conditional most-favored-nation basis.

The Franco-American Treaty of Amity and Commerce, signed in February 1778, failed to achieve the goal of equality sought by the rebellious colonies, but both countries did guarantee the right to purchase concessions granted to third parties. After the American Revolution, France attempted to negotiate an unconditional most-favored-nation treaty, but the new government insisted on the continuation of a conditional agreement partially to prevent the French from gaining unrestricted access to the developing American market. The relationship remained unchanged until 1923 when the French refused an American request for an unconditional agreement. The French government played a key role in restricting access to their automobile market after 1913 and continued to implement discriminatory trade policies after World War II. During the Eisenhower administration, the French received substantial benefits from the International Cooperation Administration for its textile industry while U.S. textile manufacturers continued to encounter restrictive barriers to the French market. During the 1970s, several American manufacturers filed accusations of dumping against the French and in 1978 stricter reporting procedures, subsequently established within the U.S. Customs Service, helped to enforce anti-dumping laws. As a major competitor in the world market, France has consistently sought to restrict access to its home market while pressing for open trade abroad.

See also: American Revolution; Dumping; Eisenhower, Dwight D. (Ike); Franco-American Treaty of Amity and Commerce.

Selected Bibliography:

Alfred E. Eckes, *Opening America's Market: U.S. Foreign Trade Policy Since 1776*, 1995.

Cynthia Clark Northrup

FRANCO-AMERICAN TREATY OF AMITY AND COMMERCE

Negotiated by Benjamin Franklin, the two-part treaty ensured trade and commerce with France as well as an alliance against Britain.

France supported the colonies early in the American Revolution, but did not publicly align itself with them until after the American victory at the battle of Saratoga. If the colonies acquired their independence, transatlantic trade would drastically change, but if the colonies failed, France would need to keep trading with England. France did not want to cut itself off from the wealth of the new world, especially from items like cotton, minerals, and other raw materials. With a victory in hand, Franklin formally opened negotiations. Soon the Treaty of Alliance and Treaty of Amity and Commerce formally bound the nations together against England.

The Treaty of Alliance gave the United States open French support, including its army, navy, and treasury. Further, each side agreed not to pursue a separate peace with England. The agreement also protected the territory France already held in North America, but the French had to agree not to acquire further possessions on the mainland.

The Treaty of Amity and Commerce covered trade issues. The agreement ensured free trade between the two nations and further stated that both countries would protect the ships of the other nation in war and peace as well as refuse aid to each other's enemies. The combined strength of the two practically ensured an American victory.

See also: American Revolution; France; Franklin, Benjamin.

Selected Bibliography:

Alfred E. Eckes, *Opening America's Market: U.S. Foreign Trade Policy Since 1776*, 1995.

Lisa A. Ennis

FRANKLIN, BENJAMIN (January 17, 1706–April 17, 1790)

One of the most respected and well-known eighteenth-century Americans; played an important role in the American Revolution.

A printer by trade, Franklin worked his entire life to achieve prosperity for himself and to improve colonial society. Well known for his inventions, publications, and organizations, he played a vital role in the American Revolution because of his position as a colonial agent in London. Born in Boston, at the age of eight Franklin entered grammar school, where he excelled, but his father removed him from school to work in the family business. He did not like this work and instead of letting Franklin become a sailor, as he desired, his father apprenticed him to his brother, who operated a printing business in Boston. At seventeen he ran away and eventually arrived in Philadelphia where, through hard work, he prospered.

In 1757, he journeyed to London to represent the Pennsylvania legislature in its attempt to tax the lands held by the Penn family. The legislature needed the revenue to defend its frontier from attack, but could only tax the land through the Penns' consent or by changing the colonial government of the colony. The Penn family agreed to tax any improved land while unsurveyed land remained untaxed. Franklin stayed in London until 1762, returned to Philadelphia, and then journeyed back to England, where he remained until 1775. During this time, the crisis between Great Britain and its American colonies started and Franklin represented the American side in London newspapers. From 1765 to 1775, he penned 126 newspaper articles that examined American views on taxation. Newspapers in Europe and the rebellious colonies reprinted the articles first published in *The London Chronicle* or the *Universal Evening Post*. Early on, Franklin misunderstood the force of the American reaction to the Stamp Act and not only willingly purchased stamps for his Philadelphia business, but also recommended that a friend become Philadelphia's stamp collector.

In his London articles, Franklin presented ad hoc arguments in the developing debate over parliament's power to tax its colonies. Although not an economist, his writings allowed people throughout England both to read and respond to the American side. In his correspondence, Franklin reiterated the American arguments of no taxation without representation, external versus internal taxes, and the economic importance of the colonies. When he returned from London, he played an important role in the Continental Congress, the American Revolution, and the Constitutional Convention. Influenced by the free trade writings of Adam Smith, Franklin argued for free trade throughout the remainder of his life.

See also: American Revolution; Continental Congress; Navigation and Trade Acts. **Vol. II**: *The Wealth of Nations*.

Selected Bibliography:

H.W. Brands, *The First American: The Life and Times of Benjamin Franklin*, 2000; Carl Van Doren, *Benjamin Franklin*, 1991.

Ty M. Reese

FREE TRADE

A classical liberal economic idea that called for free exchange of goods and services across national boundaries; once a preserve of the British, the idea now has gained wide international acceptance.

Free trade, as outlined by Scottish economist Adam Smith and other liberal thinkers, calls for the absence of barriers to the free flow of goods and services among peoples and nations. They believed that production and distribution and other aspects of trade and commerce should be left to private individuals. Free traders believed in "noninterference" as opposed to protectionism, which in the opinion of free traders, while protecting some, injured other members of the society. The United States, for most of its history, followed a highly protectionist tariff policy. With the establishment of the North American Free Trade Agreement (NAFTA), protectionism retreated, at least for the time being.

Protectionism has been the dominant economic policy of the United States since the founding of the Republic;

Congress passed exceptionally high protective tariffs after the Civil War. The Republicans championed the nineteenth-century idea of protecting domestic industries from foreign competition while Democrats such as David Ames Wells and Edward Atkinson advocated free trade. When Congress failed to adopt the idea of free trade, Democrats proposed a narrower version based on "free raw materials" with the hope that foreign competition, rather than crippling the American industries, would challenge and invigorate them to compete with the Europeans. Challenges to protectionist policies proved ineffective.

During this time, European countries, especially France and England, followed a low tariff policy. Germany's emergence, after 1871, as a major industrial power and its attempts to bolster domestic industries through the erection of tariff walls, put a damper on European free trade policies. German trade initiatives posed challenges to the American policymakers also.

The coming of age of the United States in international economic matters at the turn of the twentieth century dramatically altered U.S. and European trade relations. Several domestic and international developments engendered an atmosphere conducive for closer cooperation between low tariff Republicans and low tariff Democrats. This cooperation may have proffered an intellectual synthesis between the two groups. America, in response to the rising European tariffs, proposed an open door for trade everywhere. Nevertheless, the country kept its doors shut tight by passing high protective tariffs. Gradually, most players, except Congress, agreed on the need for a tariff revision with lower rates to compete with the Europeans.

Slightly lower tariffs in Woodrow Wilson's presidency notwithstanding, tariff rates remained high. In 1934, Congress passed the Reciprocal Trade Agreements Act (RTAA), which led to a gradual tariff reduction. The reciprocal treaties negotiated by the administration of Franklin Delano Roosevelt reduced tariffs, but only selectively. After World War II, the general worldwide trend favored reducing tariff barriers. As a result, the United States became party to the General Agreement on Tariffs and Trade (GATT) in 1948. It culminated in the World Trade Organization (WTO) of 1994.

The desire to free trade of its barriers and open markets for American exports led to an agreement on the tariff between the United States and Canada in 1989. This agreement, later expanded to include Mexico, culminated in the passage of NAFTA, signed in 1992. Winning a narrow victory in the U.S. Senate, the treaty, effective January 1994, created the second largest free trade area in the world, with over 365 million consumers.

NAFTA immediately sought to eliminate some trade barriers among the three countries and provided for the elimination of other trade restraints in the following fourteen years. The treaty also recognized the protection of intellectual property. Answering the concerns raised by many opponents, a supplementary agreement signed in 1993 placed minimum wage and environmental protection mandates on the signatory countries.

Protectionist, labor, and environmental groups vehemently opposed NAFTA. Presidential candidates like Ross Perot and Pat Buchanan also voiced their opposition. Buchanan claimed that during the last twenty years of free trade, the standard of living in America had declined. Labor organizations feared the flight of jobs to Mexico, where wages remained low and the rights of workers went largely unprotected. According to the United Auto Workers (UAW), NAFTA had displaced tens of thousands of employees in the United States; UAW further insisted that the U.S. trade deficit with Mexico and Canada had increased from $9.1 billion to $39 billion since NAFTA went into effect. Labor organizations claimed that big corporations gained at the expense of the government and ordinary people.

Opposition to the free trade movement comes from powerful and organized groups. The protests and the violence that attended the WTO meeting in Seattle, Washington, in 1999 and the Byrd amendment to the fiscal 2001 agricultural appropriations bill, called the Continued Dumping and Subsidy Offset Act, show the organizational prowess and determination of the foes of free trade. These and other signs have led many, including the Federal Reserve Board Chairman Alan Greenspan, to wonder if free trade is in retreat. The dispute between Mexico and the United States over Mexican trucking and tomatoes, and the tussle between the United States and the European Community over trade and tariffs add an interesting dimension to the debates over free trade. Korean students marching in Seoul protesting imports and demanding boycott of foreign goods and French farmers attacking McDonald's are other examples of opposition to free trade. Despite these challenges, free traders have made substantial gains in the United States and abroad. Like democracy that blossomed all over the world in the 1990s, free trade may become the new trend in international commerce. Moreover, the Internet and e-commerce have changed the ways of international trade unalterably.

See also: Atkinson, Edward; Democratic Party; General Agreement on Tariffs and Trade (GATT); North American Free Trade Agreement (NAFTA); Reciprocal Trade Agreements Act (RTAA); Republican Party; Smith, Adam; Wells, David Ames; World Trade Organization (WTO). **Vol. II**: *The Wealth of Nations*.

Selected Bibliography:

Bruce Stokes, "The Protectionist Myth," *Foreign Policy*, 1999; United Auto Workers Union, "Reforming America's Trade Policy: Serving Workers, Saving Jobs," 1997; Paul Wolman, *Most Favored Nation: The Republican Revisionists and U.S. Tariff Policy, 1897–1912*, 1992.

George Thadathil

FREE TRADE AREA OF THE AMERICAS (FTAA)

A plan to create a free trade zone of the entire Western Hemisphere.

Conceived at the First Summit of the Americas meeting in Miami in December 1994, the Free Trade Area of the Americas (FTAA) emerged as a concrete plan from the Second Summit in Santiago, Chile, in April 1998. It sought to create the largest free trade area in the world, including thirty-four countries of the Western Hemisphere, excluding Cuba, with a population of 800 million people. It would essentially extend the North American Free Trade Agreement (NAFTA) to the rest of the hemisphere by the year 2005, eliminating trade and investment barriers on nearly all goods and services traded by member nations. The Santiago meeting established nine negotiating groups to formulate frameworks and policies on market access, agriculture, investment, services, government procurement, intellectual property rights, subsidies/anti-dumping/countervailing duties, competition policy, and dispute settlement, with three additional committees to work on electronic commerce, smaller economies, and civil society participation. As with NAFTA, FTAA would include substantial protection for investors, to the extent that some fear infringement on the sovereignty of member states in regulating policy on labor and the environment. The secret nature of these negotiations has drawn criticism. At a Third Summit of the Americas meeting at Quebec in April 2001, the 900-page negotiating document remained unavailable to the press or public. Opponents argue against free trade without additional agreements to guarantee better treatment of labor and protection of the environment. They point to lower wages as a result of NAFTA, and argue that failure to include higher environmental standards costs jobs, maintains low wages in poor countries, and damages the environment while increasing the cost of patent-protected pharmaceuticals. Concerns relating to existing regional trade organizations, including the Latin American Integration Association (LAIA), the Central American Common Market (CACM), the Caribbean Common Market (CARICOM), and the Southern Cone Common Market (MERCOSUR) also exist.

Recognizing that important groups opposed the FTAA, hemispheric trade ministers meeting at San José, Costa Rica, in March 1998 established a Civil Society Participation Committee to provide opportunities for representatives of business, labor, environmental, academic, and consumer groups to present their views during the ongoing negotiations. Notwithstanding that effort, more than 30,000 protesters disrupted the Quebec meeting. Heavy police protection allowed the meeting to proceed, but violent clashes occurred between demonstrators and police outside the fenced-off meeting area. Similar protests disrupted the World Trade Organization (WTO) meetings in Seattle in December 1999, an International Monetary Fund (IMF) and WTO meeting in Washington in April 2000, and a meeting of trade ministers in Buenos Aires in early April 2001 as rising anti-globalization sentiment represented a broad spectrum of opposition to multinational corporate power. Promoters of the FTAA argue that it will reduce prices for consumers, create new markets throughout the hemisphere, and thereby expand prosperity. The United States has sought to speed up establishment of the FTAA and George W. Bush seeks trade promotion authority (formerly called fast-track legislation) to allow him to negotiate an agreement subject only to ratification of the entire treaty, rather than exposing it to modifying congressional amendments. But at Quebec, Latin American leaders rejected Bush's effort to bring the plan into operation by 2003. Some Latin American govern-

ments remain reluctant to give up tariffs, which constitute a large part of their government revenue, with Brazil and other Latin American states disinclined to relinquish their present influence in regional trade associations as well. Latin Americans also express concern about U.S. agricultural subsidies and anti-dumping laws and fear that FTAA simply replaces one form of Yankee imperialism with another.

Reacting to the Quebec protests, the thirty-four leaders from the Western Hemisphere issued a closing declaration on April 22, 2001, indicating their "commitment to hemispheric integration and national and collective responsibility for improving the economic well-being and security of our people." They adopted a plan of action "to strengthen representative democracy, promote good governance and protect human rights and fundamental freedoms [as they] seek to create greater prosperity and expand economic opportunities while fostering social justice and the realization of human potential." Their declaration recognized "the necessity to continue addressing weaknesses in our development processes and increasing human security" and promised "to increase transparency throughout government."

See also: Bush, George Herbert Walker; Countervailing duties; Dumping; Fast-track legislation; Latin America; North American Free Trade Agreement (NAFTA); World Trade Organization (WTO).

Selected Bibliography:

Mario E. Caranza, *South American Free Trade Area or Free Trade Area of the Ameri-*

cas? Open Regionalism and the Future of Regional Economic Integration in South America, 2000; Patrice Franko, *Toward a New Security Architecture in the Americas: The Strategic Implications of FTAA,* 2000; Carol Wise, ed., *The Post-NAFTA Political Economy: Mexico and the Western Hemisphere,* 1998.

Ralph Lee Woodward Jr.

FRIENDS OF THE EARTH

Concerns about the direction of the Sierra Club led its longtime executive director, David Brower, to establish this new environmental organization in 1977.

Friends of the Earth, as envisioned by its founder, would focus on international concerns, feature publications publicizing environmental causes, adopt a decentralized approach, and stand firmly against nuclear energy. Ironically, the founder of the Sierra Club delivered a statement that provided the name of the new organization. John Muir stated, "The earth can do all right without friends, but men, if they are to survive, must learn to be friends of the earth." Eventually, Brower left his new organization, but Friends of the Earth boasted chapters in scores of countries across the globe. Membership, during the 1990s, approached one million. With its transnational approach, Friends of the Earth became the first organization to warn about acid rain and to consider nuclear warfare as an issue addressed by environmentalists.

Like the Sierra Club, Friends of the Earth condemned calls by the World Trade Organization (WTO) to encourage economic liberalization at the expense of environmental regulations.

Friends of the Earth warned about the potential impact on the global ecosystem, expanding deforestation rates, the likely reaction by environmental groups, and the particular impact on forests throughout the world. The projected WTO Forest Products Agreement, Friends of the Earth noted, would threaten biological diversity with logging endangering "non-frontier forests, many of which, due to their fragmented nature and high levels of endemic species, are conservation priorities." Some tariff reductions, Friends of the Earth acknowledged, could have a positive environmental impact, removing the incentive of developing countries to ship timber instead of encouraging domestic processing. But hasty trade liberalization efforts, Friends of the Earth has suggested, would discard the opportunity "to integrate trade rules into overall sustainable development policies that preserve healthy forest ecosystems and economies."

See also: Sierra Club; World Trade Organization (WTO).

Selected Bibliography:

Robert Gottlieb, *Forcing the Spring: The Transformation of the American Environmental Movement,* 1993; Paul Wapner, *Environmental Activism and World Civic Politics,* 1996.

Robert C. Cottrell

FUR TRADE

One of the earliest major exports of North America to Europe.

The fur trade with the Iroquois Confederation brought the Dutch to the

Fur trade

Hudson Valley in the seventeenth century. This trade played a role in the development of the city of New Amsterdam (from 1664, English New York) as the major port of a hinterland that embraced the Hudson and Mohawk Valleys and the Great Lakes region. The British imperial government regulated the trade by placing furs, in 1721, on the list of enumerated commodities. At the same time, tariff preferences in Britain gave American furs an advantage over furs from northern Europe. After the American Revolution, British restrictions on furs ended, but U.S. traders faced competition from Canada in the British market. In the early nineteenth century, John Jacob Astor built a fortune by exporting furs from the West via New York. At the same time, a new branch of the fur trade opened up between the Pacific Northwest and China, where a large market existed for sea otter fur. U.S. participation in this trade paved the way for the settlement of Oregon and Washington. For most of the century, American trappers concerned themselves more with securing as large a share as possible of the fur supply in North America and with obtaining markets abroad than with tariff protection of the domestic market.

See also: American Revolution; Great Britain; Navigation and Trade Acts.

Selected Bibliography:

David J. Wishart, *The Fur Trade of the American West, 1807–1840*, 1979.

John P. Barrington

G

GALLATIN, ABRAHAM ALFONSE ALBERT (January 29, 1761–August 12, 1849)

U.S. representative from Pennsylvania and fourth U.S. secretary of the treasury.

Born on January 29, 1761, in Geneva, Switzerland, Gallatin immigrated to Boston at the age of nineteen. After teaching French at Harvard, he moved to Pennsylvania. Sent to the U.S. Senate, Gallatin called on the secretary of the treasury for a statement of debt and expenditures for each branch of the government before the Senate rejected him as a member due to his foreign birth. Gallatin returned to Washington, D.C., as a representative from Pennsylvania and received an appointment to the House Committee on Finance, the forerunner of the House Ways and Means Committee. His strong vocal opposition to Federalist spending measures aimed at distancing the United States from revolutionary France played a role in the passage of

the Alien and Sedition Acts. After Thomas Jefferson won the election of 1800, he appointed Gallatin his secretary of the treasury. Gallatin insisted on sound financial accountability, implementing accounting practices that allowed for a breakdown of receipts as well as a statement of public debt and an estimate of expected revenue. By 1809, Gallatin had managed to reduce the public debt by $14 million and the treasury maintained a surplus, even after paying $15 million for the purchase of Louisiana. In his own *Report on Manufactures*, Gallatin agreed with Hamilton's assessment concerning the need for a higher tariff to protect infant industries and advocated the use of federal revenue generated by the tariff for internal improvements such as highways and canals. After leaving office, Gallatin joined the American delegation that negotiated the Treaty of Ghent at the end of the War of 1812. He also negotiated a commercial convention with Great Britain that eliminated discriminating duties between the two countries. Establishing his residence in New York in 1817, he served as president of the National Bank of the City of New York, founded New York University and the American Ethnological Society, and held the position of president of the New York Historical Society. He died on Long Island on August 12, 1849, at the age of eighty-eight.

See also: Federalists; Hamilton, Alexander; House Ways and Means Committee; Jefferson, Thomas; War of 1812.

Selected Bibliography:

Alexander Balinky, *Albert Gallatin: Fiscal Theories and Policies*, 1958.

Cynthia Clark Northrup

GARFIELD, JAMES A. (November 19, 1831–September 19, 1881)

American legislator and twentieth president of the United States; favored a conservative monetary policy and argued for moderate protectionism.

Born in a log cabin near Cleveland, Ohio, Garfield attended a seminary and studied and taught at the Western Reserve Eclectic Institute, now Hiram College. From there he entered Williams College, where he studied the writings of Ralph Waldo Emerson and graduated with honors in 1856. Garfield returned to Hiram and took a job as the principal of the Western Reserve Eclectic Institute in 1858. He became interested in politics, spoke out against slavery, and in 1859 voters elected him as a Republican to the Ohio Senate. He studied law and gained admittance to the Ohio bar in 1860. During the Civil War, Garfield served as a major general, but left his military career to enter the U.S. House of Representatives in 1863 on the urging of President Abraham Lincoln.

Garfield served in the House from 1863 to 1880, being appointed to the Ways and Means Committee, chairing the Appropriations Committee from 1871 to 1875, and serving as minority leader from 1876 to 1880. He promoted hard money policies backed by gold, which aligned him with eastern commercial interests and pitted him against southern agrarian concerns. He opposed labor unions and maximum-hour laws. Garfield's constituency in Ohio, largely rural, influenced his support for cheap European imports. As a result, Garfield promoted moderate protectionist policies. Garfield called himself "theoretically a free trader, but practically a protectionist." On the debate over the Tariff Act of 1870, Garfield persuasively urged protectionists in the House to unite on a moderate reduction of duties on imports.

His leadership helped the Republican Party ensure protection for U.S. business, a leading issue in the 1880 presidential contest. Elected to the U.S. Senate by his home state in 1880, Garfield never had a chance to take his seat. At the Republican National Convention, the tariff issue served as a vehicle for attacking Democrats as the Republicans linked lowering tariffs with economic distress and depression. Garfield emerged as a compromise candidate and won the nomination after thirty-six ballots. As president, Garfield chose as his secretary of state expansionist James G. Blaine, who fostered a relationship with Latin America on reciprocal trade policy that paid dividends in future years. Four months after taking office, Charles J. Guiteau shot Garfield in a Washington railroad station and ten weeks later he died.

See also: Blaine, James Gillespie; Civil War (American); Emerson, Ralph Waldo; Latin America; Lincoln, Abraham; Tariff of 1870.

Selected Bibliography:

B. V. Hendrick, *The Road to Respectability: James A. Garfield and His World*, 1988; Richard McElroy, *James A. Garfield: His Life and Times*, 1986.

Marriya Bare and Artemus Ward

GARRISON, WILLIAM LLOYD (December 10/12, 1805–May 24, 1879)

Abolitionist noted for his criticism of slavery and slave owners, for advocating the immediate abolition of slavery, and for his support of numerous other reforms including free trade.

Born in Newburyport, Massachusetts, Garrison became an expert printer early in life. By 1829, he joined abolitionist Benjamin Lundy in editing *The Genius of Universal Emancipation*, but after breaking with Lundy, Garrison established *The Liberator* in 1831, which became the most notable abolitionist paper in the country. After the liberation of the slaves, in the last issue of *The Liberator* published in December 1865, Garrison announced ratification of the Thirteenth Amendment and noted the end of his vocation as an abolitionist.

Garrison then enlisted in efforts to prohibit alcohol and tobacco consumption, oppose Chinese exclusion, achieve equal rights for women, support American Indian justice, and campaign for pacifism. A lingering interest in free trade led him to promote it, and by the spring of 1869 he became actively involved. Although not a new role, his antigovernment stance, his break with the Constitution, and his struggle with Republican leadership encouraged his free trade beliefs. Earlier, as a youthful Federalist, he had endorsed Henry Clay's clamor for protective tariffs.

Garrison accepted a position as vice president of the American Free Trade League (AFTL), established in 1865, because it accompanies free speech, free press, and free institutions. The American Free Trade League opposed protective tariffs and endorsed the right of workingmen to exchange the product of their labor wherever they could obtain the most for it. In 1869, he explained his views in a letter to his son, spoke at a free trade meeting, wrote a free trade editorial explicating its purposes for *The Independent*, espoused free trade in the *Boston Journal*, and formed the Revenue League of Boston. The demise of the league in 1872 and the death of his wife in 1876 combined with debilitating health weakened Garrison. He died in New York City in 1879.

See also: American Protective Tariff League (APTL); Newspapers and media; Slavery.

Selected Bibliography:

Walter M. Merrill, *Against Wind and Tide: A Biography of William Lloyd Garrison*, 1963; John L. Thomas, *The Liberator, William Lloyd Garrison: A Biography*, 1963.

Bruce A. Glasrud

GENERAL AGREEMENT ON TARIFFS AND TRADE (GATT)

A multilateral international agreement designed to relax tariff and trade barriers after World War II.

During the postwar period, Harry S Truman wished to continue the practice of lowering tariffs initiated by the Reciprocal Trade Agreements Act (RTAA) under Franklin D. Roosevelt. The RTAA allowed the executive office to negotiate tariffs through the use of bilateral arrangements with other nations, and, by 1945, the United States had concluded thirty-two different trade agreements. The Truman administration wished to continue executive control over tariffs, but they sought a more efficient collective international approach. Because of Republican congressional gains in the 1946 mid-term elections, protectionists blocked American membership in the International Trade Organization (ITO), an organization designed to oversee these arrangements. The administration then pushed for the General Agreement on Tariff and Trade (GATT) as a stopgap measure to allow the United States to enter into multilateral trade agreements until Congress approved American membership in the ITO. Republicans accepted GATT as a modification of the RTAA, even though they rejected the creation of a new organization, but their acceptance came only after they ensured that GATT would contain safeguards. GATT included two principal protectionist precautions. The first, known as the peril point or escape clause, held that the United States could abandon its tariff agreements on certain commodities or simply seek modifications if competing imports threatened domestic American industry. The second, the anti-dumping clause, prohibited nations from flooding competitors with imports in an effort to destroy domestic industries. When it became clear that the United States would not join the ITO, GATT's rules established the standard in international trade. Indeed, it developed into something akin to an international organization and governed international trade relationships until replaced by the World Trade Organization (WTO) on January 1, 1995.

Once in place, GATT sponsored trade negotiation conferences or "rounds" designed to reduce tariff barriers and spur global economic growth. These GATT conferences made headway in lowering tariffs and expanding trade, but they proceeded at a slow pace until the 1964 Kennedy Round. The initial lethargy occurred because the U.S. Congress gave the executive branch the power to negotiate item-by-item agreements only. When John F. Kennedy came into office, he sought the power to enter into broad agreements that allowed cuts across the board on all items under discussion. The 1962 Trade Agreements Act granted this increased power, and during the Kennedy Round, U.S. tariffs dropped an average of 35 percent. By the 1970s, the focus of GATT shifted away from tariffs because nations viewed nontariff barriers as the primary impediment to international trade. The Tokyo Round increased attention to nontariff barriers.

See also: International Trade Organization (ITO); Kennedy Round; Reciprocal

Trade Agreements Act (RTAA); Roosevelt, Franklin D.; Tokyo Round; Truman, Harry S; Uruguay Round; World Trade Organization (WTO). **Vol. II**: Franklin D. Roosevelt's 1932 Campaign Radio Speech; The General Agreement on Tariffs and Trade.

Selected Bibliography:

Susan Ariel Aaronson, *Trade and the American Dream: A Social History of Postwar Trade Policy*, 1996; I.M. Destler, *American Trade Politics*, 1995.

John K. Franklin

GENERAL COMMITTEE OF ONE HUNDRED

Formed in 1909 as the central committee within the National Tariff Commission Association (NTCA).

When William Howard Taft reopened the tariff question during the first year of his presidency, a group of industry officials and representatives decided to hold a convention to discuss the issue. In February 1909, delegates attended the Indianapolis Tariff Commission Convention where supporters of an independent Tariff Commission advocated authorizing such a body to investigate the cost of production of domestic and foreign goods and scientifically determine appropriate tariff rates. Supporters of the idea believed that the creation of the Tariff Commission under such terms would eliminate inconsistencies associated with congressional determination of the rates through a politicized process whereby delegations from the Treasury, Commerce, and Labor departments under the supervision of the House Ways and Means Committee arbitrarily decided duty rates. The General Committee of One Hundred, headed by John Candler Cobb, received the backing of two influential business leaders, Henry R. Towne of the Merchants Association of New York (MANY) and Herbert Miles of the National Association of Manufacturers (NAM), both of whom persuaded a large group of delegates to support the proposed commission. When the majority of attendees failed to support the measure, tariff activists met to form the National Tariff Commission Association and the General Committee of One Hundred to lobby for a Tariff Commission. Pressure exerted by this group resulted in the formation of a Tariff Board under the provisions of the Payne-Aldrich Tariff. Although the Tariff Board lacked the full authority proposed for the Tariff Commission, Congress did provide $100,000 in appropriations for the agency and appointed qualified individuals to the board. The General Committee of One Hundred continued to support the Tariff Board while working toward the creation of an independent Tariff Commission.

See also: Merchants Association of New York (MANY); Miles, Herbert Edwin; National Association of Manufacturers (NAM); Payne-Aldrich Tariff (Tariff of 1909); Taft, William Howard.

Selected Bibliography:

Paul Wolman, *Most Favored Nation: The Republican Revisionists and U.S. Tariff Policy, 1897–1912*, 1992.

Cynthia Clark Northrup

GEORGIA

An agricultural colony and state historically opposed to tariffs and trade regulation.

Chartered in 1732, the colony of Georgia developed by the end of the colonial period into an exporter of rice, though on a smaller scale than its neighbor, South Carolina. Originally an enumerated commodity under the navigation laws, colonies could export rice only to England. In 1730, just before the founding of Georgia, Parliament amended the navigation acts to allow direct exports of rice from the American colonies to southern Europe, so Georgia enjoyed a high degree of free trade for what became its major staple. Parliament relaxed trade restrictions further by removing all duties on the importation of rice into Great Britain in 1772. The Revolutionary War and independence prevented Georgia from enjoying the benefit from this concession, but the removal of the duties helps explain the significant amount of loyalist sentiment in the colony. After the Revolution, cotton rapidly became Georgia's main export crop, with much of it sold in Great Britain. In the 1820s, Georgia joined other southern states to oppose the American System of high protective tariffs designed to foster U.S. industry. South Carolina based this opposition in part on fears that high tariffs would increase the price of manufactured articles, but also on concerns that Britain would retaliate against U.S. exports, including cotton, if the United States excluded British manufactures. After the Civil War, some former planters in Georgia entered into partnerships with northern industrialists to set up textile factories in the upper part of the state. A pro-tariff lobby group located in the region steadily moved the state away from its solidly free trade stance in the late nineteenth and early twentieth centuries.

See also: American Revolution; American System; Civil War (American); Cotton; Great Britain; Navigation and Trade Acts.

Selected Bibliography:

Harold H. Martin, *Georgia: A Bicentennial History*, 1978.

John P. Barrington

GEPHARDT, RICHARD (January 31, 1941–)

U.S. representative from St. Louis, Missouri, who served as the majority leader and minority leader of the Democratic Party.

Gephardt often opposed President William Jefferson Clinton on a number of key trade issues. In 1993, under pressure from environmental groups and unions, especially automobile unions important in the St. Louis area, he voted against approval of the North American Free Trade Agreement (NAFTA). He came under criticism from these same groups for supporting consideration of fast-track legislation and agreeing not to use his position as majority leader to influence other votes.

Gephardt's middle position on NAFTA reflected conflicts between national Democratic constituencies. In 1985, Gephardt announced the formation and became the first chairman of the Democratic Leadership Council

(DLC), an organization formed in part to reestablish ties between the Democrats and business interests. In 1988, he launched an unsuccessful bid for his party's presidential nomination. Although remaining close to the DLC, which generally favored the international economic policies of the Clinton administration, he opposed many of the president's free trade initiatives.

Shortly after the NAFTA vote, Gephardt requested that the Clinton administration withdraw its request to add Chile to the NAFTA accord, a step toward the goal of forming a Free Trade Area of the Americas. In 1999, he announced his opposition to legislation, eventually passed, to extend Most Favored Nation status to China, a prerequisite to the latter's admission to the World Trade Organization (WTO). Gephardt had asked for the legislation to include a provision to require the United States to vote against lending to China by international institutions if that country violated human rights, labor, or environmental standards, but the Clinton administration claimed this would violate WTO rules. His opposition to NAFTA and normalization of trade relations with China did not extend to the issuance of punitive threats to other Democrats in the House of Representatives, but it forced Clinton to rely heavily on votes from the opposition Republican Party to pass these parts of his trade agenda.

See also: Chile; Clinton, William Jefferson (Bill); Democratic Party; Fast-track legislation; Free trade; Free Trade Area of the Americas; Human rights; Most Favored Nation (MFN); North American Free Trade Agreement (NAFTA); Republican Party; World Trade Organization (WTO).

Selected Bibliography:

Hermann von Bertrab, *Negotiating NAFTA: A Mexican Envoy's Account*, 1997.

Daniel C. Hellinger

GERMANY

A nation whose unification and rapid rise to the status of a great power and world economic leader in the late nineteenth century derived from the establishment of high protective tariffs that sometimes influenced American tariff history.

The Zollverein (Customs Union), an organization of German states established in the second quarter of the nineteenth century to replace tariff barriers between its members with a single set of duties at the union's common border, preceded the united German Empire founded in 1871. Advocates of the Zollverein, such as Friedrich List, frequently cited the United States as a prime example of a regional union that facilitated its members' economic development through such policies as tariff protection. The success of the Zollverein and the efficiency of the Prussian bureaucracy that administered it helped to set the stage for Prussia's unification of Germany. During the depression of the 1870s, a massive influx of agricultural imports from the United States, Russia, and Argentina led German farming interests to make common cause with heavy industry in pressing for a system of high tariffs across the board. In response, Germany adopted new customs duties in 1879, becoming Europe's leader in rejecting free trade and establishing protectionist policies. The resulting round of tariff increases and, from the early 1890s, attempts to negotiate reciprocal tariff reduction agreements between countries, had the effect of drawing the debate over tariffs in the United States into a broader context of international considerations than had prevailed previously. After World War I, Germany's aggressive, highly coordinated efforts to expand international sales of manufactured goods and, in the 1930s, to protect domestic markets, heavily influenced tariff policies in the United States. After World War II, American economic and political pressure figured among the factors leading the Federal Republic of Germany to support European economic integration and the reduction of customs duties between European states.

See also: Free trade; List, Friedrich; World War I; World War II.

Selected Bibliography:

V.R. Berghahn, *Imperial Germany, 1871–1914: Economy, Society, Culture and Politics*, 1994; V.R. Berghahn, *Modern Germany: Society, Economy, and Politics in the Twentieth Century*, 1982.

Woodruff D. Smith

GODKIN, EDWIN LAWRENCE (October 2, 1831–May 21, 1902)

Founder of *The Nation* in 1865, Godkin served as one of its editors for over three decades.

Born in County Wicklow, Ireland, Godkin attended Queen's College in Belfast and served as a journalist for the *Daily News* in London. After mi-

grating to America in 1856, he continued working for newspapers before establishing *The Nation*. In 1881, the journal merged with the *New York Evening Post*'s weekly edition. Two years later, Lawrence became editor of the *Evening Post*, taking over from Carl Schurz. Aided by William Dean Howells, the newspaper's circulation approached 10,000. At its outset, Godkin proclaimed that his publication would cheer progressive causes. Soon, *The Nation* acquired a reputation for backing women's suffrage, civil rights, and public education. Godkin continued championing those issues, while condemning the political corruption of Tammany Hall, in the pages of the *Evening Post*.

Godkin highlighted the tariff issue in his editorials. Although opposed to protectionism, Godkin initially felt compelled to mute his criticisms of the tariff because of promises he had made to stockholders of *The Nation* that it would "not . . . be a free trade paper." Responding to various criticisms, Godkin, in a letter to stockholders on August 23, 1865, acknowledged, "I have been long known to be a freetrader." At the same time, he declared, he had deemed it "expedient to avoid making *The Nation* 'the organ' of any particular school of economists." Nevertheless, Godkin supported tariff reform and remained close to leading members of the American Free Trade League. In an article in the *Princeton Review* in 1887, Godkin warned that protectionist policy would result in a loss of American identity, maldistribution of wealth, and deprivation for the masses. Godkin died in England on May 21, 1902.

See also: American Free Trade League (AFTL); Free trade; *The Nation*; Protectionism.

Selected Bibliography:

William M. Armstrong, ed., *The Gilded Age Letters of E.L. Godkin*, 1974; Ogden Rollo, ed., *Life and Letters of Edwin Lawrence Godkin*, 1972.

Robert C. Cottrell

GOOD NEIGHBOR POLICY

President Franklin D. Roosevelt's Latin American policy.

A retreat from the interventionist U.S. policy toward Latin America, the Good Neighbor Policy began during the administration of Herbert Hoover led by the efforts of Secretary of State Henry L. Stimson, but Americans associate the policy more properly with the administration of Franklin Roosevelt. Roosevelt pledged, in his first inaugural address on March 4, 1933, to "dedicate this nation to the policy of the good neighbor." Application of this new approach to Latin America became apparent at the seventh Inter-American Conference in Montevideo in December 1933 when Secretary of State Cordell Hull endorsed the principal of nonintervention. The Reciprocal Trade Agreement Act of 1934 further indicated the desire of the United States to expand trade relations with Latin America. This act allowed negotiated tariff reductions with individual countries of as much as 50 percent. A new Export-Import Bank provided credit for U.S. businesses overseas, where inadequate services from commercial banks existed, and later it extended credit to foreign commercial interests as well. The Good Neighbor Policy thus emphasized trade expansion over the preoccupation with debt collection that had characterized earlier administrations.

Beginning with Cuba in 1934, the United States signed reciprocity agreements with fifteen Latin American countries, eleven of them before 1940. These policies brought substantially lower tariffs and greatly improved the climate for U.S. business interests throughout Latin America. Roosevelt completed the withdrawal of U.S. troops from the Caribbean with the removal of the Marines from Nicaragua in 1933 and Haiti in 1934. The United States ended its protectorate in Cuba with the abrogation of the Platt Amendment in 1934, and signed a new Panama Canal treaty more favorable to Panama in 1936. By August 1936, Roosevelt could say with pride, "In the whole of the Western Hemisphere our good-neighbor policy has produced results that are especially heartening," as he pledged to extend the "same sort of mutual trust" that the United States and Canada enjoyed "throughout the Americas." He declared further that "The American republics to the south of us have been ready always to cooperate with the United States on a basis of equality and mutual respect, but before we inaugurated the good-neighbor policy there was among them resentment and fear because certain administrations in Washington had slighted their national pride and their sovereign rights." At the 1936 Inter-American Conference in Buenos Aires, the United States formally accepted the principal of nonintervention. Trade between the United States and Latin America grew notably. Both regions sought new markets as they recovered from the Great Depression. The Good Neighbor Policy mirrored the New Deal at home. Roosevelt implemented more sympathetic policies toward Bolivia, Mexico, and Venezuela in their disputes with U.S. oil companies, thereby improving relations with Latin America on the eve of World War II. Rejecting the interventionist approaches of earlier administrations, Roosevelt recognized the right of Latin American governments to manage their natural resources in their own ways, while protecting U.S. economic and strategic interests through diplomacy and economic policy. The United States offered economic, technical, and military aid to Latin American governments, as well as intercultural exchanges, especially after the outbreak of World War II, using financial leverage in place of direct military intervention. The Good Neighbor Policy helped assure the support of nearly all the Latin American states during World War II and considerably advanced inter-American cooperation. Abandoning earlier U.S. efforts to make over Latin America in the North American image, Roosevelt showed less concern with promoting democratic government and willingly recognized and supported dictatorships in the Dominican Republic, El Salvador, Guatemala, Honduras, Nicaragua, and elsewhere. Latin American economic nationalists often charged the U.S. policy with economic and cultural imperialism.

Inter-American cooperation continued after World War II, but the United States abandoned the noninterventionist pledge. The United States meddled in Argentine politics in 1946 in an unsuccessful effort to prevent the election of Juan Domingo Perón, supported a revolution in Costa Rica in 1948, acquiesced in the overthrow of the Guatemalan government in 1954, assisted Cuban dissidents in the Bay of Pigs invasion in 1962, and subsequently became involved in other Cold War interventions in the internal affairs of Chile, Brazil, Panama, and other Latin American states.

See also: Cold War; Cuba; Great Depression; Hull, Cordell; Latin America; Panama Canal; Reciprocal Trade Agreements Act (RTAA); Roosevelt, Franklin D.; World War II.

Selected Bibliography:

Mark T. Gilderhus, *The Second Century: U.S.–Latin American Relations since 1889*, 2000; Frederick B. Pike, *FDR's Good Neighbor Policy: Sixty Years of Generally Gentle Chaos*, 1995; Bryce Wood, *The Dismantling of the Good Neighbor Policy*, 1985.

Ralph Lee Woodward Jr.

GORE, ALBERT ARNOLD, JR. (March 31, 1948–)

Vice president who argued for the passage of the North American Free Trade Agreement (NAFTA).

Born in Washington, D.C., on March 31, 1948, Al Gore grew up in political circles. His father served several terms, first as a congressman, and then senator from the state of Tennessee. After graduating from high school, Gore attended Harvard University in 1969 before enlisting in the army from 1969 to 1971. During the Vietnam conflict his duties focused primarily on reporting news from the front. He returned to Tennessee after his tour and accepted a position as a reporter for *The Tennessean*, where he continued to work while attending Vanderbilt University. He received a degree in law before entering politics. In 1976, he ran for and won a seat in the U.S. House of Representatives, an office he held until 1984, when he became a senator.

During the 1988 presidential campaign, he sought the nomination of the Democratic Party but lost to Massachusetts governor Michael Dukakis. In 1991, he voted for the use of force against Iraq in the Persian Gulf War, one of the few Democratic senators to vote in this manner. As the presidential campaign of 1992 neared, it appeared that the nomination would go to Governor William Jefferson Clinton of Arkansas. Clinton persuaded Gore to run with him as the Democratic vice-presidential candidate. After the election, which Clinton and Gore won, the sitting president George H.W. Bush concluded the North American Free Trade Agreement. Before the Senate ratified the treaty, the Clinton-Gore administration assumed control of the government. Democrats, pressured primarily by labor, opposed NAFTA and many believed that the executive branch would veto the treaty if the Senate did ratify it. Surprisingly, Clinton assumed a positive tone toward NAFTA, but refused to debate the issue. Instead he sent Gore to debate Ross Perot, the leading opponent of NAFTA, who ran unsuccessfully for president in 1992 as an independent candidate. Gore's performance embarrassed and discredited Perot and the protectionists. He argued that the imposition of high trade and tariff barriers during the 1930s, after the passage of the Hawley-Smoot Tariff Act, resulted in the worldwide depression. He then pointed out that Perot's new project, Alliance Airport just north of

Fort Worth, Texas, had received a classification as a free trade zone and that appeared hypocritical. The Gore-Perot debate helped generate support for the passage of NAFTA, a treaty ratified by the Senate in 1993. After serving under Clinton for two terms, Gore ran against George W. Bush for president in 2000. Following his loss in the disputed election, Gore retired from public office temporarily.

See also: Bush, George Herbert Walker; Clinton, William Jefferson (Bill); North American Free Trade Agreement (NAFTA); Perot, Henry Ross. **Vol. II**: Gore-Perot Debate over the Ratification of the North American Free Trade Agreement.

Selected Bibliography:

David Maraniss, *The Prince of Tennessee: The Rise of Al Gore*, 2000; Debra J. Saunders, *The World According to Gore*, 2000; Bill Turque, *Inventing Al Gore: A Biography*, 2000.

Cynthia Clark Northrup

GORMAN, ARTHUR PUE (March 11, 1839–June 4, 1906)

U.S. senator who co-sponsored the Wilson-Gorman Tariff bill in 1894.

Born in Woodstock, Maryland, Gorman became a page in the U.S. House of Representatives and then the Senate. Over the next fifteen years, he held a succession of positions in the Senate, including assistant doorkeeper and postmaster. During this period, he served as Senator Stephen Douglas's private secretary and accompanied Douglas on the 1858 series of campaign debates with Abraham Lincoln. Later, Gorman developed a close friendship with President Andrew Johnson, but this relationship resulted in Gorman's being dismissed from his Senate position in 1866. From 1869 to 1888, Gorman served in the Maryland legislature and helped create a political organization that controlled state politics during most of the next thirty years. In 1880, the state legislature selected him to the first of four terms as a U.S. senator. Four years later, he managed Grover Cleveland's first presidential campaign and in 1888 he supported an effort to establish an equivocal tariff plank in the Democratic platform.

In 1894, Congressman William L. Wilson introduced a tariff bill that called for some genuine reductions in duties. Republican leaders in the Senate filibustered the bill, and Gorman worked out a compromise that added 634 amendments. Many rates moved higher, and sugar, iron ore, and coal disappeared from the free list. The bill stalled in the House-Senate conference committee as the public became impatient. President Cleveland declared the bill inadequate, stating that it amounted to "party perfidy and party dishonor." But Senate Democrats denounced Cleveland's description. Gorman expressed his anger at Cleveland, whom he had consulted at every point as he devised the compromise bill. Cleveland subsequently allowed the bill to become law without his signature. Democrats would not get another chance at tariff reform until Woodrow Wilson's administration began in 1913. Gorman died of a heart attack in Washington, D.C., on June 4, 1906.

See also: Cleveland, Stephen Grover; Lincoln, Abraham; Wilson, William L.; Wilson-Gorman Tariff (Tariff of 1894).

Vol. II: Grover Cleveland's 1887 State of the Union Address. **Vol. III**: Tariff of 1894 (Wilson-Gorman Tariff).

Selected Bibliography:

John R. Lambert Jr., *Arthur Pue Gorman*, 1953.

Steven E. Siry

GRADY, HENRY W. (May 24, 1850– December 23, 1889)

An advocate of a moderate tariff, and the best-known spokesman of the so-called "New South," meaning a South free from both slavery and cotton monoculture, with a willingness to come to terms with postbellum life without relinquishing that section's fundamentally conservative temper.

Born in Athens, Georgia, on May 24, 1850, southerners deeply respected Grady and over the course of his life they seriously entertained his name as a prospective vice-presidential candidate and as a Senate candidate from Georgia. He became part owner and managing editor of the *Atlanta Constitution*.

As a figure intensely concerned with the economic rehabilitation and diversification of the American South, Grady took a particular interest in the tariff question. He remained a moderate on the issue. While he acknowledged that a regime of free trade had benefited the cotton-dominated economy of the antebellum South, he believed that some of the more diverse agricultural products of the New South, as well as its fledgling industries, owed part of their prosperity to tariff protection. The well-being of the New South demanded "a happy medium between the two extremes of free trade and ultra-protection," and by the election of 1884, his *Constitution*, once a pure free-trade organ, had begun to consider the issue from the point of view of pragmatism rather than ideology.

The 1884 presidential election, contrary to Grady's expectations, did not turn on the tariff issue. Four years later, on the day following Grover Cleveland's defeat in an election in which the tariff issue had featured prominently, the *Constitution* ran an editorial entitled "The Tariff Question Did the Mischief." A loyal Democrat, Grady would later remark that the tariff question had been "imprudently forced" in that campaign. Despite his continuing disagreement over the tariff, he indicated in 1889 that he would support Cleveland in the election of 1892. He died in Atlanta on December 23, 1889.

See also: Cleveland, Stephen Grover; Newspapers and media.

Selected Bibliography:

Raymond B. Nixon, *Henry W. Grady: Spokesman of the New South*, 1943.

Thomas E. Woods Jr.

GREAT BRITAIN

One of the chief trading competitors of the United States.

During the 1600s and the 1700s, Great Britain dominated the trade policy of the American colonies, passing a series of navigation acts that economically benefited the mother country. After the American Revolution, the United States attempted to negotiate a trade agreement with Britain, but Lord Sheffield and King George III opposed measures that provided the United States with any trade advantage. Shortly thereafter, Parliament prohibited any trade between the United States and the British West Indies. Frustrated by attempts to negotiate an agreement with Great Britain under the Articles of Confederation, John Adams urged American leaders to form a stronger federal government with authority to initiate trade measures. After the ratification of the Constitution, Secretary of State Thomas Jefferson advocated the use of retaliatory measures to counter British policies, but Hamilton insisted that such a policy would hinder trade and the collection of import duties, income necessary for the functioning of the government. Division over the issue led to the introduction of a bill by James Madison that called for a schedule of duties on items manufactured in countries without a trade agreement with the United States. President George Washington, to resolve the situation, appointed John Jay to negotiate with the British. Although Jay successfully resolved territorial issues, he failed to impress on the British the need for a trade treaty. The British continued to dominate world trade and refused to lower tariff barriers. After the War of 1812, the British initiated a policy of dumping goods on the American market in an effort to eliminate U.S. competition that had developed during the conflict. American officials responded by creating the American System that included a shift from a revenue to a protective tariff.

American tariff rates remained high until Democrats gained control of Congress, and when rates declined in 1857, the British government espoused the doctrine of free trade, hoping to encourage the United States to lower rates further. During the late nineteenth century, while the British government pursued free and open trade, emerging economic powers like the United States and Germany refused to lower tariff barriers. Consequently, British economic growth declined between 1870 and 1913 in comparison with other industrial countries. British prime minister Joseph Chamberlain stated that free trade had ruined the British home market. When Woodrow Wilson urged Congress to lower rates in the Underwood-Simmons Tariff Act, the British government expressed approval and hoped that the United States had started down the path toward free trade.

After World War I, the British abandoned free trade for a policy of imperial preferences that threatened the future trade expansion of the United States. This policy reduced the impact realized worldwide after the passage of the Hawley-Smoot Tariff Act. During the Great Depression, Secretary of State Cordell Hull offered to reduce tariff rates with Great Britain in exchange for the elimination of imperial preferences on specific items. Britain feared that any agreement with the United States would mean a lowering of rates with Germany under the Most Favored Nation provision. As a result, American rates declined substantially while the British instituted only minor revisions.

The post–World War II international community moved toward free trade with the signing of the General Agreement on Tariffs and Trade (GATT) and the United States proposed the formation of the International Trade Organization (ITO). To secure British support for the new organization, American trade representatives offered to reduce rates from 25 percent to 20 percent on half of the rates in exchange for the elimination of sixty-five items covered under the Ottawa preferential rate system. When opposition with Britain threatened to end talks without an agreement, the United States accepted terms that opened the American rubber market in exchange for a 25 percent reduction of the preferential rates. But these reductions never occurred because Great Britain continued to operate under balance-of-payment difficulties and the United States agreed to suspend tariff reductions of foreign countries experiencing this financial problem. Having twice failed to achieve a balanced trade agreement with Great Britain, U.S. negotiators called off talks in Torquay, England, in 1951 when the British refused to offer substantial concessions. The continuation of talks under GATT and British participation in the European Economic Community have resulted in the gradual reduction of the preferential system in favor of freer trade, but primarily with other European countries.

See also: American System; General Agreement on Tariffs and Trade (GATT); Great Depression; Hawley-Smoot Tariff (Tariff of 1930); International Trade Organization (ITO); Madison, James; Navigation and Trade Acts; Underwood-Simmons Tariff (Tariff of 1913); War of 1812; Washington, George.

Selected Bibliography:

Ian M. Drummond and Norman Hillmer, *Negotiating Freer Trade*, 1989; Alfred E. Eckes, *Opening America's Market: U.S. For-*

eign Trade Policy Since 1776, 1995; Richard N. Kottman, *Reciprocity and the North Atlantic Triangle, 1932–1938*, 1968.

Cynthia Clark Northrup

GREAT DEPRESSION

Although the stock market crash of October 1929 marked the beginning of the Great Depression, many international financial factors contributed to the longest and most severe economic depression in U.S. history.

The decade of the 1930s opened with increased tariff legislation because of the passage of the Hawley-Smoot Tariff Act of 1930. European and Asian countries responded with their own increase in tariff rates against the United States. President Herbert Hoover signed the Hawley-Smoot Tariff Act despite the collective warning of over 1,000 economists. This act increased custom duties and raised trade barriers at a time when the international community needed relief from the Great Depression. By January 1931, seventeen European nations entered into a Geneva tariff truce, but excluded the United States.

Political arguments continued within the United States between manufacturing and agricultural interests. Many manufacturing companies feared foreign competition and felt the need for high protective tariffs to restrict foreign imports, although some industries, such as automobile manufacturers, desired a free international market. Farming interests, though desperately in need of economic relief, realized that farmers needed foreign markets because of U.S. agricultural overproduction.

Franklin D. Roosevelt campaigned against high tariff rates in the presidential race of 1932 and called for reciprocal trade agreements. The London Economic Conference in the summer of 1933, an effort by the Roosevelt administration to encourage international cooperation, proved largely ineffective in lowering tariff duties. Diplomatic work continued under Secretary of State Cordell Hull and the Good Neighbor Policy toward Latin American countries.

President Roosevelt signed the Reciprocal Trade Agreements Act of 1934 (RTAA) on June 12, 1934, which amended the Hawley-Smoot Tariff Act by giving the executive branch further power to negotiate up to 50 percent increases or decreases in the tariff rate for future international trade agreements. The RTAA encouraged the United States to act as part of an international economic community and resolved the long-running low versus high tariff debates.

Tariffs or trade agreements also entered the 1936 presidential campaign. By that year, the United States had reached bilateral reciprocal agreements with Cuba, Belgium, Haiti, Sweden, Brazil, Colombia, Honduras, and Canada. After 1935 the United States initiated and later completed further trade agreements with Switzerland, Nicaragua, Guatemala, France, Finland, Costa Rica, El Salvador, Czechoslovakia, and Ecuador. The Good Neighbor Policy successfully increased trade in the Western Hemisphere, especially in Latin America. In 1938, the trade agreement with the United Kingdom, signed on November 17, 1938, completely reversed the protectionist trend.

In the early 1930s, Congress passed high tariffs designed to discourage imports, but many countries wanted to leave the export market open. By the late 1930s, many previously high tariff barriers lowered for imports, but Congress placed new restrictions on the export of war-related materials.

See also: Good Neighbor Policy; Hawley-Smoot Tariff (Tariff of 1930); Hoover, Herbert; Hull, Cordell; Latin America; London World Economic Conference; Reciprocal Trade Agreements Act (RTAA); Roosevelt, Franklin D.

Selected Bibliography:

Michael A. Butler, *Cautious Visionary: Cordell Hull and Trade Reform, 1933–1937*, 1998; John M. Dobson, *Two Centuries of Tariffs: The Background and Emergence of the U.S. International Trade Commission*, 1976.

Lisa L. Ossian

GREELEY, HORACE (February 3, 1811–November 29, 1872)

Journalist, U.S. representative, and presidential candidate.

Born on February 3, 1811, in Amherst, New Hampshire, Greeley apprenticed with the proprietor of the *Northern Spectator* in East Poultney, Vermont, at an early age. A few years later, Greeley sought his fortune in New York City, where he arrived practically penniless in 1831. After taking a variety of printing-related jobs, Greeley started a literary journal entitled the *New Yorker*. Eventually his involvement in Whig politics allowed him to found the New York *Tribune*, one of the most successful daily newspapers in the country, on the eve of the Civil War.

Although Greeley spent a brief time

in Congress from 1848 to 1849 and ran unsuccessfully for Congress on other occasions, his principal participation in the American political scene revolved around his editorial pen at the *Tribune*. Even though he was identified with the Whig Party, Greeley often expressed a radical streak in his beliefs. A proponent of workers' rights and an opponent of all types of monopoly, Greeley initially embraced the ideas of French philosopher Charles Fourier and his American proponent Albert Brisbane. A fervent opponent of slavery, Greeley later belonged to the radical wing of the Republican Party.

Greeley's views on the tariff resulted from his Whiggish economic ideas and his humanitarian concern for the American working class. He viewed a protective tariff as crucial for the country since high rates would protect American agricultural products as well as stimulate industrial development and diversification. Equally important, Greeley examined the impact of the tariff on the American workers. Looking at the wretchedness of the English working class, Greeley believed that the brutality of a laissez-faire economic system created their condition. A protective tariff, Greeley reasoned, might insulate and protect the working class from the harshness of free trade.

Beginning with his support of the Whig tariff of 1842 and his denunciation of the Walker Tariff of 1846, Greeley continued to support protective tariffs throughout his political career. In 1872, tired of the policies of Ulysses S. Grant, Greeley broke with his party and joined other dissidents in the formation of the Liberal Republican Party. Devoted to civil service reform and the end of Reconstruction in the South, the

Liberal Republicans also believed in low tariffs. While dissident Republicans mentioned Greeley as a possible presidential nominee, he would not abandon his views on the protective tariff. Eventually, the party abandoned its demand for tariff reduction and nominated Greeley as its candidate. After suffering an overwhelming defeat at the hands of President Grant, an exhausted and disappointed Greeley passed away on November 29, 1872.

See also: Adams, Charles Francis; Newspapers and media; Tariff of 1842; Tariff of 1846 (Walker's Tariff); Whig Party.

Selected Bibliography:

Glyndon G. Van Deusen, *Horace Greeley: Nineteenth-Century Crusader*, 1953.

Bruce Tap

GREENBACK MOVEMENT

Nineteenth-century U.S. political movement.

A product of agrarian discontent in the years following the Civil War, greenbackism embodied the idea that the federal government should continually maintain or increase the paper currency supply to meet the expanding demands of the U.S. economy. Greenbackers, who took their name from the wartime legal-tender treasury notes issued by the federal government, argued that an inflated currency would wipe out farm debts contracted during times of high prices and thus offer financial relief to struggling farmers. Influenced in part by the writings of Alexander Campbell of Illinois, a protégé of antebellum currency reformer Edward Kellogg, greenbackism spread rapidly among farmers and laborers, particularly after the Panic of 1873.

Failing to convince the Democratic Party to adopt their views, greenbackers created their own party composed primarily of midwestern and southern farmers. The Greenback Party emerged with a platform based on the reform of national monetary policy through bimetallism and the issuance of paper currency not backed by gold. The party hoped eventually to bring American farmers and laborers together under the banner of anti-monopolism. In 1876, the Greenback Party held its first national convention in Indianapolis, Indiana, and nominated New York industrialist Peter Cooper for president. Cooper received over 80,000 popular votes, but no electoral votes. Two years later, greenbackers united with members of labor to form the Greenback-Labor Party. In return for labor's support, greenbackers advocated reduced working hours, the establishment of a labor bureau in the federal government, and the reduction of Chinese immigration. The new party collected over one million votes and sent fourteen representatives to Congress during mid-term elections. Hoping to broaden its appeal among the dissatisfied as the 1880 presidential contest approached, the party endorsed women's suffrage, the federal regulation of interstate commerce, and a graduated income tax. Passage of the Bland-Allison Act (1878), allowing freer coinage of silver, and a general economic upturn eased much of the discontent that fueled the Greenback-Labor Party, dooming it to extinction. In 1880, James B. Weaver ran for president under the Greenback-Labor banner, collecting just over 300,000 votes.

Civil War general Benjamin Butler garnered less than 200,000 votes as the party's 1884 nominee, and soon afterward the Greenback-Labor Party ceased to exist. Some members joined the Union Labor Party in 1888, while others drifted back into the two major parties. During the 1890s, many became members of the Populist Party.

See also: Populists.

Selected Bibliography:

Lawrence Goodwyn, *The Populist Movement: A Short History of the Agrarian Revolt in America*, 1978; Robert C. McMath, *American Populism: A Social History, 1877–1898*, 1993.

Ben Wynne

GROSS NATIONAL PRODUCT (GNP)

Indicator of a nation's economic activity.

The gross national product (GNP) equals the total market value of the goods and services generated by a nation in a designated accounting period, usually a year. Calculation of the GNP is made prior to the deduction of depreciation or consumption in capital. The nation's GNP is the same as the gross domestic product (GDP), except that the GDP does not account for any income earned from foreign investments.

Cynthia Clark Northrup

H

HAMILTON, ALEXANDER (January 11, 1755–July 12, 1804)

First secretary of the treasury of the United States.

Born the illegitimate son of a Scottish peddler on the island of Nevis, Alexander Hamilton spent his early life working as a clerk in merchant houses throughout the Caribbean. When still a boy, he sought his fortune in America. He first studied at an academy in New Jersey and later attended King's College in New York City. When the Revolutionary War broke out, he threw himself into the patriot cause. He wrote important pamphlets in support of the revolution, served as an aide to General Washington, and fought bravely at the Battle of Yorktown. After the war, he married Elizabeth Schuyler, the daughter of General Phillip Schuyler, one of the wealthiest men in New York. He took up the practice of law in New York City, and also served his state as a representative to Congress in 1782 and 1783.

Like George Washington and James Madison, Hamilton soon became concerned over the growing debts of the nation. He remained convinced that only a stronger national government could save the country from financial ruin. Hamilton attended the Annapolis Convention in September 1786, and one year later served as a delegate from New York to the Constitutional Convention in Philadelphia. There he proposed a model of national government based on the political system of Great Britain. Although the delegates rejected most of his proposal, he became an ardent supporter of the Constitution during the ratification process. Along with James Madison and John Jay, he authored *The Federalist Papers*, a series of newspaper articles that brilliantly defended the principles underlying the Constitution.

After the financier Robert Morris turned down the position of secretary of the treasury, the newly elected president George Washington offered the job to Hamilton. He served in the post for nearly six years, and worked tirelessly to place the nation he had helped to create on a firm financial setting. In a series of important reports submitted to Congress, Hamilton carefully laid out his plans for the nation's economy. First he proposed a program known as funding and assumption. The U.S. government would pay all debts incurred by the nation during the American Revolution at full value. The nation would also assume the remaining state debts. Next Hamilton called for the creation of the Bank of the United States. Both the American government and private investors would own stock in the new institution. The bank would control the nation's credit while its notes would serve as the nation's currency. Hamilton also proposed the establishment of a mint to coin money, along with a duty on imported spirits and an excise on domestic whiskey to generate revenue. Finally, Hamilton laid out specific measures that the Congress should implement to encourage manufacturing, including premiums, bounties, and protective tariffs.

Hamilton quickly made an enemy of Washington's secretary of state Thomas Jefferson. Hamilton won Jefferson's support for funding and assumption by promising to build the new federal capital along the Potomac River in Virginia. Jefferson objected to most of Hamilton's remaining financial program. He believed that Hamilton favored policies that benefited the wealthiest Americans at the expense of average citizens such as farmers, tradesmen, and laborers. The conflict between Hamilton and Jefferson led to the creation of America's first two-party system, with Hamilton's sup-

porters known as the Federalists and Jefferson's followers known as the Democratic-Republicans.

Exhausted from political wrangling, embarrassed by scandals, including an affair with a married woman named Maria Reynolds, and in desperate need of money to support his growing family, Hamilton left public service and returned to private law in New York City. He remained interested in politics, and defended many cases in the New York Supreme Court that guaranteed the freedom of the press against most libel suits. When Thomas Jefferson and Aaron Burr deadlocked in the 1800 presidential race, Hamilton threw his support to Jefferson because he considered Burr a dangerous man. After Hamilton worked to defeat Burr in the race for governor of New York, Burr challenged him to a duel in the summer of 1804. Hamilton shot in the air, but Burr took deadly aim. After spending an agonizing day in terrible pain, Hamilton died on July 12, 1804, with his burial in the graveyard of Trinity Church near Wall Street. Though less well known than beloved leaders like George Washington and Thomas Jefferson, Hamilton's economic nationalism has remained a model for politicians as different as Henry Clay, Abraham Lincoln, and Franklin D. Roosevelt.

See also: American Revolution; Clay, Henry; *The Federalist* (Federalist Papers); Madison, James; Washington, George. **Vol. II**: *The Federalist* (Federalist Papers); *The Wealth of Nations*; *Report on Manufactures*. **Vol. III**: Tariff of 1790; Tariff of 1792; Tariff of 1794; Tariff of 1816.

Selected Bibliography:

Mary-Jo Kline, ed., *Alexander Hamilton: A Biography in His Own Words*, 1973.

Mary Stockwell

HAMILTON, JAMES (May 8, 1786–November 15, 1857)

Politician, planter, and businessman best known for his leadership of the South Carolina nullification movement.

Born in the low country of South Carolina to James Hamilton, a Revolutionary War hero, and Elizabeth Lynch, half sister of Thomas Lynch, a signer of the Declaration of Independence, Hamilton spent his youth on the family rice plantation and later in Newport, Rhode Island, and Dedham, Massachusetts, where he attended school. Hamilton also studied law with William Drayton in Charleston, South Carolina.

Before taking leadership during the nullification controversy, Hamilton served in the South Carolina legislature (1819–1823) and as intendant (mayor) of Charleston, where he oversaw Charleston's official response to Denmark Vesey's slave conspiracy.

Once a supporter of broad federal powers and a protective tariff, Hamilton moved decisively toward states' rights and antitariff views as a member of the U.S. House of Representatives. He embraced nullification in 1828 and organized a pro-nullification political party in the state following his election as governor in 1830. In November 1832, he presided over the convention that nullified the highly protectionist tariffs of 1828 and 1832. Following the passage of the 1833 compromise tariff, Hamilton urged its acceptance and successfully pushed for repeal of the Nullification Ordinance in March 1833.

After the nullification episode, Hamilton diverted his energies from elective politics to business and diplomatic pursuits. He founded a Charleston mercantile house in the mid-1830s and also operated a bank. As a planter, he raised rice in South Carolina, cotton in Georgia and Alabama, and sugarcane in Texas. The Republic of Texas dispatched him to Europe in 1839 to negotiate a loan on its behalf, and, although he never landed the loan, Hamilton obtained diplomatic recognition for Texas from the Dutch and British in 1840.

Failed cotton speculation and unreimbursed diplomatic expenditures left Hamilton deeply in debt by the early 1840s. While traveling to Texas in November 1857 to seek partial payment for his diplomatic labors, he drowned in a steamship accident off the coast of Louisiana.

See also: Calhoun, John Caldwell; Nullification; South Carolina *Exposition* and *Protest*.

Selected Bibliography:

Edward Stanwood, *American Controversies in the Nineteenth Century*, 1967; Robert Tinkler, *"Ashes of Greatness": Politics and Reputation in the Antebellum World of James Hamilton*, 1999.

Robert Tinkler

HANCOCK, JOHN (January 12, 1737–October 8, 1793)

Prominent Boston merchant, patriot, and president of the Continental Congress.

Born in Braintree, Massachusetts, Hancock graduated from Harvard in 1754 and quickly entered his uncle's mercantile business, the House of Hancock, where he trained to take over the company upon his uncle's death. The crisis that began with the Stamp Act hurt his business and helped him move toward politics. In 1765, voters elected him as a Boston selectman and from 1769 to 1774 he served as a member of the Massachusetts General Court. During 1774 and 1775 he presided over the first and second Provincial Congress before becoming a member of the Continental Congress in 1775. He spent the next five years in Congress, the first three as president.

When he inherited the House of Hancock, New England merchants routinely smuggled over one million gallons of molasses per year and, while he viewed the Sugar Act as a hindrance to trade, he did not complain. When parliament passed the Stamp Act, he participated in the growing resistance movement and warned his English agent of the negative economic consequences. As the problems between the colonies and England increased, Hancock started to neglect his business as he developed into a patriot leader. He became a supporter of non-importation because he saw the economic opportunities in this policy, and in April 1768 he encountered trouble with customs officers over his ship *Lydia*. In the early 1770s, as the problems persisted, Hancock continued to develop into an important leader. In 1774, the English attorney general decided to charge Samuel Adams, Dr. Joseph Warren, Dr. Benjamin Church, and Hancock with treason. Soon after, Hancock signed the Declaration of Independence and became a leader in the Continental Congress. In 1788, he presided over the Massachusetts Convention that ratified the Constitution. He also became governor of Massachusetts. On October 8, 1793, Hancock died in Quincy, Massachusetts.

See also: American Revolution; Colonial administration; Continental Congress; Molasses; Navigation and Trade Acts; Protests; Smuggling; Tea.

Selected Bibliography:

Harlow Giles Unger, *John Hancock: Merchant King and American Patriot*, 2000.

Ty M. Reese

HANCOCK, WINFIELD S. (February 14, 1824–February 9, 1886)

Civil War officer turned presidential candidate who lost the 1880 election over tariff issues.

Major General Hancock gained national prominence while fighting in the American Civil War at Antietam and Gettysburg. The Democratic Party considered him a viable candidate for the presidency as early as 1864, but they did not nominate Hancock until the 1880 election, in which he ran against Republican congressman James Garfield. As centrists, both Hancock and Garfield held similar positions on campaign issues. Generally, the Republican and Democratic Parties lacked internal cohesion over the issue of tariffs, yet Republicans generally favored high tariffs while Democrats favored tariffs for revenue purposes only. During the election of 1880, the tariff emerged as one of the most important issues because of crafty Republican campaign strategies. Maine's senator James G. Blaine persuaded Garfield to emphasize the benefits of protective tariffs when attacking the allegedly free trade Hancock. Republicans also attacked Hancock's shoddy record of political experience. These two campaign strategies dovetailed together neatly when the *Daily Guardian*, a New Jersey newspaper, reported a gaffe in Hancock's tariff position. Republicans derided Hancock for his assertion that "the tariff question is a local question," claiming that Hancock's faux pas demonstrated that he lacked both an understanding of the issues and concern for American workers and businesses. Democrats rushed to assert that Hancock had intended his statement to mean that citizens themselves should resolve the divisive tariff issue through their locally elected congressional representatives and that even Congressman Garfield had advocated such a position. Their defense met with no avail, and on November 7, 1880, voters showed the contentiousness of the tariff controversy by blocking Winfield S. Hancock's bid for the presidency by only 10,000 votes.

See also: Civil War (American); Garfield, James A.

Selected Bibliography:

Philip B. Kunhardt Jr., Philip B. Kunhardt III, and Peter W. Kunhardt, *The American President*, 1999.

Josh Pratt

HARMON, JUDSON (February 3, 1846– February 22, 1927)

Attorney general of the United States and governor of Ohio who in 1912 un-

successfully sought the Democratic Party's presidential nomination as an advocate of tariff reform.

After graduating from Denison University in 1866 and the Cincinnati Law School in 1869, Harmon became a member of the Democratic Party and served as a judge of the common pleas court and then the superior court in Cincinnati. Retiring from the judiciary, Harmon joined a prominent Cincinnati law firm and specialized in railroad law. He subsequently became a leading advisor to President Grover Cleveland on patronage matters. Appointed by Cleveland as attorney general of the United States in 1895, Harmon prosecuted several important antitrust cases, including the first application of the Sherman Anti-Trust Act to railroads.

Elected as governor of Ohio in 1908, he headed an administration that attacked graft and corruption, supported amendments to the U.S. Constitution for a federal income tax and the direct election of U.S. senators, endorsed a workman's compensation act, and favored other reform measures. In 1910, Harmon won reelection as governor by defeating Warren G. Harding, despite former president Theodore Roosevelt's support of his opponent. Old-line Democrats now favored Harmon for the Democratic Party's presidential nomination in 1912. Harmon advocated tariff revision in keeping with his view that government should substantially limit the taxpayers' burden. But Harmon failed to gain the Democratic Party's presidential nomination in 1912; the delegates nominated Woodrow Wilson. When Harmon's term as governor ended in 1913, he taught at the University of Cincinnati's law school and resumed his law practice in Cincinnati, where he died in 1927.

See also: Cleveland, Stephen Grover; Personal income tax (Sixteenth Constitutional Amendment); Roosevelt, Theodore; Wilson, Thomas Woodrow.

Selected Bibliography:

Hoyt Landon Warner, *Progressivism in Ohio, 1897–1917*, 1964.

Steven E. Siry

HARRISBURG CONVENTION OF 1827

Meeting of protectionists in Harrisburg, Pennsylvania, to agitate for an increase of the duty rate, primarily on wool and woolens.

Early in 1827, the House of Representatives passed a woolens bill that called for a high protective rate, but the Senate defeated the measure. Protectionists in Congress persisted in their efforts, arranging for meetings in various states and a general convention, held in Harrisburg during the summer months. Although the majority of the newspaper editors, manufacturers, and politicians who attended advocated a high tariff on wool, the attendees included other products as a means of increasing support for their cause. The convention demanded protective rates for cotton, hemp, flax, iron, glass, and various agricultural goods as well as wool and woolens. The group insisted on an *ad valorem* rate on woolens of 40 percent with a gradual increase to 50 percent, while wool, starting at a rate of twenty cents a pound would increase two-and-a-half cents per pound every year until the rate reached fifty cents a pound. Since the majority of attendees at Harrisburg supported John Quincy Adams, the convention provided Andrew Jackson and his followers with the opportunity to politicize the tariff issue, a strategy that ultimately resulted in the passage of the Tariff of Abominations and the Nullification Crisis.

See also: Adams, John Quincy; Jackson, Andrew; Nullification; Tariff of 1828 (Tariff of Abominations); Wool and woolens.

Selected Bibliography:

Frank W. Taussig, *The Tariff History of the United States*, 1931.

Cynthia Clark Northrup

HARRISON, BENJAMIN (August 20, 1833–March 13, 1901)

Endorsed the highest tariff in American history to date during his term as the twenty-third president of the United States.

After graduating from Ohio's Miami University in 1852, Harrison gained admittance to the bar two years later. He then moved to Indiana and joined the newly created Republican Party in 1856. During the Civil War, he rose to the rank of brigadier general in the Union army. In 1880, voters elected Harrison to the U.S. Senate, where he received national attention as an advocate of high tariff rates and generous pensions for Union veterans. In 1888, he emerged as the compromise candidate at the Republican National Convention. President Grover Cleveland established the primary issue in the election when he devoted his entire annual message of 1887 to an ardent recommendation for reforming the tariff.

National government revenues, 60 percent from tariff duties, remained significantly greater than expenditures. Cleveland contended that this meant unnecessary taxation and that the unspent revenue could dampen economic growth. But Harrison responded with a vigorous defense of the protective tariff. Although Cleveland had the most popular votes, Harrison received a majority of the electoral votes and won the election.

Despite his staunch protectionist position during the campaign, as president, Harrison pushed for some lower rates, yet he also advocated the idea of reciprocity whereby trade agreements reciprocally lowered duties on noncompeting products. Reciprocity appealed to consumers since they would pay lower prices, but it also potentially benefited manufacturers and farmers by creating a larger foreign market for their products. The Republican leaders maneuvered the McKinley Tariff of 1890 through Congress, which resulted in the highest tariff in American history to that point. The tariff had two features that especially differentiated it from previous tariffs: reciprocity and the promotion of new industries, particularly the tinplate industry. Republicans insisted that the McKinley Tariff would benefit workers through higher wages, but prices immediately rose faster than wages. Emphasizing the problems with the tariff, the Democrats trounced the Republicans in the 1890 congressional elections and Harrison lost his reelection bid to Grover Cleveland in 1892. Harrison retired to Indiana, where he practiced law until his death in 1901.

See also: Cleveland, Stephen Grover; McKinley Tariff (Tariff of 1890). **Vol. II**: Grover Cleveland's 1887 State of the Union Address; Benjamin Harrison's 1889 State of the Union Address. **Vol. III**: Tariff of 1890 (McKinley Tariff).

Selected Bibliography:

Homer Socolofsky and Allan Spetter, *The Presidency of Benjamin Harrison*, 1987.

Steven E. Siry

HAWAII

South Pacific kingdom that became economically linked to the United States in the nineteenth century through a reciprocity agreement that provided for the duty-free importation of Hawaiian sugar.

During the 1840s, Britain and France threatened Hawaii's independence, prompting King Kamehameha III to place the kingdom under the protection of the United States in 1851. Later, the U.S. Senate failed to ratify an 1855 reciprocal trade agreement with Hawaii, which the Franklin Pierce administration negotiated to bind the islands economically to the United States. Secretary of State William Seward obtained a similar agreement from the Hawaiians during the administration of Andrew Johnson, but again Congress rejected the agreement. Finally, in 1885, Secretary of State Hamilton Fish concluded a reciprocity agreement that passed Congress. The agreement, opposed by Chairman Justin Morrill, Daniel Voorhees, and Nelson Aldrich, allowed the duty-free importation of Hawaiian sugar at the expense of domestic producers and European sugar beet producers. Although the passage of the bill cost the American taxpayers $12.8 million, a form of restitution materialized two years later when the United States obtained a naval base at Pearl Harbor. An attempt to annex the islands failed during the administration of Grover Cleveland. In 1893, during Benjamin Harrison's term as president, American sugar producers in Hawaii temporarily overthrew the monarchy of Queen Lilioukaliani, but the U.S. government failed to recognize the self-proclaimed republic. President William McKinley formally annexed the islands in 1898 and two years later Hawaii achieved territorial status. In 1959, Hawaii became the fiftieth state of the United States. The desire to annex the Hawaiian Islands beginning in the mid-nineteenth century prompted officials to use economic incentives and trade relations to achieve their ultimate objective.

See also: Cleveland, Stephen Grover; Harrison, Benjamin; Imperialism; McKinley, William; Morrill, Justin S.; Pierce, Franklin.

Selected Bibliography:

Merze Tate, *The United States and the Hawaiian Kingdom: A Political History*, 1965.

Cynthia Clark Northrup

HAWLEY, WILLIS C. (May 5, 1864–July 24, 1941)

Republican from Oregon who served in the U.S. House of Representatives for thirteen terms.

Born near Monroe, Oregon, on May 5, 1864, Willis Chatman Hawley attended country schools, graduated from Willamette University in 1888 with a law degree, and gained admittance to the Oregon bar in 1893. As a professor of history and economics, Hawley served Willamette University as president from 1893 to 1902.

Elected to Congress in 1907, Hawley headed the House Committee on Ways and Means for the Seventieth and Seventy-first Congresses. Described as a high protectionist who personified the orthodox high-tariff Republican ideal, as chairman he introduced a bill in 1929 that ignored President Herbert Hoover's previously suggested tariff limitations. This bill, which would later be called the Hawley-Smoot Tariff Act of 1930, revised the Fordney-McCumber Act of 1922, and Hawley proudly attached his name to the 1930 tariff act. After many economists and political opponents argued that the tariff deepened the Great Depression, Hawley lost his House position in the Democratic landslide of 1932 and returned to Oregon, where he resumed practicing law until his death on July 24, 1941.

See also: Fordney-McCumber Tariff (Tariff of 1922); Hawley-Smoot Tariff (Tariff of 1930); House Ways and Means Committee. **Vol. II**: Herbert Hoover's Statement of Intention to Approve the Hawley-Smoot Tariff Act. **Vol. III**: Tariff of 1922 (Fordney-McCumber Tariff); Tariff of 1930 (Hawley-Smoot Tariff).

Selected Bibliography:

John M. Dobson, *Two Centuries of Tariffs: The Background and Emergence of the U.S. International Trade Commission*, 1976.

Lisa L. Ossian

HAWLEY-SMOOT TARIFF (TARIFF OF 1930)

Protective tariff that raised trade barriers to a record high at the beginning of the Great Depression.

Signed into law on June 17, 1930, and designed to strengthen the economy by excluding foreign competition, Congress passed the Hawley-Smoot Tariff Act under protest from some industries such as the automobile manufacturers who desired a place on the free list. Willis C. Hawley, a Republican representative from Oregon and chairman of the House Ways and Means Committee, and Reed Smoot, a Republican senator from Utah and chairman of the Senate Finance Committee, sponsored the legislation.

Originally, the House of Representatives concentrated on revising the tariff rates of the Fordney-McCumber Act of 1922, but in the Senate Smoot decided to investigate the entire House schedule, opening up the process to tariff lobbyists and creating a great deal of "logrolling" (political favors) between senators and districts. Ultimately, the legislative process produced nearly 20,000 pages of testimony in public hearings from 2,443 witnesses. The process filled 2,800 pages of the *Congressional Record*, with 4.5 million official words spoken in the Senate alone during the six months of debate. The result levied duties on nearly 21,000 items of commerce.

A compromise reached between the House and the Senate as to rate schedules preceded a second agreement reached late in June that gave the president the power to flex rates on specifications supplied by the Tariff Commission limited to a 50 percent increase or decrease in the stated rate. President Hoover, pleased with this compromise, believed his Tariff Commission could then conclude more adequate and just tariff rates.

President Hoover, who had campaigned in 1928 to adjust the tariff rates to benefit the farmers' economic situation, did not completely support the final tariff bill produced by Congress because he felt it represented manufacturing interests rather than agriculture. Although over 1,000 economists warned the president about the consequences of an increase in tariff rates, Hoover signed the bill anyway. This tariff had been a record breaker: the longest to produce and the quickest to sign.

The Hawley-Smoot Tariff Act of 1930 triggered a reaction overseas, with many countries establishing high tariff barriers. Subsequently, international trade drastically declined during the beginning of this decade of economic depression. This act increased custom duties and raised trade barriers at a time when international commerce suffered as a result of the Great Depression.

See also: Fordney-McCumber Tariff (Tariff of 1922); Great Depression; Hawley, Willis C.; Hoover, Herbert; House Ways and Means Committee; Senate Finance Committee; Smoot, Reed; Tariff Commission. **Vol. II**: Joseph Ridgway Grundy's Speech in Favor of the Hawley-Smoot Tariff; Protest of American Economists over the Hawley-Smoot Tariff; Daniel Frederic Steck's Iowa Speech Against the Hawley-Smoot Tariff; Herbert Hoover's Statement of Intention to Approve the Hawley-Smoot Tariff Act; Andrew W. Mellon's Defense of the Hawley-Smoot Tariff for Economic Recovery; James Watson's Radio Address in Support of the Hawley-Smoot Tariff; Franklin D. Roosevelt's 1932 Campaign Radio Speech; Herbert Hoover's Response to Franklin D. Roosevelt. **Vol. III**: Tariff of 1922 (Fordney-McCumber Tariff); Tariff of 1930 (Hawley-Smoot Tariff).

Selected Bibliography:

Harold B. Hinton, *Cordell Hull: A Biography*, 1942; Milton R. Merrill, *Reed Smoot: Apostle in Politics*, 1990; E.E. Schattschneider, *Politics, Pressures, and the Tariff: A Study of Free Private Enterprise in Pressure Politics, as Shown in the 1929–1930 Revision on the Tariff*, 1935.

Lisa L. Ossian

HAY, JOHN MILTON (October 8, 1838– July 1, 1905)

Secretary of state from 1898 to 1905 under William McKinley and Theodore Roosevelt.

Born in Salem, Indiana, and raised in Warsaw, Illinois, Hay attended Illinois State University and Brown University before studying law and being admitted to the bar in 1861. He worked on Abraham Lincoln's nomination and election campaigns, then took a position as Lincoln's private secretary. After serving as a commissioned officer in the U.S. Army, he accepted a series of diplomatic assignments in Paris, Vienna, and Madrid. He worked as night editor of the *New York Tribune* in 1870, resigned from the newspaper in 1875, and served as assistant secretary of state from 1879 to 1881. He then turned his attention to business and writing.

In 1898, President William McKinley appointed Hay as his secretary of state, a position he would retain until his death in 1905. Hay played an important role in improving relations with Great Britain by cooperating with it on a policy toward China, on the construction of a Central American canal, and in resolving a dispute over the boundary of Alaska.

In 1899 and 1900, Hay, working with the British diplomats, authored the Open Door Notes. Arguing for free trade, Hay's first note called for equal commercial opportunities within the various foreign powers' spheres of influence in China. The second sought a solution that would preserve the territorial and administrative integrity of China.

In 1900, he helped author the Hay-Pauncefote Treaty in which Great Britain agreed that the United States could independently build and administer, but not fortify, a canal across Central America. The Senate rejected the treaty, but passed a second Hay-Pauncefote Treaty (1901) that omitted reference to fortifications. A third canal treaty, the Hay-Herran Treaty, negotiated with Colombia, would have awarded the United States control of a six-mile-wide Canal Zone in return for a $10 million payment and rental fee of $250,000 a year. Although ratified by the U.S. Senate, Colombia rejected the treaty. After Panama declared its independence, the United States signed the Hay-Bunau-Varilla Treaty in 1904 with Panama, expanding U.S. rights in the Canal Zone and effectively making the new country a protectorate of the United States.

John Hay, while still serving as secretary of state, died at age sixty-seven in Newbury, New Hampshire.

See also: Lincoln, Abraham; McKinley, William; Open Door Notes; Panama Canal.

Selected Bibliography:

Kenton J. Clymer, *John Hay: The Gentleman as Diplomat*, 1975; Howard I. Kushner and Anne Hummel Sherrill, *John Milton Hay: The Union of Poetry and Politics*, 1977.

John D. Coats

HAYES, JOHN L. (April 13, 1812–April 18, 1887)

Served as the representative for the New England Iron Masters in their petition to change the Tariff of 1846.

Born in South Berwick, Maine, Hayes entered Dartmouth at the age of fifteen. His primary interests focused on natural history and geology, but on graduation he entered his father's law practice. Admitted to the New Hampshire bar in 1835, he then moved to Portsmouth to begin his career and family. As the circuit court clerk for New Hampshire, Hayes continued to write and study geology. He also played a crucial role in the wool-growing and -manufacturing industry urging the passage of the Tariff of 1867 that protected wool and wool products. In 1861, President Abraham Lincoln appointed him chief clerk for the U.S. Patent Office, a position he held until the end of the Civil War. After the war, Hayes served as editor of the *Bulletin of the National Association of Wool Manufacturers* and received an appointment as the head of the Tariff Commission in 1882. He spent the last years of his life writing and studying. Hayes died in Cambridge, Massachusetts.

See also: Tariff Commission; Tariff of 1846 (Walker's Tariff); Tariff of 1867.

Selected Bibliography:

Edward Stanwood, *American Tariff Controversies in the Nineteenth Century*, 1967.

Lisa A. Ennis

HAYNE, ROBERT Y. (November 10, 1791–September 24, 1839)

South Carolina senator best known for his support of free trade, states' rights, and the doctrine of nullification.

Born in Colleton District, South Carolina, Hayne joined the South Carolina bar in 1812 and voters elected him to the state legislature in 1814. In 1822, he won a seat in the U.S. Senate on a "tariff for revenue" platform and quickly gained prominence in Democratic Party circles.

As a senator, Hayne emerged as one of the most vocal opponents of protectionism and justified his opposition on both constitutional and economic grounds. He believed that the U.S. Constitution did not grant Congress the authority to implement protective tariffs for the encouragement of certain industries and, if left unchecked, northern manufacturing interests would ultimately demand an end to all foreign commerce. Hayne warned that protective tariffs, while strengthening the manufacturing sector at the expense of the South, would also contribute to increased sectionalism.

Increasingly, the tariff issue became intertwined with issues of states' rights, nullification, and slavery. In January 1830, hoping to gain western support for a lower tariff, Hayne debated Senator Daniel Webster of Massachusetts on the nature of the federal union. Hayne argued that the union, primarily an association of sovereign states, had the authority to nullify federal laws, including tariffs, within their boundaries. In 1832, Hayne gave up his Senate seat to become governor of South Carolina during the Nullification Crisis. As governor, he urged South Carolinians to ignore President Andrew Jackson's order to comply with federal attempts to collect import duties, and backed down only after accepting Henry Clay's compromise Tariff Act of 1833. After the Nullification Crisis, Hayne retired from politics to devote more time to the railroad business. He died on September 24, 1839, in Asheville, North Carolina.

See also: Clay, Henry; Democratic Party; Free trade; Jackson, Andrew; Nullication; Protectionism; Sectionalism; Tariff of 1833 (Compromise Tariff); Webster, Daniel. **Vol. II**: Andrew Jackson's Message to Congress on the Nullification Crisis; Daniel Webster's Speech Defending His Support of the Tariff of 1828; Henry Clay's 1832 Speech in Favor of the American System; Proclamation to the People of South Carolina; Robert Young Hayne's 1832 Speech in Favor of the American System. **Vol. III**: Tariff of 1832; Tariff of 1833.

Selected Bibliography:

Dall Forsythe, *Taxation and Political Change in the Young Nation 1781–1833*, 1977.

William C. Barnhart

HICKENLOOPER AMENDMENT

Amendment to the Foreign Assistance Act of 1962 introduced by Senator Bourke B. Hickenlooper that tied U.S. foreign assistance programs to the protection of U.S. overseas assets.

This amendment required the president to suspend all economic assistance to any country that expropriated the property of a U.S. company, repudiated a contract with a U.S. entity, or burdened a U.S. enterprise with discriminatory taxes or restrictive administrative requirements. It specified not only direct forms of economic aid, but also import quotas and other legislation that benefited the offending country. Affected countries had six months in which to take significant steps to reimburse U.S. companies for the value of their property, contract, or tax payments.

The amendment gained immediate support from U.S. business interests. Supporters argued that the measure produced benefits in two ways. First, it would protect overseas investments and, second, it would lead to greater U.S. investment in Latin America—a major goal of President John F. Kennedy's Alliance for Progress. But President Kennedy opposed the amendment's interference with his freedom to direct the nation's foreign affairs.

The Hickenlooper Amendment inspired two closely related pieces of legislation. In 1971, an amendment by Democratic congressman Henry Gonzalez of Texas strengthened the Hickenlooper legislation by giving the U.S. government the authority to stop multilateral bank loans to nations that expropriate U.S.–owned properties. Yet the Gonzalez Amendment weakened the legislation by allowing the president of the United States to waive the law's provisions if he considered such action in the national interest. In 1994,

Congress passed legislation sponsored by Republican senator Jesse Helms of North Carolina that made the punitive provisions of the Hickenlooper and Gonzalez Acts mandatory.

Over almost four decades, the Hickenlooper Amendment has effectively protected U.S. overseas investments. Although rarely invoked, the very existence of the legislation provides a powerful policy tool and deterrent to nations considering expropriation of U.S. assets.

See also: Alliance for Progress; Foreign policy; Latin America.

Selected Bibliography:

Paul E. Sigmund, *Multinationals in Latin America: The Politics of Nationalization*, 1980.

John D. Coats

HIDES AND SKINS

Important items of trade that emanated from all British colonies in North America.

Americans used hides, especially tough, waterproof, flexible deer hides, in the early modern world for clothing, as containers, and for decorative purposes. One of the first types of trade to take place in any colony with neighboring Indians involved the trading of hides, skins, and furs, helping the colonies through their early, uncertain days. The trade in deer hides produced the greatest long-term effect on the economy in South Carolina and Georgia, more than in any other colonies. The use of the term "buck," to mean a dollar, originated in these southern-most mainland colonies where colonists used buckskins and doeskins as a

form of currency. For most of the colonial period, the navigation laws did not regulate the export of hides, enabling colonists to sell in a wide range of markets in Europe and the West Indies. Placed on the list of enumerated commodities only in 1764, from that date colonists shipped hides and skins directly to Great Britain before shipping them on to other parts of Europe. The American Revolution soon removed this restriction on hide exports, and no colony suffered any great damage because of it. In the nineteenth century, the United States gradually moved from being a net exporter to being a net importer of hides. The federal government imposed tariffs on hides to help pay for the Civil War and World War I. During periods of peace, manufacturing interests agitated for the removal of the hide tariff, while western ranchers lobbied to keep the tariff in place. Both groups enjoyed short-term victories.

See also: American Revolution; Civil War (American); Great Britain; Navigation and Trade Acts; World War I.

Selected Bibliography:

J. Leitch Wright Jr., *The Only Land They Knew: The Tragic Story of the American Indians in the Old South*, 1981.

John P. Barrington

HIGGINSON, THOMAS WENTWORTH (December 22, 1823–May 9, 1911)

Massachusetts-born intellectual who became an ordained minister in the Unitarian Church.

His determined advocacy on behalf of the abolition of slavery, women's suffrage, and temperance proved so unrelenting that even his liberal-minded Newburyport, Massachusetts, congregation grew tired of him. As Higginson himself described it, he "preached himself out of his pulpit." He approached causes in a different manner than most politically active or socially conscious intellectuals of his day. He went well beyond simply spewing forth rhetorical phrases and scribbling purple prose in supporting the causes to which he committed himself. As a man of action, he backed up his words with a willingness to act even when that placed him at considerable risk to his personal safety. Describing himself as a "Disunionist Abolitionist," he plunged headlong into the antislavery struggle of the 1850s, and twice organized mobs intent on rescuing fugitive slaves held in custody in Boston. He raised money and procured arms for free-soil settlers in Kansas. In 1859, as one of the "Secret Six" northern leaders, he contributed money to John Brown's effort to incite a slave rebellion by leading a group of antislavery activists in a raid on Harper's Ferry, Virginia. When the part the "Secret Six" played in supporting Brown became public, three of them fled to Canada, a fourth died in Europe of tuberculosis, and a fifth had a nervous breakdown before being institutionalized in an insane asylum. Only Higginson stood his ground defying the authorities to charge him, arrest him, or subpoena him to testify. The Senate investigating committee chose never to call Higginson, probably because it did not wish to give him a national platform from which to proclaim his sentiments or to strike another blow against slavery.

Higginson volunteered for service in the Union army during the Civil War, and in 1862 received the chance to command the first regiment of African Americans to be formed, the 1st South Carolina Volunteers. He took part of the regiment on a minor raid along a South Carolina river in January 1863, and afterward wrote an enthusiastic report to the War Department, which, as intended, found its way into the newspapers: "Nobody knows anything about these men who has not seen them in battle. No officer in this regiment now doubts that the key to the successful prosecution of the war lies in the unlimited use of black troops." Higginson continued to command the unit even after the redesignation of the regiment as the 33rd U.S. Colored Troops. After the war, he continued to labor for various social causes and wrote voluminously, his best-known work being his memoir, *Army Life in a Black Regiment*. In the postwar period Higginson joined other key abolitionists such as William Bryant, Ralph Waldo Emerson, Gerrit Smith, and William Lloyd Garrison, in forming the first American Free Trade League in 1865. His political activism shifted from slavery to free trade. His active encouragement of the reclusive poet Emily Dickinson, with whom he corresponded for twenty-four years, remains one of his greatest literary contributions. Higginson died in Massachusetts in 1911.

See also: American Free Trade League (AFTL); Emerson, Ralph Waldo; Garrison, William Lloyd.

Selected Bibliography:

James W. Tuttleton, *Thomas Wentworth Higginson*, 1978.

David E. Long

HOOVER, HERBERT (August 10, 1874–October 20, 1964)

Engineer, businessman, administrator, secretary of commerce, and thirty-first president of the United States.

Born in West Branch, Iowa, to Quaker parents, a succession of relatives raised Hoover after illness took his parents before his tenth birthday. As a teenager, he moved to Salem, Oregon, in the late 1880s to live with an uncle and soon found work at the Oregon Land Company, where he developed an interest in geology and mining. He entered the pioneer class of the newly founded Stanford University. Hoover, a solid though undistinguished student, developed his administrative skills through behind-the-scenes involvement in student government. On graduation in 1895 with a degree in geology, Hoover embarked on a career as a mining engineer. In 1897, at the age of twenty-three, he landed a job with the London firm of Bewick, Moering & Company and rapidly became a successful, and wealthy, international mining engineer and businessman, supervising a variety of projects all over the world.

At the onset of World War I, Hoover headed the Commission for Relief in Belgium. With America's involvement in the war, Hoover entered government service as the U.S. food administrator, which furthered his reputation as a progressive. After the war, he engaged in various efforts to assist in the economic rebuilding of Europe and, in 1920, after declaring himself a Republican, he unsuccessfully sought the party's presidential nomination. In 1921, President Harding appointed him secretary of commerce, a post he also held during the Coolidge administration. In 1928, he won the Republican nomination and the presidency.

Hoover played a major role in U.S. tariff policy in the 1920s. His views on the tariff reflected his beliefs in progressivism, nationalism, and individualism, and appear, in some respects, contradictory. He believed, on the one hand, in protectionism, especially for American agriculture. On the other hand, Hoover, as a progressive, favored the idea of a "flexible" tariff, with rates that could be "scientifically" adjusted by the Federal Tariff Commission, thus removing rate setting from the process of political logrolling.

Hoover felt that tariff protection would not only help farmers in the domestic market, but would encourage them to diversify. During the 1920s, while at the Commerce Department, Hoover realized the long-term benefit of increased imports to the United States. But, for Hoover, tariff policy remained only a part of a comprehensive approach to postwar economic reconstruction. Hoover argued that tariffs alone had little impact on foreign purchasing power. He believed that the volume of imports depended more on internal prosperity than on tariff rates and argued that protection helped maintain domestic prosperity. Under Hoover's leadership the Commerce Department claimed that so-called "invisible exports" such as capital outflows, money sent home by immigrants, and tourist expenditures, helped lessen the trade imbalance, making it possible for America both to maintain protection and expand trade. Hoover argued that American overseas trade had grown following the upward revisions of the Fordney-McCumber Tariff of 1922. Hoover may have overestimated the importance of such revisions and failed to recognize the negative impact that the United States's favorable merchandise trade balance had on the world economy.

Hoover's views played an important role in the election in 1928 and the passage of the Hawley-Smoot Tariff Act in 1930. During the 1928 campaign, both candidates used the tariff issue, and Hoover vigorously defended protection, arguing that the issue separated Republicans and Democrats. After his election, tariff revision became a major item. Hoover favored revision, not as a way to ameliorate depressed economic conditions, but as a way to raise rates for agriculture. He hoped for only limited revision of nonfarm schedules and supported a flexibility provision, which would allow the Tariff Commission to move more quickly in making recommendations for adjustments and enable the president to adjust individual rates by as much as 50 percent. But Congress significantly raised rates and took away the president's power under the flexibility provision. Hoover saved the flexibility provision by threatening a veto, and signed the bill into law, despite the raising of nonfarm rates. The bill did much more harm than good for the Republican Party, Hoover, and the nation. The flexibility provision had little impact and the increased rates provoked retaliation that lessened

international trade as the depression deepened. The passage of the Hawley-Smoot Tariff Act contributed to Hoover's loss in 1932 to Franklin Roosevelt and has had an impact on Hoover's historical reputation.

See also: Fordney-McCumber Tariff (Tariff of 1922); Great Depression; Hawley, Willis C.; Hawley-Smoot Tariff (Tariff of 1930); Smoot, Reed; Tariff Commission; World War I. **Vol. II**: Protest of American Economists over the Hawley-Smoot Tariff; Daniel Frederic Steck's Iowa Speech against the Hawley-Smoot Tariff; Herbert Hoover's Statement of Intention to Approve the Hawley-Smoot Tariff Act; Andrew W. Mellon's Defense of the Hawley-Smoot Tariff for Economic Reform; James Watson's Radio Address in Support of the Hawley-Smoot Tariff; Franklin D. Roosevelt's 1932 Campaign Radio Speech; Herbert Hoover's Response to Franklin D. Roosevelt. **Vol. III**: Tariff of 1922 (Fordney-McCumber Tariff); Tariff of 1930 (Hawley-Smoot Tariff).

Selected Bibliography:

Martin Fausold, *The Presidency of Herbert Hoover*, 1985; Ellis Hawley, ed., *Herbert Hoover as Secretary of Commerce: Studies in New Era Thought and Practice*, 1981; Joan Hoff Wilson, *Herbert Hoover: Forgotten Progressive*, 1975.

Michael J. Anderson

HOUSE WAYS AND MEANS COMMITTEE

Oldest standing committee in the U.S. Congress, dating back to 1802.

The first Congress established a Ways and Means Committee as a select committee, but disbanded it during the tenure of Alexander Hamilton as U.S. secretary of the treasury. The most prestigious committee in the U.S. House of Representatives, its members serve on no other committees and important pieces of legislation that move to the floor do so under a "closed rule," with the rationale that the complexity of legislation precludes the feasibility of floor amendments. For many years, House Ways and Means handled all committee assignment decisions for the Democratic Party in the U.S. House of Representatives. Until 1919, except for a thirty-year interim from 1865 to 1895 when the chair of the House Appropriations Committee served in the capacity, the chair of the Ways and Means served initially as de facto and later official floor leader. Since 1919, the floor leader has served on no committees. A major component of the committee's jurisdiction includes revenue legislation involving both taxes and tariffs. Tariffs, until the twentieth century, constituted the main source of income for the United States and tariff bills for most of the nation's history constituted the bulk of the legislative work of the U.S. Congress. Generally, northerners, attempting to safeguard local industries, introduced protectionist petitions to the committee. Petitions frequently dealt with specific products such as wool, cigars, chrome, and even the apparel of immigrants. Following the establishment of the Senate Finance Committee in 1816, interest groups appealed to the committee to modify measures deemed unsatisfactorily structured in their view by the House Ways and Means Committee. The complexity of the committee has increased considerably over the past thirty years.

During the tenure of Arkansas Democrat Wilbur Mills as committee chair from 1958 to 1974, power concentrated in his hands; following his relinquishment of the position after the revelation of his involvement with stripper Fannie Fox, power moved to the subcommittees. This dispersion of power to subcommittees mirrored a trend throughout Congress that a huge influx of freshman Democrats elected in 1974 hastened. Now U.S. trade representatives work directly with a number of committee members. Since the Republican takeover of the U.S. House of Representatives in the aftermath of the 1994 elections, seniority in the committee has dramatically weakened.

See also: Congress (United States); Senate Finance Committee.

Selected Bibliography:

National Archives and Records Administration, *Guide to the Records of the United States House of Representatives at the National Archives 1789–1989. Bicentennial Edition*, 1989.

H. Michael Tarver

HULL, CORDELL (October 21, 1871– July 23, 1955)

Secretary of state under President Franklin D. Roosevelt.

Born in rural Tennessee, Hull graduated from the Law Department of Cumberland University and served as captain in the Spanish-American War, as a circuit judge, and as a U.S. representative. Elected to the Senate in 1931, he served until 1933.

Hull constantly studied the tariff, starting as a young boy during the Mills Tariff Bill debate in 1888. Hull's maiden congressional speech attacked high tariffs and monopolies. In 1906, he prepared a bill to repeal tariff duties on antitoxin and diphtheria serum. He also introduced a series of single tariff bills rather than the entire schedule designed to embarrass stand-pat Republicans, but President William Taft vetoed them. Hull denounced the tariff increase of the Payne-Aldrich Tariff of 1909.

As part of the Underwood-Simmons Tariff Act of 1913, Hull drafted House income tax legislation for the overall bill. Although this act lowered tariffs, World War I impeded international trade benefits. By 1916, Hull revised his view of high tariffs as a domestic evil and began espousing the idea that high tariffs prevented international commerce and ultimately peace.

Hull, having lost his reelection bid in 1920, did not participate in the passage of the Fordney-McCumber Tariff Act of 1922. Reelected the next term, he spent several years attacking the act, stating that tariff revision would lower domestic production and increase foreign markets. In April 1929, he delivered his longest tariff speech, attacking the pending Republican bill as protectionist and exorbitant. From 1923 to 1933 he continued to introduce, though unsuccessfully, reduced tariff legislation.

President Franklin D. Roosevelt appointed Hull as his secretary of state in March 1933. The 1934 London Economic Conference attempted international economic cooperation, but Hull still operated under the restrictions of the Hawley-Smoot Tariff Act. The Reciprocal Trade Agreements Act (RTAA) of 1934 successfully allowed for greater international economic cooperation and Hull used the flexibility granted to the executive branch by Congress to renegotiate many of the highest rates in the Hawley-Smoot Tariff Act. The reciprocal treaties, along with Roosevelt's Good Neighbor Policy, improved relations with Latin America during the 1930s. The Renewal of the Trade Agreements Act in 1937 passed Congress by an impressive margin: 285–101 in the House and 58–24 in the Senate. Hull continued to serve as secretary of state until 1945, when he received the Nobel Peace Prize.

See also: Fordney-McCumber Tariff (Tariff of 1922); Hawley-Smoot Tariff (Tariff of 1930); London World Economic Conference; Mills Bill; Reciprocal Trade Agreements Act (RTAA); Underwood-Simmons Tariff (Tariff of 1913).

Selected Bibliography:

Michael A. Butler, *Cautious Visionary: Cordell Hull and Trade Reform, 1933–1937*, 1998; Harold B. Hinton, *Cordell Hull: A Biography*, 1942; Cordell Hull, *The Memoirs of Hull*, 1948.

Lisa L. Ossian

HUMAN RIGHTS

The focus on human rights shifted with the lowering of trade barriers.

In the twentieth century, human rights acquired near-universal appeal, despite frequent violations. At the same time, the process of globalization accelerated, calling into question the likelihood that the world would universally sustain human rights. Globalization afforded the possibility that new types of hierarchies and stratification might ensue, which could result in a diminution and not an expansion of human rights. The future, analysts suggested, promised no mere replication of the older division between the northern and southern halves of the globe, nor would it generally involve developed versus developing nations. Rather, a new configuration loomed in which heightened economic competition could lead to a reduction of labor rights, environmental regulations, and social services. During the 1990s, the chasms between wealthier and poorer countries deepened, with a major redistribution of resources taking place. Yet even in the more affluent lands, theorists increasingly propounded that social welfare policies precluded nations from competing on an even keel with less generous states. International financial institutions like the World Bank championed neoclassical liberal economics as the means to better the plight of people across the globe.

In the last decade of the twentieth century, social and political activists increasingly charged that globalization associated with developments like the North American Free Trade Agreement (NAFTA), the General Agreement on Tariffs and Trade (GATT), and the World Trade Organization (WTO) threatened human rights of the most elementary sort. These included labor protections, environmental regulations, and even civil liberties that seemed secondary considerations for the architects of trade policies. Inevitably, protests developed challenging trade policies; the most striking example in the United States occurred in Seattle in late 1999 as delegates to the WTO meeting gathered. Demonstrators protested,

with police arresting hundreds of people, and millions of dollars in property damage ensued. Officials aborted the opening ceremonies, while the trade talks themselves went nowhere. Protest groups had put forth the Global Sustainable Development Resolution, calling for international cooperation to prevent multinational corporations from violating human rights, democracy, and the environment. The resolution presumed the requirement of the worldwide regulation of great corporate entities, but envisioned such regulation furthering decentralized control.

See also: Environmental issues; General Agreement on Tariffs and Trade (GATT); Labor; North American Free Trade Agreement (NAFTA); Protests; World Trade Organization (WTO).

Selected Bibliography:

Tony Evans, ed., *Human Rights Fifty Years On: A Reappraisal*, 1998.

Thomas E. Woods Jr.

HUME, DAVID (April 26, 1711–August 25, 1776)

Philosopher of the Scottish Enlightenment who espoused the principles of free trade and who supported independence for the American colonies.

Born in Edinburgh, Hume defended free trade against mercantilist and protectionist arguments in his essays "Of the Balance of Trade" and "Of the Jealousy of Trade." An outspoken opponent of Britain's trade-related wars, Hume argued that free trade on its own yielded more prosperity than war.

Colonists in British North America

read and admired Hume's work *Political Discourses*, published in 1752. Benjamin Franklin praised "Of the Jealousy of Trade" as promoting "the Interest of Humanity," and hoped that it might serve to abate "the Jealousy that reigns here of the Commerce of the colonies, at least so far as such Abatement may be reasonable."

In 1768, Hume recommended independence for the American colonies, long before most Americans themselves had considered the possibility. Prominent Englishmen worried that if the American colonies broke free from the array of tariffs and regulations that England had imposed on their trade, the results would be devastating to the mother country. Hume, on the other hand, suggested that American independence would have an insignificant impact on British commerce. He wrote in 1775 that a "forced and every day more precarious Monopoly of about 6 or 700,000 Pounds a year of Manufactures, was not worth contending for" and "that we should preserve the greater part of this Trade even if the Ports of America were open to all Nations." Interacting with America on the basis of independence and free trade remained, in Hume's view, the only realistic and rational path for Britain to take. Hume died of cancer in Edinburgh on August 25, 1776.

See also: American Revolution; Franklin, Benjamin; Free trade.

Selected Bibliography:

Donald W. Livingston, *Philosophical Melancholy and Delirium: Hume's Pathology of Philosophy*, 1998.

Thomas E. Woods Jr.

I

IACOCCA, LIDO ANTHONY (LEE) (October 15, 1924–)

Automobile executive from Allentown, Pennsylvania.

In 1946, Iacocca began his association with the Ford Motor Company and eventually developed the Mustang model. He served as president of Ford from 1970 to 1978, when the automobile maker fired him. He then accepted a position as the president, CEO, and chair of the failing Chrysler Corporation in 1978. Through a series of layoffs, cutbacks, hard-selling advertising that included his personal "pitches," and a government loan guarantee, he restored the company to profitability.

Until the 1980s, automobile manufacturers displayed little interest in establishing protectionist tariffs on their products. In March 1981, the Reagan administration negotiated voluntary export restraints set at 1.68 million cars annually. For ideological reasons, the administration refused to go further.

As the years passed, the number of Japanese cars imported increased and, by 1984, their makers had built factories in the United States.

Iacocca started out as a free trader, but after his experience with Chrysler, he became the only vocal protectionist among the Big Three. By mid-1986, Iacocca had earned a reputation as a "Japan basher," calling for government protection or "fair trade." He stated that the Japanese used various techniques to introduce cars into the American economy. His attacks continued until early 1992, with little change in government policy. Iacocca retired from Chrysler in 1992.

See also: Automobile industry; Japan.

Selected Bibliography:

Lee Iacocca, with William Novak, *Iacocca: An Autobiography*, 1984; Doron P. Levin, *Behind the Wheel at Chrysler: The Iacocca Legacy*, 1995.

Russell M. Magnaghi

IMPERIALISM

A term that came into common use in the late nineteenth century to refer to a wide range of expansionary activities undertaken by nation-states, including the establishment and exploitation of colonies, the extension of informal economic and political hegemony over other countries or regions, and the conduct of foreign policy with these forms of expansion as a principal objective.

The invention of the term coincided with the race for colonies among the great powers between the 1870s and World War I, an event in which the United States played a significant, if secondary, role. Advocates of vigorous expansion and its opponents, as well as historians seeking to explain past empires in terms of contemporary concerns, employed the term in the United States as elsewhere. In the Marxist-Leninist vocabulary of the Cold War, "imperialism" meant the "highest stage of capitalism," making the United States an "imperialist" state.

A complicated relationship has existed between imperialism and tariffs in American history. As part of the "First British Empire" before the American Revolution, the colonies operated under a system of commercial regulations that included customs duties, but legislators and policymakers had not consistently worked out the role of tariffs within the system. In general, British customs duties applied to imports into Britain from the colonies, although Parliament frequently abated them in cases of particular products or in special circumstances. Colonies could not levy duties on exports or imports on their own accounts. In the economic thinking of Alexander Hamilton and

his followers in the early years of the Federal Republic, tariffs played a central role as a means of promoting development. Market expansion through the acquisition of additional territory complemented a protectionist tariff policy, although not necessarily as a primary aim. On the other hand, many expansionists, such as some of the southern "Warhawks" of 1812, did not favor a policy of protective tariffs. Indeed, throughout the nineteenth century, Americans whose views would eventually be called "imperialist" divided on the issue of tariffs in practically every period. Tariff issues did not play a major role in the events leading to the expansion of the United States in the Mexican War, although the annexation of the new areas required a re-examination of the tariff question.

During the last quarter of the nineteenth century, many Americans, paying close attention to the intense competition among the major European powers to obtain economic hegemony over world markets and global territorial empires to support it, came to the conclusion that the United States needed to embark on a similar course or risk the curtailment of its economic development. In particular, Americans feared that European industrial countries would deprive the United States of commercial access to parts of the world where its next external markets and investment areas lay. As in Europe, such thinking, connected to a large and inconsistent array of new intellectual constructs that portrayed the globe as a theater of conflict among peoples and races, accepted the notion that only the most vigorous and expansionary would survive. And, as in Europe, the fashion for such thinking created opportunities for special interest groups, parties, and politicians to seek support for their particular concerns by linking them to the ideology of the "New Imperialism." In this context, the United States, after 1890, commenced its relatively brief career as an aggressive colonial power, acquiring, among other territories, Hawaii, a share of Samoa, and its booty from the Spanish-American War of 1898: the Philippines, Guam, Puerto Rico, and temporarily Cuba. The war to maintain control of the Philippines after 1898 helped to undermine the appeal of formal colonialism for most Americans, but the idea that the U.S. government should actively support American interests, with force if necessary, in areas in which those interests remained dominant and in which local government appeared weak, unstable, unfriendly, or too closely aligned with some other power, remained a strong influence on policy for most of the twentieth century.

A complex relationship of tariffs to turn-of-the-century American imperialism existed. Advocates of a system of informal U.S. hegemony in the Western Hemisphere, such as James G. Blaine, suggested a modified version of a customs union whereby the American republics would lower or remove tariffs between each other and maintain substantial duties on extra-hemispheric imports. Insufficient support, even among proponents of aggressive U.S. imperialism, for taking the risks to particular industries that this proposal would entail existed in the United States or elsewhere. The idea of building a tariff policy specifically around an effort to create an informal American empire by setting a very high general rate and then systematically lowering the rates for cooperative "partners" similarly failed to overcome the fears of particular interest groups. Throughout the twentieth century, the United States frequently adjusted tariffs in a piecemeal fashion for areas under U.S. control or in which powerful interest groups, such as the sugar industry, had substantial investments.

See also: American Revolution; Blaine, James Gillespie; Capitalism; Cuba; Hamilton, Alexander; Hawaii; Latin America; Sugar; War of 1812; World War I.

Selected Bibliography:

David Healy, *U.S. Expansionism: The Imperialist Urge in the 1890s*, 1970; Walter LaFeber, *The New Empire: An Interpretation of American Expansion 1860–1898*, 1963.

Woodruff D. Smith

INDUSTRIAL REVOLUTION

The rapid development of manufacturing that began in the mid-eighteenth century as a result of the introduction of new or improved machinery and a shift toward methods of mass production.

In chronological terms, historians have divided this process into two periods: the first occurring in England between 1750 and 1850, and the second occurring in the United States, parts of continental Europe, and Japan from the 1870s to the 1920s. Perhaps the most important question concerning the emergence of industrial practices involves those factors that appear to have made England the first industrial power.

In Marxian terms, industrialization, like capitalism, requires four essential elements: land (including workshops and/or factories); labor (the existence of a landless population that is dependent on wage earning for survival); capital (including, in varying interpretations, investment of money or the infrastructure of production itself); and entrepreneurship (the insight and will necessary to bring together the other three factors of production in a systematic, productive fashion). Finally, to these elements one must add the role of a sympathetic state.

Traditional scholarship emphasizes the independent drive of the profit-seeking entrepreneur drawing on the money resources of a spendthrift, "savings-oriented" populace, predominantly rural, for borrowing or investment for various enterprises. More recent scholarship has revealed that state policy contributed significantly to industrialization. Laws helped create the environment in which various manufacturing sectors might flourish. Tariff barriers helped to protect Bastiat's "infant industries" from the cheaper products of foreign competitors and their imports. "Bounties" and tax incentives subsidized or reduced the cost of improvements in, or the introduction of, innovative machinery. And, finally, state action against skilled workers and proto-unions helped create a more "governable" and stable workforce for the new factories. Although Adam Smith frequently stressed the notion of laissez-faire and the powerful "invisible hand" of market forces present as neutral contributors to industrialization, a closer reading indicates that he favored protection and state subsidies, opposed intervention in the labor market on behalf of entrepreneurs and against the working classes, and understood all too well the role of state trade and monetary policies and their positive effects on the growth and stability of capital markets.

The role of the state in bridging the gap between the theory and application of the sciences remains important. In the words of Simon Kuznets, "The sustained growth of population and product was made possible by the increasing stock of tested knowledge." Further, he argues, "One might define modern economic growth as the spread of a system of production . . . based upon the increased application of science, that is, an organized system of tested knowledge."

Less than a century later, the United States, Germany, France, Japan, and Russia all benefited from their comparative backwardness vis-à-vis England by borrowing, as they had throughout the nineteenth century, the skill, technology, capital, and even entrepreneurial acumen to equal and quickly surpass the accomplishments of industrialized England. In the end, domestic policy and practice proved important, but not wholly sufficient, to industrialize. England became the leader by borrowing in various key sectors certain techniques, knowledge, and the machinery of industrialization itself—a practice followed by all later industrial powers. The transnational dissemination of knowledge that made the resulting phenomenon of mass production possible in the mid-eighteenth century or the late nineteenth century helped produce the Industrial Revolution.

See also: Germany; Great Britain; Japan; Smith, Adam.

Selected Bibliography:

Simon Smith Kuznets, *Economic Change: Selected Essays in Business Cycles, National Income, and Economic Growth*, 1953; Leonard N. Rosenband, *Papermaking in Eighteenth-Century France: Management, Labor, and Revolution at the Montgolfier Mill, 1761–1805*, 2000; Charles Wilson, *England's Apprenticeship, 1603–1763*, 1965.

David J. Weiland III

INFANT INDUSTRIES

America's first manufacturing enterprises.

Although most Americans engaged in farming during the colonial and early national periods, many "infant" or beginning industries also developed. People in New England found the rocky soil too poor for farming and turned instead to shipbuilding and rum distilleries to make their fortunes. The valuable fur trade along the Hudson River Valley made New York a center of the hat industry. Rich deposits of coal and iron ore on the eastern slopes of the Appalachian Mountains made ironworks a profitable business throughout the middle colonies and the upper South. Most farmers carried on the manufacture of wool cloth as an occupation during the winter months.

Manufacturers in England soon became concerned about the growing competition from infant industries in the colonies. In the seventy-five years before the American Revolution, Parliament passed a series of manufacturing acts to regulate these businesses. The Wool Act of 1699 banned the export of wool textiles from the colonies. The Hat Act of 1732 placed similar restrictions on hats. The Iron Act of 1750 allowed the colonies to produce pig and bar iron only. This last measure had the most direct effect on colonial industry since America produced nearly one-seventh of the world's iron by 1775.

British interference with colonial manufacturing contributed to the American Revolution. During the war, dramatic growth took place in industries related to the war effort, especially gun production. Small workshops throughout the colonies kept the Continental Army well supplied. Gun manufacturing continued as an important industry throughout the early history of the nation. Through the gun trade Eli Whitney developed the innovative use of interchangeable parts.

Despite the growth of these early industries, most American leaders believed that the United States would remain an agricultural nation. Only Alexander Hamilton, the first secretary of the treasury, advocated the development of America into a major industrial power. In his Report on Manufactures he described the many industries already thriving in the United States. These industries ranged from leather, iron, and lumber to carriage-making, rope and naval stores, and distilleries. Hamilton proposed the use of bounties, premiums, and protective tariffs to encourage industries already under way and to foster new ones.

While his foresight proved remarkable, Hamilton missed the one infant industry that would become the true beginning of modern American manufacturing. He argued that the production of cotton cloth would never gain importance in the United States. Contrary to this prediction, cotton manufacturing became the bridge between the infant industries of the early national period and the modern industries of the Civil War era and beyond. The Browns, a wealthy family of merchants, began the production of cotton thread in their factories in Rhode Island. Later, Francis Cabot Lowell and the Boston Associates set up factories throughout New England that manufactured cotton cloth. The methods employed by Lowell established the foundation of modern manufacturing throughout the nation.

See also: Cotton; Hamilton, Alexander; Iron; Report on Manufactures.

Selected Bibliography:

Thomas Cochran, 200 Years of American Business, 1977.

Mary Stockwell

INSULAR CASES

Series of U.S. Supreme Court cases that confirmed the right of the federal government to place tariffs on goods entering the United States from its territories.

The cases, first considered by the Court in 1900, dealt with the extent to which the Constitution and Bill of Rights applied to U.S. territories. The Court heard cases on whether the U.S. government could tax imports from territories gained in the Treaty of Paris that ended the Spanish-American War. In the first of the insular cases, *DeLima v. Bidwell* (1901), a slim 5–4 majority opinion written by Justice Henry B.

Brown, held that American tariff duties no longer applied to sugar imported from Puerto Rico. Brown relied on the Dingley Tariff Act of 1897, which taxed "all articles imported from foreign countries," in his decision. Brown also stated that Puerto Rico no longer fell under the classification of "foreign" when Spain ceded it to the United States in the treaty. But in *Dooley v. United States* (1901), the Court held that exports to Puerto Rico remained taxable under Congress's war powers since a military governor administered the territory.

In *Downes v. Bidwell* (1901), Brown struggled for a coherent standard, stating that while territories failed the "foreign" test, neither were they of "the United States." In a concurrence, Justice Edward D. White built on his dissent in *DeLima* and articulated the "incorporation doctrine." The doctrine answered the question "Does the constitution follow the flag?" White said that the more a territory became "incorporated" into the American political community, the greater the protection of constitutional guarantees for the territory's inhabitants. This approach, then accepted as precedent, influenced later cases such as *Hawaii v. Mankichi* (1903) and *Dorr v. U.S.* (1904), when a majority of the Court adopted White's incorporation doctrine. The Court reflected the national split between imperialists, who viewed expansionism as a part of the nation's manifest destiny and a valid action for a world power such as the United States, and anti-imperialists, who saw such action as hypocritical, establishing the same type of colonial hierarchy that the United States, as a sovereign nation, had intended to escape at its founding.

Overall, the justices sought to allow the greatest leeway for the elected branches to act in foreign affairs.

See also: Dingley Tariff (Tariff of 1897); Imperialism; Wilson-Gorman Tariff (Tariff of 1894).

Selected Bibliography:

Victor A. Canto, *The Determinants and Consequences of Trade Restrictions in the U.S. Economy,* 1986; James E. Kerr, *The Insular Cases: The Role of the Judiciary in American Expansionism,* 1982; Winfred Lee Thompson, *The Introduction of American Law in the Philippines and Puerto Rico 1898–1905,* 1989.

Carolyn E. Ginno and Artemus Ward

INSURGENTS

Opposed the direction of tariff reform proposed by President William Howard Taft during the debate over the Payne-Aldrich Tariff.

The rise of the Republican Insurgents, a group of midwestern Republicans led by Robert M. LaFollette, Albert B. Cummins, Jonathan Dolliver, and George Norris, called for the creation of a bipartisan commission to investigate cost of production for domestic and foreign manufacturers and report their findings to the president, who would be authorized to suspend tariff duties if the commission identified the existence of monopolistic pricing. Designed to protect proprietary producers and American consumers, Taft rejected the idea of a tariff commission and favored instead the moderate reduction of tariff rates only. In December 1908, as Congress debated the Payne-Aldrich Tariff, the alternative views created a split among Republicans. While Taft, speaking in Winona, Minnesota, characterized the new tariff act as the best bill ever passed by the Republicans, Insurgents continued to criticize the measure. Throughout the duration of the Taft administration, the Insurgents voted against the president on other pieces of legislation and during the election of 1912, they campaigned against Taft. After Wilson won the election, the Insurgents continued to impact society by shifting their energies to such issues as social reform and a new toleration of labor. The tariff revision debate had created a force that continued to impact the development of the United States for the next twenty years.

See also: Cummins, Albert Baird; Dolliver, Jonathan; LaFollette, Robert Marion; Payne-Aldrich Tariff (Tariff of 1909); Taft, William Howard; Tariff Commission.

Selected Bibliography:

Paul Wolman, *Most Favored Nation: The Republican Revisionists and U.S. Tariff Policy, 1897–1912,* 1992.

Cynthia Clark Northrup

INTERNATIONAL CHAMBER OF COMMERCE (ICC)

International organization of business executives founded in 1919 to promote an open international trade system.

Founded at the end of World War I in 1919, the International Chamber of Commerce (ICC) functions under a federal structure with the World Council that represents all members like a general assembly. The council elects a president and vice president for two-year terms. The president nominates a secretary general, whom the council approves. The secretary general works with the various commissions in which the majority of the policymaking decisions occur.

With members from over 130 countries, the ICC addresses the concerns of the business community, coordinates efforts, and supplies information to government agencies around the world. The promotion of free trade remains of particular importance to organization members. Although policies formulated by the ICC have no binding authority on its members, the rules govern thousands of business transactions daily. The ICC's Court of Arbitration settles disputes between its members. In addition to establishing trade policies, the ICC also provides information on financial services, information technologies, telecommunications, marketing techniques and ethics, the environment, transportation, competition law, and intellectual property.

See also: Aldrich, Winthrop; World War I.

Selected Bibliography:

George L. Ridgeway, *Merchants of Peace: The History of the International Chamber of Commerce*, 1959.

Cynthia Clark Northrup

INTERNATIONAL FREE TRADE ALLIANCE

Organization founded in 1872 by Abraham L. Earle that advocated the complete elimination of all tariff duties.

In the post–Civil War period, Congress resisted efforts to reduce the high tariff rates imposed by the Morrill Tariff as an emergency wartime financing measure. By the 1870s, political activists like Edward Atkinson, David A. Wells, and Horace Greeley initiated a tariff reform movement that pushed for a gradual reduction of the tariff over a period of several years. Americans who believed in free trade formed alliances such as the International Free Trade Alliance. Founded in New York City by a government worker, the organization refused to associate with the tariff reformers, calling instead for the immediate abolition of all tariffs. Protectionists successfully depicted these free traders as reactionaries who threatened the security and prosperity of the country. The International Free Trade Alliance existed for a short three-year period before internal disagreements resulted in its dissolution. Other free trade organizations formed after 1875, but most of them ended as quickly as the International Free Trade Alliance. These groups did succeed in promoting the concept of free trade, an idea that politicians would implement after World War II.

See also: Atkinson, Edward; Free trade; Greeley, Horace; Morrill Tariff (Tariff of 1861); Wells, David Ames.

Selected Bibliography:

Joanne Reitano, *The Tariff Question in the Gilded Age: The Great Debate of 1888*, 1994.

Cynthia Clark Northrup

INTERNATIONAL HARVESTER

Major American manufacturer of heavy farm machinery.

Founded by Cyrus P. McCormick, who patented his reaper in 1834, the first McCormick factory opened in Chicago in 1847. Following destruction of the plant in the Great Chicago Fire of 1871, the family rebuilt the McCormick Harvesting Machine Company and, in 1902, merged with four other harvester manufacturers to become International Harvester.

McCormick first introduced his equipment into the Russian market during the 1850s, when the country invested in agricultural technology that would make it a competitive exporter of food products to other European nations. International Harvester failed to compete successfully for sales in Russia until after the depression of 1893. By 1898, sales in Russia accounted for 18 percent of the company's overall foreign sales. In that year, the Russian government abolished tariffs on foreign farm machinery, boosting sales 15 percent in 1899 and 91 percent in 1900. By 1901, the Russian market accounted for 30 percent of all sales outside North America. Agrarian lobbyists had put pressure on the Russian government to enact the tariff exemption and International Harvester made it work to its advantage.

In 1903, the tariff exemption expired and company officials feared a reduction in Russian sales. The Russian government responded with a promise of tariff exemption if International Harvester established a Russian factory. A company legal advisor, Roberts Walker, warned that Russian workers in his estimation, although lazy and only half as productive as American workers, worked for half the wages. The American market had become saturated, prompting International Harvester to take advantage of the new offer of tariff exemption and begin manufacturing in Russia.

See also: McCormick, Cyrus.

Selected Bibliography:

Fred V. Carstensen, *American Enterprise in Foreign Markets: Studies of Singer and International Harvester in Imperial Russia*, 1984.

Kathleen A. Tobin

INTERNATIONAL MONETARY FUND (IMF)

Key institution in the post–World War II Bretton Woods System charged with preserving relatively free trade.

Nearing the conclusion of World War II, the United Nations held its Monetary and Financial Conference at Bretton Woods, New Hampshire, in 1944 to find a solution to the dilemma of rebuilding a devastated Europe. One of the results of this conference, the International Monetary Fund (IMF), emerged as a key institution in the international monetary system and has remained so in the present day. The IMF's mission gradually evolved into three broad policy goals: to generate exchange-rate stability, to reconcile a nation's macroeconomic policy with its international balance of payments, and to preserve relative free trade and payments in the world economy. The IMF planned to meet the latter goal by providing short-term loans with three to five years' maturities to countries with temporary balance of payments deficits. Such loans should help reduce the likelihood that a country would impose tariffs or other restrictions on international trade to meet its balance of payments. The IMF embodies the ideals of economic liberalism, striving for economic stability and development through trade that flows with minimal national barriers.

See also: Bretton Woods Conference.

Selected Bibliography:

Richard Stubbs and Geoffrey R.D. Underhill, eds., *Political Economy and the Changing Global Order*, 1994.

Josh Pratt

INTERNATIONAL TRADE COMMISSION (ITC)

Successor organization to the Tariff Commission that took the new name in 1975 to recognize that the old Tariff Commission had been doing more than just tariff work.

The Tariff Commission had also conducted import/export studies and examined general world trade issues. The establishment of the International Trade Commission (ITC), along with a budget independent of the Office of Management and Budget, helped to increase the distance between the commission and the White House. Congress established the ITC with an annual authorization and annual appropriation. As originally constituted, no more than three of the six commissioners could belong to any one party. A 1974 law changed the term from six to nine years and limited the members to one term. Under the rotating chairmanship, the person in his or her last eighteen months became chairperson and the next closest to thirty-six

months became vice chair. Currently, the commissioners serve overlapping terms of nine years each, with a new term beginning every eighteen months. The president selects the chairperson and vice chairperson from different parties for two-year terms.

The commission gave up control over adjustments on behalf of individuals or firms, but retained responsibility for rulings on the escape clause as applied to entire industries. The guiding law of 1974 said that the negative impact might occur as a result of something other than the trade agreement. The commission determines the appropriateness of relief and the president decides what relief to apply. Congress can force the president to apply relief. The commission received limited powers to act unilaterally and consider the general welfare instead of the specific industry, but also has the obligation to observe proper administrative procedures, including open meetings. The ITC also fulfills investigative and housekeeping duties, including the rationalization and standardization of tariff schedules, and has responsibility for defending against anti-dumping and unfair trade practices, including intellectual property such as copyright and patent infringement.

A staff of 365 analysts, investigators, economists, and experts in specific industries support the ITC.

See also: Tariff Commission.

Selected Bibliography:

John M. Dobson, *Two Centuries of Tariffs*, 1976; Judith Goldstein, *Ideas, Interests, and American Trade Policy*, 1993.

John Herschel Barnhill

INTERNATIONAL TRADE ORGANIZATION (ITO)

Unsuccessful attempt to create a comprehensive code of rules for international trade and to translate into practice the commitment to free trade and economic cooperation spelled out in the 1941 Atlantic Charter.

Businessman Philip Cortney, a staunch advocate of pure free trade, led the opposition that resulted in the defeat of the International Trade Organization (ITO). He warned in his influential book *The Economic Munich*, published in 1949, of the needless ITO bureaucracy and implied that an authentic regime of free trade did not require international agencies. Wilhelm Röpke, an accomplished and well-known free-market economist, strenuously opposed the ITO for this very reason.

William Diebold Jr., a State Department official and an economist for the Council on Foreign Relations in the 1940s, observed that while he expected the opposition of protectionists, the power and influence of people he called "perfectionists" burst unexpectedly on the American political scene. According to Cortney and his allies, the ITO charter, among other things, seemed to commit the United States to a Keynesian-style "full employment" policy, replete with the economic planning and controls that were anathema to conservatives. Moreover, they believed that the proposed ITO, so full of exceptions and escape clauses, would produce a negligible or even positively illiberal effect on international trade.

Of course, protectionist arguments against the ITO also appeared, originating from a variety of protected industries. Some protectionists used other arguments as well as pointing, for instance, to the American Bar Association's warnings regarding the unconstitutionality of delegating such considerable authority to a supranational institution.

The successful opposition defeated the ITO. In December 1950, President Harry S Truman withdrew the charter from Congress, and the following year Dean Acheson testified that the president should not resubmit the charter. With the United States no longer behind the ITO, other countries lost interest as well.

The World Trade Organization (WTO), worked out in the 1990s, proceeded according to the ITO model and so did the criticism. Protectionists opposed it, but the perfectionists reappeared as well, with such free-market organizations as the Competitive Enterprise Institute and the Ludwig von Mises Institute explicitly comparing the WTO to the ITO and warning conservatives and libertarians that the organization would move toward regulation and government planning and not freer trade.

See also: Keynes, John Maynard; Truman, Harry S; World Trade Organization (WTO).

Selected Bibliography:

Susan Ariel Aaronson, *Trade and the American Dream: A Social History of Postwar Trade Policy*, 1996.

Thomas E. Woods Jr.

IRON

The most used of metals; malleable, rusts in moist air, and occurs combined in most igneous rocks.

During the colonial era, miners exploited deposits in Virginia and Massachusetts. In the early nineteenth century, Americans discovered iron in Alabama, Missouri, in Michigan's Upper Peninsula, and finally on the Mesabi Range and neighboring ranges in Minnesota. These latter developments became the major sources of American iron ore and fueled American industrialization prior to 1900. Americans used iron, processed as pig iron, for pots, kettles, and fireback. With repeated heating and hammering, pig iron turned into wrought iron, which had more varied uses.

The Iron Act of 1750 forbade the construction of mills in the colonies, but allowed the shipment of pig iron to England. Pennsylvania became a major producer of iron and passed a protective tariff to foster its nascent iron industry. In 1789, the first tariff passed under the Constitution included iron products and that of 1816 favored pig iron, along with hammered and rolled bars.

Although prior to 1776 the United States produced 15 percent of the world's output, it lagged technologically behind Europe. By the 1850s, Americans imported large quantities of iron for industrial purposes. Few efforts to place high protective tariffs on iron occurred until after 1870, when steel dominated the market.

The question of imported iron and steel remains a major problem. The dumping of iron ore and semifinished steel imports poses a potential national security threat to the United States. In 2001, the Commerce Department began investigating the ramification of this policy and congressmen from Michigan and Minnesota sought remedies.

See also: Industrial Revolution; Navigation and Trade Acts.

Selected Bibliography:

Robert B. Gordon, *American Iron, 1607–1900*, 1996; Stewart H. Holbrook, *Iron Brew: A Century of American Ore and Steel*, 1939.

Russell M. Magnaghi

ISOLATIONISM

A reaction against the internationalism of the Progressive era, isolationism gained momentum in the United States during the years between the two world wars from 1919 to 1941.

Based on American exceptionalism and disillusionment with American involvement in World War I, isolationism's proponents expressed strong aversion to assuming American responsibilities abroad, including joining military and political alliances, taking on foreign economic commitments, signing international agreements, and becoming entangled with the affairs of other countries. Isolationists preferred that America devote itself to its own concerns. They often called for using every possible means, including implementing high protective tariffs, to ensure U.S. self-interests and neutrality.

See also: Progressives; Protectionism.

Selected Bibliography:

Walter LaFeber, *The New Empire: An Interpretation of American Expansion 1860–1898*, 1963.

Guoqiang Zheng

J

JACKSON, ANDREW (March 15, 1767–June 8, 1845)

Seventh president of the United States; in office during the Nullification Crisis of 1832 and 1833.

Born in Waxhaw Settlement in the Carolinas on March 15, 1767, Jackson, a hero of the War of 1812, briefly served the state of Tennessee both in the House of Representatives and the Senate. After losing the presidential election of 1824 to John Quincy Adams, he ran again and won in 1828.

Before Jackson took office, Adams signed the Tariff Act of 1828 into law. The tariff, also known as the Tariff of Abominations, placed high protectionist duties on imports. The Tariff Act of 1832, passed four years later, dropped some duties, but still aroused the frustration of southerners, including Jackson's vice president, John C. Calhoun, and Calhoun's home state of South Carolina. In protest, South Carolina issued a Nullification Ordinance, stating that, as of February 1, 1833, the state would no longer collect the tariff.

Jackson favored lower tariffs prior to the crisis because he viewed tariff revenue chiefly as a means to lower the debt. With the debt eliminated, he believed Congress should reduce the tariff to avoid a surplus. When the crisis with South Carolina first began, he supported Gulian C. Verplanck in his suggestion to cut duties in half, but the Verplanck Tariff, doomed to failure by late January, never passed.

As time went on, Jackson became angered by South Carolina's attitude and by the behavior of Calhoun. In his Nullification Proclamation, released in January 1833, the president declared that states had no right to infringe on the federal government in this way. Not long after his proclamation, Jackson asked for a Force Bill authorizing him to use the military to enforce the tariff in South Carolina.

At the same time, Senator Henry Clay put forward his compromise tariff, which quickly supplanted the Verplanck Bill. Jackson paid little attention, being more interested in his Force Bill than Clay's efforts. He believed that force, not compromise, would defeat nullification. Both bills passed through Congress and then were forwarded to the president for signature into law. Willingly, he signed both, but gave away his preferences by signing the Force Act first.

Jackson died at the Hermitage, his home in Nashville, Tennessee, on June 8, 1845.

See also: Calhoun, John Caldwell; Clay, Henry; Clay's Compromise; Force Act; Nullification; Tariff of 1828 (Tariff of Abominations); Tariff of 1832.

Selected Bibliography:

Donald B. Cole, *The Presidency of Andrew Jackson*, 1993; Robert V. Remini, *The Life of Andrew Jackson*, 1988.

Adrienne Caughfield

JACKSONIANISM

Under the direction of Andrew Jackson and Martin Van Buren, the newly established Democratic Party ushered in a dramatic shift in American political history.

Jacksonianism witnessed a coalition of southern and western agriculturalists with northern Republicans. Blending states' rights with nationalism, Democrats forged an effective party dedicated to reforming the country.

From 1820 to 1840, immigration in eastern states swelled the population from 7.2 million to 10.7 million as western states jumped from 2.2 million to 6.4 million. The era produced marked gains for the common man, who identified with Jackson's backcountry origin. As president, "Old Hickory" espoused democratic principles and displayed a serious commitment to those values. Jacksonians maintained that they could fulfill the promise of the nation only as a majority. They also promised the people access to the government. To this end, Jackson concluded that the president represents all the citizens in the country and must protect their interests. As president, Jackson used the veto more than all his predecessors to protect the people. His conception of the executive office changed the notion of the presidency, giving it significantly greater power.

Jackson also made strategic use of patronage. In an effort to reform government, Jackson removed about 10 percent of federal employees. His critics decried his use of the "spoils system," but Jackson maintained that offices exist to serve the people and individuals sympathetic to the will of the majority should fill them.

Jacksonians also sought to impact the economy. In the most bitterly fought political contest of the period, Jackson eliminated the Bank of the United States, arguing that it created a special privilege for wealthy Americans at the expense of the common man. For similar reasons, Jackson also instituted a hard currency policy and thwarted government-sponsored internal improvement initiatives. His strict economic policies resulted in a balanced budget for the first time in American history. Jacksonians also sought to provide cheap land for westerners and provide them with relief from creditors. These efforts culminated in mixed results. While Jackson reveled in a balanced budget and the destruction of the Bank of the United States, his hard currency policies and the inadequacy of state banks fostered economic crisis, eventually resulting in the Panic of 1837.

In foreign affairs, Jacksonians pursued a more conciliatory course. By lowering tariffs, Jackson earned widespread support from southern planters. These wealthy Democrats remained in the party even after Jackson's strong nationalist stance in thwarting Calhoun's doctrine of nullification. Lower tariffs also spurred England to reopen West Indies ports to American commerce. Diminished tariff revenues, however, ultimately hampered response to the Panic of 1837.

Jacksonianism, like Andrew Jackson, dominated the era, enjoying widespread support from the American public. Not all citizens benefited, but the spirit of the age, nonetheless, influenced the Populist and Progressive initiatives of the twentieth century.

See also: Jackson, Andrew; Nullification; Van Buren, Martin. **Vol. II**: Henry Clay's 1832 Speech in Favor of the American System; South Carolina Ordinance of Nullification; Proclamation to the People of South Carolina; Andrew Jackson's Message to Congress on the Nullification Crisis; Force Act. **Vol. III**: Tariff of 1828 (Tariff of Abominations); Tariff of 1832; Tariff of 1833 (Compromise Tariff).

Selected Bibliography:

Robert Remini, *Andrew Jackson and the Course of American Empire*, 1977.

Dallas Cothrum

JAPAN

One of the world's largest economic powers, Japan has a population of approximately 120 million and a territory that consists of four main islands—Hokkaido, Honshu, Sikoku, and Kyushu—and a series of lesser islands stretching along the eastern edge of mainland East Asia. Japan's nearest mainland neighbor includes Russia to the north, South Korea to the west across the Korea Strait, China further to the west, and Taiwan to the southwest.

Beginning with the Meiji Restoration of 1868, Japan became the first nation in Asia to embark on the road of developing modern industrial economy. Yet, with a surplus population and a crisis of cultural priorities forced by rapid modernization, plus lack of natural resources for growing industrialism, Japan adopted militaristic expansionism in East and Southeast Asia. For the purpose of establishing a colonial empire, Japan went to war with Russia in 1905 and pursued a policy of military occupation in China from 1931 to 1945. Driven by its dream for a "Greater East Asia Co-Prosperity Sphere," Japan allied with Nazi Germany and Fascist Italy during World War II and started the Pacific War in 1941.

After its crushing defeat and unconditional surrender in August 1945, Japan fell under American occupation until 1951 and experienced essentially democratic reforms under General Douglas MacArthur, Supreme Commander Allied Powers (SCAP), which in part laid the foundation for Japan's later recovery and resurgence. Allied with the United States during the Cold War, Japan pursued a foreign policy of international neutralism and sought rapid economic development. The economic surge of the 1960s advanced Japan to the third greatest industrial nation in the world, with an average real growth of thirteen percent a year. By 1972, Japan's GNP reached $290 billion. By the early 1980s, Japan became the second largest economic power, ranking only behind the United States. Trade remains central to the Japanese economy. Short of needed natural resources to support its industrial economy, Japan has pursued an aggressive export trade policy, but protected its domestic market with relatively high tariffs and restricted nontariff barriers for many products. As a result, Japan achieved favorable balance of trade with many countries and harvested dramatic trade surpluses, especially with the United States, its largest trade partner. Japan's "unfair trade practices" have strained U.S.–Japanese economic relations. To reduce trade deficit and economic tension with Japan, Washington has mounted constant pressure on Japan to open their markets, set guarantee-oriented trade, and increase the appreciation of the yen, the Japanese currency.

See also: Protectionism; Trade deficits; World War II.

Selected Bibliography:

Andrew Boltho, *The Japanese Economy*, 2000; Lonny E. Charlice and Mark Tilton, *Is Japan Really Changing Its Ways?*, 2000

Guoqiang Zheng

JEFFERSON, THOMAS (April 13, 1743–July 4, 1826)

Third president of the United States and founder of the Democratic-Republican Party; his primary platform included opposition to the Hamiltonian plan for protective tariffs.

Born on Shadwell plantation in what is now Abermarle County, Virginia, Thomas Jefferson's early education included studying the classics in their original languages under private tutors. In 1760, he entered the College of William and Mary and pursued a liberal arts education, finishing in two years and reportedly studying fifteen hours each day. After a five-year apprenticeship, Jefferson gained admission to the Virginia bar in 1767. From 1769 to 1774, he represented his home county of Abermarle in the Virginia House of Burgesses and politically aligned himself with those men who opposed British colonial administration policies.

Jefferson eagerly attended the first Continental Congress, where leaders charged him with the task of writing the Declaration of Independence in 1776. In his draft of that document, Jefferson outlined the American colonists' complaints concerning England's restrictions against trade. Jefferson condemned the British Crown for cutting off American trade to all parts of the world and for imposing taxes without the people's consent. He argued that Britain's mercantilist policies had violated the colonists' rights as loyal British subjects. Britons, living in England, did not sustain the same limitations of trade as their American cousins.

Like most of his fellow Americans,

Jefferson believed a nation founded on republican principles required a free trade system to develop and maintain a healthy economy. Free trade, in the eighteenth century, offered participation in foreign trade without discriminating tariffs or other prohibitive practices. British mercantilist policies reserved important American resources for England and controlled the importation of foreign goods. Jefferson and others believed that the concept of republicanism included the idea that America must remain an agricultural society until the new republic became well established. They absorbed into their theories the significance of foreign markets and free trade to American agriculture. The seemingly unlimited potential for agricultural expansion in North America, Jefferson contended, would require the opening of abundant foreign markets in which to sell surplus products. In the spirit of this expectation, Americans opened their ports to world trade after declaring independence from Great Britain in 1776.

Jefferson threw himself into the political scene of the new nation, serving first as a member of the Virginia House of Delegates from 1776 to 1779 and then as governor from 1779 to 1781. In 1783, he represented Virginia for two years in the Continental Congress. He then became U.S. minister to France, a position he held until 1789 when he returned to the United States to accept President George Washington's cabinet appointment as secretary of state.

The issue of free trade and tariff rates became part of the growing conflict in the 1790s between Jefferson and Secretary of the Treasury Alexander Hamilton. Jefferson, the committed republican agrarian, protested Hamilton's plan to encourage immediate advancement of American manufacturing through discriminatory trade policies. Jefferson believed that Hamilton's plan would favor England over France and northern manufacturers over western and southern agrarians. Protective tariffs would benefit northern commerce and thus threaten the longevity of an agrarian economy essential to the republican experiment.

In 1793, Jefferson prepared a report for Congress on "The Privileges and Restrictions on the Commerce of the United States in Foreign Countries." The report presented the facts of America's disadvantages in foreign ports. Jefferson also sought to answer how the United States could best remove, modify, or counteract the restrictions on their commerce and navigation. The ideal, Jefferson suggested, would be freedom from all shackles everywhere. He argued that every country should produce that which nature had best fitted it to produce, and freedom to exchange with others mutual surpluses for mutual wants. For those countries refusing to relinquish prohibitive duties and other restrictive policies, Jefferson recommended economic warfare. America's free commerce and navigation, Jefferson argued, should not be given in exchange for restrictions, but rather counter prohibitions and limitations.

When Washington retired after two terms as president, Jefferson chose to seek the nation's highest office representing his republican ideals and leading the new Federalist opposition party, the Democratic-Republicans, against John Adams. Coming in second to Adams in the 1796 election, Jefferson became the vice president. Bored with the lack of responsibility in his post, he compiled *A Manual of Parliamentary Practice*, which the U.S. Senate still uses today. In 1800, he again ran for the presidency and this time defeated John Adams to become the only vice president to win two full terms as president.

As the third executive leader of the United States, Jefferson acquired much of the trans-Mississippi west in the Louisiana Purchase of 1803. He then authorized the famed Lewis and Clark expedition, which explored the newly obtained territory. In 1807, he signed the law that would, effective January 1, 1808, prohibit the importation of slaves into the United States. Yet throughout his presidency the issue of free trade loomed large.

In 1806, Jefferson found it necessary to employ economic warfare. The renewal of the Napoleonic wars, a great battle for supremacy between England and France, presented the United States with trade and navigation difficulties. In 1806, Britain threw up a blockade of the European continent, preventing American ships from trading with any European country. Jefferson retaliated with the Non-Importation Act, closing United States ports to certain British goods. The act failed to induce better treatment for American ships in foreign ports. The president again relied on economic warfare when he passed the Embargo Act of 1807, which stopped all trade between the United States and Europe. Jefferson believed that being deprived of American resources would lead Britain and France to stop harassment of U.S. ships. A similar action had been successful during the Revolution but

U.S. goods were not as crucial to European nations as they had been then. The embargo hurt the South and the West as well as New England and failed to restore free trade with Europe.

Jefferson retired to his Monticello plantation in Virginia after the inauguration of his Republican protégé, James Madison. Retirement did not preclude him from accomplishing great things. When the British destroyed his beloved national library during the War of 1812, Jefferson, in serious debt, sold his personal and voluminous library to the government. His collection formed the bulk of the newly restored Library of Congress. He also founded the University of Virginia and acted as the principal architect of several of its buildings. Serving as the first rector of the university, he also handpicked its faculty.

Thomas Jefferson died from complications of an enlarged prostate at 12:50 P.M. on July 4, 1826, the fiftieth anniversary of Independence. Jefferson had designed his own tomb and wrote the inscription under which his body rests. It reads simply: "Here was buried Thomas Jefferson, Author of the Declaration of Independence, of the Statute of Virginia for Religious Freedom, and Father of the University of Virginia." An agrarian republican and states' rightist to the end, at his behest his tomb bears no mention of his two terms as president.

See also: Adams, John; American Revolution; Colonial administration; eralists; Hamilton, Alexander; Jeffersonianism; Madison, James; Navigation and Trade Acts; War of 1812; Washington, George.

Selected Bibliography:

Dumas Malone, *Jefferson and His Time*, 1948–1981; Norman K. Risjord, *Thomas Jefferson*, 1994; Garrett Ward Sheldon, *The Political Philosophy of Thomas Jefferson*, 1991.

Carol Terry and Elaine C. Prange Turney

JEFFERSONIANISM

Federalists' opposition policies that dominated the politics of the early republic from 1800 to 1824 and struggled over the constitutional issues of a protective tariff.

Proponents of a southern way of life articulated by Thomas Jefferson and his ideological heirs James Madison and James Monroe, Jeffersonians advocated limited government involvement in the economy. At heart, they sought to protect the institution of slavery and correctly understood that only the central government could challenge the South's "peculiar institution." Jeffersonians believed that by limiting the powers of the national government, it could not assume vast powers and thus overawe the states and their domestic institutions. Because the Constitution said nothing about a tariff, Jeffersonians insisted Congress could not levy duties on imports.

The Jeffersonians formed as an opposition party to Alexander Hamilton and the Federalist Party in the early 1790s. Federalists, constituting the major commercial and financial elements in the Northeast, championed a vigorous national government as the best way to enhance economic opportunity. The economy of the North, rapidly transformed from a commercial orientation to one favoring industry, required a protective tariff to enhance the marketability of its goods. In simple terms, the economies of the North and South headed in different directions and the development of a dynamic industrial-capital economy in the North threatened the slave-based agricultural society of the South. The struggle between Jeffersonians and Hamiltonians culminated in the election of 1800 in which Jefferson defeated the Federalist candidate, John Adams, for the presidency. Circumstances, however, did not allow the Jeffersonians to follow a pure constitutional course on the tariff issue. The nation did not so much win as survive the War of 1812. In 1816, a Jeffersonian Congress acknowledged the need for an American industrial base and passed a tariff to bring this about.

See also: Adams, John; Federalists; Hamilton, Alexander; Jefferson, Thomas; Madison, James; Monroe, James; Slavery; War of 1812.

Selected Bibliography:

Drew McCoy, *The Elusive Republic: Political Economy in Jeffersonian America*, 1980.

David S. Brown

K

KASSON TREATIES

Attempt to reduce the high tariff rates of the Dingley Tariff by concluding a series of reciprocity treaties.

In 1898, the Kasson Committee, headed by John A. Kasson who had served as the envoy extraordinary and minister plenipotentiary to Austria-Hungary from 1877 to 1881 and Germany from 1884 to 1885, negotiated a series of trade agreements. Under Section 3 of the Dingley Tariff, Congress authorized the president to negotiate reciprocity agreements on specific items such as argol, champagnes, and paintings, while Section 4 provided for a two-year period during which the president could reduce duties by as much as 20 percent or place items on the free list. President William McKinley, who advocated the use of reciprocity agreements, instructed the Kasson Committee to reduce specific tariff rates with countries that maintained a high rate on American goods. Perceived as a bargaining tool that would

reduce duties on noncompeting items, negotiators quickly learned that Europe refused to consider such restrictions. The National Association of Manufacturers (NAM) initially supported the treaties, marking the first time a business association encouraged the reduction of tariff rates in the post–Civil War period. NAM leaders such as Theodore Search and James Deering persuaded members to accept and work for the passage of the Kasson treaties as a means of increasing American exports to countries around the world. Kasson concluded agreements with France, Portugal, Germany, Italy, Switzerland, Spain, Bulgaria, Great Britain, and the Netherlands that reduced the rates of foreign countries on American products by an average of 25 percent while only reducing import tariffs by an average of 8 percent. The treaties reached the Senate in 1901. Before a vote on ratification occurred, the business community expressed concern that the agreements benefited large exporters while harming the average businessman. The disagreement over the treaties publicized during the National Reciprocity Convention, coupled with McKinley's death, doomed the Kasson treaties, which never made it out of the Senate Foreign Relations Committee for a vote before the entire Senate.

See also: Dingley Tariff (Tariff of 1897); McKinley, William; National Association of Manufacturers (NAM); Senate Finance Committee.

Selected Bibliography:

Alfred E. Eckes, *Opening America's Market: U.S. Foreign Trade Policy Since 1776*, 1995; Paul Wolman, *Most Favored Nation: The Republican Revisionists and U.S. Tariff Policy, 1897–1912*, 1992.

Cynthia Clark Northrup

KENNEDY, JOHN F. (May 29, 1917–November 22, 1963)

Thirty-fifth president of the United States.

Born into a prominent family in the Boston suburb of Brookline, Massachusetts, Kennedy attended Harvard University and graduated with honors in 1940. During World War II, he served aboard a PT boat in the South Pacific. He received the Navy and Marine Corps medal for saving his crew after a Japanese destroyer sank his boat. Kennedy began his political career once the war ended. A member of the Democratic Party, he entered Congress as a representative from Massachusetts in 1947. In 1952, he ran for the Senate and won. As a senator, Kennedy sponsored bills that supported New England industry, notably fishing and textiles. In 1960, Kennedy ran for the presidency and, in a close election, defeated the Republican candidate, Richard M. Nixon.

As president, Kennedy began his New Frontier program. The Kennedy administration created the Peace Corps and decreased American military reliance on nuclear weapons by bolstering the conventional military. Civil rights became the dominant domestic issue during the Kennedy administration, and the president urged Congress to pass laws against segregation. In foreign affairs, Kennedy ordered the disastrous Bay of Pigs Invasion of Cuba, and after discovering Soviet nuclear weapons on the island, he blockaded Cuba, thereby precipitating the Cuban Missile Crisis in October 1962. Despite tense relations with the Soviets, the Kennedy administration managed to sign a nuclear test ban treaty with the communists in July 1963.

In terms of trade, Kennedy established the Alliance for Progress in 1961 to aid Latin American nations, but concern with the European Common Market dominated Kennedy's trade policies. During the Dillon Round of General Agreement on Tariffs and Trade (GATT) negotiations in 1961, the Kennedy administration managed to accomplish little because of restraints placed on the executive's ability to negotiate tariffs during the Eisenhower presidency. As a result, American agricultural goods failed to gain significant access to the European Economic Community (EEC). After the Dillon Round, Kennedy pressured Congress into passing the Trade Expansion Act of 1962 to increase the negotiating power of the president. The act ended the cumbersome requirement that forced the executive office to negotiate tariffs on an item-by-item basis and instead allowed broad deals on many items at once. It also allowed the president to alter tariffs by as much as 50 percent rather than the previous 15 percent.

Kennedy planned to continue the trend of lowering tariffs, but to secure the passage of the Trade Expansion Act, he allowed protective tariffs for cotton textiles. Kennedy also created the office of Special Representative for Trade Negotiations (STR) to assure passage of the act. With the creation of the new office to conduct all of America's tariff negotiations, the State Department lost that power. This step appeased members of Congress who feared the State Department held too much power. The Trade Expansion Act revitalized America's tariff negotiations, and its success became apparent in GATT's Kennedy Round. Unfortunately, an assassin's bullet killed Kennedy in Dallas, Texas, before the negotiations began.

See also: General Agreement on Tariffs and Trade (GATT); Kennedy Round; Trade Expansion Act of 1962. **Vol. II**: The General Agreement on Tariffs and Trade; Alliance for Progress.

Selected Bibliography:

Irving Bernstein, *Promises Kept: John F. Kennedy's New Frontier*, 1991; David Burner, *John F. Kennedy and a New Generation*, 1988.

John K. Franklin

KENNEDY ROUND

One of two major rounds of negotiations to reduce trade barriers under the General Agreement on Tariffs and Trade (GATT).

Held in Geneva, Switzerland, from May 1964 to June 1967, the Kennedy Round continued the process of lowering tariff and trade barriers begun under GATT in 1947. The round addressed several problems, including the reduction of duties by up to 50 percent on most products instead of negotiating different rates for all items, covering agricultural commodities as well as industrial products, discussion of additional trade barriers other than duty rates, and the future of negotiations with less-developed countries. After three years of bargaining, negotiators agreed to a 35 percent reduction on industrial goods over a five-year period. The reduction did not apply to the steel or textiles industries. The United States reduced its tariff rate on chemicals by 50 percent while Great Britain and other European countries lowered the rate by 24 percent to compensate for the American Selling Price, a method of appraising duties based on the market price in the United States. The average rate on agricultural products decreased between 15 and 18 percent. Other important agreements reached included the acceptance of a uniform anti-dumping code and an understanding that developed nations would not negotiate reciprocity agreements with less-developed nations since reciprocal trade always benefits the industrialized country. During the five-year period of implementation following the passage of the agreement, the U.S. trade surplus gradually decreased, and since 1972 the United States has experienced a trade deficit.

See also: General Agreement on Tariffs and Trade (GATT); Great Britain.

Selected Bibliography:

Ernest H. Preeg, *Traders and Diplomats: An Analysis of the Kennedy Round Negotiations under the General Agreement on Tariffs and Trade*, 1970.

Cynthia Clark Northrup

KEYNES, JOHN MAYNARD (June 5, 1883–April 20, 1946)

British economist who challenged the classical economic theories in *The General Theory of Employment, Interest and Money*.

Born in Cambridge, England, Keynes attended Eton College before teaching economics at Cambridge and working for the British Treasury. After World War I, he achieved international fame for his sharp criticism of the Versailles Treaty. In *The Economic Consequences of the Peace*, published in 1919, he stressed that Germany could never pay the war reparations demanded by the victors and argued that the treaty would destabilize European affairs. After resigning from public service over the issue, Keynes returned to teaching. During the Great Depression, as mass unemployment affected industrial countries around the world, Keynes published *General Theory*, a book in which he argued that unemployment would not decrease by lowering wages. President Franklin D. Roosevelt agreed with Keynes's assessment concerning the need for deficit spending to end the Great Depression.

The passage of the Hawley-Smoot Tariff Act of 1930 raised questions about tariffs. Keynes stated that the use of tariffs to reduce domestic consumption of foreign goods offered an alternative to his preferred solution of adjusting trade through exchange-rate devaluation. In September 1931, the British government devalued the pound, but increased the tariff rate. Keynes disagreed with the policy on the basis that other countries would likely retaliate against Great Britain. As his nation moved closer to war with Hitler, he supported the use of the tariff as the less contradictory means of increasing government revenue for the impending increase in military expenditures. He attended the Bretton Woods Conference in 1944 and after World War II he rejoined the British Treasury.

See also: Great Depression; Roosevelt, Franklin D.

Selected Bibliography:

Robert Skidelsky, *John Maynard Keynes*, 2000.

Cynthia Clark Northrup

KNOW-NOTHING PARTY

A nativist political organization that gained influence in U.S. politics between 1852 and 1856.

Actually named the American Party, it acquired the sobriquet of Know-Nothing because the Supreme Order of the Star-Spangled Banner decreed that its various nativist fraternal societies combined in 1850 adopt a strict code of secrecy, including the use of the password "I know nothing" if anyone questioned members about the order's motives, purpose, and program. The Know-Nothing Party emerged in opposition to the post-1846 influx of Roman Catholic immigrants from Europe, especially those from Ireland and Germany, believing that the Catholics loyal to the Pope in Rome would undermine American democracy and that immigrants caused an increase in poverty, crime, and disorder in urban areas. Its platform demanded the use of government power to preserve a Protestant society in America by excluding Catholics or the foreign-born from holding public office; passing more restrictive naturalization laws that would force immigrants to wait not five but twenty-one years before becoming naturalized citizens; and administering literacy tests for voting. By relating immigration restrictions to economic improvements for working Americans, the Know-Nothings appealed to native-born American workers and farmers, who felt their jobs and ways of life threatened by cheap labor and the unfamiliar culture of the foreigners. Although economic programs seldom concerned the party, some Know-Nothings in northern states wanted high tariffs to protect American working people.

Reorganized as a new American Party after the election of 1852, the Know-Nothing Party won national prominence because the two major parties, the Whigs and the Democrats, had begun to divide over the slavery issue. In the off-year elections of 1854, the party won control of the state government in Massachusetts and polled more than 40 percent of the vote in Pennsylvania and New York. Also fractionalized by the slavery issue, the Know-Nothings disintegrated as a national party following the presidential election of 1856.

See also: Democratic Party; Whig Party.

Selected Bibliography:

Tyler Anbinder, *Nativism and Slavery: The Northern Know Nothings and the Politics of the 1850s*, 1992.

Guoqiang Zheng

KNOX, PHILANDER CHASE (May 6, 1853–October 12, 1921)

Wealthy Republican corporate lawyer, attorney general of the United States, and secretary of state.

Born in Brownsville, Pennsylvania, Knox served as attorney general of the United States under both Presidents William McKinley and Theodore Roosevelt. William Howard Taft appointed him as his secretary of state in 1909, a post he held until 1913. Highly respected by both Roosevelt and William Howard Taft, Knox supported "dollar diplomacy," a policy that he employed to forestall political instability in Latin America and China that resulted from economic collapse. Instead of military intervention, Knox advocated American economic intervention to maintain order, or what became known within the Taft administration as using dollars instead of bullets.

Besides dollar diplomacy, Knox participated in the tariff revision movement that appeared at the turn of the twentieth century. Although not advocates of free trade, tariff revisionists opposed high protectionism and argued for lowering tariffs because the economic policies of the United States, such as the promotion of an Open Door or equal access to markets and high domestic tariffs, proved inconsistent with high tariff barriers. Knox and Taft entrusted the State Department's Bureau of Trade Relations (BTR) with the responsibility of formulating policy in tariff negotiations, and appointed men to the BTR who generally agreed with the notion that tariff reduction would make the United States more competitive in the international market.

Knox and the BTR rankled the Treasury Department's Tariff Board, empowered by the Payne-Aldrich Tariff to help in formulating tariff policy by investigating production costs at home and abroad, by excluding the board from tariff negotiations. President Taft ordered the BTR to include the Tariff Board in negotiations, but while nego-

tiating the treaties within the framework of Payne-Aldrich, both sides disagreed on the matter of granting a foreign power a minimum tariff without concessions from those countries. Taft and Knox resolved these differences after lengthy consultations. Philander Knox died in Washington, D.C., in 1921.

See also: Payne-Aldrich Tariff (Tariff of 1909); Roosevelt, Theodore; Taft, William Howard.

Selected Bibliography:

Paul Wolman, *Most Favored Nation: The Republican Revisionists and U.S. Tariff Policy, 1897–1912*, 1992.

Stephen G. Craft

L

LABOR

Historically ambivalent in its long-term position, the American labor movement has alternated between neutrality on the issue of the tariff, to favoring low tariffs, to opposing the General Agreement on Tariffs and Trade (GATT) and the North American Free Trade Agreement (NAFTA).

As early as the 1840s, protectionists argued the Pauper Labor Theory in which the tariff helped maintain the standards of living for the American worker. But labor organizations and unions often interpreted the tariff in terms of their own self-interests. The Knights of Labor organized to help all workers, whether skilled or unskilled, male or female, white or black. Striving to achieve highly idealistic goals such as the abolition of the wage system, the Knights initially took a neutral position on the tariff. As the union declined in membership and its organization got smaller, the Knights opposed high tariffs, arguing that these trade barriers favored industrial businessmen instead of American workers.

The American Federation of Labor, on the other hand, consistently remained ambivalent in its attitude toward tariffs. Organized to help skilled workers and concentrating on bread-and-butter issues like wages and working conditions, the AFL remained mostly neutral in its position on protectionism, often seeking to avoid the issue if at all possible. In recent times, the union has taken stronger stands on protecting American workers by demanding the improvement of foreign labor standards. The Industrial Workers of the World (Wobblies) took a much clearer position on the tariff. Organized to help migrants, foreign workers, and the casual, the Wobblies saw the tariff as having no substantive significance whatsoever in regard to improving the American worker's standard of living.

The Congress of Industrial Organizations (CIO), the next major union to organize, enhanced the growth of industrial unionism throughout the basic industries in the United States. The CIO favored a reduction in the tariff schedules and supported reciprocity treaties with foreign nations. When the AFL and CIO joined forces in 1955, the new AFL-CIO saw the tariff issue in a different light.

Just as the major unions addressed the issue of tariffs, the leaders of these labor organizations expressed their views freely. Samuel Gompers, founder and longtime leader of the AFL, always made it clear that the labor movement should remain neutral in taking any stand on protectionism. His successor, William Green, maintained Gompers's neutrality stand but also favored free trade.

Philip Murray and Walter Reuther of the CIO favored free trade and consistently spoke out in favor of this position during the 1950s. When the AFL and CIO amalgamated in 1955, George Meany became president of the AFL-CIO. Meany initially responded to the issue by calling together experts to study the tariff question and make recommendations. Once completed, he announced his intention to leave the tariff issue alone.

While the labor unions and their leaders expressed their opinions, specific unions, both local and international, developed their own positions on the tariff. Individual unions tended to define their own interests as to whether a tariff would help members. Unions that frequently favored high tariffs included those who joined Matthew Woll's America's Wage Earners Protective Conference. Initially attracting a fair amount of support, the conference lost its membership by 1950.

Although the hatters, potters, boot and shoe workers, and textile unions did support its position, they did not join its ranks.

Those either opposing high tariffs or favoring free trade included unions whose workers became involved in the export trade. If the unions calculated that they had an advantage over foreign competition, they felt comfortable calling for no tariffs or free trade. Such unions as the seaman's, mine workers, musicians, locomotive engineers, and teamsters fit into this category. Unions that favored reciprocity treaties included the textile workers, sheet metal workers, firemen, and machinists. Finally, some unions changed their position, like the mine workers who supported high tariffs on oil but none on coal.

Today, the AFL-CIO has taken a clearly consistent stand on the question of protectionism. As the United States and the world enter into global trade markets, the effects of treaties on the American worker have become more and more pronounced, at least as far as the labor movement is concerned. The AFL-CIO, as a result, has openly opposed and continues to fight against the North American Free Trade Agreement and the General Agreement on Tariffs and Trade. As the union movement declined in membership and power from the 1960s on, the AFL-CIO became more and more vocal about protecting their members. Today, the union demands that any agreement signed with a foreign nation include provisions to raise foreign wages and foreign labor standards. Only in this way do they believe American workingmen and -women can protect their jobs and sustain an acceptable standard of living. In the 1990s and the election of 2000, the AFL-CIO went all out to get their members to support the candidates the union wanted, especially those who opposed fast-track agreements that President William Jefferson Clinton had consistently asked Congress to approve. In the thinking of the AFL-CIO, American jobs remain at risk and the federal government should use its powers to protect American workers from foreign countries that rely on low-wage labor and unacceptable labor standards. Such a position has come full circle, given the labor movement's traditional stand of neutrality on the tariff, favoring low tariffs, or endorsing free trade and reciprocity agreements.

See also: American Federation of Labor (AFL); Clinton, William Jefferson (Bill); Congress of Industrial Organizations (CIO); Fast-track legislation; General Agreement on Tariffs and Trade (GATT); North American Free Trade Agreement (NAFTA).

Selected Bibliography:

Robert D. Leiter, "Organized Labor and the Tariff," *Southern Economic Journal*, 1961; James Shoch, "Contesting Globalization: Organized Labor, NAFTA, and the 1997 and 1998 Fast-Track Fights," *Politics and Society*, 2000.

Michael V. Namorato

LaFOLLETTE, ROBERT MARION
(June 14, 1855–June 18, 1925)

Politician, presidential candidate, and one of the principal leaders of the U.S. Progressive movement.

Born in Primrose, Wisconsin, La-Follette graduated from the University of Wisconsin in 1879. He practiced law and from 1885 to 1891 he served as a Republican member of the U.S. House of Representatives. As a congressman, his eloquent defense of high tariffs, a key issue among pro-business Republicans, won him a seat on the powerful House Ways and Means Committee. LaFollette played a prominent role in the passage of the McKinley Tariff of 1890, which established high tariffs and helped pave the way for William McKinley's presidential run. In 1891, LaFollette lost a bid for a fourth term in Congress, a defeat he blamed on a lack of support from leaders of his state's Republican machine.

LaFollette returned to Wisconsin as the populist movement peaked. Wisconsin farmers blamed their financial difficulties on eastern capitalists who, they claimed, controlled credit too tightly and set unreasonable railroad rates. In this political climate, La-Follette remained loyal to the Republican Party, but abandoned its conservative base. Whether through an ideological conversion or out of political expedience, LaFollette built his own reform-oriented political organization based on the support of farmers, small businessmen, professionals, and intellectuals, all of whom believed that concentrated wealth in the east denied them access to the political system. Elected governor of Wisconsin in 1900 and reelected in 1902 and 1904, he successfully promoted a number of reforms, including the implementation of a primary system, increased regulation of railroads and other corporations, a civil service law, and compensation for workers injured on the job. In 1905, he won a seat in the U.S. Senate.

On his return to Washington, La-Follette began promoting national reforms as a leader of the Progressive wing of the Republican Party. While he had advocated increasing import duties as a congressman, Senator La-Follette embraced tariff reduction, an important progressive concern. He argued that protectionism encouraged the growth of business monopolies harmful to the economic and political infrastructure of the United States. As a result, LaFollette condemned the Republican-sponsored Dingley Tariff of 1897 and worked against the Payne-Aldrich Tariff, although it still passed in 1909. In 1912, he and two other Republican senators voted for the Underwood-Simmons Tariff Act, a downward tariff revision promoted by President Woodrow Wilson. Refusing to compromise his position, LaFollette later fought against the Fordney-McCumber Tariff, another Republican-sponsored bill that increased import duties.

In 1922, LaFollette won reelection to a fourth term in the Senate, but by that time he had alienated most of his fellow Republicans. In 1924, he ran on an independent campaign for president under the banner of the Progressive Party, receiving 17 percent of the popular vote. A few months after the election, he died of heart failure in Washington, D.C., at the age of seventy. In 1957, the U.S. Senate voted LaFollette one of the five outstanding senators of all time.

See also: Fordney-McCumber Tariff (Tariff of 1922); House Ways and Means Committee; Insurgents; Progressives; Republican Party.

Selected Bibliography:

David P. Thelen, *Robert M. LaFollette and the Insurgent Spirit*, 1976; Nancy C. Unger, *Fighting Bob LaFollette: The Righteous Reformer*, 2000.

Ben Wynne

LATIN AMERICA

Most of the Western Hemisphere located south of the United States; colonized by Spain, Portugal, and France.

Spain ruled most of this region from the sixteenth through the eighteenth century, except for Brazil, a country ruled by the Portuguese from 1500 to 1580 and then again from 1640 to 1822. Other European powers established smaller colonies in the region, especially in the Caribbean. Spain and Portugal followed mercantilist policies that excluded foreign trade with their colonies. French, English, and Dutch traders nevertheless carried on much contraband trade with them, and in the eighteenth century some of this trade became legal. Trade between English North America and Latin America began in the seventeenth century. Ports from Boston to Charleston participated in illegal trade with Latin America and also became buccaneering havens. The trade in slaves and sugar between New England, Africa, and the West Indies became especially important in the eighteenth century. During the 1790s, as Spain became dependent on neutral shipping, U.S. trade with Latin America rose significantly. With Latin American political independence by 1822, most of the new nations, encouraged by Great Britain, pursued free trade policies, although they continued to depend on import duties as their principal source of government revenue. The United States recognized the independent Latin American nations before any other nation outside the region. In 1823, the Monroe Doctrine declared the special interest of the United States in the region, but U.S. trade with Latin America remained slim compared with that of Great Britain, the exception being sugar imports from the continuing Spanish colony of Cuba.

After the Civil War, the United States greatly increased the number of consuls in the region and instructed them to promote U.S. trade. Secretary of State James G. Blaine hosted the First International Conference of American States and helped establish the Pan American Union with its headquarters in Washington, D.C., in 1889. Negotiation of trade agreements with Latin American states accompanied U.S. investment, which moved heavily first into Cuba and Mexico and subsequently into other Latin American nations. The McKinley Tariff of 1890 provided for reciprocity treaties. Several such accords with Latin American states followed. The Wilson-Gorman Tariff of 1894 nullified the agreements, but the Dingley Tariff of 1897 restored this feature. World War I permitted further expansion of U.S. trade with Latin America, although high tariffs in both the United States and Latin America restricted the growth of such trade through the Great Depression. Meanwhile, U.S. military and economic intervention in many of the states of the Caribbean created rising animosity to-

ward the United States. President Franklin D. Roosevelt adopted the Good Neighbor Policy, which revived reciprocity with the Reciprocal Trade Agreements Act (RTAA) of 1934. U.S. relations with Latin America improved, with a revitalization of inter-American cooperation that brought substantial Latin American support to the Allies in World War II.

After the war, the United States continued to promote inter-American solidarity, but within a Cold War context. The Organization of American States (OAS) replaced the Pan-American Union, and U.S. investment and trade with the region once more soared upward. Abandoning its non-interventionist pledges of the Good Neighbor era, the United States intervened politically in the internal affairs of Argentina in 1946, Costa Rica in 1948, Guatemala in 1954, Cuba in 1962, Brazil in 1964, Chile in 1973, and Nicaragua in the 1980s, and economically throughout the hemisphere. It imposed a trade embargo on Cuba from 1960 on. The Inter-American Development Bank opened in 1960 to improve credit for Latin American economic development. With the Alliance for Progress, beginning in 1961, the U.S. Agency for International Development (AID) stepped up its economic assistance programs in the region. Yet the United States faced rising economic nationalism in Latin America throughout the twentieth century. With encouragement from the U.N. Economic Commission for Latin America (ECLA), many countries sought to protect native industries through import substitution and protective tariffs. Through a combination of foreign aid, subsidies, and trade agreements, the United States nevertheless increased its trade with Latin America, although its percentage of the trade declined as European and Asian traders increased their shares. A number of regional efforts at common markets also developed in Latin America from the 1950s on. In 1994, the United States formed the North American Free Trade Agreement (NAFTA) with Canada and Mexico, largely eliminating tariffs among these three nations. Subsequently, it has tried to extend this program to the entire hemisphere with the Free Trade Area of the Americas (FTAA). This effort faced stiff opposition from labor and environmental protection interests who charged that NAFTA and FTAA promoted business interests with too little concern for protection of the environment and the well-being of the population in general.

See also: Alliance for Progress; Blaine, James Gillespie; Chile; Cold War; Cuba; Dingley Tariff (Tariff of 1897); Economic Commission for Latin America (ECLA); Free Trade Area of the Americas (FTAA); Good Neighbor Policy; Great Britain; Great Depression; McKinley Tariff (Tariff of 1890); North American Free Trade Agreement (NAFTA); Organization of American States (OAS); Reciprocal Trade Agreements Act (RTAA); Roosevelt, Franklin D.; Sugar; Wilson-Gorman Tariff (Tariff of 1894); World War I; World War II. **Vol. II**: William McKinley's 1888 Speech on Tariff Benefits for Labor; Franklin D. Roosevelt's 1932 Campaign Radio Speech; Alliance for Progress; The Enterprise for the Americas Initiative; Presidential Debate over the North American Free Trade Agreement; Gore-Perot Debate over the Rat-

ification of the North American Free Trade Agreement. **Vol. III**: Tariff of 1894 (Wilson-Gorman Tariff); Tariff of 1897 (Dingley Tariff).

Selected Bibliography:

Victor Bulmer-Thomas, *The Economic History of Latin America Since Independence*, 1994; Mark T. Gilderhus, *The Second Century: U.S.–Latin American Relations since 1889*, 2000; Lars Schoultz, *Beneath the United States: A History of U.S. Policy Toward Latin America*, 1998.

Ralph Lee Woodward Jr.

LEASE, MARY ELIZABETH CLYENS (September 11, 1853–October 29, 1933)

Political activist associated with the Populist Party.

Born in Ridgeway, Pennsylvania, Mary Elizabeth graduated from St. Elizabeth's Academy in Allegany, New York, in 1868. She moved to Kansas and married Charles Lease. In 1874, the couple moved to Dennison, Texas, where Lease gave birth to four of her five children.

In Dennison, Lease studied law and joined the temperance movement. She proved a gifted speaker and in 1885, after a move back to Kansas, gained admittance to the bar. Shortly thereafter, Lease committed her efforts to progressive causes. She joined the Knights of Labor, ran for office on the Union Labor ticket, and then followed the Farmers' Alliance to its rebirth as the People's (or Populist) Party. She played a prominent role in the Populist Party's 1892 Omaha Convention and distinguished herself as a stump speaker who clearly laid the blame for common people's economic problems at the feet of eastern business elites. She often advised farmers to "raise less corn and more hell."

Following the failure of the Populist movement, Lease moved to New York City, wrote for Joseph Pulitzer's *New York World*, and lectured for the New York Board of Education. She made a brief return to the political arena in support of Theodore Roosevelt's bid for the presidency in 1912, but by the start of World War I, Lease had left the political stage. She died in Callicoon, New York, in 1933.

See also: Populists; Roosevelt, Theodore.

Selected Bibliography:

Dorothy Rose Blumberg, "Mary Elizabeth Lease, Populist Orator: A Profile," *Kansas History*, 1978; Richard Stiller, *Queen of the Populists: The Story of Mary Elizabeth Lease*, 1970.

John D. Coats

LEE, HENRY (February 4, 1782–February 6, 1867)

Authored *Report of the Committee of the Citizens of Boston and Vicinity, Opposed to a Further Increase of Duties on Importations*, in which he attacked protectionist tariffs.

Born in Beverly, Massachusetts, on February 4, 1782, Lee dropped out of college early to enter business. Traveling to Calcutta in 1811, Lee remained in India, where he established trading acquaintances. A student of political economy, he opposed some of the viewpoints presented by supporters of the American System. He also wrote for Condy Raguet's *Free-Trade Advocate*, a Philadelphia publication. Lee turned his attention to the tariff, an issue very strong in New England. Woolen manufacturers supported protectionist tariffs because they faced strong competition from overseas. Merchants and traders who opposed these tariffs chose Henry Lee to write the almost 200-word *Report*, which is sometimes called the "Boston Report." Edward Stanwood, in his *American Tariff Controversies in the Nineteenth Century*, argued that "no more powerful document was ever produced in this country." The document challenged the ideas that the government should protect manufactures and that protective duties result in lowering prices. Lee's document further attacked the idea that the British government made sudden alterations in their system of duties, after the United States passed its tariff of 1824. Lee further pointed out that the British began petitioning for this change in 1820 and passed legislation lowering the tariff even before they had heard of the American bill.

Daniel Webster's disappointing response to the "Boston Report" appears in the congressional debate on the Tariff Act of 1828. He admitted that the British did not lower their tariff in response to the Tariff of 1824, but argued that "the effect of that reduction, on our manufactures, was the same precisely as if the British act had been designed to operate against them, and for no other purpose."

In 1832, South Carolina gave its eleven electoral votes for vice president to Henry Lee.

See also: Tariff of 1824; Tariff of 1828 (Tariff of Abominations); Webster, Daniel.

Selected Bibliography:

Edward Stanwood, *American Tariff Controversies in the Nineteenth Century*, 1967; U.S. Senate, 20th Congress, 1st session, *Register of Debates*, 1828.

David E. Walker

LILIUOKALANI, LYDIA PAKI KAMEKEHA (September 2, 1838–November 11, 1917)

Last monarch of the Hawaiian Islands.

Born into the island kingdom's royal family, she ascended the throne in 1891 after the death of her brother, King David Kalakaua. Kalakaua, who had ascended the throne in 1874, inherited an island that had been transformed by the creation and expansion of the sugar industry by foreign planters. The planters represented a powerful interest group in the islands, and the king would significantly weaken native rule when he transferred political power to foreign residents in 1887.

The sugar trade closely tied Hawaii to the United States. The Hawaiian government secured a Treaty of Reciprocity in 1875, renewed in 1881, that allowed tariff-free entry of island sugar to U.S. markets in exchange for Hawaii's agreement not to transfer economic or territorial rights to a third country. The U.S. government revoked the Treaty of Reciprocity and ended Hawaiian sugar's tariff-free entry into the U.S. market as part of the protectionist McKinley Tariff of 1890. The tariff's threat to the sugar industry plunged the islands into economic crisis.

In this turbulent environment, Liliuokalani took the throne and attempted to restore a degree of the monarchy's power through the nationalist Oni Pa'a (Stand Firm) movement. Her efforts won the enmity of American planters, and their concerns regarding the new queen, economic insecurity, and their own American nationalism, caused them to conspire against her. In January 1893, white planters overthrew Liliuokalani in a nearly bloodless coup and immediately sent a delegation to Washington to request annexation by the United States. Political complications in Washington delayed the annexation process, but the short-lived Republic of Hawaii gave way when the U.S. Congress approved annexation and territorial status for Hawaii on July 7, 1898.

Liliuokalani spent some time under house arrest in 1895, but regained her freedom that same year after abdicating the throne. As a private citizen she gained acclaim as a native songwriter. She died in Honolulu in 1917.

See also: Congress (United States); Hawaii; McKinley Tariff (Tariff of 1890); Sugar.

Selected Bibliography:

Merze Tate, *The United States and the Hawaiian Kingdom: A Political History*, 1965.

John D. Coats

LINCOLN, ABRAHAM (February 12, 1809–April 14, 1865)

Sixteenth president of the United States.

Born on February 12, 1809, in Hardin County, Kentucky, the son of Thomas and Nancy Hanks Lincoln, the Lincoln family moved to southern Indiana shortly after his birth. Spending a large share of his childhood and adolescence in Indiana, Lincoln also became familiar with the routine of subsistence agriculture.

In 1831, he migrated with his family to Illinois, settling a few miles west of Decatur. After the young Lincoln left his father's home, he settled in New Salem and won a seat in the state legislature. Moving to nearby Springfield, he studied law and became partners with prominent Whig attorney John Todd Stuart. Lincoln remained in Springfield until he won the presidential election of 1860. During his time in Springfield, he wed Mary Todd and raised a family, established a successful legal practice with partner William H. Herndon, and continued as an important local Whig politician serving terms in the state legislature as well as a single term in the U.S. House of Representatives.

During the 1850s, Lincoln abstained from political matters until the Kansas-Nebraska Act of 1854 reinvigorated his career. Instrumental in the success of the Illinois Republicans, the party chose Lincoln to contest the reelection of Democratic senator Stephen A. Douglas in 1858. Although Lincoln lost the race, he earned a national reputation primarily as the result of the series of debates that the two candidates held throughout the state. Lincoln's performance in the 1858 campaign helped secure him the Republican presidential nomination in 1860. His election to the presidency in 1860 precipitated the secession crisis that led to the outbreak of civil war between the North and South. Presiding over the nation during four tumultuous years, Lincoln's patience and perseverance helped secure the triumph of the Union as well

as the abolition of slavery. His assassination by John Wilkes Booth on April 15, 1865, left the newly reunited nation leaderless as it entered the important period of political reconstruction.

Lincoln's early life shaped his views of the tariff. Lincoln rejected the subsistence ethic, embracing instead the tenets of the newly emerging market economy. Lincoln remained enthralled with the views of Whig statesman Henry Clay, whose economic program, the American System, endorsed government-sponsored internal improvements, a national bank, and protective tariffs as a means of facilitating the development of a market economy.

Although Lincoln read the works of many economists, the views of Whig thinker Henry Carey proved influential in shaping his position on the tariff. Lincoln viewed the protective tariff as necessary to stimulate and protect domestic industry. To the charge that protective tariffs artificially raised prices and harmed consumers, Lincoln argued that the rich, producers, and consumers should share the cost of tariffs equally. If Americans allowed low-priced foreign goods to flood the market, a disproportionate amount of American labor, Lincoln argued, would be wasted on transporting foreign goods to and from markets. A low tariff would also allow cheaper goods to undercut domestic manufacturing, promoting unemployment and idleness. Indeed, Lincoln agreed with fellow Republican critics of the Buchanan administration when they linked the economic downturn of 1857 to Buchanan's gradual downward revision of the tariff.

Early in his political career, Lincoln focused more on the protective tariff than he did on the controversial issue of slavery. As the Republican presidential nominee in 1860, his position on protective tariffs gained him the support of the Pennsylvania delegation, a state whose iron foundries desperately sought relief from cheaper English imports. Lincoln supported the Morrill Tariff that raised rates from 19 percent to 36 percent. Although the measure passed just prior to his inauguration, Lincoln supported three subsequent revisions of this tariff during the war that revised rates upward to 47 percent.

Lincoln's position on protective tariffs remained consistent throughout his political career. As part and parcel of the Whig economic philosophy he embraced, Lincoln endorsed and argued for protective tariffs as a state legislator, as an unsuccessful candidate for the U.S. Senate, and as president of the United States.

See also: American System; Carey, Henry Charles; Civil War (American); Clay, Henry; Morrill Tariff (Tariff of 1861); Republican Party; Whig Party.

Selected Bibliography:

David Herbert Donald, *Lincoln,* 1995; Allen C. Guelzo, *Abraham Lincoln: Redeemer President,* 1999.

Bruce Tap

LINEN

A branch of the textile industry that has generally failed to thrive in the United States despite favorable legislation.

During the colonial period, linen weaving remained the only type of textile manufacture not reserved for the mother country by the imperial government. In an attempt to take advantage of this opportunity, a group of religious and other public figures persuaded the Massachusetts authorities to set up a linen factory in Boston in 1751 to employ the poor. This first foray into large-scale textile manufacturing in English America did not thrive: Massachusetts could not compete with the cheaper linen manufactured by another of Britain's colonies, Ireland, and the factory went bankrupt in 1759. The colonies did profit from the supply of flaxseed to Irish linen weavers, in accordance with the general scheme of the British navigation laws, that the New World should supply the empire with raw materials. After the Revolution, and even after the War of 1812, investors focused on cotton and woolen textile production, leaving the linen industry largely neglected, except for the small-scale manufacture of coarse grades of material. In the later part of the nineteenth century, the general drive to promote all branches of manufacture included the linen industry, and the tariff on linens became higher and higher, reaching above 50 percent by 1890. Even so, the United States continued to manufacture only coarse linens, and into the twentieth century foreign suppliers dominated the American market for finer grades despite high tariff barriers.

See also: American Revolution; Navigation and Trade Acts; War of 1812.

Selected Bibliography:

Gary B. Nash, *The Urban Crucible: Social Change, Political Consciousness, and the Origins of the American Revolution*, 1979.

John P. Barrington

LIST, FRIEDRICH (Baptized August 6, 1789–November 30, 1846)

German economist, journalist, politician, and promoter whose arguments in favor of protective tariffs and state-sponsored economic development and against the free trade doctrines of Adam Smith and David Ricardo exercised great influence in Germany and the United States.

Born in Reutlingen, Germany, List pursued a highly successful career in the Württemberg civil service that culminated in a professorship at the University of Tübingen. His activities as a liberal journalist and politician led to his dismissal from state service in 1818. He became the leader of a national organization lobbying the German states to form a customs union (Zollverein). Charged in 1822 with political offenses, he fled abroad, but returned to Württemberg for a brief imprisonment before immigrating to the United States in 1825. While in America, List participated in railroad and other development projects and took part in debates over American tariff policy. After returning to Germany in 1830, he worked as a freelance journalist, promoting railway construction, the expansion of the Zollverein, and German political unification. His book *Das Nationale System der politischen Ökonomie*, published in 1841, presented an important argument for economic protectionism. The book influenced Americans as well as Germans. List committed suicide in Kufstein, in the Austrian Alps, in 1846.

An extremely important figure in the history of German economics, List influenced national policy from the time of his death until the end of the twentieth century. He affected U.S. tariff history in two respects. First, during his stay in the United States he supported the American System and developed ideas derived from Alexander Hamilton and Henry C. Carey to new levels of sophistication. In addition, his presentation of the infant industries argument for selective protection of key industrial sectors, and the way in which he embedded that argument in an analysis of the process of economic development within national economies, provided strong theoretical support for tariff protection frequently cited in the United States throughout the second half of the nineteenth century.

See also: American System; Carey, Henry Charles; Free trade; Germany; Hamilton, Alexander; Ricardo, David; Smith, Adam.

Selected Bibliography:

W.O. Henderson, *Friedrich List: Economist and Visionary 1789–1846*, 1983.

Woodruff D. Smith

LOBBYING

Attempts by campaigners or representatives of special interest groups to influence the U.S. Congress on particular issues such as tariff rates.

Lobbyists have sought to increase duties on imported items since the early nineteenth century. Industries concentrated in a general geographic region, which allowed for easier communication among numerous companies, participated in the lobbying process more actively than those spread out over several states. The wool and woolens industry in New England pushed for higher tariff on woolen items as early as 1816. The steel industry, located primarily in western Pennsylvania, hired lobbyists to exert pressure on Congress to increase rates on imported metals to protect their market.

The most successful era of lobbying occurred between 1861 and 1913. During this time, the Republican-dominated Congress continued to raise duty rates as well as add items to the dutiable list. Not surprisingly, this period corresponds to the rise of big business. The efforts of lobbyists proved effective—so effective that a reform movement, led by farmers, emerged to challenge the giant monopolies that had formed under the protective umbrella of high tariffs.

The last successful lobbying efforts for increased tariffs occurred in 1930. President Herbert Hoover asked Congress for a revision of the tariff schedule to assist debt-ridden farmers. Although the House of Representatives passed a bill that included high trade barriers for agriculture, Senator Reed Smoot called for a complete revision of the tariff, opening up the process to lobbyists. By the time the Hawley-Smoot Tariff passed both houses of Congress, rates of hundreds of manufactured items had increased as well. The impact of lobbying on international trade relations proved disastrous, depressing trade at a time when nations around the world struggled to pull out of the Great Depression.

In the post–World War II period, lobbyists have continued to play a role in trade debates, but their emphasis has changed. Instead of pushing for higher tariffs, lobbyists argue that the free trade relations established by such agreements as the North American Free Trade Agreement (NAFTA) have led to violations of human rights and the need to address environmental issues. Organizations such as the World Wildlife Fund and the Sierra Club, as well as unions like the AFL-CIO, pressured Congress to delay ratification of agreements until all the participating governments cooperated by including provisions that addressed these issues.

See also: American Federation of Labor–Congress of Industrial Organizations (AFL-CIO); Dingley Tariff (Tariff of 1897); Hawley-Smoot Tariff (Tariff of 1930); North American Free Trade Agreement (NAFTA); Payne-Aldrich Tariff (Tariff of 1909); Populists; Sierra Club; U.S. Steel Corp.; Wool and woolens; World Wildlife Fund.

Selected Bibliography:

Kenneth Goldstein, *Interest Groups, Lobbying, and Participation in America*, 1999; Elizabeth Sanders, *Roots of Reform: Farmers, Workers, and the American State, 1877–1917*, 1999; Mark A. Smith, *American Business and Political Power: Public Opinion, Elections, and Democracy*, 2000.

Cynthia Clark Northrup

LODGE, HENRY CABOT (May 12, 1850–November 9, 1924)

American statesman best known for his isolationist foreign policy and opposition to the Treaty of Versailles and the League of Nations.

Born in Boston, Massachusetts, Lodge graduated from Harvard University in 1871 and Harvard Law School in 1875. In 1876, he became the recipient of Harvard's first Ph.D. in political science. During his early career, Lodge wrote many books as a historian, including biographies of Alexander Hamilton and Daniel Webster. He first entered politics as a Republican member of the Massachusetts House of Representatives, where he served from 1880 to 1886. In 1886, Lodge won a seat in Congress, serving in the House of Representatives until 1893 when voters elected him to the Senate, where he would serve out the rest of his political career. As chairman of the Senate Foreign Affairs Committee and Senate majority leader, Lodge emerged as the leading opponent of the Treaty of Versailles and the League of Nations.

Early in life, Lodge favored free trade principles, but by the early 1880s he became a dedicated protectionist and would remain so throughout the rest of his life. Lodge credited his conversion to protectionism to his reading of Hamilton's *Report on Manufactures*. Throughout his political life, Lodge viewed protectionism as an essential component of American nationalism and connected support for high tariffs with the growth of home industries that would make the United States less dependent on foreign countries. Although he supported the McKinley Tariff (1890) that raised import duties by 50 percent, he did not categorically accept all its provisions. Moreover, he believed that Congress had raised some of the duties too high. But he viewed the McKinley bill as the only

one with a chance to gain congressional support. In 1908, Lodge became a member of the Senate Finance Committee and helped draft the Payne-Aldrich Tariff in 1909. On retiring from the Senate, Lodge returned to Cambridge, where he died in 1924.

See also: Congress (United States); Free trade; Hamilton, Alexander; McKinley Tariff (Tariff of 1890); Payne-Aldrich Tariff (Tariff of 1909); Protectionism; *Report on Manufactures*; Senate Finance Committee; Webster, Daniel.

Selected Bibliography:

John Garraty, *Henry Cabot Lodge: A Biography*, 1953; William Widenor, *Henry Cabot Lodge and the Search for an American Foreign Policy*, 1980.

William C. Barnhart

LONDON WORLD ECONOMIC CONFERENCE

Meeting held June 12 through July 24, 1933, in London for the ostensible purpose of increasing trade through tariff reduction, currency stabilization, and reduction of World War I debts.

The primary participants—Britain, France, and the United States—pursued different strategies for economic recovery. Thus, their goals at the conference proved fundamentally incompatible, making failure inevitable. In 1931, Britain left the gold standard and erected tariffs favoring the empire and the "sterling bloc." Britain wanted to raise prices and depreciate the pound, but would not accept an unbalanced budget or public works program. France remained on the gold standard, erected tariffs to deny Britain the advantage of currency depreciation, and refused to countenance price increases for fear of inflation. America raised tariffs significantly, left the gold standard in April 1933, and initiated a program of inflation and public works known as the New Deal.

President Franklin D. Roosevelt subordinated the conference to domestic recovery. He wanted the conference to produce only vague, inoffensive resolutions and appointed delegates with different experience in economic affairs. Secretary of State Cordell Hull drafted a reciprocal trade bill, but FDR feared this might jeopardize recovery legislation and dropped the proposed agreement. The decision crushed Hull's hope that the conference might reach a general agreement on tariff reciprocity. Conference delegates focused on currency stabilization and reached a preliminary agreement to stabilize the dollar. Roosevelt rejected the accord. The gold bloc countries then asked him to use the Federal Reserve to limit currency fluctuation due to speculation. FDR feared that such a move would lead to permanent stabilization and jeopardize his recovery program. He vetoed the proposal in a sharp public message on July 3, and the conference broke up without any significant results.

Afterward, the world divided into a gold bloc, a dollar bloc, and a sterling bloc, each of which tried to beggar the other. International trade collapsed and did not recover until after World War II.

See also: Great Depression; Hull, Cordell; Roosevelt, Franklin D.

Selected Bibliography:

Robert Dallek, *Franklin D. Roosevelt and American Foreign Policy, 1932–1945*, 1979; Herbert Feis, *Characters in Crisis*, 1966; Raymond Moley, *After Seven Years*, 1939.

James David Perry

LONGWORTH, NICHOLAS (November 5, 1869–April 5, 1931)

Republican congressman from Ohio, considered one of the leading experts on tariff law in the U.S. House of Representatives; he played a key mediating role during debates over the Payne-Aldrich, Fordney-McCumber, and Hawley-Smoot Tariffs.

A fourth-generation member of one of Cincinnati's oldest and wealthiest families, celebrated for his charm and wit, and the husband of Theodore Roosevelt's outspoken daughter Alice, Longworth dominated Washington society as one of the "social lions" for a quarter century, a circumstance that has generally obscured his considerable abilities and accomplishments as a parliamentary manager. Elected to the city Board of Education in 1898, the Ohio House of Representatives in 1899, and the state Senate in 1901, he advanced to the U.S. Congress in 1903. Longworth served on both the Committee on Foreign Affairs and the Ways and Means Committee, where he advocated limited government, moderately high tariff duties, and low domestic taxes. During the fight over the Payne-Aldrich Tariff, Longworth played an important role as mediator between the high-protectionist Stalwart and strong reductionist Insurgent wings of his own party. The first main-

stream Republican to oppose the reelection of "Czar" Joseph G. Cannon as
Speaker in 1910, and an outspoken
critic of the seniority system, he lost his
bid for reelection during the Democratic sweep of 1912. Restored to the
House in 1914, he emerged as one of
his party's workhorses, becoming majority leader in 1923 and Speaker in
1925. Although generally an avid
"New Era" Republican during the
1920s, Longworth steadily enhanced
his reputation as both strong leader
and effective conciliator, earning the
nickname "Genial Czar." His open opposition to prohibition resulted in his
party denying him the presidential
nomination in 1928, while his coalition-
building efforts failed to prevent the
passage of the Hawley-Smoot Tariff,
the "worst tariff bill in the nation's history" and "protectionism's last hur-
rah." Worn out from the exertion and
contention of the tariff fight, Longworth died of pneumonia while visiting friends in Aiken, South Carolina.

See also: Cannon, Joseph Gurney;
Fordney-McCumber Tariff (Tariff of
1922); Hawley-Smoot Tariff (Tariff of
1930); House Ways and Means
Committee; Insurgents; Payne-Aldrich
Tariff (Tariff of 1909); Roosevelt, Theodore.

Selected Bibliography:

Donald C. Bacon, "Nicholas Longworth:
The Genial Czar," *Masters of the House: Congressional Leadership Over Two Centuries*,
1998; Clara Longworth de Chambrun, *The
Making of Nicholas Longworth*, 1933; William
Hard, "Nicholas Longworth," *American Review of Reviews*, 1925.

John D. Buenker

LOWELL, FRANCIS CABOT (April 7, 1775–August 10, 1817)

Manufacturer and entrepreneur who
established the basic pattern of textile
production in the nineteenth century.

Born in Newburyport, Massachusetts, Lowell graduated from Harvard
in 1793. In 1810, seeking to learn more
about the textile industry, he went on
a fact-finding tour of Great Britain's
leading textile mills and took notes on
the design plans of various power
looms. On his return to Massachusetts,
Lowell, along with a brilliant me-
chanic, Paul Moody, designed and patented a power loom based on the
models he had seen in Britain. With
several partners, Lowell formed the
Boston Manufacturing Company in
1814 and proceeded to construct a textile factory in Waltham, located on the
Charles River just outside Boston. In
the first textile factory in America,
Lowell integrated all steps in the manufacturing process, from spinning to
weaving, under one roof.

Lowell sought to make New England a center of both textile production
and trade. Although the embargoes in
place during the War of 1812 stimulated the growth of American manufacturers, the war's end brought a flood
of cheap goods, especially British and
Indian cloth, into the American market.
In 1816, to protect American-made
cloth from foreign competition, Lowell
journeyed to Washington, D.C., to
lobby for a protective tariff. He enlisted
the support of southern representatives, especially John C. Calhoun, then
an economic nationalist, and William
Lowndes of South Carolina. Their efforts culminated in the Tariff Act of

1816, which levied a 25 percent duty on foreign cloth and fostered a temporary alliance of New England manufacturers and southern cotton producers. Frail and sickly throughout his life, Lowell died in Boston on August 10, 1817, at the age of forty-two.

See also: Calhoun, John Caldwell; Great Britain; Lowndes, William Jones; Tariff of 1816; Textiles; War of 1812.

Selected Bibliography:

Robert Dalzell, *Enterprising Elite: The Boston Associates and the World They Made*, 1987; Robert Sobel, *The Entrepreneurs: Explorations Within the American Business Tradition*, 1974.

William C. Barnhart

LOWNDES, WILLIAM JONES
(February 11, 1782–October 27, 1822)

South Carolina representative known for shepherding the first peacetime protective tariff through Congress in 1816.

The son of Sarah Jones and Rawlins Lowndes, president of South Carolina during the Revolution, Lowndes grew up on Horseshoe Plantation near Jacksonborough, Colleton District, South Carolina. Later he spent three years in an English boarding school before returning home to continue his studies in Charleston and take up the law.

Lowndes served in the South Carolina legislature before his election to the U.S. House of Representatives, where he distinguished himself as a leader of the nationalist Republican faction. During his congressional ca-

reer, he allied with John C. Calhoun and Henry Clay to support measures to strengthen the nation's economy and defenses. Their push for a tougher maritime policy toward Great Britain contributed to war in 1812 and earned the trio the sobriquet "War Hawks." Recognizing Lowndes's leadership qualities, President James Monroe offered to appoint him secretary of war in 1817, but the South Carolinian preferred to remain in Congress.

As chairman of the House Ways and Means Committee, Lowndes steered the Tariff Act of 1816 through Congress. The act set duties as high as 25 percent on imported cotton and wool goods. The law also introduced the "minimum-value" principle that valued cheap imported cotton cloth, some costing as little as six cents per square yard, at a minimum value of twenty-five cents.

Although Lowndes clearly accepted the principle that Congress could enact a protective tariff, he regarded the highly protective 1816 law as a temporary measure to assist American manufacturers damaged by the post-war dumping of British goods on the domestic market. Within a few years, Lowndes considered continued protection for manufacturers no longer necessary. Moreover, he believed that by diverting the flow of capital and labor from their natural courses into less productive channels, the tariff might become harmful. Thus, he opposed the Tariff Act of 1820.

Lowndes narrowly lost the race for Speaker of the House in 1820, but the next year the South Carolina legislature unanimously nominated him for president of the United States for the 1824 election. Lowndes preferred Calhoun for that post and so refused to accept the nomination.

Soon thereafter, Lowndes came down with tuberculosis. He resigned from Congress in May 1822 so that he might go abroad to restore his health. While en route to England that October, he succumbed to the disease and was buried at sea.

See also: Calhoun, John Caldwell; Clay, Henry; Monroe, James; Tariff of 1816; Tariff of 1820.

Selected Bibliography:

Norris W. Preyer, "Southern Support of the Tariff of 1816—A Reappraisal," *Journal of Southern History*, 1959; Carl J. Vipperman, *William Lowndes and the Transition of Southern Politics, 1782–1822*, 1989.

Robert Tinkler

M

MACLAY, WILLIAM (July 20, 1737–April 16, 1804)

First senator for the state of Pennsylvania; he voiced his opposition to certain measures in Congress, particularly Alexander Hamilton's financial proposals, and authored a journal that provides the most comprehensive account of debates during the First Congress from 1789 to 1791.

Born in Chester County, Pennsylvania, Maclay served in a variety of positions and posts before entering Congress. He was a lieutenant in the third battalion during the French and Indian War and was stationed in various stockades on the road to Fort Pitt. After the war, he studied law and worked as a surveyor. He also represented the interests of the Penn family throughout the state. During the American Revolution, he fought with the Continental Army at Trenton and Princeton. When the hostilities ceased, Maclay received an appointment to the Supreme Executive Council, to the Court of Commons Pleas as a judge, as a deputy surveyor, and as a commissioner of navigation of the Susquehanna River.

In January 1789, the Pennsylvania legislature elected him to the first U.S. Senate to serve the short term along with Robert Morris, who served the full six-year term. In Congress, Maclay, who refused to be intimidated by the presence of George Washington in the chambers, argued that the president should not attend Senate meetings. He also raised objections on other issues. While Thomas Jefferson served as U.S. ambassador to France, Maclay laid the foundation for a loyal opposition that would transform the American political system with the election of 1800. When Hamilton proposed a single schedule for all tariff duties, Maclay opposed the measure, arguing that the United States should show gratitude to those countries that had recently assisted during the American Revolution. Maclay called for a discriminatory policy that would benefit friendly nations while punishing enemies.

After retiring from Congress, Maclay returned to Harrisburg and served in the state legislature. Maclay, who died in 1804, left a journal of all Senate debates conducted during the First Congress. In 1880, George Washington Harris published and edited Maclay's journal, a source that provides a wealth of information on the issues and personalities that shaped the early republic.

See also: American Revolution; Hamilton, Alexander; Washington, George.

Selected Bibliography:

William Maclay, *The Diary of William Maclay and Other Notes on Senate Debates*, 1988.

Cynthia Clark Northrup

MADISON, JAMES (March 31, 1751– June 28, 1836)

Political theorist and fourth president of the United States; he identified himself as "the friend to a very free system of commerce."

Born in Port Conway of King George County, Virginia, Madison grew up on Montpelier Plantation in the heart of the Blue Ridge Mountains. After studying with a private tutor, he chose to attend the College of New Jersey (now Princeton), where, after only two years, he graduated with a liberal arts education. Although he studied law, Madison had no intention of practicing, and appeared destined to a life of politics. He sought and won his first elected post in 1772 and remained in public life

until the end of his second term as president in 1816.

Like most of the founding generation, Madison had specific beliefs about tariffs and trade. He described restriction of trade as unjust and impolitic, yet he also recognized that in establishing the new nation, exceptions might have to be made. He did not object to government regulation of trade or protective tariff policies as long as such measures proved temporary. Madison proposed the first tariff bill (1789) discussed before Congress after the adoption of the U.S. Constitution. As a compromise measure to placate both Hamiltonian Federalists and Jeffersonian Republicans, Madison presented the tariff bill as a means to regulate trade and raise revenue. The final measure revised and passed by Congress also provided some protection for American industry. In 1790, Alexander Hamilton introduced a revenue-raising package that included collecting duties on imported wine, spirits, tea, and coffee, as well as a domestic excise tax on the same items. Congress bitterly opposed the domestic taxation, but appeared willing to consider the tariff. Again Madison stepped in with a compromise bill that increased import duties, but left domestic taxes untouched.

Madison had always suggested that a policy of commercial discrimination would best serve the United States. This policy would distinguish between nations that had participated in commercial treaties with the United States and those that had refused. Trading partners would enjoy special tonnage and tariff duties. Madison especially regretted the commercial ties between the American and British economies. He saw the extensive credit offered by Britain to American merchants over the years as crippling to the nation's commerce. He hoped that, by supporting France and other cooperative nations with favorable trade policies, the United States could distance itself from the injurious system of British mercantilism. As a consequence, he aimed his proposed Tariff Act of 1794 directly at Great Britain, suggesting that an increased tariff would force Great Britain to welcome U.S. merchants into its ports.

Madison clearly targeted Great Britain in his discriminating trade theories. Desiring to establish a strong American republic, and believing that the only way to achieve that goal would be with a free, virtuous, and independent population, Madison emphasized the dangers of dependence. According to republican theory, dependence brought venality and corruption, for both the individual and the nation. Madison pointed out that Britain, as a commercial and manufacturing nation, remained filled with the laboring poor and suffered from a densely populated, debauched society, victims of a corrupt political system. America, on the other hand, promised the abundance of natural resources and markets to become truly independent. American economic independence, he argued, need not rest on protective tariffs or even on extensive domestic manufactures. Madison meant for discrimination in trade duties to serve as a temporary measure. He foresaw an international order in which commerce would flow freely in natural channels. To achieve such a goal, Madison knew that all nations

would have to comply. With his commercial discrimination policy, Madison attempted to induce compliance from Britain.

When Britain and France renewed their hostilities in 1803, the United States found itself once again squeezed out of international trade. Through the British Parliament's Rule of 1756 and Orders in Council and Napoleon's Berlin and Milan Decrees, both nations threatened to blockade nonbelligerent trade. In addition, Britain began impressing American seamen into the Royal Navy at an alarming rate. Years of aggravation and several failed attempts to gain control of the trade situation caused President Madison to declare war on Great Britain in 1812. After the war ended in a relative stalemate in 1815, Great Britain began dumping goods on the American market. A postwar recession ensued. In an effort to help U.S. manufacturers recover, the Madison administration passed America's first truly protective tariff in 1816, just as Madison retired from public service. His final political gesture included signing into law the notorious Tariff Act of 1816 and the charter of the Second Bank of the United States. He retired to Montpelier, where he died from complications related to rheumatism on June 28, 1836. Madison's effort to pass the 1816 tariff opened a trade controversy that politicians would debate in earnest until the mid-twentieth century.

See also: Federalists; Hamilton, Alexander; Jefferson, Thomas; Jeffersonianism; Tariff of 1789; Tariff of 1790; Tariff of 1794; Tariff of 1816; War of 1812. **Vol. II**: *The Federalist* (Federalist Papers). **Vol. III**: Tariff of 1789; Tariff of 1790; Tariff of 1794; Tariff of 1816.

Selected Bibliography:

Lance Banning, *The Sacred Fire of Liberty: James Madison and the Founding of the Federal Republic*, 1995; J.C.A. Stagg, *Mr. Madison's War: Politics, Diplomacy, and Warfare in the Early Republic, 1783–1830*, 1983.

Carol Terry and Elaine C. Prange Turney

MALTHUS, THOMAS (February 14, 1766–December 23, 1834)

English economist, Anglican minister, and demographer best known for his 1798 *Essay on the Principle of Population as It Affects the Future Improvement of Society*, in which he warned that rapid population growth would tax the food supply.

Malthus grew up in a prosperous family. His father had a close friendship with David Hume. Schooled at home until his 1784 admission to Jesus College, Cambridge, he became a fellow in 1793 and took his holy orders in 1797. Beginning in 1805, he taught as a professor of history and political economy at the East India Company's college in Hertfordshire, and in 1819 he became a Fellow of the Royal Society. As an empiricist, Malthus, who was greatly influenced by the realities of life in England, disagreed with the theoretical belief of perfecting society.

In 1798, Malthus presented a dire picture of the future in his *Essay on the Principle of Population*. In the *Essay*, Malthus argued that population growth occurred exponentially while the food supply grew arithmetically. As the population grew, it would tax the land and poverty would increase. This unstoppable population growth destroyed any chance of perfecting or improving society. Although war, famine, and disease occasionally checked population growth, they only provided a limited solution. For Malthus, the only true checks included vice, within which he included birth control, and self-restraint. Because of the criticism generated by the publication of his *Essay*, Malthus examined the United States of America, where land and resources remained plentiful, and estimated that its population doubled every twenty-five years. He then argued that Europe failed to achieve the same growth rate because of the numerous checks on population growth. His ideas made poverty seem unavoidable and unstoppable, and thus reinforced David Ricardo's Iron Law of Wages and made charity a hopeless enterprise. In his *Essay*, he countered the argument that the elimination of taxes would benefit the poor because the cost of goods would diminish, but so would wages. For Malthus, taxation decreased demand and that decreased production. Malthus's ideas had important consequences for Europe's poor since he argued that relief must include moral restraint. Many people interpreted his ideas as meaning charity only increased the problem of poverty because it allowed poor people to reproduce beyond their available resources.

See also: Hume, David; Ricardo, David.

Selected Bibliography:

Samuel Hollander, *The Economics of Thomas Robert Malthus*, 1997; William Petersen, *Malthus*, 1979.

Ty M. Reese

MASSACHUSETTS

A colony and state with a well-developed commercial and manufacturing economy.

In colonial times, Massachusetts benefited from the protection given by the navigation laws to ships built in the colonies with colonial sailors serving as the crew. As a result, Massachusetts developed a major shipbuilding industry and mercantile sector, which enabled merchants to accumulate capital to an extent unusual for a colony. Under British rule, Massachusetts established a variety of legal and profitable trade routes: exporting fish to southern Europe and foodstuffs and timber products to the West Indies, while importing sugar from the West Indies for manufacture into rum. Massachusetts merchants also profited from carrying a variety of merchandise from colony to colony. After the American Revolution, the British closed the West Indies to U.S. ships and Massachusetts merchants experienced a severe slump. The Massachusetts mercantile sector experienced difficulties until the wars following the French Revolution opened up trade with European colonies in the Caribbean, and Massachusetts's commerce boomed. Hurt by Jefferson's embargo, and then by the War of 1812, many Massachusetts merchants began investing in industrial enterprises, especially in woolen textiles. After peace returned, Massachusetts remained divided on the tariff issue, fearing damage to its shipbuilding and mercantile interests if tariffs hindered their trans-Atlantic trade, yet desiring protection for its woolen textiles, which faced stiff competition from British imports. By the end of the 1820s, the shifting balance between manufacturing and shipping in the Massachusetts economy helped to place the state in the protectionist camp and explained its support for the Whig and, later, Republican Parties. In the twentieth century, the move from dependence on selling textiles to the domestic market to manufacturing a variety of high-tech goods for export led Massachusetts to espouse the lowering of world trade barriers.

See also: American Revolution; Jefferson, Thomas; Navigation and Trade Acts; War of 1812.

Selected Bibliography:

Richard D. Brown, *Massachusetts: A Bicentennial History*, 1977.

John P. Barrington

MAXIMUM-MINIMUM TARIFF

A tariff system in which a foreign country sets both levels of tariff autonomously without modification by international agreement.

The higher or "maximum" level applies to imports from countries that have signed reciprocal tariff reduction agreements with the country employing such a system. The concept of the Maximum-Minimum Tariff, introduced by Spain in 1877 and copied by France in 1892, became embodied by the United States in the Payne-Aldrich Tariff of 1909. Bowing to public opinion, President William Howard Taft convened a special session of Congress in 1909 for the purpose of tariff revision. Republican members of Congress responded to business pressures to expand the export market by giving tariff negotiators greater flexibility. Under the new Payne-Aldrich Tariff, U.S. tariffs averaged 19.3 percent.

During the subsequent administration of Democrat Woodrow Wilson, passage of the Underwood-Simmons Tariff Act resulted in the United States unilaterally lowering the average tariff rate to 9.1 percent. The idea, as enacted by Spain, called the regular tariff the maximum tariff, and the lowest rate that a country could expect as a result of tariff negotiations was called the minimum tariff.

See also: Payne-Aldrich Tariff (Tariff of 1909); Taft, William Howard; Wilson, Thomas Woodrow.

Selected Bibliography:

William A. Lovett, Alfred E. Eckes Jr., and Richard L. Brinkman, eds., *U.S. Trade Policy: History, Theory, and the WTO*, 1999.

Henry B. Sirgo

McADOO, WILLIAM G. (October 31, 1863–February 1, 1941)

U.S. secretary of the treasury.

Born near Marietta, Georgia, McAdoo began to practice law in New York City in 1892. In 1902, he became president of the Hudson and Manhattan Railroad Company and built the first traffic tunnel under the Hudson River. In 1912, McAdoo, a Wilson supporter, served as the chairman of the Democratic National Committee. During the campaign, he wrote articles discussing and defending Wilson's economic policies. McAdoo called for the election of new officials not affiliated with the monopoly of manufacturers. After Wilson won the election, McAdoo

became secretary of the treasury, serving from 1913 to 1918. In 1914, he married Wilson's daughter, Eleanor Randolph Wilson. McAdoo also received an appointment as the director general of U.S. railroads, a wartime position, from 1917 to 1919. Dale Shook contends that McAdoo's endeavors reflected his "ambition, a desire for prestige and respect, a sense of public service, and a secondary goal of making money."

As secretary of the treasury, the president directed McAdoo to revise tariff law—a high-priority item in the Wilson administration. McAdoo believed that tariff laws remained overprotective and did not encourage development of new industries. The tariff laws also resulted in higher prices and lower wages, he contended. The Underwood-Simmons Tariff Act of 1913 resulted in lower duties on imports and removed, among other items, tariffs from wool, sugar, steel rails, and iron ore. To replace the lost revenue, the bill proposed a graduated income tax, which the Constitution's Sixteenth Amendment, ratified in 1913, provided.

McAdoo also participated in the creation of a Federal Reserve Board. Working with congressional leaders, he wanted a government bank that would diminish Wall Street banking interests' power. At the same time, McAdoo believed that government involvement should encourage individual initiative. McAdoo's ideas and actions raised his popularity and the trust of the public. Shook compared McAdoo's role to that of an assistant president in charge of both the creation of policy and of nonpolitical affairs administration.

During World War I, McAdoo actively supported wartime efforts. In his speech titled "American Rights," he argued, "God has called us as a champion of freedom and democracy." In addressing economic needs, he contended that accepting Germany's attempt to create a zone of about 500 miles in which Americans could not sail their ships would bring about disaster to America's farms, manufactories, mining interests, and labor interests.

McAdoo ran unsuccessfully for president in 1920 and 1924. When McAdoo and Attorney General A. Mitchell Palmer deadlocked at the 1920 Democratic convention, delegates selected Governor James Cox of Ohio. When McAdoo and Governor Alfred E. Smith of New York deadlocked in 1924, John W. Davis won the nomination. McAdoo served as U.S. senator from California from 1933 to 1938. He died on February 1, 1941, in Washington, D.C.

See also: Federal Reserve Bank; Personal income tax (Sixteenth Constitutional Amendment); Underwood-Simmons Tariff (Tariff of 1913); Wilson, Thomas Woodrow; World War II.

Selected Bibliography:

Dale N. Shook, *William G. McAdoo and the Development of National Economic Policy: 1913–1918*, 1987.

David E. Walker

McCLEARY, JAMES THOMPSON (February 5, 1853–December 17, 1924)

U.S. representative from Minnesota.

Born in Ingersoll, Ontario, Canada, on February 5, 1853, McCleary attended McGill University in Montreal before immigrating to the United States. He served as the superintendent of the Pierce County, Wisconsin, schools until 1811, when he moved to Minnesota. He continued his career in education before winning a seat in the House of Representatives, where he served from March 4, 1893 to March 3, 1907. During the debates over tariff revision in 1905 and 1906, many Republicans supported a downward revision of the tariff. McCleary opposed his fellow Republicans who supported these changes and introduced a bill that would have set the Dingley Tariff rates as the minimum. He also allowed a 25 percent penalty levied against any country that refused to extend the favored-nation tariff rates to the United States. Henry Cabot Lodge proposed a similar bill. When the first session of the Fifty-ninth Congress adjourned, neither bill had reached the floor for debate. During the break, President Theodore Roosevelt and Secretary of State Elihu Root negotiated an agreement with Germany that eliminated some of the criticism over the use of the Maximum-Minimum Tariff. When Congress reconvened, both bills failed to pass. During the election held in November 1906, McCleary lost his reelection bid primarily because of his stance against Republican revisionism. Roosevelt appointed him as second postmaster general, a position he held from March 4, 1907 to September 15, 1908. After retiring from public office, he served as the secretary of the American Iron and Steel Institute in New York City until 1920 and then moved to California before returning to Wisconsin, where he died in 1924.

See also: Dingley Tariff (Tariff of 1897); Germany; Lodge, Henry Cabot; Maximum-Minimum Tariff; Roosevelt, Theodore; Root, Elihu.

Selected Bibliography:

Paul Wolman, *Most Favored Nation: The Republican Revisionists and U.S. Tariff Policy, 1897–1912*, 1992.

Cynthia Clark Northrup

McCORMICK, CYRUS (February 15, 1809–May 13, 1884)

Inventor, philanthropist, and pioneer in the mechanization of agriculture.

Born in Rockbridge County, Virginia, of Scots-Irish descent, McCormick received little in the way of formal education, but apprenticed under his father who experimented with farm machinery, including unsuccessful attempts to build an automatic reaper. In 1834, McCormick patented his own mechanical reaper that would replace the use of the sickle and cradle and spur a vast increase in American grain production. To better market his new machine to the growing number of midwestern farmers, McCormick established a manufacturing center in Chicago, Illinois, in 1847. By the 1850s, McCormick sold over 1,000 reapers a year. He soon gained international recognition due to successful demonstrations of his machine at the Crystal Palace Exhibition in 1851 and the International Exposition in Paris during 1855.

Although a leading manufacturer, McCormick generally opposed protective tariffs, especially by 1915 when he supported the Tariff Commission League's effort to reduce rates. As a southerner by birth, he identified with agrarian interests and remained suspi-

cious of any policies that favored the creation of a manufacturing elite and made the northeast economically and politically dominant. In the 1860s and 1870s, McCormick emerged as a leading figure in Illinois state politics, serving at various times as chairman of the state Democratic committee. Unafraid of competition from foreign producers of reapers, and mindful of the linkage between the success of the small grain farmer and his own prosperity, McCormick supported the National Grange in its demands for lower tariffs in the 1870s. To expand the foreign market for American grain, McCormick also helped form the Mississippi Valley Society to promote trade relations between England and the Mississippi valley. He died in Chicago on May 13, 1884.

See also: American farmers; Free trade.

Selected Bibliography:

Craig Canine, *Dream Reaper*, 1995; William Hutchinson, *Cyrus Hall McCormick*, 1968.

William C. Barnhart

McDUFFIE, GEORGE (August 10, 1790–March 11, 1851)

Democratic representative and senator from South Carolina.

Born in Columbia County, Georgia, McDuffie graduated from South Carolina College, now the University of South Carolina, in 1813. He studied law before entering the South Carolina State House of Representatives in 1818. Elected to the U.S. House of Representatives in 1820, he served as the chairman of the House Ways and Means Committee and as a manager during the impeachment proceedings against District Judge James H. Peck of Missouri in 1830. As the representative from South Carolina, he opposed the passage of the Tariff of Abominations and accepted Clay's Compromise. He remained a strong supporter of the states' rights argument espoused by John C. Calhoun in the South Carolina *Exposition* and *Protest*. He resigned in 1834 to become the governor of South Carolina from 1834 to 1846. After serving as president of the board of trustees for South Carolina College, he filled the position of U.S. senator on the resignation of William C. Preston. Reelected in 1842, he chaired the Committee on Foreign Relations during the Twenty-ninth Congress. McDuffie died in 1851 at his Cherry Hill home.

See also: Calhoun, John Caldwell; Clay's Compromise; Nullification; South Carolina *Exposition* and *Protest*.

Selected Bibliography:

Edwin Green, *George McDuffie*, 1936.

Cynthia Clark Northrup

McDUFFIE, JOHN (September 25, 1883–November 1, 1950)

Member of the U.S. House of Representatives from Alabama and co-author of the McDuffie-Tydings Act that granted independence to the Philippines.

Born in River Ridge, Alabama, McDuffie attended Southern University and graduated from Alabama Polytechnic Institute in 1904. In 1908, he received a law degree from the University of Alabama. Voters elected him to the Alabama House of Representatives in 1907 and in 1911 he became a prosecuting attorney. In 1918, he won a seat in the U.S. House of Representatives as a Democrat.

McDuffie served as the Democratic whip in the House from 1930 to 1932. He lost a contest for Speaker to Henry Rainey of Illinois. During the administrations of Herbert Hoover and Franklin Roosevelt, he chaired the House Economy Committee and the House Insular Affairs Committee from 1933 until he left Congress in 1935. Working with Senator Millard Tydings of Maryland, his counterpart in the Senate, McDuffie drafted the McDuffie-Tydings Act of 1934, legislation that granted independence to the Philippines.

President Roosevelt appointed him as a U.S. judge for the Southern District of Alabama in 1935. He remained in that position until he died on November 1, 1950, in Mobile, Alabama, after a long illness.

See also: Hoover, Herbert; McDuffie-Tydings Act; Roosevelt, Franklin D.; Tydings, Millard E.

Selected Bibliography:

Ralph Neal Brannen, *John McDuffie: State Legislator, Congressman, Federal Judge, 1883–1950*, 1975.

John David Rausch Jr.

McDUFFIE-TYDINGS ACT

Legislation that provided for Philippine independence; drafted by Representative John McDuffie and Senator Millard Tydings.

In 1933, the Philippine Senate refused to ratify the Hare-Hawes-Cutting

Act, which had become law over the veto of President Herbert Hoover. Hare-Hawes-Cutting specified a date for Philippine independence from the United States for the first time. Working with Filipino political leader Manuel Quezon, Representative John McDuffie, chairman of the House Territories Committee, and Senator Millard Tydings, chairman of the Senate Territories Committee, crafted a bill similar to the one rejected by the Philippine Senate in 1933.

The introduction of the McDuffie-Tydings Independence Act occurred in both houses of Congress on March 14, 1934. The House bill resembled the Hare-Hawes-Cutting Act with a few minor changes. According to the proposed legislation, trade relations between the Philippines and the United States would continue unchanged for five years with a few exceptions. The United States would levy full tariffs on Philippine imports of sugar, coconut oil, and manila hemp. After the Philippines became independent, the full tariff would apply to goods exported from the Philippines. The immigration laws of the United States that excluded Asians would apply to all persons born in the Philippines after independence. The House approved the bill on March 19. The Senate passed the bill after defeating a number of amendments altering the date of Philippine independence. President Franklin Roosevelt signed the bill into law on March 24, 1934. The Philippine Senate ratified the measure on May 1, 1934. Filipinos elected delegates to a constitutional convention on July 10. President Roosevelt approved the new constitution on March 23, 1935. The Philippines remained a commonwealth for ten years, until July 4, 1946. In 1939, Congress approved amendments to the trade provisions of McDuffie-Tydings to benefit the Philippines.

See also: Hoover, Herbert; McDuffie, John; Roosevelt, Franklin D.; Sugar; Tydings, Millard E.

Selected Bibliography:

Garel A. Grunder and William E. Livezy, *The Philippines and the United States*, 1973; Caroline H. Keith, *"For Hell and a Brown Mule": The Biography of Senator Millard E. Tydings*, 1991.

John David Rausch Jr.

McKENNA, JOSEPH E. (August 10, 1843–November 21, 1926)

American legislator and jurist from California who supported high tariffs and protection for western railroad and other business interests.

Born in Philadelphia to Irish immigrants, McKenna moved to Benicia, California, with his family in 1855. Educated in parochial schools, he gained admittance to the bar in 1865 and served as district attorney for Solano County from 1866 to 1870. A Republican, he won a seat in the state legislature in 1875 and stayed there until 1876. After two narrow defeats, he won election to the U.S. House of Representatives in 1885.

In Congress, McKenna supported high tariffs and promoted pro-business policy positions as a member of the powerful Ways and Means Committee chaired by William McKinley. In his four terms as a member of the House, he championed the extension of railroad land grants, passed legislation improving port facilities, and restricted the freedoms of Chinese laborers. He submitted pro-business amendments to the McKinley Tariff of 1890 to restrict foreign spirits.

On the recommendation of his political mentor, California senator Leland Stanford, President Benjamin Harrison appointed McKenna to the U.S. Court of Appeals for the Ninth Circuit. He left that post in 1897 to serve as attorney general under President William McKinley, but after only a few months, the president nominated him to the U.S. Supreme Court. Because of his ties to Stanford and western railroad interests, the Senate delayed his nomination for four months. Eventually he received confirmation and went on to serve on the Court for twenty-seven years. Justice McKenna exhibited a strong nationalist jurisprudence, upholding federal police powers such as the Pure Food and Drug Act of 1906 and the Mann Act of 1910, which prohibited the transportation of women across state lines for immoral purposes. In failing health, he was persuaded by his colleagues to step down from the Court. He died a year later at the age of eighty-three on November 21, 1926, in Washington, D.C.

See also: Harrison, Benjamin; McKinley, William; McKinley Tariff (Tariff of 1890).

Selected Bibliography:

Brother Matthew McDevitt, *Joseph McKenna: Associate Justice of the United States*, 1946; James F. Watts Jr., "Joseph McKenna" *The Justices of the United States Supreme Court 1789–1969: Their Lives and Major Opinions*, 1969.

Artemus Ward

McKINLEY, WILLIAM (June 29, 1843– September 14, 1901)

A strong advocate of protectionism as both a U.S. representative and president who symbolized industrial nationalism while not favoring business trusts.

Born in Niles, Ohio, McKinley attended Allegheny College. After dropping out for health reasons in 1860, McKinley distinguished himself in the Civil War, achieving the rank of major. He then studied law, settled in Canton, Ohio, and married Ida Saxton, the daughter of a wealthy banker. His friendship with Rutherford B. Hayes secured his career as an Ohio politician. He represented Ohio in the House for most of the years between 1877 and 1891, building for himself a reputation as a champion of American industry.

He enhanced this reputation when, as the chairman of the House Committee of Ways and Means, he proposed the McKinley Tariff of 1890. Although the Democrats won the congressional elections, and McKinley lost his seat in the House, later that year after exploiting public fears of raising prices, McKinley became governor of Ohio in 1891 and again in 1893. As governor, McKinley enjoyed the support of laborers whose jobs remained protected by his tariff policy. Although he once used the National Guard to stop a labor riot in Akron, he did not favor more harsh measures against labor unions. His popularity in Ohio, his friendship with powerful industrialist Mark Hannah, his reputation as an avid protectionist, and a Democratic administration weakened by economic depression opened the door for McKinley to win the presidency.

In 1896, he faced Democrat William Jennings Bryan, whose call for inflationary measures to benefit American farmers attracted Populists to his platform. McKinley campaigned from his front porch while Hannah gathered his support in America's industries. In what appeared to be an epic struggle between industrial and agricultural interests, as well as creditors' versus debtors' interests, McKinley won the presidency with 271 electoral votes while Bryan received 176. His 600,000-vote margin was the largest since 1872.

Although the campaign had been a battle over domestic policy, foreign concerns dominated his administration. The Spanish-American War of 1898 and the Filipino insurrection that followed occupied most of his energy as president. But before foreign concerns diverted his attention, McKinley and the Republican-dominated Congress passed the highly protective Dingley Tariff in 1897. They hailed it as an act to raise government revenue, but Democrats saw it as a shameless payoff to big businesses. Industrialists who contributed heavily to the McKinley campaign certainly did so as an investment. Although this measure appeared reminiscent of the highly protective McKinley Tariff, no similar public outcry against the bill occurred, especially after Americans turned their interest to the war. Taking advantage of their political stronghold, McKinley and the congressional Republicans passed another measure favored by business— the Gold Standard Act of 1900. To garner western support for the bill, the door remained open for international bimetallism, later rejected by the European Community. The McKinley ad-

ministration had effectively derailed Populist plans to inflate U.S. currency.

Later that year, imperialism dominated the presidential election. Again, McKinley faced Bryan. The two stood on the same domestic issues they had in 1896, but Bryan added an anti-imperialistic tone. McKinley won his reelection bid with an even greater plurality of votes. However, in September 1901, while speaking on America's role in the world at the Pan American Exposition in Buffalo, Leon Czolgosz, a crazed anarchist, assassinated him.

See also: Bryan, William Jennings; Dingley Tariff (Tariff of 1897); House Ways and Means Committee; Populists; Protectionism. **Vol. II**: Benjamin Harrison's 1889 State of the Union Address; Samuel J. Randall's 1888 Speech on Tariff Benefits for the Wealthy. **Vol. III**: Tariff of 1890 (McKinley Tariff); Tariff of 1897 (Dingley Tariff).

Selected Bibliography:

Lewis L. Gould, *The Presidency of William McKinley*, 1980; H. Wayne Morgan, *William McKinley and His America*, 1963.

Matt McCook

McKINLEY TARIFF (TARIFF OF 1890)

Legislation proposed by Representative William McKinley and passed in 1890 raising the general level of tariffs to one of its highest points in U.S. history.

Responding to the pressure to reduce the surplus in the treasury while still protecting U.S. industries, McKinley proposed this high tariff to cut American imports and lower government revenue. Emboldened by the 1888 election of Benjamin Harrison, which they perceived as a mandate for protectionism, Republicans believed that consumers would accept a reduction in table item duties, even when faced with increases in other products. Thus, the McKinley tariff lowered rates on certain items and added many to the free list, including tea, raw sugar, coffee, and molasses. At the same time, it raised the average level of tariffs to 50 percent of the cost of the product. Republicans hoped that by putting table items on the free list, they could point to tangible results in their efforts to reduce tariffs.

Although many of the tariff rates appeared friendly to farmers—such as the increased rate on imported cotton from 30 percent to 50 percent—American industries benefited most from the bill. Adding raw sugar to the free list benefited American sugar manufacturers as much as consumers. McKinley demonstrated his commitment to infant American industries by raising duties on tin plates. Protectionists considered such encouragement of small and nonexistent American industries the most enlightened aspect of the bill. Although the United States had no carpeted wools industry, McKinley placed high duties on them since many clothing and combed woolen traders had formerly disguised their products as carpeted wool to avoid tariffs on the higher quality wools. McKinley also demonstrated his political acumen in getting the bill passed. To appease American sugar farmers who did not want sugar on the free list, the bill provided that American sugar farmers receive $6 million to $7 million. To garner support for his measure from

western Democrats, McKinley and many other Republicans agreed to support the Sherman Silver Purchase Act.

Although much of his protective philosophy surfaced in the bill, one important amendment did not bear his fingerprints, nor did it meet with his approval. Senator James G. Blaine, not nearly as confident in the public mandate for protectionism, wanted a reciprocity agreement attached to the tariff bill. Instead of adding sugar to the free list, Blaine favored using the duty on sugar and other items as leverage in trading with other nations. He preferred giving the president the power to remove or reduce duties for certain nations if those nations made similar gestures. But Nelson Aldrich managed to get approval for a reciprocity plan that worked in the opposite way. The Aldrich Amendment allowed the president the power to impose retaliatory measures against products of other nations that levied unfair tariffs on the United States, rather than allowing him to remove existing tariffs. This amendment signaled the beginning of the use of reciprocity clauses in a tariff bill.

The bill in its final form passed the House on September 27, 1890, and the Senate on September 30 of the same year. Voting occurred almost exclusively along party lines, with most Republicans supporting the bill and Democrats opposing it. The anticipated increase in food and clothing prices caused the Republicans to lose overwhelmingly in the congressional elections of 1890. William McKinley lost his House seat. Grover Cleveland's election in 1892 gave the Democrats control of both houses of Congress and the presidency. It seemed to tariff reformers to signal public disapproval of protective tariffs.

See also: Aldrich, Nelson W.; Blaine, James Gillespie; Cleveland, Stephen Grover; Harrison, Benjamin; McKinley, William; Wools and woolens. **Vol. II**: Benjamin Harrison's 1889 State of the Union Address; Samuel J. Randall's 1888 Speech on Tariff Benefits for the Wealthy. **Vol. III**: Tariff of 1890 (McKinley Tariff).

Selected Bibliography:

Edward S. Kaplan and Thomas W. Ryley, *Prelude to Trade Wars: American Tariff Policy, 1890–1922*, 1994; Tom E. Terrill, *The Tariff, Politics, and American Foreign Policy 1874–1901*, 1973.

Matt McCook

McMILLIN, BENTON (September 11, 1845–January 8, 1933)

U.S. representative who first proposed a personal income tax as a means of lowering the tariff without the loss of revenue.

Born in Monroe County, Kentucky, in 1845, McMillin attended Philomath Academy, Tennessee, studied law at the University of Kentucky, and practiced as an attorney until he joined the Tennessee State House of Representatives in 1874. Between 1879 and 1899, he served in the U.S. House of Representatives. He attended every Democratic National Convention between 1876 and 1932, with the exception of 1920. The Democratic Party drew on his campaign and oratorical skills for national electoral races.

As a ranking member of the Ways and Means Committee, McMillin ve-

hemently represented the southern sectional interest in lower tariffs. He also supported the creation of an income tax. He advocated such a levy both as a means to redistribute wealth and as an important step in lowering trade restrictions. The federal government at the time depended heavily on tariffs, which served as its major source of revenue; an income tax would thus diminish government dependence on import duties and make their reduction more palatable financially. In 1894, McMillin surreptitiously included an income tax provision in the Wilson-Gorman Tariff Act. The Supreme Court declared this law invalid in 1895, demanding that such a tax be enacted by constitutional amendment. In 1899, McMillin resigned from Congress to serve as governor of Tennessee.

His policy preferences endured. Young Tennesseean Cordell Hull later claimed to have "learned many of my political lessons [at] Benton McMillin's feet." McMillin's fervent support for lower tariffs and the income tax significantly influenced Hull's views on these issues. In 1907, Hull won the same Tennessee seat in Congress formerly occupied by McMillin. Following in his mentor's footsteps, Hull drafted the provision that led to the ratification of the first income tax law in U.S. history in 1913.

See also: Personal income tax (Sixteenth Constitutional Amendment); Wilson-Gorman Tariff (Tariff of 1894).

Selected Bibliography:

Edward Stanwood, *American Tariff Controversies in the Nineteenth Century*, 1967.

Jamie Miller

MELLON, ANDREW W. (March 24, 1855–August 26, 1937)

American financier, philanthropist, and U.S. secretary of the treasury.

Born in Pittsburgh, Pennsylvania, Mellon studied at Western University, now the University of Pittsburgh, before joining his father's bank in 1874. In 1884, his father retired and Mellon assumed control over the financial institution and spent the next three decades building a financial empire by providing loans to the growing industrial companies of the region. Recognizing changes in technology and surrounding himself with bright, ambitious businessmen, Mellon formed several large companies such as the Aluminum Company of America (Alcoa), Gulf Oil Company, and Union Steel Company, that later merged with the United States Steel Corporation, the American Locomotive Company, and the Union Trust Company. He resigned as president of the Mellon National Bank in 1921 to accept an appointment as secretary of the treasury in 1921, serving in this capacity until 1932. During his tenure in office, Mellon successfully advocated the reduction of income taxes and surtaxes. Even though the government received less revenue, Mellon managed to reduce the national debt from $24,298,000,000 in 1920 to $16,185,000,000 in 1930. Although a supporter of lower personal taxes, Mellon pushed for an increase in tariffs. He championed a two- to five-cent-per-pound increase on aluminum imports, and after Congress increased the rate in 1922, the price of domestic aluminum rose three cents per pound. Critics charged Mellon with using his position in the cabinet for personal gain at the expense of average Americans. When Mellon left office after the election of Franklin D. Roosevelt, he served as the U.S. ambassador to Great Britain from 1932 to 1933. As a philanthropist he founded the Mellon Institute of Industrial Research in Pittsburgh, providing the institution with a gift of $10 million, and then donated his entire art collection, along with funds for the construction of the National Gallery of Art to house the masterpieces, to the public in 1937. Mellon died in Southampton, New York, on August 26, 1937.

See also: Carnegie, Andrew; Personal income tax (Sixteenth Constitutional Amendment); Trusts. **Vol. II**: Andrew W. Mellon's Defense of the Hawley-Smoot Tariff for Economic Recovery; Franklin D. Roosevelt's 1932 Campaign Radio Speech. **Vol. III**: Tariff of 1922 (Fordney-McCumber Tariff); Tariff of 1930 (Hawley-Smoot Tariff).

Selected Bibliography:

Philip H. Love, *Andrew W. Mellon: The Man and His Work*, 1929; Oswald Garrison Villard, *Free Trade—Free World*, 1947.

Cynthia Clark Northrup

MERCANTILISM

The mercantile system that characterized the political economy of most European states from the sixteenth through the eighteenth century.

Mercantilism emerged with the rise of nation-states and the centralization of authority as feudal systems declined. Although variations in specific policies existed, mercantilist policy favored the interests of the state, especially with respect to overseas colonies and foreign trade. Government regulation of industry and commerce placed national aims above local or individual interests in efforts to strengthen national power and prosperity through the establishment of favorable balances of trade, while developing agriculture and industry and reducing dependence on foreign sources. Mercantilist policy also encouraged the creation of strong merchant marines, formation of overseas trade monopolies, and population growth.

Portugal and Spain initiated such policies in the formation of their empires in the sixteenth century, and others followed their model with modifications. Spain emphasized the acquisition of precious metals from its American mines along with a monopolistic trading system that tried, unsuccessfully, to exclude foreigners from the trade. With the draining of specie from Europe to the East in the preceding centuries, bullionism became the monetary policy of mercantilism as Spain welcomed the gold and silver of Latin America. Spain developed its colonial empire with a primary concern for maintaining a favorable balance of precious metals, equating the amassing of gold and silver with national wealth. Luis Ortiz's *Memorial al Rey para prohibir la salida del oro* (Report to the King on prohibiting the export of gold), published in 1558, articulated this view at the beginning of the reign of Philip II. The conservation and increase of the supply of precious metals became the basic principle of commercial policy, but enormous defense expenditures and the failure to develop domestic industry eventually converted Spain

from one of Europe's richest countries to one of its poorest. French and English mercantilism in the seventeenth century also favored monopolistic companies, but provided greater flexibility in foreign and colonial trade and proved more successful in stimulating home industry. These nations recognized that they could not always control the flow of precious metals and that wealth could be gained from trade itself. But they closely regulated companies engaged in overseas trade in an attempt to preserve national advantage. Navigation laws, corn laws, and protective tariffs characterized English mercantilist policies.

The mercantilists assumed a fixed amount of wealth in the world, and that international trade created the means by which that wealth moved from one nation to another. Notable proponents of mercantilism in the seventeenth century, although not using the term, included Jean-Baptiste Colbert in France, Antonio Serra in Italy, and Thomas Mun in England. Mun's brief *England's Treasure by Foreign Trade*, published in 1664, influenced English policy. These writers emphasized expansion of trade as a source of wealth and stressed removing some restrictions on the flow of precious metals. Adam Smith first used the term "mercantilism" in his *Wealth of Nations* in 1776, referring to the mercantile system that he described as currently employed by the imperial powers, but which he criticized strongly in favor of laissez-faire policies of freer trade. Other early critics of mercantilism included Sir William Petty and Sir Dudley North, who pointed out that, while trade required money, the hoarding of precious metals deterred trade. David

Hume, in his *Political Discourses* in 1753, challenged the contention of mercantilists who argued that the gain of each nation must occur at the expense of others.

Mercantilism served the development of capitalism in the early modern period, for it encouraged population growth and accumulation and investment of capital in trade and manufacturing in the metropolis. It thus contributed to the early stages of the Industrial Revolution. At the same time, it contributed to underdevelopment in colonial regions because of the restrictions it imposed on colonial freedom of trade and industry. Under mercantilism, the mother country restricted colonial development of any economic activity that did not serve the interest of the mother country. North American colonists thus opposed British navigation laws and especially the mercantilist restrictions imposed following the Seven Years' War. Mercantilist policies thus caused the American Revolution. After independence, strong mercantilist sentiments arose in the United States, especially in the northern states that sought to protect infant industries from the competition of the more industrialized European nations.

In the late eighteenth century, under the pressure of physiocratic economic philosophy and free trade policies, mercantilism began to diminish. François Quesnay, especially in his *Tableau économique* (Economic picture), published in 1758, led the physiocratic attack on mercantilism and greatly influenced the more comprehensive view on economic systems by Adam Smith, which laid the foundations for modern capitalism. Yet mercantilist policies persisted in many countries, including the United States,

well into the nineteenth and twentieth centuries in an effort to encourage and protect native agriculture and manufacturing. Great Britain, with its maritime superiority, led the movement for free trade in the nineteenth century. Tariff wars continued throughout the century, but a movement toward lower tariffs and reciprocity gained at the beginning of the twentieth century. Following World War I, a "new mercantilism" prevailed with a rise in measures that restrained international trade. This trend culminated in the Great Depression, after which a trend toward lower tariffs and international trade agreements culminated in the General Agreement on Tariffs and Trade (GATT) in 1947.

See also: Capitalism; General Agreement on Tariffs and Trade (GATT); Great Britain; Great Depression; Hume, David; Industrial Revolution; Navigation and Trade Acts; Smith, Adam.

Selected Bibliography:

Robert B. Ekelund and Robert B. Tollison, *Politicized Economies: Monarchy, Monopoly, and Mercantilism*, 1997; Lars Magnusson, ed., *Mercantilist Economics*, 1993; John J. McCusker and Russell R. Menard, *The Economy of British America, 1607–1789*, 1985.

Ralph Lee Woodward Jr.

MERCHANTS ASSOCIATION OF NEW YORK (MANY)

Group that supported the creation of a tariff commission.

Formed in the mid-1890s, this organization of New York merchants addressed many issues ranging from water problems within the city to problems associated with importing and exporting. During the early 1900s, the group argued against reciprocity treaties on the basis that no particular industry would willingly sacrifice itself for the benefit of others; therefore, this type of agreement would not succeed. When Herbert Miles initiated a campaign for a scientific tariff commission, the Merchants Association of New York (MANY) supported the movement.

During the 1909 Indianapolis Tariff Commission Convention, several members of MANY spoke to the delegates, including Henry R. Towne, a cost-accounting expert. Towne presented his paper "The Neutral Line," which called for a tariff commission with rate-setting influence that would scientifically examine the comparative costs of production of U.S. and foreign products. He emphasized the need to keep the cost down on basic household items and food as a means of preventing labor unrest. "If tariffs were forced to toe 'the neutral line,'" Towne hypothesized, "traditional and social harmonies might be restored." Towne's speech convinced many delegates of the need for a tariff commission that would base rates on specific data. The convention passed a resolution calling for the establishment of a commission, but then another resolution stated that until the formation of the commission, tariff negotiations should continue as before. The second resolution took some of the power out of the first one. The MANY continued to push for the creation of the Tariff Commission.

See also: Miles, Herbert Edwin; Tariff Commission.

Selected Bibliography:

Thomas Pryor Gore, *A Permanent Tariff Commission: An Address delivered before the Merchants' Association of New York, on December 9, 1915, relative to the establishment of a Permanent Tariff Commission*, 1916; Paul Wolman, *Most Favored Nation: The Republican Revisionists and U.S. Tariff Policy, 1897–1912*, 1992.

Cynthia Clark Northrup

METCALF, EDWIN D. (August 21, 1876–September 30, 1949)

Chairman of the National Association of Agricultural Implements and Vehicle Manufacturers (NAAIVM); opposed Herbert Miles's argument for a Tariff Commission.

Born in Springfield, Massachusetts, on August 21, 1876, Metcalf owned a majority of the D.M. Osborne Harvester Company of Auburn, New York. He represented International Harvester on the Special Tariff Committee of NAAIVM that Herbert Miles chaired. When the committee issued a final report on tariffs, Metcalf agreed that independent manufacturers had the need to purchase cheaper raw materials and had the right to do so. Although he represented one of the largest trusts at that time, Metcalf supported the findings as a way of deflecting criticism against big business. One of the major issues of the day focused on the ability of large companies such as International Harvester to purchase raw materials like steel from other big companies such as U.S. Steel at lower prices than the midsize enterprises. Although the larger companies refused to lower prices, the committee agreed that manufacturers needed access to raw materials from foreign countries. This required a reduction of tariff rates on these goods.

Although he encouraged Miles to testify before Congress, when Metcalf testified, he argued that the smaller companies did not require a reduction in tariffs, a change that would open foreign competition against International Harvester and his own company. Instead, he emphasized that these firms could compete in the international market by specializing in specific markets and using the existing drawback legislation. Metcalf died on September 30, 1949, in Auburn, New York.

See also: International Harvester; Miles, Herbert Edwin; Tariff Commission.

Selected Bibliography:

Paul Wolman, *Most Favored Nation: The Republican Revisionists and U.S. Tariff Policy, 1897–1912*, 1992.

Cynthia Clark Northrup

MEXICO

A country populated and intermittently dominated by numerous indigenous groups in the centuries before 1519, Mexico was seized by Spain following a widespread indigenous conflict, civil war, and a smallpox epidemic lasting from 1519 to 1521.

From 1524 to 1821, the resulting Spanish colony, named New Spain, remained governed by a series of crown-appointed viceroys from Mexico City, the site of the former Aztec capital of Tenochtitlan. The administrative expanse under the supervision of colonial Mexico City encompassed much of the Caribbean, the territories from modern-day Florida west to New Orleans, north to Missouri, west to San Francisco, California, and south through Central America to modern-day Costa Rica. Spain added to this vast area the Philippines and several islands in the Western Pacific by the end of the sixteenth century.

During the colonial period, Mexico played a key role in financing Spanish foreign policy through a series of taxes on the indigenous population (such as *tributo*), on internal as well as international commerce, and, most important, on the mining of precious metals: gold and silver. Until the 1680s, Mexican silver production placed second only to that of Potosí in Bolivia. From the 1680s to independence, Mexican silver mining served as the cornerstone for Spanish imperial policy. Although never as generally important as direct taxes on mineral production, indigenous levies, and revenues from a royal tobacco monopoly, tariffs such as the *almojarifazgo* nonetheless signaled the interdependence of mining and international trade, both in the Atlantic and Pacific.

Throughout the colonial era, the Spanish crown and its representatives abroad—a number of merchant guilds (*consulados*) based in Seville, Mexico City, Veracruz, and a few other steadily populated and strategically located areas in Spanish America—controlled trade in Mexico. Until 1754, these guilds collected the taxes and tariffs. From 1754 to the 1770s, a new royal tax bureaucracy grew steadily, manned largely by *criollos*, Spaniards born in

Mexico. The era of the 1780s to independence saw a steady effort by the Spanish crown to significantly dilute the creole presence in both regional and royal government. The regular appointment of *peninsulares*—loyal and trustworthy Spaniards born in Spain—steadily replaced Mexican creoles in many key positions.

For most of the first fifty years after independence, Mexico experienced continuous political instability and foreign invasion. During this time, war with the United States, direct and indirect, combined with a series of one-sided treaties, cost Mexico the northern half of the country, and created the borders that exist today between the two countries.

By the late 1860s, following a devastating civil war, Mexican liberals led by Benito Juárez and later Porfirio Díaz, pushed through a series of economic reforms that brought railroads, industry, a revival and expansion of the mining sector, and a return to policies closely emulating those of the mercantilist-dominated colonial period: the export of raw materials and the import of manufactured goods from a rapidly industrializing United States and Western Europe. The social cost of these policies ran high. Between 1910 and 1920, Mexico experienced another civil war—the Mexican Revolution—that profoundly altered the structure, if not the character, of government for the rest of the twentieth century. Ruled by a single group, the Institutional Revolutionary Party (PRI) for the next eighty years, Mexico nationalized numerous key economic sectors, most notably the foreign capital-dominated oil industry, and carried out a wide-reaching policy of land reform. However, the Mexican economy ultimately remained tied to the demands and oscillations of international markets, especially through their ties to the United States.

By the late 1960s, the PRI, the supposed guardians of revolutionary ideals, focused more on big business and foreign economic interests than on the needs of their own people. Despite growing cynicism and dissatisfaction, the PRI retained power for another two decades, presiding over a massive borrowing program in the era of the post-1973 boom in oil prices. When the oil bubble burst in 1981, Mexico found itself saddled with an enormous debt burden, unending economic crises, and frequent currency devaluations.

Led by a series of U.S.-educated economists from the mid-1980s to the end of the century, Mexico entered into negotiations with the United States and Canada for the creation of the still controversial North American Free Trade Agreement (NAFTA) to end tariff barriers between the three countries. Although it is still too soon to determine the full ramifications of the agreement, Mexico has enjoyed enormous growth in its manufacturing sector along the border with the United States due to the large disparity in wages between the two countries. It is along this border that Mexico produces tariff-free consumer goods for U.S. markets, goods manufactured in the United States as recently as two decades ago.

See also: Latin America; North American Free Trade Agreement (NAFTA); Salinas de Gortari, Carlos; Silver.

Selected Bibliography:

Jan Bazant, *A Concise History of Mexico from Hidalgo to Cárdenas, 1805–1940*, 1977; Michael C. Meyer and William L. Sherman, *The Course of Mexican History*, 1979; John Womack Jr., *Zapata and the Mexican Revolution*, 1969.

David J. Weiland III

MILES, HERBERT EDWIN (November 21, 1860–August 6, 1939)

Most vocal proponent of a downward tariff revision and the establishment of a tariff commission.

Born in Waupaca, Wisconsin, on November 21, 1860, Miles worked his way up to the top of the agricultural implements industry. He served as the president of the Racine-Sattley Company of Racine, Wisconsin, a firm formed in 1909. With over 1,500 employees in his Wisconsin and Illinois plants, Miles operated a medium- to large-sized business that manufactured farm wagons, buggies, and plows. He joined the ranks of many other self-made millionaires who benefited from a high tariff. Most medium-sized companies had their foreign competition taxed at a rate of 20 to 45 percent *ad valorem*.

Miles, an officer of the National Association of Agricultural Implement and Vehicle Manufacturers (NAAIVM), led a group of sales managers from the implements industry in negotiations with U.S. Steel in March 1906. The group blamed the big trusts for increases in the cost of materials that undermined their relationship with the average farmer. They asked for an industry quantity discount to twenty-six dollars a ton, a decrease of four dollars a ton.

Representatives of U.S. Steel finally agreed to a one-time reduction to twenty-eight dollars a ton for fifteen days. Then the price increased back up to thirty dollars a ton. Although several members believed that the agreement might lead to other concessions, executives from U.S. Steel quickly destroyed that belief. Tensions between entrepreneurs and big businesses continued to increase and the NAAIVM officials decided to push for a downward revision of the tariff and the establishment of a scientific tariff commission as a means of stabilizing their position in the domestic market.

The NAAIVM joined forces with the stronger National Association of Manufacturers in 1905. The leader of NAM, James W. Van Cleave, appointed Miles as his delegate to handle the tariff commission issue. Both men spoke to numerous crowds and wrote about the need for an independent tariff commission that would base tariff rates on a cost comparison between domestic and foreign production. Miles wanted the Congress to authorize broad powers for the commission, including the ability to summon witnesses, examine business records, and issue subpoenas. Miles believed that a tariff commission would eliminate legislative barriers and help even out the tax burden among all Americans. Other members of the Republican Party joined Miles, including many of the Insurgents like Robert LaFollette and Albert J. Beveridge. When the legislation reached Congress for the establishment of a tariff commission in 1908, Speaker of the House Joseph Cannon helped defeat the bill. Although the movement failed temporarily, Republicans began to accept the concept of a scientific approach to the determination of tariff rates. Republicans who wanted a downward revision of the tariff helped ensure the passage of the Payne-Aldrich Tariff.

Miles died in Madison, Wisconsin, on August 6, 1939, and will always be remembered as the father of the Tariff Commission.

See also: Insurgents; National Association of Manufacturers (NAM); Roosevelt, Theodore; Taft, William Howard.

Selected Bibliography:

Nahum Isaac Stone, *One Man's Crusade for an Honest Tariff: The Story of Herbert E. Miles, Father of the Tariff Commission*, 1952; Paul Wolman, *Most Favored Nation: The Republican Revisionists and U.S. Tariff Policy, 1897–1912*, 1992.

Cynthia Clark Northrup

MILL, JOHN STUART (May 20, 1806–May 8, 1873)

Nineteenth-century British philosopher and economist.

As the son of noted philosopher James Mill, young John Stuart Mill followed the teachings of Jeremy Bentham, the founder of utilitarianism. Bentham taught that correct actions promote the greatest happiness for the greatest number of people. Although owing much to the training of his father and the philosophy of Bentham, Mill broke with a strict application of the principle of utility to human life. He stressed that the quality of happiness mattered as much as the quantity of happiness. He also taught that correct actions always promote the development of each and every individual.

His brand of utilitarianism placed a greater emphasis on personal development and the progress of all humanity.

While one of the most brilliant philosophers of his day, Mill remained a businessman. Like his father before him, he worked for much of his life as the director of the British East India Company. During his tenure, he developed significant insights into the principles that govern international trade. His first principle explained the distribution of gains from international trade. Economists of the day struggled to develop a method of calculating gains from trade between nations. Mill proposed that gains must be understood in terms of reciprocal demand. A nation offers as much of an exported good as another nation willingly accepts. Mill described this balance as the equilibrium price. At the ideal equilibrium price, imports demanded by one nation always equal the exports supplied by another nation.

Mill knew that the equilibrium price remained an abstract concept rarely achieved in actual practice. His second principle of international trade explained that gain in foreign trade almost always tips away from the equilibrium price in favor of one nation or the other. Mill described this imbalance as the elasticity of demand. The principle comes into play when one nation demands more products of another nation than it is willing to sell. In such a case, the producing nation will enjoy a more favorable balance of trade than the purchasing nation.

He added one further principle related to tariffs. He argued that an import duty inevitably raises the price of imported goods within a nation. The higher price in turn reduces the sale of imported goods both in overall quantity and overall revenue. Eventually, the revenue that a foreign nation earns on its exports no longer covers the value of its imports. The foreign country loses gold and the prices of its goods fall. In contrast, prices rise in the country imposing the tariff. Domestic goods sell in a greater volume at a higher cost, while prices also rise on goods sold abroad. But even with such a principle that described the value of tariffs, Mill consistently warned against prohibitive tariffs that set rates so high that they stopped all imports as well as exports. He also argued that changes in income affect the balance of trade just as much as changes in prices.

See also: East India Company; Protectionism.

Selected Bibliography:

Henry William Speigel, *The Growth of Economic Thought*, 1971.

Mary Stockwell

MILLS, ROGER Q. (March 30, 1832– September 2, 1911)

Member of the U.S. House of Representatives and U.S. Senate from Texas known for his opposition to Prohibition and high tariffs.

Born in Todd County, Kentucky, Mills received an academy education before moving to Texas in 1849. He gained admittance to the bar in 1852 and established a practice in Corsicana, Texas. Mills entered local politics as a member of the Whig Party. In the 1850s, he changed to the American Party and then the Democratic Party.

During the Civil War, Mills served as an officer in the Confederate Army.

Elected to the U.S. House of Representatives in 1872, Mills began a twenty-six-year career in Congress. His platform included a call for an end to Reconstruction, additional spending on frontier defense, and funding for the expansion of railroads and ports in Texas. He opposed Prohibition, working to defeat a state constitutional amendment on the ballot in 1887. As chairman of the House Ways and Means Committee in the Fiftieth Congress, Mills wrote the Mills Bill. The House easily approved the legislation that included relatively moderate reductions in tariff rates in July 1888. The protectionist Senate, controlled by the Republican Party, defeated the measure.

The defeat of the Mills Bill made tariff reform a campaign issue in the presidential election of 1888. Mills campaigned across the country in support of tariff reductions and the Democratic candidate for president, Grover Cleveland. After the Democrats lost the 1888 presidential election, the tariff issue lost its place on the national political agenda, replaced by free silver. Still speaking on the need to reduce tariffs, Mills lost a contest for Speaker of the House in 1891. The Democrats in the Texas legislature elected him to the U.S. Senate in 1892 and reelected him in 1893. In the Senate, Mills continued to support tariff reductions. He also supported the revolt in Cuba, but opposed the acquisition of Hawaii.

Mills retired from the Senate in 1899 after losing some of his popularity because he would not support free silver coinage. He returned to his ranch in

Corsicana, Texas, where he died on September 2, 1911.

See also: Blaine, James Gillespie; Cleveland, Stephen Grover; Cuba; Democratic Party; Hawaii; House Ways and Means Committee; McKinley, William; Prohibition; Reagan, John Henninger; Reconstruction; Silver; Whig Party; Wilson, William L.; Wilson-Gorman Tariff (Tariff of 1894).

Selected Bibliography:

Alwyn Barr, *Reconstruction to Reform: Texas Politics, 1876–1906*, 1971.

John David Rausch Jr.

MILLS BILL

Proposed legislation designed to reduce tariff rates in 1888.

Following the failure of the Tariff of 1883 and the Morrison Bill of 1886 to reduce customs duties, the Democratic administration of Grover Cleveland attempted its own tariff reform. Cleveland had addressed the subject of the tariff in his messages to Congress, but devoted his December 1887 speech to the growing treasury surplus and his own views that the tariff represented inequitable taxation and a bar to economic expansion. Additionally, Cleveland and the Democrats wanted a reform of the tariff before the 1888 election so that they could concentrate on the issue of the gold standard.

With Cleveland's support, Roger Mills, a representative from Texas, introduced a reform bill to Congress in the spring of 1888. Unfortunately, he argued for a 7 percent reduction biased toward products that would benefit the southern economy, like manufactured iron goods, glass, and fine quality cotons and woolens, while sugar, rice, iron ore, and cheap cotton cloth remained protected. A party-line vote in the house resulted in the bill's passage, but the Republican majority, who introduced their own bill, eventually let both bills die at the expiration of the congressional session, deliberately stalling Mills's bill in the Senate. Much of the blame for the Mills Bill's failure belongs to President Cleveland, who failed to aggressively promote the bill aside from advocating a "campaign of public education" on tariff reform, as well as to the obvious regional bias of the legislation, which made it unpopular with northern politicians.

See also: Cleveland, Stephen Grover; Mills, Roger Q.; Tariff of 1883 (Mongrel Tariff).

Selected Bibliography:

Tom E. Terrill, *The Tariff, Politics, and American Foreign Policy 1874–1901*, 1973; Richard E. Welch Jr., *Presidencies of Grover Cleveland*, 1988.

Margaret Sankey

MOBILIZATION ON DEVELOPMENT, TRADE, LABOR, AND THE ENVIRONMENT (MODTLE)

Coalition of labor, development, and environmental groups formed to oppose aspects of the proposed North American Free Trade Agreement (NAFTA).

International debate over NAFTA began in 1991 and continued even after the treaty's ratification in 1993. Much of this concern centered on whether such an agreement would allow U.S. businesses to exploit the relatively weak labor and environmental laws of Mexico and damage its social infrastructure. Mobilization on Development, Trade, Labor, and the Environment (MODTLE) was formed in 1991 as a coalition of labor, environmental, consumer, religious, agricultural, human nd development groups that opposed the proposed trade agreement. Although MODTLE never opposed international trade growth, the organization felt that NAFTA would undermine social and environmental standards and proposed criteria that they felt must be included as provisions in NAFTA to preserve Mexico's internal integrity. MODTLE's criteria included enforcement of fair labor practices, development of increased workplace health and safety standards, social infrastructure investment, preservation of stringent environmental standards, prevention of environmental dumping, and commitment to human rights. Since NAFTA's approval in late 1993, MODTLE has continued to monitor the impacts of NAFTA on Mexico's population and environment.

See also: Fast-track legislation; North American Free Trade Agreement (NAFTA).

Selected Bibliography:

Jeff Faux and Thea Lee, *The Effect of George Bush's NAFTA on American Workers: Ladder Up or Ladder Down?*, 1992.

Josh Pratt

MOLASSES

A thick, dark to light brown syrup separated from raw sugar in sugar manufacture into various grades.

The use of molasses dates back to 1493 when Columbus introduced it to the West Indies. It became an important product in colonial trade because colonists produced rum, a popular drink in the colonies, from molasses. The Molasses Act of 1733 imposed a heavy tax on sugar and molasses coming from everywhere except for the British Caribbean sugar islands. Due to widespread evasion of the tariff, Parliament lowered the rate in 1764.

Until World War I, molasses remained the most popular sweetener in the United States. After the war, sugar prices plummeted, displacing molasses and maple syrup. The government protected the importation of molasses through protective tariffs going back to the first tariff in 1789. In the years prior to the Civil War, tariffs allowed the sugar plantations in the South to flourish. In 1850, one-half of the sugar consumed in the United States originated in the South. Subsequent tariffs included provisions dealing with sugar and molasses. Since 1934, the United States has almost continuously restricted the quantity of sugar and molasses imported.

Today, exporters of molasses to the United States include nations in Africa, Asia, Europe, and South America. The Omnibus Trade and Competitiveness Act of 1988 regulates the amount of molasses imported into the United States through the Secretary of Agriculture.

See also: Civil War (American); Navigation and Trade Acts.

Selected Bibliography:

J. Carlyle Sitterson, *Sugar Country: The Cane Sugar Industry in the South, 1753–1950*, 1953.

Russell M. Magnaghi

MONROE, JAMES (April 28, 1758–July 4, 1831)

Fifth president of the United States and defender of economic nationalism.

Born in Westmoreland County, Virginia, James Monroe inherited his father's estate, finished studies at Campbelltown Academy, and entered the College of William and Mary, all in 1774 at the young age of sixteen. Feeling the call of the American Revolution, he dropped out of college in 1775 to join the Continental Army and rose to the rank of major. He never completed his education, but instead studied law under the brilliant tutelage of Thomas Jefferson.

Monroe's vast and distinguished political career included a seat in the U.S. Senate from 1790 to 1794, followed by a two-year stint as U.S. minister to France. From 1799 to 1802, and again for three months in 1811, he served as governor of Virginia. In the Madison administration, Monroe served both as secretary of state from 1811 to 1817 and secretary of war from 1814 to 1815. He also negotiated the Louisiana Purchase as a special envoy with U.S. minister to France Robert R. Livingston in 1803. In 1816, he won the presidential election, continuing the legacy of both the so-called Virginia dynasty and the Jeffersonian Republicans, serving until 1824.

As president, Monroe presided over the nation during the Era of Good Feelings, a brief period of unremarkable political partisanship that came to a sudden halt with the Panic of 1819 and the controversy over Missouri's admission to statehood in 1820. In 1823, aided by the able diplomatic skills of his secretary of state, John Quincy Adams, Monroe issued his now-famous and often-invoked Monroe Doctrine in which he exposed his economic nationalist sentiments by declaring a European hands-off policy in the Western Hemisphere.

The passage of the Tariff Act of 1816, Great Britain's continued dumping of cheap goods into the American market, and the plunge from postwar recession into full-blown depression all worked in concert, creating the need for strong economic policy. True to his Republican roots, Monroe had, in his first administration, gained new territory in Florida and west to the Pacific, settled United States–Canadian boundary disputes with Great Britain, and had internal improvements vetoed. But in his second inaugural address he promised a moderately protective tariff and committed to addressing the serious trade issues with Great Britain.

In the Commercial Convention of 1815, the United States and Britain had agreed to open up commercial freedom and prohibit discriminatory duties against each other's ships. Yet Britain refused to adjust its colonial navigation laws that restricted U.S. trade with British colonial holdings in the New World. With this action, the British had revived its triangular trade and in so doing had quite literally restricted America's direct trade to Great Britain. By 1816, more than half of U.S. tonnage never left American ports. In March 1817, Britain further frustrated the Americans by restricting the importation of West Indies produce in U.S. vessels. Monroe's response harked back to previous Jeffersonian policies as he first declared a policy of nonimportation, followed in May 1820 with a nonintercourse action against British vessels trading in the Western Hemisphere. To the delight of American policymakers, these actions appeared to cripple Britain's trade and actually caused the great empire to revise its 160-year-old navigation laws. Reciprocity appeared close at hand as Great Britain loosened its policies in favor of U.S. trade.

Late in 1823, Congress interrupted the brief tranquility in Anglo-American relations by asking Monroe to approve a highly protective tariff bill. When Britain received the news of the Tariff Act of 1824, it responded in kind, with new tonnage duties imposed on all U.S. cargo entering British colonial ports. Monroe responded to this overture and other international events with his economically motivated doctrine demanding a noncolonization policy in the Western Hemisphere. The Monroe Doctrine would become the president's economic legacy and would set the stage for nearly all future U.S. international economic and diplomatic policy.

Monroe retired from public life at the end of his second presidential term and died of heart failure on July 4, 1831, the third of the first five presidents to die on the most important commemorative day in American history.

See also: Jefferson, Thomas; Jeffersonianism; Madison, James; Navigation and Trade Acts; Tariff of 1816; Tariff of 1818; Tariff of 1820; Tariff of 1824.

Selected Bibliography:

Harry Ammon, *James Monroe: A Biography*, 1991; George Dangerfield, *The Awakening of American Nationalism, 1815–1828*, 1965.

Elaine C. Prange Turney

MONTESQUIEU, CHARLES-LOUIS DE SECONDAT, BARON DE LA BRÈDE ET DE (January 18, 1689–February 10, 1755)

Eighteenth-century French political philosopher who wrote *The Spirit of Laws* and commented on the "Spirit of Commerce."

Born into a military family ennobled by the French crown for services in the sixteenth century, Montesquieu studied law at the University of Bordeaux, graduating in 1708. Having married a wealthy woman and inherited the family estate of his uncle, the young philosopher practiced law, attended to his business interests, and studied the sciences. In 1721, he published his first work, *Persian Letters*, followed by several other works, including *The Spirit of Laws*, written in 1750. In this work, he classified the three forms of government, discussed the separation of powers, and insisted that climate influenced the type of political system that developed within each country. Montesquieu also commented on trade and the "Spirit of Commerce," arguing that commerce between nations eliminates the prejudices that lead to war. David Hume, Charles Bonnet, and other philosophers of the Enlightenment praised Montesquieu's work, although his critics succeeded in persuading the pope to place the book on the *Index Librorum Prohibitorum* one year after its publication. Montesquieu died in Paris on February 10, 1755.

See also: Hume, David.

Selected Bibliography:

Alfred E. Eckes, *Opening America's Market: U.S. Foreign Trade Policy Since 1776*, 1995;

Charles Louis Montesquieu, *The Spirit of the Laws*, 1989.

Cynthia Clark Northrup

MORRILL, JUSTIN S. (April 14, 1810– December 28, 1898)

U.S. representative and senator who introduced the Morrill Tariff legislation during the Civil War.

Born on April 14, 1810, in the small Vermont village of Strafford, Morrill, a prosperous merchant, retired from business at the relatively young age of thirty-eight. In the early 1850s, Morrill began dabbling in politics and voters eventually nominated and elected him as a Whig representative to Congress in 1854. Although Morrill took his seat in Congress as a Whig, he promptly switched to the Republican Party shortly after his election to Congress. Between his service in the House and U.S. Senate, Morrill would spend over forty years in elective office.

As a legislator, Morrill gained notoriety for sponsoring the Morrill Act of 1862, which created the land grant universities in the United States. Designed to provide practical, scientific education for the farming population, the Morrill Act allowed states to establish universities through the sale of public lands. Each state received a grant of 30,000 acres for every senator and representative in Congress.

His financial views reflected his Whig economic antecedents. Considered an expert on finance, Morrill's committee assignments reflected his colleagues' confidence in his economic expertise. For many years, he served as a member of the House Ways and Means Committee, succeeding Thaddeus Stevens as chair from 1865 to 1867. In the Senate, Morrill routinely received assignments to the Senate Finance Committee, which he chaired from 1877 to 1879, 1881 to 1893, and again in 1898. A proponent of sound currency and the gold standard, Morrill remained wary of paper currency and led the fight to retire greenbacks after the Civil War.

The Morrill Tariff remains his most significant contribution to the tariff. Introduced into Congress in the winter of 1859, the Morrill Tariff, originally designed to restore *ad valorem* duties to the level of the 1846 Walker Tariff, sought to relieve financial distress created in the aftermath of the Panic of 1857. Morrill, with the aid of a few Republican colleagues on the House Ways and Means Committee, almost exclusively wrote the act. Passed by the House on May 10, 1860, the Senate defeated the measure when low-tariff southern Democrats opposed it. With the advent of secession, the control of Congress passed to the Republican Party and the measure eventually passed in the Thirty-sixth Congress. Lincoln signed it into law on March 2, 1861.

Although the act appeared to restore rates to 1846 levels, in reality, the law became much more protectionist than even Morrill desired. The act substituted specific duties for *ad valorem* rates, but established rates for specific duties considerably higher than those rates. Congress established particularly high rates on such items as iron and wool. The Morrill Tariff went through several revisions during the Civil War and provided a significant source of wartime revenue and also established the principle of compensatory duties—high tariff rates exclusively designed to protect American manufacturers from foreign competition.

Morrill's experience with tariff legislation did not end with the Morrill Tariff. For instance, he played a significant role in the passage of the Tariff of 1883. While protectionist in spirit, the provision actually lowered tariff rates by 5 percent. After a long and distinguished career in American politics, Morrill passed away on December 28, 1898.

See also: Civil War (American); House Ways and Means Committee; Morrill Tariff (Tariff of 1861); Republican Party; Senate Finance Committee; Whig Party.

Selected Bibliography:

William B. Parker, *The Life and Public Services of Justin Smith Morrill*, 1971.

Bruce Tap

MORRILL TARIFF (TARIFF OF 1861)

Named after its principal architect, Vermont representative Justin S. Morrill, this act raised rates to finance the Civil War.

Introduced into the House of Representatives on March 12, 1860, proponents advertised the tariff as "a bill to provide for the payment of outstanding Treasury Notes, to authorize a loan, to regulate and fix duties upon imports, and for other purposes." Practically speaking, the intent of the Morrill Tariff focused on reversing what Republicans and other manufacturing interests saw as a dangerous trend toward free trade. Since the tariff of 1857

had lowered *ad valorem* duties, the iron, cotton, and woolen industries, largely represented by the newly formed Republican Party, had lobbied for an upward revision of the tariff.

As envisioned by Morrill and the House Ways and Means Committee, the proposed tariff would enact specific duties on certain items instead of an across-the-board *ad valorem* duty. Although proponents of the bill argued that the general rates would equal the moderate Walker Tariff of 1846, in reality, Republicans inflated the specific duties levied on many items, particularly iron and woolen manufactures, with the former done to attract Pennsylvania into the Republican Party and the latter to entice several western states.

Because the Democrats still controlled Congress, the Morrill Tariff, passed by the House in May 1861, met defeat by southern Democrats in the Senate. When many of these Democrats left the Senate during the secession crisis of 1861, Republicans found they had the necessary votes to carry the measure. Signed into law on March 2, 1861, Congress passed the measure just two days prior to Abraham Lincoln's inauguration.

Congress immediately amended the Morrill Tariff once war broke out between the North and the South, particularly as fueling the Union war effort required additional revenue. An act passed on August 5, 1861, levied duties on commodities such as tea, sugar, and coffee, while increasing duties on a variety of other items. On December 24, 1861, another act raised duties recently levied on tea, sugar, and coffee. By the end of the decade, duties increased to an average rate of 47 percent, the highest in American history to that date.

The Morrill Tariff reestablished the principle of protection for American industry. The domination of the government by the Democratic Party since the administration of Andrew Jackson had resulted in a policy of low tariffs for almost thirty years. The Morrill Tariff not only reversed that trend, but also ushered in a period of protective tariffs that would last throughout the nineteenth century.

See also: Civil War (American); Lincoln, Abraham; Morrill, Justin S.; Tariff of 1846 (Walker Tariff).

Selected Bibliography:

William B. Parker, *The Life and Public Services of Justin Smith Morrill*, 1971; Sidney Ratner, *The Tariff in American History*, 1972.

Bruce Tap

MOST FAVORED NATION (MFN)

Status or treatment accorded to nations engaged in international transactions in the areas of trade, investment, foreign exchange, intellectual property, diplomatic immunity, and the recognition of foreign judicial awards.

The MFN treatment in international trade means that an extending country treats the recipient no less favorably than any other country. More precisely, it denotes the extension by a country of any concessions, privileges, or immunities granted, or yet to be granted, in a trade agreement to one country that is, or will be, the "most favored" to all countries to which it accords MFN treatment. The United States enacted legislation in 1998 to replace the misleading term "most favored nation" with "normal trade relations" or another appropriate term.

Because MFN status gives its holder a guarantee against certain forms of selective discrimination by the granting country, it remains crucial for the establishment and maintenance of equality of competitive opportunities in international trade. Thus, the terms "most favored nation" and "nondiscriminatory" are often used interchangeably. In practice, when a country receives MFN status from another country, the latter's imports remain taxed at concessional, rather than full, rates. The MFN treatment thus often means that the recipient's products sell at a lower price and with greater competitiveness in the extending country's markets.

Although generally better than the minimum standard required under customary international law, MFN status does not put a foreign partner on an equal footing with domestic nationals. This permits countries some flexibility in the execution of their domestic administrative practices and policies concerning trade. MFN clauses in international agreements fall into several categories: unilateral or reciprocal, conditional or unconditional, limited (by territory, time, or substantive scope) or unlimited (general).

MFN remains a core principle of most trade agreements championed and signed by the United States since World War II and forms the bedrock of multilateralism in international transactions. The United States currently accords general MFN treatment to its foreign trading partners through three often overlapping avenues. One uses a bilateral, intergovernmental compact, such as a "commerce, friendship, and navigation (CFN)" treaty, or an executive agreement in both countries to accord reciprocal MFN status. In a second process, the United States accords MFN treatment to members of the World Trade Organization (WTO), which, as a rule, mandates that all members receive MFN treatment. In the third, the United States specifically accords to all foreign countries any concessions in duty rates or other forms of import restrictions agreed to in reciprocal negotiations conducted under the Reciprocal Trade Agreements Act (RTAA). This U.S. legislation, first enacted in 1934 and now contained in Section 126 of the Trade Act of 1974 provides no specific procedure for extending MFN status to a country (except in the case of restoration of the status), because all countries other than those to which MFN treatment is specifically denied by law enjoy MFN status.

MFN status served as an instrument of economic warfare during the Cold War. The United States deviated from its principle of general application when President Harry S Truman, as required by Section 5 of the Trade Agreements Extension Act of 1951, suspended the application of MFN tariff rates to the Soviet Union and all countries or areas under the control of international communism, with the exception of Yugoslavia. The suspended countries faced an increase of tariff rates to the levels enacted by the Hawley-Smoot Tariff Act of 1930.

Title IV of the Trade Act of 1974 allows the suspended countries to regain or temporarily gain MFN tariff status if they conclude a trade agreement with the United States that contains a reciprocal MFN clause and complies with the requirements of the act's free

emigration (Jackson-Vanik) provision. Congress can change the MFN status of a country through legislation.

See also: Reciprocal Trade Agreements Act (RTAA); World Trade Organization (WTO).

Selected Bibliography:

United Nations, *Most Favored-Nation Treatment*, 1999.

Sayuri Shimizu

MULRONEY, BRIAN (March 20, 1939–)

Prime minister of Canada who negotiated the North American Free Trade Agreement (NAFTA) with the United States and Mexico.

Born in Baie-Comeau, Quebec, Mulroney received his education at a private school in New Brunswick. He earned a degree from St. Francis Xavier University in 1959 and a law degree from Laval University in 1964. He gained admittance to the bar in Quebec in 1965.

Mulroney proved unsuccessful in his first foray into politics when he lost the election for Progressive Conservative Party leader to Joe Clark in 1976. In 1977, he received an appointment as president of the Iron Ore Company of Canada. Elected leader of the Progressive Conservative Party in 1983, he defeated former prime minister Joe Clark. In 1984, Mulroney became prime minister after his party won 211 of the 282 seats in the Canadian House of Commons.

In 1985, he began free trade negotiations with the United States. The Progressive Conservative Party won a second majority in the 1988 elections, the first back-to-back victory for the party in thirty-five years. In October 1988, he concluded a free trade agreement with the United States. The Liberal Party made opposition to the agreement a key part of its campaign, but Mulroney won the election and put the free trade agreement into effect. This agreement preceded another agreement on acid rain reached with the United States in 1991.

While working to have NAFTA ratified by the House of Commons in 1993, he resigned as Progressive Conservative leader. He did not seek reelection in the October 1993 elections in which his party lost all but two seats. The following Liberal government eventually ratified NAFTA.

See also: Canada; Free trade; Mexico; North American Free Trade Agreement (NAFTA).

Selected Bibliography:

Frederick W. Mayer, *Interpreting NAFTA: The Science and Art of Political Analysis*, 1998.

John David Rausch Jr.

N

NADER, RALPH (February 27, 1934–)

American lawyer and consumer advocate.

A graduate of Princeton and Harvard Law School, Nader researched automotive designs while in Cambridge. In 1959, in an article titled "The Safe Car You Can't Buy," published by *The Nation*, Nader declared, "It is clear Detroit today is designing automobiles for *style*, cost, performance, and calculated obsolescence, but not—despite the 5,000,000 reported *accidents*, nearly 40,000 fatalities, 110,000 permanent disabilities, and 1,500,000 injuries yearly—for safety." Nader soon became known as the nation's leading consumer advocate, particularly following his publication in 1965 of *Unsafe at Any Speed*, which again targeted the car industry. Goaded by Nader's revelations, Congress subsequently passed the National Traffic and Motor Vehicle Safety Act. Nader soon carried out studies of other industries, including meat, poultry, coal mining, and natural gas, which led to additional legislation. Aided by his Nader's Raiders, a band of consumer activists, Nader established a series of public interest groups that sought to hold both corporations and government bodies responsible for lax enforcement of environmental and consumer protection measures. In 1992, 1996, and 2000, Nader carried out Third Party bids for the presidency in an attempt to highlight the alliance between big business and government.

As a determined opponent of international trade agreements, Nader opposed the North American Free Trade Agreement (NAFTA), the General Agreement on Tariffs and Trade (GATT), and the World Trade Organization (WTO). As he saw matters, "GATT . . . and WTO is [*sic*] a massive global regulatory system concocted by corporations, lawyers and their minions without any accountability. It's an autocratic system." Nader condemned the timber companies that had reduced equatorial forests; the great fishing fleets that "had reduced the ocean catch for the first time in history"; "the fossil fuel giants" that had contaminated "the air, water and land of 3rd World countries along with automobile manufacturers." Nader's group, Public Citizen, accused the WTO of abridging the ability of nations to establish legislation regarding the environment, health, and labor. The WTO amounted to, in his estimation, "a slow-motion coup d'etat over democratic governance worldwide."

See also: General Agreement on Tariffs and Trade (GATT); North American Free Trade Agreement (NAFTA); World Trade Organization (WTO).

Selected Bibliography:

Robert D. Holsworth, *Public Interest Liberalism and the Crisis of Affluence: Reflections on Nader, Environmentalism, and the Politics of a Sustainable Society*, 1980; Ralph Nader, ed., *The Case Against Free Trade: GATT, NAFTA and the Globalization of Corporate Power*, 1993.

Robert C. Cottrell

THE NATION

Unlike its founder, E.L. Godkin, who had been a staunch proponent of free trade, the late-twentieth-century version of *The Nation* viewed with disdain proposals by government and corporate leaders to foster economic liberalism.

In the post–World War II era, the journal sharply criticized the General Agreement on Tariffs and Trade (GATT) and the North American Free Trade Agreement (NAFTA), along with the World Trade Organization (WTO), warning that such mechanisms endangered environmental regulations, labor laws, and basic human rights. By contrast, *The Nation* viewed as a hopeful development the outpouring of protests in the midst of a WTO meeting in Seattle in 1999. The journal suggested that "the promise of Seattle" offered the possibility of a new movement in which disparate folk "united by the spirit of smart, playful optimism" could challenge corporate and political elites. In contrast to the general media, *The Nation* refused to dismiss the protestors as "Luddite wackos." William Greider of *The Nation* considered the WTO symbolic of globalization, which the protestors contested on behalf of "voiceless people" across the globe.

The Nation insisted on the accountability of American corporations, which would require the establishment of "minimum standards for corporate behavior on environmental protection, labor issues and human rights." Companies that failed to adhere to such standards, the journal suggested, should have to pay "penalty tariffs" for "profiteering on human suffering and ecological despoliation." *The Nation* also declared that the United States should insist on the protection of workers' rights in countries that produced goods for the American market. The journal asserted that corporations setting up shop in other nations should remain accountable. Such responsibility, *The Nation* asserted, extended to the dumping of toxic wastes in the Amazon River.

See also: General Agreement on Tariffs and Trade (GATT); North American Free Trade Agreement (NAFTA); World Trade Organization (WTO).

Selected Bibliography:

The Nation, 1865–present.

Robert C. Cottrell

NATIONAL ASSOCIATION OF MANUFACTURERS (NAM)

National business organization designed to promote the interests of manufacturers by protecting the U.S. market for American producers while simultaneously attempting to exploit possible foreign markets through tariffs, reciprocity treaties, and, most recently, rules-based trading.

Founded in 1895, the NAM's constitution defined its goals as promoting the industrial interests of America, fostering domestic and foreign commerce, protecting individual rights, and improving relations between employers and employees. Throughout its history, NAM has consistently pursued policies that opposed governmental intervention in the economy as well as any efforts to promote the independent trade union movement. NAM, as one of the most patriotic business organizations functioning at the time, helped foster the pro-business climate in the United States throughout the 1920s. But once the Great Depression began and Franklin D. Roosevelt became president, NAM became one of the most outspoken critics of the New Deal in its legislative actions such as the Wagner Act, calls for increased corporate taxation, reform of the Supreme Court, and fostering of the union movement. During World War II, NAM accepted the action of the government, but after 1945 it led the business world in calling for limits on federal intervention in the American economy and restrictions on union activities.

Although NAM has historically favored tariffs, it has had difficulty in defining or endorsing any specific rate schedules. To resolve this difficulty, it strongly favored reciprocity treaties. In recent years, NAM has supported the North American Free Trade Agreement (NAFTA), the General Agreement on Tariffs and Trade (GATT), and the World Trade Organization (WTO). Essentially, NAM has supported and will sustain whatever it believes will promote the growth of American manufacturers.

See also: Free trade; General Agreement on Tariffs and Trade (GATT); Great Depression; North American Free Trade Agreement (NAFTA); Roosevelt, Franklin D.; World Trade Organization (WTO); World War II. **Vol. II**: James Watson's Radio Address in Support of the Hawley-Smoot Tariff; Franklin D. Roosevelt's 1932 Campaign Radio Speech; The General Agreement on Tariffs and Trade.

Selected Bibliography:

Wallace Bennett, "The Very Human History of 'NAM,' " 1949; Jerry Jasinowski, *NAM: The Manufacturing Revolution and the New Economy*, 1995; Albert Steigerwalt, *The National Association of Manufacturers, 1895–1914*, 1964.

Michael V. Namorato

NATIONAL CIVIC FEDERATION

Organization founded in 1900 by midwestern newspaper editor and economist Ralph Easley; dedicated to seeking "harmonious relations between employers and wage earners" by bringing together representatives of both camps to solve the pressing industrial relations problems of the time.

While committed to serving as a forum for labor-related issues, the organization carefully avoided taking any stand on the controversial tariff and trade issues of the day. Easley aimed to fashion a middle way between the extremism of late nineteenth-century laissez-faire capitalism and the radicalism appealing to many workers in the face of rapid industrialization. The federation devoted itself, in particular, to organizing trade agreements between various businesses and labor organizations. Other concerns included a campaign against child labor and the promotion of "welfare work." The federation drew a wide variety of members from all sectors of American life, including former President Grover Cleveland, Senator Marcus Hanna, Archbishop John Ireland, and AFL president Samuel Gompers. With an ideologically diverse membership and lofty goals such as creating labor peace, the federation explicitly sought to avoid divisive issues such as the tariff debate. The organization's mouthpiece, *The National Civic Federation Review*, published between 1903 and 1920, assiduously avoided any reference to trade issues. By World War I, the issue of Bolshevism increasingly occupied the organization, which continued to function into the 1940s—although with declining effectiveness.

See also: Cleveland, Stephen Grover; Communism; Labor; World War I.

Selected Bibliography:

Ralph Easley, "The Work of the National Civic Federation," *Harper's Weekly Magazine*, 1904.

Edmund F. Wehrle

NATIONAL CONFERENCE FOR THE EXPANSION OF FOREIGN TRADE

Coalition of government and private leaders that endorsed lower tariffs, freer trade, and a commission on tariffs.

High tariffs came under attack in the early years of the twentieth century as revisionists expressed concern that protectionism contributed to a variety of domestic ills. They believed that duties on imports encouraged the depletion of domestic natural resources, discouraged foreign trade, and granted congressionally ordained monopolies to some American industries. While some manufacturing sectors ardently resisted lowering tariffs for fear that foreign trade violated their self-interest and European competition could ruin their business, the more radical tariff and antitrust revisionists strove to create an inclusive coalition of proponents for tariff reform.

Efforts to form a coalition of tariff commission proponents culminated in 1907 when more than 900 delegates gathered for the National Conference for the Expansion of Foreign Trade (also called the National Convention for the Extension of the Foreign Commerce of the United States) in Washington, D.C. The function included such noteworthy backers as Secretary of State Elihu Root and Secretary of Commerce and Labor Oscar S. Straus, and it had the support of House Speaker Joseph C. Cannon and President Theodore Roosevelt. Roosevelt even endorsed a tariff revision speech given by Secretary Root and created speculation that he might favor tariff reform.

The seminal work of the convention included the members' endorsement of a tariff commission. This permanent commission would include a nonpartisan advisory panel that would study U.S. trade relations with foreign nations as well as recommend modifications to customs duties. The coalition formed at the convention continued to press for tariff commission legislation and tariff reform in Congress.

See also: Cannon, Joseph Gurney; Roosevelt, Theodore; Root, Elihu; Tariff Commission.

Selected Bibliography:

Paul Wolman, *Most Favored Nation: The Republican Revisionists and U.S. Tariff Policy, 1897–1912*, 1992.

Josh Pratt

NATIONAL COUNCIL OF COMMERCE

Quasi-governmental business organization with many powerful members involved in the tariff debate.

Herbert E. Miles sought to sustain revisionist pressure on Congress after he testified on the need for moderate tariff reform in December 1908. He felt that President William Taft relied heavily on tariff revisionists' efforts as well as outspoken Republicans for his attempts to lower tariffs. Miles acted quickly to arrange to become President

Taft's first choice for an appointment to the position of the secretary of commerce and labor.

Miles's confidence in his candidacy stemmed from his ties to the National Council of Commerce, a semigovernmental business organization created by Oscar S. Straus, his predecessor under President Theodore Roosevelt. The National Council on Commerce gave Miles a forum to interact with important figures involved with the tariff debate. It provided him with experience in the political arena, legitimacy as a tariff reformer sensitive to business interests, and connections to influential people involved in the tariff issue. In fact, Gustav H. Schwab, a central figure in the Merchants Association of New York (MANY) and chairman of the National Council of Commerce, had recently appointed Miles to a prestigious position on the advisory committee.

See also: Merchants Association of New York (MANY); Miles, Herbert Edwin; National Council of Commerce; Roosevelt, Theodore; Taft, William Howard.

Selected Bibliography:

Paul Wolman, *Most Favored Nation: The Republican Revisionists and U.S. Tariff Policy, 1897–1912*, 1992.

Josh Pratt

NATIONAL FOREIGN TRADE COUNCIL (NFTC)

Foreign trade organization that supported bank cooperation as well as industrial export cooperation in foreign expansion.

During the second decade of the twentieth century, a major controversy developed over whether banks or exporting industries seeking to do business in foreign markets should receive official approval that would allow them to cooperate with one another. The National Foreign Trade Council (NFTC) allied itself with banks involved in foreign expansion as well as foreign trade organizations like the Association of Machinery and Equipment Appraisers to press for greater freedom for firms to cooperate when operating in international markets. The NFTC backed bank cooperation, but felt that developing America's international commercial and investment potential necessitated export cooperation among industrial firms as well. In 1914, the NFTC pressured Congress to modify the Sherman Antitrust Act to make it harmonious with the enhanced banking cooperation privileges provided for in the Federal Reserve Act. The NFTC also supported a resolution in 1914 calling for a modification of antitrust laws to allow cooperation in foreign markets. The group felt unsure about whether export cooperation required definite legal guarantees; some of its members believed that current laws and regulations already permitted foreign trade cooperation as long as it did not interfere with domestic trade.

See also: Federal Reserve Bank.

Selected Bibliography:

Paul Wolman, *Most Favored Nation: The Republican Revisionists and U.S. Tariff Policy, 1897–1912*, 1992.

Josh Pratt

NATIONAL RECIPROCITY LEAGUE (NRL)

Short-lived national group formed by the tariff revisionist organizations that was intended to lobby Congress on issues of tariff reciprocity, maximum and minimum tariffs, and a tariff commission.

Tariff revisionists in the early twentieth century strove to encourage movements to lower duties and end tariff-generated trusts through the creation of organized industrial and commercial associations. These associations included the National Live Stock Association (NLSA), the National Association of Agricultural Implement and Vehicle Manufacturers (NAAIVM), and the Merchants Association of New York (MANY). From these organizations, the revisionists then formed powerful national lobbying groups that could transmit their message directly to Congress and the voters. The specific lobbying arms of these organizations included the American Reciprocal Tariff League (ARTL), the National Tariff Commission Association (NTCA), and the National Reciprocity League (NRL).

Industry leaders, dismayed at the failure of the National Reciprocity Convention to ensure the passage of a reciprocity treaty with France, attempted to preserve reciprocity by founding the National Reciprocity League in 1902. The organization featured as leaders such notables as former ambassador John A. Kasson and former NAAIVM president H.C. Staver. The NRL published *National Reciprocity* magazine and agitated for reciprocity with Cuba to force American corporations into foreign competition.

The revisionists working within the NRL supported expansion into foreign markets, but often disdained the radical, antibusiness tenets traditionally associated with revisionism. They argued that analytical, scientific procedures must determine tariff policy. The best way to achieve such policies, the early twentieth-century revisionists believed, came from expanding reciprocity, legislating dual tariffs, and creating a tariff commission.

Tariff revisionists had many uses for groups such as the NRL. They provided a forum through which the revisionists' message could reach the people and influence government policy simultaneously. They also used the NRL to develop a creed of reciprocity, to encourage a system of maximum and minimum tariffs, and to support the creation of a scientific tariff commission. Additionally, the NRL promoted the doctrine that tariff rates should rest firmly on comparative costs of production.

See also: Kasson treaties; Merchants Association of New York (MANY); National Tariff Commission Association (NTCA).

Selected Bibliography:

Paul Wolman, *Most Favored Nation: The Republican Revisionists and U.S. Tariff Policy, 1897–1912*, 1992.

Josh Pratt

NATIONAL TARIFF COMMISSION ASSOCIATION (NTCA)

Lobby group that played an influential role in the development of the Tariff Board in the prewar era.

Revisionist groups participated in industrial and agricultural organizations in the early 1900s, and these organizations then developed national lobbying groups that could pursue revisionist ideals in Washington. The National Tariff Commission Association (NTCA) ranked among the most influential. The NTCA worked for tariffs based on reciprocity and the largely theoretical concept of comparative costs of production. It also lobbied for a tariff commission that would root its decisions in scientific norms and a policy of maximum and minimum tariffs. Although the NTCA strove to avoid the appearance of partisanship, it did work openly in support of President William Taft's Republican tariff policies.

The NTCA gained momentum in its causes in 1909 when Herbert E. Miles recruited influential people to serve on its executive committee. The Tariff Board endeavored to link itself with the NTCA, whose goals then included supporting Tariff Board investigations and legitimizing the board as a full-fledged tariff commission. NTCA support for the Tariff Board came despite its official statement, which urged a tariff commission without the power to directly set laws or rates.

Both the Tariff Board and the NTCA became concerned with the relationship between the government and foreign trade constituencies in February 1910. The NTCA favored a tariff commission modeled similarly to the only existing permanent tariff commission at that time, Germany's Imperial Commission for the Elaboration of Economic Measures. The NTCA felt that such a model would allow its members to influence the board without being accused of employing overtly partisan politics. It also appreciated the organization of the model around industrial cleavage instead of political party lines. Later the NTCA recommended multiple investigations and travel by board members to review the European tariff commission.

See also: Germany; Maximum-Minimum Tariff; Taft, William Howard.

Selected Bibliography:

Paul Wolman, *Most Favored Nation: The Republican Revisionists and U.S. Tariff Policy, 1897–1912*, 1992.

Josh Pratt

NAVIGATION AND TRADE ACTS

Series of acts passed to regulate trade within the empire for the benefit of Great Britain.

England first regulated Virginia tobacco exports by executive action of the crown. A 1621 order required that Virginia export tobacco directly to England and, to protect customs revenue, Parliament forbade the growing of tobacco in the British Isles. During the Interregnum, reacting to Holland's cheaper freight rates, Parliament passed the Navigation Act of 1651. According to that law, any vessel bringing imports from America, Africa, or Asia to England, its colonies, or Ireland would have an English captain, a mostly English crew, and arrive in an English-built ship, with "English" including English Americans.

After the Restoration, Charles II nullified the 1651 law, but Parliament promptly reenacted and extended its provisions by passing the 1660 Navi-

gation Act, requiring that English ships, with an English captain and at least three-quarters of the crew of English birth, transport all imports and exports. Unlike the 1651 law, the 1660 act "enumerated" major colonial products, such as tobacco, sugar, cotton, indigo, ginger, fustic, and dye woods, that could only be exported to England or another English colony. Other products enumerated later included rice, rum, molasses, and naval stores. From 1730 on, rice could be exported to Europe south of Cape Finisterre.

The Staple Act of 1663 required that European products arrive in the colonies via England, except for salt used by northern fishing colonies, wine from Madeira and the Azores, and Irish or Scottish indentured servants, horses, and provisions. The Union of 1707 ended limitations on Scotland.

The Plantations Duty Act of 1673 closed a loophole whereby enumerated goods had been sent from one colony to another and then to a foreign country. Parliament imposed a prohibitive tax on enumerated goods shipped from one colony to another instead of to England. To prevent colonial manufactures competing with British producers, laws forbade the exporting of finished woolens and fur hats and the construction of new iron mills.

The trade laws benefited British merchants and increased customs revenues by funneling taxable trade through Britain. They affected the American colonies in a complex manner. The resentment of Virginian tobacco growers at the exclusion of cheaper Dutch freighters contributed to Bacon's Rebellion of 1676. The violation of the navigation acts by Massachusetts merchants led the crown to void the original charter of the colony in 1684. In the eighteenth century, before the French and Indian War, a general acceptance of the trade acts existed, except for persistent violation of the 1733 Molasses Act. After Parliament passed the American Revenue Act of 1764, known as the Sugar Act, complaints about Britain's imperial system escalated, but American protests in the years before the American Revolution centered on the fact that the Sugar Act, Stamp Act, and Townshend Revenue Act raised revenue in America instead of regulating trade. Benjamin Franklin, Thomas Jefferson, and other colonists realized that the navigation acts imposed an indirect levy on Americans by forcing them to trade with and through Britain regardless of cost, but the First Continental Congress, while protesting parliamentary taxation, "cheerfully" accepted navigation acts "for the purpose of securing the commercial advantages of the whole empire to the mother country." In the 1780s and 1790s, American trading patterns remained much the same. The restrictions on manufactures proved insignificant in the eighteenth century, when America lacked the capital and labor for intensive manufacturing. The navigation acts did not prevent the colonies from experiencing great growth in wealth and population during the colonial period.

See also: American Revolution; Great Britain; Mercantilism; Sugar.

Selected Bibliography:

Charles McLean Andrews, *The Colonial Period of American History*, 1938; Oliver M. Dickerson, *The Navigation Acts and the American Revolution*, 1951; John J. McCusker and Russell R. Menard, *The Economy of British North America, 1607–1789*, 1985.

Joseph A. Devine

NEWSPAPERS AND MEDIA

Newspapers and the media have played a role in informing the American public about tariff issues as well as shaping public opinion on the topic.

During the eighteenth century, the primary role of editors remained the reporting of factual information. Because the Constitutional Convention delegates debated the levying of duties, but without any public debate, the papers could only serve in the capacity of informant. The shift in emphasis occurred during and after the War of 1812, when politicians reopened the controversy over a protective tariff. *Niles' Register* gained prominence as the most influential newspaper in the nation by focusing on the tariff, with editors across the country reprinting important articles. The paper, published in Baltimore, maintained an objective stance by reporting both sides of the argument, but the editorials, written by Hezekiah Niles, supported a protective tariff that would benefit the manufacturers of the Northeast. The success of the *Niles' Register* encouraged editors to take strong positions on issues of national and local importance, transforming the industry in the process.

In most cases, geographic location determined what side the paper supported on the tariff issue. Southern papers, true to a long-standing hatred for import taxes that affected the South more than the North, opposed the tariff while northern papers supported it. In the post–Civil War period, the dominant political party also influenced the paper's position. By the 1900s, some southern newspapers, like the *Dallas News*, opposed the tariff even after the Democratic Party acquiesced on the subject. The *News* editorialized that southerners who approved of the tariff sought to profit from the corruption as northerners had done for years.

Newspapers helped shape public opinion. Two publications that provided extensive coverage of the tariff issues of the day through political cartoons were *Puck* and *Judge*. Papers like the *New York Times* influenced the public, especially after Congress passed the Hawley-Smoot Tariff Act of 1930. The paper's coverage created the impression that the act raised rates to the highest in American history and helped cause the Great Depression. After World War II, newspapers published articles in favor of free trade, usually warning of the disastrous effect that high duties had on the international community after the passage of Hawley-Smoot. The option to withdraw from any agreement if trade situations changed drastically remained the primary concern of both Congress and the American people. Newspapers focused on the fact that the General Agreement on Tariffs and Trade (GATT) included the ability of signatories to terminate GATT participation. Since the widespread use of television starting in the 1960s, the electronic media has also helped mold public opinion and enabled lawmakers to pass free trade legislation such as the Kennedy Round, the North American Free Trade Agreement (NAFTA), and the World Trade Organization (WTO).

See also: Constitutional Convention; General Agreement on Tariffs and Trade (GATT); Great Depression; Hawley-Smoot Tariff (Tariff of 1930); Niles, Hezekiah; North American Free Trade Agreement (NAFTA); War of 1812.

Selected Bibliography:

Alfred E. Eckes, *Opening America's Market: U.S. Foreign Trade Policy Since 1776*, 1995; Ralph Halstead Parker, "The History of the Dallas Morning News," 1930.

Cynthia Clark Northrup

NILES, HEZEKIAH (October 10, 1777–April 2, 1839)

Editor and newspaper publisher who favored a protective tariff and used his publication, *The Niles Register*, to promote the passage of the Tariff of 1828.

Born in Jefferis' Ford, Chester County, Pennsylvania, in 1777, Niles was raised as a Quaker. At the age of seventeen he entered into an apprenticeship with a printer in Philadelphia. Three years later, he moved to Wilmington, Delaware, before settling down in Baltimore to become the editor of the *Baltimore Evening Post* from 1805 to 1811. That same year he started another paper, initially called the *Weekly Register* and later known as *Niles' Weekly Register*, which he published until 1836. During the debate over the Tariff of 1828, also known as the Tariff of Abominations, Niles promoted the American System. As a proponent of business and manufacturing interests, he argued that a high tariff would benefit the economy. He maintained a balanced and certain objectivity in his reporting by printing the extremes of both sides of the argument.

His clear prose and reliance on facts and statistics resulted in many editors from around the country reprinting his stories, a common practice during the nineteenth century. Niles shaped the opinions of countless Americans on the issue of protectionism versus free trade, convincing them of the need for a high tariff. His newspaper remains the best resource for analyzing the debate over the tariff between 1811 and 1836. Niles died in Wilmington, Delaware, on April 2, 1839.

See also: American System; Newspapers and media; Tariff of 1828 (Tariff of Abominations).

Selected Bibliography:

Edward Stanwood, *American Tariff Controversies in the Nineteenth Century*, 1967.

Cynthia Clark Northrup

NON-CONSUMPTION MOVEMENT

A chief weapon used by the colonists in their efforts to resist British economic coercion and gain independence in the New World.

In the aftermath of the French and Indian War, a growing spirit of American nationalism clashed "with the increasing centralization of the British Empire." In September 1767, word reached the American colonies that Parliament had passed the Townshend Acts. Led by James Otis, colonists adapted a series of resolutions calling on the people of Boston "to extricate themselves from their financial embarrassments by manufacturing for themselves a long list of articles, including wearing apparel and furnishings, coaches, anchors, cordage, loaf sugar, malt liquors, cheeses, watches, and

jewelry." The non-consumption movement strove to avoid the violence that accompanied the enforcement of the Stamp Act. However, New Englanders opposed paying the new duties.

Although Otis and his radical Boston associates fired the initial salvo, John Dickinson's *Letters from a Farmer in Pennsylvania to the Inhabitants of the British Colonies*, appearing that December, ignited support for a revival of non-importation agreements. In his famous *Letters*, Dickinson conceded the "right of Parliament not only to regulate but even to suppress commerce and industry in the colonies." Yet he strongly "denied its authority to levy internal or external taxes." Perceived as a threat to colonial liberty, opposition to the Townshend duties rapidly spread with "varying degrees of thoroughness and effectiveness."

The non-consumption movement, which started in Boston, had its chief impact in New England. But non-importation measures spread to New York in April 1768 and to Philadelphia by September. Most of the protests occurred in the northeast. In some instances, confrontation led to violence. Mobs terrorized Tory merchants who refused to join the movement. The leadership of the movement soon passed from the Whig merchants to "the radical Sons of Liberty who insisted that it be protracted until all colonial grievances, not merely the Townshend duties, had been redressed."

British merchants felt the economic impact. The Townshend duties, enacted to alleviate British taxpayer burdens, brought in no more than 3,500 pounds while the business loss to the British public amounted to 7,250,000 pounds. Any hope of securing revenue from the colonies by internal and external taxation ceased to exist by the end of 1768. In 1769, Parliament repealed all the Townshend duties except the tax on tea.

Interestingly, parliamentary concession failed to achieve the desired colonial demand. New York merchants, angered by Newport's flouting of the non-importation agreements and suspicions about Boston's intentions, opened their ports to all British merchandise except tea. Although Boston and Philadelphia attempted to continue the non-consumption policy, New York's defection led to the collapse of the boycott.

The non-consumption movement set off the policy of economic coercion of the mother country. The formation of the Continental Association in 1774 continued the actions first initiated by Otis and Dickinson. In October 1774, colonists approved a "non-importation, non-exportation, and non-consumption Association affecting all trade relations with the Mother Country," along with the warning that it would remain in force until officials addressed all grievances. This movement served notice on King George III "that the exercise of his prerogatives must be consistent with American ideas about the nature of their liberties on the one hand, and the limitations of his authority, on the other." Such action marked the colonists' determination to establish an independent nation in the New World.

See also: American Revolution; Navigation and Trade Acts.

Selected Bibliography:

Charles McLean Andrews, *The Colonial Period of American History*, 1938; Lawrence Henry Gipson, *The Coming of the Revolution, 1763–1775*, 1962; Michael Kammen, *Empire and Interest: The American Colonies and the Politics of Mercantilism*, 1970; Curtis P. Nettels, "British Mercantilism and the Economic Development of the Thirteen Colonies." *Journal of Economic History*, 1952; Arthur M. Schlesinger, *The Colonial Merchants and the American Revolution, 1763–1776*, 1918; Esmond Wright, *Fabric of Freedom*, 1961.

Chuck Howlett

NORTH AMERICAN FREE TRADE AGREEMENT (NAFTA)

A reduced-tariff trade agreement between the United States, Canada, and Mexico.

Following his election in 1988 as president of Mexico, Carlos Salinas de Gotari conferred with newly elected U.S. president George Herbert Walker Bush. Soon thereafter, Mexican officials proposed a free trade agreement between the two countries. Reversing its traditional trade policy, Mexico sought to attract foreign capital to finance more rapid economic growth. The United States had recently completed a free trade agreement with Canada in 1988, but remained cool toward free trade with Mexico. The Bush administration welcomed the initiative, seeking formation of a U.S.-dominated trade block that would counterbalance those forming in Europe and Asia. Negotiations, begun in 1991, led to an agreement in August 1992, which Bush, Salinas, and Canadian prime minister Brian Mulroney signed on December 17, 1992. The North American Free Trade Agreement (NAFTA) provided for reduced tariffs, with a goal of establishing a free trade zone of North

America that would serve some 370 million people with $6.5 trillion worth of production. Powerful domestic interest groups in all three nations prevented it from becoming an absolute free trade zone, but NAFTA immediately removed all duties on most goods between the three nations and called for elimination over a period of fifteen years of most other tariffs and barriers to investment across these borders. The NAFTA agreement also provided for freer movement across borders for people, including visitors for business purposes, traders and investors, company employees providing managerial and executive services, and a broad range of professionals. Opposition to NAFTA existed in all three countries. Ross Perot, a candidate for the U.S. presidency in 1992, made it an issue in the election of that year, charging that it would cost many jobs in the United States, and even after the election, the U.S. Congress remained reluctant to ratify or implement the agreement. In response to opposition from affected groups, NAFTA promised cooperation on labor and environmental issues among the three countries. A strong promotional effort by President William Jefferson Clinton overcame enough of the congressional opposition to win ratification and implementation of the agreements in November 1993, and the treaty went into effect on January 1, 1994. The issue of job loss in the United States and Canada proved less severe than originally feared by opponents, and in the United States the increased imports from Mexico and Canada led to the creation of some new jobs. In fact, NAFTA brought less rapid economic change to any of the countries than anticipated by supporters or opponents, but it did lead to greater cooperation between Mexican, Canadian, and U.S. companies, labor unions, and environmentalists on a wide range of issues. By the beginning of the twenty-first century, notable increases in trade had occurred and Mexico had become, after Canada, the second largest trading partner of the United States. NAFTA also stimulated rapid economic growth in Mexico.

Chapter 11, a controversial part of NAFTA, contains a provision that gives investors the right to sue national governments in special international trade tribunals of the World Bank and United Nations for monetary damages for violations of NAFTA provisions. Designed to protect NAFTA investors, opponents have used this provision to challenge national and local laws and governmental policies. In one of the largest of such suits, the Canadian Methanex Corporation in 1999 sued the U.S. government for $970 million, arguing that California's ban on methyl tertiary butyl ether (MTBE), a gasoline additive, violated the company's NAFTA investor rights. A similar case in 1998 by the U.S. Ethyl Corporation against the Canadian government settled out of court. Corporations had filed more than fifteen cases by 2002. And in Canada, United Parcel Service has sued the Canadian national postal service, charging unfair competition under the NAFTA agreement. These suits have brought charges that NAFTA undermines national sovereignty. Concern for labor standards and environmental protection have caused continuing opposition to NAFTA, with charges that it favors business interests at the expense of other segments of the society and that it tends to widen the gap between the rich and poor, rather than contributing to general prosperity. Canadians have complained that NAFTA has drawn skilled workers away from their country into the United States. The exports of other countries of the Americas, notably in the Caribbean region, have suffered as they compete with duty-free Mexican exports to the United States and Canada. Plans to expand North America into a more general Western Hemisphere free trade zone with the Free Trade Area of the Americas (FTAA) continue.

See also: Bush, George Herbert Walker; Canada; Clinton, William Jefferson (Bill); Fast-track legislation; Free Trade Area of the Americas (FTAA); Labor; Mexico; Mulroney, Brian; Perot, Henry Ross; Salinas de Gortari, Carlos. **Vol. II**: Enterprise for the Americas Initiative; Presidential Debate over the North American Free Trade Agreement; Gore-Perot Debate over the Ratification of the North American Free Trade Agreement.

Selected Bibliography:

John R. MacArthur, *The Selling of "Free Trade": NAFTA, Washington, and the Subversion of American Democracy*, 2000; William A. Orme Jr., *Understanding NAFTA: Mexico, Free Trade and the New North America*, 1996; Carol Wise, ed., *The Post-NAFTA Political Economy: Mexico and the Western Hemisphere*, 1998.

Ralph Lee Woodward Jr.

NORTH–SOUTH CONFLICT

Referring to disagreements arising from economic disparity in the international economy between wealthier nations largely found in the Northern Hemisphere and poorer nations disproportionately found in the Southern Hemisphere.

The terminology offers an alternative to other dichotomous classifications, such as "developed" and "underdeveloped," or "center" and "periphery." Some use the term "South" instead of "Third World," a term regarded as a residual catch-all phrase, anachronistic since the end of the Cold War.

The South encompasses 80 percent of the world's population, but commands only 20 percent of its wealth, giving rise to what the economist Robert Heilbroner called "a politics of mutual suspicion and struggle." The disparity is often attributed historically to the mercantilist practices of colonialism and neocolonialism. In the period between the post–World War II wave of decolonization and the rise of neoliberal economic policies and trade liberalization of the 1980s, diplomats from the South and certain academic currents questioned the utility of the doctrine of comparative advantage for achieving the goal of economic development. They developed the neo-Marxist theory of "dependency," rooted in the axiom of unequal exchange and the work of Raul Prebisch and his followers at the United Nations Economic Commission for Latin America. Their theory that the export of primary export commodities in exchange for manufactured goods resulted in chronically disadvantageous terms of trade for the South received recognition by Third World scholars such as Samir Amin.

The success of the Organization of Petroleum Exporting Countries in raising the price of oil and regulation of supply in the "OPEC decade" of 1974 to 1983 convinced many poor countries of the effectiveness of similar cartels. These organizations and the United Nations Conference for Trade and Development (UNCTAD) seek to revise the terms of trade in favor of the South. At its highpoint of success, many nations of the South asserted sovereign control over their natural resources, nationalized key mining and energy sectors, and reached preliminary agreements to stabilize commodity prices with buffer stocks. However, internal disputes among nations of the South, the impact of the debt crisis, and the weakening of OPEC brought a retreat from these achievements. UNCTAD abandoned the goal of stabilizing commodity prices and accommodated itself to neoliberal trade and development policies.

See also: Cold War; Conseil Intergouvernemental des Pays Exportateurs de Cuivre (CIPEC); Copper; Mercantilism; Oil; Organization of Petroleum Exporting Countries (OPEC); Prebisch, Raul; Third World; United Nations; World War II.

Selected Bibliography:

Samir Amin, *Accumulation on a World Scale: A Critique of the Theory of Underdevelopment*, 1974; Robert Heilbroner, *An Inquiry into the Human Prospect*, 1991.

Daniel C. Hellinger

NULLIFICATION

The extreme states' rights doctrine that gained prominence in the early 1830s when South Carolina invoked it to oppose protective tariffs.

Drawing on the compact theory of the U.S. Constitution laid down in the Virginia and Kentucky Resolutions, Nullifiers argued that a state could declare any federal law null and void if the state judges declared the act unconstitutional.

Support for nullification in South Carolina developed gradually during the 1820s. Following the War of 1812, neo-Federalist nationalists such as John C. Calhoun and William Lowndes dominated South Carolina's politics. They construed the Constitution broadly and supported protective tariffs. By the mid-1820s, states' rights and anti-tariff sentiment overcame neo-Federalism as distress gripped the cotton economy. Although overproduction and competition from western cotton-producing areas accounted for most of their troubles, Carolina cotton growers blamed their woes on the tariff. Rice planters, too, disliked the higher prices for imported manufactured goods that the tariff brought. Agriculturalists also feared that angry Europeans would retaliate against higher duties by buying their cotton and rice elsewhere. Compounding matters, many Carolinians became convinced that a federal government with broad powers might someday threaten slavery.

In 1828, Calhoun argued that a convention of the people, like that which ratified the federal Constitution, could nullify the tariff and check federal abuses. James Hamilton agreed and, as governor from 1830 to 1832, organized the States Rights and Free Trade Association, a statewide network of pro-nullification clubs. Through the association, Nullifiers educated ordinary citizens about their preferred remedy for the state's ills. Their campaign succeeded. In 1832, Nullifiers gained the two-thirds legislative majority necessary to call a convention. On November 24, 1832, the convention passed an ordinance nullifying the Tariff Act of 1828 and the Tariff Act of 1832, as well as threatening secession should the federal government act against the state.

The next month, President Andrew Jackson declared his intention to enforce the tariff, and South Carolina prepared its militia for action. Meanwhile, anti-nullification Unionists within the state drilled their own troops. To avert disaster, Calhoun and Henry Clay pushed the compromise Tariff Act of 1833 through Congress. Legislators also adopted the Force Act, which authorized the president to use the military if necessary to enforce the tariff laws. In March 1833, South Carolina's convention delegates met again to accept the compromise tariff, repeal their Ordinance of Nullification, and, for good measure, nullify the Force Act. Jackson ignored the second nullification and the crisis ended without bloodshed.

See also: Calhoun, John Caldwell; Clay, Henry; Clay's Compromise; Force Act; Hamilton, James; Jackson, Andrew; Lowndes, William Jones; South Carolina *Exposition* and *Protest*; Tariff of 1828 (Tariff of Abominations); Tariff of 1832. **Vol. II**: Henry Clay's 1832 Speech in Favor of the American System; South Carolina *Exposition*; South Carolina *Protest*; South Carolina Ordinance of Nullification; Proclamation to the People of South Carolina; Andrew Jackson's Message to Congress on the Nullification Crisis; Force Act. **Vol. III**: Tariff of 1828 (Tariff of Abominations); Tariff of 1832; Tariff of 1833 (Compromise Tariff).

Selected Bibliography:

Richard E. Ellis, *The Union at Risk: Jacksonian Democracy, States' Rights, and the Nullification Crisis*, 1987; William W. Freehling, *Prelude to Civil War: The Nullification Controversy in South Carolina, 1816–1836*, 1965.

Robert Tinkler

O

OIL

Replaced coal as the most important source of energy after the invention of the internal combustion engine, becoming the most important commodity of the twentieth century.

Experts have disagreed over the extent to which markets versus political forces determine the price of oil. Oil, an exhaustible resource with great military and geostrategic value found in the subsoil under different property regimes and varying costs of recuperation, has developed into an industry that attracts rent-seeking and regulation.

World War I demonstrated the importance of oil to mechanized warfare and produced a scramble for influence and leases among the companies of the victorious European powers in the middle eastern colonies and the Caucuses. By contrast, the United States relied mostly on domestic reserves until the 1950s. Standard Oil Company controlled 80 percent of refining capacity in the United States in the 1880s, but the Supreme Court, using antitrust legislation, broke it into three enterprises in 1911. In 1928, the major American and European companies, known as the "Seven Sisters," formed the International Petroleum Cartel (IPC) to regulate competition for leases and markets. Because of antitrust laws, the IPC did not cover the United States, but during the Great Depression the main foreign companies, Shell (Anglo-Dutch) and British Petroleum, agreed not to compete with American companies for the U.S. market. After 1930, U.S. companies and independent drillers achieved voluntary regulation via the Interstate Oil Compact Commission and, under the guise of conservation, by the Texas Railroad Commission. For the next forty years, these arrangements kept oil prices stable, but gradually rising.

While restricting foreign oil in the U.S. market, the Seven Sisters expanded production abroad. After Mexican nationalization in 1938 and

Venezuela's 1943 increase in royalties and taxes, the American companies moved to wrest concessions from European domination in the Middle East. By the 1950s, low-cost oil from abroad, even with a 10 percent tariff and added transportation costs, began to displace American oil in the home market. In 1958, the Eisenhower administration, under pressure from the Texas oil lobby, imposed import quotas. These lasted fourteen years and further depleted U.S. reserves.

These U.S. restrictions generated a diplomatic reaction from abroad. In 1959, Venezuela offered to open its domestic market to U.S. exports in exchange for privileged access to the American oil market. When the United States rejected the offer and abrogated a 1939 reciprocal trade agreement, Venezuela approached Saudi Arabia, the largest and lowest cost producer, to join it in convening the founding conference of the Organization of Petroleum Exporting Countries (OPEC) in Baghdad in 1960. OPEC exploited favorable circumstances to raise oil prices fourfold in 1973 and 1974, tenfold by 1981.

The consuming countries responded to the OPEC challenge with increased energy efficiency, development of non-OPEC-controlled fields, and cooperative oil diplomacy through an International Energy Administration. After 1981, prices began to fall, reaching their nadir around nine dollars per barrel in 1986. Even though the production and trading of oil occurred under a more liberal regime than ever before, consumption began to outstrip supply again in the 1990s. In 2000, rising heating oil and gasoline prices induced the Clinton administration to release thirty million barrels from strategic reserves.

Increased cooperation among OPEC producers, the anticipated return of Iraqi production excluded since the 1991 Gulf War, integration of oil from former Soviet Republics into the world market, and pressure to reduce carbon dioxide emissions to cope with global warming and other environmental threats left uncertainty about the future of the liberalized oil regime of the early twenty-first century.

See also: Clinton, William Jefferson (Bill); Coal; Eisenhower, Dwight D. (Ike); Foreign Policy; Great Depression; Latin America; Organization of Petroleum Exporting Countries (OPEC); World War I.

Selected Bibliography:

Morris Albert Adelman, *The Genie Out of the Bottle: World Oil Since 1970*, 1995; Bernard Mommer, *Foundations of Fiscal Regimes in Oil*, 1998.

Daniel C. Hellinger

OPEN DOOR NOTES

U.S. policy against the abrogation of international trade and investment in China by any nation.

By the second half of the nineteenth century, Japan, Germany, Great Britain, France, and other European powers had carved for themselves spheres of interest throughout China. Although America's Chinese trade volume had increased since the Opium War in 1840, U.S. imperialist designs had progressed at a slower pace than her European and Japanese counterparts. At the dawn of the twentieth century, the

United States had relatively little Chinese trade or influence compared to Japan and the European powers.

Fearful of losing the trade with China altogether because of foreign powers and seeking to avoid the levying of discriminatory tariffs and other commercial barriers against the United States, Secretary of State John Hay proclaimed the Open Door Policy in 1899. The Open Door Notes asked all nations with spheres of influence in China to agree to the following provisions: grant equal treatment to all commerce and navigation within a nation's sphere of influence, apply the Chinese tariff to all goods shipped or landed in Chinese ports regardless of the nationality of the merchant, and eliminate the higher harbor dues and higher railroad charges against a nation conducting business in another nation's sphere of influence. Although this policy lacked enforceability and the foreign powers in China responded evasively to Hay's request, he declared the Open Door Policy official in 1900.

Hay feared that the antiforeigner Boxer Rebellion of 1900 would give foreign powers a reason to overturn the Open Door Notes and strengthen their spheres of influence in China, so the United States paid homage to the policy by sending troops as part of the multinational coalition to suppress the Boxer Rebellion. Later, as Russia and Japan fought the Russo-Japanese War over Chinese territorial ambitions, President Theodore Roosevelt worried that the belligerents would disrupt American commerce in China under the Open Door Notes, so he induced the warring parties to make peace.

In 1909, President William Taft supplemented the Open Door Notes with the policy of dollar diplomacy, which increased U.S. trade abroad by supporting American enterprises and investments in China. In 1909, Japan and Russia violated the Open Door Policy without U.S. retaliation, and American commercial enterprises began to reduce their investment in China. By 1913, President Wilson's policies all but abandoned the Open Door Notes, which became relevant again only as an attempted check on Japanese ambitions prior to World War II.

See also: Hay, John Milton; Roosevelt, Theodore; Taft, William Howard.

Selected Bibliography:

Jonathan D. Spence, *The Search for Modern China*, 1999.

Josh Pratt

ORGANIZATION OF AMERICAN STATES (OAS)

A regional association of nations.

The Organization of American States (OAS) grew out of a series of inter-American conferences that began in 1890 and became known as the Pan-American Union in 1910. On April 20, 1948, participants at the Ninth International American Conference in Bogotá, Colombia, dissolved the Pan American Union and signed the OAS Charter. OAS goals include protecting the security of the hemisphere, peaceful settlement of disputes between member states, and the promotion of economic, cultural, and military cooperation among members. The OAS later expanded to include Canada and the Caribbean nations. As of 2002, the organization had thirty-five member states. Based in Washington, D.C., the OAS has interests in a host of areas, ranging from cultural exchanges and education to trade relations and the promotion of human rights and democratic government.

During the Cold War, the United States viewed the OAS primarily as a means to protect the Western Hemisphere from communist influence. With U.S. leadership, the OAS, following the Cuban Missile Crisis, dropped Cuba to a nonvoting status in 1962. Although the OAS denounced unilateral intervention, it would narrowly approve an inter-American force to replace U.S. troops who had intervened in the Dominican Republic in 1965. Latin American member nations would seek independence from U.S. leadership in the 1970s, as evidenced by the refusal in 1979 of the OAS to mediate between the U.S.-backed Somoza dynasty and Sandinista rebels in Nicaragua.

With a history of promoting free trade and economic integration in the hemisphere, the OAS has sponsored a number of initiatives in those areas. Perhaps the most prominent of these initiatives is the Inter-American Development Bank (IDB), a regional development institution established in 1959. The bank began with twenty member nations and in 1999 had forty-six members. The IDB's charter calls for it to finance the borrowing member nations, assist private investors, and provide assistance in building development plans and projects. IDB lending grew from $295 million in 1961 to $10 billion in 1998.

The OAS includes several other economically oriented institutions. The Economic Commission for Latin America (ECLA), founded in 1948 as one of five regional commissions of the United Nations, has contributed mainly in the area of economic theory, where it has debated the merits of import substitutions, examined the external debt problem, and has most recently engaged the idea of social equity. In 1995, the OAS launched the Free Trade Unit to support an effort to create a Free Trade Area of the Americas (FTAA). The Free Trade Unit works with the OAS Special Committee on Free Trade to coordinate information of trade policies and seek methods to promote effective economic coordination within the region.

In addition to trade issues, in the 1990s, the OAS increased its efforts to promote human rights and democracy through the Inter-American Commission on Human Rights and electoral observation missions.

See also: Canada; Cold War; Cuba; Economic Commission for Latin America (ECLA); Free Trade Area of the Americas (FTAA); Latin America.

Selected Bibliography:

L. Ronald Scheman, *The Inter-American Dilemma: The Search for Inter-American Cooperation at the Centennial of the Inter-American System*, 1988.

John D. Coats

ORGANIZATION OF PETROLEUM EXPORTING COUNTRIES (OPEC)

Organization of Third World exporters seeking to regulate the pricing and supply of oil.

In response to falling prices and the decision of the United States in 1958 to impose quotas on oil imports, Venezuela's Minister of Mines and Hydrocarbons, Juan Pérez Alfonzo, called the father of OPEC, approached Saudi Arabian Sheik Abdullah Tariki about forming such an organization. In 1960, they convened representatives of Iraq, Iran, and Kuwait at the founding conference of the Organization of Petroleum Exporting Countries (OPEC). Algeria, Indonesia, Nigeria, United Arab Emirates, Qatar, and Libya joined later. Norway and Mexico hold observer status.

OPEC initially offered cooperation with consuming countries, which showed little interest. In 1968, members declared "permanent sovereignty" over natural resources, becoming a Third World battle cry in the global North–South conflict. OPEC members thereby asserted their right to control levels of production. In 1969, at the initiative of Libya's Muammar Qaddafi, they established a reference price system for calculating taxes and royalties. The companies had lost control over supply and pricing.

Few recognized OPEC's gathering power, but, by 1970, eleven members controlled 73 percent of the world's oil production. During the 1973 Yom Kippur War, Arab countries (not OPEC) declared an embargo against Israel and its Western allies. Oil prices increased fourfold; they would rise tenfold by 1981. Consuming countries responded with measures to increase non-OPEC production and cut wasteful consumption. The International Energy Agency formed to coordinate their responses. OPEC attempted to maintain prices through quotas, but members often cheated. By 1986, prices per barrel plunged to nine dollars, 25 percent of their levels five years earlier. Many

predicted OPEC's demise, but in 1999 members had regained some of their market share and agreed on new quotas.

See also: Latin America; Mexico; Third World.

Selected Bibliography:

Stephen G. Rabe, *The Road to OPEC: United States Relations with Venezuela: 1919–1976*, 1982.

Daniel C. Hellinger

ORIGINS OF POLITICAL PARTIES

In part, the result of disagreements over tariff levels.

The first party system of the new republic, which pitted Federalists against Democratic-Republicans and lasted from the 1790s to the War of 1812, arose in part over differing opinions on the tariff issue brought to light when Treasury Secretary Alexander Hamilton introduced his fiscal plan for the new nation, which included a protective tariff. Federalists embraced Hamilton's plan, which also included federal assumption of state-induced American Revolution debts, an excise tax on wine and spirits, and the creation of a national bank, among other things. Under the leadership of Thomas Jefferson and James Madison, the Democratic-Republican Party formed in opposition to Washington's Federalist administration and its principal domestic and foreign policies: Hamilton's fiscal plan and John Jay's 1795 treaty with Great Britain. Members of both parties agreed that the federal government desperately needed adequate revenue, but they disagreed on exactly what role the tariff should play in securing it. Hamilton believed that a good tariff strategy would protect America's infant industries. Jefferson opposed the tariff because he believed that the future of the country lay in its agricultural production, not in its industrial development. The constituencies of both parties had reservations about the tariff. The merchants and seaport communities that supported the Federalists, but feared that high tariffs would impede overseas trade, on which mercantile profits and full employment in the ports depended. The farming communities that supported the Democratic-Republicans also disliked high tariffs because they did not want to see a steep rise in the cost of manufactured goods. In an effort to raise revenue while supporting their respective party members, the Federalists and Republicans reached a compromise in the passage of the moderate Tariff Act of 1789. The issue continued to incite debate between the parties until the post–War of 1812 recession caused the Republican administration of James Madison to pass into law the United States's first highly protective tariff in 1816.

Tariffs played an even greater role in dividing voters and politicians during the second party system between Democrats and Whigs from the 1830s to the 1850s. Whigs adhered to Henry Clay's American System, which advocated the development of the U.S. economy along modern, industrial lines. Clay sought the protection of infant industrial enterprises in the United States against foreign, especially British, imports, through very high tariff rates.

Just after the War of 1812, strong nationalist feelings meant that Clay won broad support for his tariff plan and, starting with the Tariff Act of 1816, tariff levels rose higher and higher. Over time, agricultural regions began to protest against high tariffs that raised the price of imported manufactured goods. By the 1830s, tariffs had become one of the most important factors defining political divisions in the United States. When northern Republicans passed the Morrill Tariff during the Civil War, they had little Democratic opposition because of the absence of southern congressmen.

After the war, the two emerging parties consistently debated the tariff issue, with Republicans supporting high protective tariffs and Democrats fighting to lower tariffs and greatly expand the free list. The tariff issue dominated presidential elections throughout the late nineteenth and early twentieth centuries, exacerbated exclusively by partisan politics. In the later part of the twentieth century, a Third Party developed over several economic issues. The new Reform Party under the leadership of business leader Ross Perot challenged the efficacy of the proposed passage of the North American Free Trade Agreement (NAFTA).

See also: American System; Calhoun, John Caldwell; Clay, Henry; Democratic Party; Tariff of 1816; Whig Party.

Selected Bibliography:

Henry L. Watson, *Liberty and Power: The Politics of Jacksonian America*, 1990.

John P. Barrington

P

PANAMA CANAL

A 51-mile ship canal through the Isthmus of Panama linking the Atlantic and Pacific Oceans.

Conceived as early as 1535, the Panama Canal became a reality in 1914, replacing a railway that a U.S. company had constructed in 1855. Ships sailing between the East and West Coasts of the United States saved about 8,000 nautical miles. Voyages between one coast of North America and the other coast of South America saved up to 3,500 miles, and ships sailing between Europe and the Orient saved up to 2,000 miles. In the late nineteenth century, mosquito-borne diseases and insufficient capital contributed to French failures to complete the canal, as well as to an unsuccessful U.S. effort in Nicaragua. The Spooner Act of 1902 authorized the U.S. government to acquire the French concession and property, but failure to secure Colombian approval delayed the U.S. effort. Thus, in 1903, President Theodore Roosevelt recognized Panamanian secession from Colombia and promptly negotiated the Hay-Bunau-Varilla Treaty with Panama. In addition to rights to build the canal, the United States received, in perpetuity, a ten-mile-wide Panama Canal Zone, and in 1904 Panama became a U.S. protectorate. The Panama Canal Act of 1912 established regulations and tolls for the canal operation. British objection to a provision of that act that exempted American coastal trade from tolls as a violation of the Hay-Pauncefote Treaty of 1904 resulted in the repeal of that provision in 1914, when the canal opened to ships of all nations under U.S. administration. Goods passing through the canal paid no duties unless destined for the Republic of Panama. The Hull-Alfaro Treaty of 1936 ended Panama's protectorate status and granted other concessions to Panama. During World War II, Panama granted the U.S. military bases in Panama. The Eisenhower-Remón Treaty of 1955, following riots in Panama, recognized Panamanian titular sovereignty over the canal zone and promised resolution of other contentious issues, but implementation of this treaty moved too slowly to satisfy Panamanian nationalists, especially after Egypt seized the Suez Canal in 1956. New protests in 1964 ultimately led to the 1978 Torrijos-Carter Treaties, by which the United States transferred the canal to Panama on December 31, 1999, with the guarantee that the canal would remain open and neutral to all nations.

See also: Roosevelt, Theodore; World War II.

Selected Bibliography:

John Major, *Prize Possession: The United States and the Panama Canal, 1903–1979*, 1993.

Ralph Lee Woodward Jr.

PATTEN, SIMON NELSON (May 1, 1852–July 24, 1922)

American economist and social philosopher known for his strong views on economic nationalism and protectionism at the turn of the twentieth-century.

Born in Cossayuna, New York, Patten grew up on his father's farm in Sandwich, Illinois. Raised by a strict father and a stepmother, he enrolled in Jennings Seminary in Aurora and became quite interested in philosophy and social science, two areas he continued to explore at Northwestern University and later Halle, Germany, under the tutelage of Johannes Ernst Conrad. Plagued briefly by eyesight problems, he received his Ph.D. in 1878. By 1888, he accepted a chair of political economy at the University of Pennsylvania Wharton School.

A fairly prolific author, Patten led the growing institutional movement in economics, assisting in the attack on the classical economics of David Ricardo and Thomas Malthus. Patten strongly adhered to his belief in the abundance of nature and the human capability to exploit it. He persistently argued that economics, the science of optimism, could point the way to progress only with the rejection of laissez-faire and the harnessing of industrialism. Interdisciplinary approaches to the American economy remained necessary to study its intricacies. For Patten, the twentieth century symbolized the age of surplus.

Given these axioms of modern economics, Patten offered traditional arguments for protectionism. He thought that the United States needed to seek its own economic future and protect its industries. Patten not only passed on his opinions on tariffs and economics to his students, such as Rexford G. Tugwell, he also promulgated them as president of the American Economics Association in 1908. His major works, especially *Premises of Political Economy*, published in 1885, *Theory of Social Forces*, published in 1896, and *New Basis of Civilization*, published in 1907, expounded his beliefs. A highly successful and remembered teacher, Patten died on July 24, 1922.

See also: Malthus, Thomas; Ricardo, David; Tugwell, Rexford G.

Selected Bibliography:

Allan Gruchy, *Modern Economic Thought: The American Contribution*, 1947; Rexford G.

Tugwell, ed., *Essays in Economic Theory*, 1924.

Michael V. Namorato

PAYNE, SERENO E. (June 26, 1843–December 11, 1914)

Member of the U.S. House of Representatives from New York and drafter of the Payne-Aldrich Tariff of 1909.

Born in Hamilton, New York, Payne received an academy education. He graduated from the University of Rochester in 1864 and then read law. He gained admittance to the New York bar in 1866. Payne participated in Republican Party politics, giving his first political speech in 1864. From 1867 to 1882, he held a number of local offices. In 1882, Payne won a seat in the U.S. House of Representatives.

In 1889, Payne received an appointment to the House Ways and Means Committee, which initiated all tax legislation. He worked hard and participated in writing and defending the McKinley Tariff of 1890 and the Dingley Tariff of 1897. He strongly opposed the Wilson-Gorman Tariff of 1894, the work of Democratic congressmen. Payne became chairman of the committee in 1899 when Nelson Dingley died. He also became Republican floor leader. Payne had an opportunity to serve as Speaker of the House when David Henderson of Iowa retired in 1903, but division in the New York delegation cost him some support. Joseph Cannon of Illinois won the Speakership and Payne remained floor leader.

The Republican Party platform of 1908 called for a reduction in tariff rates. In 1909, the newly inaugurated President William Howard Taft called a special session of Congress to act on the tariff issue. As chair of the Ways and Means Committee, Payne drafted a tariff revision bill that met Taft's specifications. He introduced the bill into the Sixty-first Congress with a speech lasting nine and a half hours. Despite some vocal opposition in the chamber, the bill passed the House largely as Payne had drafted. More conservative Republicans significantly amended the bill in the Senate.

The Republican Party lost control of the House in the 1910 election in part due to the unpopularity of the Payne-Aldrich Tariff. Payne played a much less significant role in the tariff debate as a minority member of the committee. Not long after being reelected to another term in Congress, he died on December 11, 1914, in Washington, D.C.

See also: Aldrich, Nelson W.; Democratic Party; Dingley Tariff (Tariff of 1897); House Ways and Means Committee; LaFollette, Robert M.; Payne-Aldrich Tariff (Tariff of 1909); Republican Party; Senate Finance Committee; Taft, William Howard. **Vol. II**: Inaugural Address of William Howard Taft; William Howard Taft's Winona Speech; William Howard Taft's 1912 Acceptance Speech. **Vol. III:** Tariff of 1890; Tariff of 1894; Tariff of 1897; Tariff of 1909.

Selected Bibliography:

Paul Wolman, *Most Favored Nation: The Republican Revisionists and U.S. Tariff Policy, 1897–1912*, 1992.

John David Rausch Jr.

PAYNE-ALDRICH TARIFF (TARIFF OF 1909)

A largely unsuccessful attempt at tariff reform co-authored by Representative Sereno Payne and Senator Nelson Aldrich.

Tariff reform had largely been ignored since the passage of the Dingley Tariff in 1897. In response to tariff reformers within the party, the Republican Party platform of 1908 pledged to reduce tariff rates. Many Progressive Republicans saw tariff reduction as one way to break up trusts. In 1909, newly inaugurated President William Howard Taft sought to fulfill the pledge and called a special session of Congress to work on tariff rates.

Representative Sereno Payne, a Republican from New York and chairman of the House Ways and Means Committee, drafted a bill that met President Taft's wishes. The bill would have the effect of equalizing the costs of production at home and abroad. It also delegated some power to the president, including language that allowed Taft to create a nonpartisan, fact-finding tariff board. Payne included provisions reducing the tariff on pulp and paper, a move popular with publishers. The bill passed the House largely as Payne had drafted.

In the Senate, Nelson Aldrich, a Republican from Rhode Island and chairman of the Senate Finance Committee, reported that a bill with tariff rates higher than the bill had passed the House. The restoration of duties on goods placed on the tariff-free list by the House and *ad valorem* rates replaced by specific duties occurred because the method provided a more efficient way to protect industry. Progressive Republican senators, including Robert M. LaFollette of Wisconsin, attacked Aldrich's bill and attracted much press attention. An attempt to amend an income tax onto the bill proved particularly noteworthy. Despite the controversy and after eleven weeks of debate, the Senate approved the bill by a vote of 45 to 34.

During the summer of 1909, the House and Senate versions of tariff reform went to a conference committee in an attempt to reach a compromise. President Taft and Representative Payne forced the Senate conferees to accept some reductions. By this time, the Progressive Republicans and the press, which had lost the fight for cheap newsprint, had stigmatized the bill. At best, the Payne-Aldrich Tariff provided an incremental change in the direction of reducing tariff rates. The compromise bill lowered 650 tariff schedules, raised 220, and left 1,150 unchanged. It also provided the president with the power to increase rates by adding a 25 percent tax on the value of an import to retaliate against a country that was "unduly discriminatory" to American products.

The legislation, called "the best tariff law in Republican history" when signed by President Taft in 1909, provided the Democratic Party with an issue to use to win control of the House of Representatives in the 1910 congressional elections.

See also: Aldrich, Nelson W.; Democratic Party; Dingley Tariff (Tariff of 1897); House Ways and Means Committee; LaFollette, Robert Marion; Payne, Sereno E.; Republican Party; Senate Finance Committee; Taft, William Howard. **Vol. II**: Inaugural Address of William Howard Taft; William

Howard Taft's Winona Speech; William Howard Taft's 1912 Acceptance Speech. **Vol. III:** Tariff of 1897 (Dingley Tariff); Tariff of 1909 (Payne-Aldrich Tariff).

Selected Bibliography:

Judith Goldstein, *Ideas, Interests, and American Trade Policy*, 1993; Paul Wolman, *Most Favored Nation: The Republican Revisionists and U.S. Tariff Policy, 1897–1912*, 1992.

John David Rausch Jr.

PEEK, GEORGE N. (November 19, 1873–December 17, 1943)

Businessman, farm leader, and champion of equality for American farmers in the world market.

Born in Polo, a small town in northern Illinois, Peek and his family moved to a farm near Oregon, Illinois, in 1895. He entered Northwestern University in 1891, staying one academic year. Deere and Webber, a branch of the John Deere Plow Company in Minneapolis, hired Peek in 1893. In 1901, he became general manager of the John Deere Plow Company branch in Omaha. By 1914, he received a promotion to vice president of sales and worked at company headquarters in Moline, Illinois. Peek served on the War Industries Board (WIB) during World War I.

In 1921, Peek and General Hugh S. Johnson, a former colleague on the WIB, published a pamphlet titled "Equality for Agriculture." Farmers, buying manufactured goods at high prices caused by protective tariffs, sold their own produce at low prices on the world markets. The program outlined by Peek and Johnson would use the force of the federal government to prop up the prices for farm commodities at levels equal to those of the "golden period" of 1910 to 1914. Peek spent more than a decade trying to get his plan enacted into law, finally succeeding in getting the concept of farm equity included in the Agricultural Adjustment Act of 1933.

A Republican, Peek campaigned among farmers to support Democratic nominees Al Smith and Franklin Roosevelt in the elections of 1928 and 1932, respectively. After Roosevelt signed the Agricultural Adjustment Act into law, the president rewarded Peek by naming him the administrator of the program. After only seven months, President Roosevelt asked him to resign after Peek conflicted with Secretary of Agriculture Henry Wallace. In an attempt to make amends, Roosevelt named him president of the Export-Import Bank. He resigned from that position in 1935. Peek remained a vocal critic of the New Deal for the rest of his life. He died in Rancho Santa Fe, California, on December 17, 1943.

See also: Agricultural Adjustment Act (AAA); Baruch, Bernard Mannes; Great Depression; Roosevelt, Franklin D.; World War I.

Selected Bibliography:

Gilbert C. Fite, *George N. Peek and the Fight for Farm Parity*, 1954.

John David Rausch Jr.

PEOPLE'S REPUBLIC OF CHINA (PRC)

The world's most populous nation, with 1.2 billion people, and third largest in terms of area (3,696,100 square miles); a growing economic power with increasing importance for U.S.

trade and investment during the last quarter of the twentieth century.

Proclaimed in October 1949 when the Communist Party of China (CPC) took power, the PRC adopted the Soviet model of centralized state and planning economy in the early 1950s. When China failed to afford Soviet-type capital-intensive industrialization through the advancement of heavy industry, the CPC leader Mao Zedong decided to formulate a Chinese approach to achieving speedy industrial and agricultural development by mobilizing the enormous manpower of China. But his Great Leap Forward and People's Commune movements implemented between 1958 and 1960, designed to achieve Mao's utopia, only caused disastrous consequences. To carve a Chinese model of Communism, he launched ultra-leftist political movements, but they had damaging consequences on China after 1957. The Great Cultural Revolution, beginning in 1966 and ending in 1976 when Mao died, brought the PRC to near political and economic collapse.

The post-Mao CPC under Deng Xiaoping pursued pragmatism for China's modernization; in 1979 it initiated continuous economic reforms in the name of building "socialism" with Chinese characteristics by preserving the CPC power of policy decisions while bringing in market mechanism into Chinese economy. Through economic decentralization and by opening up to foreign investments, China has improved productivity, comprehensive national strength, and people's living standards. Since 1980, the Chinese GDP has grown by an annual average of 9.5 percent. In 1997, the World Bank ranked China's economy as third in the world after the United States and Japan.

Exports to the United States and American investment in Chinese technology, which the PRC government has encouraged by using selective protective tariffs and income taxes, remain vital to China's economic growth. Since 1980, the United States has become the foremost market for Chinese exports and China has generated an increasing trade surplus—more than $40 billion in 1998. Meanwhile, American investment in China has been growing rapidly. In 1997, Americans invested in 22,240 Chinese projects totaling $35.17 billion. Despite the trend toward greater economic intercourse with China, the United States has long been protesting China's unfair trade practices such as high tariffs and market closings to certain American industries, and piracy of intellectual property rights, especially in U.S. movies, computer software, and CDs, for they allegedly produced an unfavorable balance of trade between the two countries. Contention on these issues led the United States to threaten tariff retaliation against China in 1992. To avoid a trade war, the two countries negotiated and signed the 1992 Intellectual Property Protection Memorandum. Three years later, China promised to lower the contentious tariff barriers and open markets to several American products in exchange for American support of China's entry into the World Trade Organization (WTO). To better relations, the U.S. Congress voted in 2000 to give China a permanent Most Favored Nation (MFN) status.

See also: Cold War; Communism; World Trade Organization (WTO).

Selected Bibliography:

Jonathan D. Spence, *The Search for Modern China*, 1999; Ranbir Vohra, *China's Path to Modernization*, 2000.

Guoqiang Zheng

PEROT, HENRY ROSS (June 27, 1930–)

American businessman and presidential candidate who opposed the lowering of tariff barriers through the formation of free trade zones such as the North American Free Trade area.

Born in Texarkana, Texas, Perot attended Texarkana Junior College before entering the U.S. Naval Academy in 1949. After receiving his commission in 1953, he served four years before leaving the military to work as a salesman for International Business Machines (IBM). In 1962, he formed his own corporation, Electronic Data Systems (EDS). Perot made his fortune after taking the company public in 1968. In 1992, Perot ran for president on an independent party ticket against George Herbert Walker Bush, the Republican incumbent, and William Jefferson Clinton, the Democratic governor of Arkansas. After Clinton won the election, the North American Free Trade Agreement (NAFTA), signed under the Bush administration, reached the Senate for ratification. In an attempt to win support for its passage and silence opponents of the measure, the White House arranged a debate between Vice President Al Gore and Ross Perot in 1993. Gore presented Perot with photographs of Senator Reed Smoot and Representative Ellis Hawley and argued that the high Hawley-Smoot Tariff resulted in the Great

Depression. He then pointed out that Ross Perot owned Alliance Airport, a free trade zone in Fort Worth, Texas. The debate helped persuade senators to pass NAFTA. Although Perot ran for president again in 1996 as the Reform Party candidate, he received only 8 percent of the popular vote as opposed to the 19 percent he had managed to win in the previous election. Perot currently resides in Dallas, Texas.

See also: Bush, George Herbert Walker; Clinton, William Jefferson (Bill); Free trade; Gore, Albert Arnold, Jr.; North American Free Trade Agreement (NAFTA). **Vol. II**: Presidential Debate over the North American Free Trade Agreement; Gore-Perot Debate over the Ratification of the North American Free Trade Agreement.

Selected Bibliography:

William Crotty, ed., *America's Choice: The Election of 1992*, 1993; Todd Mason, *Perot: An Unauthorized Biography*, 1990.

Cynthia Clark Northrup

PERSONAL INCOME TAX (SIXTEENTH CONSTITUTIONAL AMENDMENT)

This amendment reads: "The Congress shall have power to lay and collect taxes on incomes, from whatever source derived, without apportionment among the several States, and without regard to any census or enumeration."

Issues concerning taxes have always proven contentious for Americans. Article I, Section 9 of the U.S. Constitution says that "No Capitation, or other direct, Tax shall be laid, unless in Proportion to the Census or Enumeration." Critics argue that the personal income tax, the most direct kind of taxation, constitutes a regressive tax, since the poor would pay proportionally more of their income to the government for taxes than would the rich. But the federal government needed the tax money to keep operating, expand its services, and provide assistance to citizens in times of natural disaster or economic collapse. With the earlier example of Great Britain using income taxes to pay for government expenditures during the Napoleonic Wars, the Union government in 1861 instituted an income tax during the American Civil War that lasted until 1872. The Wilson-Gorman Tariff Act of 1894 included an income tax provision that the Supreme Court struck down in *Pollock v. Farmers' Loan and Trust Company* in 1895. Perceived as socialistic and anti-American, citizens feared that this act forced redistribution of income.

An economic recession in 1907 found the federal government without the financial means to quickly ease the situation. A complex political battle in Congress in 1909 created the conditions that led to the federal income tax. Senate Republican leader Nelson Aldrich of Rhode Island, in an effort to thwart the Bailey-Cummins income tax amendment to his Payne-Aldrich Tariff Bill, proposed a separate constitutional amendment, thinking it would fail. Much to his chagrin, many members of Congress felt otherwise. In July of that year, Congress passed the amendment overwhelmingly by a vote in the Senate of 77 to 0, with the House of Representatives passing the measure by a vote of 318 to 14. Alabama ratified the amendment first. When Wyoming, the thirty-sixth state, approved the amendment on February 13, 1913, the constitutional amendment received the approval of enough states to become law. Eventually, forty-two of the forty-eight states ratified the amendment. During this period, the Supreme Court, in *Flint v. Stone Tracy Co.*, decided in 1911, unanimously upheld the legality of a corporate income tax. An eight-page amendment to the Underwood-Simmons Tariff Act, passed on October 3, 1913, provided the enabling legislation. Representative Cordell Hull, who later became secretary of state under President Franklin Roosevelt, drafted the legislation. In the middle of the 1950s, a serious movement in Congress to repeal or modify the amendment proved unsuccessful. This amendment not only repealed the *Pollock v. Farmers' Loan* Supreme Court decision, but it became the keystone to the federal income tax structure. Although widely criticized and sometimes evaded, the vast majority of American citizens pay their share of the tax. With a shift to free trade and the reduction of tariffs, Americans generally accepted the need for some level of income taxation for the government to function; disputes arise over how much to charge, and what exemptions to offer.

See also: Aldrich, Nelson W.; Underwood-Simmons Tariff (Tariff of 1913); Wilson, Thomas Woodrow.

Selected Bibliography:

George D. Schrader, "Constitutional History of the Income Tax," *Georgia State Bar Journal*, August 1970; Jerold L. Waltman, *Political Origins of the U.S. Income Tax*, 1958.

Daniel K. Bleweit

PIERCE, FRANKLIN (November 23, 1804–October 8, 1869)

Fourteenth president of the United States.

Born in Hillsborough, New Hampshire, Pierce attended Bowdoin College, graduating in 1824. He practiced law and entered politics as a Democratic member of the New Hampshire legislature. He served in the U.S. House of Representatives, the U.S. Senate, and as a general during the Mexican War. Pierce did not pursue the nomination for president in 1852, but the Democratic convention of that year chose him after separate attempts to nominate James Buchanan, Stephen Douglas, and William Marcy failed. Nominally known for his pro-slavery views and his support for the Compromise of 1850, the Democratic leadership chose him in part because he proved acceptable to the convention's southern delegates. In the general election, Pierce handily defeated the Whig nominee, war hero Winfield Scott.

Pierce, an amiable man, proved ill suited to handle the rigors of the presidency as sectional tensions mounted. His attempts to maintain national harmony met with little success as debates over slavery intensified. During his administration, the Ostend Manifesto became public, enraging many northerners, and the Kansas-Nebraska Act sparked a bloody civil war in Kansas. He nominated James Guthrie as his secretary of the treasury, one of his strongest cabinet appointees. An honest, hardworking administrator, Guthrie quickly became one of his chief advisors on financial matters. On Guthrie's recommendation, Pierce signed economic legislation that included a moderate reduction of the tariff. As president, Pierce continued supporting Democratic policies, including tariff reduction, but sectional difficulties and his own indecisiveness made it impossible for him to maintain party unity. He alienated many Democrats and the party chose James Buchanan as its nominee for president in 1856. After leaving the White House, Pierce retired from public life. He died in Concord, New Hampshire, on October 8, 1869.

See also: Democratic Party.

Selected Bibliography:

Larry Gara, *The Presidency of Franklin Pierce*, 1991.

Ben Wynne

PINCKNEY, CHARLES COTESWORTH (February 25, 1746–August 16, 1825)

South Carolina lawyer, Revolutionary War officer, diplomat, and politician.

Born in South Carolina, Pinckney received his education in England, returned to the colony in 1769, began his law practice, and was elected to the local assembly. He served during the American Revolution, rising to the rank of brigadier general. As a delegate at the Constitutional Convention in 1787, Pinckney firmly supported the position that a strong central government provided the best course for the new nation. Despite this view, he argued against giving Congress the right to impose taxes on exports, believing that this position would compromise his state.

Rather than simply revising the Articles of Confederation, delegates to the Constitutional Convention decided to write a new constitution, one that would correct all the apparent weaknesses that existed in the Articles. Fiscal policy proved the one major weakness: The federal government needed the authority to collect revenues from the states. While Pinckney supported in theory the idea of granting Congress such power, he felt that the specific plan proposed by Congress would jeopardize the political and economic viability of his state.

Many delegates supported a plan that granted Congress the right to tax exports. Pinckney believed that this placed a great economic burden on his state since South Carolina derived most of its income from exporting plantation staples. This meant that his state would contribute a greater share of revenue than other states that exported fewer commodities. Pinckney thought that the plan for apportioning representation already hurt South Carolina since Congress proved reluctant to count slaves, a substantial part of their overall wealth. He argued that taxation based on wealth required full representation. Other convention delegates agreed with this logic and voted against granting Congress the power to tax exports.

In 1796, Pinckney received an appointment as minister to France, but the French revolutionary regime refused to grant him entry. In 1800, Pinckney ran as the Federalist candidate for president and their nominee for vice president in 1804 and 1808, but lost on all three occasions. For the rest of his life, he practiced law in Charleston and served occasionally in the leg-islature. Pinckney died in Charleston at the age of seventy-nine.

See also: Constitutional Convention; Federalists; Slavery.

Selected Bibliography:

William Peters, *A More Perfect Union: The Making of the U.S. Constitution*, 1987.

Virginia Jelatis

PIRATES

Individuals or groups who robbed vessels on the high seas.

Lacking the resources, economic insight, or political initiative to compete directly with Catholic Spain's colonial endeavors, its Western European rivals—the Dutch, French, and English—resorted to isolated and concerted attacks on Spanish ports and ships in pursuit of the riches of empire. The Dutch Sea Beggars, French buccaneers, and English pirates, acting on behalf of their respective governments or for their own enrichment, wrought intermittent havoc in the Caribbean, Gulf of Mexico, and along both coasts of South America.

During the second half of the sixteenth and the early part of the seventeenth centuries, piracy along the "Spanish Main" created the need for small outposts for resupply in the Bahama, Windward, and Leeward Islands, points from which would-be attackers could await the treasure-laden ships of the Spanish. These ports also served as way stations for the smuggling of goods from Europe to Spanish America to more regularly meet colonial consumer demand during the lengthy periods between

Spain's biennial arrivals of its own merchant fleets. By the beginning of the seventeenth century, Spain reached an accord with England to end state-sponsored raids, an agreement extended to include all the major powers of Western Europe by the end of the century.

Although diplomacy brought an end to peacetime attacks, declarations of war led to frequent renewals of piracy. In addition, "lawless" individuals or privateers continued to hijack ships and raid ports throughout the early modern period. These attacks remained increasingly limited to a handful of pirates, yet governments failed to reach an agreement concerning smuggling. In fact, just the opposite proved true. A foreign ship claiming sanctuary from inclement weather or the need for repairs or supplies could gain entry into "enemy" ports where trade followed.

So-called buccaneers also played an important role in the American Revolution, supplementing the limited resources of the colonial navy with regular raiding of British merchant ships. In the early part of the nineteenth century, the fledgling U.S. Navy protected mercantile interests in the region by heeding the call into action against the Barbary corsairs of the Mediterranean.

Ultimately, the advent of the steam engine in the first half of the nineteenth century drastically reduced the effectiveness of pirates. Ships powered by steam could easily outrun or catch raiders. In 1856, the Declaration of Paris brought a formal end to "letters of marque" among most maritime nations. Piracy continues in different parts of the world, including pockets of the Caribbean and in a flourishing state in Southeast Asia.

See also: Great Britain; Latin America.

Selected Bibliography:

Alexandre Olivier Exquemelin, *The Buccaneers and Marooners of America: Being an Account of the Famous Adventures and Daring Deeds of Certain Notorious Freebooters of the Spanish Main*, 1891; Clarence Henry Haring, *The Buccaneers in the West Indies in the XVII Century*, 1910; Marcus Buford Rediker, *Between the Devil and the Deep Blue Sea: Merchant Seamen, Pirates, and the Anglo-American Maritime World, 1700–1750*, 1987.

David J. Weiland III

POLK, JAMES K. (November 2, 1795–June 15, 1849)

Eleventh president of the United States, member of the House of Representatives, Speaker of the House, and governor of Tennessee.

Born in North Carolina, Polk and his family moved to Tennessee in 1806. He entered the University of North Carolina in 1815 and graduated first in his class. He studied law in Nashville and in 1820 gained admittance to the Tennessee bar. He served in the state House of Representatives from 1823 to 1825 and was elected to the U.S. House of Representatives in 1825, where he supported Andrew Jackson. As a member of the House, he backed Jackson during the fight over nullification. As chairman of the House Ways and Means Committee, he influenced the decision to remove federal deposits from the second Bank of the United States. In 1839, he resigned as Speaker of the House to run for governor of

Tennessee to prevent a Whig takeover of the government in that state. In 1841 and again in 1843, a Whig candidate defeated him for the governorship.

The Democratic convention in 1844 chose him over Martin Van Buren as the presidential candidate and he won the campaign on the platform of the annexation of Texas and the reoccupation of Oregon with an electoral vote of 170 to 105 over Whig candidate Henry Clay. He announced that he would serve only one term and set about to name a strong cabinet of James Buchanan, Robert J. Walker, William L. Marcy, and George Bancroft. He put forth four objectives for his presidency: reduction of the tariff, reinstatement of the Independent Treasury System, settlement of the Oregon boundary dispute, and acquiring more western territory. All of these measures he achieved before he retired to his home in Nashville, where he died in June 1845.

See also: Clay, Henry; Jackson, Andrew; Nullification; Van Buren, Martin; Walker, Robert John.

Selected Bibliography:

Paul H. Bergeron, *The Presidency of James K. Polk*, 1987; John S.D. Eisenhower, *So Far from God: The U.S. War with Mexico, 1846–1848*, 2000; Charles A. McCoy, *Polk and the Presidency*, 1960; Charles G. Sellers Jr., *James K. Polk, Jacksonian, 1795–1843*, 1957.

Robert P. Sutton

POPULISTS

A social and political force that existed from 1889 to 1896 and challenged the materialism of the day.

Populism grew out of the settlement of the west. Railroads promised easy wealth to lure immigrants. Heavy rains led to rich harvests in the early 1880s. Migrating families borrowed from eastern banks and land values skyrocketed until 1887, when abundant rains halted and land values plummeted. In the South, the post–Civil War banking collapse left little capital. Farmers accepted merchants' goods in exchange for a lien on crops. If the crops failed to cancel the debt, the farmer remained in bondage for another year. Some blamed the resulting overproduction for low prices.

Farmers saw money-supply expansion as the solution to their problems. Unlimited coinage of silver and gold became the chief feature of the Populist program, which embodied agrarian grievances and demands, including the abolition of national banks and the direct government issuance of paper money to the people, suppression of trusts and combines, railroad regulation, equitable taxation, market regulations, tariff reductions, "rigid enforcement of public rights in every corporate franchise," and the acceptance of effective popular participation in political decisions. While some Populists advocated free trade, others took a "tariff for revenue only" position.

In 1890, the Populists overwhelmed Republicans "by a tidal wave of popular anger." The McKinley Tariff Act dominated the national debate. The silver-coinage issue spurred the western political revolution. In 1892, James B. Weaver ran as the candidate of the Populist Party that had been formed in 1891 under the name People's Party. He received more than one million popular votes and twenty-two electoral votes. Between 1892 and 1896, conditions favored the continued growth of the party. Business depression followed the Crisis of 1893, while the repeal of the silver purchase clause of the Sherman Act antagonized people in the West and South who believed that the free coinage of silver would cure their ills. Some Populists argued that the power to create money proved so important that both major political parties would create sham political issues, such as tariffs, so that they could ignore the economic despair.

By 1896, the Democratic Party would adopt free silver in order to absorb the Populists. William Jennings Bryan's "Cross of Gold" speech at the Democratic National Convention committed the party to the free coinage of silver. Bryan became the candidate of both Democrat and Populist Parties, but he lost the first U.S. election in which the campaign lines distinguished between rich and poor. Almost all Populists became Democrats after 1896 because the Democratic Party had adopted the Populists' issues. After 1912, the Populist Party ceased to exist.

See also: American farmers; Bryan, William Jennings; Democratic Party; McKinley Tariff (Tariff of 1890); Republican Party.

Selected Bibliography:

Peter H. Argersinger, *Populism and Politics: William Alfred Peffer and the People's Party*, 1974; John D. Hicks, *The Populist Revolt: A History of the Farmer's Alliance and the People's Party*, 1931; Stanley B. Parsons, *The Populist Context: Rural Versus Urban Power on a Great Plains Frontier*, 1973; Norman Pollack, ed., *The Populist Mind*, 1967.

Theo Edwin Maloy

PREBISCH, RAUL (Unknown month and date, 1901–)

South American economist.

Born in Argentina in 1901 to a German immigrant father and a native Argentine mother of Spanish descent, Prebisch earned an advanced degree in economics at the University of Buenos Aires in 1923, at the age of twenty-two. Pursuing a dual career throughout his life as an educator and public servant, he began his academic career as a professor of political economy. In the mid-1920s, he took up a post as deputy director of statistics for the Argentine government, and soon rose to the position of director of economic research for the Argentine National Bank. From there he moved to the post of undersecretary of finance from 1930 to 1932, before serving as advisor to the Ministries of Finance and Agriculture between 1933 and 1935. In 1935, he headed the organization of the Argentine Central Bank, serving as its director-general from 1935 to 1943. This experience led him to Mexico, where he assisted in the organization of their Central Bank. Throughout this period, he continued to serve on the faculty of the University of Buenos Aires. In 1948, Prebisch left the university to serve as advisor to the United Nations' newly formed Economic Commission for Latin America. In 1950, he received an appointment as the executive secretary of the commission. In later years, he also served as an advisor to the United Nations' CEPAL and UNCTAD organizations.

Through his role with ECLA, Prebisch first offered a different approach to the resolution of Latin America's economic problems on a more visible stage. Drawing on Keynesian thought, the historical school of economics, and the writings of Central European institutionalists, Prebisch led the way to the formation of Dependency Theory, or Structuralism. From the outset, he challenged classical assumptions of linear or stage theories of economic development by proposing a series of reforms, targeting what he considered not "underdevelopment" but "bad development."

Seeking Latin American answers to Latin American problems, Prebisch and his adherents advocated focused, domestic consumer–oriented industrialization in concert with governmental policies of protectionism known as Import Substitution Industrialization (ISI). His specific concern focused on the redress of the historical results of a series of policies and realities—industrial, production, and socioeconomic—that were inherently colonial, resulting in an orientation toward the export of primary products and generally unbalanced growth. Because of these distorted national institutions and structures, Third World countries remained defenseless before the draw of First World finance and capitalism. This yielded a state of "dependency" on First World manufacturing and "core-periphery relationships."

See also: Capitalism; Economic Commission for Latin America (ECLA); Third World.

Selected Bibliography:

United Nations Economic Commission for Latin America, *The Economic Development of Latin America and Its Principal Problems*, 1950.

David J. Weiland III

PRESIDENTIAL CAMPAIGNS

Election contests between opposing political parties for the presidency.

Presidential election campaigns have often involved debate over tariff and trade issues, sometimes influencing the outcome of the election. The first time the tariff became a major issue in a presidential campaign occurred in the 1828 rematch between John Quincy Adams and Andrew Jackson. Jackson and his supporters argued that Adams favored a tariff that benefited New England manufacturers. The claim appeared valid after the Hartford Convention, attended mainly by supporters of John Quincy Adams, approved a higher tariff. Adams signed into law the Tariff of 1828, also known as the Tariff of Abominations, after Congress passed the legislation. During the presidential campaign later that same year, Jackson argued for a "judicial tariff" while pointing at Adams's record of increasing duty rates for the benefit of one class.

During the election of 1844, James K. Polk raised the issue of tariff reduction. His opponent, John Tyler, lost the election primarily on the issue of the annexation of Texas. After his inauguration, Polk instructed his secretary of the treasury, Robert Walker, to issue a report on manufactures to Congress. Walker recommended a reduction of the tariff as a means of reducing a treasury surplus.

The tariff played a dominant role in the campaign between Grover Cleveland and Benjamin Harrison in 1888. Cleveland had devoted his entire State of the Union address to the tariff just prior to the election, sparking debate among free traders, tariff reformers, and protectionists. Republicans advocated the continued use of high protective tariffs despite a huge surplus. Prosperous times and a strong resistance to change resulted in Cleveland's losing the election, but four years later, as economic difficulties seized the nation, he won a second term. Although Congress debated a tariff reduction, the outcome proved disappointing. Cleveland refused to sign the Wilson-Gorman Tariff, letting it pass into law without his signature.

The tariff also influenced the outcome of the election of 1912. During the Taft administration, Congress passed the Payne-Aldrich Tariff, a bill that Taft declared "The best bill ever passed by Republicans." Many within the Republican Party, including former president Theodore Roosevelt, disagreed with his assessment. Consequently, Roosevelt decided to run against Taft in the election of 1912, a move that split the Republican Party and assured a Democratic victory. Woodrow Wilson, the Democratic candidate, had campaigned on the reduction of the tariff. After his election, Congress passed the Underwood-Simmons Tariff Act, along with the enabling legislation for the Sixteenth Amendment that allowed the collection of personal income taxes.

During the Great Depression and World War II, Americans accepted the need for tariff reduction to stimulate international trade and prevent future conflicts. The tariff issue faded to the background during presidential campaigns until the election of 1992. President George Herbert Walker Bush had just signed the North American Free Trade Agreement (NAFTA) and the Senate had not debated the treaty prior to the November election. Bush supported the reduction of the tariff while the Democratic candidate, William Jefferson Clinton, personally indicated his support, although his party remained somewhat reluctant. A Third Party candidate, H. Ross Perot, vehemently opposed passage of NAFTA. A debate between Perot and Clinton's running mate Al Gore helped win the support of enough Democrats to ensure ratification of the agreement after the election.

See also: Adams, John Quincy; Bush, George Herbert Walker; Clinton, William Jefferson (Bill); Insurgents; Jackson, Andrew; North American Free Trade Agreement (NAFTA); Payne-Aldrich Tariff (Tariff of 1909); Perot, Henry Ross; Polk, James K.; Roosevelt, Theodore; Taft, William Howard; Tyler, John; Wilson, Thomas Woodrow.

Selected Bibliography:

Alfred E. Eckes, *Opening America's Market: U.S. Trade Policy Since 1776*, 1995.

Cynthia Clark Northrup

PROGRESSIVES

Political movement of the early 1900s that advocated the destruction of trusts through the reduction of tariffs.

Theodore Roosevelt's election as president in 1904 ratified America's post-1896 social politics. Roosevelt advocated "legislative control of the great corporations commonly called trusts." For his first legislative accomplishment, he created the Bureau of Corporations in the Department of Commerce and Labor. Roosevelt proved that he could use the Sherman Anti-Trust Act against illegal combinations in restraint of trade. Congress passed pure food and meat inspection bills and gave the Interstate Commerce Commission power to prescribe railroad rates. Roosevelt's interests included swollen fortunes, inheritance taxes, race suicide, international peace, national defense, outdoor life, simplified spelling, child labor, naval development, and Latin American relations. The Progressive movement gained national recognition.

In 1908, Roosevelt did not seek reelection. The Republican Party nominated William Howard Taft and praised Roosevelt's achievements. Both parties appealed to the Progressive sentiment throughout the country.

Although Roosevelt created progressivism, Robert M. LaFollette holds the distinction of being the first Republican to understand the internal conflict within the party between public interests and private business. As Wisconsin governor, he pursued adequate and proper taxation of commission-regulated railroads. Entering the U.S. Senate in 1906, he initiated a movement to take party control away from leaders who acted subservient to railroads and industrial corporations.

In 1909, LaFollette, joining a small group of Republican senators, refused to vote for the Payne-Aldrich Tariff Act. In the 1908 campaign, the Republican Party pushed for the reduction of the tariff. Western Republican senators opposed passage of the Payne-Aldrich bill, and when Taft described the tariff as "the best that had ever been passed," a break developed between the Progressives and the president.

In the 1910 campaign, Progressive Republicans attacked party leaders who accused them of disloyalty. The Demo-

crats made massive gains, with Progressives holding the western Republican seats. A Democrat-Progressive coalition controlled most issues in Congress. When Taft vetoed the farmer's free list, the wool tariff, and the cotton tariff bills, most Progressives joined the Democrats in unsuccessfully attempting to override the vetoes.

The Progressives attacked Taft as deserting Roosevelt's policies, especially concerning the Payne-Aldrich Tariff. In 1912, Progressives divided on who could block Taft's renomination. When they urged LaFollette to withdraw in favor of Roosevelt, a bitter personal feud ensued. After Taft won renomination, a new Progressive Party nominated Roosevelt, who ran against Taft and Democrat Woodrow Wilson. Calling for social and industrial justice, the Progressive platform declared, "The supreme duty of the Nation is the conservation of human resources." The platform emphasized industrial health and accidents, child labor, wage standards, women's labor, hours and days of labor, convict labor, industrial education, and industrial research. With LaFollette privately supporting Wilson, the Democrats won.

Roosevelt sought both the Republican and Progressive nominations in 1916. When the parties could not unite, Roosevelt urged the nomination of Henry Cabot Lodge, an opponent of the Progressives. The Republicans nominated Charles Evans Hughes, the Progressives nominated Roosevelt, but he declined the nomination, and Wilson won reelection. The Progressive Party had died.

Drifting farther to the political left, LaFollette's 1924 presidential campaign as the candidate of the Conference for

Progressive Political Action failed because of insufficient financial support, difficulty in getting on ballots, and charges of radicalism. By the 1920s, Progressivism assumed a peripheral position to the values of a decade of Prohibition and bathtub gin, prosperity and profit, growth and speculation.

See also: Democratic Party; LaFollette, Robert Marion; Lodge, Henry Cabot; Payne-Aldrich Tariff (Tariff of 1909); Republican Party; Roosevelt, Theodore; Taft, William Howard.

Selected Bibliography:

J. David Gillespie, *Politics at the Periphery: Third Parties in Two-Party America*, 1993; Fred E. Haynes, *Third Party Movements Since the Civil War: With Special Reference to Iowa*, 1966; Amos R.E. Pinchot, *History of the Progressive Party 1912–1916*, 1958; Steven J. Rosenstone, Roy L. Behr, and Edward H. Lazarus, *Third Parties in America: Citizen Response to Major Party Failure*, 1984.

Theo Edwin Maloy

PROHIBITION

The Eighteenth Amendment (the Volstead Act) outlawed the manufacture, sale, barter, transport, import, export, delivery, and possession of intoxicating liquor.

The law became operational on January 17, 1920, despite a presidential veto, by an overwhelming majority in both Congress and the states. Thirteen years later, support for its repeal proved equally overwhelming. Prohibition appealed to those who sought to impose a strict moral order on a country whose most recent migrants, including the Irish, Germans, and Italians, brought with them unwhole-

some habits associated with the consumption of whiskey, beer, and wine. Known as "the woman's war" against liquor, it also won the support of many industrialists, whose profits and productivity declined with intoxicated workers on the assembly line.

The Anti-Salon League and its Ohio spokesman Wayne Wheeler exerted an enormous influence over both Congress and the political parties. In 1920, Wheeler reminded the Republican Party that it had "always stood for law and order." Delegates noted the dry voting record of a senator from Ohio, Warren Harding, and chose him as the Republican presidential candidate. Thus began one of the most corrupt administrations in the history of the United States. Corruption ravaged the agencies with dry law responsibilities. Harding's "Ohio gang" became, in part, a criminal network for the systematic protection of bootleggers.

Some of the short-run consequences of Prohibition appeared encouraging, and the death rate from alcoholism dropped significantly. Halfway through the Prohibition era, Henry Ford declared that "if booze ever comes back to the U.S. I am through with manufacturing." A high percentage of acknowledged "drys" won election to Congress in 1928. But the medium-run consequences of Prohibition proved disastrous. At the end of the 1920s, 32,000 speakeasies operated in New York alone. By 1927, as many as 50,000 people had died from poisoned liquor and hundreds of thousands suffered from blindness or paralysis. Newspapers portrayed Wheeler in cartoons and editorials as a poisoner.

A growing majority of Americans favored repeal and the end of Prohibition arrived rapidly. John D. Rockefeller withdrew his financial support for the Anti-Salon League and in 1932 published a letter complaining that "drinking has generally increased" and "a vast army of lawbreakers has been recruited and financed on a colossal scale." Within a few days of Franklin Roosevelt's election victory, Congress passed a resolution rendering the Eighteenth Amendment void.

Neighbors of the United States all benefited from Prohibition. The authorities intercepted less than 5 percent of illegally imported liquor. The Internal Revenue Bureau calculated that in 1920, Americans consumed 25 million gallons of illegal liquor, with another 30 million gallons legally consumed for "medicinal" purposes. The government lost approximately $32 million in import duties and domestic taxes. The effects of the depression compounded this fiscal disaster, leaving Pierre Dupont to both complain and exaggerate that a tax on liquor would "permit the total abolition of income tax, both personal and corporate." By 1940, annual excise tax from alcohol exceeded a billion dollars.

Prohibition provides a textbook study of the consequences of attempting to repeal the laws of supply and demand. As Al Capone put it, "I make my money by supplying a public demand." While bootleggers distilled illegal alcohol to meet this demand, some "madmen in authority" distilled "their frenzy" from the intoxicating drug of moral righteousness. Others simply practiced hypocrisy. Harding's White House effectively became a speakeasy, where privileged guests feasted on copious amounts of whiskey.

Described by President Calvin Coolidge as "the greatest social experiment of modern times," government-sponsored Prohibition proved a colossal failure. The emergence of "the invisible government" of organized crime remains its lasting legacy.

See also: Great Depression; Roosevelt, Franklin D.

Selected Bibliography:

Edward Behr, *Prohibition: The 13 Years that Changed America*, 1997; Justin Steuart, *Wayne Wheeler, Dry Boss: An Uncensored Biography of Wayne B. Wheeler*, 1928.

Robert Leeson

PROTECTIONISM

Economic practice that places the interests of the United States above all others.

Although protectionism can incorporate a number of measures such as restrictive quotas on foreign products, it often implements high tariffs to discourage imports and encourage American production. Protectionism has its roots in the mercantilist policies of England and France during the seventeenth and eighteenth centuries when they sought to protect their own respective interests by implementing regulations on trade. From the establishment of the United States as a new and independent nation, Congress has periodically implemented and debated protectionism as a key component of economic policy.

Alexander Hamilton, the first secretary of the treasury, proposed protectionist policies in 1791 in his Report on Manufactures to Congress. He recommended high tariffs on foreign imports with revenue used to subsidize American manufacturing. He argued the necessity of such investment to ensure America's future economic strength. President George Washington, and others who considered his recommendations too extreme, failed to see the immediate potential for industrial development. But the War of 1812 demonstrated to many policymakers a need to look out for U.S. economic interests. Still dependent on foreign products, the United States had been drawn into that war by trade disputes with Great Britain and France. Determined to prevent the United States from falling into that position again, Congress embarked on a program of protectionism based on a high tariff.

Early nineteenth-century economic nationalism inspired criticism of Adam Smith's philosophy of free trade, giving rise to "America first" protectionist investment. The protective tariff intensified sectionalism during the antebellum period, as the South saw the North as benefiting from it unfairly. Investing increasingly in agriculture, the South depended on the import of manufactured goods and open trade relations with countries that purchased cotton and tobacco, and protested investment of revenue in northern manufacturing. The sectionalist debate over the tariff aided in shifting policy toward a "revenue only," instead of a protectionist, policy. However, the post–Civil War era saw a renewed embrace of protective tariffs. Between 1871 and 1913, the average tariff never dipped below 38 percent. While economists argued whether protectionism or free trade would benefit America more, the na-

tion experienced unprecedented industrial expansion.

From Abraham Lincoln to Herbert Hoover, Republicans generally supported protectionism, claiming it promoted American prosperity and job security, while Democratic sympathies lay more clearly with free trade, or at least with "revenue only" tariffs. This partisan debate came to a head in 1932, when Franklin Roosevelt and fellow Democrats charged that the Hawley-Smoot Tariff Act, enacted under Hoover in 1930, had in fact deepened the effects of the Great Depression. Seeking to protect the economy after the stock market crash of 1929, Republicans succeeded in passing this legislation raising the tariff to 59 percent, which Democrats claimed initiated a downward spiral of the global economy. In 1947, twenty-three nations, including the United States, entered into the General Agreement on Tariffs and Trade (GATT), a reciprocal trade agreement in which some 100 nations held membership by 1990. Economic downturns and increased foreign competition during the 1970s and beyond prompted new demands for protectionist measures; however, GATT generally limited protectionism through the second half of the twentieth century.

See also: Great Britain; Hamilton, Alexander; Hawley-Smoot Tariff Act (Tariff of 1930); Report on Manufactures; Tariff of 1828 (Tariff of Abomintions); War of 1812.

Selected Bibliography:

Alfred E. Eckes, *Opening America's Market: U.S. Foreign Trade Policy Since 1776*, 1995; Martha L. Gibson, *Conflict Amid Consensus in American Trade Policy*, 2000; Judith Goldstein, *Ideas, Interests, and American Trade Policy*, 1993; David A. Lake, *Power, Protection, and Free Trade: International Sources of U.S. Commercial Strategy, 1887–1939*, 1988.

Kathleen A. Tobin

PROTESTS

Strong disapproval of any number of issues, including legislation concerning the tariff.

Throughout American history, protests have occurred on numerous occasions after officials enacted tariff legislation. Trade restrictions passed by Parliament brought verbal protests from the colonists. The passage of the Tea Act resulted in colonists dumping 342 chests of tea into the harbor during the Boston Tea Party in defiance of the crown. The American Revolution provides the best example of colonial protest over trade barriers.

After independence, Americans continued to voice their opposition to what they deemed oppressive taxation. The high tariff rates established by the Tariff of 1828, also known as the Tariff of Abominations, created divisions between the South and the North that led to the Nullification Crisis. John C. Calhoun, in his *South Carolina Exposition*, protested the enactment of federal legislation for the benefit of one section of the country. Arguing that the states had the right to nullify any federal law, Calhoun brought the country to the brink of war. With President Andrew Jackson threatening to use military force if necessary, Henry Clay engineered a compromise that prevented the potential crisis.

After the Civil War, when the tariff rates remained at the high wartime levels, farmers protested the effect of the tariff. The agrarian movement promoted the development of the Populist Party to formally challenge the Republican position on high tariffs. The Populists also voiced opposition to other issues, many of which the Progressives enacted at the turn of the twentieth century.

In the post–World War II period, a shift toward free trade has resulted in a new variety of protest. Instead of the tariff reformers and free traders of previous generations, we now have modern protesters, including environmentalists and labor unions, seeking to address problems arising from the establishment of free trade zones such as the North American Free Trade Agreement (NAFTA). Protesters also criticize the establishment of the World Trade Organization (WTO), pointing out continued violations of human rights and disregard for the environment in countries throughout the world.

Protests, originally centered on economic issues, have shifted to social and cultural issues in the twentieth century. Although the focus changed, protesters continue to gravitate to trade and tariff issues as a means of promoting their own agendas.

See also: American Revolution; Calhoun, John Caldwell; Clay, Henry; Jackson, Andrew; Navigation and Trade Acts; North American Free Trade Agreement (NAFTA); Nullification; Populists; Progressives; South Carolina *Exposition* and *Protest*; Tea; World Trade Organization (WTO).

Selected Bibliography:

Alfred E. Eckes, *Opening America's Market: U.S. Trade Policy Since 1776*, 1995.

Cynthia Clark Northrup

PULITZER, JOSEPH (April 10, 1847–October 29, 1911)

One of the greatest newspaper owners and editors in American history.

Born and raised in Budapest, Hungary, Pulitzer immigrated to the United States in 1864 and served in the Union Army during the Civil War. After the war, he worked as a journalist in St. Louis, and won a seat in the Missouri state legislature in 1869 as a Republican. Pulitzer would permanently shift his allegiance to the Democratic Party in 1872 after the failure of Horace Greeley and the Liberal Republican Party.

Professionally, he moved from journalist, to editor, to owner of a series of newspapers, most notably the *St. Louis Post-Dispatch*. In 1883, he moved his newspaper interests to New York City, where he bought the *New York World*. His newspapers embraced sensationalist journalism that relied on exposés, investigative reporting, sports pages, and illustrations to reach a broad audience. The newspaper closely followed the political line drawn by its owner and soon became the largest Democratic newspaper in the country. Pulitzer strongly backed Grover Cleveland's successful candidacy in 1884. He also won election to Congress that same year but, citing the demands of his newspapers, resigned from Congress in April 1886.

Pulitzer and his editorial staff joined the Democratic Party in attacking the high protectionist tariffs imposed by Republican administrations. In his call for tariff reduction, he embraced the idea of revenue tariffs while rejecting the use of duties to protect U.S. industries.

By 1896, a fierce battle between Pulitzer's *World* and William Randolph Hearst's *New York Morning Journal* erupted. In a practice known as yellow journalism, both papers would sensationalize events in Cuba to boost sales. Together they helped mobilize public opinion behind U.S. intervention in Cuba and profited from the rise in circulation caused by the Spanish-American War in 1898.

Despite his failing health, Pulitzer remained actively involved in the management of his papers until his death in Charleston, South Carolina, in 1911. In his will he established the Pulitzer Prizes for journalism.

See also: Cleveland, Stephen Grover; Newspapers and media.

Selected Bibliography:

W.A. Swanberg, *Pulitzer*, 1967.

John D. Coats

Q

QUAY, MATTHEW STANLEY
(September 30, 1833–May 28, 1904)

Prominent political boss of the late nineteenth century who ensured congressional passage of the McKinley Tariff in 1890.

Born in Dillsburg, Pennsylvania, Quay graduated from Jefferson College in 1850 and received admittance to the bar in 1854. The following year he entered politics in Pennsylvania, where the Republican Party had just formed. When the Civil War began, he briefly served as a colonel in the 134th Pennsylvania infantry and won the Medal of Honor at Fredericksburg. He later served as a military agent in Washington, D.C., the chief of transportation and telegraphs in Pennsylvania, and secretary to the governor. The latter position and Quay's association with Simon Cameron's political machine provided the foundation for Quay to gain state and national offices.

Elected in 1887 to the first of three terms in the U.S. Senate, he served as Republican national chairman in 1888 and co-managed Benjamin Harrison's successful presidential campaign. Quay put together a campaign organization that emphasized, in the industrial states, the continuing need for a protective tariff. Although the tariff created a treasury surplus, the Republican-controlled Congress passed the McKinley Tariff, which raised rates to the highest level in American history to that point. Quay strongly favored the tariff bill partly because of his many promises to industrialists during the 1888 campaign. He ensured passage of the McKinley Tariff by gaining southern support through a compromise proposal that prevented a vote on a federal elections bill concerning African Americans' right to vote.

During Grover Cleveland's second term as president, William L. Wilson, the Democratic chairman of the House Ways and Means Committee, managed to shepherd a bill through the House of Representatives that lowered the tariff rates. But in the Senate, Quay and other protectionist senators used the unlimited debate rule to block passage of the measure. Quay initiated a filibuster that lasted for two months and two days. To end the filibuster, Democratic senator Arthur Pue Gorman worked out a compromise that accepted hundreds of changes in the proposed tariff schedule. President Cleveland, outraged at these changes, let the Wilson-Gorman Tariff become law without his signature. Quay continued to serve in the Senate, except for a nine-month period beginning in 1900 and continuing into 1901. Hailed by fellow boss Thomas Platt as the "ablest politician this country has ever produced," Quay died in Beaver, Pennsylvania, in 1904.

See also: Cleveland, Stephen Grover; Harrison, Benjamin; House Ways and Means Committee; McKinley Tariff (Tariff of 1890); Wilson-Gorman Tariff (Tariff of 1894).

Selected Bibliography:

James A. Kehl, *Boss Rule in the Gilded Age: Matt Quay of Pennsylvania*, 1981.

Steven E. Siry

R

RANDALL, SAMUEL JACKSON
(October 10, 1828–April 13, 1890)

Elected to the U.S. House as a Democrat in 1862, reelected for thirteen additional terms, rose to be Speaker of the House, and fought members of his party when he supported protectionism and relatively high tariffs.

Born in Philadelphia, Pennsylvania, into an active Whig family, Randall married Ann Worrell and entered Philadelphia politics in 1851 as a Whig. He switched to the Democratic Party later on when his party imploded.

Randall opposed Republican Reconstruction efforts, arguing that the Union had never dissolved and therefore needed no rebuilding. His ability at parliamentary obstruction led to coinage of a new term, "Samrandallism." This obstructionist ability served him in good stead when, as Speaker, his procedural rulings and committee appointments guarded legislation that kept high protective tariffs on American manufactures. At odds with fellow Democrats over fiscal policy, when the party won control of the House in 1883, members refused to reelect Randall as Speaker. In the same year, as chairman of the powerful Appropriations Committee, he worked to lower government expenditures and controlled legislation that required funding. In the 1884 presidential election, he worked to block the tariff reductionist statement in the Democratic Party platform and apparently exerted considerable influence on the newly elected President Cleveland as a protectionist until 1887, when Cleveland moved more toward free trade.

Randall also angered his party when, in 1884 and 1886, he led forty other Democrats in defeating a tariff reduction bill proposed by William R. Morrison and incurred the wrath of Grover Cleveland when he fought to kill the administration-backed Mills Tariff Bill. In retribution, Cleveland deprived

Randall of his control over Democrat patronage in Pennsylvania.

Randall died in Washington, D.C., with interment in Laurel Hill Cemetery, Philadelphia, Pennsylvania.

See also: Civil War (American); Cleveland, Stephen Grover; Democratic Party; Mills Bill; Whig Party. **Vol. II**: Grover Cleveland's 1887 State of the Union Address.

Selected Bibliography:

Albert V. House, "The Political Career of Samuel Jackson Randall," 1935.

Glynn Ingram

RANDOLPH, JOHN (June 2, 1773–June 24, 1833)

Virginia planter and renowned orator who advocated agrarian rights throughout his service in the House of Representatives and the Senate.

Born at the family tobacco plantation Bizarre in Virginia, Randolph grew up the youngest son of a prosperous and powerful family. He attended school at Princeton and Columbia College in New York before returning home in 1794 to assume control of his property in Roanoke. Taking a seat in the House of Representatives in 1799 as a Republican, he served there until elected to the Senate. True to the old Republican program of advocating a simple agricultural economy and showing hostility toward federal control of trade and industry, Randolph opposed embargoes and the Bank of the United States. He also emerged as the foremost opponent of the tariff. To Randolph, a tariff designed expressly to exclude foreign products remained unconstitutional, but one created specifically to raise revenue that also provided incidental protection, although foolish, would fall within the intentions of the founders. Defending agrarian society, Randolph charged that farmers bore the brunt of taxation and needed relief from the economic oppression of manufacturers. He spoke against the tariff of 1824, condemning it for being frankly protective and brutally indifferent to the already troubled southern agricultural interests. Randolph, a slaveholder personally opposed to slavery, also charged that the tariff would harm slaves by making it prohibitively expensive for slaveholders to provide for them. Elected to the Senate in 1825 to fill a vacancy, Randolph served from December 26, 1825, to March 3, 1827. Voters then reelected him to the House of Representatives for a two-year term. From May to September 1830, Randolph served as the U.S. minister to Russia. After his return, he won reelection to the House of Representatives in 1833, but served only three months before he succumbed to a lung ailment in Philadelphia on June 24, 1833. He freed his slaves on his death, but his will became the subject of a court contest with a jury ruling that in the later years of his life, Randolph no longer functioned with a sane mind.

See also: Slavery; Tariff of 1824.

Selected Bibliography:

Russell Kirk, *Randolph of Roanoke: A Study in Conservative Thought*, 1951.

Caryn E. Neumann

RAYMOND, DANIEL (Unknown month and day, 1786–Unknown month and day, 1849)

Lawyer known principally for his writings in political economy.

Raymond first achieved notoriety with his pamphlet *The Missouri Question* in 1819, in which he supported the abolition of slavery. In this work, he pointed out the threat to white supremacy of black population growth under slavery.

His *Thoughts on Political Economy*, published in 1820, became the first major work of economic theory by an American and remains his principal contribution to policy development. He approached the subject differently than the contemporary English and French classical economists. He realized that national wealth does not simply equal the sum of all individual wealth. This led him to the belief that political economy should focus more on increasing the productive power of the nation than its static wealth, such as property.

Raymond saw national wealth as being increased by "effective" labor—labor that created permanent improvements, enhancing the nation's capacity. He disagreed with Adam Smith, who believed that the wealth of a nation increased if it accumulated a surplus of produce in excess of consumption. In fact, this surplus output does not contribute to wealth unless bought by consumers. If consumers fail to buy the output, then the government has a responsibility to avoid the effects of the resulting downturn in the economy. Raymond saw the best way of achieving this as the creation of public monopolies through such devices as trade treaties and tariffs. The resulting increase in prices would, in his view, stimulate businesses that would then hire more workers, and in turn labor would buy up the accumulation of surplus goods. Tariffs raise prices, but the revenues from these high prices remain within the country and are not lost. He believed that tariffs should be highest on goods that employed the largest number of people.

See also: Slavery; Smith, Adam.

Selected Bibliography:

Joseph Dorfman, *The Economic Mind in American Civilization*, 1946.

Tony Ward

REAGAN, JOHN HENNINGER (October 8, 1818–March 6, 1905)

U.S. representative, senator, and Confederate postmaster general known in part for his efforts at tariff reduction.

Born in Sevierville, Tennessee, Reagan, the son of a farmer, moved to Texas as a young man. In 1846, he launched his political career with his election as a county judge, afterward serving in the state legislature and as a district judge. Elected to Congress in 1857, Reagan served in the House until January 1861, when he resigned his seat in the aftermath of the election of Abraham Lincoln. He served as postmaster general for the Confederacy throughout the war.

Following his capture by Union forces and a brief imprisonment, Reagan began a political comeback that included his election to Congress in 1874. Reelected five times, he left his seat in 1887 to take office as a U.S. senator, a position he held until his resignation in

June 1891. In his postwar political career, he gained notoriety primarily for his work for the regulation of railroads, yet he also became one of the more prominent advocates on tariff reform. Reagan believed that protective tariffs fostered monopolies and thus contributed to the inequality of wealth in the United States—with tariff reform prices would drop and the enrichment of only the few at the expense of the masses would be hampered. Reagan emphasized the tariff issue while campaigning for Grover Cleveland in 1884 and 1888, and in the latter year he cited the protective system and its benefits to monopolies in proposing a bill to regulate trusts. A strong opponent of the McKinley Tariff bill, Reagan labeled it as class legislation and warned that if passed, it had the potential to wreak havoc with the two-party system.

Reagan resigned his Senate seat to serve as chairman of the Texas Railroad Commission. In his later years, he also helped found the Texas Historical Association and finished his memoirs. He died in Palestine, Texas.

See also: Civil War (American); Cleveland, Stephen Grover; Trusts.

Selected Bibliography:

Ben H. Procter, *Not Without Honor: The Life of John H. Reagan*, 1962.

Ed Bradley

RECIPROCAL TRADE AGREEMENTS ACT (RTAA)

Legislation designed to authorize the president to reduce the high rates of the Hawley-Smoot Tariff on a reciprocal basis with foreign countries.

On June 12, 1934, Congress passed an amendment to the Hawley-Smoot Tariff. The Reciprocal Trade Agreements Act (RTAA) authorized the president to enter into tariff negotiations with foreign governments and to increase or decrease the tariff rates by as much as 50 percent. Widely regarded as the handiwork of Secretary of State Cordell Hull, a believer in trade liberalization, the RTAA signaled a watershed in U.S. trade policy for two reasons. First, Congress delegated to the president the power to set tariff rates by negotiating bilaterally with foreign government on the principle of reciprocity. By providing for executive agreements rather than treaties, Congress made Senate ratification of such trade agreements unnecessary. Duties would apply to imports from all foreign countries unless the president found evidence of discriminatory treatment by a foreign country against a U.S. business. Thus, the Most Favored Nation (MFN) policy, followed since 1922 in U.S. commercial treaties, remained in these executive agreements.

Although President Franklin D. Roosevelt had, in effect, requested permanent negotiating authority, Congress set a time limit that allowed for the retention of congressional control over the tariff-setting process. Under the 1934 act, the president could request that Congress renew the authority after three years. To prevent the reduction of tariffs on products that would suffer injurious or unfair competition from overseas suppliers, Congress inserted a provision requiring that private citizens receive an opportunity to argue their case in public hearings before the president initiates tariff negotiations.

The general framework set up by the 1934 act underwent several important shifts after World War II. Under the auspices of the General Agreement on Tariffs and Trade (GATT), a shift occurred from bilateral to multilateral agreements. In 1962, Congress transferred the responsibility for conducting trade negotiations from the Department of State to the White House Special Trade Representative. The United States also moved from a product-by-product method to a linear reduction formula by which tariffs on an entire product sector could be reduced.

See also: General Agreement on Tariffs and Trade (GATT); Hull, Cordell; Most Favored Nation (MFN); Roosevelt, Franklin D.

Selected Bibliography:

Robert A. Pastor, *Congress and the Politics of U.S. Foreign Economic Policy 1929–1976*, 1980.

Sayuri Shimizu

RECONSTRUCTION

The process of recreating the nation following the Civil War.

While politicians and people focused most of their attention during Reconstruction on other issues, tariff policy can illuminate the economic dimensions of Reconstruction and help explain internal divisions within the Republican Party during the 1870s. With Republicans in firm control of Congress at the end of the war, they had fashioned tariffs to suit their policy of using the federal government to promote economic development. At the beginning of Reconstruction, Republicans hoped to use federal power to refashion the economy of the defeated South to make it resemble the successful North. Because protective tariffs sheltered the developing southern industrial base, a wide consensus within the party, North and South, supported protection. Meanwhile, the Democratic Party, desiring a speedy end to Reconstruction, objected to the use of federal power to transform the South.

The early Republican economic consensus during Reconstruction waned. As economic issues became more important than civil rights or southern policy in the 1870s, party unity fractured. Disgruntled by corruption and government favors to business, the Liberal Republican Movement of the 1870s favored free trade rather than traditional Republican protectionism. Liberal Republicans denied the orthodox Republican doctrine that protective tariffs increased prosperity for all Americans. Instead, they charged that high tariffs produced class legislation, designed to favor specific groups at the expense of the public. Although Liberal defections weakened Republican ranks, the Panic of 1873 significantly reduced the popularity of the Republican Party and called its economic program, including protectionism, into question. When Democrats captured the House of Representatives in 1874, they inaugurated an era of divided government in which one party rarely controlled both houses of Congress. Under such conditions, tariff policy changed little; Republicans could not extend protection, but neither could Democrats significantly cut rates.

See also: Civil War (American); Congress (United States); Democratic Party; Free trade; Greeley, Horace; Presidential campaigns; Protectionism; Republican Party.

Selected Bibliography:

Eric Foner, *Reconstruction: America's Unfinished Revolution, 1863–1877*, 1988.

Christopher M. Paine

REED, THOMAS BRACKETT (October 18, 1839–December 7, 1902)

U.S. congressman and Speaker of the House; known for his procedural reform of the House of Representatives and his staunch support of protectionism.

Born in Portland, Maine, Reed served in the navy, the state legislature, and as Maine's attorney general before his first election to Congress in 1876. Quickly becoming a leader in the Republican Party, Reed served three terms as Speaker. He loyally supported the Republican stance on tariff issues. A thorough, orthodox protectionist, he believed that the prosperity of American workers, the health of the national economy, and the success of the Republican Party all depended on a high tariff. Reed made his greatest contributions to the Republican economic program as the leader of the party in Congress from 1885 to 1899. With Republicans in the minority, Reed opposed the Mills Bill, which lowered tariffs in 1888, and also led the fight against the Wilson-Gorman Tariff of 1894. When Republicans commanded a majority in the House, his leadership proved indispensable to passing protective legislation. In his first term as Speaker, Reed reformed House rules to reduce the ability of the minority to obstruct legislation. As a result of the "Reed Rules," the Republican majority passed the McKinley Tariff of 1890 and other significant legislation. By making the House majority's ability to pass legislation the main question of the session, Reed solidified the narrow Republican majority. Although he did not work on the details of tariff legislation, his reform of parliamentary procedure allowed Republicans to enact higher tariffs to protect American business in 1890 and in 1897. Disgusted with Republican acceptance of imperialism following the Spanish-American War, Reed retired from politics in 1899. After entering private law practice, he suddenly fell ill while visiting Washington, D.C., and died there on December 7, 1902.

See also: Congress (United States); McKinley Tariff (Tariff of 1890); Protectionism; Wilson-Gorman Tariff (Tariff of 1894).

Selected Bibliography:

William A. Robinson, *Thomas B. Reed, Parliamentarian*, 1930.

Christopher M. Paine

RELIGION

An important factor in trade regulation during the colonial period.

The navigation laws of Great Britain, designed primarily to create a fleet of skilled seamen, provided a flow of easily taxable products into England to help the government meet the cost of defending the empire. After the Glorious Revolution, France remained the chief enemy of England, with Spain a close second. English wars, along with the mercantilist system that helped support those wars, acquired a strong religious tone. Most American colonists shared the concern about keeping the wealth and strength of the Catholic powers in check. The religious dimension to international conflict in the period helped the colonists accept the restraints of the navigation acts because they supported imperial defense. Colonists also celebrated the positive balance of trade between the British Empire and its Catholic foes. Jonathan Edwards saw the export of fish by New Englanders to Spain as a sure way of weakening the Spanish economy and depriving the Spanish monarchy of part of its means of waging war on Protestants. However, during the Revolutionary War, the United States depended on French and Spanish aid, and after the war sought a multitude of trade partners to reduce dependence on trade with Great Britain. As a result, the religious aspect of trade and trade regulation diminished.

One other connection between religion and trade regulation in the colonial period concerned the import of indentured servants. In 1698, South Carolina passed laws excluding the importation of Irish Catholics as servants who could turn into a security risk. Maryland imposed stiff taxes on the importation of Irish-Catholic servants after 1704 to reduce the strong Catholic influence in that colony.

See also: Great Britain; Navigation and Trade Acts.

Selected Bibliography:

Linda Colley, *Britons: Forging the Nation, 1707–1837*, 1992.

John P. Barrington

REPORT ON MANUFACTURES

Alexander Hamilton's report on congressional aid to manufacturing.

On January 8, 1790, President George Washington spoke to Congress on the relationship between manufacturing and national defense. He argued that manufacturing essential items like military supplies remained necessary for the safety of the nation. One week later, Congress ordered Secretary of the Treasury Alexander Hamilton to prepare a report on how the government could promote manufacturing in the United States. Hamilton worked on the report for nearly two years. He studied the economic ideas of Adam Smith and David Hume. The works of French finance minister Jacques Necker also greatly influenced him. After four drafts, Hamilton finally presented his Report on Manufactures to Congress on December 5, 1791.

In his opening remarks, Hamilton argued against those who believed America must remain a nation of farmers. He countered that manufacturing would bring more wealth to the nation than farming ever could. It would make use of the natural talent that most Americans had for invention. As Americans created new machines and related products, more and more people could be put to work. Women, children, and newly arrived immigrants would gladly work to make more money for themselves and their families. These new opportunities would allow all Americans to develop their individual talents.

Hamilton next argued against those who said that America must use all of its economic resources to move west, and thus import its manufactured goods from Europe. He urged Americans to look at the political realities of the day. Constant wars along with the economic policies of most European nations disrupted the free flow of trade across the Atlantic, making it imperative that America develop manufacturing simultaneously with its westward advance.

Hamilton concluded that manufacturing would not develop on its own in America. Only the national government could raise the massive amounts of capital necessary for manufacturing to take hold in the country. Protective tariffs should be placed on rival foreign goods. To grant premiums for excellence in manufacturing, he proposed the establishment of a national board with bounties or cash payments awarded to manufacturers who produced the most necessary items. Lastly, Congress should take every measure to improve transportation in the country. Knowing that some might argue these actions unconstitutional, Hamilton concluded that Congress had the power to promote manufacturing under the "necessary and proper" clause of Article I of the Constitution.

See also: Hamilton, Alexander; Hume, David; Smith, Adam. **Vol. II**: *The Wealth of Nations*; *Report on Manufactures*. **Vol. III**: Tariff of 1792; Tariff of 1816.

Selected Bibliography:

Alexander Hamilton, *The Papers of Alexander Hamilton*, 1963.

Mary Stockwell

REPORT ON THE BANK

Alexander Hamilton's plan for a national bank.

Secretary of the Treasury Alexander Hamilton issued his *Report on the Bank* to Congress in December 1790. The report gave further recommendations on placing the American nation on a firm financial basis. Its main theme focused on the creation of the Bank of the United States. According to Hamilton, the United States needed a national bank for several reasons. The bank would increase the active capital available to the United States. This capital could be invested in both trade and industry. The bank would also provide loans to the government in emergencies. Finally, all the great commercial nations of the world had national banks. If America wished to join their ranks, then the country must establish a national bank.

Hamilton proposed that Congress charter the Bank of the United States for a twenty-year period that could be renewed. The bank would issue $10 million in stock at a cost of $400 per share. The American government would own 20 percent of the stock, while private investors would purchase the remaining 80 percent. A twenty-five-member Board of Directors would govern the bank. Each director held stock in the bank and all were citizens of the United States. The government would appoint five of the directors. The twenty-five members of the Board of Directors would choose the president of the bank.

Congress debated Hamilton's recommendations for two months and then approved the first charter of the Bank of the United States. Most congressmen agreed with Hamilton's arguments concerning the value of a national bank. Large sums of money would become available for both public and private credit. The government would find its operations more stable.

In turn, it could promote commerce and industry. Trade, agriculture, and manufacturing would flourish.

Before signing the bill that chartered the bank, President George Washington asked Alexander Hamilton and Thomas Jefferson to write opinions on whether Congress had the power to create a national bank. Hamilton argued for a "loose" interpretation of the Constitution. He believed that Congress could create a national bank just as it could raise taxes, regulate trade, and provide for the common defense. Jefferson argued for a "strict" interpretation of the Constitution. He believed that Congress could not create a national bank because the Constitution did not give this power specifically to Congress. Washington agreed with Hamilton and signed the bill, turning the Bank of the United States into law in February 1791.

See also: Congress (United States); Hamilton, Alexander; Washington, George.

Selected Bibliography:

Alexander Hamilton, *The Papers of Alexander Hamilton*, 1963.

Mary Stockwell

REPORT ON THE PRIVILEGES AND RESTRICTIONS ON THE COMMERCE OF THE UNITED STATES IN FOREIGN COUNTRIES (REPORT ON PRIVILEGES)

Report presented to Congress by the Jefferson administration discussing trade relations between the United States and Europe.

Written by the Jefferson administration and submitted to Congress on December 16, 1793, the *Report on Privileges* first describes American trading relationships with Spain, Portugal, France, Great Britain, the United Netherlands, Denmark, and Sweden, as well as with their respective colonies, and later suggests steps to counterbalance the effects of foreign tariffs on American businesses. At this time, the United States exported breadstuffs, tobacco, rice, and wood in the greatest amounts. Great Britain purchased the most American exports, taking in approximately twice as many American goods as the second largest trading partner, France, and more than four times as many goods as Spain or Portugal. However, American imports from these nations lacked proportion with exports; the United States imported the most goods from Great Britain, who supplied seven times as many goods as France and fifty times as many as Spain.

American firms faced barriers to trading with these nations and especially with their colonies. The report notes that Europeans imposed heavy barriers to trade in Europe and prohibited much American commerce in their colonies. Friendly agreements promoting free trade with these nations or, if necessary, countervailing tariffs and other nontariff barriers provided the solution to this dilemma, the report claimed. The Jefferson administration emphasized in the *Report on Privileges* that friendly agreements remained likely and desirable, but it also outlined steps for implementing countervailing tariffs and barriers and left to Congress the decision on which of these measures to implement.

See also: France; Great Britain; Jefferson, Thomas.

Selected Bibliography:

Edward S. Kaplan, *The Bank of the United States and the American Economy*, 1999.

Josh Pratt

REPUBLICAN PARTY

Political party associated with high protective tariffs until the twentieth century, when the party pursued a policy of free trade.

The longest-running line of issue cleavage between the major parties in U.S. politics started over the tariff, with the Democratic Party from its formation in 1792 to 1955 advocating low tariffs and its major opposition party urging high tariffs. The Democratic Party has traditionally centered on recent immigrant groups, low-income groups, and intellectuals. The Federalist Party, which became the Whig Party and then the Republican Party, remained the party of merchants and manufacturers. U.S. manufacturers until the 1970s saw little to gain and much potential harm from the lowering of tariff barriers. The Republican Party, while sociologically the heir to the Federalists and the Whigs, functions as a distinctly separate party from the one founded in Jackson, Michigan, and Ripon, Wisconsin, in 1854. The Whig Party, unable to cope with the issue of slavery, disintegrated. Former Democrats and Whigs joined the Republican Party, which fielded its first presidential candidate in 1856, and whose nominee in 1860, former Whig Abraham Lincoln, won the presidency with

39.8 percent of the total popular vote cast on a platform that stated the following:

> **Tariff.** That, while providing revenue for the support of the general government by duties upon imports, sound policy requires such an adjustment of these imports as to encourage the development of the industrial interests of the whole country.

As late as 1928, the Republican platform on which President Herbert Hoover would stand when he signed the Hawley-Smoot Tariff Act of 1930 reaffirmed the protective tariff as fundamental to the nation's political life. The Hawley-Smoot Tariff Act, widely perceived as exacerbating the Great Depression, contributed to the Republican loss of the White House until 1952 when internationalist and former supreme allied commander Dwight D. Eisenhower won the election. His main rival for the 1952 Republican presidential nomination, U.S. senator ("Mr. Republican") Robert Alfonso Taft of Ohio, espoused isolationism. Patrick J. Buchanan, the last major representative of isolationist and protectionist thinking in the Republican Party to seriously compete for its presidential nomination, did win the New Hampshire Republican primary in 1996, but left the party in 2000 and ran in the general election as the nominee of the Reform Party. Ironically, Buchanan's presence on the ballot possibly contributed to the inauguration of increased international trade advocate, Republican George W. Bush of Texas, as president of the United States.

See also: Democratic Party; Federalists; Free trade; Protectionism; Republican Party.

Selected Bibliography:

Gerald M. Pomper, "The Presidential Election," *The Election of 2000*, 2001.

Henry B. Sirgo

RICARDO, DAVID (April 18, 1772– September 11, 1823)

English economist, best known for his Iron Law of Wages and his 1817 *Principles of Political Economy and Taxation*, who embraced laissez-faire ideas.

Ricardo's father became wealthy through the London Stock Exchange and at the age of fourteen he entered the family business. Initially influenced by Adam Smith's *Wealth of Nations*, Ricardo developed friendly relationships with James Mill, Jeremy Bentham, and Thomas Malthus. In 1819, through his extensive land holdings in Gloucestershire, he became a member of the House of Commons.

Ricardo's Iron Law of Wages, his most influential idea, stated that, if the forces of supply and demand determined wages, they would maintain themselves at a subsistence level. In 1815, Ricardo became involved in England's corn law controversy and argued that only landed gentlemen benefited from taxing imported grain. The tariff decreased the profits of manufacturers. His *Principles* examined the laws that governed distribution among the classes while developing a labor theory of value in which the labor utilized in production determined the value of a commodity. He argued that taxes and tariffs increased the price of the taxed commodity, while the price of the nontaxed commodity remained the same. The tax hurt the manufacturer of the goods as well as consumers who had to pay more. Ricardo's *Principles* influenced the development of classical economics. In 1823, he became ill with an ear infection, retired from Parliament, and died.

See also: Malthus, Thomas; Smith, Adam.

Selected Bibliography:

John P. Henderson, *The Life and Economics of David Ricardo*, 1997.

Ty M. Reese

ROBBER BARONS

Term used to refer to American industrial and financial magnates of the nineteenth century who became wealthy by questionable means, such as exploitation of natural resources, governmental influence, and labor.

Following the U.S. Civil War, Americans turned their energies toward the development of the vast resources of the nation, and many of the men who furnished the industrial leadership during that time became known as robber barons. In general, these magnates made millions of dollars—by monopolizing trade in one or two industries with the help of high protective tariffs—in the process of developing the transportation, communication, and manufacturing industries in the post–Civil War years. The term attempted to denote criminal nobility (hence, "robber" and "baron"), suggesting that these men achieved their wealth through theft from others. Generally viewed as immoral, greedy, and corrupt, the robber barons often utilized illegal business practices and treated their workers cruelly. Classic examples of the robber barons are J.P. Morgan, Cornelius Vanderbilt, Jay Gould, Andrew Carnegie, and John Rockefeller. Toward the end of their lives, many of these men became philanthropists, funding colleges, museums, scholarships, and libraries.

See also: Carnegie, Andrew; Civil War (American); Cleveland, Stephen Grover.

Selected Bibliography:

Thomas B. Brewer, ed., *The Robber Barons: Saints or Sinners?*, 1970.

H. Michael Tarver

ROOSEVELT, FRANKLIN D. (January 30, 1882–April 12, 1945)

Thirty-second president of the United States and the only president elected to office for four terms.

Born in Hyde Park, New York, on January 30, 1882, Roosevelt received his education at Harvard and Columbia Law School. He decided to enter politics at an early age. Elected first to the New York State Senate, during World War I, Wilson appointed him as assistant secretary of the navy. In 1920, he ran as vice president on the Democratic ticket, but lost to Warren G. Harding, who called for "a return to normalcy." Elected president of the United States during the dark days of the Great Depression, FDR realized that Herbert Hoover's program, the Reconstruction Finance Corporation, would not work due to its voluntary

nature. Roosevelt and his staff initiated a bold governmental experiment popularly known as the New Deal. The legislative program, the National Industrial Recovery Act, focused on three major goals: relief, recovery, and reform. Roosevelt's policymakers attempted to achieve these national goals through direct government intervention in the economy, both domestic and international.

Internationally, the Roosevelt administration looked on with dismay at the failure of the June 1933 London Economic Conference. The conference had "marked the last opportunity of democratic statesmen to work out a cooperative solution to common economic problems, and it ended in total failure." Fascist nations such as Germany, Italy, and Japan turned away from international liberalism, seeking instead territorial acquisition in the form of captive markets.

Addressing the growing problem of international disorder became the primary mission of Secretary of State Cordell Hull. Hull, "a hard-bitten, hot-tempered Tennessee mountaineer," supported appeasement within administration circles. He personally believed that lower tariffs could promote the cause of internationalism. His economic thinking remained "a blend of Adam Smith and the cotton South." Hull proclaimed himself an ardent follower of " 'Locke, Milton, Pitt, Burke, Gladstone, and the Lloyd George school.' "

Hull recognized the increasing threat of fascism as a formidable barrier to nations adopting free trade principles. Hull quickly advanced the idea, "once favored by Blaine and McKinley, of reciprocity—of empowering the president, free of the pressures of congressional logrolling, to negotiate agreements with other nations to lower duties." It marked a bold departure from protectionist policies of the 1930 Hawley-Smoot Tariff Act. Initially, Roosevelt balked at Hull's proposal "as impolitic." But FDR also had become increasingly "disturbed by the extreme economic nationalist course the nation was pursuing" and asked Congress, in early March 1934, for the necessary authority to negotiate new tariff agreements.

Business interests and Republican congressmen greeted the president's request with vociferous opposition. However, Democratic strength in the Senate led to the June approval of the Reciprocal Trade Agreements Act (RTAA). With Hull's initiative, the Roosevelt administration now offered to negotiate special trade agreements to lower tariffs with any country.

In the Reciprocal Trade Agreements Act of 1934, Congress authorized the president to raise or lower existing tariffs by as much as 50 percent without Senate approval. A nation that lowered its tariffs on U.S. goods would, in turn, receive more favorable tariffs on goods sent to the United States. The act enabled Roosevelt and his staff to bargain, or reciprocate, with other countries at their discretion. The act also included the important Most Favored Nation clause. This component offered any country the opportunity to gain the most preferential treatment in any tariff agreement. The act helped stimulate American business by improving trade relations with other nations. It did not, however, solve the Great Depression. World War II did that. The agreements worked out with Canada and Great Britain proved particularly noteworthy. The increase of trade between these two countries and the United States provided an economic foundation for the political cooperation that ultimately became so vital to the allied effort during World War II.

Prior to his death on April 12, 1945, in Warm Springs, Georgia, Roosevelt witnessed numerous negotiated and signed reciprocal trade agreements with other countries. In fact, by 1940, Hull had signed twenty-two such agreements. The 1934 RTAA promoted a more liberal trade policy that not only "won some political good will, especially in Latin America," but also "served as an instrument of economic warfare against the fascist powers." Roosevelt's leadership in developing more liberal tariff policies served the nation well during one of its most trying times.

See also: Germany; Great Britain; Great Depression; Hoover, Herbert; Hull, Cordell; London World Economic Conference; Reciprocal Trade Agreements Act (RTAA); Smith, Adam. **Vol. II**: Herbert Hoover's Statement of Intention to Approve the Hawley-Smoot Tariff Act; Franklin D. Roosevelt's 1932 Campaign Radio Speech; Herbert Hoover's Response to Franklin D. Roosevelt. **Vol. III**: Tariff of 1930 (Hawley-Smoot Tariff).

Selected Bibliography:

Grace Beckett, *The Reciprocal Trade Agreements Program*, 1951; Robert Ferrell, *American Diplomacy in the Great Depression*, 1957; Richard N. Kottman, *Reciprocity and the North Atlantic Triangle, 1932–1938*, 1968; William E. Leuchtenburg, *Franklin D. Roosevelt and the New Deal, 1932–1940*, 1963; Arthur M. Schlesinger Jr., *The Coming of the*

New Deal, 1988; Richard Synder, "Commercial Policy as Reflected in Treaties from 1931 to 1939," *American Economic Review*, 1940; Power Yung-Chao Chu, *A History of the Hull Trade Program, 1934–1939*, 1957.

Chuck Howlett

ROOSEVELT, THEODORE (October 27, 1858–January 6, 1919)

Twenty-sixth president of the United States; he modernized the office but did little with the tariff.

Born in New York City, Roosevelt came to national prominence as a hero of the Spanish-American War. His enormous popularity led to his selection as vice president under William McKinley. He became president when McKinley died of a gunshot wound in New York. Strong in foreign policy and a noted environmentalist, the twenty-sixth president receives credit for being one of the most successful chief executives of the United States. While noted for reforming government and business, Roosevelt refused to address trade issues. At Harvard and during the early years of his political life, Roosevelt had flirted with the notion of free trade. Once in office, he followed protectionist policies. In his first annual message as president, Roosevelt described reciprocity trade agreements as handmaidens of protection. To Roosevelt, reciprocity could only be achieved safely if it occurred "without injury to our home industries." He dropped McKinley's campaign promise that called for such agreements and argued that duties should remain high enough to protect the American worker. The tariff remained as the central economic policy of the Republicans. Safeguards against reducing protective duties remained in place during the Roosevelt administration, making reciprocity little more than a gesture. In 1902, Roosevelt proposed that a body of experts make recommendations to Congress about revisions in particular schedules as needed, but he never put this idea into practice. Late that same year, William Howard Taft, the governor general of the Philippines, asked Roosevelt to help the ailing Filipino economy by lowering American duties on Filipino products. The House of Representatives passed a 50 percent cut in the customs rate, but the relief bill stalled in the Senate. Roosevelt warned that congressional failure to pass the bill would demonstrate irresponsibility, but the president did not throw his weight behind the proposal and it died. Allowing protectionists to dominate the issue of trade made sense to Roosevelt because other foreign and domestic issues absorbed him. His biographer suggests that the president preferred to reap the short-range political benefits of caution on the issue and to pursue topics, such as railroad regulation, that he found less tedious. Roosevelt's decision about reciprocity also reflected his own uncertainty and lack of confidence about the tariff, as well as his refusal to risk his political future. The question of the tariff would continue to fester. William Howard Taft, Roosevelt's successor, reopened the tariff debate, and during the next four years the Republican Party split over the issue. Roosevelt returned to the political scene in 1911 as the candidate for the Progressive Bull Moose Party, running against Taft and Woodrow Wilson. After losing the election, he retired from public service and died of a coronary embolism on January 6, 1919.

See also: McKinley, William; Progressives; Taft, William Howard. **Vol. II**: William McKinley's 1888 Speech on Tariff Benefits for Labor; Inaugural Address of William Howard Taft; William Howard Taft's Winona Speech; William Howard Taft's 1912 Acceptance Speech; Theodore Roosevelt's Bull Moose Acceptance Speech.

Selected Bibliography:

Lewis L. Gould, *The Presidency of Theodore Roosevelt*, 1991.

Caryn E. Neumann

ROOT, ELIHU (February 15, 1845–February 7, 1937)

American lawyer, statesman, and Nobel Peace Prize winner.

Born in Clinton, New York, in 1845, Root attended New York University, graduating in 1867. After establishing a reputation as a leading corporate lawyer, he served as the U.S. attorney for the southern district of New York, where he met Theodore Roosevelt. Two years later, he returned to private practice. In 1899, President William McKinley appointed Root as the secretary of war, a position he held until 1904. He reformed and reorganized the War Department and established the War College. After the Spanish-American War, Root supported the Platt Amendment and advocated the establishment of civilian governments in Puerto Rico and the Philippines. In 1905, Roosevelt appointed Root to the position of secretary of state. Although Roosevelt remained reluctant to tackle the tariff issue, Root maintained that the Republican Party should reduce the duty rates established under the Dingley Tariff. He noted that representatives from industries such as shoes, glass, and steel had indicated that the industries no longer required high tariffs and that a continuation of the current tariff schedule would lead to charges of cut-price exporting, or dumping, by large American corporations. He argued that the failure to address the issue would result in charges by Gold Democrats that the Roosevelt administration, in an era of antitrust sentiment, continued to support big business. While secretary of state, Root also negotiated several treaties with foreign countries, including the Root-Takahira Agreement, and authored the Open Door Notes. In 1909, after the election of William Howard Taft, Root served as a senator from New York until 1915. In 1912, he received a Nobel Peace Prize for his efforts for international peace. After World War I, he supported the creation of the League of Nations and the World Court. He died in New York City on February 7, 1937.

See also: Dingley Tariff (Tariff of 1897); McKinley, William; Open Door Notes; Roosevelt, Theodore.

Selected Bibliography:

Richard William Leopold, *Elihu Root and the Conservative Tradition*, 1954; Paul Wolman, *Most Favored Nation: The Republican Revisionists and U.S. Tariff Policy, 1897–1912*, 1992.

Cynthia Clark Northrup

ROSTENKOWSKI, DANIEL (January 2, 1928–)

A protégé of the late mayor Richard J. Daley, Rostenkowski decided to forego a rise in the U.S. House Democratic Party leadership, although he had managed the successful 1972 campaign of Tip O'Neill for the position of majority leader, and instead pursued and indeed reached the chairmanship of the House Ways and Means Committee.

Like Mayor Daley, Rostenkowski remained more of a pragmatist than an ideologue and sought to further the interests of the Chicago U.S. House district that he represented. When Rostenkowski faced difficult Democratic primaries in 1992 and 1994, in part as a result of a disadvantageous redistricting, he received the support of Richard J. Daley's son and successor, Mayor Richard M. Daley. Rostenkowski maintained a pragmatic approach as chairman of the House Ways and Means Committee when addressing such topics as trade and tariffs, a classically distributive public policy area. Although a loyal Democrat, Rostenkowski demonstrated little concern about issues of interest to organized labor and about such perennial twentieth-century Democratic policy proposals as national health insurance. His work as chair of the Ways and Means Committee proved indispensable to President William Jefferson Clinton as the president sought to secure congressional approval of the North American Free Trade Agreement (NAFTA). Rostenkowski, sensitive to the needs of his own district, recognized the concerns of members of Congress when changes in tariff policy threatened to disturb economic and political interests in their districts.

When the Republicans took control of the U.S. House in 1995 for the first time in forty years, a Republican candidate defeated Rostenkowski in his home district. The Republican, a lawyer who had never held elective office, won partly as a result of an indictment against Rostenkowski that forced him to relinquish his chairmanship to Sam Gibbons (D-FL). The year 1996, besides witnessing the electoral vanquishment of his 1994 Republican rival, also saw Rostenkowski plead guilty to two counts of mail fraud. Although sentenced to seventeen months in prison and fined $100,000, President Clinton later pardoned Rostenkowski on December 22, 2000.

See also: Clinton, William Jefferson (Bill); House Ways and Means Committee; North American Free Trade Agreement (NAFTA).

Selected Bibliography:

Richard E. Cohen, *Rostenkowski: The Pursuit of Power and the End of the Old Politics*, 2000.

Henry B. Sirgo

RUM

Distilled liquor, made from molasses; played a significant role in colonial trade.

Rum, a by-product of the sugar industry in the West Indies, remained important in New England, New York, and Pennsylvania. In Massachusetts and Rhode Island, it became the largest manufacturing industry in the eighteenth century and an important article in both domestic and overseas trade. Early New England trade with the Caribbean exchanged lumber and fish for molasses, which distilleries then converted to rum. While locals consumed most of the rum, it also became linked, especially from Newport, Rhode Island, to the triangular slave trade between New England, West Africa, and the Caribbean. English colonial rum also competed with French cognac for the Indian fur trade. The cheaper, locally produced rum provided the English with an advantage over the French-produced cognac. In the Caribbean, New Englanders found it more profitable to trade with the French, Spanish, or Dutch islands. England frowned on this illegal trade. In a 1733 Molasses Act, the English Parliament placed a nine-pence-per-gallon tariff on non-British molasses, but inadequate enforcement allowed New Englanders to continue to smuggle non-British molasses for rum production. Attempts to enforce a lower, but still objectionable, tariff in the Sugar Act of 1764 led to bitter resistance in New England and became one of the causes of the American Revolution. Rum smugglers, important to the growth of colonial shipping, accounted in part for advances in the design of fast-sailing ships that could outrun British customs officials.

See also: American Revolution; Navigation and Trade Acts; Sugar.

Selected Bibliography:

John McCusker, *Rum and the American Revolution: The Rum Trade and the Balance of Payments of the Thirteen Continental Colonies*, 1989.

Ralph Lee Woodward Jr.

S

SALINAS DE GORTARI, CARLOS
(April 3, 1948–)

President of Mexico who negotiated the North American Free Trade Agreement (NAFTA).

Salinas overcame rising opposition from both the left and the right to win the presidency in a disputed election by a bare 50.4 percent majority, thus continuing the long domination of Mexico by the Revolutionary Institutional Party (PRI). Salinas had deep roots in the PRI. His father had served as a cabinet minister and a senator of the party and his mother remained an active feminist leader in the PRI. Although raised and educated in the capital city, his family came from the small town of Agualeguas near the Río Grande and he spent enough time at the family ranch for his political career to become associated with the northern part of the country. In 1978, Salinas earned a Ph.D. in economics at Harvard University, where he learned U.S. economic and business practices. As

an economic advisor and government official in the PRI governments from 1971 forward, he served as minister of planning under President Miguel de la Madrid Hurtado from 1982 to 1988. As president, Salinas continued the neoliberal policies of de la Madrid with considerable privatization of government-owned resources and services. Salinas promoted closer trade relations with the United States and development of the Mexican–U.S. border region. His most notable achievements include NAFTA, adopted in 1992, which went into effect on January 1, 1994. One of his primary motives in reversing Mexico's traditional protectionist policies focused on attracting more foreign capital for economic growth. Despite this victory, his government suffered numerous difficulties, including the devastating Hurricane Gilbert in 1988, serious decline in the value of the Mexican peso, and an uprising of the Zapatista National Liberation Army in the southern state of

Chiapas. Charges of corruption and fraud in his family left him in disgrace by the end of his term and he moved to Europe. He defended his administration in a lengthy memoir, *México: un paso difícil a la modernidad*, bitterly criticizing his successor, Ernesto Zedillo.

See also: Bush, George Herbert Walker; Mexico; North American Free Trade Agreement (NAFTA).

Selected Bibliography:

Philip L. Russell, *Mexico Under Salinas*, 1994.

Ralph Lee Woodward Jr.

SAY, JEAN-BAPTISTE (January 5, 1767–November 15, 1832)

French political economist and journalist known for his "Law of Markets" ("products are paid for with products"; i.e., aggregate demand in an economy cannot exceed or fall below aggregate supply in that economy), first presented in his *Treatise on Political Economy* in 1803.

This notion formed the basis for the division between the classical economists David Ricardo and Thomas Malthus in the controversy over the possibility of general commodity gluts. In his writings, Say, considered an optimist and ardent supporter of free trade, popularized Adam Smith's ideas.

Born in Lyons, France, to middle-class Huguenot parents, Say spent most of his early life in London and Geneva. When a young man, he returned to Paris and worked for a life insurance company. He became the leading member of a group of influential free-market intellectuals, and the first editor of the group's journal, *La Decade Philosophique*. At the end of the Napoleonic Wars, Say held a chair of political economy at the College de France.

Unlike Smith, Say focused more on the "economic man" than on moral philosophy. He regarded political economy as a practical endeavor for the assistance of industry, and thus placed the risk-taking entrepreneur at the center of his approach. In his 1803 *Treatise*, he vehemently opposed protection, basing his opposition on Smithian economic analysis, and asserted that free trade and peace go hand in hand. And this, while other opponents of protection, such as Bastiat, relied on humor and a more humanistic approach to convey the same message.

In addition to his 1803 *Treatise*, Say's better-known works include *Cathechism of Political Economy*, published in 1815, *Letters to Mr. Malthus*, translated in 1821, in which he attacked the "deplorable consequences" of "importation duties," and *Cours complet d'economie politique practique*, published in 1823. Say's influence remained widespread not only on the continent, but also in Britain and Russia, and even extended to the United States, where his admirers included Thomas Jefferson and James Madison. He died in Paris on November 15, 1832.

See also: Malthus, Thomas; Ricardo, David; Smith, Adam.

Selected Bibliography:

R.R. Palmer, ed., *J.B. Say: An Economist in Troubled Times*, 1997; Joanne Reitano, *The Tariff Question in the Gilded Age: The Great*

Debate of 1888, 1994; Thomas Sowell, *Say's Law: An Historical Analysis*, 1972.

Warren Young

SAYRE, FRANCIS B. (April 30, 1885– March 29, 1972)

Assistant secretary of state associated with the passage of the Reciprocal Trade Agreements Act (RTAA).

Born in South Bethlehem, Pennsylvania, in 1885, Sayre studied at Williams College and Harvard Law School. In 1913, he married Jessie Woodrow, the daughter of President Woodrow Wilson. Between 1919 and 1933, he served as a professor at Harvard Law School, departing briefly to serve as advisor in foreign affairs to the government of Siam. President Franklin D. Roosevelt appointed him assistant secretary of state in 1933. In the State Department he worked closely with Cordell Hull to devise, pass, implement, and renew the RTAA of 1934. Both critics and supporters at the time alleged that he believed in the reciprocal trade program much the way Saint Augustine believed in God. Indeed, he worked tirelessly over the course of six years to promote and strengthen the new approach to trade. He delivered countless speeches and paced the corridors of Capitol Hill to campaign for lower tariffs negotiated through reciprocal trade agreements.

Sayre also sought to transform the RTAA steadily during the 1930s from an inward-looking, emergency measure, to a more internationalist, permanent program. Although initially he and Hull sold the policy as an urgent treatment designed to open foreign markets for American surpluses, over time they began to bill it as a cornerstone of American foreign economic policy. Sayre argued in congressional testimony that lower trade barriers, nondiscrimination, and reciprocity contributed to international stability and ultimately diminished the likelihood of war. He apparently invented the aphorism "If goods do not cross boundaries, armies will." In 1939, Sayre left the State Department to serve as high commissioner to the Philippines.

See also: Hull, Cordell; Reciprocal Trade Agreements Act (RTAA); Roosevelt, Franklin D.

Selected Bibliography:

Michael A. Butler, *Cautious Visionary: Cordell Hull and Trade Reform, 1933–1937*, 1998.

Jamie Miller

SCHWAB, CHARLES M. (February 18, 1862–September 19, 1939)

Protégé of Andrew Carnegie; an unusually skilled businessman well known for his support of a protective tariff on steel.

Born in Loretto, Pennsylvania, Schwab went to work for Andrew Carnegie as a young man, rising through the ranks to become the president of Carnegie Steel in 1897. Not long after his mentor retired and sold Carnegie Steel to J.P. Morgan—who went on to combine it with other companies to create U.S. Steel—a combination of professional differences with the new board of directors and exhaustion resulting from personal dissipation led Schwab to resign in 1904. That same year, he reestablished himself, in direct competition with his old firm, when he assumed control over Bethlehem Steel, which he had purchased as a private investment while at U.S. Steel. He transformed it into an extraordinarily efficient and prosperous firm. From 1905 to 1920, Bethlehem's labor force doubled every five years.

Schwab argued that the protective tariff contributed significantly to national prosperity as well as to the high wages that American steel workers enjoyed. With much of his clientele in the eastern United States, he feared European competition—and therefore favored the tariff—more than did U.S. Steel, most of whose sales occurred west of Pittsburgh. Since rail transport of steel remained quite costly, U.S. Steel enjoyed protection from the impact of foreign competition. Bethlehem enjoyed no such luxury.

At the same time, Schwab fought against tariffs on iron ore, in large part because Bethlehem Steel relied on Cuban mines for its ore, whereas U.S. Steel had its primary source in the Mesabi Range, near Lake Superior.

Despite Schwab's warnings of economic catastrophe, Congress passed the low Underwood-Simmons Tariff Act in 1913. The economic repercussions it had for Schwab and for American steel production in general were compounded by the stimulus of World War I, which began the following year. Schwab went on to support the Hawley-Smoot Tariff of 1930. He died bankrupt in New York on September 19, 1939.

See also: Carnegie, Andrew; Iron; Underwood-Simmons Tariff (Tariff of 1913).

Selected Bibliography:

Robert Hessen, *Steel Titan: The Life of Charles M. Schwab*, 1975.

Thomas E. Woods Jr.

SECOND REPORT ON PUBLIC CREDIT

Alexander Hamilton's recommendation to use the tariff and excise taxes to pay the national debt.

In August 1790, Congress asked Secretary of the Treasury Alexander Hamilton to prepare a second report on measures needed to secure the public credit of the United States. Four months later, Hamilton presented his recommendations to Congress. He explained that the United States had recently assumed $21,500,000 in state debts. The interest on this debt exceeded $788,333 and would begin to accrue after 1791. The federal government owed another $38,291 in interest on the original debt. The national government needed to raise $826,624 as quickly as possible.

Hamilton suggested the collection of additional revenue by creating three new taxing categories for distilled spirits with higher duty rates. The first category would include distilled spirits imported from overseas. Duties on these items would range from eight to fifteen cents per gallon. The second category would include distilled spirits made in the United States from imported materials such as molasses and sugar. These items would be charged from eleven to thirty cents per gallon. Finally, the third category would include distilled spirits made in the United States from American materials. Duties on these items would range from nine to twenty-five cents per gallon. Hamilton also recommended a yearly tax of sixty cents on all domestic stills that made spirits for public sale. If a still made spirits only for the consumption of the owner and his family, then it would not be taxed.

Hamilton knew that the taxes he recommended would not be popular. Much would depend on the vigilance of the tax collectors and the integrity of the taxpayers. But in his opinion, taxes on consumption of distilled spirits seemed preferable to direct taxes on land or houses. Hamilton also reminded Congress that Massachusetts, Connecticut, and Pennsylvania already collected similar taxes with few problems. Even at the lowest possible rates for each category, the government could raise enough revenue in only one year to meet the immediate financial needs of the nation. Furthermore, any excess amounts collected could be applied to the sinking fund. Hamilton urged Congress to implement these recommendations along with the ones that would shortly follow in his report on the establishment of a national bank as the surest means available to establish the sound public credit of the American nation.

See also: Hamilton, Alexander; *Report on Manufactures*.

Selected Bibliography:

Alexander Hamilton, *The Papers of Alexander Hamilton*, 1963.

Mary Stockwell

SECTIONALISM

As a primary source of political debate in the United States since the founding of the republic, economic and trade policies contributed to the sectional tensions in antebellum America that eventually produced civil war.

Although not exclusively influenced by the slavery issue, most sectional disputes of the antebellum period stemmed from the growing philosophical and economic contrast between the South's commitment to slavery-based agriculture and the North's to free labor. As the gulf between the two sections widened through the first half of the nineteenth century, the tariff became one of the nation's most divisive political issues. Conventional wisdom in the North held that a high tariff provided one of the most effective ways to spur industrial growth. In the agricultural South, politicians and the public alike came to despise the "Yankee Tariff," which they believed unfairly denied southerners access to more reasonably priced goods.

Economic differences between the two sections emerged following the ratification of the Constitution as national political factions developed around Alexander Hamilton and Thomas Jefferson. As George Washington's treasury secretary, Hamilton became the young nation's leading protectionist, arguing with other Federalists that protection remained an economic necessity to encourage domestic manufacturing and establish a strong central government. Jefferson and his Democratic-Republican allies in the South opposed Hamilton's economic measures, arguing for smaller government and reduced governmental interference. They viewed Hamilton's plans as unduly favorable to northern commercial interests at the expense of southern agriculture.

While debates over protection took on a sectional character, the issue would not become truly divisive for some time. Congress enacted only mildly protectionist tariffs between 1789 and 1816, and, as conflict with Great Britain flared, nationalist "war hawks" in Congress like Henry Clay and John C. Calhoun supported protection as a means to aid industry and thus reduce American dependence on British goods. But toward the end of the second decade of the nineteenth century, events began changing the nature of the tariff question, particularly in the South. The financial panic of 1819 caused a sharp drop in agricultural prices, damaging the southern economy. At the same time, southern fears of becoming a national minority in Congress were coming to the fore during debates over statehood for Missouri. Congressional reapportionment after the 1820 census also worked to the advantage of the West and Middle Atlantic regions, where pro-tariff sentiment was on the rise. In 1822, the Denmark Vesey insurrection conspiracy, though quickly suppressed, heightened fears in the South that similar slave rebellions might take place. As a result, most southern political leaders, including Calhoun, began using states' rights rhetoric as they collectively defended their section's ambiguous "way of life," which had become hopelessly intertwined with the peculiar institution.

After 1820, southern leaders focused increasingly on northern enthusiasm for the tariff as proof of a concerted effort to deny the South its constitutionally guaranteed rights within the Union. Led by Calhoun, southern politicians widely denounced the higher protective tariff of 1824 as oppressive and a blatant abuse of federal power. Louder protests came four years later when Congress again raised tariff rates. The 1828 measures, which southern critics called the Tariff of Abominations, raised rates on manufactured goods to about 50 percent of their value, providing significant protection for New England cloth manufacturers. Lacking an industrial base, the South gained no benefits from the tariff and stood to suffer because of increased prices on goods that the region did not produce. Southern politicians railed against these alleged fiscal abuses, and the Tariff of 1828 became the foundation for the Nullification Crisis.

Constant protest against the 1828 measures led to a revision of the tariff four years later. Although the Tariff of 1832 lowered customs duties somewhat, it left high rates on manufactured cloth and iron. Far from satisfied with the new tariff, Calhoun used its passage to take a political stand. Under his leadership, South Carolina called a special Nullification Convention in 1832 to address the issue. The convention declared both the 1828 and 1832 tariffs null and void, and forbade the collection of customs duties in the state. The resulting political crisis threatened the stability of the Union, and President Andrew Jackson in turn threatened to use military force to make South Carolina comply with the federal law. Clay and Calhoun averted armed conflict by negotiating the so-called Compromise Tariff of 1833. The new measures provided for a gradual reduction of certain high duties. While the crisis passed, the nullification controversy ushered in a new political era. It marked the emergence, for the first time, of an organized, articulate, and determined pro-slavery interest in national politics.

Tariff reduction under the 1833 compromise measures lasted for only a short time. An extended economic depression that lasted from 1837 to 1843 led to an increase in customs duties and allowed the Whig Party to make significant political gains during the period. The Whig platform included a commitment to a high tariff designed to stimulate the economy along the model of Clay's American System. The plan eventually collapsed as Democrats, with a strong power base in the South, regained control of the government and the economy improved. In 1847, Mississippian Robert Walker, James K. Polk's treasury secretary, led an effort that reduced customs duties. Southern Democrats welcomed tariff reduction, yet it created tension with Democrats in the North, many of whom supported a modest protection program. The result further isolated the South from the rest of the nation.

For the remainder of the antebellum period, the tariff became a less prominent issue in terms of strict economic debate due to the economic boom of the 1850s, but many southerners still perceived the issue in sectional terms. As the slavery debate intensified, southern politicians repeatedly referred to the tariff in their rhetoric, painting it as a vital component of a northern conspiracy against the South that allegedly had been going on for decades. After an economic downturn in 1857, Republicans responded with calls for higher tariffs, cementing the issue in southern minds with the party of Abraham Lincoln.

See also: American System; Calhoun, John Caldwell; Clay, Henry; Clay's Compromise; Hamilton, Alexander; Jefferson, Thomas; Labor; Tariff of 1828 (Tariff of Abominations); Walker, Robert John.

Selected Bibliography:

Richard E. Ellis, *The Union at Risk: Jacksonian Democracy, States' Rights, and the Nullification Crisis*, 1987; Lacy K. Ford, *The Origins of Southern Radicalism*, 1988; William W. Freehling, *The Road to Disunion: Secessionists at Bay, 1776–1854*, 1990.

Ben Wynne

SENATE FINANCE COMMITTEE

Recognizing the importance of revenue, Congress established the Senate Finance Committee and the House Ways and Means Committee to supervise matters pertaining to government revenues and the U.S. Treasury.

The Senate Finance Committee's charge has evolved in response to the increasing scope and complexity of the U.S. government's revenue-generating activities, which now include internal taxes, tariffs and import quotas, and customs collection. Since the initial enactment in 1934 and subsequent renewals of the Reciprocal Trade Agreements Act, the Senate Finance Committee has worked with the executive branch in regulating foreign trade and protecting American business interests abroad. Toward these goals, the committee sponsors public hearings on all reciprocal trade agreements, problems stemming from foreign trade that affect American workers, and legislation relating to investment policy and taxation of savings, interest, and dividends.

The committee also exercises indirect authority over the nation's agricultural policy through its jurisdiction over legislation on sugar and sugar imports.

The accelerating globalization of the U.S. economy since the late nineteenth century has created new responsibilities for the Senate Finance Committee. It holds jurisdiction over multinational corporations, balance of payments, and measures bearing on overseas revenue sources for the U.S. Treasury. The proliferation of American involvement in economic, particularly financial, institutions in the post–World War II period also added to the committee's supervisory functions. The African Development Bank, the Inter-American Development Bank, the Private Investment Corporation, the International Monetary Fund (IMF), and the U.S. Export-Import Bank all come under the committee's purview.

As the New Deal American polity assumed added administrative and service functions, the Senate Finance Committee acquired jurisdiction over new programs insofar as tax revenues supported them. It exercises indirect authority over federal debts, social security, employment and labor measures, legislation affecting job opportunity and basic skills training programs, pension and pension reform legislation, health programs financed by taxes or trust funds, legislation concerning welfare programs, child support enforcement, child welfare, child care, foster care, adoption assistance, supplemental security income, unemployment compensation, and insurance and social services for the elderly and persons with disabilities. The committee also investigates private and self-employed pension plan problems and

oversees the Pension Benefit Guaranty Corporation. It participates in the supervision of Medicare and Medicaid and studies national health program proposals.

Through its authority over legislation on taxes and credits for public financing of federal elections, the committee plays a key role in election financing. The committee's jurisdiction also covers legislation dealing with the interrelationship among federal, state, and local governments, including revenue-sharing legislation, legislation on tax-exempt foundations and charitable funds, and legislation concerning changes in enforcement of tax laws.

The Senate Finance Committee discharges its responsibilities through five subcommittees: Health Care, International Trade, Long Term Growth and Debt Reduction, Social Security and Family Policy, and Taxation and IRS Oversight. The chairperson and ranking minority member are nonvoting, ex officio members of all subcommittees of which they are not regular voting members.

See also: House Ways and Means Committee; Reciprocal Trade Agreements Act (RTAA).

Selected Bibliography:

Ballard C. Campbell, *The Growth of American Government*, 1995.

Sayuri Shimizu

SIERRA CLUB

Organization founded by naturalist John Muir to protect the Sierra Nevada mountain range.

The Sierra Club immediately fought

to prevent a reduction of the size of Yosemite National Park. Subsequently, the Sierra Club opposed efforts to dam Hetch Hetchy Valley in Yosemite, Yellowstone National Park, and the Grand Canyon. The organization also backed the setting aside of various preserves as additional national parks and the carving out of national monuments. Lobbying by the Sierra Club has resulted in the protection of wilderness lands in Alaska. The Sierra Club convinced the World Bank to kill a half-a-billion-dollar loan to Brazil, which sought to develop major portions of the Amazon. During the 1990s, the Sierra Club helped to prevent a weakening of the Endangered Species Act. By that point, the Sierra Club focused on ozone depletion, toxic chemicals, and global warming. Located throughout the United States and Canada, the membership of the Sierra Club approached 400,000 as the twentieth century neared its end.

Like many other environmental groups, the Sierra Club opposed efforts by the World Trade Organization to expand its operations. The Sierra Club warned against attempts to weaken environmental regulations and labor rights in a rush to further economic liberalization. The Sierra Club applauded the Clinton administration's support for the discarding of fishery subsidies, which had helped lead to a reduction in the ocean catch. At the same time, the organization called for the reexamination of "other environmentally damaging subsidies" pertaining to forests, fossil fuels, and nuclear power. Trade policy, the Sierra Club argued, must "consider reasonably foreseeable impacts on a global scale." Furthermore, a review of the General Agreement on Tariffs and Trade and other international trade concords, the Sierra Club insisted, must occur to determine "environmental impacts of trade policy."

See also: Environmental issues; General Agreement on Tariffs and Trade (GATT); North American Free Trade Agreement (NAFTA); World Trade Organization (WTO).

Selected Bibliography:

Michael Cohen, *The History of the Sierra Club 1892–1970*, 1988.

Robert C. Cottrell

SILVER

One of the most important commodities in the history of world exchange, the discovery of silver in the Americas inaugurated truly global trade for the first time.

Experiencing a shortage of precious metals to trade for Asian luxury items by 1500, silver from Mexico and Bolivia arriving after the 1540s brought Europeans the commodity of greatest value to their most important trading partners, China and India, during the second half of the sixteenth century. Until the early twentieth century, the likes of the Spanish American silver peso and the U.S. "trade dollar" remained essential components in the acquisition of Asian luxury items such as silk, porcelain, tapestries, rugs, various textiles, and even gold.

As a cornerstone of early developments in Western economic thought, the importance of silver is reflected in the doctrines of mercantilism, bullionism, and the writings of numerous political economists until the mid-nineteenth century. Notions of a balance of payments and a trade deficit originate with the emergence of American silver on international markets in the sixteenth century.

For the Spanish of the early modern era, silver remained as important as it was for the Mughals of India or the Ming and Qing dynasties of China. Silver from Potosí in the modern-day Bolivia (then Upper Peru) and the less productive, but more numerous mines of Mexico or New Spain financed the late sixteenth-century wars of religion between Catholics and Protestants and Spain's participation in the Thirty Years War from 1618 to 1648.

Between 1600 and 1700, the world market price of silver declined precipitously. The enormous increase in volume of this circulating medium of exchange, combined with a glut in European and American markets of Chinese and Indian luxury textiles, brought the value of the white metal down to a point of equilibrium between East and West. From a peak of 7 or 8:1 in relation to gold in 1550 in both China and India, the rate of exchange in Asia fell to 14 or 15:1 by the early eighteenth century, roughly equal to the prevailing rates across western Europe. From 1700 to 1900, silver–gold exchange rates in Asia virtually paralleled those of Europe, signaling the end of an age.

If its importance in international trade waned after 1700, it retained great importance for colonial British America and the early economy of the post-independence United States, as well as its money supply. There it circulated, as in Asia, as legal tender until 1854. Moreover, the Spanish American silver peso served as the model for the U.S. silver dollar, and Wall Street continued to echo this relationship until the end of the twentieth century. On Wall Street stock prices were daily reported to the eighth or sixteenth of a dollar despite the absence of official, equivalent currency denominations, reflecting the earlier Spanish fractional currencies of the real (an eighth of a peso) and the half real (a sixteenth). Even early U.S. paper currency demonstrated the significance of Spanish American silver, from the days of the Continental Currency backed by "Spanish milled dollars" to the U.S. paper dollar, or "Silver-back."

Ultimately, the importance of silver, both in trade and U.S. monetary policy, declined to the point that, by the end of the nineteenth century, the Populists and their candidate, William Jennings Bryan, fought unsuccessfully against the rise of an international and domestic gold standard, with a manifesto calling for a fixed silver–gold exchange rate and the free coinage of silver to increase the monetary supply. Thrice they tried. Thrice they failed. The Age of Silver had ended.

See also: Bolivia; Mercantilism; Mexico; Populists.

Selected Bibliography:

Peter Bakewell, ed., *Mines of Silver and Gold in the Americas*, 1997; Lawrence Goodwyn, *The Populist Movement: A Short History of the Agrarian Revolt in America*, 1978; Earl J. Hamilton, *American Treasure and the Price Revolution in Spain, 1501–1650*, 1934.

David J. Weiland III

SIMMONS, FURNIFOLD McLENDEL (January 20, 1854–April 30, 1940)

Representative and senator from North Carolina who co-sponsored the Underwood-Simmons Tariff.

Born on his family plantation in North Carolina, Simmons attended Wake Forest College before graduating from Trinity College (which later became Duke University) in Durham, North Carolina. After studying for the bar and practicing law, Simmons ran as a Democrat for Congress in 1887. He failed in his reelection bid in 1888 and 1890, but President Grover Cleveland appointed him to the position of collector of internal revenue in North Carolina. In 1900, Simmons was elected as senator of North Carolina. After the election of the Democrat Woodrow Wilson in 1912, Simmons helped to sponsor the Underwood-Simmons Tariff Act, which lowered tariff rates. Republicans agreed to the passage of the act under the condition that the states ratify the Sixteenth Amendment, making a personal income tax constitutional. The Underwood-Simmons Tariff remained in effect for a short period of time, but the outbreak of World War I resulted in tariff rates once again rising with the passage of the Fordney-McCumber Tariff. Duty rates reached record highs with the passage of the Hawley-Smoot Tariff in 1930. After passage of Hawley-Smoot, Simmons lost the reelection bid. He returned to New Bern, North Carolina and lived there until his death in 1940.

See also: Underwood-Simmons Tariff (Tariff of 1913); Underwood, Oscar Wilder.

Selected Bibliography:

J. Fred Rippy, ed. *F.M. Simmons: Statesman of the New South*, 1936.

Cynthia Clark Northrup

SIMPSON, JEREMIAH ("SOCKLESS JERRY") (March 31, 1842–October 23, 1905)

Kansas farmer, rancher, and politician whose colorful nickname was inspired by a newspaper poem.

Born in Westmoreland County, New Brunswick, Canada, Simpson and his family moved to New York during his childhood. He served as a sailor and had risen to the rank of captain on the Great Lakes ships before briefly joining the army during the Civil War.

In 1879, Simpson moved his family to Kansas, where he farmed and ranched at Medicine Lodge. Forced into debt in 1886 due to the terrible winter that killed his cattle, he joined many others in the same situation. Agricultural depression engulfed the entire state of Kansas. Although a Republican, he participated in a number of third parties and eventually became a member of the Populist Party. With Democratic support, he won election to Congress in 1890, 1892, and 1896.

In Congress, Simpson served as the floor leader of the Populists and earned a reputation as one of the keenest and disconcerting members. He supported free trade, having been influenced by Henry George's *Protection or Free Trade* in 1886. As a stunt, Simpson got the book published in the *Congressional Record*. The Government Printing Office distributed over a million copies at a cost of five-eighths of a cent each.

Simpson never lost a chance to attack the protectionist Republicans and Democrats. One of his classic remarks was: "Why spend money on harbors to promote foreign trade, then build a tariff wall to obstruct foreign trade? Why not let the foreigner flounder in the harbor?" Over the years, Simpson gave numerous lengthy speeches in Congress attacking the tariff question and the sugar duty.

After being defeated in 1898 for a fourth term, he briefly published a newspaper, *Jerry Simpson's Bayonet* (Wichita) to attack opponents and maintain political visibility. Later, he moved to New Mexico, but eventually returned to Kansas and died in Wichita on October 23, 1905.

Simpson's legacy remains that of an agitator whose brilliant political skills allowed him to articulate his populist principles.

See also: Populists.

Selected Bibliography:

Peter H. Argersinger, "No Rights on this Floor: Third Parties and the Institutionalization of Congress," *Journal of Interdisciplinary History*, 1992; Carleton Beals, *The Great Revolt and Its Leaders: The History of Popular American Uprisings in the 1890s*, 1968.

Russell M. Magnaghi

SLAVERY

A system of forced labor that dispersed Africans throughout the Americas to labor on the land.

As European settlement of the Americas started, the abundance of land and resources made the New World economically attractive. The shortage of laborers created a problem for most settlements, especially in areas where the plantation system developed. The attempt to solve this labor shortage commenced with the enslavement of the Native Americans, then indentured servants from Europe, and finally African slaves. Slaves quickly became important to America's economic development because their labor produced cash crops such as tobacco, sugar, molasses, and rum, which quickly became profitable trade items. In North America, tobacco production created a demand for slaves. Cash crops became very valuable to the various European states colonizing the Americas, and their exchange occurred through the development of mercantilism. For Great Britain, tobacco became extremely valuable, and at times Parliament taxed the commodity at rates of 100 percent. The value of these cash crops caused Great Britain to create a series of navigation laws that economically defined and controlled its American colonies.

The total number of Africans brought to the Americas exceeded eleven million, with five million going to Spanish America and Brazil, four million to the West Indies, 400,000 to North America, and around 200,000 to Europe. The African slave trade and slavery created an elaborate system of tariffs, duties, and taxes. Not only did slaves produce taxed commodities but, on importation, Parliament taxed the slaves themselves. For the British Empire, colonists commonly paid a ten-pound sterling duty on every slave imported.

For North America, the American

Revolution not only created political independence, but also began a sectional split since many northern states abolished slavery while the southern states continued the practice. This created a problem in the Constitutional Convention because, as they debated the issue of regulating trade, the debate over the slave trade arose. The question focused on whether Congress should tax imported slaves. Some argued that the ⅗ Clause of the Constitution would encourage the importation of slaves, making it necessary to tax them. While they argued the political and economic side of slavery and the slave trade, the issue that they sought to avoid involved the morality of slavery in a nation founded on freedom. A special committee recommended that Congress do nothing concerning the importation of slaves until 1800, but tax newly imported slaves. After debating the committee's report, Congress reached a compromise that became part of Article 1, Section 9 of the Constitution. This section prohibited the importation of slaves after 1808 and allowed a tax of up to ten dollars per person on imported slaves until then. In 1808, the external slave trade ended, but the internal trade remained, along with the smuggling of slaves into the United States.

See also: American Revolution; Colonial administration; Continental Congress; Great Britain; Mercantilism; Navigation and Trade Acts; Rum; Sugar.

Selected Bibliography:

Ira Berlin, *Many Thousands Gone: The First Two Centuries of Slavery in North America*,
1998; Herbert S. Klein, *The Atlantic Slave Trade*, 1999.

Ty M. Reese

SMITH, ADAM (Baptized June 5, 1723–July 17, 1790)

Scottish political economist known for his work titled *An Inquiry Into the Nature and Causes of the Wealth of Nations*, published in 1776, which challenged the principles of mercantilism and argued for the development of a capitalist system based on free trade.

Born in Kirkcaldy, Fife, Scotland, Smith attended Oxford before receiving an appointment as a professor of logic at Glasgow University in 1751. Within the year, he occupied the chair of moral philosophy, teaching such topics as law, political economy, and ethics. In 1759, he wrote *Theory of Moral Sentiments*, establishing the proper conduct for human interaction under God.

In 1776, his most important work, *Wealth of Nations*, received acclaim while he was living in London. After discussing the division of labor, the role of the government, and the demands of the market, Smith focused on trade and duties. Arguing that a country, like an individual, displays a lack of prudence for manufactured items produced less expensively elsewhere, he also stated that the only exceptions to free trade are when the industry is necessary for national defense of the country or if a similar tax exists on the domestic manufactured item. According to Smith, the naval strength of Great Britain contributed substantially to the defense of the country; therefore, the navigation acts proved acceptable.

Smith justified the use of trade restrictions or prohibitions for purposes of retaliation and to prevent disorder. Domestic monopolies established for the benefit of merchants and manufacturers inhibit a return to free trade and result in the formation of powerful interest groups. When addressing the issue of duties established for government revenue, Smith recommended duties on luxury items since the rich voluntarily pay the tax. He also suggested that an import tax yields a diminished benefit for the state after the expense of enforcement. An increase in smuggling, the salaries of customs and excise officials, and the discouragement of certain industries combine to negatively offset the benefits of the revenue. Smith's theories impressed the American colonials during the revolution, and afterward Alexander Hamilton relied on the *Wealth of Nations* when establishing the political economy of the United States.

In 1778, Smith accepted the post of commissioner of customs in Edinburgh, Scotland. He resided with his mother and an unmarried cousin. After a short illness, he died on July 17, 1790.

See also: American Revolution; Capitalism; Colonial administration; Free trade; Great Britain; Mercantilism; Navigation and Trade Acts; Smuggling. **Vol. II:** *The Wealth of Nations.*

Selected Bibliography:

Athol Fitzgibbons, *Adam Smith's System of Liberty, Wealth, and Virtue: The Moral and Political Foundation of the* Wealth of Nations, 1995; Peter McNamara, *Politician Economy and Statesmanship: Smith, Hamilton, and the Foundation of the Commercial Republic*, 1998.

Cynthia Clark Northrup

SMITH, GERRIT (March 6, 1797– December 28, 1874)

Dedicated reformer, philanthropist, and free trader.

Born to wealth and prestige, during his lifetime Smith expanded on that inheritance. As a devout Presbyterian, he supported many of the social causes of his day, including vegetarianism, women's suffrage, the temperance movement, and prison reform. But his primary cause, and the one for which he would be best remembered, remains the abolition of slavery. He helped fugitive slaves escape into Canada, on one occasion having led an antislavery mob that broke a runaway slave out of jail in Syracuse, New York; gave away more than 3,000 farms in upstate New York to indigent blacks and poor whites; and encouraged "free-soil" settlement in Kansas following the passage of the Kansas-Nebraska Act. He helped found the Liberty Party and served a term in the U.S. House of Representatives as an antislavery independent from 1853 to 1854. He remained a longtime admirer of John Brown, a devotion that inspired him to finance Brown's work, specifically his plan to invade the South and arm the slaves. In the aftermath of Brown's raid in 1859, it became known that the "Secret Six," a group of prominent northerners who had provided Brown with funding to support his project, included Smith. The news received sensational publicity nationwide, causing three of the six to flee the country, fearing arrest. Smith suffered a breakdown, requiring his confinement for several weeks in a Utica insane asylum. He died in New York City in 1874.

See also: Bryant, William Cullen; Emerson, Ralph Waldo; Garrison, William Lloyd; Greeley, Horace; Higginson, Thomas Wentworth; Slavery.

Selected Bibliography:

Ralph V. Harlow, *Gerrit Smith: Philanthropist and Reformer*, 1939.

David E. Long

SMOOT, REED (January 10, 1862–February 9, 1941)

Republican senator from Utah for thirty years, and an apostle of the Mormon Church for forty-one years.

Born in Salt Lake City, Utah, Smoot attended church schools and later graduated from Brigham Young University. He entered business and made a sizable fortune. Smoot, selected by the Utah legislature, received an appointment to the U.S. Senate on January 20, 1903, and again in 1909. Smoot won popular Senate elections in 1914, 1920, and 1926, but lost in 1932. By 1930, he received recognition as the "dean of the Senate."

Senator Smoot became a tariff expert not from innovative trade ideas, but as a diligent rate-maker and student of the schedules, often called "a walking encyclopedia" of tariff facts and figures. He strove to find a scientific tariff based on facts, certain and predictable. He faced criticism for supposed bias to the Utah sugar industry and became known as a "sugar senator."

Smoot turned from his father's Democratic Party in 1888 to the Republican policy of protection. His first tariff issue involved opposition to the Philippine Bill in 1906 that eliminated duties against the island. Smoot worked on the Underwood-Simmons Tariff Act in 1913 under President Woodrow Wilson and added minor modifications, but voted against this low-tariff act. Smoot remained active in the Emergency Tariff of 1921 and worked as Senator Porter McCumber's assistant in the Fordney-McCumber Act of 1922.

Smoot reached the chairmanship of the Senate Finance Committee in 1923, earning a reputation as a watchdog for his relentless searches for waste. He headed the Hawley-Smoot Act of 1930 and so dominated the tariff investigations that many called the act the Smoot-Hawley Tariff.

Although the Hawley-Smoot Tariff Act bears partial blame for the Great Depression, Smoot insisted from 1930 to 1932 that economic conditions would have been worse had Congress not adjusted the Fordney-McCumber Act with the 1930 tariff revision. Smoot lost his Senate position in the Democratic landslide of 1932.

See also: Fordney-McCumber Tariff (Tariff of 1922); Hawley-Smoot Tariff (Tariff of 1930); Senate Finance Committee; Underwood-Simmons Tariff (Tariff of 1913). **Vol. II**: Woodrow Wilson's Democratic Nomination Acceptance Speech. **Vol. III**: Tariff of 1913 (Underwood-Simmons Tariff); Tariff of 1922 (Fordney-McCumber Tariff); Tariff of 1930 (Hawley-Smoot Tariff).

Selected Bibliography:

Milton R. Merrill, *Reed Smoot: Apostle in Politics*, 1990.

Lisa L. Ossian

SMUGGLING

The practice of illegally transporting goods across borders, generally as secret contraband.

Smuggling often occurs when the law prohibits the transport of goods, as with African slaves after the slave trade ended, with alcohol under Prohibition, and with the illicit drug and arms trade in recent years. But, in early American history, the imposition of high tariffs often encouraged smuggling to avoid paying duties.

First reports of such smuggling occurred in England in 1275, when the crown imposed a customs duty on wool. In the New World, the Spanish crown first prosecuted smugglers in the sixteenth century after capturing these bootleggers transporting valuable cargoes of gold, silver, pearls, and sugar through the Caribbean without registering the goods or paying required taxes. As other European nations competed for economic interests among their colonies in the Americas, regulatory tariffs intensified smuggling. During the eighteenth century, heralded as the "golden age" of smuggling, smugglers commonly transported luxury items such as tea, coffee, rum, and silk—items heavily taxed by the crown.

Although common in England, smuggling grew rampant in the West Indies and New England colonies. American colonists found it easier to trade with the French, Spanish, and Dutch directly, refusing to obey regulations requiring that trade with other countries take place through the mother country to ensure the payment of proper duties. In the years leading up to the American Revolution, customs offices and officials experienced numerous attacks because they symbolized British colonial oppression. The embrace of free trade in the first years of the Republic removed duties. As a result, smuggling and the demand for smugglers' services declined.

See also: Free trade; Mercantilism; Pirates.

Selected Bibliography:

John Paxton and John Wroughton, *Smuggling*, 1971; Neville Williams, *Contraband Cargoes: Seven Centuries of Smuggling*, 1959.

Kathleen A. Tobin

SOCIALISM

The word *socialism* appeared during the seventeenth century, describing proposals to substitute social control for individual control of life and work.

Before 1850, American socialism operated as a humanitarian rather than a political or economic movement. Utopian Socialist groups established communities supposedly free from industrial society's evils. Nineteenth-century German working-class emigrants established modern scientific, or Marxian Socialism, in the United States. Founded as the Social Democratic Working-Men's Party of North America in 1874, the Socialist Labor Party of North America dominated American socialism for twenty years.

In the 1890s, the Social Democratic Party of America organized. Becoming the Socialist Party in 1901, it won an encouraging presidential vote for Eugene V. Debs in 1912. The political growth came with the elimination of Marxist language and the adoption of the ideas of traditional American radicalism. The Socialist Party demanded collective ownership of railroads, the telephone and telegraph system, grain elevators, stockyards, and the banking system. Not until 1948 did the Socialist Party declare in its platform, "The United States should support all efforts to establish customs unions as a first step in the direction of a world-wide outlawry of trade barriers." American socialism has emphasized almost every issue except tariff and trade.

Socialists failed to bring together radicals of the West and the liberal labor forces of the industrial centers. When Socialists could not gather a significant vote during the Great Depression, it became apparent that the movement would never become a major force in American politics. The party's survival rested on Debs and Norman M. Thomas, leaders who functioned more as preachers than politicians or economists. By the mid-twentieth century, no important American socialist political movement existed, although the Socialist Party, U.S.A., still nominates candidates.

See also: Free trade; Labor.

Selected Bibliography:

Fred E. Haynes, *Social Politics in the United States*, 1970; William B. Hesseltine, *The Rise and Fall of Third Parties: From Anti-Masonry to Wallace*, 1948; Kirk H. Porter and Donald Bruce Johnson, *National Party Platforms: 1840–1960*, 1961; David A. Shannon, *The Socialist Party of America: A History*, 1955.

Theo Edwin Maloy

SOUTH CAROLINA *EXPOSITION* AND *PROTEST*

Two distinct documents that together played a key role in the nullification struggle between South Carolina and the federal government over tariff policy.

The *Protest* briefly summarized the South Carolina legislature's complaints about the Tariff Act of 1828, while the much longer *Exposition*, originally drafted by John C. Calhoun, expounded the political theory that justified state nullification of a federal law.

Adopting a strict constructionist perspective, Calhoun's *Exposition* pointed out that the U.S. Constitution did not specifically grant Congress the power to enact a tariff for any purpose other than for raising revenue. Therefore, protective tariffs designed to encourage manufacturing remained unconstitutional. Moreover, such tariffs discriminated against citizens in South Carolina and other southern agricultural states; the reliance of southerners on heavily taxed imported goods meant that they bore the bulk of the tariff's burden without receiving any appreciable benefits.

After establishing the unconstitutionality and unfairness of protectionism, Calhoun devoted the remainder of the *Exposition* to the remedy that South Carolina could opt to oppose a pro-tariff congressional majority. Influenced by Thomas Jefferson's Kentucky Resolution of 1798, Calhoun argued that, through the constitutional compact of 1787, the sovereign states established the federal government as their mere agent to accomplish a few specific functions on their behalf. If the federal government ever exceeded the very limited terms of its constitutional agency—as it had, Calhoun believed, in passing a protective tariff—then a state could rectify matters by exercising its superior authority. Acting through a convention representing the essential sovereignty of its people, a state could nullify a federal law it deemed unconstitutional. Calhoun called this process the "state veto." The "veto" would stand, he suggested, unless reversed by three-fourths of the states, the number required for amending the Constitution.

The South Carolina legislature did not formally adopt Calhoun's *Exposition*, but it ordered 4,000 copies of an edited version printed. Legislators did adopt the *Protest*, essentially a series of anti-tariff resolutions.

See also: Calhoun, John Caldwell; Jefferson, Thomas; Nullification; Tariff of 1828 (Tariff of Abominations). **Vol. II**: South Carolina *Exposition*; South Carolina *Protest*; South Carolina Ordinance of Nullification; Proclamation to the People of South Carolina; Andrew Jackson's Message to Congress on the Nullification Crisis. **Vol. III**: Tariff of 1828 (Tariff of Abominations).

Selected Bibliography:

William W. Freehling, *Prelude to Civil War: The Nullification Controversy in South Carolina, 1816–1836*, 1965; Clyde N. Wilson and W. Edwin Hemphill, eds., *The Papers of John C. Calhoun X, 1825–1829*, 1977.

Robert Tinkler

SPRINGER, WILLIAM McKENDREE (May 30, 1836–December 4, 1903)

Democrat from Illinois best remembered as chairman of the U.S. House of Representatives Ways and Means Committee and chairman of the Committee on Territories, and sponsor of the 1888 Springer Bill.

Born in New Lebanon, Indiana, Springer moved with his family to Jacksonville, Illinois, in 1848. He graduated from the University of Indiana at Bloomington in 1858, gained admittance to the Illinois bar in 1859, and practiced law in Lincoln and Springfield. He won a seat at the Illinois state constitutional convention in 1862 and later to that state's House of Representatives for two terms in 1871 and 1872. Elected to the U.S. House of Representatives as a Democrat in 1875, he served nine terms in that body until March 3, 1895, when he lost a reelection bid.

Charles F. Crisp (D-Ga.) named Springer as the chair of the House Ways and Means Committee after Springer supported his successful bid for Speaker of the House. He pushed through several minor tariff revisions during this time, but his reputation rests on his detailed use of parliamentary procedures and rules of debate.

The Springer Bill of 1888 called for the opening of Oklahoma to settlement. The measure met defeat in the U.S. Senate, but it later passed as an attachment to the Indian Appropriation Bill. President Grover Cleveland signed the bill into law on March 2, 1889, two days before he left office. President Benjamin Harrison issued the proclamation on March 22 that opened the land to settlement at noon on April 22, 1889. Two million acres of land became available that day in an area that would become the forty-sixth state.

See also: Cleveland, Stephen Grover; Harrison, Benjamin; House Ways and Means Committee.

Selected Bibliography:

Edward Stanwood, *American Tariff Controversies in the Nineteenth Century*, 1967.

Margaret Sankey

SPRINGER BILL

Failed attempt to reduce the tariff through a series of "pop-gun" bills.

After the failure of the Mills Bill to enact a full-tariff reform, William M. Springer, an Illinois Democrat and newly appointed chairman of the House Ways and Means Committee, introduced a plan among tariff reform Democrats to attack the tariff on separate commodities and goods. Fiercely opposed by Mills, who advocated a wholesale reform of the tariff, Springer introduced a measure, also known as the "Cheap Clothes Bill" to provide free wool and greatly reduce the duty of finished woolen goods. This, he supposed, would neither "alarm industry or embarrass trade" while it would attack the tariff at its weakest points—along with other bills that asked for free iron, coal, and other products—and force members of Congress to debate and vote on each bill on its own merits. This plan would also drive a wedge between industries whose lobbies had banded together to pressure Congress against changing the tariff because each would seek to protect itself. Although this tactic cut down on the amendments and debate that had plagued the Mills Bill, eighty-two speeches were entered on this bill, and

it ultimately failed to pass in the House of Representatives.

See also: Mills Bill; Springer, William McKendree.

Selected Bibliography:

William McKinley, *The Tariff in the Days of Henry Clay and Since*, 1970; Frank W. Taussig, *The Tariff History of the United States*, 1967.

Margaret Sankey

STEEL

Commercial iron that contains carbon in any amount up to 1.7 percent as an essential alloying constituent; remains malleable when under suitable conditions, and differs from cast iron in its malleability and lower carbon content.

Steel became a major industry during the 1870s and 1880s. Because it relied on sophisticated imported technology covered by European patents, a small group of businessmen controlled the industry. They obtained the patents and operated through a few heavily capitalized firms. Its market remained limited to large purchasers closely allied to the industry. Furthermore, the steel producers formed combinations to protect their industry. Carnegie Steel Company, which became the nucleus of U.S. Steel in 1901, provides the best example of this development.

Working in a major industry in the United States, the steel producer secured protective tariff legislation more easily than earlier iron producers. The American Iron and Steel Association from the beginning lobbied for a protective tariff. As a result, prior to 1900, the rates on rails remained specific and not *ad valorem*. Although designed to stabilize prices, the tariff resulted in the opposite—overproduction. Between 1875 and 1920, American steel production increased from 380,000 tons to sixty million tons annually, and the United States became the world leader.

Although the industry grew by the 1950s, it began to lose ground to the rest of the world. Within a decade, the richer and easily worked deposits dwindled, forcing producers to rely on beneficiation to enrich ores and convert them into pellets.

Today the steel industries of Europe and Asia provide keen competition. In the late twentieth century, U.S. producers grew concerned that the dumping of iron ore and semifinished products would harm national security. They called for investigations and protectionist remedies.

See also: American Iron and Steel Institute (AISI); U.S. Steel Corp.

Selected Bibliography:

Christopher G.L. Hill, *Steel Phoenix: The Fall and Rise of the U.S. Steel Industry*, 1997; Thomas R. Howell, William A. Noellert, Jesse G. Krier, and Alan William Wolff, eds., *Steel and the State: Government Intervention and Steel's Structural Crisis*, 1988.

Russell M. Magnaghi

STEVENS, THADDEUS (April 4, 1792– August 11, 1868)

Influential lawyer and legislator.

Born in Danville, Vermont, the son of Joshua Stevens and Sarah Morrill Stevens, Thaddeus Stevens graduated from Dartmouth College in 1814. He relocated to Pennsylvania, eventually moving to Gettysburg, where he began a lucrative law practice. Entering politics in the 1830s, Stevens served several terms in the Pennsylvania legislature as an anti-Mason. In 1848, voters elected him to Congress as a Whig representative.

An important player in the formation of the Republican Party, Stevens won election to Congress again in 1859 and served continuously until his death in 1868. As chairman of the House Ways and Means Committee, he played an important role in financing the war. He also played a significant role in the crusade against slavery and other important wartime legislation. After the war, Stevens became a determined advocate of radical Reconstruction and a persistent critic of President Andrew Johnson. Stevens argued for impeachment and served as chairman of the House managers who prosecuted the case before the Senate. On August 11, 1868, just a few months after the impeachment trial, Stevens passed away.

As a representative in Congress, Stevens spoke out often in favor of protective tariffs. In 1852, for instance, he denounced the Walker Tariff of 1846 as a pro-British measure that promoted the illusory belief of free trade. According to Stevens, a nation could only advance its interest through the principle of protection. While a high tariff would obviously benefit industry, it would also help workers through providing jobs and farmers by setting higher duties on agricultural products. In a speech at Lancaster, Pennsylvania, in 1858, Stevens criticized the Buchanan administration for the economic downturn of 1857, arguing that idle workshops proved "the effects of free trade." He expressed his position on the tariff in numerous house speeches. On February 25, 1861, he outlined his views to the House when speaking on the Morrill Tariff. "I admit that the principle of the Republican Party, with regard to this tariff matter . . . is not to tax tea and coffee, but to tax those things which, by being taxed, afford not only a revenue, but a protection to home industry."

As chairman of the House Ways and Means Committee during the Civil War era, Stevens served as an influential member of Congress. A good deal of his influence derived from his ability to secure legislation favorable to the principle of protection, such as the Morrill Tariff of 1861. Signed into law on March 2, 1861, the tariff substituted specific duties in place of *ad valorem* duties and raised overall protective rates to 37 percent. When rates increased in 1862 and 1864, Stevens, as chair of the Ways and Means Committee, played an important role in guiding the legislation through the House. After the war, Stevens continued to endorse a high protective tariff and resisted efforts to repeal wartime tariff legislation.

See also: Civil War (American); Free trade; House Ways and Means Committee; Morrill Tariff (Tariff of 1861); Tariff of 1846 (Walker's Tariff).

Selected Bibliography:

Beverly Wilson Palmer and Holly Beyers Ochoa, eds., *The Selected Papers of Thaddeus Stevens*, 1998; Hans Trefousse, *Thaddeus Stevens: Nineteenth Century Egalitarian*, 1997.

Bruce Tap

SUB-TREASURY PLAN

An American proposal to assist farmers by giving them loans for crops.

In the late nineteenth century, farmers experienced severe financial difficulties and laid the blame for their economic woes on the financial system of the United States. With the sub-treasury plan, farmers hoped to eliminate credit as a factor in American economic life and enable the conduct of business on a cash basis. The plan would allow the government to issue a cheap and plentiful currency directly to producers in short-term loans based not on gold and silver holdings, of which farmers had none, but on wealth produced by the common folk. The sub-treasury plan was first proposed at the 1889 national meeting of the National Farmers' Alliance and Industrial Union. These populists argued that every county in the United States producing over $500,000 worth of agricultural products each year should have a sub-treasury office with facilities for storing certain nonperishable agricultural products. At the time that a farmer delivered his crop, the product would be graded and classed. The farmer would receive a certificate of deposit, and money equal to 80 percent of the local current value of the crop loaned to the warehouse storage owner at 1 percent interest annually. If farmers failed to redeem their products within a year, the sub-treasury official auctioned them off to the highest bidder to satisfy the debt. To its proponents, the sub-treasury properly ordered the financial system by favoring producers over idle speculators. Populists argued that the plan guaranteed farmers a fair share of the wealth that they produced and would encourage them to produce even more. By eliminating the ability of a few to manipulate the currency, the extremes of wealth in the country would also end. With the collapse of the Populist Party in 1896, the notion of a sub-treasury faded away as well, but in 1916 Progressives incorporated some of the elements of the sub-treasury in the Warehouse Act.

See also: American farmers; Populists; Progressives.

Selected Bibliography:

Bruce Palmer, *"Man Over Money": The Southern Populist Critique of American Capitalism*, 1980.

Caryn E. Neumann

SUGAR

A major commodity in U.S. trade with the Caribbean region.

In the colonial period, British West Indian sugar produced wealth for British investors that helped fuel the industrial revolution. Sugar's by-product, molasses, provided the basis for a substantial New England rum industry. The Molasses Act of 1733 and Sugar Act of 1764 sought, unsuccessfully, to stop New Englanders from smuggling molasses from the non-British islands. After the American Revolution, U.S. sugar imports from Cuba rose steadily, especially after 1818 when Spain allowed Cuba to trade legally with the United States. By the 1850s, Cuba exported more sugar than any other country, with the United States its principal market. The Ten Years War, fought from 1868 to 1878, seriously damaged Cuban sugar production and European beet sugar gained a significant share of the U.S. market, but after the war a thorough technological renovation of the Cuban sugar, along with preferential treatment by U.S. tariffs, allowed it to regain a large share of the U.S. sugar market. A favorable tariff agreement between the United States and Germany had supported imports of beet sugar, but reciprocity treaties with Hawaii in 1875 and Spain in 1883 favored sugar imports from Hawaii and Cuba. The McKinley Tariff of 1890 led to a new reciprocity treaty with Spain, but the Wilson-Gorman Tariff of 1894 terminated it. The Cuban War for Independence, fought from 1895 to 1898, once more disrupted Cuban production, but, following that war, U.S. investment poured into Cuban sugar production and refining, and the Cuban Reciprocity Treaty of 1902 gave Cuba a preferential place within the U.S. market. Cuba provided 95 percent of U.S. sugar imports in the early twentieth century, as the United States rejected German efforts to gain Most Favored Nation treatment for its sugar. A government subsidy protected domestically produced sugar, principally in Louisiana and Hawaii. A new reciprocity treaty with Cuba in 1934 established quotas for Cuban sugar, which continued until the U.S. embargo on Cuban trade in 1960. Modifications of the 1934 agreement by the Sugar Acts of 1946 and 1948 increased the Cuban sugar quota, but required an increase in Cuban imports of U.S. rice. Thereafter, many other tropical regions of the Caribbean region and elsewhere rapidly increased their production of sugar for the U.S. market.

See also: Hawaii; McKinley Tariff (Tariff of 1890); Wilson-Gorman Tariff (Tariff of 1894).

Selected Bibliography:

Sidney W. Mintz, *Sweetness and Power: The Place of Sugar in Modern History*, 1985.

Ralph Lee Woodward Jr.

SUMNER, WILLIAM GRAHAM
(October 30, 1840–April 12, 1910)

One of the most outspoken opponents of protective tariffs of the late nineteenth and early twentieth centuries.

Born in Paterson, New Jersey, into a family of working-class immigrants, his friends and relatives knew Sumner as a studious and intellectually rigorous young man. As vice president of the American Free Trade League (AFTL), he wrote and spoke extensively on the subject, devoting more of his attention to the tariff than to any other issue of the day. Sumner accepted a position at Yale University as a professor of political and social science in 1872, and toward the end of his life served as president of the American Sociological Society.

His laissez-faire outlook resulted in his passionate commitment to free trade, but his criticism of protectionism went beyond its curtailment of individual liberty. The protective system, in his view, remained economically inefficient and even morally offensive. Business interests, he argued, agitated for protective policies to save themselves "the trouble and annoyance of business competition and . . . be assured profits in their undertakings by the State, that is, at the expense of their fellow citizens."

A practical man, Sumner focused more on popularizing the case against tariffs than on adding to the existing edifice of laissez-faire economic theory. He published his *Lectures on the History of Protection* in 1877 in a number of newspapers, including the *New York Times*. In Sumner's view, the objectionable aspect of tariffs included the harm caused to consumers by raising domestic prices, an argument he made again and again. Because tariffs remained an indirect and hidden tax, in his opinion, they remained all the more mischievous and reprehensible.

Sumner won converts to the cause among his students—a suggestion borne out by annual polls of Yale's graduating seniors who, by a margin of four to one, consistently favored free trade. He died in Englewood, New Jersey, on his way to a meeting of the American Sociological Society.

See also: American Free Trade League (AFTL); Consumerism.

Selected Bibliography:

Bruce Curtis, *William Graham Sumner*, 1981.

Thomas E. Woods Jr.

T

TAFT, WILLIAM HOWARD
(September 15, 1857–March 8, 1930)

Twenty-seventh president of the United States and tenth chief justice of the U.S. Supreme Court.

Born in Cincinnati, Ohio, Taft graduated from Yale University in 1878. Two years later, he received a law degree and soon entered Republican politics, serving in appointed posts in his home state. In 1890, President Benjamin Harrison appointed him solicitor general of the United States and two years later as judge of the U.S. Sixth Circuit Court of Appeals. From 1901 to 1904, Taft served as governor of the Philippines before joining Theodore Roosevelt's cabinet as secretary of war from 1904 to 1908. Taft accepted the Republican nomination for president in 1908 as Roosevelt's handpicked successor. In the general election, he defeated Democrat William Jennings Bryan.

The Progressive wing of the Republican Party held high hopes for Taft's

administration. The new president's inaugural address gave special emphasis to the need for downward tariff revision, a primary Progressive demand, and Taft called Congress into special session to address the issue. Progressive Republicans became disillusioned quickly. Although Taft proposed legislation reducing tariff rates, he failed to support his original position in the face of opposition from his party's conservative leadership. Taking a strictly legal point of view, Taft argued that direct involvement by the president in legislative matters violated the constitutional doctrine of separation of powers. A few months later, Taft suffered a major political defeat when the Republican Congress passed the Payne-Aldrich Tariff of 1909, keeping tariff rates high.

Taft fell out of favor with liberal Republicans and his break with Theodore Roosevelt led to the creation of Roosevelt's separate Progressive (Bull Moose) Party. Taft received the Republican nomination for president in 1912, but the division within his party allowed Democrat Woodrow Wilson to win the White House. After leaving office, Taft served for eight years as a law professor at Yale. In 1921, he realized a lifelong dream when President Warren G. Harding appointed him Chief Justice of the U.S. Supreme Court. Taft resigned from the Court in February 1930 and died a month later in Washington, D.C.

See also: Harrison, Benjamin; McKinley, William; Payne-Aldrich Tariff (Tariff of 1909); Progressives; Republican Party. **Vol. II:** Benjamin Harrison's 1889 State of the Union Address; William McKinley's 1888 Speech on Tariff Benefits for Labor; Inaugural Address of William Howard Taft; William Howard Taft's Winona Speech; William Howard Taft's 1912 Acceptance Speech. **Vol. III:** Tariff of 1909 (Payne-Aldrich Tariff).

Selected Bibliography:

Edward S. Kaplan and Thomas W. Ryley, *Prelude to Trade Wars: American Tariff Policy, 1890–1922*, 1994.

Ben Wynne

TARIFF COMMISSION

Governmental organization that advised the president on rates.

The Progressives established the Tariff Commission to rationalize the tariff process and reduce to a reasonable level the highly protective tariffs of the Republican era. Although Congress had established the Office of the Commissioner of Revenue in 1866, efforts to set up a tariff commission did not occur until 1882 and again in 1888. The first formal board, legislated in 1909, acted as an advisory body to the president. The 1917 act established the current structure, but Congress retained the rate-making power until the 1930s when Congress authorized the president to adjust rates on a reciprocal basis.

The Tariff Commission, responsible for determining costs of production in the United States and overseas, advised the president on raising and lowering rates by up to 50 percent to equalize costs between U.S. manufacturers and foreign competitors. The president had the right to ignore the commission's advice. Between 1922 and 1930, Warren Harding, Calvin Coolidge, and Herbert Hoover made only thirty-seven changes, thirty-two increases, and five decreases. Rates decreased on paintbrush handles, bobwhite quails, mill feeds, phenol, and cresylic acid. The executive branch refused to grant fifteen additional requests. Between 1930 and 1939, the ITC examined 101 requests, with the president issuing twenty-five increases and thirty-one decreases while refusing forty-five petitions. The Hawley-Smoot Tariff Act reorganized the commission and provided higher salaries for members. The president also received additional power under Hawley-Smoot to raise rates against goods from countries discriminating against the United States.

The Tariff Commission conducts escape clause investigations at the request of the president or Congress. A 1942 agreement with Mexico had included a provision that the United States could withdraw any concession at any time if it caused serious harm to domestic producers of the same or a like product. This clause, included by Harry S Truman through an executive order in 1947, established a standard implemented by Congress in 1951 for all current or future agreements. The president had the right to ignore investigation results, but had to offer an explanation to Congress for the denial. Congress could override a presidential decision with a two-thirds vote. In 1955, Congress redefined an industry to include each product of a multiproduct firm and allowed the finding of injury, even if caused by something other than the imports.

After 1948, the Tariff Commission fixed the minimum rates necessary to protect domestic producers, the so-called peril points. Congress repealed these thresholds in 1949, reinstated them in 1951, and finally replaced them in 1962 with more flexible "probable economic impacts" of concessions. Under the Trade Act of 1974, the Tariff Commission became the International Trade Commission.

See also: Hawley-Smoot Tariff (Tariff of 1930); International Trade Commission (ITC); Progressives; Republican Party. **Vol. II**: Herbert Hoover's Statement of Intention to Approve the Hawley-Smoot Tariff Act. **Vol. III**: Tariff of 1909 (Payne-Aldrich Tariff).

Selected Bibliography:

John M. Dobson, *Two Centuries of Tariffs*, 1976; Judith Goldstein, *Ideas, Interests, and American Trade Policy*, 1993.

John Herschel Barnhill

TARIFF OF ABOMINATIONS

See Tariff of 1828.

TARIFF OF 1789

First tariff act passed under the U.S. Constitution.

In 1789, the ratification of the U.S. Constitution created a new federal government that faced many problems and challenges, including the creation of a revenue system that would provide for the government's operating expenses while allowing it to service the debt from the American Revolution. Although the new federal government desperately needed income, it also faced the problem that any new level of taxation would compete with numerous state and local systems. Congress quickly realized that its revenue needed to come from tariffs since Americans imported a large number of manufactured commodities along with raw materials such as molasses, with many of these goods arriving on foreign ships. James Madison played an important role in pushing the Tariff Act through Congress, but only after great debate and conflict. Many of the northern states, interested in developing their own manufacturing industries, demanded high protective tariffs, while numerous southern states, which were experiencing a revival in the slave-based plantation system because of cotton, saw low tariffs as being in their best interest. At the same time, the rum-producing New England states demanded a low tariff on molasses while southern states argued that such a luxury commodity should have a high tariff. Madison attempted to work around these concerns by stressing the national interest over the regional or local. The Tariff of 1789 passed after both sides agreed to a compromise. Congress taxed most goods at 5 percent, but some duties ranged as high as 50 percent. The act also increased the duty on molasses two and one-half cents per gallon.

See also: American Revolution; Federalists; Hamilton, Alexander; Madison, James; Rum. **Vol. III**: Tariff of 1789.

Selected Bibliography:

Reginald Horsman, *The New Republic: The United States of America, 1789–1815*, 2000.

Ty M. Reese

TARIFF OF 1790

First tariff bill recommended by Alexander Hamilton.

In January 1790, the newly appointed secretary of the treasury Alexander Hamilton submitted his first recommendations to Congress regarding the tariff. He reported that the nation needed nearly $3 million to pay for government operating expenses and the interest on foreign and domestic debts. Hamilton suggested an increase in duties on imported wines, distilled spirits, tea, and coffee, along with an excise tax on domestic spirits.

The first attempt to pass Hamilton's suggestions in Congress failed. Most representatives accepted the recommendations on increases in the tariff, but bitterly opposed the excise tax on domestic spirits. James Madison of Virginia took the lead in crafting a new bill that only included increases on import duties. Madison's Tariff of 1790 quickly passed both the House and Senate and became law in September 1790.

The bill raised duties on all articles specified in the Tariff of 1789 by 50 percent and placed larger increases on imported wines, distilled spirits, tea, coffee, and spices. The bill also included some protection for American manufacturers of rope and steel. The duty on hemp, the basic raw material for making rope, dropped from sixty to fifty-four cents per hundredweight. The duty on tarred cordage rose from ninety cents to one dollar and fifty cents per hundredweight. Duties on steel increased from fifty-eight to seventy-five cents per hundredweight. Several unenumerated articles charged at 5 percent in the Tariff of 1789 appeared on the enumerated list at anywhere from 7 to 10 percent. Congress also levied higher duties on all manufactured goods.

Hamilton incorporated his recommendations for an excise tax on domestic spirits into a separate bill in 1792. This act placed an excise tax of nine to twenty cents per gallon on domestic distilled spirits. This measure sparked the Whiskey Rebellion in western Pennsylvania.

See also: Hamilton, Alexander; Madison, James. **Vol. II**: *Report on Manufactures*. **Vol. III**: Tariff of 1790.

Selected Bibliography:

Edward Stanwood, *American Tariff Controversies in the Nineteenth Century*, 1967.

Mary Stockwell

TARIFF OF 1792

First tariff bill to incorporate Alexander Hamilton's recommendations on manufacturing.

In his first State of the Union message to Congress in January 1790, President George Washington encouraged the promotion of manufacturing in the United States. He specifically argued that the production of military supplies would render Americans "a free people . . . independent of others." One week after Washington delivered his message, Congress ordered Secretary of the Treasury Alexander Hamilton to recommend a plan to promote American industries. Hamilton responded in December 1791 with his *Report on Manufactures*, in which he included thirty specific recommendations.

Congress examined Hamilton's recommendations during the debate over the Tariff of 1792. Washington had asked Congress to raise more money for the protection of the western frontier. A confederation of Ohio tribes had defeated an American army led by General Arthur St. Clair in November 1791. Washington needed to raise a new army to defeat the tribes and open the Ohio region for settlement. Hamilton reported that Congress must appropriate $525,950 to equip the additional troops. This money could come from three possible sources. The sale of shares in the Bank of the United States could generate funds, the government could borrow the money, or an increase in taxes could provide revenue. Hamilton recommended the final option and asked Congress to increase import duties in the Tariff of 1792.

Although the new tariff began as an emergency revenue measure, it soon became an instrument for incorporating recommendations made in Hamilton's *Report on Manufactures*. In the final bill that became law in May 1792, Congress incorporated twenty-six of Hamilton's original thirty recommendations. Congress also included other important additions, including a tax on imported raw cotton while increasing the rate from fifty-four cents to one dollar per hundredweight. Congress also raised the duty on iron.

See also: Hamilton, Alexander; *Report on Manufactures*. **Vol. III**: Tariff of 1792.

Selected Bibliography:

Edward Stanwood, *American Tariff Controversies in the Nineteenth Century*, 1967.

Mary Stockwell

TARIFF OF 1794

James Madison's attempt to use the tariff for foreign policy purposes.

James Madison acted as the driving force behind the Tariff of 1794. He proposed a general increase in the tariff as commercial retaliation against Great Britain. Madison hoped that higher tariffs would force Great Britain to open its ports to American shipping. The Committee of the Whole debated Madison's recommendations, but never forwarded them to Congress for a vote. The debate did inspire a new drive to increase the tariff to support the public credit. William Smith of South Carolina had objected to Madison's original proposals, but now asked Secretary of the Treasury Alexander Hamilton to make specific recommendations on the matter to Congress.

Hamilton responded by informing the committee that he projected a deficit of $425,633 for the 1794 fiscal year. He also anticipated the need for an additional $650,000 to support the army of General Anthony Wayne in Ohio. Hamilton argued that interruption in commerce with Great Britain would lead to a loss of $1,300,000 in revenue from duties collected at the existing rates. He estimated that the country needed nearly $2,400,000 in extra revenue and recommended that Congress borrow $1 million. He relied on excise taxes on carriages, auctions, manufactured snuff, and sugar to compensate for the balance. Other recommendations included stamp duties levied on retail liquor dealers, a direct tax on land, and an increase in the tariff.

The Committee of the Whole debated Hamilton's recommendations, rejecting the direct tax on land, but approving all the other measures. The House debated the recommendations and eliminated the stamp duty, but approved the new excise taxes, along with the tariff increases. Representatives from Pennsylvania defeated an additional three-cents-per-bushel duty on salt and defended an increase on the duty on coal. The tariff became law in June 1794.

See also: Hamilton, Alexander. **Vol. III**: Tariff of 1794.

Selected Bibliography:

Edward Stanwood, *American Tariff Controversies in the Nineteenth Century*, 1967.

Mary Stockwell

TARIFF OF 1796

Tariff used to raise revenues for the American government.

Between 1794 and 1816, Congress passed twenty-four bills modifying the tariff. With few exceptions, these measures increased duties on imports to raise revenues for the American government. They also made slight modifications in methods of tariff collection and in the time allowed to pay duties. The Tariff of 1795 provides a good example of the typical changes made during this period. Congress simplified the duties on sugar and tea while modifying the method for charging *ad valorem* rates. Under the new tariff act, the point of export, instead of import, determined the rate of duty, ensuring the calculation of the tariff at the point of highest value.

The Tariff of 1796 followed this same pattern. Several congressmen worried about the excessive duties on wines, distilled spirits, and tea. They argued that these tariffs should only remain in effect until the United States retired the debt. In the final tariff bill of 1796, Congress decided to limit the duties on wine, distilled spirits, and tea to only one more year. To speed the process of debt payment, Congress raised duties on sugar, molasses, tea, cocoa, velvet, and muslin during the following year. The trend continued in 1800, when a new tariff bill increased duties on sugar, sugar candy, molasses, wine, and all goods imported at *ad valorem* rates of 10 percent.

Tariffs also increased during this period to pay for military expenses. Congress raised all *ad valorem* rates by 2 percent in 1804 to pay for the war against the Barbary pirates. Similarly, during the War of 1812, Congress doubled all import duties to pay for the war effort. The higher duties were to remain in effect until one year after the conclusion of peace with Great Britain.

See also: Great Britain; Protectionism; War of 1812. **Vol. III**: Tariff of 1796.

Selected Bibliography:

Edward Stanwood, *American Tariff Controversies in the Nineteenth Century*, 1967.

Mary Stockwell

TARIFF OF 1816

First major attempt to use the tariff to protect American industries.

Like previous tariffs, this bill began as a revenue measure originally intended to pay for the War of 1812, but differed in that the act specifically protected America's infant industries. Manufacturing had grown rapidly during the War of 1812. But, at the end of the war, businessmen worried that England would flood America with cheap goods. Francis Lowell, a Massachusetts cotton manufacturer and founder of the Boston Associates, led the fight to keep foreign products out of American markets.

The new tariff set duties of 25 percent on all cotton and woolen textiles and on manufactured iron. Hammered bar iron entered the country with a duty of forty-five cents per hundredweight, with the duty on rolled bar, sheet, hoop, and rod iron set at one dollar and fifty cents per hundredweight. Congress established an *ad valorem* rate of 20 percent on pig iron, 30 percent on paper, leather, and hats, and 15 percent on all other manufacturers' items.

The tariff's most controversial issue involved setting the minimum price for cotton imports. Most cotton cloth imported directly from England cost twenty-five cents per yard, with cheaper cloth available from India. Even with higher tariff rates, Indian cloth cost less to buy than American cloth. Lowell convinced Congress to add a clause to the tariff stating that imported cotton cloth worth less than twenty-five cents per yard would be valued at twenty-five cents per yard and charged duties accordingly.

The new tariff created no sectional rifts. While the greatest support came from middle and western states, even southerners like John C. Calhoun endorsed the measure as the best way to unite the nation. Ironically, the strongest opposition came from Lowell's own state of Massachusetts. Here merchants feared higher tariff rates would damage their commerce.

See also: Cotton; Iron; Protectionism; War of 1812. **Vol. II**: *Report on Manufactures*. **Vol. III**: Tariff of 1816.

Selected Bibliography:

Frank William Taussig, *The Tariff History of the United States*, 1967.

Mary Stockwell

TARIFF OF 1818

First tariff to draw sectional support and opposition.

A downturn in the American economy led congressmen from middle and western states to demand an increase in tariff rates. The end of the Napoleonic Wars in Europe and the War of 1812 in America continued to affect the nation. Overseas markets for American agricultural products dried up as Europe, at peace for the first time in thirty years, raised enough food to feed itself. Farm and land prices plummeted throughout the western states. England continued to dump cheap manufactured goods on American shores. Unable to compete, businesses throughout the northern states declared bankruptcy.

Representatives from New York, New Jersey, Pennsylvania, Ohio, and Kentucky called for increased tariff rates that would create a home market for American farm products and at the same time protect American industries. Farmers asked for tariffs on wool, hemp, wheat, corn, and flax. They also demanded an increase in rates on imported rum and brandy to protect their own home-brew industries. Cotton and iron manufacturers demanded higher rates on all manufactured products.

The Tariff of 1818 extended the rates of 25 percent set for cotton and woolen textiles until 1826, instead of decreasing to 20 percent in 1819 as originally stipulated. More significant increases on iron products included a duty of fifty cents per hundredweight on pig iron, with higher duties on casting, anchors, nails, and spikes.

Support for this tariff fell across sectional lines. Middle and western states voted overwhelmingly for the bill. Southern states opposed the measure, and feared that all future tariffs would favor northern economic interests. The measure divided New Englanders. Most states approved the measure, but Massachusetts continued to oppose protective tariffs. Merchants in Boston especially feared that increased tariff rates would damage their commerce.

See also: War of 1812; Wool and woolens.

Selected Bibliography:

Frank William Taussig, *The Tariff History of the United States*, 1967.

Mary Stockwell

TARIFF OF 1820

First tariff crafted by Henry Clay.

Speaker of the House Henry Clay of Kentucky carefully crafted the Tariff of 1820 to protect northern and western economic interests, a measure required to bring the nation out of its continuing economic slump. Manufactured goods from Britain continued to flood American markets. Domestic textile and iron manufacturers could not compete against these cheap imports. European agriculture continued to recover, leaving western farmers with no overseas markets. Prices for staples like wheat and corn continued to fall, while land prices from Ohio westward plummeted. In Clay's opinion, only a drastic increase in tariff rates could prevent further economic decline.

Clay's bold new proposed tariff raised overall *ad valorem* rates from 12 to 25 percent. Duties on cotton and woolen imports would rise from 25 to 33 percent. Rates on ready-made clothing, hats, bonnets, and caps would go up from 30 to 40 percent. Duties on forged iron bars would increase from seventy-five cents per hundredweight to one dollar and twenty-five cents per hundredweight. Rates on almost all other imports would rise between 20 and 100 percent. The higher taxes would apply to sugar, molasses, coffee, and salt. Related bills would shorten the amount of time allowed to pay duties and would tax the sale of imported goods at public auctions.

The bitter debate on the tariff divided along sectional lines. Congressmen from most northern states supported the measure, while those from southern states unanimously voted against it. Southerners worried that higher tariffs would make imported goods too expensive to buy. More important, they feared Britain would retaliate by banning the import of American cotton. Although the measure passed in the House, it failed in the Senate by one vote. Senator Harrison Gray Otis of Massachusetts cast the deciding vote against the measure, fearing higher tariffs would damage the commercial interests of his state.

See also: Clay, Henry; Cotton; Wool and woolens.

Selected Bibliography:

Frank William Taussig, *The Tariff History of the United States*, 1967.

Mary Stockwell

TARIFF OF 1824

Tariff that put Henry Clay's American System into action.

Despite the failure of the Tariff of 1820, Speaker of the House Henry Clay remained convinced of the necessity of protective tariffs for the development of the national economy. Protective tariffs played an important role in his American System. This plan promoted national legislation to stimulate manufacturing in the North as well as farming and transportation in the west. As both sections prospered, Clay believed the American nation would also prosper.

Clay's proposed tariff increased the rates set in 1818 and incorporated many of the changes first advocated in 1820. The minimum price of imported cotton cloth increased from twenty-five cents to thirty cents per yard, with an average duty of over 50 percent. The duty on imported woolens rose to 30 percent, with a planned increase to 33⅓ percent in 1825. Duties on most iron products jumped from 20 to 25 percent and climbed to nearly 35 percent on window glass, while six separate schedules determined the tax on glass containers. Eleven specific rates, along with an *ad valorem* rate of 40 percent, covered paper products. Congress placed leather, beef, bacon, cheese, wheat, and flour on the dutiable list and increased rates sharply on imported building materials.

Both the Congress and the nation divided over the passage of the new law. Most northerners supported the high protective tariffs, while southerners completely opposed the legislation. Senator Robert Hayne of South Carolina warned that the South would never accept tariffs that only supported northern and western interests. Massachusetts joined the South in opposing the bill. Daniel Webster argued that the tariff may be unconstitutional and would most certainly damage the commercial interests of his state. But Henry Clay argued even more persuasively that the protective tariffs would secure a prosperous future for all Americans. The tariff passed both the House and Senate in close votes and became law in May 1824.

See also: American System; Clay, Henry; Hayne, Robert Y.; Webster,

Daniel. **Vol. II**: Henry Clay's 1832 Speech in Favor of the American System. **Vol. III**: Tariff of 1824.

Selected Bibliography:

Jonathan Pincus, *Pressure Groups and Politics in Antebellum Tariffs*, 1977.

Mary Stockwell

TARIFF OF 1828 (TARIFF OF ABOMINATIONS)

Highly protectionist tariff that eventually led to the Nullification Crisis.

Since the early nineteenth century, the United States had flirted with the idea of protection. High-quality European goods, particularly from Great Britain, entered the U.S. market at lower prices than American goods. This made it difficult for struggling native entrepreneurs to make a profit or stay solvent. A protectionist tariff would place high duties on various imports, giving domestic producers a better chance to compete. Henry Clay endorsed a protectionist tariff to fend off the British and promote his American System.

Many historians label the Tariff of 1816 the first protectionist tariff. Interest in the tariff grew after the Panic of 1819, particularly in the agricultural middle and western states. Merchants in New England disliked the tariff, primarily because their shipping industries relied on many imports for survival. Southerners also disapproved of the tariff, sensing a link between slavery and free trade. Support of the tariff therefore depended more on region than party affiliation during the 1820s.

In this period, a fledgling textile industry developed that included woolen goods. Woolen manufacturers represented the strongest element in the push for a protectionist tariff and asked specifically to have a tariff placed on wool and woolens. Massachusetts congressman Daniel Webster endorsed their cause in the House of Representatives, and by 1827 a bill for a tariff on woolens had emerged.

During the summer of 1827, delegates attended a convention in Harrisburg, Pennsylvania, to discuss the tariff. Organized by manufacturers and others who supported a protectionist tariff, members of the convention argued for duties on wool and agricultural goods. Jacksonian Democrats, who supported the tariff, argued that supporters of President John Quincy Adams had put together the meeting in an attempt to lure protectionists to his side. Jacksonians and Adamsites had been at war since Andrew Jackson lost to Adams in the presidential election of 1824. During the political rematch of 1828, Jackson and his supporters, wrangling for votes, willingly used the tariff in an attempt to make Adams and his followers look bad.

On January 31, 1828, Jacksonians sent a tariff bill to the House of Representatives that was so obnoxious that few, if any, would vote for it. Jackson wanted the measure to fail. The bill focused on goods that New England needed, including molasses and hemp. It also targeted pig iron, which no one had requested protection for. New Englanders would refuse to accept the duties, as high as 50 percent in some cases, while southerners would call the bill a "bitter pill" for northeastern manufacturers and men of commerce.

Jacksonians agreed not to add any amendments to the bill. Once it came to a vote, New Englanders and southerners would vote against it, allowing the measure to fail even though northern Jacksonians voted for it. As a result, no tariff would be passed and the supposedly pro-tariff Adams Whigs would look bad as a result.

The vote proceeded without amendments, as planned in the House. As expected, most southerners voted against the tariff, while congressmen from the middle and western states approved it to appease their constituents. In New England, the vote was twenty-three for the tariff to thirty-nine against it. However, due to the number of New Englanders who approved the tariff, it passed the House and moved on to the Senate. The Democrats, unsurprised, assumed it would pass the House only to wither in the Senate.

In the Senate, the unthinkable happened. Senator Martin Van Buren sponsored an amendment to lower the duty on woolens to 45 percent *ad valorem*. The Senate bandied other amendments, but senators only approved this one amendment. All the others failed by a vote of twenty-two to twenty-four. In this case, Van Buren's support, along with one other senator, passed the amendment by two votes. The amendment suddenly made the tariff bill more acceptable to New England senators.

The vote in the Senate followed along similar lines to the House vote. Almost the entire South voted against the tariff, except both Kentucky senators, including Henry Clay, and one senator each from Tennessee and Louisiana. Again, the middle and western states voted for the bill. New England's senators remained almost equally divided. The difference came when Daniel Webster threw his support in favor, stating the woolens amendment as his reason. The tariff passed the Senate by five votes and President John Quincy Adams signed it into law on May 19, 1828.

The passage of the bill stunned Jacksonians. Their plan to have the tariff bill fail should have worked. Its southern opponents had labeled it a "bill of abominations," and when the tariff became law, the name stuck. The Tariff of Abominations remained the target of southern fury over the next four years while Congress worked to lower the various duties. Eventually, Congress passed the Tariff of 1832, but even that remained too protectionist for men like John C. Calhoun, who led his state of South Carolina in renouncing the tariff and threatening to ignore it after February 1, 1833. What began as political manipulation very nearly ended in secession.

See also: Calhoun, John Caldwell; Clay, Henry; Clay's Compromise; Force Act; Jackson, Andrew; South Carolina *Exposition* and *Protest*; Tariff of 1816; Tariff of 1832; Webster, Daniel. **Vol. II**: Henry Clay's 1832 Speech in Favor of the American System; South Carolina *Exposition*; South Carolina *Protest*; South Carolina Ordinance of Nullification; Proclamation to the People of South Carolina; Andrew Jackson's Message to Congress on the Nullification Crisis; Force Act. **Vol. III**: Tariff of 1816; Tariff of 1824; Tariff of 1832; Tariff of 1833.

Selected Bibliography:

Irving H. Bartlett, *John C. Calhoun: A Biography*, 1993; Merrill D. Peterson, *The Great*

Triumvirate: Webster, Clay, and Calhoun, 1987.

Adrienne Caughfield

TARIFF OF 1832

The legislation that reduced the extremely high levels of the Tariff of 1828.

In essence, the 1832 act returned national tariff policy to that established by the Tariff of 1824, but many southerners still found even this milder form of protectionism objectionable. Indeed, South Carolina responded to the passage of the 1832 act by implementing nullification.

Because the 1828 law caused such rancor in the South, where it was widely reviled as the Tariff of Abominations, Congress attempted to lower rates. After decreasing tariffs on a few items in 1830, legislators produced a more comprehensive revision in the act passed on July 14, 1832. For instance, this tariff did away with the "minimum value" principle first introduced in 1816; no longer would Congress tax cheap woolen and cotton goods at the more expensive rate. Overall, the 1832 law reduced the average tariff on dutiable goods to about 33 percent from the nearly 50 percent average under the 1828 law.

Most regions of the country embraced the 1832 tariff. Even in antitariff South Carolina, three of the state's nine congressmen supported the measure as an amelioration of the 1828 act. But many New Englanders who remained dependent on trade rather than manufacturing opposed the tariff.

The strongest opposition came from South Carolina. Since the mid-1820s, leading Palmetto State politicians declared a protective tariff of any kind unconstitutional. Only a tariff level of approximately 20 percent, enough to generate revenue for the federal government's needs, would pass muster with them. Because the 1832 tariff included protectionist measures, South Carolina governor James Hamilton organized a special state convention in November 1832 that nullified the law and threatened secession. In response, Congress passed the Tariff of 1833, which reduced tariffs further and promised a revenue-only standard in ten years.

See also: Nullification; South Carolina *Exposition* and *Protest*; Tariff of 1816; Tariff of 1824; Tariff of 1833. **Vol. II**: Henry Clay's 1832 Speech in Favor of the American System; South Carolina *Exposition*; South Carolina *Protest*; South Carolina Ordinance of Nullification; Proclamation to the People of South Carolina; Andrew Jackson's Message to Congress on the Nullification Crisis. **Vol. III**: Tariff of 1816; Tariff of 1824; Tariff of 1832; Tariff of 1833 (Compromise Tariff).

Selected Bibliography:

William W. Freehling, *Prelude to Civil War: The Nullification Controversy in South Carolina, 1816–1836,* 1965; Sidney Ratner, *The Tariff in American History,* 1972.

Robert Tinkler

TARIFF OF 1833 (COMPROMISE TARIFF)

Direct consequence of the nullification controversy between South Carolina and President Andrew Jackson.

In the confrontation, the state of South Carolina, led by John C. Calhoun, threatened to nullify the Tariff Act of 1828 and the Tariff Act of 1832, and to secede from the Union if the president tried to enforce the statutes. On December 9, 1832, Jackson responded to the threat by issuing his "Proclamation to the People of South Carolina." He asserted that no state had the right to secede because "secession does not break a league, but destroys the unity of a nation." It ended with a clear statement that "disunion by armed force is *treason*." The president backed up the proclamation with a request to Congress for authority to collect the tariffs. Congress passed the Force Act, called the Bloody Bill in South Carolina, in January 1833, empowering him to override the nullification ordinance.

But while these threatening developments unfolded, congressmen developed compromise measures behind the scenes. Secretary of the Treasury Louis McLane and others persuaded the House Ways and Means Committee on January 8 to report out a bill that asked for immediate and significant tariff reductions and the gradual lowering of the duties by 50 percent by 1834. Although Henry Clay remained reluctant to support any tariff reduction, as an ardent nationalist he feared the consequences of South Carolina, indeed the entire South, going against the Force Act. For these and other motives, not the least of which was the political credit he would receive for settling the crisis, he conferred with John Tyler, John C. Calhoun, John J. Crittenden, and others, and worked out the Compromise Tariff of 1833.

Introduced by Clay in the Senate on February 12, 1833, the tariff measure reduced in two-year intervals over the next decade to a general level of 20 percent by July 1, 1842. Protectionists amended the bill to provide for the valuation of goods at the port of entry. The measure contained some drawbacks, including the provision of *ad valorem* duties only, uneven reductions, and the use of an arbitrary figure of 20 percent. But with Clay's adroit leadership, the bill passed the House on February 26 by a vote of 119 to 85, and the Senate on March 1 by a vote of 29 to 16. Jackson signed the bill into law on March 2, 1833. South Carolina immediately nullified the Force Act, but accepted the Compromise Tariff of 1833 by rescinding the original ordinance nullifying the Tariffs of 1828 and 1832. The crisis had ended.

See also: Calhoun, John Caldwell; Clay, Henry; Clay's Compromise; Force Act; Jackson, Andrew; Tariff of 1828 (Tariff of Abominations); Tariff of 1832. **Vol. II**: Henry Clay's 1832 Speech in Favor of the American System; South Carolina *Exposition*; South Carolina *Protest*; South Carolina Ordinance of Nullification; Proclamation to the People of South Carolina; Andrew Jackson's Message to Congress on the Nullification Crisis; Force Act. **Vol. III**: Tariff of 1828 (Tariff of Abominations); Tariff of 1832; Tariff of 1833 (Compromise Tariff); Tariff of 1842.

Selected Bibliography:

Robert V. Remini, *Henry Clay: Statesman for the Union*, 1991; John G. Van Deusen, *The Economic Bases of Disunion in South Carolina*, 1921; Glyndon G. Van Deusen, *The Jacksonian Era 1828–1848*, 1992.

Robert P. Sutton

TARIFF OF 1841

Act that signaled another bitter fight between President John Tyler and the Whigs.

This act focused on the tariff and the distribution of federal lands among the states. Henry Clay proposed raising the tariff to alleviate the government's growing debt of $11 million and using the sale of public lands to help individual states balance budgets. Tyler agreed with the legislation, but warned that he would not support a tariff that violated the Compromise Tariff of 1833.

The act drafted called for the suspension of distribution wherever tariff duties exceeded 20 percent. The second part of the act called for a 20 percent increase on items either on the free list or taxed less than 20 percent. Clay supported distribution because it would generate revenue and create a vehicle for further taxation, but Tyler proved unwilling to consider distribution as a means of raising money beyond what the treasury needed, which he considered a violation of the Compromise Tariff of 1833. Clay's primary concern revolved around protection, while Tyler saw distribution as a relief measure from the states with protection as a minimal concern.

Tyler agreed to suspend the Compromise in light of the debt problem, but refused to repeal it; he vetoed the provisional bill, stating that it violated both the Compromise and Distribution Acts. Congress then passed a permanent bill calling for the 20 percent increase and distribution. Tyler vetoed the bill again. His actions launched an effort to impeach him, but no resolution passed and Congress eventually offered a bill that excluded the distribution clause.

See also: Calhoun, John Caldwell; Force Act; Jackson, Andrew; Nullification; Tariff of 1828 (Tariff of Abominations); Tariff of 1832; Tyler, John. **Vol. II**: South Carolina Ordinance of Nullification; Proclamation to the People of South Carolina; Andrew Jackson's Message to Congress on the Nullification Crisis; Force Act. **Vol. III**: Tariff of 1828 (Tariff of Abominations); Tariff of 1832; Tariff of 1833 (Compromise Tariff).

Selected Bibliography:

Oliver Perry Chitwood, *John Tyler: Champion of the Old South*, 1939.

Lisa A. Ennis

TARIFF OF 1842

Indirect consequence of the Tariff Act of 1833.

This revenue measure ended the secession controversy over nullification by calling for the reduction of the tariff to a 20 percent level over a period of ten years. Because of declining government revenues during the 1830s and the financial dislocation caused by the Panic of 1837, the national debt by 1842 had reached a colossal figure for the day of $13,500,000, and continued to increase. Politicians of both major parties considered a national deficit an abomination and urged Congress to attack the problem by increasing the tariff to provide the government with much needed revenue. A more pressing financial crisis loomed because, due to the vague wording of the Tariff Act of 1833, congressmen questioned if the federal government had any authority to collect revenue duties after June 30 of that year.

Millard Fillmore of the House Ways and Means Committee introduced a bill to raise the tariff to the level of the Tariff Act of 1832, or 33 percent. But President John Tyler vetoed this so-called Little Tariff because it failed to suspend distribution of federal monies to the states. Under the distribution clause of the Pre-emption Act of 1841, states received 90 percent of the proceeds from the sale of western lands, with funds divided among the states according to population, but when tariff rates exceeded 20 percent, the distribution would cease. In his veto message, John Tyler did agree to the principle of "incidental" protection. Encouraged, the House of Representatives began discussion on what would be the Tariff of 1842. But to the consternation of the Whigs, after the bill passed both houses of Congress by narrow votes, the president immediately vetoed it for the same reasons he had vetoed the Little Tariff: the bill kept the tariff over 20 percent while it continued distribution to the states. In response, John Quincy Adams, chair of a Select Committee of the House, issued a report asking for an amendment to the Constitution to give Congress the power to overturn presidential vetoes by a simple majority vote and hinted at impeaching Tyler. Although the House accepted his report, it had no effect on changing the two-thirds vote to override the president, and the veto stood. Having no alternative, the House then passed another tariff bill without the distribution clause for a sectional vote: The Middle Atlantic and New England representatives sup-

ported the bill while the South and southwest opposed the legislation; those from the midwest divided over the issue, but most representatives supported the bill. Tyler signed it into law on August 30, 1842. The tariff put the rates up to the 1832 level of 33 percent. But the new statute vacated the distribution clause of the Pre-emption Act of 1841.

See also: Nullification; Tariff of 1832; Tariff of 1833; Tyler, John. **Vol. II**: South Carolina Ordinance of Nullification; Proclamation to the People of South Carolina; Andrew Jackson's Message to Congress on the Nullification Crisis; Walker's Report. **Vol. III**: Tariff of 1832; Tariff of 1833 (Compromise Tariff); Tariff of 1842.

Selected Bibliography:

Samuel F. Bemis, *John Quincy Adams and the Union*, 1956; Glyndon G. Van Deusen, *The Jacksonian Era 1828–1848*, 1992; Leonard D. White, *The Jacksonians: A Study in Administrative History 1829–1861*, 1954.

Robert P. Sutton

TARIFF OF 1846 (WALKER'S TARIFF)

Democratic compromise tariff that helped win the 1844 election.

During the election of 1844, the Democratic Party had made a bargain: If the South would support internal improvements, the Northwest would support reduction of the Tariff of 1842, which then stood at 33 percent. The South received their tariff reduction in the form of the Tariff Act of 1846, known as the Walker Tariff after President James K. Polk's secretary of the treasury Robert J. Walker, who issued a controversial report urging the reduction of the duties. The Northwest failed to receive the promised internal improvements. President Polk, when Congress assembled in December 1845, requested a revenue tariff bill with minor protection. He believed that Congress should tax everyday items at a lower rate because he feared an increased surplus of revenue in the treasury. He did want such minor protection equally applied to agriculture, manufacturing, commerce, and labor. On April 14, 1846, the House Ways and Means Committee sent Congress a revenue bill based on the president's request and on the Walker Report. Walker proposed a general *ad valorem* duty of about 25 percent and commodities schedules that included rates on luxuries ranging from 100 percent duties down to some on the free list.

Protracted debate on the tariff ensued. Opponents feared the loss of much needed revenue to underwrite the War with Mexico, then in progress. Others argued that the measure would deprive northern manufacturers of much needed protection from foreign competition, disrupt the business community, and force American workers to compete with cheap European labor. Whigs lined up against the bill, preferring instead to stay with the Tariff Act of 1842. Some northern Democrats, especially from Pennsylvania and New York, opposed it, as well as members of the party from Virginia. Supporters condemned the Tariff Act of 1842 as riddled with favoritism for the rich and powerful. Many duties in the 1842 law discriminated against the poor. Its proponents argued that the Walker Tariff would not hurt American industry and would, instead, produce a salutary effect on the economy.

The Walker Tariff passed the House on July 3 by a margin of 114 to 94, with eleven Democrats from Pennsylvania and four from New York voting against the bill. The South, including two Whigs, voted fifty-six in favor of the measure and only twenty against it, most of the latter from Kentucky and Tennessee. The Senate voted on July 6 and divided evenly; only the vote of Vice President George M. Dallas broke the tie. Even so, the Senate accepted an amendment by Daniel Webster that prevented undervaluation of imports before returning the bill to the House for a final vote. The House accepted the bill with the amendment, and on July 31 President James K. Polk signed it into law.

The Tariff of 1846 failed to have the negative impact on the economy predicted by its opponents. But it proved significant in other respects. It revived the support toward free trade, challenged by the Tariff of 1842, which continued until the Civil War. More significant, the sectional agreement between the South and Northwest that passed the 1846 tariff signaled the high-water mark of the political alliance in the Democratic Party between these two sections. Afterward, it began to crumble.

See also: House Ways and Means Committee; Polk, James K.; Tariff of 1842; Walker, Robert John; Walker's Report; Webster, Daniel. **Vol. II**: Walker's Report. **Vol. III**: Tariff of 1842; Tariff of 1846 (Walker's Tariff).

Selected Bibliography:

Charles G. Sellers Jr., *James K. Polk: Jacksonian, 1795–1843*, 1957; James P. Shenton, *Robert John Walker*, 1961.

Robert P. Sutton

TARIFF OF 1857

Reflected the concern of the Democratic Party with reducing tariffs and using them for revenue but not protection.

Influenced by the Democrats' belief in the proper purpose of taxation, the Tariff Act of 1857 lowered the *ad valorem* rates on the eight schedules set by the Tariff Act of 1846. Duties placed on each class of articles fell and the free list expanded. Most rates dropped by 20 to 25 percent from the 1846 levels; the top rate, charged on liquor and spirits, fell more steeply, from 100 percent *ad valorem* to 30 percent. The act also modified the schedules of 1846 slightly, with most items receiving lower-rated classifications.

Most imports faced lower duties under the Tariff of 1857. The act reduced duties on iron, clothing, and most household goods from 30 to 24 percent. Rates on many other raw materials needed for industry dropped from 20 to 15 percent. Clothing manufacturers, hurt by reductions on imported clothes, welcomed the addition of raw wool valued under twenty cents per pound to the free list. Libraries and scientific societies also benefited from the expanded free list; books, instruments, and other equipment for their use received exemptions from the tariff. Of course, Democrats retained coffee and tea, the two imported items most Americans consumed, on the free list.

Yet the act also reduced duties on luxury imports such as fine food, wine, spirits, and cigars.

The Tariff of 1857 drew wide approval from Democratic circles and ex-Democratic free traders like editor William Cullen Bryant. But later in 1857, economic depression gripped the United States and protectionists blamed the new rates for the Crisis of 1857. The Tariff of 1857 emerged as a heated political issue in parts of the country—particularly Pennsylvania—in the 1860 campaign, helping Republicans capture the presidency.

See also: Bryant, William Cullen; Coffee; Crisis of 1857 (Panic of 1857); Democratic Party; Free trade; Presidential campaigns; Protectionism; Republican Party; Tariff of 1846 (Walker's Tariff); Taxation; Tea; Wool and woolens. **Vol. III**: Tariff of 1846 (Walker's Tariff); Tariff of 1857.

Selected Bibliography:

George Minot and George P. Sanger, eds., *The Statutes at Large and Treaties of the United States of America*, 1859.

Christopher M. Paine

TARIFF OF 1861

See Morrill Tariff (Tariff of 1861).

TARIFF OF 1862

Passed to increase revenue during the Civil War.

On most items, the Tariff Act of 1862 established taxes based on quantity rather than value. The act set higher duties in two ways. Some rates in the Tariff Act of 1861 increased on commodities such as sugar, molasses, tobacco, chocolate, and raw cotton. On other items, the Act of 1862 levied taxes on top of the old rates. Iron, alcoholic beverages, wool, clothing, china, and furs faced new duties in addition to those set by the Tariff of 1861. The law also toughened enforcement. Invoices filed with customs officials acquired the force of oaths; false documentation thus could become perjury. Penalties for inaccurate and false filings increased as well, reflecting the government's wartime need to maximize revenue.

Passage of the Tariff of 1862 would have been impossible without the Civil War. With southern delegations no longer in Congress, Republicans had sufficient majorities to set tariff policy to their liking. Thanks to the tremendous cost of the war and the resulting need for more revenue, protectionist Republicans won allies inside the party for a steep tariff. The Tariff of 1862 also rewarded loyal businessmen who backed the war and the party with the financial incentive of protection. The Tariff of 1862 fit into a larger Republican economic program that Congress passed that year. Republicans hoped to use the new tariff, homestead legislation, and the creation of a transcontinental railroad to develop the American economy through industrialization and settlement of the West. The Tariff of 1862 had a dual purpose. First, it raised revenue to pay for the war. Second, it exemplified the Republican program of using government to assist economic development, helping to transform the United States into a modern, industrial nation.

See also: Civil War (American); Congress (United States); Cotton; Iron; Lincoln, Abraham; Morrill, Justin S.; Morrill Tariff (Tariff of 1861); Protectionism; Republican Party; Sugar; Taxation; Wool and woolens. **Vol. III**: Tariff of 1861 (Morrill Tariff); Tariff of 1862.

Selected Bibliography:

George Minot and George P. Sanger, eds., *The Statutes at Large and Treaties of the United States of America*, 1863.

Christopher M. Paine

TARIFF OF 1864

Passed to increase revenue during the Civil War.

The Tariff Act of 1864 followed the general pattern of the Tariff Act of 1862, using specific duties for most basic imported items and supplementing them with *ad valorem* rates where needed. Rates increased across the board, especially on iron products and wool. The act also broadened the reach of tariffs by removing tea from the free list and eliminating the exemptions for scientific material imported for educational purposes instituted in the Tariff Act of 1857. For goods facing *ad valorem* rates, the Tariff of 1864 added costs of brokerage, shipping, and similar expenses to the value of the goods. By taxing these charges, the government moved to collect the maximum revenue possible. To protect American shipping, the act further assessed an extra 10 percent charge on all goods coming to the United States on foreign-owned vessels. The government also received the benefit of the doubt in questionable cases; collectors would have wide discretion to determine the correct applicable duties.

The Tariff Act of 1864 continued the policy of the Republican Party established in previous Civil War tariff legislation. The necessity of increasing revenue to pay for the war meshed nicely with economic goals. During the war, Republicans frequently used the federal government to transform the nation economically as well as politically. The Tariff of 1864 extended the principle of protection by increasing duties and penalizing merchants who did not use American ships. This additional protection rewarded businessmen who had supported the party and the war. Crass political concerns also shaped the Tariff of 1864. With a presidential campaign looming later in the year, Republicans intended the Act of 1864 to help energize their base and secure votes in swing states such as Pennsylvania and New Jersey.

See also: Civil War (American); Iron; Presidential campaigns; Republican Party; Tariff of 1857; Tariff of 1862; Tea; Wool and woolens. **Vol. III**: Tariff of 1857; Tariff of 1862; Tariff of 1864.

Selected Bibliography:

George Minot and George P. Sanger, eds., *The Statutes at Large and Treaties of the United States of America*, 1866.

Christopher M. Paine

TARIFF OF 1865

Passed to make slight adjustments to the Tariff Act of 1864.

To streamline the collection of *ad valorem* duties, the Tariff Act of 1865 repealed all provisions taxing the costs of shipping, warehousing, and brokering imports. Instead of using this value-added method provided for in the 1864 law, the 1865 act set market value as the standard for determining the cost of imported items. The 1865 law also raised rates on certain imports. Despite the growing need for iron for railroad construction, especially for the transcontinental lines, the Tariff Act of 1865 raised duties on railroad iron by ten cents per hundredweight. Rates on cotton increased from three to five cents per pound. Liquors and spirits also faced stiff additional taxes on top of the already high rates set in 1864.

Although an adjustment to existing rates rather than a general reformulation of tariff policy, the Tariff Act of 1865 illustrates certain concerns of the Republican Party in the last weeks of the Civil War. With much of the Confederacy under federal control, manufacturers could rely on a steady supply of southern cotton. Increasing duties on imported cotton helped protect loyal southern farmers without disrupting production of cotton goods. By increasing rather than lowering rates on railroad iron, Republicans continued to favor American iron makers, even at the expense of railroads. Building a railroad to California and rebuilding lines in the defeated South took a backseat to protectionism. Increased rates on liquor served as a politically easy sin tax on wealthier citizens; rural Republicans could also express their growing distaste for alcohol by taxing it more heavily. The act's provision that colonists pay for legal judgments for defaulted taxes in coin also protected government revenue from a drop in the value of the wartime paper currency.

See also: Civil War (American); Cotton; Morrill Tariff (Tariff of 1861); Protectionism; Republican Party; Tariff of 1862; Taxation. **Vol. II**: John Sherman's 1865 Speech in Favor of Increased Tariffs. **Vol. III**: Tariff of 1861 (Morrill Tariff); Tariff of 1862; Tariff of 1865.

Selected Bibliography:

George Minot and George P. Sanger, eds., *The Statutes at Large and Treaties of the United States of America*, 1866.

Christopher M. Paine

TARIFF OF 1866

Designed to regulate imports of tobacco and alcohol and to provide for the collection of statistics on American trade.

The Tariff Act of 1866 established the Bureau of Statistics inside the Department of the Treasury. The new bureau received the responsibility of collecting information on commerce, navigation, and manufacturing. Using required, regular reports to Congress, the Bureau of Statistics would provide useful information to both government and business. The Tariff Act of 1866 also set additional regulations on alcohol and tobacco, including minimum quantities for importation, higher duties, stricter packaging requirements, and inspection stamps. The new regulations reduced the loss of revenue from tariff evasion. Also, to reduce government expenditure, the law repealed all fishing bounties.

To streamline commerce, the act allowed free transit for goods through certain American ports to Mexico or to Canada. In exchange, American shippers could send their goods from one part of the United States along approved routes through Canada or Mexico to other American destinations without having to face additional taxation. The law also corrected a flaw in the Republican reasoning in the Tariff Act of 1865. Because southern states had failed to produce sufficient cotton following the end of the Civil War, the Tariff of 1866 lowered duties to three cents per pound to maintain a steady supply for northern mills.

The Tariff Act of 1866 reflected the Republican Party's belief that the federal government should assist economic development. The new Bureau of Statistics would provide valuable information to businessmen and allow future government policies based on sound knowledge and rational principles. Instituting duty-free transit through Canada and Mexico, as well as giving the same privilege to goods passing through the United States, allowed businessmen to cut costs and increase profits without significantly diminishing government revenue.

See also: Canada; Congress (United States); Cotton; Exports; Fish; Mexico; Republican Party; Smuggling; Tariff of 1865; Taxation. **Vol. III**: Tariff of 1865; Tariff of 1866.

Selected Bibliography:

George Minot and George P. Sanger, eds., *The Statutes at Large and Treaties of the United States of America*, 1868.

Christopher M. Paine

TARIFF OF 1867

Concerned trade in raw wool and woolen goods.

The Tariff Act of 1867 attempted to classify imported wool by type into three broad categories: clothing wool, combing wool, and carpet wool. To ensure consistency in gradation, the law required all customhouses to maintain samples of each kind. Clothing and combing wool faced a combination of specific and *ad valorem* duties, according to their value, with carpet wool taxed by the pound according to value. The Tariff of 1867 increased the duties on raw wool, helping to protect American farmers. To protect the woolen industry, raw wool already washed or scoured faced double or triple duties.

The Tariff Act of 1867 also increased duties on a variety of finished woolen goods. The law placed high specific duties on most items and attached *ad valorem* rates between 35 and 50 percent. Although manufacturers disliked tariffs on raw wool, they could hardly complain; the act extended generous protection against foreign competition in finished goods. The Republican Party, still in firm control of Congress during 1867, changed tariffs on wool to reflect their philosophy of protectionism. Rates set by previous tariff acts had extended adequate protection to most American industries, but tariffs on wool had remained a sharp point of contention between farmers and manufacturers. The Republican majority reconciled the competing interests of these groups by giving both what they wanted. With the Tariff Act of 1867, protectionist Republicans bid for the votes of businessmen, workers, and farmers, especially those in northern swing states and new western states during the presidential campaign of 1868. Although few voters would respond solely to higher tariffs on wool, the act could do Republicans no harm and possibly much good at the polls. Crass electoral considerations once again merged with Republican protectionist philosophy.

See also: American farmers; Congress (United States); Presidential campaigns; Protectionism; Republican Party; Wool and woolens. **Vol. III**: Tariff of 1867.

Selected Bibliography:

George Minot and George P. Sanger, eds., *The Statutes at Large and Treaties of the United States of America*, 1868.

Christopher M. Paine

TARIFF OF 1870

Moderate bill passed largely as a compromise between protectionists and tariff reformers, both within the Republican Party.

David A. Wells, chair of the National Revenue Commission and a former protectionist, reported that tariffs hindered U.S. exports. Although the continual growth in exports seemed to falsify his claim, many newly elected Republicans responded to his call for tariff reform. An attempt to pass a tariff bill similar to the one that failed in 1867 died after its postponement in 1868. When Republicans gained control of both houses of Congress and the presidency in 1869, conservative Republicans saw an opportunity to strengthen the protective tariff. But many Republicans no longer supported protectionism, particularly those individuals from the West who did not benefit from protective tariffs as much as those in the industrial East. Instead, they believed that tariffs did not need to be raised or abolished.

Congress addressed the tariff issue again during the second session of the Forty-first Congress in 1870. On February 1, Robert Schenck, chairman of the House Ways and Means Committee, proposed a bill that affected a smaller number of classes of merchandise than prewar tariffs. This proposed bill reduced the duties on many table items and certain raw materials. Specifically, the act reduced tariff rates for tea from twenty-five cents to fifteen cents per pound, coffee from five cents to three cents per pound, low-grade sugar from three cents to .0175 cents per pound, and pig iron from nine dollars to seven dollars per ton. Additionally, it added 137 items to the free list, including ivory, Indian rubber, non-manufactured lumber, and rags for making paper. Although revenue reformers did not think the moderate reduction in rates went far enough, most of them voted for the bill. Because debate over the tariff bill slowed its progress, Schenck attached every part of the tariff bill to the internal revenue legislation under consideration. By doing so, he assured passage in the House on June 6 with a vote of 153 to 55. On July 5, the Senate passed the bill with forty-three ayes and only six nays. The president signed it into law on July 14.

The Tariff of 1870 did not produce the result that revenue reformers or protectionists expected. High duties on cotton, wool, and silk did not slow the growth of imports to the United States. In fact, imports increased, even for those items whose protective rates remained high. Consequently, government revenue increased. This in turn made the demand for tariff reduction and the decrease of the government surplus all the more urgent.

See also: Cotton; House Ways and Means Committee; Tariff of 1867; Tariff of 1872; Wells, David Ames; Wool and woolens.

Selected Bibliography:

Edward Stanwood, *American Tariff Controversies in the Nineteenth Century*, 1967.

Matt McCook

TARIFF OF 1872

Bill that lowered average tariff rates 10 percent in response to a perceived public demand for immediate tariff reform.

Faced with attacks from major Republican newspapers denouncing protectionism and a growing liberal Republican movement unhappy with President Ulysses S. Grant's Reconstruction policies, financially conservative Republicans feared the collapse of America's protective tariff system. Therefore, many of them agreed to reduce tariffs moderately to make the principle of protective tariffs more palatable. Even the staunch protectionist James G. Blaine responded to the threat by appointing men favorable to reduction to the House Ways and Means Committee.

Protectionists objected to the proposed bill, but realized the need to appease reformers. The Senate dealt with other issues while the House debated and passed a second heavily amended bill abrogating the duty on tea and coffee. The Senate passed the bill, with extensive changes in the rates of duties on a variety of articles. Seeing that the new bill represented an altogether different measure, the House struck down the Senate bill, claiming that the Constitution required all bills involving revenue to originate in the House, and started over. After considerable debate over the constitutionality of Senate revenue initiatives, the final version of the bill passed the House 149 to 61 on May 20. Dissenters included both extreme protectionists and free traders who refused to budge. The Senate accepted the bill eleven days later with a vote of forty-nine to three. The tariff bill became law on June 6, 1872.

Although the Tariff Act of 1872 only moderately reduced duties, the United States lost over $29 million in annual revenue and talk of tariff overthrow seemed to quiet. Democrats used the tariff issue in an attempt to regain power just as liberal Republicans used it to replace those in control of their party. Opposing the reelection of Grant in 1872, liberal Republicans supported Horace Greeley, a journalist known for defending protectionism. After the Panic of 1873, the tariff reform issue took a backseat to other issues. Protectionism stayed strong for another eight years, signaling the failure of the liberal Republican movement.

See also: Blaine, James Gillespie; Greeley, Horace; House Ways and Means Committee; Tariff of 1870. **Vol. III**: Tariff of 1872.

Selected Bibliography:

Edward Stanwood, *American Tariff Controversies in the Nineteenth Century*, 1967.

Matt McCook

TARIFF OF 1883 (MONGREL TARIFF)

An unsuccessful attempt by the Republican administration of Chester A. Arthur to seize the issue of customs reform for their party and make moderate changes before losing control of Congress to the Democratic Party.

Spurred by a presidential address that pointed out the almost embarrassing treasury surplus, a commission was formed to study the existing tariff and recommend reforms. Although hard-line protectionists like John L. Hayes dominated the commission, the resulting report advised an average 20 to 25 percent cut in the tariff and a greatly enlarged free list, as well as changes in customs administration that closely mirrored recently passed reforms to the civil service.

The House Ways and Means Committee, controlled by protectionists, revised the report upward, as did the Senate Finance Committee. The Finance Committee's bill passed easily in the Senate, and, subsequently, the Senate agreed to conference it with the Ways and Means Committee to find a compromise acceptable to both houses. The revision passed the Joint Committee by a close vote of 32 to 31, and then passed the House in a 152 to 116 vote on March 3, the last full day of the congressional session. The result of the intended reform proved slight—from the 20 to 25 percent reduction advocated at the beginning, the final bill encompassed only a 1.47 percent reduction in the tariff rate and quickly acquired the name Mongrel Tariff for its motley mix of compromises that ultimately pleased no lobby group and had little effect on the economy. The Tariff of 1883, however, did cause a flurry of political maneuvering in the newspapers and magazines, beginning one of the great mass media campaigns of modern American politics.

See also: Cleveland, Stephen Grover; House Ways and Means Committee; Senate Finance Committee. **Vol. II**: Grover Cleveland's 1887 State of the Union Address. **Vol. III**: Tariff of 1883 (Mongrel Tariff).

Selected Bibliography:

Thomas C. Reeves, *Gentleman Boss: The Life of Chester Alan Arthur*, 1975; Edward Stanwood, *American Tariff Controversies in the Nineteenth Century*, 1903.

Margaret Sankey

TARIFF OF 1890

See McKinley Tariff (Tariff of 1890).

TARIFF OF 1891

Attempt by Democrats to lower the tariff one item at a time.

In an 1890 speech to Congress, President Benjamin Harrison sang the praises of the Tariff of 1890. Congress placed more goods than ever on the free list. Harrison went on to say that no evidence existed proving the taxes created a hardship on anyone or retarded commerce in any way. The Democratic majority took Harrison's speech as an invitation to pursue more legislation and entered a vigorous tariff campaign.

Democrats planned to divide the proposed tariff into separate pieces of legislation and pass each bill individually. An important aspect of the Democratic strategy involved an effort to inform the public about the positive aspects of the bills. William M. Springer, the best-known advocate of tariff reductions, proposed the items individually, causing his Republican opponents, who called his small bills pop-guns, to never take him seriously.

Democrats shrewdly chose items that appealed to specific geographical regions or particular groups. For instance, to appeal to the southern states, one bill proposed making cotton-packaging goods such as bagging, the machines to make bagging, ties, and cotton gins duty free. Other items, each with their own pop-gun bill, included putting wool on the free list and lowering the duty on wool products, added binding twine to the free list, and abolishing the duties on tin plates and lead ores.

The House referred the twelve little bills to the Senate's Committee on Finance. This committee reported back on each in a lengthy report detailing all the reasons that none of the twelve should be law. The battle would continue on, and would influence the outcome of the 1892 presidential election.

See also: McKinley Tariff (Tariff of 1890); Senate Finance Committee; Springer, William McKendree. **Vol. III**: Tariff of 1890 (McKinley Tariff).

Selected Bibliography:

Edward Stanwood, *American Tariff Controversies in the Nineteenth Century*, 1967.

Lisa A. Ennis

TARIFF OF 1894

See Wilson-Gorman Tariff (Tariff of 1894).

TARIFF OF 1895

Proposed tariff legislation that reduced duties on wool but retained rates above the 1890 level.

President Grover Cleveland sent a message to Congress on December 20, 1895, concerning a large withdrawal of gold from the national treasury. Cleveland warned of the seriousness of the withdrawal and recommended immediate action, adding that Congress should not recess until it had dealt with the issue. Cleveland did not offer any ideas or guidelines indicating what form of relief he had in mind. The Republican Congress developed a temporary revision of the tariff calling for more revenue.

To cope with the immediacy of the issue, Speaker Thomas B. Reed appointed Nelson Dingley as chairman of the Committee on Ways and Means. Dingley's committee reported back on December 26. The proposed bill increased the duty on wool, but included a proviso that kept the duties below the Act of 1890. Because of the emergency situation, the House reported on the bill and voted on that same day, passing the measure by a vote of 228 to 83. But when the bill reached the Senate's Committee on Finance, a delay ensued. The Senate preferred free silver instead of an increase in revenue generated by a tariff. They then offered a revised bill for consideration.

See also: Dingley, Nelson, Jr.; Dingley Tariff (Tariff of 1897); House Ways and Means Committee; Populists.

Selected Bibliography:

Edward Stanwood, *American Tariff Controversies in the Nineteenth Century*, 1967.

Lisa A. Ennis

TARIFF OF 1896

Failed tariff legislation involving the issuance of free silver.

The Senate's Committee on Finance offered a revision to the Tariff Act of 1895 calling for free silver coinage as a source of revenue instead of increased tariffs. The committee's chairman, Senator Justin S. Morrill, who had repeatedly opposed free silver, wrote the report on the substitution. The Senate never seriously pursued the bill. Opponents defeated several motions to bring the bill up for a resolution.

Further, the Senate realized that the president would veto any free silver bill. Colorado senator Henry Teller, leader of the free silver Republicans, openly criticized the Senate, stating that senators never had any intention of dealing with the free silver issue. The bill remained tabled for the duration of the Fifty-fourth Congress and free silver continued to evoke heated discussions and became a major issue in the following presidential campaign.

See also: Morrill, Justin S.; Senate Finance Committee.

Selected Bibliography:

Edward Stanwood, *American Tariff Controversies in the Nineteenth Century*, 1967.

Lisa A. Ennis

TARIFF OF 1897

See Dingley Tariff (Tariff of 1897).

TARIFF OF 1909

See Payne-Aldrich Tariff (Tariff of 1909).

TARIFF OF 1913

See Underwood-Simmons Tariff (Tariff of 1913).

TARIFF OF 1922

See Fordney-McCumber Tariff (Tariff of 1922).

TARIFF OF 1930

See Hawley-Smoot Tariff (Tariff of 1930).

TARIFF REFORM

Efforts to reduce the tariff rates.

During the Civil War, tariff schedules increased to record high levels, partly to produce revenues for the insatiable military machine. American industry had profited from this protection and hesitated to relinquish the sheltering benefits in peacetime. The high duties continued to increase the amount of revenue collected at the customhouses, and by 1881 the Treasury reported an annual surplus amounting to an embarrassing $145 million. Most of the government's income, in those pre–income tax days, derived from the tariff.

Congress could reduce the vexatious surplus in two ways. One option called for spending the surplus on pensions and "pork-barrel" bills and thus currying favor with veterans and other self-seeking groups. The other alternative meant lowering the tariff, something big industrialists vehemently opposed. In 1871, Congress attempted to address the demands of tariff reformers after the publication of

a report written by David A. Wells, special commissioner for the revenue, that generated support for a downward revision. The following year, Congress authorized a reduction in some of the rates, but generally duties remained high.

The next attempt at reform occurred during the administration of Grover Cleveland. Rejecting the advice of Democratic politicians who warned him of the inherent risks, Cleveland decided to challenge protectionism. "What is the use," he insisted, "of being elected or reelected unless you stand for something?" With characteristic bluntness, Cleveland devoted his annual State of the Union address to the subject of the tariff. Traditionally, the annual message of the president had always provided a review of the events of the previous year. Cleveland broke that tradition, generating an electric response within Congress. Democrats appeared deeply depressed by the obstinacy of their chief, while Republicans rejoiced at his apparent recklessness. The old warrior James G. Blaine gloated, "There is one more President for us in [tariff] protection." For the first time in years, a real issue divided the two parties and would dominate the upcoming presidential election of 1888. Although Cleveland lost the election to Benjamin Harrison, he won his reelection bid in 1892.

After the turn of the century, tariff reformers focused on the development of a tariff commission that could scientifically analyze the cost of production of both domestic and foreign goods to ensure a fair and equitable tariff. Reaching a peak during the administration of William Howard Taft, the reform movement lost momentum after the passage of the Sixteenth Amendment, which allowed the collection of personal income taxes, and the Fordney-McCumber Tariff, which lowered duty rates substantially. Although rates increased in the interwar period, after World War II the general shift toward free trade has resulted in the development of protectionist groups instead of tariff reformers.

See also: Cleveland, Stephen Grover; Insurgents; Taft, William Howard; Tariff Reform Movement; Wells, David Ames.

Selected Bibliography:

Edward Stanwood, *American Tariff Controversies in the Nineteenth Century*, 1967.

Albert Atkins and
Cynthia Clark Northrup

TARIFF REFORM MOVEMENT

Agitation for the reduction of tariff rates from 1868 to 1872.

As the nation recovered from the Civil War, tariff rates remained high. A commission, appointed to evaluate the financial situation, analyzed the tariff schedules. In 1869, the head of the commission, David A. Wells, issued his annual report. He concluded that the high rates harmed both manufacturers and consumers and called for the lowering of the duties. Democrats, anxious to embrace an issue that would shift attention away from the difficulties incurred by the Civil War, seized the opportunity. Arguing that the tariff had generated a surplus and demanding a reduction, they placed the Republicans in a difficult position. At the

same time, charges of corruption permeated the administration of Ulysses S. Grant and Democrats managed to establish a connection between corruption and the tariff.

By 1871, Congress began addressing the issue, partly to prevent the Democrats from capitalizing on the issue during the upcoming presidential election. The House of Representatives passed a measure that reduced taxes on items such as coffee, tea, and coal, but when the bill reached the Senate, the Senate Finance Committee completely altered it. After a constitutional debate over the power of the Senate to generate revenue measures, Congress finally passed the Tariff Act of 1872, which moderately reduced the rates. Although imports continued to increase, tariff revenues declined by $28 million for the year. The reduction of the surplus, along with the Democratic nomination of Horace Greeley, a staunch protectionist, ensured the reelection of Grant in 1872.

See also: Greeley, Horace; Tariff of 1872; Wells, David Ames.

Selected Bibliography:

Edward Stanwood, *American Tariff Controversies in the Nineteenth Century*, 1967.

Cynthia Clark Northrup

TAXATION

America moves from the tariff to the income tax.

Before the American Revolution, most colonists acknowledged England's right to control trade through external taxes, but they denied any power on the part of Parliament to levy internal taxes. They believed that this power resided solely in the colonial assemblies. The matter became a divisive one after the French and Indian War. Great Britain accumulated enormous debts prosecuting the war. Parliament levied heavy taxes on the citizens of Great Britain to pay for the war debt. The American colonists paid higher taxes primarily to support the many redcoats newly deployed along the western frontier. In 1765, Parliament laid the Stamp Act on the thirteen American colonies. The law required a tax on nearly every paper transaction, including wills, contracts, deeds, newspapers, and even playing cards.

Riots broke out throughout the colonies as Britain attempted to collect the stamp tax. Colonial leaders like James Otis of Massachusetts argued for maintaining the sharp distinction between internal and external taxes. He also gave the battle cry for the American Revolution with his famous demand for no taxation without representation. Although Parliament repealed the Stamp Act, Britain continued to uphold its right to lay both internal and external taxes on the colonies. Americans countered that only the duly elected representatives of the people could lay taxes on them. This tradition became a founding principle of the United States of America.

After the revolution ended, the question of taxation again came to the forefront. The nation and the individual states remained deeply in debt from the war. Some states like Massachusetts raised property taxes to pay off the debt. Many people could not pay the higher taxes, and some even joined

Daniel Shays in his attack on state courts responsible for foreclosing on farmers for back taxes. The national government set up under the Articles of Confederation proved unable to respond to the crisis because Congress lacked the power to tax. The desperate situation led to the adoption of the Constitution that finally gave the national government the ability to tax.

The first Congress used the tariff to raise money for government operations. The Tariff of 1789 laid a 5 percent duty on all foreign products entering the nation, along with slightly higher rates on items such as hemp and glass. Alexander Hamilton proposed more taxes when he became the first secretary of the treasury. His plan for funding and assumption to pay off the nation's debts required higher tariffs as well as an excise tax on domestic whiskey. Most of Hamilton's plans won the support of Congress, but the new excise tax led to the Whiskey Rebellion in western Pennsylvania in the summer of 1794.

The tariff remained the most important tax for revenue in the United States throughout the nineteenth century. During the antebellum period, the use of the tariff as a protection for American industry and for revenue became an issue as divisive as internal taxation before the American Revolution. Many tariffs protected northern and western interests at the expense of southern ones. The battle over the tariff led to the development of the theory of nullification that in turn helped to bring about the Civil War. During the conflict, both the North and South used new methods of taxation. The Union turned to the income tax in August

1861, laying a tax of 3 percent on all yearly incomes of $800 or more. Later, the rate increased to 10 percent on all yearly incomes of $10,000 or more. Without the financial resources of the North, the South used a tax in kind. Southerners turned over 10 percent of their farm goods, including cotton, to the Confederate cause.

After the Civil War, many Americans believed that the income tax provided the best way to fund government operations. The Supreme Court disagreed, and, in 1894, struck down the income tax as unconstitutional. The Court ruled that the Constitution restricted congressional taxes to those levied according to population and those strictly apportioned among the states. Reformers continued to demand a graduated income tax on both individuals and corporations as the only fair system of taxation for modern America. In 1913, Congress won the power to levy an income tax through the Sixteenth Amendment. As the income tax increased in revenue, the government no longer needed the tariff to fund federal operations. Tariffs have continued to fall in favor of free trade as revenue from income taxes continues to rise.

See also: American Revolution; Civil War (American); Great Britain; Hamilton, Alexander; North American Free Trade Agreement (NAFTA); Personal income tax (Sixteenth Constitutioinal Amendment).

Selected Bibliography:

W. Elliott Brownlee, *Federal Taxation in America: A Short History*, 1996.

Mary Stockwell

TAYLOR, ZACHARY (November 24, 1784–July 9, 1850)

Hero of the Mexican War, twelfth president of the United States, and tenuous advocate of protective tariffs.

Born to an elite Virginia family, Taylor proved successful in plantation agriculture and as a military leader. Throughout his life, he effectively managed his private finances without relying on relief laws or inflated currency. In 1807, Taylor joined the army and participated in Black Hawk's War and the Seminole War. During the Mexican War, he defeated an enemy outnumbering his force by a margin of three to one in a series of engagements in Texas and northern Mexico. His efforts, though tactically amateurish, garnered him national recognition and thrust him into politics.

Despite a lack of experience, Taylor emerged as a national candidate for the Whigs in 1848. He appealed to "Cotton Whigs," northern industrialists needing southern cotton, who favored tariff protection. Southern Whigs and even some Democrats supported Taylor for his pro-slavery stance. Finally, antislavery leaders found his opposition to the expansion of slavery attractive.

Taylor, who had never voted prior to his election, brought a caretaker's approach to the presidency. He promised to allow Congress to determine domestic policy and only veto measures clearly unconstitutional. As a result, Taylor interfered little with the Democrat-dominated Congress that favored a continuation of James K. Polk's policies of lowered tariffs. During his sixteen months in office, Taylor dedicated his efforts to saving the Union through the Compromise of 1850. Taylor died from gastroenteritis prior to the passage of the compromise.

See also: Polk, James K.; Whig Party.

Selected Bibliography:

Elbert B. Smith, *The Presidencies of Zachary Taylor and Millard Fillmore*, 1988.

Dallas Cothrum

TEA

A commodity whose taxation played an important role in the American Revolution.

As the thirteen American colonies grew and developed in the eighteenth century, tea consumption increased as the social ritual of tea drinking crossed class boundaries. In 1766, England's king, George III, allowed William Pitt to form a government that faced intense parliamentary opposition. Charles Townshend emerged as the speaker for Pitt's ministry in the House of Commons and he oversaw the passage of the 1767 Townshend Revenue Act that imposed duties on selected colonial imports. One of these duties fell on tea. Townshend wanted to use the income from these tariffs to pay colonial judges and governors, and not just for the general revenue. This act renewed the controversy first initiated by the Stamp Act as the colonists rejuvenated their policy of non-importation and refined their arguments concerning internal versus external taxes and "no taxation without representation." After the Boston Massacre occurred, England's new minister, Lord North, decided on a path of modification over enforcement or repeal. Because the tariff on tea provided three-quarters of the revenue raised by the act, Parliament repealed all the duties except for the one on tea. This allowed the crisis to dissipate. The problem concerning tea reemerged in 1773 when Parliament passed the Tea Act in an attempt by Lord North to save the East India Company. This act made tea cheaper in the colonies because it repealed tariffs on tea in Great Britain, yet it gave the East India Company a monopoly over the colony tea trade. In Boston, the landing of tea instigated the 1773 Boston Tea Party in which colonists threw 342 chests of tea into the harbor. Britain responded by passing the 1774 Coercive (Intolerable) Acts that pushed the colonies toward independence.

See also: American Revolution; Colonial administration; East India Company; Great Britain; Navigation and Trade Acts.

Selected Bibliography:

Benjamin Woods Labaree, *The Boston Tea Party*, 1968.

Ty M. Reese

TECHNOLOGY

Recent arguments call for a tariff on technology.

Throughout U.S. history, advances in technology have impacted the economic policy and development of the country. But, on many occasions, other countries, such as Great Britain, already owned the technology. The designs of the spinning jennies and looms of the Lowell textile factories originated in England. A distinct shift in this pattern occurred in the post–World War II period. The need for increased military technology during the war and even afterward, as the United States entered the Cold War and the space age, propelled advances in technologies. With most of the other industrial countries of the world recovering from financial ruin, the United States held a temporary monopoly on the new technology. Technology transfers occurred that ultimately reduced the revenue of the government as multinational companies controlled this commodity. Under the tax laws of the United States, these companies deduct the amount of taxes charged by foreign countries for profits earned overseas. The loss of income caused by the tax credit has generated a call for the use of a tariff to compensate for the difference. Although the government has not implemented such a tariff, the continued development of technology could ultimately lead to some form of taxation to prevent excessive foreign investment.

See also: Taxation.

Selected Bibliography:

Robert D. Tollison and Thomas D. Willett, "Foreign Investment and the Multinational Corporation," *Tariffs, Quotas, and Trade: The Politics of Protectionism*, 1979.

Cynthia Clark Northrup

TEXTILES

When Samuel Slater established his spinning mill in Pawtucket, Rhode Island, in 1790, he began the American textile industry.

Without British competition, during the War of 1812, American textiles grew rapidly from 80,000 spindles in 1811 to 500,000 in 1815. The amount of cotton needed to meet the requirements of the industry grew from 500 bales in 1800, to 10,000 in 1810, and 90,000 in 1815. This demand remained limited to industrial-scale yarn spinning. Weaving, still a home industry in 1810, occurred predominantly in Georgia, a state that produced more cotton cloth than Rhode Island, and North and South Carolina, the states with the largest number of looms. Virginia, South Carolina, and Georgia produced more homespun goods than the other states and territories combined. Not until 1814 did Francis C. Lowell of Waltham, Massachusetts, open a mill that used the power loom. Factory manufacturing of cloth took some years after that to overtake home weaving. As American textiles industrialized, English textiles, made from American cotton and sometimes shipped by New England merchants, dominated American markets. The nascent New England textile industry needed protection from the more developed English industry. Beginning in 1816, protective tariffs split the industrial Northeast from the agricultural regions, especially the South, and New England merchants and shippers. The 1816 act raised tariffs an average of 42 percent over prewar levels to pay war debts and protect fledgling industries. Cotton textile rates included a 25 percent *ad valorem* assessment on higher grades of cloth and a minimum valuation on cheaper grades. All goods cheaper than twenty-five cents per yard received a minimum assessment of 6.25 cents. British manufacturing had advanced so much that the price of a yard of coarse cotton cloth dropped from roughly thirty cents in 1815 to under ten cents in 1830. The

Tariff of 1816 effectively kept out all lower grade textiles, which was the quality that American mills produced. Over the next thirty years, especially after 1828 and the Tariff of Abominations, protection remained a driving force in good and bad economic times. Even Henry Clay's compromise measure of 1833, with its 20 percent reductions in the overall *ad valorem* rate by 1842, proved too complex, cumbersome, and ineffective. By 1842, the shortage of money created by the Panic of 1837 forced Congress to reduce the tariff rates back to 1832 levels. Finally, in 1846, the Walker Tariff lowered rates to a level unseen since 1816. The downward trend continued until the Republicans revived protection in the late 1850s. The Panic of 1857 helped fuel protectionist sentiment by farmers in the Midwest and workers in the East. By then the textile industry had developed to a competitive stage.

The Civil War created a cotton shortage in both New England and England. Some mills modernized, and some developed techniques for using lesser grades and waste. Some shut down. Between 1868 and 1870, New England capacity rose 12 percent, but the American textile industry moved south in search of cheaper labor. Manufacturers enjoyed a lighter tax and legislative burden—and bigger profit. At the same time, the transcontinental railroad linked the West and East coasts, and the new immigration began. Internal demand began utilizing much of the cotton crop. Still, Republicans controlled the government most of the time between the Civil War and the Great Depression. Protection continued almost uninterrupted until the Underwood-Simmons Tariff Act under the Democrat Woodrow Wilson. The Republican victory in 1921 produced the Fordney-McCumber Tariff that returned textile tariffs to pre-Underwood levels. With Franklin Roosevelt, American policy shifted from tariffs to nation-to-nation negotiations. The United States began setting import quotas, claiming that imports either threatened national security or, under the agricultural adjustment acts of 1937, 1948, and 1949, proved harmful to American farmers. In 1948, the government easily shut off all imports of raw cotton. In 1956 and 1957, America got Japan to limit its exports of textiles. The 1961 and 1962 Agreements on Cotton Textiles formalized the arrangement for the world's textile producers. The cotton textile agreements produced initial dislocation that required 115 unilateral quotas in the first year. The industry stabilized as more countries became signatories, and imports only doubled in the 1960s while exempt synthetics grew 1,700 percent. The 1974 Multifiber Textile Arrangement and the Textile Surveillance Body tried to stabilize growth of synthetics, but America had 650 separate quotas by 1985. In the 1960s and 1970s, Japan accepted more American textiles. In 1975, the United States imported $233.3 million worth of textiles; in 1985, $892 million. Cheap labor and newer equipment elsewhere meant the only option available remained to specialize in high-quality textiles until the competition matched American quality.

See also: Cotton; Fordney-McCumber Tariff (Tariff of 1922); Lowell, Francis Cabot; Nullification; Tariff of 1816; Underwood-Simmons Tariff (Tariff of 1913); War of 1812.

Selected Bibliography:

John M. Dobson, *Two Centuries of Tariffs*, 1976; Judith Goldstein, *Ideas, Interests, and American Trade Policy*, 1993; Nancy Kane, *Textiles in Transition*, 1972; Sidney Ratner, *The Tariff in American History*, 1972.

John Herschel Barnhill

THIRD WORLD

First coined by Georges Balandier in his 1957 book, *Tiers Monde*, in reference to the conference of Asian and African nations at Bandoeng, the concept of a "Third World" of nations increasingly came to represent those poorer or underdeveloped countries of the world, including Latin America.

Against the backdrop of the Cold War, the initial designation of Third World signified political and economic distinctions between a capitalist First World, a communist Second World, and a nonaligned, underdeveloped remainder. In general, the Third World contrasts with the capitalist, industrialized West because of a significantly lower standard of living, low wages, poor working conditions, nutritional inadequacies, endemic public health crises, high illiteracy rates, and rampant corruption.

During the period from the 1950s through the 1980s, the Cold War between Western capitalism and the United States and an Eastern Communist Bloc led by the U.S.S.R. turned hot, most commonly in the Third World. In Korea, Vietnam, Cuba, Angola, Afghanistan, Central America, and the Middle East, East and West tested each other's resolve with increasingly sophisticated conventional weaponry that was either loaned, sold, or used by the United States and the U.S.S.R. to curry favor and test the "balance of power" in a global chess match played out under the shadow of nuclear war.

During the last quarter of the twentieth century, and particularly after the collapse of the Soviet bloc in 1989, the Third World received increasing attention of a different sort. Overpopulation, deforestation, the spread of AIDS, industrial growth and its environmental consequences, enormous foreign debt burdens, regional conflicts driven by ethnic and religious differences, and the threatened proliferation of nuclear weapons have refocused the attention of both East and West. While competition for favor continues, international conferences on the environment, population growth, women's rights, health, and the end of trade barriers have dominated discussions and differences between a developed First World and developing Third World.

See also: Cold War; North–South Conflict.

Selected Bibliography:

Andre Gunder Frank, *Capitalism and Underdevelopment in Latin America: Historical Studies of Chile and Brazil*, 1967; David S. Landes, *The Wealth and Poverty of Nations: Why Some Are So Rich and Some So Poor*, 1998.

David J. Weiland III

THURMAN, ALLEN GRANBERRY (November 13, 1813–December 12, 1895)

U.S. representative and senator who ended his political career as Grover Cleveland's vice-presidential running mate in 1888.

Born in Lynchburg, Virginia, Thurman moved with his family to Chillicothe, Ohio, in 1815. He ran as a Van Buren Democrat from Ohio in 1844 and entered the Twenty-ninth Congress as the youngest representative. Thurman voted with his party on land and expansion issues and worked to lower the protective tariff. After serving one term, he declined to run in 1846 and did not reenter national politics until elected as a U.S. senator from Ohio in 1868, and reelected in 1874. A loyal Democrat, Thurman received the honor of serving as the president pro tempore of the Senate in the Forty-sixth Congress.

While in Congress, he earned a varied reputation on fiscal policy; in the antebellum period he championed hard money and opposed national banks; and in the 1870s he opposed expansion of the Civil War–issued greenback. A strongly loyal Democrat, he consistently supported his party's attack on protective tariffs, gaining special recognition for marshaling legal arguments against taxes on imports and exports. He died in Columbus, Ohio, with his interment in Green Lawn Cemetery.

See also: Cleveland, Stephen Grover.

Selected Bibliography:

John S. Hare, *Allen G. Thurman: A Political Study*, 1933.

Glynn Ingram

TIN ORE

A strategic mineral important to the waging of World War I and World War II.

Tin ore remains an important mineral at the beginning of the twenty-first century. Indium tin oxide, when co-deposited with magnesium fluoride, provides a protective coating for solar arrays of spacecraft in geosynchronous orbit that does not impair solar cell performance. The use of tin oxide film potentially allows the development of gas sensors used to detect hydrocarbons (CxHy) and nitrogen oxides (Nox) at a variety of temperatures.

Although tin ore deposits exist in Alaska and the kingdom of Saudi Arabia, since the 1500s, Bolivia has played an important role in the production of the strategic mineral of tin ore, becoming the nation most dependent on it for the maintenance of its domestic economy and its position in international trade. Like many political jurisdictions that depend on mineral extraction, Bolivia has exhibited a lack of economic diversification that has resulted in negative externalities. Consequently, fluctuations in world demand for tin ore have wreaked havoc with its economy. During World War I and II, Bolivia prospered, based on its tin exports, only to be pauperized following the conclusion of both wars. Bolivia has always maintained low tariff barriers to maximize its tin exports and has not seen the need to develop a manufacturing sector or to grow much of its own food. The lack of diversification in the Bolivian economy has occurred because tin elites, as well as members of the traditional agricultural elite, have not welcomed the sharing of power that a diversified economy, concomitant with a diversified interest group structure, would entail.

See also: Bolivia; World War I; World War II.

Selected Bibliography:

Ricardo Godoy, *Mining and Agriculture in Highland Bolivia: Ecology, History, and Commerce Among the Jukumanis*, 1990.

Henry B. Sirgo

TOBACCO

One of the first major exports of English America, and one of the most taxed.

In 1617, the first significant shipment of tobacco arrived in England from Virginia. Tobacco exports boomed and tobacco cultivation spread to Maryland, North Carolina, and, for a time, the West Indies. The Navigation Act of 1660 introduced a duty of two pence per pound on tobacco imported to England from Virginia, raised in 1685 to five pence. The act also prohibited the export of colonial tobacco to any European destination except England. Over the colonial period, economic regulation and taxation restricted the market for American tobacco. After the American Revolution, tobacco, freed from British imperial regulations, carried a tax as a foreign import when it entered Great Britain. Robert Morris and Thomas Jefferson succeeded in winning concessions from France for U.S. tobacco imports in the 1780s, while exports to other nations, especially the Netherlands, boomed. U.S. tobacco farmers faced no danger from foreign imports, so tobacco has not received significant tariff protection from the U.S. government. However, it became the object of excise taxation, both in the War of 1812 and in the Civil War. Since the Civil War, Congress has subjected tobacco to an excise tax, with reduced rates in peacetime, and higher levels in World War I and II.

See also: American Revolution; Civil War (American); France; Jefferson, Thomas; War of 1812; World War I; World War II.

Selected Bibliography:

Edmund Morgan, *American Slavery, American Freedom: The Ordeal of Colonial Virginia*, 1975.

John P. Barrington

TOKYO ROUND

A series of multilateral negotiations under the General Agreement on Tariffs and Trade (GATT) that had the goal of achieving the expansion and liberalization of world trade.

When the trade negotiations began in Tokyo on September 7, 1973, the participating countries planned to cut the remaining body of tariffs by as much as 60 percent and to reform the network of nontariff barriers that also severely impeded trade. The general thrust of the negotiations focused on increasing the openness, certainty, and non-arbitrariness of the rules governing international trade. The United States, the European Community, Japan, and Canada attended as the major participants in the Tokyo Round. Divisions among the ranks of developing countries reduced the impact of their participation in the negotiations, but these nations lacked the influence they had enjoyed during the Kennedy Round. To a great extent, the Tokyo

Round succeeded in liberalizing trade. The customs valuation code eliminated the American Selling Price (ASP), an unresolved problem in the last round, but maintained the protection offered by the ASP through increased tariffs. The American wine-gallon tax had served as a long-standing trade problem and the elimination of this tariff constituted one of the most important deals of the round. Additionally, the negotiations achieved a 35 percent average weighted tariff reduction on the imports of developing countries. The Tokyo Round concluded in Geneva with the accords signed immediately by twelve nations, including all the industrialized countries that had participated. The developing countries of Hungary and Argentina accepted the agreements, yet most Third World nations rejected the accords. Nevertheless, the Tokyo Round concluded the most comprehensive and far-reaching negotiations since the creation of GATT in 1947.

See also: General Agreement on Tariffs and Trade (GATT); Kennedy Round.

Selected Bibliography:

Gilbert R. Winham, *International Trade and the Tokyo Round Negotiation*, 1986.

Caryn E. Neumann

TRADE ACT OF 1974

Amendment to the Hawley-Smoot Tariff dealing with trade in the service sector.

The Trade Act of 1974 amended section 301 of the Tariff Act of 1930 to include trade in services. Section 301 defines the principal statutory authority under which the United States may impose trade sanctions against foreign countries that maintain acts, policies, and practices that violate or deny U.S. rights or benefits under trade agreements or are unjustifiable, unreasonable, or discriminatory and burden or restrict U.S. commerce.

A section 301 investigation may be commenced in one of two ways: An interested party files a petition with the U.S. Trade Representative (USTR) or the USTR self-initiates an investigation. The USTR must publish its determination to initiate an investigation, or reasons for not initiating in the case of a petition, in the *Federal Register*. After public comments, public hearings, consultation with foreign governments, and/or formal dispute settlements, the USTR must conclude its investigation and publish in the *Federal Register* a determination of whether the foreign practice is actionable under section 301. In addition, Sections 201 through 204 of the Trade Act of 1974 authorize the president to take action when the importation of a particular product into the country occurs in such large quantities as to cause injury or threaten serious injury to a domestic industry, even if dumping or subsidies remain a nonissue. Under these sections, the U.S. International Trade Commission assesses claims of injury to U.S. industries and recommends relief, if appropriate, to the president. Relief could take the form of increased tariffs or quotas on imports and/or adjustment assistance for the domestic industry.

See also: Countervailing duties; Dumping; Hawley-Smoot Tariff (Tariff of 1930).

Selected Bibliography:

Alfred E. Eckes, *Opening America's Market: U.S. Trade Policy Since 1776*, 1995.

Albert Atkins

TRADE AGREEMENT ACT OF 1979

Implemented the trade agreements negotiated at the Tokyo Round of the General Agreement on Tariffs and Trade (GATT) and further liberalized trade.

The Tokyo Round of GATT negotiations conducted between September 1973 and April 1979 pressured the United States to modify its laws and procedures in favor of freer trade. Congress, during the Carter administration, drafted the Trade Agreement of 1979 to implement the policies of the Tokyo Round and make U.S. laws consistent with the multilateral trade agreement. One of the major provisions of the act prohibited U.S. government agencies from setting standards that created unnecessary obstacles to foreign businesses conducting commerce in the United States. Another required the makers of U.S. trade policy to extend consideration to international agreements and make such agreements the basis of policy whenever possible. The legislation also modified antidumping as well as countervailing laws. It granted extensions to the authority of the president to negotiate nontariff barriers with other nations. It also required the executive branch to restructure its trade functions to comply with the Tokyo Round negotiations.

The Trade Agreement Act of 1979 restricted the capacity of the United States to negotiate trade agreements with foreign nations in a variety of ways. The act prohibited the government from considering America's political relationship with the foreign trading partner's government. The act also disallowed any consideration of the treatment of U.S. manufacturers or the government by foreign nations.

As a consequence of the Trade Agreement Act, for the first time in its history, the United States vigorously enforced its unfair trade laws. After the act took effect, the number of antidumping orders issued skyrocketed from twenty-one between 1976 and 1980 to thirty-four between 1981 and 1985 and 118 between 1986 and 1990. A similar trend emerged in countervailing duty orders, with nine orders issued between 1975 and 1980, twenty-four from 1981 to 1985, and thirty-seven from 1986 to 1990.

See also: General Agreement on Tariffs and Trade (GATT); Toyko Round.

Selected Bibliography:

Alfred E. Eckes, *Opening America's Market: U.S. Foreign Trade Policy Since 1776*, 1995.

Josh Pratt

TRADE AGREEMENTS EXTENSION ACT

Legislation that extended reciprocal trade agreements, established in 1934 and renewed in 1937, as an amendment to the Hawley-Smoot Tariff of 1930.

Congress renewed the Hawley-Smoot Tariff periodically until 1962 when the Trade Expansion Act replaced the tariff legislation. The 1934 law allowed the president to reduce tariffs by 50 percent. The Trade Agreements Extension Act of 1945 authorized the president to reduce tariffs by 50 percent of the 1945 rate instead of the 1934 rate. Effectively, with the two, the president could reduce rates by up to 75 percent from the 1934 level. Legislation of 1956 limited further reductions to 20 percent.

In 1945, the negotiating process shifted from bilateral tariff reduction to multilateral conferences at which participants would integrate all their demands into the trade structure. The 1945 act authorized the United States to send delegates to conferences with the authority to reduce tariffs. The first conference, held for the purpose of creating the International Trade Organization (ITO) to oversee multilateral trade and tariffs, drafted a charter, but Congress failed to approve it. In 1947, conferees from twenty-three nations drafted the General Agreement on Tariffs and Trade (GATT) at Geneva, prohibiting various acts that interfered with free trade. It also included the escape clause whereby the United States could back out of an agreement that it deemed harmful. The U.S. Tariff Commission administered GATT for the United States. The 1948 act defined peril points and set up a multilateral trade agreement. Free trade areas, such as the Common Market and the European Economic Community, hampered U.S. trade relations.

See also: General Agreement on Tariffs and Trade (GATT); Hawley-Smoot Tariff (Tariff of 1930); International Trade Organization (ITO); Tariff Commission.

Selected Bibliography:

John M. Dobson, *Two Centuries of Tariffs*, 1976; Judith Goldstein, *Ideas, Interests, and American Trade Policy*, 1993.

John Herschel Barnhill

TRADE ASSOCIATIONS

Membership organizations that promote the mutual economic interests of industry- or product-related business firms.

At the company level, trade associations provide services too expensive for individual firms, including advertising the industry; managing human resources; standardizing industrial procedures; collecting and analyzing economic data; hosting seminars, trade shows, and conventions; and providing discount rates for insurance, legal consulting, and training. By disseminating legal and market information, they encourage fair and informed trade practices. Trade associations also serve as an important link between firms and government by lobbying local and federal legislative bodies to enact beneficial economic policy.

Some trade associations, such as the National Association of Cotton Manufacturers, formed in the mid-nineteenth century, but they did not become widely popular until the twentieth century. Early associations organized to fix prices and establish trade zones, but antitrust legislation forced them into new areas such as cooperative lobbying, market research, and standardization. A group of Cincinnati machine tool-makers who feared that federal protectionist policies would harm their international export business founded the most significant national association, the National Association of Manufacturers (NAM), in 1895. NAM encouraged American economic growth by advocating foreign reciprocity agreements, workplace safety, public economic education, and tax reform. In 1917, NAM led American industrial associations in organizing the National Industrial Conference Board (NICB), National Safety Council, and the National Industrial Council (NIC). Economic prosperity during World War I and the enactment of Franklin Roosevelt's National Industrial Recovery Act spurred association growth; by 1938, the number of American trade associations had grown from 2,000 in 1919 to over 7,000. By 1956, the numbers increased to nearly 12,000, including 700 regional, 3,300 state, and more than 7,000 local associations. Influential industrial associations included the National Machine Tool Builders Association, formed in 1902, the American Iron and Steel Institute, formed in 1908, and the American Farm Bureau Federation, formed in 1919.

Throughout the twentieth century, NAM influenced the development of federal free trade legislation, successfully lobbying for enactment of the Trade Expansion Act, the North American Free Trade Agreement (NAFTA), and the reestablishment of China's Most Favored Nation status. The rapid globalization of commerce in the late twentieth century led to establishment of the World Trade Organization (WTO), which served as an international industrial association aimed at reducing trade barriers.

See also: American Iron and Steel Institute (AISI); Most Favored Nation (MFN); National Association of Manufacturers (NAM); North American Free Trade Agreement (NAFTA); Trade Expansion Act of 1962; Trade Expansion Act of 1968; World Trade Organization (WTO).

Selected Bibliography:

Joseph F. Bradley, *The Role of Trade Associations and Professional Business Societies in America*, 1965; Charles S. Mack, *Executive Handbook of Trade and Business Associations: How They Work and How to Make Them Work Effectively for You*, 1991.

John Grady Powell

TRADE DEFICITS

Difference between the amount of imports into a country and the amount of goods exported by that country.

Bullionists and mercantilists in Western Europe during the sixteenth and seventeenth centuries first expressed their concern over trade deficits in their writings. By the eighteenth century, an emerging group of political economists challenged the importance of such concerns. The focus on trade deficits, increasingly and cogently articulated, followed the developments in formation of national accounts and the field of accounting in general. The debates that followed have continued through the nineteenth century to the present.

Governments attempt to enhance the importation of bullion through international trade by selling more or at greater profit than one buys in international markets. In this pursuit, policy advocates and politicians, particularly in industrialized or industrializing states, view national prosperity in terms of the small or large firm. Like a private business, success remains measured by the yardstick through the year-end accounting of the balance sheet.

Adam Smith argued that the balance of trade and trade deficits should be of lesser concern than questions of national economic development. In other words, trade deficits, viewed as investments, contribute to or cause domestic prosperity. Despite this, the government continues to issue quarterly reports of trade deficits that seemingly have little impact on the larger economy of a given state.

See also: Balance of trade; Smith, Adam.

Selected Bibliography:

Mark Blaug, *Economic Theory in Retrospect*, 1985; Charles Wilson, *England's Apprenticeship, 1603–1763*, 1965.

David J. Weiland III

TRADE EXPANSION ACT OF 1962

Proposed by President John F. Kennedy as a means of opening worldwide trade and preventing the expansion of communism during the post–World War II period.

The formation of the European Community (EC) as a trading bloc resulted in the lowering of tariffs between member states in Europe. Fearing that the United States and Great Britain would lose access to the lucrative European markets, Kennedy encouraged Great Britain to join the EC and decided to pursue a policy of Atlantic cooperation between the United States and the organization. After French president Charles de Gaulle prevented the approval of Britain's application for membership, Kennedy asked Congress

to authorize a measure that would allow the president broad authority to reduce existing tariffs. In the proposal sent to Congress in January 1962, Kennedy requested the authority to reduce rates by up to 50 percent in exchange for reciprocal concessions, the inclusion of across-the-board cuts instead of item-by-item reductions, and the elimination of tariffs on items if the United States or the British Common Market produced at least 80 percent of the world's production. Opposition to the measure included fears that the elimination of safeguards would adversely affect domestic producers and workers. The bill passed Congress on June 28, 1962, by a vote of 299 to 125 in the House of Representatives and 78 to 8 in the Senate. The act provided the president with an expansion of trade–negotiating power and shifted U.S. policy toward freer trade at the expense of domestic producers. The passage of the Trade Expansion Act led to the U.S. participation in the Kennedy Round.

See also: European Community (EC); Kennedy, John F.

Selected Bibliography:

Alfred E. Eckes, *Opening America's Market: U.S. Foreign Trade Policy Since 1776*, 1995.

Cynthia Clark Northrup

TRADE EXPANSION ACT OF 1968

Bill that would have expanded President Johnson's authority to make tariff adjustments.

Protectionist sentiment challenged the movement toward freer trade in American politics during the 1960s as increased imports threatened the economic livelihood of domestic companies. Although Congress enacted no new tariffs during this era, the United States increased nontariff barriers against Japanese imports, devalued the dollar, and worked vigorously to stimulate U.S. exports. The expiration in 1967 of the Trade Expansion Act of 1962 hindered President Lyndon Johnson's ability to lower tariffs and promote greater American trade. To remedy this situation, on May 28, 1968, Johnson submitted to Congress a bill that would have granted the president the authority to reduce tariffs for two more years. This bill promoted the reduction of trade barriers and ran counter to the protectionist policies that some legislators in this era favored. The proposed legislation called for allowing the president to adjust tariffs through June 30, 1970. Second, it expressed the desire to remove the American Selling Price valuation system, thereby lowering foreign tariffs on American chemicals, automobiles, and tobacco. Third, it authorized payment for America's share of General Agreement on Tariffs and Trade (GATT) expenses. Next, the legislation loosened the eligibility requirements for federal assistance to businesspersons and workers facing serious financial difficulties due to the increased imports, and it extended similar assistance provisions to the Automotive Trade Act of 1965. The House Ways and Means Committee held hearings on President Johnson's Trade Expansion Act of 1968, as well as other trade bills, for eighteen days in June and July 1968. However, the committee elected to take no further action on the legislation, which prevented the bill from being voted on by the House and effectively defeated it.

See also: General Agreement on Tariffs and Trade (GATT); Trade Expansion Act of 1962.

Selected Bibliography:

U.S. Department of State, *Foreign Relations of the United States 1964–1968*, 1998.

Josh Pratt

TRADE ORGANIZATION CONFERENCE

International conference of twenty-three countries initiated by the United States, held in Geneva, Switzerland, that resulted in the substantial reduction of customs tariffs and elimination of discriminatory measures in international trade on a multilateral basis.

A number of international as well as domestic post–World War II conditions favored a large-scale American initiative on the liberalization of international trade. As the world economic leader, the United States had accumulated about 50 percent of the world's production by 1947 and continued to support the expansion of international trade. The 1945 renewal of the Reciprocal Trade Agreements Act (RTAA) allowed the Truman administration to reduce by half any tariff rates through agreements with foreign countries while protecting American industries. By 1947, the United States had negotiated bilateral economic agreements, including handling of war debts with twenty-nine countries, which envisaged the reduction or binding of duties on commodities on about 70 percent of all dutiable imports. The postwar U.S. economic prosperity and prospects of the large-scale expansion of American exports stimulated the increasing domestic acceptance of the value of free trade as a powerful factor of economic growth.

Internationally, the postwar economic recovery demanded multinational cooperation, revival of world trade, and removal of elements of economic nationalism such as trade barriers, particularly protective tariffs. No immediate danger to the American market from additional imports existed due to the postwar economic ruin in major world industrial countries. Thus, the United States could negotiate lower tariffs with foreign countries in exchange for the reduction of American import duties.

In the war years and thereafter, the United States actively promoted the concept of general agreement for the conduct of world trade, including reduction of tariffs and an idea of a permanent international organization to oversee the new rules of international commerce during international economic negotiations, including the Bretton Woods Conference. On December 13, 1945, the U.S. Department of State proposed a preliminary meeting of an International Trade Conference to discuss reciprocal lowering of tariffs. Later, on September 19, 1946, the Department of State released a draft of the International Trade Organization Charter detailing a code of international commerce. The place, schedule, and agenda of the conference, officially named the International Conference on Trade and Employment, received approval during the meeting of the preparatory committee of the representatives of seventeen countries in London in November 1946.

The General Agreement on Tariffs and Trade (GATT), signed by delega-

tions of twenty-three countries representing nineteen different customs areas, remains the legacy of the Geneva conference. The agreement, which integrated previous bilateral trade agreements, envisaged the most significant tariff reduction in history and included the unconditional Most Favored Nation clause as a norm of trade treaties affecting from 65 to 70 percent of world trade. It also called for the liberalization of customs procedures, elimination of quotas or import licenses, and it limited the right of nations to subsidize their exports.

The American delegation led by Undersecretary of State for Economic Affairs William L. Clayton managed to gain or confirm the reduction of import duties by the United Kingdom, Canada, Australia, and western European powers on a number of U.S. exports, including grains, fresh and canned fruits and vegetables, dried and condensed milk, meat, canned salmon, cigarettes, raw cotton, aircraft, automobiles, motorcycles, tractors, machine tools, office machines, radios, electrical goods, and other manufactures. Many U.S. exports benefited from the reduction or elimination of some of the imperial preferences by the British Commonwealth countries. In return, the United States introduced or confirmed the tariff reductions on so-called noncompetitive items, such as English woolens and worsteds, leather goods and chinaware, Scotch and Canadian whiskey, Belgian and French laces, French wines, perfumery, and lingerie, Dutch bulbs, Irish linens, as well as imported beef and veal, copper, butter, cement, wheat, bauxite, manganese ore, textile machinery, and steel products.

In the summer of 1947, the U.S. Congress put the Geneva conference in jeopardy, adopting the wool bill, which increased the duty on the imported wool. President Harry S Truman, strongly supported by Secretary of State George C. Marshall and former secretaries of state Henry L. Stimson and Cordell Hull, vetoed the bill, saving the Geneva agreement despite protests from representatives of the mountain states.

Initially considered an interim trade arrangement pending the formation of an international trade organization, the subsequent failure of this scheme resulted in GATT developing into an effective forum for expanding multilateral trade negotiations while ensuring U.S. influence in world trade.

See also: General Agreement on Tariffs and Trade (GATT); World War II.

Selected Bibliography:

Robert E. Hudec, *The GATT Legal System and World Trade Diplomacy*, 1990; Thomas W. Zeiler, *Free Trade, Free World: The Advent of GATT*, 1999.

Peter Rainow

TRUMAN, HARRY S (May 8, 1884– December 26, 1972)

Thirty-third president of the United States.

Born in Lamar, Missouri, Truman served in the U.S. Army during World War I, and after the war returned to Missouri to try his hand in business. Having little luck, Truman entered politics and received support from the Democratic Pendergast machine in Kansas City. In 1922, voters elected him as a judge of Jackson County, Missouri, and he entered the national political arena after his election to the U.S. Senate in 1934. In 1944, Franklin D. Roosevelt selected Truman as his vice-presidential candidate, and after Roosevelt won his fourth term, Truman took office in 1945. After Roosevelt died on April 12, 1945, Truman became the president of the United States and immediately had the responsibility of presiding over the nation during the final months of World War II. In the postwar period, Truman oversaw the initial stages of the Cold War, and committed American troops in the Korean War. Domestically, he pushed for the Fair Deal, an attempt to continue many of Roosevelt's New Deal policies. However, after the Republicans gained control of both houses of Congress following the 1946 elections, many of his efforts met resistance.

The tariff policy of the Truman administration sought to continue tariff reductions begun by the Roosevelt administration. In an effort to continue eliminating trade barriers, the president wanted the United States to join the International Trade Organization (ITO), but protectionist Republicans blocked American membership. The Truman administration then focused its efforts on the General Agreement on Tariffs and Trade (GATT). Truman linked tariffs and international trade concerns to the Cold War. A key element of the Marshall Plan in 1947 included grants to help rebuild European nations devastated by the war. Truman, like other Cold War presidents, put foreign policy over domestic economic interests. Fearing the Democrats would sacrifice domestic industry to gain anticommunist allies, Republicans continued to harass his trade agenda. Under pressure, Truman created the independent Tariff Commission to investigate complaints from domestic industries and to make appropriate recommendations about tariff policies.

In the 1952 election, Truman lost to Republican Dwight D. Eisenhower. After vacating the Oval Office, he retired to Independence, Missouri, where he died on December 26, 1972.

See also: Cold War; General Agreement on Tariffs and Trade (GATT); International Trade Organization (ITO); Roosevelt, Franklin D.; World War II.

Selected Bibliography:

Robert Ferrell, *Harry S Truman: A Life*, 1994; William E. Pemberton, *Harry S Truman: Fair Dealer and Cold Warrior*, 1989.

John K. Franklin

TRUSTS

Large corporations that benefited from high tariffs.

Prior to the Civil War, industry in the United States remained relatively small compared to other industrial countries such as Great Britain. Although Congress had implemented a protective tariff to assist domestic manufacturers, the rates fluctuated as Democrats fought for the reduction of rates when the treasury experienced surpluses. A transformation within the industrial sector commenced during the Civil War as the government raised tariff rates to record high levels to finance the war expenditures. Beginning with the Morrill Tariff and continuing into the twentieth century, rates remained high. In addition to providing funds for the federal government, the high tariffs created a barrier for businesses, effectively shielding them from the threat of foreign competition. The lack of enforceable legislation to curb the worst abuses domestically, combined with the use of the tariff against imports, allowed businesses such as Standard Oil, U.S. Steel, International Harvester, and many others to expand until they dominated their respective markets. Determined to protect their interests, the owners of these large trusts courted senators and representatives. The influence of the railroad companies grew to such proportions that Congress became known as the "Railroad Lobby." After the turn of the century, writers like David Phillips, author of "Treason of the State," who linked seventy-five of the ninety senators to the trusts, and Ida Tarbell, the author who exposed the practices of John D. Rockefeller, provided ammunition for the trust-busters of the Progressive Era. As the government initiated a series of cases against the trusts under President Theodore Roosevelt, the power of the giant corporations dwindled. The dissolution of the interlocking directorates and the loss of political influence as senators sought to please voters after the passage of the Seventeenth Amendment allowed for the direct election of senators led to a short-lived attempt to reduce duty rates with the Underwood-Simmons Tariff Act. Although rates soared again after World War I, the power of the trusts had been broken, and after World War II the United States moved toward free trade.

See also: Civil War (American); International Harvester; Underwood-

Simmons Tariff (Tariff of 1913); U.S. Steel Corp.

Selected Bibliography:

Robert C. Kochersberger, ed., *More than a Muckraker: Ida Tarbell's Lifetime in Journalism*, 1994; Charles Edward Russell, *Doing Us Good and Plenty*, 1914.

Cynthia Clark Northrup

TUGWELL, REXFORD G. (July 10, 1891–July 21, 1979)

Prominent academic and New Dealer known for his outspoken views on the causes of the Great Depression.

Born in Sinclairville, New York, Tugwell received his professional training in economics at the University of Pennsylvania's Wharton School. Serving briefly at the American University Union in Paris in 1917, he later went into academics at Columbia University and quickly climbed the professorial ladder. During the 1920s, Tugwell wrote prolifically on the inequities of the American economic system, the economy's failure to achieve abundance, laissez-faire, technological obsolescence, and the need for planning. When Herbert Hoover failed to alleviate the economic crisis during the Great Depression, Tugwell advocated domestic allotment rather than tariffs or marketing agreements for farm recovery. By 1932, he gained entrance into the Brain Trust of the Roosevelt administration, where he served as an agricultural advisor and speechwriter. After Roosevelt's victory, Tugwell served in the U.S. Department of Agriculture and the Resettlement Administration.

As a professional economist in the 1920s, Tugwell expressed his views on the Hawley-Smoot Tariff and McNary-Haugenism. In his opinion, neither one of these programs offered any significant hope of alleviating farm distress since they both failed to address the fundamental problem in agriculture—overproduction. For that reason, Tugwell, the New Deal administrator, supported the domestic allotment provisions of the Agricultural Adjustment Act. He also strongly called for the implementation of a permanent land-use planning program as evidenced by the Resettlement Administration.

Eventually, Tugwell's outspoken views cost him his New Deal position in 1936. From 1938 to 1941, he served as chairman of the New York City Planning Commission. Between 1941 and 1946, he governed Puerto Rico and, after 1947, he returned to academics and wrote prolifically on a wide range of topics, including planning, the atomic bomb, the New Deal, and the need for a new American Constitution. He died in Santa Barbara, California.

See also: Hawley-Smoot Tariff (Tariff of 1930); Roosevelt, Franklin D.

Selected Bibliography:

Michael V. Namorato, *Rexford G. Tugwell: A Biography*, 1988; Michael V. Namorato, *The Diary of Rexford G. Tugwell: The New Deal Years*, 1992.

Michael V. Namorato

TWAIN, MARK (Pseudonym for Samuel Langhorne Clemens; November 30, 1835–April 21, 1910)

Arguably his nation's greatest author, Mark Twain contributed *The Adven-*

tures of *Tom Sawyer*, *The Adventures of Huckleberry Finn*, and *The Mysterious Stranger*, among many other works, to the pantheon of American literature.

Through his novels, short stories, essays, and public lectures, Twain called into question the materialism of the Gilded Age, America's racial practices, and U.S. imperialism. Raised in Hannibal, Missouri, Twain worked as a printer's apprentice, a journeyman printer, and a riverboat pilot before briefly serving in the Confederate Army. Moving to Carson City, Nevada, with his brother Orion, Twain unsuccessfully prospected for gold and silver before becoming a reporter. A succession of well-received books eventually poured forth, ranging from *The Gilded Age* in 1873 to *Life on the Mississippi* in 1883 to *A Connecticut Yankee in King Arthur's Court* in 1889. Financial setbacks resulted in the bankruptcy of his publishing company, but Twain rebounded through international travels that made him a still more celebrated figure. With his economic difficulties and the deaths of his daughter and wife, a more pessimistic outlook took hold of Twain, but his popularity continued unabated.

Twain seldom referred directly to the tariff, an issue that haunted politicians throughout the course of the nineteenth century. Increasingly, he condemned the protectionist policies favored by the Republican Party. In *Tom Sawyer Abroad*, which appeared in 1894, Twain's protagonist declared that tariffs amounted to "just hogging." Tom went on to predict that Congress would soon tax God's blessings as "there warn't nothing foreign that warn't taxed!" The following year,

Twain inscribed the following passage in his notebook: "The man that invented protection belongs in hell." As Twain saw matters, the tariff merely raised prices for the western sector of the United States. At the same time, tariff policies constantly shifted: "The law is changed and the man is robbed by his own government." The support of tariffs provided to the trusts angered Twain most of all. "We swept slavery and substituted Protection," he charged. The Republican Party remained largely to blame for this: "By a system of extraordinary tariffs it has created a number of giant corporations in the interest of a few rich men & by most ingenious & persuasive reasoning it has convinced the multitudinous and grateful unrich that the tariffs were instituted in their interest."

See also: Protectionism; Republican Party.

Selected Bibliography:

Philip S. Foner, *Mark Twain: Social Critic*, 1958; Justin Kaplan, *Mr. Clemens and Mark Twain: A Biography*, 1966.

Robert C. Cottrell

TYDINGS, MILLARD E. (April 6, 1890–February 9, 1961)

U.S. representative and senator from Maryland who co-sponsored the McDuffie-Tydings Act of 1934 granting independence to the Philippines.

Born in Havre de Grace, Maryland, Tydings earned an engineering degree from Maryland Agricultural College in 1910. While working for the Baltimore and Ohio Railroad, he enrolled in the University of Maryland law school, completing his law degree in 1913. He was admitted to the bar and established a legal practice in Havre de Grace.

Elected to the Maryland House of Representatives in 1915, Tydings eventually became its Speaker. Voters elected him to the Maryland Senate in 1921 and he successfully campaigned as a Democrat for election to the U.S. House of Representatives in 1922. Tydings won a seat in the U.S. Senate in 1926, becoming one of the youngest members of that body. He gained national attention for his work to repeal Prohibition and as chairman of the Territories and Insular Possessions Committee; he co-authored the McDuffie-Tydings Act that gave independence to the Philippines.

Conflict marred the remainder of his career in the Senate. He survived a "purge" attempt by President Franklin Roosevelt in 1938. In his 1950 reelection campaign, Tydings fell victim to a negative campaign financed by Senator Joseph McCarthy, a Republican from Wisconsin. Tydings had criticized McCarthy for the latter senator's methods in investigating communism in the federal government. In an attempt to return to the Senate, he won the Democratic primary in 1956, but fell ill and never fully recovered. Tydings died at his farm Oakington, near Havre de Grace.

See also: McDuffie, John; McDuffie-Tydings Act; Prohibition; Roosevelt, Franklin D.

Selected Bibliography:

Caroline H. Keith, *"For Hell and a Brown Mule": The Biography of Senator Millard E. Tydings*, 1991.

John David Rausch, Jr.

TYLER, JOHN (March 29, 1790–January 18, 1862)

Tenth president of the United States.

Born near Williamsburg, Virginia, on the family plantation in Charles City County, Tyler graduated from the College of William and Mary in 1807 and read law under his father, the governor of Virginia, from 1808 to 1811. He became a member of the Virginia House of Delegates in 1810, served on the state's Executive Council from 1815 to 1816, and won a term as governor of Virginia in 1825. Elected to the U.S. House of Representatives in 1817, Tyler also served in the Senate from 1827 to 1836. While in the Senate, he opposed Andrew Jackson's stand against South Carolina in the fight over nullification, particularly the extreme language of the "December Proclamation." In 1833, he opposed the removal of federal deposits from the Bank of the United States, calling Jackson "reckless and headstrong." In 1834, he resigned his seat when the Virginia legislature instructed him to vote in favor of Thomas H. Benton's resolution to expunge the censure of Jackson from the Senate journal. In 1836, he accepted the nomination of Maryland Whigs for the vice presidency and received the vote of forty-seven electors.

The Whig Party chose him as the vice-presidential candidate in the 1840 election, running him with William Henry Harrison on the slogan of "Tippecanoe and Tyler too!" When Harrison died on April 4, 1841, Tyler became the first vice president to succeed to the presidency. But he quickly became involved in serious disagreements with leaders of the Whig Party, especially Henry Clay. Tyler vetoed twice Clay's bill to recharter a national bank and opposed the Whig efforts to pass a protective tariff. When Clay then bottled up all appropriations bills, and thereby threatened the federal government with bankruptcy, Tyler reluctantly signed the Tariff Act of 1842. By then all of Tyler's cabinet, including Secretary of State Daniel Webster, had resigned. For the remaining two years in office, Tyler devoted all of his attention to the acquisition of Texas, which, after the victory of James K. Polk in the election of 1844, he accomplished by a joint resolution of Congress on March 3, 1845. Tyler remained in private life until he became a member of the Confederate Congress in 1861. He died in Richmond the following January.

See also: Calhoun, John Caldwell; Clay, Henry; Clay's Compromise; Jackson, Andrew; Nullification; Polk, James K.; Tariff of 1842 (Compromise Tariff); Webster, Daniel; Whig Party.

Selected Bibliography:

Oliver Perry Chitwood, *John Tyler: Champion of the Old South*, 1939; Robert Gunderson, *The Log-Cabin Campaign*, 1977; Robert J. Morgan, *A Whig Embattled: The Presidency Under John Tyler*, 1974; Norma Lois Peterson, *The Presidencies of William Henry Harrison and John Tyler*, 1989; David M. Pletcher, *The Diplomacy of Annexation: Texas, Oregon, and the Mexican War*, 1985; Robert Seager, *And Tyler Too*, 1963.

Robert P. Sutton

U

UNDERWOOD, OSCAR WILDER (May 6, 1862–January 25, 1929)

U.S. representative from Birmingham, Alabama, who sponsored the Underwood-Simmons Tariff Act of 1913.

Elected to the U.S. House of Representatives in 1894, Underwood served as chairman of the House Ways and Means Committee, where he favored internationalism and free trade and supported President Woodrow Wilson. He failed to secure the Democratic presidential nomination in 1912 and as a U.S. senator unsuccessfully sought the Democratic presidential nomination in 1924. Underwood encouraged a Senate Judiciary Committee investigation into grassroots efforts of the tariff lobby to oppose Wilson's favored tariff legislation, an act that strengthened the bonds between himself and the president. Indeed, he campaigned vigorously for Wilson in the 1912 election, particularly in areas heavily populated by Italian Americans who thought highly of Underwood because he favored the removal of tariffs on lemons. Late in March 1913, the very month President Wilson took the oath of office, Underwood presented him with draft tariff legislation produced by the Ways and Means Committee. After Underwood emerged from a two-hour session on April 1, he announced an agreement on a bill that greatly expanded the free list. After Underwood worked out a compromise with U.S. senator Furnifold M. Simmons of North Carolina, the bill received approval on September 9, 1913. Underwood's relations with President Woodrow Wilson cooled after he moved to the U.S. Senate in 1915 and assumed the position of Senate majority leader. Underwood, along with Henry Clay, holds the distinction of leading his party in both chambers. He died in 1929, the year before the passage of the highly restrictive Hawley-Smoot Tariff that embodied the antithesis of his political philosophy.

See also: House Ways and Means Committee; Simmons, Furnifold McLendel; Underwood-Simmons Tariff (Tariff of 1913).

Selected Bibliography:

Evans C. Johnson, *Oscar W. Underwood: A Political Biography*, 1980.

Henry B. Sirgo

UNDERWOOD-SIMMONS TARIFF (TARIFF OF 1913)

First successful attempt in the post–Civil War period to reduce tariff rates, passed by Congress along with the Sixteenth Amendment, which allowed for the collection of a personal income tax.

From the Civil War through 1912, only one Democratic president, Grover Cleveland, won the White House, and during his administration he attempted to reduce the tariff downward. In 1912, Democratic candidate Woodrow Wilson won the election and immediately pushed for several progressive reforms, including the formation of the Federal Reserve Bank and a complete revision of the tariff. Congress debated the reduction of duties and, in an effort to negate the proposed legislation, Republicans proposed the inclusion of a constitutional amendment that provided for a modest personal income tax to replace lost government revenue. Believing that the measure could not pass a final vote and that the states would never ratify the amendment, Republicans supported the Underwood-Simmons Tariff Act in 1913. Congress passed the bill, decreasing the average tariff rate from 41 to 27 percent and placing over one hundred items on the free list. The tariff remained in effect for a short period before the outbreak of World War I and the disruption of international trade. When the war ended, the Republican-dominated Congress raised rates to a new high to discourage the importation of foreign goods during the postwar recession.

See also: Cleveland, Stephen Grover; Democratic Party; Fordney-McCumber Tariff (Tariff of 1922); Personal income tax (Sixteenth Constitutional Amendment); Republican Party; Simmons, Furnifold McLendel; Underwood, Oscar Wilder; Wilson, Thomas Woodrow; World War I. **Vol. II**: Woodrow Wilson's Democratic Nomination Acceptance Speech. **Vol. III**: Tariff of 1913 (Underwood-Simmons Tariff).

Selected Bibliography:

Evans C. Johnson, *Oscar W. Underwood: A Political Biography*, 1980.

Cynthia Clark Northrup

UNION LABOR PARTY

A workingmen's political party that dominated San Francisco politics until a corruption scandal destroyed it.

After the end of a citywide strike in which police protected strikebreakers, some labor leaders called for the formation of a party to enable unions to elect the mayor. The platform of the Union Labor Party (ULP) called for public ownership of utilities, better schoolhouses, arbitration of industrial disputes, exclusion of all Asians, segregation of Asians in schools, and the abolition of the poll tax. The ULP tasted victory in its first election in November 1901. The balloting provided a referendum on the right of unions to organize and establish a closed shop, and on the question of whether labor or capital should control government. The ULP won control of the mayor's office and the board of supervisors. For the next decade, the party elected candidates for mayor in four out of five elections, but never succeeded in establishing a statewide party. When some of the ULP leaders exhibited sudden wealth, the San Francisco graft prosecutions of 1906 commenced. Prosecutors charged these leaders with accepting bribes from representatives of residential developments as well as taking money from telephone company, cable car, and trolley operators. During 1907 and 1908, the courts convicted several ULP men, including Mayor Thomas Schmitz and Boss Abraham Ruef, dealing labor's prestige a heavy blow. A tendency to blame the party's disgrace on unionism as a whole existed when people knew little or nothing about the ULP except for its name.

See also: Labor.

Selected Bibliography:

Jules Tygiel, "Where Unionism Holds Sway: A Reappraisal of San Francisco's Union Labor Party," *California History*, 1983.

Caryn E. Neumann

UNITED NATIONS

Organizational body of nations that mediates global issues such as human rights, world peace, world hunger, and trade between countries.

The United Nations (UN) kept trade flowing between countries through negotiations, helping to avoid the high tariffs of the 1930s. Trade prior to the

1930s remained uneven between countries. To level the playing field, the United States passed the Hawley-Smoot Tariff of 1930. This act raised rates on imports in order to protect interests at home. U.S. trade partners reciprocated with similar tariffs. Nations at this time also negotiated trade on a one-to-one basis, usually granting one side an unfair advantage. Unfortunately, these issues constricted trade greatly.

World War II and its end brought about the formation of several organizations under the UN to deal with problems that arose from the war as well as problems that occurred before the war. In 1947, fifty countries gathered to draft a charter for an International Trade Organization (ITO) that would mediate over trade issues. Many of the countries agreed on the charter in March 1948, but the U.S. Congress ignored President Harry S Truman and the United Nations because of the corporate interests at home.

In 1947, twenty-three nations, including the United States, adopted some of the ITO charter in Geneva, Switzerland. After the meeting, UN members established a new organization in lieu of the ITO, the General Agreement on Tariffs and Trade (GATT). GATT took over negotiations on world trade and tariffs in January 1948. In 1955, GATT proposed the formation of a governing body for trade and President Dwight D. Eisenhower petitioned the U.S. Congress to sign the agreement, but it refused.

Members of GATT held several round negotiations after 1955. At the Dillon Round from 1960 to 1962, members reached an agreement on reducing industrial tariffs by 20 percent. The United States began preparing for greater concessions at the next round of negotiations. Next came the Kennedy Round negotiations, which brought about even more change than that of its predecessor. The United States and fifty-two other countries agreed to cut certain tariffs by 50 percent, and installed an anti-dumping clause that allowed countries to impose additional duties on unfairly priced imports. The Tokyo Round from 1973 to 1979 allowed loopholes and vacillation on previous trade agreements and tariff policies. The Uruguay Round from 1986 to 1993 proved successful at lowering industrial tariffs between Canada, the United States, the European Community, and Japan. A problem arose with agricultural trade between the United States and the European Community at these negotiations. In April 1994, 117 GATT members signed a final agreement that included four basic principles: reduce tariffs; eliminate certain nontariff barriers and subsidies; trade in services, investment, and intellectual property; and encourage discipline for agriculture.

See also: Dumping; General Agreement on Tariffs and Trade (GATT); Great Depression; Hawley-Smoot Tariff (Tariff of 1930); Kennedy Round; Toyko Round; Uruguay Round; World Trade Organization (WTO).

Selected Bibliography:

Alfred E. Eckes, *Opening America's Market: U.S. Foreign Trade Policy*, 1995.

Shannon Daniel O'Bryan

U.S. CHAMBER OF COMMERCE

Formed in 1912, the U.S. Chamber of Commerce promoted the idea of a tariff commission with broad subpoena powers and the authority to conduct cost-of-production investigations.

The U.S. Chamber of Commerce originally operated as the National Council of Commerce (NCC), formed in 1907 under the administration of Theodore Roosevelt. The NCC functioned as a quasi-governmental business advisory council within the Department of Commerce and Labor. Herbert Miles argued that Congress should grant the NCC the authority to discuss political issues such as tariffs and trade, a function initially denied. When Miles proposed the modification of the NCC's function, President William Howard Taft severed the NCC's government links after appointing John Candler Cobb to reorganize the Council. In 1912, the NCC became the U.S. Chamber of Commerce, an independent business lobbying group. Freed from restrictions placed on government agencies, the Chamber of Commerce supported the formation of a Tariff Board to investigate production costs and question industry officials on matters relating to the tariff. President Woodrow Wilson opposed the creation of such a board until 1915, when circumstances created by World War I resulted in his supporting the establishment of a Tariff Commission. Today, the U.S. Chamber of Commerce includes over 3,000,000 businesses, 830 business associations, and eighty-seven American Chambers of Commerce overseas.

See also: Miles, Herbert Edwin; Roosevelt, Theodore; Taft, William Howard; Wilson, Thomas Woodrow.

Selected Bibliography:

Paul Wolman, *Most Favored Nation: The Republican Revisionists and U.S. Tariff Policy, 1897–1912*, 1992.

Cynthia Clark Northrup

U.S. INTERNATIONAL TRADE COMMISSION

An independent, nonpartisan, quasi-judicial federal agency that provides Congress and the president with trade advice, analyzes the impact of imports on American businesses, and initiates actions against unfair trade practices such as patent, trademark, or copyright violations.

Established as an independent agency by the Trade Act of 1974 on January 3, 1975, the U.S. International Trade Commission (USITC) researches and investigates foreign trade and tariffs. The predecessors of the USITC include the U.S. Tariff Commission (1916–1974), the Cost of Production Division of the Bureau of Foreign and Domestic Commerce of the Department of Commerce (1913–1916), the Tariff Board (1909–1912), and the Tariff Commission of the Department of the Treasury (1882).

Designed to advise the executive and legislative branches and promote a sound and informed trade policy, the USITC investigates complaints by domestic industries and agricultural interests claiming injury from excessive quantities of imports or lower-priced competition from abroad. The commission generates reports for the presi-

dent, who decides whether or not to take any formal action.

See also: Tariff Commission.

Selected Bibliography:

John M. Dobson, *Two Centuries of Tariffs: The Background and Emergence of the U.S. International Trade Commission*, 1976.

Cynthia Clark Northrup

U.S.–NAFTA COALITION

Organization of private businesses that worked together for the promotion and passage of the North American Free Trade Agreement (NAFTA).

Formed under the first Bush administration, by 1993, the coalition comprised 2,300 U.S. companies and lobbying groups, with thirty-five leading corporations acting as the organizing force throughout all fifty states. AT&T, IBM, General Electric, DuPont, Nike, Textron, Kodak, Allied Signal, Texas Instruments, and American Express participated in the organization. Initially, James Robertson of American Express and Kay Whitmore of Kodak assumed leadership responsibilities, but after they both resigned as the top executives of their companies Lawrence Bossidy of Allied Signal and Jerry Junkins of Texas Instruments directed the organization. Formed prior to the signing of the agreement, the group remained relatively inactive until officials resolved the issues and then initiated a campaign to win the support of smaller businesses as well as the public for the passage of NAFTA. Working with the Mexican negotiating team, they identified population centers that would experience the greatest impact as a result of NAFTA and conducted a grassroots campaign to persuade people of the benefits of the treaty. The activity and support of the U.S.–NAFTA Coalition helped ensure congressional approval of fast-track legislation and the ratification of NAFTA.

See also: Fast-track legislation; North American Free Trade Agreement (NAFTA).

Selected Bibliography:

Hermann von Bertrab, *Negotiating NAFTA: A Mexican Envoy's Account*, 1997.

Cynthia Clark Northrup

U.S. STEEL CORP.

The U.S. Steel Corp. was incorporated in New Jersey in 1901, the first billion-dollar corporation in the United States, and established its headquarters in Pittsburgh, Pennsylvania.

After a rocky start due to government antitrust action, U.S. Steel began to acquire other steel, cement, and mineral companies. Over the years, the company merged many times. U.S. Steel Co. joined with the U.S. Steel Corp. in 1953. During the 1960s, U.S. Steel bought foreign plants, chemical and petroleum companies, distilleries, and financial corporations. In 1991, the corporation underwent restructuring, with the Marathon Group assuming responsibilities for the exploration and production of crude oil and natural gas, and the U.S. Steel Group producing and selling steel and related material such as coke and taconite pellets. U.S. Steel, with joint ventures in Canada, Japan, Mexico, Russia, Slovakia,

and South Korea, dominates steel production worldwide.

Beginning in the early 1980s, U.S. Steel and other major steel companies joined forces against foreign producers, whom, they alleged, dumped goods and used unfair subsidies to introduce cheap steel into the U.S. market. As a result, the Reagan administration arranged voluntary restraint agreements with foreign nations. Failure to renew the agreements and a multinational steel agreement in 1992 left the industry unprotected against imports. These problems continued through the 1990s. In 1993, Thomas J. Usher, president of U.S. Steel Group, stated that the countervailing duty and anti-dumping laws failed to provide adequate protection. In October 1999, President William Jefferson Clinton signed a loan package into law that critics at home and abroad called a form of subsidy. U.S. Steel and other steel-makers continue to face this ongoing struggle of foreign competition dumping subsidized steel onto the American market.

See also: Carnegie, Andrew; Mellon, Andrew W.; Trusts.

Selected Bibliography:

Douglas A. Fisher, *Steel Serves the Nation, 1901–1951, The Fifty Year Story of United States Steel*, 1951.

Russell M. Magnaghi

URUGUAY ROUND

Eighth round of negotiations held since the General Agreement on Tariffs and Trade (GATT) went into effect in January 1948.

Initiated in September 1986 at a

meeting of GATT ministers held in Punta del Este, Uruguay; negotiations successfully concluded on December 15, 1993. Ministers representing most of the 125 nations that participated in the Uruguay Round signed the agreement on April 15, 1994, in Marrakesh, Morocco. A major impasse on agricultural subsidies and intellectual property rights nearly derailed the Uruguay Round in the early 1990s.

Since 1934, Congress has delegated authority to the president to negotiate tariff agreements and then accepts or rejects the package as a whole. All presidents from Franklin D. Roosevelt through George W. Bush have advocated increased international trade and an overall reduction in tariffs and other trade barriers. This proved true of Ronald Reagan, George Herbert Walker Bush, and William Jefferson Clinton, all of whom served during the Uruguay Round negotiations. The Uruguay Round permanently altered the world trading system in such a way that it replaced GATT with the World Trade Organization (WTO). As influential as GATT had been, the agreement had a provisional existence and no institutional foundation. That the Uruguay Round took such a long time to negotiate is not surprising given that most Americans have never been enthusiastic about expanding trade and that the United States between 1980 and 1990 shifted from the position of being the world's greatest creditor nation to that of being the greatest debtor nation. Indeed, the World Trade Organization remains controversial. Alfred E. Eckes has written that "U.S. trade negotiators, pursuing a trade-policy agenda supporting the interests of large multinational corporations eager to expand further abroad, yielded effective sovereignty to an international commercial organization (the WTO)." When the WTO officially opened with a meeting on November 29, 1999, in Seattle, Washington, protesters from environmental organizations and labor unions demonstrated outside. U.S. proposals dealing with anti-dumping rules and agricultural subsidies drew opposition from many nations. Consequently, President Clinton and other WTO leaders decided to adjourn the meeting with nothing accomplished.

See also: Bush, George Herbert Walker; Clinton, William Jefferson (Bill); General Agreement on Tariffs and Trade (GATT); Kennedy Round; World Trade Organization (WTO).

Selected Bibliography:

William A. Lovett, Alfred E. Eckes Jr., and Richard L. Brinkman, eds., *U.S. Trade Policy: History, Theory, and the WTO*, 1999.

Henry B. Sirgo

V

VAN BUREN, MARTIN (December 5, 1782–July 24, 1862)

Eighth president, secretary of state, and senator.

Throughout his political career, Martin Van Buren faced the tariff as a major issue. A product and master of machine politics in New York State, Van Buren played an instrumental role in the 1824 election in which John Quincy Adams won the presidency; then, after falling out with Adams, as the leader of the 1828 coalition that elected Andrew Jackson. Trapped between New York wool producers and manufacturers, he avoided voting on the Tariff of Abominations, but ultimately voted for higher protection for wool cloth after being pressured. As Jackson's secretary of state and chief advisor, he cobbled together the Democratic machine that would be so successful in the 1832 campaign. Jacksonian political rhetoric stressed the primacy of the common citizen over privilege, exemplified in the

crushing of the Bank of the United States, but the defection of Vice President John C. Calhoun allowed Van Buren to engineer a shift in policy around South Carolina's attempted nullification of the tariff. With Daniel Webster, Van Buren moved the Jacksonians into a nationalist policy, but later worked with Calhoun and Henry Clay to pass a compromise tariff in 1833. Resigning as secretary of state, Van Buren received the nomination for vice president in 1832 and then succeeded Jackson as president in 1836.

Unfortunately, Van Buren faced the economic panic of 1837 soon after taking office. Refusing to alter the tariff, he drew fire for promising only an independent treasury system for the United States, not large-scale government aid. Facing unpopularity and party defections, Van Buren lost the 1840 election to William Henry Harrison. The annexation of Texas and Van Buren's opposition to it sank his chances as a Democratic candidate in

1844, but as an elder statesman he led a faction of "Barnburners" to political influence and patronage under Polk. Although Van Buren lost the 1848 election, the Free-Soilers supported him. After traveling in Europe, Van Buren retired to Kinderhook, New York, where he died in 1862.

See also: Adams, John Quincy; Calhoun, John Caldwell; Clay, Henry; Jackson, Andrew; Tariff of 1828 (Tariff of Abominations); Wool and woolens.

Selected Bibliography:

Donald B. Cole, *Martin Van Buren and the American Political System*, 1984; John Niven, *Martin Van Buren: The Romantic Age of American Politics*, 1983.

Margaret Sankey

VENEZUELA

South American nation of fifteen million inhabitants, located east of Colombia along the northern coast of South America.

Venezuela has transacted a significant amount of trade with the United States since a major oil strike in 1922. From 1930 to World War II, Venezuela exported more oil than any other country in the world. In 1936, in response to proposals in the U.S. Congress to double oil tariffs, Venezuelan and U.S. diplomats negotiated the Reciprocal Trade Agreement of 1939. Venezuela gained privileged access to the U.S. market in exchange for lowering barriers to U.S. manufacturers in its growing market fed by petroleum export earnings.

In the 1950s, domestic U.S. oil producers faced rising costs after the exhaustion of easily extracted reserves, and pressured the Eisenhower administration to restrict cheaper Venezuelan and Middle Eastern imports. Venezuela sought to retain access to the U.S. market by incorporating itself into the U.S. Interstate Oil Compact Commission. The Eisenhower administration rejected Venezuelan overtures; in 1959, it abrogated the 1939 treaty. Venezuela then persuaded Saudi Arabia to join its call for the first conference of the Organization of Petroleum Exporting Countries (OPEC) in Baghdad in 1960.

During the "OPEC decade" of 1973 to 1983, Venezuela nationalized its oil industry. After prices collapsed in the 1980s, the country continually violated the quotas set by OPEC in an effort to maintain prices. In 1997, Venezuela won a ruling from the World Trade Organization that anti-pollution regulations issued by the U.S. Environmental Protection Agency discriminated against its oil exports. President Hugo Chávez, a nationalist former military officer elected in 1998, and Ali Rodríguez, minister of energy and hydrocarbons until becoming president of OPEC in 2000, successfully convinced OPEC to reinvigorate the quota system and implement a policy of adjusting supply to banded pricing. The second summit of heads of state of OPEC took place in Caracas in 2000, forty years after the first.

See also: Oil; Organization of Petroleum Exporting Countries (OPEC).

Selected Bibliography:

Stephen G. Rabe, *The Road to OPEC: United States Relations with Venezuela, 1919–1976*, 1982.

Daniel C. Hellinger

VEST, GEORGE G. (December 6, 1830–August 9, 1904)

Democrat from Missouri who served in the U.S. Senate from 1879 to 1903.

Vest served as the chairman of the Committee on Public Buildings and Grounds in the Fifty-third Congress. Best known for guiding Democratic Senate efforts that resulted in over 600 amendments being added to the Wilson-Gorman Tariff Act of 1894, Vest effectively helped turn it into a high tariff act that President Grover Cleveland refused to sign, choosing to let it become law without his signature.

Born on December 6, 1830, in Frankfort, Kentucky, Vest graduated from Centre College in 1848 and from Transylvania University in Lexington, Kentucky, with a law degree in 1853 before moving to Boonville, Missouri, in 1856. A Democratic presidential elector in 1860, he won a seat in the Missouri State House of Representatives that same year. In 1862, he received an appointment as a colonel and judge advocate general for Confederate forces in Missouri under Major General Sterling Price. In 1865, Vest won a seat in the Confederate Senate, resigning his seat in the House of Representatives of the Confederate Congress, which he held from February 1862 to January 1865. After the end of the Civil War, he returned to the practice of law and in 1877 moved to Kansas City.

Voters elected Vest to the U.S. Senate in 1879, where he succeeded James Shields. He served from March 4, 1879 to March 3, 1903, when he retired due to poor health. While in the Senate, he served on the Senate Finance Committee and encountered criticism for allowing amendments to the proposed tariff bill of 1894. Although he repeatedly denied the inclusion of additional amendments, the final bill contained many changes that Vest stated he knew nothing about at the time of his previous testimony. Senator Vest opposed the Treaty of Paris, ending the Spanish American War, due to the Philippines becoming an American "colony." In a resolution opposing the treaty, Vest said, "that under the Constitution . . . no power is given to the Federal Government to acquire territory to be held and governed permanently as colonies." He died in Sweet Springs, Missouri.

See also: Wilson-Gorman Tariff (Tariff of 1894).

Selected Bibliography:

Edward Stanwood, *American Tariff Controversies in the Nineteenth Century*, 1974.

Scott R. DiMarco

VETO POWER OF THE PRESIDENT

The Constitution of the United States gives the president the power to veto congressional legislation.

Once Congress passes a law, the president has three options: (1) sign the bill into law, (2) allow the bill to become law by not taking action for ten days, or (3) veto, or reject, the bill. In the last case, the president must give Congress a rationale for rejecting the bill. Congress can still save a vetoed bill by overriding the veto by a two-thirds majority in each chamber. The president may also carry out a pocket veto by withholding his signature from a bill if Congress adjourns within ten days of submitting said bill.

The presidential veto remains a very effective check on congressional power, for in U.S. history Congress has successfully overridden vetoes only 4 percent of the time. The very threat of a veto is often sufficient to cause Congress to reconsider its position. Historically, presidents have used the veto sparingly until after the Civil War, when the executive branch assumed a more active role in legislative issues. Grover Cleveland used the veto by allowing the Wilson-Gorman Tariff of 1894 to pass into law without his signature, signifying his disapproval of the measure. The president rarely uses the veto on tariff-related issues.

Congress has effectively countered the veto power of the president by creating omnibus bills that feature widely popular legislation, but also contain elements the president may oppose. In the Constitution's veto provision, the president must choose to veto or pass into law the entire bill. Attempts to create a line-item veto power for the president have failed, most recently with the U.S. Supreme Court overturning a provision that would allow the president to propose rescinding funds in appropriations bills in the 1998 case *Clinton v. New York City.*

See also: Civil War (American); Constitutionality.

Selected Bibliography:

Robert J. Spitzer, *The Presidential Veto,* 1988.

John D. Coats

VIRGINIA AND KENTUCKY RESOLUTIONS

Laid out the compact theory of the U.S. Constitution on which key opponents of the protective tariff relied beginning in the 1820s.

James Madison and Thomas Jefferson drafted the Virginia and Kentucky Resolutions, respectively, to protest the Alien and Sedition Acts, which a Congress dominated by Federalists passed and President John Adams signed into law in 1798. The resolutions originally served primarily to rally Jeffersonian Republicans against their political opponents, but became the touchstones of states' rights supporters for years to come.

Jefferson's draft of the Kentucky Resolutions argued that the states created an agent of limited powers—the federal government—to carry out specific tasks under the U.S. Constitution. If the federal government ever tried to assume powers not expressly delegated to it, a single state, as a party to the original compact, could judge such an act unconstitutional and refuse to enforce it. As Jefferson put it, "Where powers are assumed which have not been delegated, a nullification of the act is the rightful remedy."

The Kentucky legislature passed a version of Jefferson's resolutions in November 1798 that did not use the term "nullification." In February 1799, the legislature defied denunciations of its earlier resolutions by passing another set that explicitly claimed the right of nullification for states.

Although based on the compact theory as well, the resolutions adopted by the Virginia legislature in December 1798 failed to enunciate a clear remedy for a state to pursue if the federal government overstepped its constitutional authority. To be sure, a state could "interpose for arresting the progress of the evil" of unconstitutionally expansive federal power, but the form such interposition should take remained vague. The Virginia Resolutions seemed only to call on other states to join the Old Dominion in protesting to Congress.

In the late 1820s, Jefferson's stronger states' rights stance strongly influenced the supporters of nullification as shown in the *South Carolina Exposition* and *Protest*. Still, an aged Madison denied that the resolutions he and his fellow Virginian had penned in 1798 allowed for state nullification of any federal law as envisioned by John C. Calhoun and James Hamilton.

See also: Adams, John; Calhoun, John Caldwell; Federalists; Jefferson, Thomas; Madison, James; Nullification; South Carolina *Exposition* and *Protest*.

Selected Bibliography:

Drew R. McCoy, *The Last of the Fathers: James Madison and the Republican Legacy*, 1989.

Robert Tinkler

VOORHEES, DANIEL WOLSEY (September 26, 1827–April 10, 1897)

Lawyer, representative, and senator.

Born in Butler County, Ohio, Voorhees and his family moved to Indiana soon after his birth, settling in Fountain County near the town of Covington. Trained as a lawyer, Voorhees eventually chose politics as his vocation, and voters elected him to represent the seventh Indiana congressional district. He served in the House of Representatives from 1861 to 1866, and then from 1869 to 1873, and represented Indiana in the U.S. Senate from November 1877 to March 1897. He died in Washington,

D.C., but was buried in Terre Haute, Indiana, where he had made his home since 1857.

As a midwestern Democrat, Voorhees began his political career as a representative of the agrarian West, a proponent of free trade, and a vociferous critic of protective tariffs. During the Civil War, he became one of the principal critics of the Lincoln administration known as Copperheads. Critical of Union war aims that included goals such as the abolition of slavery, Voorhees, and Copperheads like him, vigorously opposed Republican economic policies, particularly the Morrill Tariff. During the Civil War, many of his constituents had experienced a disruption of normal trading patterns with the South due to the closing of the Mississippi River. Forced to ship through the Great Lakes and via railroads, many farmers experienced dismay over rising costs of transportation. Since the Morrill Tariff, and its subsequent revisions in 1862 and 1864, raised the level of protection for many goods, spokesmen like Voorhees denounced the tariff as a measure designed exclusively to benefit eastern manufacturing interests while "subjecting the great agricultural West to onerous and unequal burdens." He continued his criticism of Republican tariff policy throughout the war.

After the war, Voorhees would serve another twenty-four years in Congress as a respected Senator and, during the presidency of Grover Cleveland, chair of the Senate Finance Committee. In the post–Civil War period, Voorhees gradually moved away from the position of an agrarian radical. He never joined the populist crusade for the unlimited coinage of free silver, remaining a "gold democrat" who endorsed the financial policies of Grover Cleveland. Voorhees remained consistent in his opposition to the protective tariff. In 1894, for instance, he played an important role in guiding the Wilson-Gorman Tariff through Congress, a tariff that put several commodities on the free list as well as reduced average duties on products from the much higher McKinley Tariff of 1890.

See also: Civil War (American); Cleveland, Stephen Grover; Morrill Tariff (Tariff of 1861); Senate Finance Committee.

Selected Bibliography:

Leonard S. Kenworthy, *The Tall Sycamore of the Wabash, Daniel Wolsey Voorhees*, 1936; Frank L. Klement, *The Copperheads in the Middlewest*, 1960.

Bruce Tap

W

WAGES

Compensation earned by workers for their labor.

In the preindustrial era, Western labor compensation included a mixture of local and craft custom and traditions. Wages typically consisted of some combination of a nominal monetary payment and a further payment in kind of reciprocal goods and services that might include food, shelter, or clothing. The inclusion of a payment in kind through the early modern period offered employees a generalized shelter against the period's steady inflationary trend upward. Intermittently, negotiations between employer and employees for changes in the level of compensation, either decreases or increases, frequently signaled the abrogation of custom on the part of one side or the other, resulting in lockouts or walkouts and an end to production.

The rise of industrial capitalism from the mid-eighteenth century onward brought a series of changes to the nature and form of labor compensation. A steadily growing alliance between state and entrepreneur, along with the emergence of machine-based production, weakened the position of labor vis-à-vis employers. With increasing state protection against recalcitrant labor acts such as the Anti-Combination Acts in England and France, Adam Smith's caution about the detrimental role of state intervention in the labor market and its negative impact on laborers became increasingly evident. Lockouts increased, while walkouts became less effective; this was the result of the declining value of craft-specific skills capable of being performed by less contentious machines.

During the first half of the nineteenth century, political economists such as Thomas Malthus and David Ricardo engaged in a series of public debates over the validity of Say's Law, which claimed that without detrimental secular intervention, economic growth would progress steadily to the benefit of all in a given society. For his part, Malthus famously argued that growth remained limited by a finite pool of resources and unchecked population growth, ultimately leading to the "optimum theory of population" a century later. In contrast, Ricardo responded with a "one-factor theory of value" that, despite his own misgivings, articulated the role of wages in the price of goods and their circulation at market (his primary concern) and with his later "Iron Law of Wages."

After the mid-nineteenth century, certain aspects of the theories and understandings of this "School of Classical Economics" and "Political Economy" came under attack by Karl Marx. Although Marxian economics has long since been discounted, the basic ideas surrounding the role and value of work in the industrial production process continue to shape the wage debate to this day. Marx introduced the concept of the alienation of the industrial workforce through the process of proletarianization, the reduction of the value of a laborer's work to the money wage he or she received. By reorganizing labor to meet the demands of machine production, the elimination of the value of craft and skill reduced labor to a simple input in the emergence of capitalism. In essence, Marx took the earlier Theory of Labor Value and restated it in terms of a larger process of production and its impact on the laboring class. Instead of concentrating on the impact of wages on market price, Marx focused on the reorientation of society in general to a unique system of production: wage labor and industrialization. Marx's Theory of Surplus Value thus signaled the end of custom and tradition in compensation

in the face of the increasing dominance of technological inputs. The sale of labor in this new system added value to the end product, but limited the ability of the working classes in the new factory system to share in the resulting profits. Thus, the sale of labor for the money-wage could not readily translate into a uniform rise in a national standard of living for both worker and entrepreneur.

During the late nineteenth and early twentieth centuries, the understanding of wages revolved around the social and mathematical implications of Marx's vision. The post-Marxian neoclassical era of economics saw the rise of state socialism, or the direct intervention of government as mediator between labor and entrepreneur, and the accompanying rise and legitimization of labor unions. John Maynard Keynes and Knute Wicksell influenced this change by advocating state intervention in the economy to redress the resulting imbalance of capitalism and thereby balance the scales for the greater good of all.

The post–World War II period brought another shift, with a rightist co-optation of Smithian notions of laissez-faire. During the last thirty years, this misinterpretation of Adam Smith has accompanied a right-wing critique and a shift in the understanding of the role of wages and international terms of the resulting political debate. This controversy includes a critique of the welfare state, the reification of the free market, and a return to the fundamentals of Say's Law. In particular, the use of state power to regulate the economy and manage business cycles, along with the advocacy of growth and attempts to control inflation through control of monetary policy, have epitomized the theories of Milton Friedman and the practice of politicians such as Ronald Reagan and his policy of "trickle-down" economics. Driven in large measure by high wages in the industrialized West, the neoclassical critique has also led to a shift in production from the industrialized nations to the Third World, where lower wages more than compensate for increased transportation costs and tariffs. Despite resulting unemployment and a shift from a production to a service economy, politicians and theorists have pursued the proliferation of transnational free trade zones and the further demise of the traditional, wage-earning domestic working class.

See also: Capitalism; Free trade; Keynes, John Maynard; Malthus, Thomas; Ricardo, David; Smith, Adam; Third World.

Selected Bibliography:

Mark Blaug, *Economic Theory in Retrospect*, 1985; Maurice Herbert Dobb, *Wages*, 1956.

David J. Weiland III

WALKER, ROBERT JOHN (July 19, 1801–November 11, 1869)

U.S. senator, secretary of the treasury, and governor of the Kansas Territory.

Born in Northumberland, Pennsylvania, Walker received a master's degree from the University of Pennsylvania in 1822 and became a supporter of Andrew Jackson's campaign for the presidency in 1824. In 1826, he joined his brother in Natchez, Mississippi, practiced law, and entered local poli-

tics. Elected to the Senate in 1836 as a Democrat, he became an outspoken leader for the annexation of the Republic of Texas. In 1842, voters reelected him to another term in the Senate. Two years later he published *Letter of Mr. Walker, of Mississippi, relative to the Annexation of Texas*, in which he stressed that the Republic of Texas could become a "funnel" through which slaves could escape to freedom in Mexico.

During the 1844 Democratic convention, Walker played an instrumental role in denying Martin Van Buren the candidacy by restoring the two-thirds majority rule to win the nomination. Van Buren's defeat opened the way for James K. Polk, who, Walker claimed, received the nomination with his support and that of Andrew Jackson. Polk appointed Walker as secretary of the treasury, and while in that position he published Walker's Report condemning the Tariff Act of 1842 as discriminating "in favor of the rich, and against the poor." The following year, he worked hard for the successful adoption of a new tariff bill that he composed, the Tariff Act of 1846. That same year, Walker successfully advocated the reestablishment of the Independent Treasury System, abolished under the presidency of John Tyler, and the enactment of the Warehousing Act that established bonded warehouses where imports remained free of charge until the sale of the goods. As an expansionist, he approved of the Treaty of Guadalupe Hidalgo and the acquisition of the huge western territories from Mexico. Before leaving office in 1849 after Zachary Taylor's election, Walker persuaded President Polk to create the Interior Department, thereby dividing the jurisdictions of the Treasury and the Land Office.

In 1856, he returned to politics by letting James Buchanan use his home in Washington as campaign headquarters. In March 1857, Buchanan appointed Walker governor of the Kansas Territory, where he supported the antislavery Kansans. Walker returned to Washington to convince Buchanan not to support the pro-slavery faction, but, failing that, he resigned as governor. During the Civil War, he supported the North, and in Europe he sold over $150 million in U.S. war bonds. During Reconstruction, he unsuccessfully challenged the Reconstruction Acts of 1867 in the Supreme Court and advised President Andrew Johnson to back the Radical Reconstruction measures. Soon afterward, his health began to fail and, unable to practice law, he fell deeply in debt and had to sell his Washington home to satisfy his creditors. In the fall of 1869, he died in the nation's capital.

See also: Jackson, Andrew; Polk, James K.; Tariff of 1842; Tariff of 1846 (Walker's Tariff); Taylor, Zachary; Tyler, John; Van Buren, Martin; Walker's Report. **Vol. II**: Walker's Report. **Vol. III**: Tariff of 1842; Tariff of 1846 (Walker's Tariff).

Selected Bibliography:

James P. Shenton, *Robert John Walker*, 1961.

Robert P. Sutton

WALKER'S REPORT

Twenty-page report to Congress written by Secretary of the Treasury Robert Walker, arguing for the lowering of duties.

Walker submitted his report in response to a request from President James K. Polk, who sought a reduction of the Tariff Act of 1842. In addition to repeating arguments that the president had advanced in his message on the tariff in December 1845, Walker added other significant reasons for the change downward. He stated at the beginning of his report that "no more money should be collected than is necessary for the wants of the government, economically administered." He wanted to abolish all specific duties and condemned the Tariff Act of 1842 with its discriminatory rates as unjust. He believed that a tariff must treat all sections and social classes equally and argued that protectionism penalized the planter and farmer because it deprived them of the opportunity to purchase cheap foreign goods with income from agricultural exports. Speaking against protectionism, he stated that it only benefited the manufacturers through "profits and dividends extracted from the many, by taxes upon them, for the benefit of the few." Although he proclaimed that he felt no ill will "against manufacturers," only "opposition to the protective system, and not to classes or individuals," he remained clearly prejudiced against factory owners. He believed that the factory owner, obsessed with profits, planned to keep wages depressed and would soon drive the American working class to rebellion. According to Walker, the American worker must have a better chance to compete with foreign labor to raise its standard of living. He insisted on free trade; it was

America's greatest challenge. "Let our commerce be as free as our political institution," he wrote, and "nation after nation will . . . follow our example."

Although these points had merit, Walker's other arguments exhibited flaws. For example, he wrongly asserted that the price on an import, when increased by a duty, automatically raised the price of an American product. He erred in predicting that the protective tariff system would collapse when and if England repealed her duties on our agricultural commodities. As an ardent Jeffersonian, he exclaimed that "agriculture is our chief employment; it is best adapted to our situation, and if not depressed by the tariff would be most profitable." American agriculture, he claimed, unfettered by foreign tariff duties, could feed the hungry of the world.

See also: Polk, James K.; Tariff of 1842. **Vol. II**: Walker's Report. **Vol. III**: Tariff of 1842; Tariff of 1846 (Walker's Tariff).

Selected Bibliography:

James P. Shenton, *Robert John Walker*, 1961; Robert J. Walker, *Report from the Secretary of the Treasury, On the State of the Finances, December 3, 1845*, 1846.

Robert P. Sutton

WALKER'S TARIFF

See Tariff of 1846 (Walker's Tariff).

WAR OF 1812

America's second War of Independence, which resulted in the passage of protective tariffs.

In June 1812, President James Madison asked Congress to declare war on Great Britain. Madison and his supporters in Congress, known as the War Hawks, had many complaints against the British. First and foremost, England had interfered with America's trade on the high seas for nearly two decades. In an effort to stop all commerce with Napoleon, the British navy had captured hundreds of American ships. Equally important, the English had impressed many American sailors into the royal navy. British officers boarded American ships at gunpoint and removed any sailors thought to be English citizens. Finally, Madison suspected the British army in Canada of helping the Shawnee chief Tecumseh organize his Indian confederation against the United States along the western frontier. Tecumseh had united dozens of tribes in his effort to stop America's westward advance. He hoped that the British would help him win a separate Indian nation north of the Ohio River for all the tribes.

Although Congress declared war as Madison requested, the country divided over the wisdom of this action. Many in New England refused to fight against their greatest trading partner, Great Britain. Representatives from throughout the region met in Hartford to condemn "Mr. Madison's War" and to discuss possible secession from the Union. In contrast, the War Hawks never wavered in their support for the war, and now boldly called for the conquest of Canada and the final defeat of the Indians along the entire western frontier. But despite their support, they could lay out no specific plans on how to conquer Canada or the Indians. Similarly, most men from the South and West openly supported the war, but they had little military experience and even less willingness to pay the taxes necessary for a sustained conflict.

President Madison struggled to propose a coherent military strategy and raise the necessary funds for financing the war. The military plans involved sending three armies into Canada. One army under Revolutionary War general William Hull marched from Detroit into Ontario. Another crossed into Canada along the Niagara frontier. The final army ascended the Hudson River Valley and advanced toward Montreal. To pay for the war, Congress doubled tariff rates across the board. This increase would remain in effect until one year after cessation of hostilities with Great Britain. Wealthy Americans also loaned millions of dollars to the American government. The funds, never sufficient to finance the war, forced the nation near bankruptcy throughout the conflict, even though Congress raised the tariff to a record high rate.

The opening year of the War of 1812 proved a disaster for the Americans. In July, General Hull surrendered Detroit to the combined British and Indian forces led by Isaac Brock and Tecumseh. British and Indian forces captured the American posts of Fort Wayne, Fort Dearborn, and Fort Michillimackinac. Instead of taking Canada, Americans faced the prospect of losing the Old Northwest from the Ohio Valley to the Mississippi River to the British and their Indian allies. Similarly, the two-pronged attack on Canada along the Niagara frontier and the Hudson River Valley failed in October 1812, when American militiamen refused to leave their home states and fight on Canadian soil.

The tide turned in favor of the Americans throughout much of 1813. Madison appointed William Henry Harrison as head of the army in the Northwest and Andrew Jackson as commander of the army in the Southwest. Oliver Hazard Perry received orders to build a fleet of American ships at Erie, Pennsylvania, and to defeat the British navy on the Great Lakes. Harrison turned back the invading British and Indians led by Tecumseh at Fort Meigs along the Maumee River by the summer of 1813. Perry's fleet soundly defeated the British navy at Put-in-Bay on Lake Erie near Sandusky in September 1813. By October, Harrison forced the British and Indians into western Ontario. His army defeated Tecumseh at the Battle of the Thames. Tecumseh died in the fighting, breaking Indian resistance on the northwestern frontier. Later, in Alabama, Jackson defeated the last of Tecumseh's allies in the brutal Creek War.

Despite these American victories, Great Britain went on the offensive in 1814. The French forced the abdication of Napoleon and exiled him to Elba. His defeat freed troops and equipment for service on the American continent. Britain now planned a three-pronged attack against the United States. One army headed south from Montreal along the Hudson River Valley. Another sailed to the Chesapeake Bay, while the third assembled in the Caribbean for an attack on New Orleans. Although better trained and equipped than their American opponents, the first arm of the British invading army turned back at Plattsburgh on the western shore of Lake Champlain in

September 1814. The second army captured Washington, D.C., burning many government buildings, including the White House. But the British encountered stiff opposition at Baltimore, forcing them to retreat to the Caribbean, where they joined the forces gathering for the attack on New Orleans. General Andrew Jackson and his American forces soundly defeated the British at the Battle of New Orleans in January 1815.

As Americans celebrated the great victory at New Orleans, word arrived that the peace treaty ending the war had already been signed on Christmas Eve in 1814. John Quincy Adams, Speaker of the House Henry Clay, and former secretary of the treasury Albert Gallatin had worked tirelessly to prepare the Treaty of Ghent for nearly a year. The British demanded a separate Indian state in the Old Northwest Territory. The Duke of Wellington advised the negotiators that such a demand was impossible to defend. The British finally agreed to a *status quo ante bellum*. Although America lost many battles during the war, the nation finally won the respect of Great Britain. England would never again interfere with American trade on the high seas or help the Indians in their long war against the advancing Americans.

During the postwar period, Great Britain erected trade barriers that discriminated against U.S. manufacturers and dumped products on the American market in an effort to destroy the infant industries that had developed during the conflict. In response, legislators passed the first protective tariff, a shift in American trade policy that continued until 1933.

See also: American Revolution; France; Great Britain; Jefferson, Thomas; Madison, James; Protectionism.

Selected Bibliography:

Reginald Horsman, *The War of 1812*, 1969.

Mary Stockwell

WASHINGTON, GEORGE (February 22, 1732–December 14, 1799)

First president of the United States; he approved the first tariffs on imports and exports in the United States.

Born on the family estate in Westmoreland County, Virginia, on the Potomac River, George Washington grew up under the tutelage of his older brother Lawrence after their father died when Washington was eleven years old. He had a common education and, unlike most of the Founding Fathers, never attended college. Instead, he applied his sharp math skills to develop a surveyor's career. He served as a member of the Virginia House of Burgesses from 1759 to 1774. He also served as a delegate to the Continental Congress before being appointed commander in chief of the Continental Army, a post he held from 1775 to 1783. In 1789, the country elected Washington as the first president of the United States, the only candidate ever to garner a unanimous vote from the Electoral College.

Unlike his fellow Virginians, Washington accepted the idea that commerce and industry, rather than agriculture, could best render the United States an independent entity in the global economy. If the nation developed as an agrarian society, he warned, it would remain an economic colony of industrialized Europe. Washington believed that an increase in industry would boost the nation's economic vitality and contribute to national security. He also believed that the "general welfare" clause of the Constitution gave the government the right to manufacture arms and ammunition and assist in the construction of roads and canals over which these commodities would flow. The government, he argued, could augment industry by offering bounties, subsidies, and tariffs.

Two distinct political factions, or parties, developed during Washington's first administration. Alexander Hamilton, secretary of the treasury (1789–1795), became the spokesman of the Federalist Party, and Thomas Jefferson, secretary of state (1790–1793), led the opposing group, identified as the Democratic-Republican Party. Although he acknowledged association with neither faction, Washington demonstrated by his actions a preference for the Federalists' position. Hamilton defined the Federalist position in his financial plan for the new nation. In his plan, he revealed his ambition to increase the power of the federal government and encourage the rapid development of American industry. Jeffersonian Republicans, on the other hand, preferred that state governments retain the right to act in the best interest of their constituents. They also desired to stave off the inevitable rise of industrialization and remain an agrarian nation as long as possible. The tariff issue became a point of contention between the two groups. Being of the Federalist persuasion, Washington approved the first protective tariff on foreign imports. With the president's blessing, Congress imposed a variety of domestic excise taxes, including a duty on spirits, such as whiskey, distilled within the United States. The administration also revised the schedule of tariffs. In 1789, Washington had also approved a tax of fifty cents a ton on foreign ships entering American ports and a duty of 5 to 15 percent on the value of imported goods. The Tariff Act of 1792 raised the rates of import duties and offered some protection for American industry. As a result, customs revenue increased steadily, providing about 90 percent of the national government's income, and manufacturing received the boost it needed for rapid development, allowing numerous critics to hail the Federalist plan a success.

As the first president, Washington set a precedent when, after serving two terms, he elected to retire from public life. Nearly 140 years would pass before any man attempted to seek a third presidential term. In his 1796 published farewell message, Washington warned the nation to avoid political factions and entanglements with Europe. Upon retirement, he returned to his Mount Vernon home and played host to countless visitors anxious to meet the infamous George Washington. He died on December 14, 1799, after catching a terrible cold while riding horseback in freezing rain and snow. He left his wife Martha an estate valued at over $500,000 and instructions to free all his slaves on Martha's death.

See also: Adams, John; Federalists; Hamilton, Alexander; Jefferson, Thomas; Origins of political parties; Tariff of 1789; Tariff of 1790; Tariff of 1792; Tariff of 1794; Tariff of 1796.

Selected Bibliography:

John E. Ferling, *The First of Men: A Life of George Washington*, 1988; James Thomas Flexner, *Washington: The Indispensable Man*, 1972.

Carol Terry and Elaine C. Prange Turney

WATSON, JAMES ELI (November 2, 1864–July 29, 1948)

Republican representative and senator from Indiana known as a protectionist who advocated high tariffs.

Born and raised in Winchester, Indiana, in a community with a notable Quaker populace, Watson graduated from DePauw University in 1886 before pursuing a career in law. He relocated to Rushville, Indiana, in 1893 and voters elected him to the House of Representatives, where he served from 1895 to 1897 and then from 1899 to 1909. As a member of the House Ways and Means Committee, he supported legislation creating an information-gathering tariff commission, which Congress ultimately incorporated into the Payne-Aldrich Tariff Bill. As Republican House whip from 1905 to 1909, Watson promoted a policy of sound money and stable currency, criticized downward tariff revision, and firmly advocated immigration restriction.

Following an unsuccessful run for governor of Indiana in 1908, he served in a cabinet post in the National Association of Manufacturers (NAM) in 1909. When he failed to receive an appointment as the secretary of the Department of Commerce and Labor under President William Taft, he became a lobbyist for the NAM. Returned to Congress in 1916, Watson filled a vacant Senate seat where he remained until 1933. Favoring isolationism, he effectively blocked many of President Woodrow Wilson's foreign policy initiatives, including ratification of the Treaty of Versailles and the U.S. entrance into the League of Nations. As Senate majority leader from 1929 to 1933, he tenaciously opposed the undertakings of tariff revisionists, including those put forth by President Herbert Hoover. Fiercely protectionist, Watson recognized the scope of the U.S. home market and believed tariffs could both protect and generate profit. Following an unsuccessful campaign for reelection in 1932, he resumed the practice of law in Washington, D.C., where he died in 1948.

See also: Hoover, Herbert; National Association of Manufacturers (NAM); Payne-Aldrich Tariff (Tariff of 1909); Wilson, Thomas Woodrow. **Vol. II**: Woodrow Wilson's Democratic Nomination Acceptance Speech; Herbert Hoover's Statement of Intention to Approve the Hawley-Smoot Tariff Act; James Watson's Radio Address in Support of the Hawley-Smoot Tariff; Franklin D. Roosevelt's 1932 Campaign Radio Speech. **Vol. III**: Tariff of 1909 (Payne-Aldrich Tariff); Tariff of 1930 (Hawley-Smoot Tariff).

Selected Bibliography:

James Eli Watson, *As I Knew Them: Memoirs of James E. Watson, Former United States Senator from Indiana*, 1936.

John Marino

THE WEALTH OF NATIONS

The popular title of *An Inquiry into the Nature and Causes of the Wealth of Nations*, this masterpiece on modern economics, written by Scottish political economist Adam Smith, assailed mercantilism and advocated the development of an open, self-adjusting capitalist system based on free trade.

First published in 1776, *The Wealth of Nations* expressed the central ideas that the pursuit of self-interests by individuals benefited society as a whole; that the division of labor improved productivity and prosperity; and that economic affairs, including commerce, should operate according to their own devices—through free competition and marketplace demands. Its author argued against any private or government attempt to arbitrarily reorganize or redirect economic activities for the purpose of monopoly and special privileges. Smith especially castigated the mercantile policy of attempting to improve the balance of trade through restrictive and preferential taxation, especially the incentive-like drawbacks and bonuses that permitted fraud and smuggling harmful to both state revenue and fair trade. Meanwhile, he justified a nation's need for taxation, including the tariff, to provide resources necessary for major social requirements such as defense, public works, public assistance, and education. He defended, for instance, the navigation acts of the 1600s, which stipulated that goods brought from British overseas colonies into England arrive in British ships. He also advocated the use of trade restrictions to protect the safety of trade in general. Taxation, though necessary, should remain well proportioned in a fair and moderate manner so as to preserve the harmony between private and public interests, and help encourage an unfettered, self-regulating economic system. *The Wealth of Nations* had a far-reaching signifi-cance on modern economic literature. Smith's ideas influenced Americans during and after the Revolution of 1776 and especially inspired Alexander Hamilton in establishing a financial and economic system for the American republic.

See also: Free trade; Hamilton, Alexander; Mercantilism; Navigation and Trade Acts; Smith, Adam. **Vol. II:** *The Wealth of Nations*.

Selected Bibliography:

Peter McNamara, *Political Economy and Statesmanship: Smith, Hamilton, and the Foundation of the Commercial Republic*, 1998; Ian Simpson Ross, *The Life of Adam Smith*, 1995.

Guoqiang Zheng

WEBSTER, DANIEL (January 18, 1782– October 24, 1852)

Lawyer, U.S. representative, senator, and secretary of state under Presidents John Tyler and Millard Fillmore.

Born in New Hampshire, Webster graduated from Dartmouth College in 1891. He studied law under two Federalist senators and commenced his legal practice at Portsmouth in 1807. While in the House of Representatives, he joined the minority opposition to the War of 1812. In 1817, he moved to Boston and appeared before the U.S. Supreme Court as an attorney in such landmark cases as *Dartmouth College v. Woodward* (1819), *McCulloch v. Maryland* (1819), and *Gibbons v. Ogden* (1824). As a member of Congress, he gained national recognition as an impressive orator, a reputation that reached a pinnacle in his second reply to Senator Robert

Hayne of South Carolina in the 1830 Webster-Hayne debates over nullification. Along with Henry Clay, he formed the Whig Party in opposition to Andrew Jackson and in favor of a high protective tariff. After his wife's death in 1829, he remarried a wealthy New York merchant's daughter and purchased a farm in Marshfield, Massachusetts, where he lived the rest of his life. In 1832, he joined with Clay to recharter the Second Bank of the United States. After Jackson vetoed the legislation, Webster delivered a strong oration against the president in the Senate. During the presidency of Martin Van Buren, he vigorously fought against the establishment of the independent treasury that Congress created in 1840. Webster reflected New England's shift from a commercial economy to a manufacturing one by supporting the protective Tariff Act of 1828. He did agree to a gradual lowering of the tariff in 1833 as a means of settling the crisis over nullification.

He supported William Henry Harrison and John Tyler in the election of 1840 and Harrison appointed him to his cabinet as secretary of state. Webster supported Clay's program for the reestablishment of a national bank, internal improvements, and a protective tariff. After Harrison's death, Tyler twice vetoed the bank bills and attempted to raise the tariff several times. When Tyler's cabinet resigned in protest, Webster remained to finish the delicate negotiations with Britain over the Maine–Canada boundary, a treaty that he successfully completed in the 1842 Webster-Ashburton Treaty. In 1843, he resigned from Tyler's cabinet and returned to the Senate in 1845 as a leader of the Whig Party. He opposed the annexation of Texas and the spread of slavery.

When war broke out with Mexico in 1846, he condemned it as an unconstitutional war of expansion. He also supported the Wilmot Proviso, which prohibited the spread of slavery to territories acquired from Mexico because of the war.

When the nation became bitterly divided over the question of the future of slavery in the Mexican territory, a crucial debate occurred in the Senate in the winter of 1850. It began when Henry Clay advanced an Omnibus Bill that would admit California as a free state, create the territories of New Mexico and Utah without the Wilmot Proviso, and allow the citizens of these territories to decide the question of whether or not to establish slavery. On March 7, Webster delivered one of his most famous speeches. He argued that while Congress had the right to pass the Wilmot Proviso, it would prove unnecessary because geography prevented slavery from establishing itself in New Mexico and Utah. He condemned extremists on both sides since abolitionists in the North needlessly pushed for the Proviso and drove the South into hysterics, while states' rights hard-liners in the South insisted that Congress protect the right of slave owners to take slaves anywhere in the Union as a constitutionally protected right of property. Webster warned the South that any attempt to secede would mean war. His speech did much to gather moderate support in the North and West for compromise, and in the fall of 1850, Henry Clay introduced the final terms of the Compromise of 1850. The measures, ably guided by Stephen A. Douglas of Illinois, passed both houses of Congress. After the compromise, President Millard Fillmore appointed Webster as his secretary of state. In the cabinet, Webster began the first investigations into the possibility of constructing an interoceanic canal in Nicaragua.

In 1852, Webster challenged Fillmore as a rival Whig candidate for the presidency. The party convention rejected both men and chose General Winfield Scott instead. After the convention, Webster's health failed and he retired to his farm in Marshfield, embittered at what he saw as the callous ingratitude of American voters. He died there before the fall election and the victory of Democratic candidate Franklin Pierce.

See also: Clay, Henry; Jackson, Andrew; Nullification; Tariff of 1828 (Tariff of Abominations); Tyler, John; Van Buren, Martin. **Vol. II**: Daniel Webster's Speech Defending His Support of Free Trade; Robert Young Hayne's 1832 Speech in Support of Free Trade; Henry Clay's 1832 Speech in Favor of the American System. **Vol. III**: Tariff of 1828 (Tariff of Abominations); Tariff of 1832.

Selected Bibliography:

Merrill D. Peterson, *The Great Triumvirate: Webster, Clay, and Calhoun*, 1987; Robert Vincent Remini, *Daniel Webster: The Man and His Time*, 1997.

Robert P. Sutton

WELLS, DAVID AMES (June 17, 1828–November 5, 1898)

American economic writer, chair of the National Revenue Commission, and creator of the U.S. Bureau of Statistics, which established a system of scientific taxation in the United States.

Born in Springfield, Massachusetts, Wells studied at the Lawrence Scientific School and afterward co-published *The Annual of Scientific Discovery* with George Bliss. During the Civil War, he wrote *Our Burden and Our Strength* in which he argued that the United States possessed the ability to repay the huge national debt incurred as a result of Civil War expenditures. The following year, President Abraham Lincoln appointed him as chairman of the newly created National Revenue Commission. Congress created this commission for the express purpose of studying ways in which the United States could increase revenues to pay for the war, but by the time the commission met for the first time in June 1865, the war had ended. For the next five years, the period that Congress authorized for the commission to exist, the commissioners issued annual reports on such issues as the growth of the economy, the ability to repay the debt, and recommendations concerning the tariff. In his 1867 report, Wells maintained an ardent protectionist stance, but over the next two years he witnessed the abuses and excesses of protectionism. He believed that the high tariff harmed not only consumers, but in many instances the manufacturers that the duties were designed to protect. By 1869, Wells assumed a free trade position evident in his annual report. In addition to his *Reports of the Special Commissioner of the Revenue* from 1866 to 1869, Wells also wrote *Recent Economic Changes* in 1889 and *Theory and Practice of Taxation*, a work published in 1900 after his death. Wells died in Norwich, Connecticut.

See also: Civil War (American); Lincoln, Abraham; Protectionism.

Selected Bibliography:

Edward Stanwood, *American Tariff Controversies in the Nineteenth Century*, 1967.

Cynthia Clark Northrup

WESTERN HEMISPHERE SUBCOMMITTEE OF HOUSE INTERNATIONAL RELATIONS COMMITTEE

Functioning group within the International Relations Committee.

The House International Relations Committee ("International Relations"), more commonly referred to as the House Foreign Affairs Committee, can trace its lineage back to the Continental Congress in 1775 when Benjamin Franklin served as the chairman of the committee. The current name, first used following a large net increase in the number of House Democrats in 1975, reverted to the previous name in 1979, being replaced by International Relations following the Republican takeover of Congress in the aftermath of the 1994 national elections. The committee consists of one functional committee that deals with human rights and international organizations, and five regional committees, one of which is the Western Hemisphere Subcommittee. The committees assist members in achieving one of three major goals: reelection, influence within the chamber, or policy influence.

The International Relations Committee attracts individuals who seek to influence the formation of public policy. This is certainly true of Cass Ballenger (R-NC) who won election during the Democratically advantageous year of 1986 and also served on the policy-oriented Education and Work Force

Subcommittee that has jurisdiction over such trade-pertinent matters as the Occupational and Safety Health Administration (OSHA). He authored two pieces of OSHA reform legislation that President William Jefferson Clinton signed in 1998. The former North Carolina legislator, who came out of the plastics industry and has traveled mostly as a private citizen extensively throughout Central America and South America, advocates extending the North American Free Trade Agreement (NAFTA) to include all the nations of Central America and South America. He is an unsurprising choice to serve as chair of the Western Hemisphere Subcommittee of House International Relations Committee.

The ranking Democrat on the subcommittee, Bob Menendez of New Jersey, joined the House of Representatives in 1992 and voted for the passage of NAFTA signed by Democratic president Clinton, although opposed by Majority Leader Richard Gephardt (D-Mo.). He insisted on the importance of negotiating side agreements that protect and enhance environmental and worker safety standards. Menendez co-authored legislation that assists U.S. businesses investing overseas and authored the Small Business Protection Act that protects small businesses in the event that they make use of imports on which the United States has imposed retaliatory trade tariffs. While strongly interested in policy formulation, he remains attentive to the interests of his district, as when he worked to protect a company in Perth Amboy that produces steel wire rods from underpriced steel imports.

When regional subcommittees formed, committee members realized the necessity of a Western Hemisphere group. Canadians remain among the largest foreign investors in the United States. The importation and distribution of bananas from Central America affect U.S. cities, including Boston and New Orleans. Citgo, a Venezuelan company, maintains a large industrial presence in such metropolitan areas as Lake Charles, Louisiana.

The strengthening of subcommittees that took place in the 1970s has certainly been evident in the work of the Subcommittee on the Western Hemisphere of House International Relations Committee. The subcommittee in the One Hundred Seventh Congress, composed of six Republicans and five Democrats, mirrors the close partisan balance in the U.S. House of Representatives. The subcommittee held eight hearings in the second session of the One Hundred Sixth Congress, mainly featuring testimony on the topic of trade in the Western Hemisphere.

Political leaders for nearly seventy years stressed the importance of trade in the Western Hemisphere. President Franklin D. Roosevelt established his Good Neighbor Policy with the nations of Latin America to promote trade with those nations and ameliorate the economic impact of the Great Depression on the domestic U.S. economy. President George Herbert Walker Bush, in the early 1990s, announced his Enterprise for the Americas Initiative that embraced the establishment of a free trade area covering all of the nations of the Western Hemisphere by 2005. Among those testifying before the Western Hemisphere Subcommittee in 2000 in support of such a development were Sidney Weintraub, who holds the William E. Simon chair in political

economy at the Center for Strategic and International Studies in Washington, D.C., and Dr. Susan Kaufman Purcell, author of *The U.S. and Latin America*. Weintraub pointed out that Latin America conducts 40 percent of its foreign trade with the United States. Purcell stressed the importance of improving the prospects for democracy in Latin America and higher standards of living in the United States and Latin America. She concluded:

> For these reasons, the creation of a free trade area of the Americas should be the number one priority of the next U.S. administration's Latin American policy. All other U.S. policy initiatives pale in importance compared to the many benefits that hemispheric free trade would bring to both Latin America and the United States.

See also: Bush, George Herbert Walker; Clinton, William Jefferson (Bill); Congress (United States); Gephardt, Richard; North American Free Trade Agreement (NAFTA); Roosevelt, Franklin D.

Selected Bibliography:

John Edward Wilz, "Good Neighbor Policy," *Franklin D. Roosevelt: His Life and Times*, 1985.

Henry B. Sirgo

WHARTON, JOSEPH (March 3, 1826– January 11, 1909)

An American industrialist, founder of the Wharton School of Business, and leading authority on the manufacture of small coins.

Born to a Quaker family in Philadelphia, Pennsylvania, Wharton apprenticed in accounting before joining an elder brother in the manufacture of white lead for paint. After studying chemistry in Philadelphia, Wharton managed a mining and chemical manufacturing firm in which he developed a profitable method of refining metallic zinc. A rise in the price of zinc increased his wealth, but he left the industry in 1863 to manufacture nickel. He developed a commercially successful process for making high quality nickel and supplied the U.S. Mint with the metal for a new small coin. For almost twenty-five years, Wharton monopolized the American nickel industry. To protect his industry, Wharton lobbied Congress for high duties on nickel and enjoyed partial success when Congress increased the duty to thirty cents a pound, even though he had pushed for fifty cents. He believed that, after providing Americans with better coinage, he deserved a reward. Wharton used his profits from nickel to invest in iron, steel, and railroads. He actively participated in the American Industrial League as a means of uniting lobbyists in protecting industry. In 1881, Wharton funded the Wharton School with the understanding that professors would promote high tariffs. From 1873 until he died in Philadelphia, Wharton served as a chief lobbyist for the American Iron and Steel Association.

See also: American Iron and Steel Institute (AISI); Lobbying.

Selected Bibliography:

W. Ross Yates, *Joseph Wharton: Quaker Industrial Pioneer*, 1987.

Caryn E. Neumann

WHIG PARTY

Founded in 1834 by National Republicans; opposed to the policies of President Andrew Jackson.

Denouncing the seventh president as a monarch, the new party took its name from its British counterparts, who resisted the arbitrary authority of the English monarch in the eighteenth century.

In many respects, the evolution of a second-party system seemed inevitable. For several years, the Democratic-Republican Party had experienced tension between two factions within the party. Andrew Jackson, Martin Van Buren, and others represented the Jeffersonian tradition of strict constructionism and a weak central government, particularly when it came to sponsorship of economic development. Henry Clay, John Quincy Adams, and Daniel Webster endorsed a more Hamiltonian tradition of broad constructionism and favored a more positive relationship between the federal government and the promotion of economic development. The American Whig party emerged from the nationalist wing of the Republican Party.

The American System, formulated by Henry Clay, represented the specific economic ideas that invigorated the Whig Party. Clay developed a set of economic proposals, nationalistic in scope, that necessitated federal involvement in many aspects of the nation's economic life. Clay envisioned policies that would allow each section of the young republic to specialize in the type of economic activity for which it was best suited. The South could focus on cotton for export and to feed

New England textile factories, the Northwest could devote itself to the cultivation of wheat and other food-stuffs, while New England could continue on its path of industrial development.

The American system encouraged aggressive spending on internal improvements, especially a national system of transportation. Orderly growth and stability required the continuation of a National Bank. Andrew Jackson's veto of the recharter bill for the Second Bank of the United States became a major issue in the formation of the Whig Party. Finally, emerging American manufacturing concerns depended on protection from foreign competition, principally Great Britain, through protective tariff legislation.

Prior to 1816, the United States had adopted a modest tariff for revenue purposes only. In 1816, Congress enacted the first protective tariff to discourage the purchase of foreign goods altogether, thereby stimulating domestic manufacturing. The protective tariff reached an all-time high in the passage of the Tariff of Abominations in 1828. Just prior to the formation of the Whig Party in 1834, Henry Clay played a pivotal role in the Compromise Tariff of 1833, a measure that lowered the protective tariff as a means of diffusing the Nullification Crisis.

As the party of the protective tariffs, the Whigs experienced little success in realizing their economic goals. Although the Whig candidate William Henry Harrison captured the White House in 1840, his premature death brought Virginian John Tyler to the presidency. Tyler's commitment to the Whig economic agenda proved mar-

ginal, resulting in a presidency mired by controversy and division. While Whigs managed to raise duties to 1832 levels in the tariff of 1842, the Walker Tariff of 1846, brought about by a Democratic Congress and the Democratic administration of James K. Polk, lowered tariff rates and returned to a revenue principle as opposed to protection.

Even though the Whig Party elected Zachary Taylor to the presidency in 1848, the increasing prominence of the slavery issue as well as such ethnocultural issues as temperance detracted from the economic agenda and eventually led to the disappearance of the Whig Party by the middle of the 1850s. The Republican Party that emerged out of the political crisis co-opted many of the Whig economic ideas, including the Morrill Tariff of 1861.

See also: American System; Clay, Henry; Jackson, Andrew; Taylor, Zachary; Van Buren, Martin.

Selected Bibliography:

Daniel Walker Howe, *The Political Culture of the American Whigs*, 1979; Charles Sellers, *The Market Revolution: Jacksonian America, 1818–1846*, 1991.

Bruce Tap

WHITMAN, WALT (May 31, 1819– March 26, 1892)

American poet associated with a celebration of democracy and individual freedom.

His greatest work, *Leaves of Grass*, contains the much-praised "Song of Myself," which features "Walt Whitman, an American," humanity, the universe, and nature. "The United States themselves," Whitman wrote, "are essentially the greatest poem." Born in West Hills, New York, Whitman served as a printer's assistant, compositor, teacher, and newspaper editor before turning to journalism as a full-time occupation. Later, he worked as a carpenter and a government clerk. Politically active in Democratic Party ranks, Whitman fiercely opposed slavery and supported free-soil developments in the new territories.

Whitman consistently supported free trade. While serving as editor of the *Brooklyn Eagle*, Whitman castigated the protectionist stance of the Whigs. Such a position, he believed, remained consistent with the Democratic call for limited government and opposition to monopolies. He likened Whig support for high tariff rates to allowing slavery into the new territories or anti-immigration efforts. In June 1846, Whitman assailed the "manufacturing capitalists of the North," for their position on protection. "How nice a game they play in asking a high tariff 'for the benefit of the working men.' . . . Our American capitalists of the manufacturing orders would poor a great many people to be so rich!" Retaining his belief in free trade until the end of his life, Whitman asserted in 1888 that "it is not a fiscal, it is a moral, problem—a problem of the largest humanities." Opposing a nationalistic approach, Whitman revealed, "I am for free trade because I am for anything that will break down barriers between people: I want to see the countries all wide open."

See also: Free trade.

Selected Bibliography:

Gay Wilson Allen, *Walt Whitman Handbook*, 1946; Walt Whitman, *Complete Poetry and Collected Prose*, 1982.

Robert C. Cottrell

WILLKIE, WENDELL (February 18, 1892–October 8, 1944)

Republican candidate for president of the United States in 1940.

Born in Elwood, Indiana, Willkie received a bachelor's and a law degree from Indiana University. In 1933, he rose to the position of president of the Commonwealth and Southern Corporation, a utilities holding company in New York City. Although a Democrat, he gained national prominence as a critic of President Franklin Roosevelt's New Deal.

Willkie moved to the Republican Party in 1940 and that same year became a dark horse candidate for the Republican nomination. Grassroots "Willkie for President" clubs carried him to the Republican convention and he received the nomination on the sixth ballot.

Willkie's campaign focused on the two overarching issues of the day: World War II and Roosevelt's New Deal. He supported aid to the Allies, accepted some of Roosevelt's reforms, and called for the federal government to encourage growth in the private sector. He lost the election decisively, although he polled more votes than any Republican candidate to that time.

Following his loss, Willkie toured England, the Middle East, the Soviet Union, and China. In 1943, he wrote a best-selling book, *One World*, which condemned imperialism and advocated international cooperation through a strong international organization. He withdrew from the contest for Republican presidential nominee in 1944 during the early campaigning. He died later that year in New York City from heart failure at age fifty two.

See also: Roosevelt, Franklin D.; World War II.

Selected Bibliography:

Steve Neal, *Dark Horse: A Biography of Wendell Willkie*, 1989.

John D. Coats

WILSON, THOMAS WOODROW (December 28, 1856–February 3, 1924)

Twenty-eighth president of the United States; championed the progressive reforms of the New Freedom, including downward tariff revision to promote free enterprise.

Born to a long line of Presbyterian pastors in Staunton, Virginia, Wilson grew to boyhood in a South traumatized by the Civil War and Reconstruction. After graduation from Princeton University in 1879, he entered the law school of the University of Virginia, began his practice of law in Atlanta, and secured admission to the bar in 1882. Not finding success as a lawyer, Wilson entered Johns Hopkins University in 1883 to prepare for a teaching career and won a doctorate in political science and history in 1886. He then took successive professorships at Bryn Mawr College in Pennsylvania, Wesleyan University in Connecticut, and Princeton University; in each, he excelled in the scholarship of political science and history. Through teaching and writing, Wilson analyzed and disseminated his political views on the problems of American leadership and its impact on the structure of American national government. He argued that the separation of executive from legislative responsibility had produced failed governance in the American political system.

Wilson's election as president of Princeton University in 1902 gave him the first opportunity to apply his political theory to practice. During his tenure as president from 1902 to 1910, Wilson enforced central leadership as he reformed instructional method and curriculum, though he failed to reform undergraduate social life. After an abortive attempt in 1909 to curb the monetary influence of donors at Princeton, Wilson agreed to accept from the leading Democratic boss of New Jersey the nomination for governorship. But he rejected the task asked of him: to act as the conservative counterforce that would stem the Progressivism then at high tide. Elected governor of New Jersey in 1911, Wilson dominated the state Democratic Party and supported comprehensive reform legislation that included a corrupt practice act, the Workingmen's Compensation Act, municipal reform, reorganization of the school system, passage of antitrust laws, and the implementation of the direct primary. With his record as a reformer, Wilson undertook a nationwide Democratic contest for the White House in 1912 and, supported by William Jennings Bryan, won the nomination for the presidency. To counter the New Nationalism of the Progressive Party's nominee, Theodore Roosevelt—who championed the sweeping extension of federal regulation and welfare activity —Wilson campaigned for the New Freedom, a national program to unleash American economic dynamism and boost individual energies for creative competition. The New Freedom advocated drastic tariff reform, the reorganization of the banking and credit system to free them from monopolistic control, and the strengthening of antitrust laws to address unfair trade practices. Wilson won the presidency by polling 435 electoral votes out of 531, but gained only 42 percent of the popular vote.

As president, Wilson strengthened executive authority by pushing an ambitious legislative agenda and forcefully securing its approval from a Democratic Congress. On the day of his inauguration, March 4, 1913, Wilson called Congress into special session to redeem the Democratic Party's promise of tariff reform. Wilson argued against high tariffs, believing them to enhance the power of trusts while weakening free competition. By battling the lobbyists and inner-party opposition, Wilson forced the Underwood-Simmons Tariff Act of 1913 through Congress. This act was the first substantial downward revision of duties since before the Civil War. With the object of equalizing foreign and domestic costs, the act put iron, steel, raw wool, sugar, and certain agricultural products on the free list and reduced the rates on cotton and woolen goods. To compensate for the expected loss of revenue, Congress enacted a graduated income tax under the newly ratified Sixteenth Amendment. Wilson also pushed through Congress the Federal Reserve Act of 1913, antitrust

legislation, and the Federal Trade Commission.

The New Freedom ideals also found expression in Wilson's foreign policy, which aimed to construct new international relations along liberal-internationalist lines by calling on foreign nations to copy American-type democracy and capitalism. Such diplomacy met severe challenges, almost brought the United States into war with Mexico in 1916, and caused in part the American entry into World War I in 1917. At the war's end, Wilson failed to implement his Fourteen Points for international peace, save for the League of Nations, but even on that issue he fought a losing battle against the Republican opposition in Congress. Wilson suffered a nervous collapse in September 1919 while on a national speaking tour touting support for the League and never fully recovered. In December 1920, Wilson won the Nobel Peace Prize for his efforts at Versailles in 1919. He died in Washington, D.C.

See also: Bryan, William Jennings; Civil War (American); Democratic Party; Federal Trade Commission (FTC); Roosevelt, Theodore; Underwood-Simmons Tariff (Tariff of 1913); World War I. **Vol. II**: Theodore Roosevelt's Bull Moose Acceptance Speech; Woodrow Wilson's Democratic Nomination Acceptance Speech. **Vol. III**: Tariff of 1894 (Wilson-Gorman Tariff); Tariff of 1913 (Underwood-Simmons Tariff).

Selected Bibliography:

Kendrick Clements, *The Presidency of Woodrow Wilson*, 1992; Robert M. Saunders, *In Search of Woodrow Wilson: Beliefs and Behavior*, 1998.

Guoqiang Zheng

WILSON, WILLIAM L. (May 3, 1843– October 17, 1900)

Member of the U.S. House of Representatives from West Virginia partly responsible for the Wilson-Gorman Tariff of 1894.

Born in Jefferson County, Virginia, Wilson earned a B.A. from Columbian College (now George Washington University) in 1860 and studied at the University of Virginia for a year. During the Civil War, he served as a private in the Confederate cavalry. After the war, Wilson returned to Columbian College to study law, obtaining admittance to the bar in 1869. He started his legal practice in Charles Town, West Virginia, in 1871.

Wilson entered politics in the Democratic Party and served as a city attorney and superintendent of schools. In 1874, he campaigned unsuccessfully for a seat in the West Virginia House of Representatives. Wilson represented the state at the Democratic National Convention of 1880 and also served as a presidential elector. In 1882, he received an appointment to the office of president for West Virginia University. Wilson held that position for less than a year before voters elected him to the U.S. House of Representatives in the fall of 1882. He served for the next twelve years.

In the House, Wilson earned a reputation as a tariff reformer. He opposed the protective tariff, arguing that it created a burden on consumers. While calling for a reduction in the protective tariff, he took care to exclude West Virginia products, especially coal, from a general tariff reduction. A member of the Ways and Means Committee, he supported the Mills Bill. As committee chair, Wilson guided a bill through the House that would have reduced tariffs far below the rates set by the McKinley Tariff. The Wilson-Gorman Tariff emerged from the Senate as a weakened version of the original bill. President Grover Cleveland allowed the bill to become law without his signature.

Wilson lost his congressional seat in 1894, but returned to Washington as President Cleveland's postmaster general in 1895. After leaving the Cabinet in 1897, he became president of Washington and Lee University. Wilson died of tuberculosis on October 17, 1900, in Lexington, Virginia.

See also: Cleveland, Stephen Grover; McKinley Tariff (Tariff of 1890); Mills Bill; Wilson-Gorman Tariff (Tariff of 1894).

Selected Bibliography:

Festus P. Summers, *William L. Wilson and Tariff Reform*, 1953.

John David Rausch Jr.

WILSON-GORMAN TARIFF (TARIFF OF 1894)

Initiated for the purpose of reducing rates.

The tariff issue dominated the 1892 presidential campaign, and the victorious Democratic Party called for tariff reform. The financial panic of 1893 tempered enthusiasm for lower tariffs and the resulting Wilson-Gorman Tariff of August 1894 offered much less than many Democrats wanted. Representative William L. Wilson (D-W.Va.) sponsored the bill in the House, but Arthur P. Gorman (D-Md.), a staunch protectionist, guided the legislation through the Senate. The final act, burdened with some 634 amendments, substantially reduced the impact of the new tariff. Although it lowered some of the higher rates of the McKinley Tariff of 1890, it failed to please serious tariff reform advocates, and President Grover Cleveland allowed it to become law without his signature. Among its notable features, Wilson-Gorman ended the reciprocity provision of the McKinley Tariff, thereby invalidating a number of trade agreements concluded in the early 1890s. It abrogated the Saratoga Convention of 1891, causing a serious German protest that this tariff violated its Most Favored Nation status with the United States. Wilson-Gorman placed raw wool on the free list, and slightly lowered some rates on woolen manufactures. It included small reductions on cotton and silk goods, on pig iron, steel rails, and many other articles, as well as larger reductions on coal, iron ore, chinaware, and tin plate. To offset an anticipated drop in revenues, the act increased the tariff on raw sugar. Under the Wilson-Gorman Tariff, average rates for fiscal years 1894 to 1897 averaged 21 percent on all goods and 41 percent on dutiable goods, compared with 22 percent overall, and 59 percent on dutiable goods under the McKinley Tariff during the period 1892 to 1894. Although short-lived, this tariff initiated a process of moderating high U.S. tariffs continued by subsequent Republican and Democratic administrations, beginning with the Dingley Tariff of 1897, which restored the reciprocity feature of the McKinley Tariff. Republicans argued that Wilson-Gorman seriously undermined U.S. commercial credibility abroad. The Wilson-Gorman Act also established a federal personal income tax, but the Supreme Court later declared that provision unconstitutional in *Pollock v. Farmers' Loan and Trust Co.*

See also: Dingley Tariff (Tariff of 1897); McKinley Tariff (Tariff of 1890); Most Favored Nation (MFN); Personal income tax (Sixteenth Constitutional Amendment). **Vol. II**: Grover Cleveland's 1887 State of the Union Address; Benjamin Harrison's 1889 State of the Union Address; William McKinley's 1888 Speech on Tariff Benefits for Labor. **Vol. III**: Tariff of 1890 (McKinley Tariff); Tariff of 1894 (Wilson-Gorman Tariff); Tariff of 1897 (Dingley Tariff).

Selected Bibliography:

Festus P. Summers, *William L. Wilson and Tariff Reform: A Biography*, 1974; Paul Wolman, *Most Favored Nation: The Republican Revisionists and U.S. Tariff Policies, 1897–1912*, 1992.

Ralph Lee Woodward Jr.

WOMEN

Activists, consumers, employers, home caretakers, and laborers, women held a number of views regarding the tariff; it also affected them to varying degrees.

Tariffs raised the cost of living, especially goods women wished to purchase, whether for the household or their own dress or care. Exorbitant duties on items such as woolen dresses or prices kept high by U.S. manufacturers that faced little or no competition from foreign companies affected the purchases of women. On the other hand, the burgeoning companies hired more people, including women, thus making the tariff valuable to female workers.

Yet the women so employed worked long hours in difficult conditions for extremely low wages and frequently remained unable to purchase the desired goods that tariff advocates had promised they would be able to afford.

Although lacking a specific political method, such as the vote, to make their voices heard regarding the tariff in the nineteenth and early twentieth centuries, women met the challenge by editorializing, organizing, speaking, lobbying, and campaigning. Not surprisingly, women advocated different perspectives concerning free trade and the protective tariff. The International Council of Women asserted that men spent too much time on the tariff and not enough on rights for one-half the citizenry. Labor organizer and radical Lucy Parsons opposed a protective tariff, along with most other governmental actions, and called for free distribution of the products of labor for consumption. Populist leader Mary Elizabeth Lease equivocated somewhat on the issue and argued for free trade in the Americas, but not with Europe. Unfortunately, the debate over free trade became one of feminism versus antifeminism; protectionists demanded high tariffs because they would keep women at home, "where they belonged," with the children. Progressive reformer Charlotte Perkins Gilman countered that contention and encouraged women to seek economic independence by entering the labor force.

The mystique of domesticity, supported by the protectionists, encouraged women to maintain old-fashioned households (even without new inventions), while other women clamored for changes and entered occupations previously held by men. Proliferation of convenience goods changed the nature of domestic work; by 1890, nearly four million women worked outside the home. This occurrence instilled fear in male workers and protectionists, who resisted the destruction of the ideology of women as wives and mothers. The Republican Party exacerbated the situation by assuming that protection should maintain equality of the costs of production at home and abroad, together with a reasonable profit.

Selected Bibliography:

Carolyn Asbaugh, *Lucy Parsons, American Revolutionary*, 1976; Joanne Reitano, *The Tariff Question in the Gilded Age: The Great Debate of 1888*, 1994; Richard Stiller, *Queen of Populists: The Story of Mary Elizabeth Lease*, 1970.

Bruce A. Glasrud

WOOL AND WOOLENS

Products that played a central role in many nineteenth-century tariff controversies.

Wool and woolens appeared on the duty-free list from 1789 to 1816, when Congress placed a 15 percent duty on wool. Beginning in 1824, the rates on wool progressively increased from 25 to 50 percent over the next three years. In addition, customs officials placed a minimum valuation of twenty-five cents on wool and taxed the items accordingly. Debate within the wool industry, located primarily in Massachusetts, hampered efforts to increase the rates and prevent the importation of all wool and woolen goods. Larger manufacturers and capitalists believed that the factory system that had been used so successfully in the cotton industry would work for wool as well. Smaller manufacturers believed that only a high tariff could yield the necessary profits to sustain their business. The anti-protectionist forces gained the support of Congress and the rates remained low. The debate over wool reemerged during the Harrisburg Convention, with delegates favoring a higher tariff, but not the exclusion of all foreign imports since the domestic production of wool failed to fulfill the requirements of American factories. The passage of the Tariff of 1828, known as the Tariff of Abominations, ensured the continuance of the wool industry as tariff rates remained high. But the Compromise Tariff of 1833 ushered in an era of financial difficulty and production stoppages. Wool manufacturers struggled under the gradual reduction of rates until 1841, when the duty rate dropped to 28 percent and farmers could not sell the wool clipped from their sheep in 1842 to American factories. Debate continued over the rate for wool during the 1840s and 1850s. After the Civil War, wool appeared again in the Mills Bill of 1888, when Congress rejected a proposed increase to 40 percent. The wool industry continued to struggle until legislators placed wool on the free list in 1896. The immediate impact of this bill included the loss of $21 million in revenue, a threefold increase in the importation of wool, and the loss of a domestic market for the 80 million pounds of wool, amounting to a loss of approximately $30 million a year on this one product alone. The negative impact on the economy resulted in the restoration of wool to the dutiable list in 1897.

See also: Dingley Tariff (Tariff of 1897); Harrisburg Convention of 1827; Mills Bill; Tariff of 1816; Tariff of 1828 (Tariff of Abominations).

Selected Bibliography:

Edward Stanwood, *American Tariff Controversies in the Nineteenth Century*, 1967.

Cynthia Clark Northrup

WORLD TRADE ORGANIZATION (WTO)

The primary global institution overseeing international trade rules.

Headquartered in Geneva, Switzerland, the World Trade Organization (WTO) includes more than 130 members who account for over 90 percent of international trade. The organization's principal objective focused on ensuring that world commerce flows as smoothly, predictably, and freely as possible.

The WTO is the successor to the General Agreement on Tariffs and Trade (GATT), which provided a post–World War II framework for liberalizing international trade. In a series of protracted negotiations, known as rounds, the U.S.-sponsored GATT system proved successful at reducing trade barriers, especially protective tariffs. Three decades after GATT's establishment in 1947, the level of tariff rates, import quotas, and export subsidies in industrialized nations had been cut drastically. The average tariff in the United States, for example, declined by over 90 percent. This development stimulated world trade, investment, and economic growth.

During the 1980s, several developments threatened the GATT system.

For one, there arose a series of nontariff trade barriers known as Voluntary Export Restraints (VER). Because of their "voluntary" nature, these bilateral agreements, designed to limit exports, bypassed GATT rules. The United States, long a champion of GATT and trade liberalization, participated in VER agreements because of domestic economic problems. The combination of trade deficits and employment setbacks in key U.S. industries such as steel and automobiles led to calls for protectionism. Mounting international ill will toward Japan threatened the GATT system. Second in size only to the United States, the Japanese economy had expanded unlike any other, emerging as the world's largest exporter. Often complaining about Japan's "administrative" trade barriers, many industrialized countries maneuvered to limit Japanese imports.

Fears over a serious breakdown in the multilateral trading system brought forth a new round of trade negotiations. These talks, known as the Uruguay Round, conducted from 1986 to 1994, significantly revised the original GATT by creating new rules for promoting free trade in manufactured goods. GATT focused largely on the trade of physical goods, but the Uruguay Round also concluded landmark agreements that established trade rules for services and intellectual property. Ultimately, the Uruguay Round resulted in the creation of the WTO as the umbrella organization responsible for the implementation of these pacts by monitoring trade and by settling disputes.

The WTO has a dynamic political structure dominated by six primary bodies. The highest-ranking institution is the Ministerial Conference, which consists of political representatives from each member nation. It convenes at least once every two years. The General Council, which also acts as the WTO's Dispute Settlement Body and the Trade Policy Review Body, serves the Ministerial Conference. The official ambassador or diplomatic delegation-head in Switzerland represents WTO members on the General Council. The council gathers several times a year. The next organizational level includes Goods, Services, and Intellectual Property Councils, each reporting directly to the General Council. The WTO's final major body, the Secretariat, consists of a bureaucracy of some 500 staffers charged with supporting the various councils and committees, analyzing international trade, providing technical assistance to developing nations, and explaining WTO affairs to the media and public.

Since its creation, the WTO has experienced major successes contributing to freer and fairer trade. In February 1997, after prolonged deliberation, it helped facilitate a major telecommunications pact between sixty-eight countries, with all agreeing to abide by a common set of rules and open their markets to foreign companies. Later that same year, more nations concluded a similar agreement covering services in banking, securities, and insurance. The WTO has also succeeded as an arbiter of trade disputes, with its rulings enjoying the support of the leading economic powers. But not all has gone well. In November 1999, for example, anti-globalization groups, including organized labor and environmental advocates, gathered en masse in Seattle to protest against the WTO during a new round of trade talks. The WTO faces many such challenges in the future, but its early successes have been undeniable.

See also: Automobile industry; Buchanan, Patrick J.; Bush, George Herbert Walker; Clinton, William Jefferson (Bill); Dumping; Environmental issues; Free trade; General Agreement on Tariffs and Trade (GATT); Kennedy Round; Labor; Protectionism; Steel; Tokyo Round; Trade deficits; Uruguay Round; World War II. **Vol. II**: The General Agreement on Tariffs and Trade.

Selected Bibliography:

Bernard M. Heckman, *The Political Economy of the World Trading System: From GATT to WTO*, 1995; William A. Lovett, Alfred E. Eckes Jr., and Richard L. Brinkman, eds., *U.S. Trade Policy: History, Theory, and the WTO*, 1999; World Trade Organization, *From GATT to the WTO: The Multilateral Trading System in the New Millennium*, 2000.

Jeffrey J. Matthews

WORLD WAR I

Conflict that engulfed most of the industrialized world as a result of secret alliances and imperial ambitions.

War in Europe broke out after a Serbian national assassinated Archduke Francis Ferdinand of Austria-Hungary in 1914. When the emperor declared war on Serbia, the Serbs called on the Russian czar to fulfill his obligations under a secret alliance between the two countries. Austria-Hungary responded by relying on the German military to fight beside them in accordance with a separate unpublicized treaty between their countries. German involvement

drew the Ottoman Empire into the war; German military officers had been training Ottoman forces for several decades. When Russia called on its western ally, the Germans attacked France through neutral Belgium, bringing Great Britain into the conflict at the same time. Japan, seizing an opportune moment to expand its influence in Asia while the European powers fought among themselves, declared war on Russia, France, and Great Britain. The system of secret alliances and imperial ambitions turned the assassination into a world-changing event.

The United States maintained a policy of neutrality for the first few years of the war as President Woodrow Wilson attempted to promote his plan for the postwar period. Outlining his Fourteen Points, Wilson advocated the right of self-determination for all peoples, peace without victory, and the creation of the League of Nations. Meanwhile, German commanders, responding to a British naval blockade of the North Sea, initiated submarine warfare attacking and sinking both passenger and merchant marine ships. After the sinking of the *Lusitania* in 1916, the United States moved closer to war, but refrained from formally entering the conflict until Wilson received an intercepted telegram from the German foreign secretary Arthur Zimmermann to the German ambassador in the United States. The Zimmermann Note instructed him to contact Mexican officials should the United States declare war on Germany. In exchange for a Mexican attack on the southern U.S. border, an event that would prohibit American troops from assisting its allies in Europe, Mexico could reclaim its former territory in Texas, Arizona,

New Mexico, and California. The release of the telegram shifted public opinion in the United States and Congress quickly approved Wilson's request for a declaration of war. Once the United States entered the conflict, fighting continued for just over one year before the Germans sued for peace. The signing of the Treaty of Versailles officially ended the war, but failed to incorporate any of Wilson's Fourteen Points except for the League of Nations, an international organization that the United States refused to join.

Prior to the war, Wilson had persuaded Congress to reduce the tariff, although the passage of the Underwood-Simmons Tariff Act occurred as the states ratified the Sixteenth Amendment, which allowed for a personal income tax. Rates remained low throughout the war as Europeans, unable to produce enough for their own consumption or for export, relied on the United States for its food and military supplies. The end of the war raised fears of a flood of European imports, and Congress moved quickly to enact the Emergency Act of 1921 and the Fordney-McCumber Tariff of 1922, raising rates from an average of 15.2 percent to 36.2 percent over a two-year period. While the high tariff contributed to the prosperity of the United States during the 1920s, it also created trade imbalances that exacerbated the financial difficulties of European nations, especially Germany.

See also: Fordney-McCumber Tariff (Tariff of 1922); Underwood-Simmons Tariff (Tariff of 1913); Wilson, Thomas Woodrow.

Selected Bibliography:

Alfred E. Eckes, *Opening America's Market: U.S. Foreign Trade Policy Since 1776*, 1995; Ellis Hawley, ed., *The Great War and the Search for a Modern Order: A History of the American People and their Institutions, 1917–1933*, 1992.

Cynthia Clark Northrup

WORLD WAR II

Second world conflict; fought over unresolved issues from World War I.

At the conclusion of World War I, the Treaty of Versailles assigned the blame for the war to Germany and forced the country to pay heavy war reparations to the victors. Although initial payments occurred, the economic instability within the country, exacerbated by the Great Depression, resulted in the rise of the Nazi Party. As the United States struggled to find a solution to the ever-deepening crisis, Hitler rebuilt the German economy by focusing on military expenditures. Between 1939 and 1941, he initiated a series of conquests, each of which Great Britain and France acquiesced to after he promised to end further expansion. His invasion of Poland on September 1, 1939, ended the policy of appeasement and forced Great Britain and France to declare war on Germany two days later.

As during the first war, the United States operated under a policy of neutrality until December 7, 1941, when the Japanese attacked Pearl Harbor. During the next several months, the Japanese swept through the Pacific islands without resistance before the United States could reassert its presence. On December 8, 1941, the United

States and Great Britain declared war on Japan, whereupon the Germans declared war on the two nations. Fighting on the coast of North Africa, Sicily, Italy, and France, the United States finally forced Germany to surrender, with Russia taking the heaviest casualties for the Allies. The Japanese continued to fight after the war in Europe ended, and only when President Harry S Truman authorized the dropping of the atomic bomb on Hiroshima and Nagasaki did the nation of Japan surrender.

American officials resisted the temptation to raise tariff barriers as they had in the immediate post–World War I period. Realizing that the trade imbalances of the 1920s contributed to the second world conflict, the industrialized nations moved toward a system of liberalized trade under the General Agreement on Tariffs and Trade. Since 1947, the United States has maintained this course, even if forced to do so unilaterally. Not only did American officials believe that freer trade would prevent future international crises, they also realized that trade barriers would inhibit U.S. attempts to counter the rise of communism during the ensuing Cold War.

See also: General Agreement on Tariffs and Trade (GATT); Hawley-Smoot Tariff (Tariff of 1930); World War I.

Selected Bibliography:

Alfred E. Eckes, *Opening America's Market: U.S. Trade Policy Since 1776*, 1995; Alan S. Milward, *War, Economy and Society, 1939–1945*, 1977.

Cynthia Clark Northrup

WORLD WILDLIFE FUND

Created by a small but influential group of scientists, conservation activists, and political leaders, this organization currently operates as the world's largest privately funded group dedicated to protecting wildlife and wild lands.

In 1961, Sir Julian Huxley, a renowned biologist, and Sir Peter Scott, a vice president of the International Union for Conservation of Nature and Natural Resources (IUCN), spearheaded a campaign to marshal human and financial resources in support of the conservation movement on a worldwide scale. In September of that year, the World Wildlife Fund established the IUCN's headquarters in Morges, Switzerland, with H.R.H. Prince Bernhard of the Netherlands as its first president. Reflecting its British origins, the fund's first national affiliate opened in the United Kingdom, with H.R.H. Prince Phillip, the duke of Edinburgh as its head. The second national organization incorporated in the United States in December.

The goals of the new fund-raising organization included the maintenance of essential ecological processes and life support systems, preservation of genetic diversity, and promotion of sustainable uses of species and ecosystems. Through the 1960s and 1970s, WWF broadened its guiding philosophy from the protection of individual species to include consideration of the social and economic processes occurring outside nature reserves. Parallel to this evolution, WWF went beyond the established scientific experts, mostly North Americans and Europeans, on whom it originally relied, to cultivate professional and institutional resources in the countries where it funded field projects.

In 1985, WWF affiliated with the Conservation Foundation, a group that combined experience in policy advocacy with expertise in issues such as pollution. In 1990, the two organizations consolidated. The resulting corporation, the World Wildlife Fund, now has national affiliates and representatives in more than fifty countries and has sponsored over 13,100 projects in 157 countries. During negotiations involving the North American Free Trade Agreement (NAFTA), the World Wildlife Fund opposed passage of the treaty, arguing that the agreement lacked adequate provisions for the preservation of wildlife.

See also: Environmental issues.

Selected Bibliography:

Samuel P. Hays, *A History of Environmental Politics Since 1945*, 2000.

Sayuri Shimizu

WRIGHT, SILAS (May 24, 1795– August 27, 1847)

New York congressman and principal architect of the Tariff of 1828.

Born in Amherst, Massachusetts, Wright graduated from Middlebury College in 1815 and joined the New York State bar in 1819. After serving in the New York State Senate, he emerged as a prominent figure in the Democratic Party and the Albany Regency, a political machine that dominated New York politics in the 1830s.

Elected to the U.S. House of Representatives in 1827, Wright received an appointment to the Committee on Manufactures. Initially a supporter of protective tariffs, he helped to craft the controversial Tariff of Abominations in 1828. Wright's brand of protectionism emphasized agriculture as the most important sector of the American economy. He believed in the need to protect manufactured wool cloth, as well as agricultural items such as raw wool, a product produced in his home state of New York. Although he objected to some of its provisions, Wright also supported Henry Clay's Compromise Tariff of 1833 to help ease relations with the South.

By the end of his career, Wright changed his stance on protectionism and became a staunch supporter of revenue, rather than protective tariffs. He believed that only a revenue tariff reflected Congress's constitutional power to raise money. Following a brief tenure as governor of New York from 1845 to 1846, Wright passed away in Canton, New York.

See also: Clay, Henry; Democratic Party; Protectionism; Tariff of 1828 (Tariff of Abominations).

Selected Bibliography:

John Garraty, *Silas Wright*, 1949.

William C. Barnhart

Bibliography

BOOKS

Aaronson, Susan Ariel. *Trade and the American Dream: A Social History of Postwar Trade Policy.* Lexington: University Press of Kentucky, 1996.

Abbott, Lyman. *Henry Ward Beecher.* New York: Chelsea House, 1980.

Acheson, Sam Hanna. *Joe Bailey: The Last Democrat.* New York: Macmillan, 1932.

Adams, Samuel Hopkins. *Incredible Era: The Life and Times of Warren Gamaliel Harding.* New York: Octagon Books, 1979.

Adelman, Morris Albert. *The Genie Out of the Bottle: World Oil Since 1970.* Cambridge, Mass.: MIT Press, 1995.

Allen, Gay Wilson. *Waldo Emerson: A Biography.* New York: Viking Press, 1981.

———. *Walt Whitman Handbook.* Chicago: Packard and Company, 1946.

Ambrose, Stephen E. *Eisenhower.* New York: Simon & Schuster, 1894.

American Protective Tariff League. *The American Protective Tariff League, Organized May 1885, Principles, Constitution and By-Laws, List of Officers and Members with the President's Annual Address, List of Documents, Etc.* New York: APTL, 1889.

Amin, Samir. *Accumulation on a World Scale: A Critique of the Theory of Underdevelopment.* New York: Monthly Review Press, 1974.

Ammon, Harry. *James Monroe: A Biography.* Westport, Conn.: Meckler, 1991.

Anbinder, Tyler. *Nativism and Slavery: The Northern Know Nothings and the Politics of the 1850s.* Oxford: Oxford University Press, 1992.

Andrews, Charles McLean. *The Colonial Period of American History.* New Haven, Conn.: Yale University Press, 1938.

Araim, Amer Salih. *Intergovernmental Commodity Organizations and the New International Economic Order.* New York: Praeger, 1991.

Argersinger, Peter H. *Populism and Politics: William Alfred Peffer and the People's Party.* Lexington: University Press of Kentucky, 1974.

Armstrong, William M., ed. *The Gilded Age Letters of E.L. Godkin.* Albany: State University of New York Press, 1974.

Bibliography

Artola, Miguel. *La hacienda del Antiguo Régimen*. Madrid: Alianza/Banco de España, 1982.

Asbaugh, Carolyn. *Lucy Parsons, American Revolutionary*. Chicago: Illinois Labor History Society, 1976.

Ashley, Percy. *Modern Tariff History*. New York: H. Fertig, 1970.

Bacon, Donald C. "Nicholas Longworth: The Genial Czar," *Masters of the House: Congressional Leadership over Two Centuries*. Roger H. Davidson, Susan Webb Hammond, and Raymond W. Smock, eds. Boulder, Colo.: Westview Press, 1998.

Bailyn, Bernard. *The Ideological Origins of the American Revolution*. Cambridge: Belknap Press, 1967.

Bakewell, Peter, ed. *Mines of Silver and Gold in the Americas*. Brookfield, Vt.: Variorum, 1997.

Bakewell, Peter John. *Miners of the Red Mountain: Indian Labor in Potosí, 1545–1650*. Albuquerque: University of New Mexico Press, 1984.

Baldwin, Henry. *A General View of the Origin and Nature of the Constitution and Government of the United States*. Philadelphia: Lippincott, 1837.

Balinky, Alexander. *Albert Gallatin: Fiscal Theories and Policies*. New Brunswick, N.J.: Rutgers University Press, 1958.

Banning, Lance. *The Sacred Fire of Liberty: James Madison and the Founding of the Federal Republic*. Ithaca, N.Y.: Cornell University Press, 1995.

Barr, Alwyn. *Reconstruction to Reform: Texas Politics, 1876–1906*. Austin: University of Texas Press, 1971.

Barre, W.L. *The Life and Public Service of Millard Fillmore*. New York: B. Franklin, 1971.

Barrows, Chester. *William M. Evarts: Lawyer, Diplomat, Statesman*. Chapel Hill: University of North Carolina Press, 1941.

Bartlett, Irving H. *John C. Calhoun: A Biog-raphy*. New York: W.W. Norton, 1993.

Batra, Ravi. *The Great American Deception: What Politicians Won't Tell You About Our Economy and Your Future*. New York: John Wiley & Sons, Inc., 1996.

———. *The Myth of Free Trade: A Plan for America's Economic Revival*. New York: Charles Scribner's Sons, 1993.

Baxter, Maurice G. *Henry Clay and the American System*. Lexington: University Press of Kentucky, 1995.

Bazant, Jan. *A Concise History of Mexico from Hidalgo to Cardenas, 1805–1940*. New York: Cambridge University Press, 1977.

Beals, Carleton. *The Great Revolt and Its Leaders: The History of Popular American Uprisings in the 1890s*. New York: Abelard-Schuman, 1968.

Beckett, Grace. *The Reciprocal Trade Agreements Program*. New York: Russell and Russell, 1951.

Behr, Edward. *Prohibition: The 13 Years that Changed America*. London: BBC Books, 1997.

Belohlavek, John M. *George Mifflin Dallas*. University Park: Pennsylvania State University Press, 1977.

Bemis, Samuel F. *John Quincy Adams and the Union*. New York: Alfred A. Knopf, 1956.

Bennett, Wallace. *The Very Human History of 'NAM.'* New York: The Newcomen Society of England (American Branch), 1949.

Bergeron, Paul H. *The Presidency of James K. Polk*. Lawrence: University Press of Kansas, 1987.

Berghahn, Volker R. *Imperial Germany, 1871–1914: Economy, Society, Culture and Politics*. Providence: Berghahn Books, 1994.

———. *Modern Germany: Society, Economy, and Politics in the Twentieth Century*. Cambridge: Cambridge University Press, 1982.

Berlin, Ira. *Many Thousands Gone: The First*

Two Centuries of Slavery in North America. Cambridge, Mass.: The Belknap Press of Harvard University Press, 1998.

Bernard, Winfield E.A. *Fisher Ames, Federalist and Statesman, 1758–1808*. Chapel Hill: Published for the Institute of Early American History and Culture at Williamsburg, Virginia, by the University of North Carolina Press, 1965.

Bernstein, Irving. *Promises Kept: John F. Kennedy's New Frontier*. New York: Oxford University Press, 1991.

Bertrab, Hermann von. *Negotiating NAFTA: A Mexican Envoy's Account*. Westport, Conn.: Praeger, 1997.

Blaug, Mark. *Economic Theory in Retrospect*. New York: Cambridge University Press, 1985.

Boltho, Andrew. *The Japanese Economy*. Oxford: Oxford University Press, 2000.

Bowman, Sylvia E. *The Year 2000: A Critical Biography of Edward Bellamy*. New York: Bookman Associates, 1958.

Bradley, Joseph F. *The Role of Trade Associations and Professional Business Societies in America*. University Park: Pennsylvania State University Press, 1965.

Braeman, John. *Albert J. Beveridge: American Nationalist*. Chicago: University of Chicago Press, 1971.

Brands, H.W. *The First American: The Life and Times of Benjamin Franklin*. New York: Doubleday, 2000.

Brandt, E.N. *Growth Company: Dow Chemical's First Century*. East Lansing: Michigan State University Press, 1997.

Brewer, John. *The Sinews of Power: War, Money, and the English State, 1688–1783*. New York: Alfred A. Knopf, 1989.

Brown, Charles H. *William Cullen Bryant: A Biography*. New York: Charles Scribner's Sons, 1971.

Brown, Richard D. *Massachusetts: A Bicentennial History*. New York: W.W. Norton, 1977.

Brown, Thomas B., ed. *The Robber Barons: Saints or Sinners?* New York: Holt, Rinehart, and Winston, 1970.

Brownlee, W. Elliott. *Federal Taxation in America: A Short History*. New York: Cambridge University Press, 1996.

Bulmer-Thomas, Victor. *The Economic History of Latin America Since Independence*. Cambridge: Cambridge University Press, 1994.

Burner, David. *John F. Kennedy and a New Generation*. Boston: Little, Brown, 1988.

———. *The Politics of Provincialism: The Democratic Party in Transition, 1918–1932*. New York: Alfred A. Knopf, 1968.

Burton, Anthony. *The Rise and Fall of King Cotton*. London: A. Deutsch, 1984.

Bush, George. *All the Best, George Bush: My Life in Letters and Other Writings*. New York: Charles Scribner's Sons, 1999.

Butler, Michael A. *Cautious Visionary: Cordell Hull and Trade Reform, 1933–1937*. Kent, Ohio: Kent State University Press, 1998.

Cameron, Duncan and Mel Watkins, eds. *Canada Under Free Trade*. Toronto: James Lorimer and Company, 1993.

Campbell, Ballard C. *The Growth of American Government*. Bloomington: University of Indiana Press, 1995.

Campbell, Murray and Harrison Hatton. *Herbert E. Dow: Pioneer in Creative Chemistry*. New York: Appleton-Century-Crofts, 1951.

Canine, Craig. *Dream Reaper*. New York: Alfred A. Knopf, 1995.

Canto, Victor A. *The Determinants and Consequences of Trade Restrictions in the U.S. Economy*. New York: Praeger, 1986.

Caranza, Mario E. *South American Free Trade Area or Free Trade Area of the Americas? Open Regionalism and the*

Future of Regional Economic Integration in South America. Burlington, Vt.: Ashgate, 2000.

Carlisle, Rodney P. "Cambreleng, Churchill Caldom," *American National Biography*, John A. Garraty and Mark C. Carnes, eds. New York: Oxford University Press, 1999.

Carroll, Mollie Ray. *Labor and Politics: The Attitude of the American Federation of Labor Toward Legislation and Politics*. New York: Arno Press, 1969.

Carson, Rachel. *Silent Spring*. Boston: Houghton Mifflin, 1994.

Carstensen, Fred V. *American Enterprise in Foreign Markets: Studies of Singer and International Harvester in Imperial Russia*. Chapel Hill: University of North Carolina Press, 1984.

Chambers, William. *Political Parties in a New Nation, 1776–1809*. New York: Oxford University Press, 1963.

Charlice, Lonny E. and Mark Tilton. *Is Japan Really Changing Its Ways?* Washington, D.C.: Brookings Institution Press, 2000.

Chitwood, Oliver Perry. *John Tyler: Champion of the Old South*. New York: D. Appleton-Century Company, Inc., 1939.

Clark, Champ. *My Quarter Century of American Politics*. New York: Harper and Brothers Publishers, 1920.

Clements, Kendrick. *The Presidency of Woodrow Wilson*. Lawrence: University Press of Kansas, 1992.

Clymer, Kenton J. *John Hay: The Gentleman as Diplomat*. Ann Arbor: University of Michigan Press, 1975.

Cochran, Thomas. *200 Years of American Business*. New York: Basic Books, 1977.

Cockroft, James. *Latin America: History, Politics, and U.S. Policy*. Chicago: Nelson-Hall Publishers, 1996.

Cohen, Michael. *The History of the Sierra Club 1892–1970*. San Francisco: Sierra Club Books, 1988.

Cohen, Richard E. *Rostenkowski: The Pursuit of Power and the End of the Old Politics*. Chicago: Ivan R. Dee, 2000.

Cole, Donald B. *Martin Van Buren and the American Political System*. Princeton, N.J.: Princeton University Press, 1984.

———. *The Presidency of Andrew Jackson*. Lawrence: University Press of Kansas, 1993.

Colley, Linda. *Britons: Forging the Nation, 1707–1837*. New Haven, Conn: Yale University Press, 1992.

Congressional Quarterly's Guide to Congress. 4th ed. Washington, D.C.: Congressional Quarterly, Inc., 1991.

Conway, Moncure Daniel. *Emerson: At Home and Abroad*. New York: Haskell House Publishers Ltd., 1968.

Cook, Don. *The Long Fuse: How England Lost the American Colonies, 1760–1785*. New York: Atlantic Monthly Press, 1995.

Cooper, William J. *Jefferson Davis, American*. New York: Alfred A. Knopf, 2000.

Countryman, Edward. *The American Revolution*. New York: Hill and Wang, 1985.

Crapol, Edward P. *James G. Blaine: Architect of Empire*. Wilmington, Del.: Scholarly Resources, 2000.

Crotty, William, ed. *America's Choice: The Election of 1992*. Guilford, Conn.: Dushkin Publishing Group, 1993.

Curry, Dean C. *Global Transformation and Foreign Economic Policy: The Case of the United States–European Community Agricultural Relations, 1958–1979*. New York: Garland, 1990.

Curtis, Bruce. *William Graham Sumner*. Boston: Twayne Publishers, 1981.

Dallek, Robert. *Franklin D. Roosevelt and American Foreign Policy, 1932–1945*. Oxford: Oxford University Press, 1979.

Dalzell, Robert. *Enterprising Elite: The Boston Associates and the World They*

Made. Cambridge, Mass.: Harvard University Press, 1987.

Dangerfield, George. *The Awakening of American Nationalism, 1815–1828*. Prospect Heights, Ill.: Waveland Press, Inc., 1965.

Davies, K.G. *The North Atlantic World in the Seventeenth Century*. St. Paul: University of Minnesota, 1974.

Davis, David Howard. *Energy Politics*. New York: St. Martin's Press, 1982.

de Chambrun, Clara Longworth. *The Making of Nicholas Longworth*. New York: Ray Long and Robert R. Smith, Inc., 1933.

De Gregorio, William A. *The Complete Book of U.S. Presidents*. 5th ed. New York: Wings Books, 1994.

Destler, I.M. *American Trade Politics*. Washington, D.C.: Institute for International Economics, 1995.

———. "Trade Consensus, SALT Stalemate: Congress and Foreign Policy in the 1970s," *The New Congress*. Thomas E. Mann and Norman J. Ornstein, eds. Washington, D.C.: American Enterprise Institute for Public Policy Research, 1981.

Dickerson, Oliver M. *The Navigation Acts and the American Revolution*. Philadelphia: University of Pennsylvania Press, 1951.

Divine, Robert A. *Eisenhower and the Cold War*. New York: Oxford University Press, 1981.

Dobb, Maurice Herbert. *Studies in the Development of Capitalism*. London: Routledge & Kegan Paul, 1963.

———. *Wages*. London: J. Nisbet, 1956.

Dobson, John M. *Two Centuries of Tariffs: The Background and Emergence of the U.S. International Trade Commission*. Washington, D.C.: U.S. Government Printing Office, 1976.

Doenecke, Justus. *The Presidencies of James A. Garfield and Chester A. Arthur*. Lawrence: University Press of Kansas, 1981.

Donald, David Herbert. *Lincoln*. New York: Simon & Schuster, 1995.

Dorfman, Joseph. *The Economic Mind in American Civilization*. New York: Viking Press, 1946.

———, ed. *Two Essays by Henry Carter Adams*. New York: Augustus M. Kelley Publishers, 1969.

Dornbusch, Rudiger and Raúl Labán. *The Chilean Economy: Policy Lessons and Challenges*. Washington, D.C.: The Brookings Institute, 1994.

Drummond, Ian M. and Norman Hillmer. *Negotiating Freer Trade*. Waterloo, Ont.: Wilfrid Laurier University Press, 1989.

Duberman, Martin B. *Charles Francis Adams, 1807–1886*. Stanford, Calif.: Stanford University Press, 1968.

Eckes, Alfred E. *Opening America's Market: U.S. Foreign Trade Policy Since 1776*. Chapel Hill: University of North Carolina Press, 1995.

Eiselen, Malcolm Rogers. *The Rise of Pennsylvania Protectionism*. Philadelphia: Porcupine Press, 1974.

Eisenhower, John S.D. *So Far from God: The U.S. War with Mexico, 1846–1848*. Norman: University of Oklahoma Press, 2000.

Ekelund, Robert B. and Robert B. Tollison. *Politicized Economies: Monarchy, Monopoly, and Mercantilism*. College Station: Texas A&M University Press, 1997.

Elkins, Stanley and Eric McKitrick. *The Age of Federalism*. New York: Oxford University Press, 1993.

Ellis, Richard E. *The Union at Risk: Jacksonian Democracy, States' Rights, and the Nullification Crisis*. New York: Oxford University Press, 1987.

Evans, Tony, ed. *Human Rights Fifty Years On: A Reappraisal*. Manchester, N.Y.: Manchester University Press, 1998.

Exquemelin, Alexandre Olivier. *The Buccaneers and Marooners of America: Being an Account of the Famous Ad-*

ventures and Deering Deeds of Certain Notorious Freebooters of the Spanish Main. London: T. Fisher Unwin, 1891.

Fausold, Martin. *The Presidency of Herbert Hoover.* Lawrence: University Press of Kansas, 1985.

Faux, Jeff and Thea Lee. *The Effect of George Bush's NAFTA on American Workers: Ladder Up or Ladder Down?* Washington, D.C.: Economic Policy Institute, 1992.

Feis, Herbert. *Characters in Crisis.* New York: Little, Brown, 1966.

Ferling, John E. *The First of Men: A Life of George Washington.* Knoxville: University of Tennessee Press, 1988.

Ferrell, Robert. *American Diplomacy in the Great Depression.* New Haven, Conn.: Yale University Press, 1957.

———. *Harry S Truman: A Life.* Columbia: University of Missouri Press, 1994.

———. *The Presidency of Calvin Coolidge.* Lawrence: University Press of Kansas, 1998.

Fisher, Douglas A. *Steel Serves the Nation, 1901–1951, The Fifty Year Story of United States Steel.* New York: U.S. Steel Corp., 1951.

Fite, Gilbert C. *George N. Peek and the Fight for Farm Parity.* Norman: University of Oklahoma Press, 1954.

Fitzgibbons, Athol. *Adam Smith's System of Liberty, Wealth, and Virtue: The Moral and Political Foundation of the Wealth of Nations.* New York: Oxford University Press, 1995.

Flexner, James Thomas. *Washington: The Indispensable Man.* Boston: Little, Brown, 1972.

Flippen, J. Brooks. *Nixon and the Environment.* Albuquerque: University of New Mexico Press, 2000.

Foner, Eric. *Reconstruction: America's Unfinished Revolution, 1863–1877.* New York: Harper & Row, 1988.

Foner, Philip S. *History of the Labor Movement in the United States.* New York: International Publishers, 1975.

———. *Mark Twain: Social Critic.* New York: International Publishers, 1958.

Ford, Lacy K. *The Origins of Southern Radicalism.* New York: Oxford University Press, 1988.

Forsythe, Dall. *Taxation and Political Change in the Young Nation 1781–1833.* New York: Columbia University Press, 1977.

Frank, Andre Gunder. *Capitalism and Underdevelopment in Latin America: Historical Studies of Chile and Brazil.* New York: Monthly Review Press, 1967.

Franko, Patrice. *Toward a New Security Architecture in the Americas: The Strategic Implications of FTAA.* Washington, D.C.: CSIS Press, 2000.

Freehling, William W. *Prelude to Civil War: The Nullification Controversy in South Carolina, 1816–1836.* New York: Harper & Row, 1965.

———. *The Road to Disunion: Secessionists at Bay, 1776–1854.* New York: Oxford University Press, 1990.

Gara, Larry. *The Presidency of Franklin Pierce.* Lawrence: University Press of Kansas, 1991.

Garraty, John. *Henry Cabot Lodge: A Biography.* New York: Alfred A. Knopf, 1953.

———. *Silas Wright.* New York: Columbia University Press, 1949.

Gatell, Frank Otto. "Henry Baldwin," *The Justices of the United States Supreme Court 1789–1969: Their Lives and Major Opinions.* Leon Friedman and Fred L. Israel, eds. New York: Chelsea House, 1969.

———. "Philip B. Barbour." *The Justices of the United States Supreme Court 1789–1969: Their Lives and Major Opinions.* Leon Friedman and Fred L. Israel, eds. New York: Chelsea House, 1969.

George, Henry. *Protection or Free Trade: An*

Examination of the Tariff Question, with Regard to the Interests of Labor. New York: Robert Schalkenbach Foundation, 1991.

Gianaris, Nicholas V. *The European Community and the United States: Economic Relations.* New York: Praeger, 1991.

Gibson, Martha L. *Conflict Amid Consensus in American Trade Policy.* Washington, D.C.: Georgetown University Press, 2000.

Gilderhus, Mark T. *The Second Century: U.S.–Latin American Relations since 1889.* Wilmington, Del.: Scholarly Resources, 2000.

Gillespie, J. David. *Politics at the Periphery: Third Parties in Two-Party America.* Columbia: University of South Carolina Press, 1993.

Gipson, Lawrence Henry. *The Coming of the Revolution, 1763–1775.* New York: Harper & Row, 1962.

Godoy, Ricardo. *Mining and Agriculture in Highland Bolivia: Ecology, History, and Commerce Among the Jukumanis.* Tucson: University of Arizona Press, 1990.

Goldstein, Judith. *Ideas, Interests, and American Trade Policy.* Ithaca, N.Y.: Cornell University Press, 1993.

Goldstein, Kenneth. *Interest Groups, Lobbying, and Participation in America.* New York: Cambridge University Press, 1999.

Goodwyn, Lawrence. *Democratic Promise: The Populist Moment in America.* New York: Oxford University Press, 1976.

———. *The Populist Movement: A Short History of the Agrarian Revolt in America.* New York: Oxford University Press, 1978.

Gordon, Robert B. *American Iron, 1607–1900.* Baltimore: Johns Hopkins University Press, 1996.

Gore, Thomas Pryor. *A Permanent Tariff Commission: An Address delivered before the Merchants' Association of New York, on December 9, 1915, relative to the establishment of a Permanent Tariff Commission.* Washington, D.C.: U.S. Government Printing Office, 1916.

Gottlieb, Robert. *Forcing the Spring: The Transformation of the American Environmental Movement.* Washington, D.C.: Island Press, 1993.

Gould, Lewis L. *The Presidency of Theodore Roosevelt.* Lawrence: University Press of Kansas, 1991.

———. *The Presidency of William McKinley.* Lawrence: Regents Press of Kansas, 1980.

———. *Progressives and Prohibitionists: Texas Democrats in the Wilson Era.* Austin: University of Texas Press, 1973.

———. *Reform and Regulation: American Politics from Roosevelt to Wilson.* Prospect Heights, Ill.: Waveland Press, 1986.

Grant, George. *Buchanan: Caught in the Crossfire.* Nashville: Thomas Nelson, 1996.

Grant, James. *Bernard Baruch: The Adventures of a Wall Street Legend.* New York: Simon & Schuster, 1983.

Green, Edwin. *George McDuffie.* Columbia: State Co., 1936.

Green, Marguerite. *The National Civic Federation and the American Labor Movement, 1900–1925.* Washington, D.C.: Catholic University of America Press, 1956.

Greene, John Robert. *The Presidency of George Bush.* Lawrence: University of Kansas Press, 2000.

Gruchy, Allan. *Modern Economic Thought: The American Contribution.* New York: Augustus Kelley, 1947.

Grunder, Garel A. and William E. Livezy. *The Philippines and the United States.* Westport, Conn.: Greenwood Press, 1973.

Guelzo, Allen C. *Abraham Lincoln: Redeemer President.* Grand Rapids, Mich.: William B. Eerdmans Publishing Co., 1999.

Gunderson, Robert. *The Log-Cabin Campaign*. Westport, Conn.: Greenwood Press, 1977.

Gunter, Joseph and Konrad J. Kundig, eds. *Copper: Its Trade, Manufacture, Use and Environmental Status*. Lee, N.H.: ASM Publishers, 1998.

Gwinn, William Rea. *Uncle Joe Cannon, Archfoe of Insurgency; A History of the Rise and Fall of Cannonism*. New York: Bookman Associates, 1957.

Hamilton, Alexander. *The Papers of Alexander Hamilton*. New York: Columbia University Press, 1963.

Hamilton, Alexander, James Madison, and John Jay. *The Federalist Papers*. New York: Bantam Books, 1987.

Hamilton, Earl J. *American Treasure and the Price Revolution in Spain, 1501–1650*. Cambridge, Mass.: Harvard University Press, 1934.

Hammond, Susan Webb and Raymond W. Smock, eds. *Masters of the House: Congressional Leadership Over Two Centuries*. Boulder, Colo.: Westview Press, 1998.

Hargreaves, Mary. *The Presidency of John Quincy Adams*. Lawrence: University Press of Kansas, 1985.

Haring, Clarence Henry. *The Buccaneers in the West Indies in the XVII Century*. New York: E.P. Dutton and Company, 1910.

Harlow, Ralph V. *Gerrit Smith: Philanthropist and Reformer*. New York: H. Holt & Co., 1939.

Hart, Michael. *Fifty Years of Canadian Tradecraft: Canada at the GATT 1947–1997*. Ottawa: Centre for Trade Policy and Law, 1998.

Hawley, Ellis, ed. *The Great War and the Search for a Modern Order: A History of the American People and their Institutions, 1917–1933*. New York: St. Martin's, 1992.

———. *Herbert Hoover as Secretary of Commerce: Studies in New Era Thought and Practice*. Iowa City: University of Iowa Press, 1981.

Haynes, Fred E. *Social Politics in the United States*. New York: AMS Press, 1970.

———. *Third Party Movements Since the Civil War: With Special Reference to Iowa*. New York: Russell & Russell, 1966.

Hays, Samuel P. *A History of Environmental Politics Since 1945*. Pittsburgh: University of Pittsburgh Press, 2000.

Healy, David. *U.S. Expansionism: The Imperialist Urge in the 1890s*. Madison: University of Wisconsin Press, 1970.

Heckman, Bernard M. *The Political Economy of the World Trading System: From GATT to WTO*. New York: Oxford University Press, 1995.

Heilbroner, Robert. *An Inquiry into the Human Prospect*. New York: Norton, 1991.

Henderson, H. James. *Party Politics in the Continental Congress*. Lanham, Md.: University Press of America, 1987.

Henderson, John P. *The Life and Economics of David Ricardo*. Boston: Kluwer Academic Publishers, 1997.

Henderson, W.O. *Friedrich List: Economist and Visionary 1789–1846*. Totowa, N.J.: Frank Cass, 1983.

Hendrick, Booraemk V. *The Road to Respectability: James A. Garfield and His World*. Lewisburg, Pa.: Bucknell University Press, 1988.

Hesseltine, William B. *The Rise and Fall of Third Parties: From Anti-Masonry to Wallace*. Washington, D.C.: Public Affairs Press, 1948.

Hessen, Robert. *Steel Titan: The Life of Charles M. Schwab*. Pittsburgh: University of Pittsburgh Press, 1975.

Hicks, John D. *The Populist Revolt: A History of the Farmer's Alliance and the People's Party*. Minneapolis: University of Minnesota Press, 1931.

Hieronymi, Otto. *Economic Discrimination Against the United States in Western*

Europe, 1945–1958. Geneve: Librairie Droz, 1972.

Hill, Christopher G.L. *Steel Phoenix: The Fall and Rise of the U.S. Steel Industry*. New York: St. Martin's, 1997.

Hinton, Harold B. *Cordell Hull: A Biography*. Garden City, N.Y.: Doubleday, Doran & Company, Inc., 1942.

Hofstadter, Richard. *The American Political Tradition and the Men Who Made It*. New York: Alfred A. Knopf, 1948.

Hogan, Michael J. *Informal Entente*. Chicago: Imprint Publications, 1991.

Holbrook, Stewart H. *Iron Brew: A Century of American Ore and Steel*. New York: Macmillan, 1939.

Hollander, Samuel. *The Economics of Thomas Robert Malthus*. Toronto: University of Toronto Press, 1997.

Holsworth, Robert D. *Public Interest Liberalism and the Crisis of Affluence: Reflections on Nader, Environmentalism, and the Politics of a Sustainable Society*. Boston: G.K. Hall, 1980.

Holt, Michael. *The Rise and Fall of the Whig Party: Jacksonian Politics and the Onset of the Civil War*. Oxford: Oxford University Press, 1999.

Horsman, Reginald. *The New Republic: The United States of America, 1789–1815*. New York: Longman, 2000.

———. *The War of 1812*. New York: Alfred A. Knopf, 1969.

House, Albert V. "The Political Career of Samuel Jackson Randall." Ph.D. diss., University of Wisconsin, 1935.

Howe, Daniel Walker. *The Political Culture of the American Whigs*. Chicago: University of Chicago Press, 1979.

Howell, Thomas R., William A. Noellert, Jesse G. Krier, and Alan William Wolff, eds. *Steel and the State: Government Intervention and Steel's Structural Crisis*. Boulder, Colo.: Westview Press, 1988.

Hudec, Robert E. *The GATT Legal System and World Trade Diplomacy*. Salem, N.H.: Butterworth Legal Publishers, 1990.

Hull, Cordell. *The Memoirs of Hull*. New York: Macmillan, 1948.

Hurst, Steven. *The Foreign Policy of the Bush Administration: In Search of a New World Order*. New York: Cassell, 1999.

Huston, James L. *The Panic of 1857 and the Coming of the Civil War*. Baton Rouge, La.: State University Press, 1987.

Hutchinson, William. *Cyrus Hall McCormick*. New York: Da Capo, 1968.

Hutchison, Terrence. *Before Adam Smith: The Emergence of Political Economy (1162–1776)*. Oxford: Oxford University Press, 1988.

Hyde, Charles. *Copper for America: The United States Copper Industry from Colonial Times to the 1990s*. Tucson: University of Arizona Press, 1998.

Iacocca, Lee, with William Novak. *Iacocca: An Autobiography*. New York: Bantam Books, 1984.

Jasinowski, Jerry. *NAM: The Manufacturing Revolution and the New Economy*. Princeton, N.J.: Newcomen Society of the United States, 1995.

Jeffers, Paul H. *An Honest President: The Life and Presidencies of Grover Cleveland*. New York: William Morrow, 2000.

Jensen, Merrill. *The Articles of Confederation*. Madison: University of Wisconsin Press, 1940.

Jillson, Calvin and Rick K. Wilson. *Congressional Dynamics: Structure, Coordination, and Choice in the First American Congress, 1774–1789*. Stanford, Calif.: Stanford University Press, 1994.

Johnson, Arthur Menzies. *Winthrop W. Aldrich: Lawyer, Banker, Diplomat*. Boston: Harvard University Press, 1968.

Johnson, Claudius O. *Borah of Idaho*. New York: Longmans, Green and Company, 1936.

Johnson, Evans C. *Oscar W. Underwood: A Political Biography*. Baton Rouge:

Louisiana State University Press, 1980.

Johnson, Harry G. *Aspects of the Theory of Tariffs*. Cambridge, Mass.: Harvard University Press, 1972.

Jones, Manfred. *Isolationism in America, 1935–1941*. Ithaca, N.Y.: Cornell University Press, 1966.

Kammen, Michael. *Empire and Interest: The American Colonies and the Politics of Mercantilism*. Philadelphia: Lippincott, 1970.

Kane, Nancy. *Textiles in Transition: Technology, Wages, and Industry Relocation in the U.S. Textile Industry, 1880–1930*. Westport, Conn.: Greenwood Press, 1972.

Kaplan, Edward S. *The Bank of the United States and the American Economy*. Westport, Conn.: Greenwood Press, 1999.

Kaplan, Edward S. and Thomas W. Ryley. *Prelude to Trade Wars: American Tariff Policy, 1890–1922*. Westport, Conn.: Greenwood Press, 1994.

Kaplan, Justin. *Mr. Clemens and Mark Twain: A Biography*. New York: Simon & Schuster, 1966.

Kaufman, Burton I. *Trade and Aid*. Baltimore: Johns Hopkins University Press, 1982.

Keay, John. *The Honourable Company*. London: HarperCollins, 1993.

Kehl, James A. *Boss Rule in the Gilded Age: Matt Quay of Pennsylvania*. Pittsburgh: University of Pittsburgh Press, 1981.

Keith, Caroline H. *"For Hell and a Brown Mule": The Biography of Senator Millard E. Tydings*. Lanham, Md.: Madison Books, 1991.

Kenworthy, Leonard S. *The Tall Sycamore of the Wabash, Daniel Wolsey Voorhees*. Boston: B. Humphries, 1936.

Kerr, James E. *The Insular Cases: The Role of the Judiciary in American Expansionism*. Port Washington, N.Y.: Kennikat Press, 1982.

Kindleberger, Charles P. *The Dollar Shortage*. London: Chapman & Hall, 1950.

Kintner, Earl W. *An Antitrust Primer: A Guide to Antitrust and Trade Regulation Laws for Businessmen*. New York: Macmillan, 1973.

Kirk, Russell. *Randolph of Roanoke: A Study in Conservative Thought*. Chicago: University of Chicago Press, 1951.

Klehr, Harvey, John Earl Haynes, and Fridrikh Igorevich Firsov. *The Secret World of American Communism*. New Haven, Conn.: Yale University Press, 1995.

Klehr, Harvey and Ronald Radosh. *The Amerasia Spy Case: Prelude to McCarthyism*. Chapel Hill: University of North Carolina Press, 1996.

Klein, Herbert S. *The Atlantic Slave Trade*. New York: Cambridge University Press, 1999.

Klement, Frank L. *The Copperheads in the Middle West*. Chicago: University of Chicago Press, 1960.

Kline, Mary-Jo, ed. *Alexander Hamilton: A Biography in His Own Words*. New York: Newsweek Books, 1973.

Klotter, James C. *The Breckinridges of Kentucky, 1760–1981*. Lexington: University Press of Kentucky, 1986.

Kochersberger, Robert C., ed. *More than a Muckraker: Ida Tarbell's Lifetime in Journalism*. Knoxville: University of Tennessee, 1994.

Koenig, Louis W. *Bryan: A Political Biography of William Jennings Bryan*. New York: Putnam's, 1971.

Kottman, Richard N. *Reciprocity and the North Atlantic Triangle, 1932–1938*. Ithaca, N.Y.: Cornell University Press, 1968.

Kunhardt, Philip B. Jr., Philip B. Kunhardt III, and Peter W. Kunhardt. *The American President*. New York: Riverhead Books, 1999.

Kushner, Howard I. and Anne Hummel Sherrill. *John Milton Hay: The Union* of Poetry and Politics. Boston: Twayne Publishers, 1977.

Kuznets, Simon Smith. *Economic Change: Selected Essays in Business Cycles, National Income, and Economic Growth.* New York: W.W. Norton, 1953.

Labaree, Benjamin Woods. *The Boston Tea Party.* New York: Oxford University Press, 1968.

LaFeber, Walter. *The New Empire: An Interpretation of American Expansion 1860–1898.* Ithaca, N.Y.: Cornell University Press, 1963.

Lake, David A. *Power, Protection, and Free Trade: International Sources of U.S. Commercial Strategy, 1887–1939.* Ithaca, N.Y.: Cornell University Press, 1988.

Lambert, John R. Jr., *Arthur Pue Gorman.* Baton Rouge: Louisiana State University Press, 1953.

Landes, David S. *The Wealth and Poverty of Nations: Why Some Are So Rich and Some So Poor.* New York: W.W. Norton, 1998.

Larner, Robert J. and James W. Meehan Jr., eds. *Economics and Antitrust Policy.* New York: Quorum Books, 1989.

Lawson, Philip. *The East India Company: A History.* New York: Longman, 1993.

Leopold, Richard William. *Elihu Root and the Conservative Tradition.* Boston: Little, Brown, 1954.

Leuchtenberg, William. *The FDR Years: On Roosevelt and His Legacy.* New York: Columbia University Press, 1995.

———. *Franklin D. Roosevelt and the New Deal, 1932–1940.* New York: Harper & Row, 1963.

Levin, Doron P. *Behind the Wheel at Chrysler: The Iacocca Legacy.* New York: Harcourt Brace & Company, 1995.

Levinson, Jerome and Juan de Onís. *The Alliance That Lost Its Way: A Critical Report on the Alliance for Progress.* Chicago: Quadrangle Books, 1970.

Link, Arthur S. *Wilson: The New Freedom.* Princeton, N.J.: Princeton University Press, 1956.

Livingston, Donald W. *Philosophical Melancholy and Delirium: Hume's Pathology of Philosophy.* Chicago: University of Chicago Press, 1998.

Lloyd, Lewis E. *Tariffs: The Case for Protection.* New York: The Devin-Adair Company, 1955.

Love, Philip H. *Andrew W. Mellon: The Man and His Work.* Baltimore, Md.: F.H. Coggins and Company, 1929.

Lovett, William A., Alfred E. Eckes Jr., and Richard L. Brinkman, eds. *U.S. Trade Policy: History, Theory, and the WTO.* Armonk, N.Y.: M.E. Sharpe, 1999.

Lowery, Charles D. *James Barbour: A Jeffersonian Republican.* Alabama: University of Alabama Press, 1984.

MacArthur, John R. *The Selling of "Free Trade": NAFTA, Washington, and the Subversion of American Democracy.* New York: Hill and Wang, 2000.

Mack, Charles S. *Executive Handbook of Trade and Business Associations: How They Work and How to Make Them Work Effectively for You.* New York: Quorum Books, 1991.

Maclay, William. *The Diary of William Maclay and Other Notes on Senate Debates.* Kenneth R. Bowling and Helen E. Veits, eds. Baltimore, Md.: Johns Hopkins University Press, 1988.

Maddox, Robert James. *William E. Borah and American Foreign Policy.* Baton Rouge: Louisiana State University Press, 1969.

Magnusson, Lars. *Mercantilist Economics.* Boston: Kluwer Academic Publishers, 1993.

Major, John. *Prize Possession: The United States and the Panama Canal, 1903–1979.* New York: Cambridge University Press, 1993.

Malone, Dumas. *Jefferson and His Time.* 6 vols. Boston: Little, Brown, 1948–1981.

Maraniss, David. *The Prince of Tennessee:*

The Rise of Al Gore. New York: Simon & Schuster, 2000.

Martin, Harold H. *Georgia: A Bicentennial History*. New York: Norton, 1978.

Mason, Todd. *Perot: An Unauthorized Biography*. Homewood, Ill.: Dow Jones-Irwin, 1990.

Mayer, Frederick W. *Interpreting NAFTA: The Science and Art of Political Analysis*. New York: Columbia University Press, 1998.

McCoy, Charles A. *Polk and the Presidency*. Austin: University of Texas Press, 1960.

McCoy, Donald R. *Calvin Coolidge: The Quiet President*. New York: Macmillan, 1967.

McCoy, Drew. *The Elusive Republic: Political Economy in Jeffersonian America*. Chapel Hill: University of North Carolina Press, 1980.

———. *The Last of the Fathers: James Madison and the Republican Legacy*. Cambridge: Cambridge University Press, 1989.

McCullough, David. *John Adams*. New York: Simon & Schuster, 2001.

McCusker, John. *Rum and the American Revolution: The Rum Trade and the Balance of Payments of the Thirteen Continental Colonies*. New York: Garland, 1989.

McCusker, John J. and Russell R. Menard. *The Economy of British America, 1607–1789*. Chapel Hill: University of North Carolina for the Institute of Early American History and Culture, 1985.

McDevitt, Brother Matthew. *Joseph McKenna: Associate Justice of the United States*. Washington, D.C.: Catholic University Press, 1946.

McDonald, Forest. *Novus Orrdo Seclorum: The Intellectual Origins of the Constitution*. Lawrence: University Press of Kansas, 1985.

McElroy, Richard L. *James A. Garfield: His Life and Times*. Canton, Ohio: Daring Books, 1986.

McKinley, William. *The Tariff in the Days of Henry Clay and Since*. New York: Kraus Reprint, 1970.

McMath, Robert C. *American Populism: A Social History, 1877–1898*. New York: Hill and Wang, 1993.

McNamara, Peter. *Political Economy and Statesmanship: Smith, Hamilton, and the Foundation of the Commercial Republic*. DeKalb: Northern Illinois University Press, 1998.

McPherson, James. *Ordeal by Fire: The Civil War and Reconstruction*. New York: McGraw-Hill Higher Education, 2000.

Merrill, Milton R. *Reed Smoot: Apostle in Politics*. Logan: Utah State University Press, 1990.

Merrill, Walter M. *Against the Wind and Tide: A Biography of William Lloyd Garrison*. Cambridge, Mass.: Harvard University Press, 1963.

Meyer, Michael C. and William L. Sherman. *The Course of Mexican History*. New York: Oxford University Press, 1979.

Milward, Alan S. *War, Economy, and Society, 1939–1945*. Berkeley: University of California Press, 1977.

Minot, George and George P. Sanger, eds. *The Statutes at Large and Treaties of the United States of America*. Boston: Little, Brown, 1859.

Mintz, Sidney W. *Sweetness and Power: The Place of Sugar in Modern History*. New York: Viking Penguin, 1985.

Moley, Raymond. *After Seven Years*. New York: Harper, 1939.

Mommer, Bernard. *Foundations of Fiscal Regimes in Oil*. Oxford: Oxford Institute for Energy Studies, December 1998.

Montesquieu, Charles Louis. *The Spirit of the Laws*. New York: Cambridge University Press, 1989.

Mooney, Chase C. *William H. Crawford,*

1772–1834. Lexington: University Press of Kentucky, 1974.

Moran, Theodore H. *Multinational Corporations and the Politics of Dependence*. Princeton, N.J.: Princeton University Press, 1974.

Morgan, Arthur E. *Edward Bellamy*. New York: Columbia University Press, 1944.

Morgan, Edmund. *American Slavery, American Freedom: The Ordeal of Colonial Virginia*. New York: W.W. Norton, 1975.

Morgan, H. Wayne. *From Hayes to McKinley: National Party Politics, 1877–1896*. Syracuse, N.Y.: Syracuse University Press, 1969.

———. *William McKinley and His America*. Syracuse, N.Y.: Syracuse University Press, 1963.

Morgan, Robert J. *A Whig Embattled: The Presidency Under John Tyler*. Lincoln: University of Nebraska Press, 1974.

Morley, Morris H. *Imperial State and Revolution: The United States and Cuba, 1952–1987*. New York: Cambridge University Press, 1987.

Morrison, Rodney J. *Henry Charles Carey and American Economic Development*. Philadelphia: The American Philosophical Society, 1986.

Muzzey, David S. *James G. Blaine: A Political Idol of Other Days*. New York: Dodd, Mead & Company, 1934.

Nader, Ralph, ed. *The Case Against Free Trade: GATT, NAFTA, and the Globalization of Corporate Power*. San Francisco: Earth Island Press, 1993.

Namorato, Michael V. *Rexford G. Tugwell: A Biography*. Westport, Conn.: Praeger, 1988.

———, ed. *The Diary of Rexford G. Tugwell: The New Deal Years*. Westport, Conn.: Greenwood Press, 1992.

Nash, Gary B. *The Urban Crucible: Social Change, Political Consciousness, and the Origins of the American Revolution*. Cambridge, Mass.: Harvard University Press, 1979.

Neal, Steve. *Dark Horse: A Biography of Wendell Willkie*. Lawrence: University Press of Kansas, 1989.

Niven, John. *John C. Calhoun and the Price of Union: A Biography*. Baton Rouge: Louisiana State University Press, 1988.

———. *Martin Van Buren: The Romantic Age of American Politics*. New York: Oxford University Press, 1983.

Nivens, Allen. *Ford: The Times, The Man, The Company*. New York: Charles Scribner's Sons, 1954.

Nixon, Raymond B. *Henry W. Grady: Spokesman of the New South*. New York: Alfred A. Knopf, 1943.

Ogden, Rollo, ed. *Life and Letter of Edwin Lawrence Godkin*. Westport, Conn.: Greenwood Press, 1972.

Orme, William A. Jr. *Understanding NAFTA: Mexico, Free Trade and the New North America*. Austin: University of Texas Press, 1996.

Page, Thomas Walker. *Making the Tariff in the United States*. New York: McGraw-Hill Book Company, Inc., 1924.

Palmer, Beverly Wilson and Holly Beyers Ochoa, eds. *The Selected Papers of Thaddeus Stevens*. Pittsburgh: University of Pittsburgh Press, 1998.

Palmer, Bruce. *"Man Over Money": The Southern Populist Critique of American Capitalism*. Chapel Hill: University of North Carolina, 1980.

Palmer, R.R., ed. *J.B. Say: An Economist in Troubled Times*. Princeton, NJ: Princeton University Press, 1997.

Parker, Ralph Halstead. "The History of the Dallas Morning News." Masters thesis, University of Texas, 1930.

Parker, William B. *The Life and Public Services of Justin Smith Morrill*. New York: Da Capo Press, 1971.

Parsons, Stanley B. *The Populist Context: Rural Versus Urban Power on a Great*

Plains Frontier. Westport, Conn.: Greenwood Press, 1973.

Pastor, Robert A. *Congress and the Politics of U.S. Foreign Economic Policy 1929–1976*. Berkeley: University of California Press, 1980.

Patten, Simon Nelson. *Essays in Economic Theory*. Rexford G. Tugwell, ed. New York: Alfred A. Knopf, 1924.

Paxton, John and John Wroughton. *Smuggling*. London: Macmillan, 1971.

Pemberton, William E. *Harry S Truman: Fair Dealer and Cold Warrior*. Boston: Twayne Publishers, 1989.

Pendergrast, Mark. *Uncommon Grounds: The History of Coffee and How It Transformed Our World*. New York: Basic Books, 1999.

Pérez, Louis A. Jr. *Cuba: Between Reform and Revolution*. New York: Oxford University Press, 1995.

Peters, William. *A More Perfect Union: The Making of the U.S. Constitution*. New York: Crown Publishing, 1987.

Petersen, William. *Malthus*. Cambridge, Mass.: Harvard University Press, 1979.

Peterson, Merrill D. *The Great Triumvirate: Webster, Clay, and Calhoun*. New York: Oxford University Press, 1987.

Peterson, Norma Lois. *The Presidencies of William Henry Harrison and John Tyler*. Lawrence: University Press of Kansas, 1989.

Pickering, Mary. *Auguste Comte: An Intellectual Biography*. Cambridge: Cambridge University Press, 1993.

Pickett, William B. *Dwight D. Eisenhower and American Power*. Wheeling, Ill.: Harland-Davison, 1995.

———. *Homer E. Capehart: A Senator's Life, 1897–1979*. Indianapolis: Indiana Historical Society, 1990.

Pinchot, Amos R.E. *History of the Progressive Party 1912–1916*. New York: New York University Press, 1958.

Pincus, Jonathan. *Pressure Groups and Politics in Antebellum Tariffs*. New York: Columbia University Press, 1977.

Pike, Frederick B. *FDR's Good Neighbor Policy: Sixty Years of Generally Gentle Chaos*. Austin: University of Texas Press, 1995.

Pletcher, David M. *The Diplomacy of Annexation: Texas, Oregon, and the Mexican War*. Norwalk, Conn.: Easton Press, 1985.

Pollack, Norman, ed. *The Populist Mind*. New York: The Bobbs-Merrill Company, 1967.

Pomper, Gerald M. "The Presidential Election," *The Election of 2000*. New York: Chatham House Publishers, 2001.

Porter, Kirk H. and Donald Bruce Johnson. *National Party Platforms: 1840–1960*. Urbana: University of Illinois Press, 1961.

Prebisch, Raúl. *Towards a Dynamic Development Policy for Latin America*. New York: United Nations, 1963.

Preeg, Ernest H. *Traders and Diplomats: An Analysis of the Kennedy Round Negotiations under the General Agreement on Tariffs and Trade*. Washington, D.C.: Brookings Institute, 1970.

Preston, Diane. *The Boxer Rebellion: The Dramatic Story of China's War on Foreigners That Shook the World in the Summer of 1900*. New York: Walker, 2000.

Procter, Ben H. *Not Without Honor: The Life of John H. Reagan*. Austin: University of Texas Press, 1962.

Rabe, Stephen G. *The Most Dangerous Area in the World: John F. Kennedy Confronts Communist Revolution in Latin America*. Chapel Hill: University of North Carolina Press, 1998.

———. *The Road to OPEC: United States Relations with Venezuela: 1919–1976*. Austin: University of Texas Press, 1982.

Rader, Benjamin. *The Academic Mind and Reform: The Influence of Richard T. Ely in American Life*. Lexington: University of Kentucky Press, 1966.

Ratner, Sidney. *The Tariff in American History*. New York: D. Van Nostrand Company, 1972.

Rayback, Robert J. *Millard Fillmore: Biography of a President*. Norwalk, Conn.: Easton Press, 1959.

Rediker, Marcus Buford. *Between the Devil and the Deep Blue Sea: Merchant Seamen, Pirates, and the Anglo-American Maritime World, 1700–1750*. Cambridge: Cambridge University Press, 1987.

Reeves, Thomas C. *Gentleman Boss: The Life of Chester Alan Arthur*. New York: Alfred A. Knopf, 1975.

Reis, Jim. "John Griffin Carlisle," *The Kentucky Encyclopedia*, John E. Kleber, ed. Lexington: University of Kentucky Press, 1992.

Reitano, Joanne. *The Tariff Question in the Gilded Age: The Great Debate of 1888*. University Park: Pennsylvania State University Press, 1994.

Remini, Robert V. *Andrew Jackson and the Course of American Empire*. New York: Harper & Row, 1977.

———. *Daniel Webster: The Man and His Time*. New York: W.W. Norton, 1997.

———. *Henry Clay: Statesman for the Union*. New York: W.W. Norton, 1991.

———. *The Life of Andrew Jackson*. New York: Harper and Row, 1988.

Richardson, Heather Cox. *The Greatest Nation of the Earth: Republican Economic Policies During the Civil War*. Cambridge, Mass.: Harvard University Press, 1997.

Ridgeway, George L. *Merchants of Peace: The History of the International Chamber of Commerce*. Boston: Little, Brown, 1959.

Rippy, J. Fred, ed. *F.M. Simmons: Statesman of the New South*. Durham, N.C.: Duke University Press, 1936.

Risjord, Norman K. *Thomas Jefferson*. Madison, Wisc.: Madison House, 1994.

Robbins, Caroline. *The Eighteenth-Century Commonwealthman: Studies in the Transmission, Development, and Circumstance of English Liberal Thought*. Cambridge, Mass.: Harvard University Press, 1961.

Robinson, William A. *Thomas B. Reed, Parliamentarian*. New York: Dodd, Mead & Company, 1930.

Roche, George Charles III. *Frederic Bastiat: A Man Alone*. New Rochelle, N.Y.: Arlington House, 1971.

Rollo, Ogden, ed. *Life and Letters of Edwin Lawrence Godkin*. Westport, Conn.: Greenwood Press, 1972.

Rose, John Holland, ed. *The Cambridge History of the British Empire*. Cambridge: Cambridge University Press, 1929.

Rosenband, Leonard N. *Papermaking in Eighteenth-Century France: Management, Labor, and Revolution at the Montgolfier Mill, 1761–1805*. Baltimore, Md.: Johns Hopkins University Press, 2000.

Rosenstone, Steven J., Roy L. Behr, and Edward H. Lazarus. *Third Parties in America: Citizen Response to Major Party Failure*. Princeton, N.J.: Princeton University Press, 1984.

Ross, Ian Simpson. *The Life of Adam Smith*. Oxford: Clarendon Press, 1995.

Ross, Thomas Richard. *Jonathan Prentiss Dolliver: A Study in Political Integrity and Independence*. Iowa City: State Historical Society of Iowa, 1958.

Rossides, Eugene T. *U.S. Import and Trade Regulation*. Washington, D.C.: BNA Books, 1986.

Russell, Charles Edward. *Doing Us Good and Plenty*. Chicago: C. H. Kerr & Company, 1914.

Russell, Greg. *John Quincy Adams and the Public Virtues of Diplomacy*. Columbia: University of Missouri Press, 1995.

Russell, John A. *Joseph Warren Fordney: An*

American Legislator. Boston: The Stratford Co., 1928.

Russell, Philip L. *Mexico Under Salinas*. Austin: Mexico Resource Center, 1994.

Sanders, Elizabeth. *Roots of Reform: Farmers, Workers, and the American State, 1877–1917*. Chicago: University of Chicago Press, 1999.

Sarasohn, David. *The Party of Reform: Democrats in the Progressive Era*. Jackson: University Press of Mississippi, 1989.

Saunders, Debra J. *The World According to Gore*. San Francisco: Encounter Books, 2000.

Saunders, Robert M. *In Search of Woodrow Wilson: Beliefs and Behavior*. Westport, Conn.: Greenwood Press, 1998.

Schattschneider, E.E. *Politics, Pressures, and the Tariff: A Study of Free Private Enterprise in Pressure Politics, as Shown in the 1929–1930 Revision on the Tariff*. New York: Prentice-Hall, Inc., 1935.

Scheman, L. Ronald. *The Inter-American Dilemma: The Search for Inter-American Cooperation at the Centennial of the Inter-American System*. New York: Praeger, 1988.

Schild, Georg. *Bretton Woods and Dumbarton Oaks: American Economic and Political Postwar Planning in the Summer of 1944*. New York: St. Martin's, 1995.

Schlesinger, Arthur M. *The Colonial Merchants and the American Revolution, 1763–1776*. New York: Columbia University Press, 1918.

Schlesinger, Arthur M. Jr. *The Coming of the New Deal*. Boston: Houghton Mifflin, 1988.

Schoultz, Lars. *Beneath the United States: A History of U.S. Policy Toward Latin America*. Cambridge, Mass.: Harvard University Press, 1998.

Seager, Robert. *And Tyler Too: A Biography of John and Julie Gardiner Tyler*. Norwalk, Conn.: Easton Press, 1963.

Sellers, Charles G. Jr. *James K. Polk, Jacksonian, 1795–1843*. Princeton, N.J.: Princeton University Press, 1957.

———. *The Market Revolution: Jacksonian America, 1815–1846*. New York: Oxford University Press, 1991.

Shannon, David A. *The Socialist Party of America: A History*. New York: Macmillan, 1955.

Shaw, Ronald E. *Canals for a Nation: The Canal Era in the United States, 1790–1860*. Lexington: University Press of Kentucky, 1990.

Sheldon, Garrett Ward. *The Political Philosophy of Thomas Jefferson*. Baltimore, Md.: Johns Hopkins University Press, 1991.

Shenton, James P. *Robert John Walker*. New York: Columbia University Press, 1961.

Shook, Dale N. *William G. McAdoo and the Development of National Economic Policy: 1913–1918*. New York: Garland Publishing Inc., 1987.

Sigmund, Paul E. *Multinationals in Latin America: The Politics of Nationalization*. Madison: University of Wisconsin Press, 1980.

Sitterson, J. Carlyle. *Sugar Country: The Cane Sugar Industry in the South, 1753–1950*. Lexington: University of Kentucky Press, 1953.

Skidelsky, Robert. *John Maynard Keynes*. London: Macmillan, 2000.

Slaughter, Thomas P. *The Whiskey Rebellion: Frontier Epilogue to the American Revolution*. New York: Oxford University Press, 1986.

Smith, Elbert B. *The Presidencies of Zachary Taylor and Millard Fillmore*. Lawrence: University of Kansas Press, 1988.

Smith, Mark A. *American Business and Political Power: Public Opinion, Elections, and Democracy*. Chicago: University of Chicago Press, 2000.

Sobel, Robert. *Coolidge: An American*

Enigma. Washington, D.C.: Regnery Publishing, Inc., 1998.

———. *The Entrepreneurs: Explorations Within the American Business Tradition*. New York: Weybright and Talley, 1974.

Socolofsky, Homer and Allan Spetter. *The Presidency of Benjamin Harrison*. Lawrence: University Press of Kansas, 1987.

Sowell, Thomas. *Say's Law: An Historical Analysis*. Princeton, NJ: Princeton University Press, 1972.

Speigel, Henry William. *The Growth of Economic Thought*. Englewood Cliffs, N.J.: Prentice-Hall, Inc., 1971.

Spence, Jonathan D. *The Search for Modern China*. New York: W.W. Norton, 1999.

Spitzer, Robert J. *The Presidential Veto*. Albany: State University of New York Press, 1988.

Stagg, J.C.A. *Mr. Madison's War: Politics, Diplomacy, and Warfare in the Early Republic, 1783–1830*. Princeton, N.J.: Princeton University Press, 1983.

Stampp, Kenneth M. *America in 1857: A Nation on the Brink*. New York: Oxford University Press, 1990.

Stanwood, Edward. *American Tariff Controversies in the Nineteenth Century*. New York: Russell & Russell, 1967.

Steigerwalt, Albert. *The National Association of Manufacturers, 1895–1914*. Ann Arbor: Bureau of Business Research, University of Michigan, 1964.

Stephenson, Nathaniel W. *Nelson W. Aldrich: A Leader in American Politics*. Port Washington, N.Y.: Kennikat Press, 1971.

Steuart, Justin. *Wayne Wheeler, Dry Boss: An Uncensored Biography of Wayne B. Wheeler*. Westport, Conn.: Greenwood Press, 1928.

Stiller, Richard. *Queen of the Populists: The Story of Mary Elizabeth Lease*. New York: Crowell, 1970.

Stocking, George W. and Myron W. Watkins. *Cartels in Action: Case Studies in International Business Diplomacy*. New York: Twentieth Century Fund, 1946.

Stone, Nahum Isaac. *One Man's Crusade for an Honest Tariff: The Story of Herbert E. Miles, Father of the Tariff Commission*. Appleton, Wis.: The Lawrence College Press, 1952.

Stone, Richard Gabriel. *Hezekiah Niles as an Economist*. New York: AMS Press, 1982.

Stubbs, Richard and Geoffrey R.D. Underhill, eds. *Political Economy and the Changing Global Order*. New York: St. Martin's, 1994.

Summers, Festus P. *William L. Wilson and Tariff Reform: A Biography*. Westport, Conn.: Greenwood Press, 1974.

Swanberg, W.A. *Pulitzer*. New York: Charles Scribner's and Sons, 1967.

Sweeney, John J. and David Kusnet. *America Needs a Raise: Fighting for Economic Security and Social Justice*. New York: Replica Books, 2000.

Switzer, Jacqueline Vaughn. *Environmental Politics: Domestic and Global Dimensions*. New York: St. Martin's, 1994.

Tandeter, Enrique. *Coercion and Market: Silver Mining in Colonial Potosí, 1692–1826*. Albuquerque: University of New Mexico Press, 1993.

Tate, Merze. *The United States and the Hawaiian Kingdom: A Political History*. New Haven, Conn.: Yale University Press, 1965.

Taussig, Frank W. *Free Trade, The Tariff and Reciprocity*. New York: Macmillan, 1927.

———. *The Tariff History of the United States*. New York: Johnson Reprint Corp., 1967.

Terrill, Tom E. *The Tariff, Politics, and American Foreign Policy, 1874–1901*. Westport, Conn.: Greenwood Press, 1973.

Thelen, David P. *Robert M. LaFollette and the Insurgent Spirit*. Boston: Little, Brown, 1976.

Thomas, John L. *Alternative America: Henry George, Edward Bellamy, Henry Demarest Lloyd and the Adversary Tradition*. Cambridge, Mass.: Belknap Press, 1983.

———. *The Liberator, William Lloyd Garrison: A Biography*. Boston: Little, Brown, 1963.

Thompson, Winfred Lee. *The Introduction of American Law in the Philippines and Puerto Rico 1898–1905*. Fayetteville: University of Arkansas Press, 1989.

Tollison, Robert D. and Thomas D. Willett. "Foreign Investment and the Multinational Corporation," *Tariffs, Quotas, and Trade: The Politics of Protectionism*. San Francisco: Institute for Contemporary Studies, 1979.

Trefousse, Hans. *Thaddeus Stevens: Nineteenth Century Egalitarian*. Chapel Hill: University of North Carolina Press, 1997.

Tugwell, Rexford G., ed. *Essays in Economic Theory*. New York: A.A. Knopf, 1924.

Turque, Bill. *Inventing Al Gore: A Biography*. Boston: Houghton Mifflin, 2000.

Tuttleton, James W. *Thomas Wentworth Higginson*. Boston: Twayne Publishers, 1978.

Unger, Harlow Giles. *John Hancock: Merchant King and American Patriot*. New York: John Wiley & Sons, 2000.

Unger, Nancy C. *Fighting Bob LaFollette: The Righteous Reformer*. Chapel Hill: University of North Carolina Press, 2000.

United Nations. Economic Commission for Latin America. *The Economic Development of Latin America and Its Principal Problems*. Lake Success, N.Y.: United Nations Department of Economic Affairs, 1950.

———. *Most Favored-Nation Treatment*. New York: United Nations, 1999.

Van Deusen, Glyndon G. *Horace Greeley: Nineteenth-Century Crusader*. Philadelphia: University of Pennsylvania Press, 1953.

———. *The Jacksonian Era 1828–1848*. Prospect Heights, Ill.: Waveland Press, Inc., 1992.

Van Deusen, John G. *The Economic Bases of Disunion in South Carolina*. New York: Columbia University Press, 1921.

Van Doren, Carl. *Benjamin Franklin*. New York: Penguin Books, 1991.

Villard, Oswald Garrison. *Free Trade—Free World*. New York: Robert Schalkenbach Foundation, 1947.

Vipperman, Carl J. *William Lowndes and the Transition of Southern Politics, 1782–1822*. Chapel Hill: University of North Carolina Press, 1989.

Vohra, Ranbir. *China's Path to Modernization*. Upper Saddle River, N.J.: Prentice-Hall, 2000.

Walker, Robert J. *Report from the Secretary of the Treasury, on the State of the Finances. December 3, 1845*. Washington, D.C.: U.S. Government Printing Office, 1846.

Wall, John Frazier. *Andrew Carnegie*. New York: Oxford University Press, 1970.

Walters, Raymond Jr. *Alexander James Dallas: Lawyer, Politician, Financier 1759–1817*. New York: Da Capo Press, 1969.

Waltman, Jerold L. *Political Origins of the U.S. Income Tax*. Jackson: University Press of Mississippi, 1958.

Wapner, Paul. *Environmental Activism and World Civic Politics*. Albany: State University of New York Press, 1996.

Warner, Hoyt Landon. *Progressivism in Ohio, 1897–1917*. Columbus: Ohio State University Press, 1964.

Watson, Harry L. *Liberty and Power: The Politics of Jacksonian America*. New York: Noonday Press, 1990.

Watson, James Eli. *As I Knew Them: Memoirs of James E. Watson, Former United States Senator from Indiana*. Indianapolis: Bobbs-Merrill Company, 1936.

Watts, James F. Jr. "Joseph McKenna," *The Justices of the United States Supreme Court 1789–1969: Their Lives and Major Opinions*. Leon Friedman and Fred L. Israel, eds. New York: Chelsea House, 1969.

Welch, Richard E. Jr. *The Presidencies of Grover Cleveland*. Lawrence: University Press of Kansas, 1988.

White, Leonard D. *The Jacksonians: A Study in Administrative History 1829–1861*. New York: The Free Press, 1954.

Whitman, Walt. *Complete Poetry and Collected Prose*. New York: Viking Press, 1982.

Widenor, William. *Henry Cabot Lodge and the Search for an American Foreign Policy*. Berkeley: University of California Press, 1980.

Wiles, P.J.D. *Communist International Economies*. Oxford: Blackwell, 1968.

Williams, Neville. *Contraband Cargoes: Seven Centuries of Smuggling*. New York: Longmans, Green and Co., 1959.

Williamson, Harold Francis. *Edward Atkinson: The Biography of an American Liberal, 1827–1905*. New York: Arno Press, 1972.

Wilson, Charles. *England's Apprenticeship, 1603–1763*. London: Longmans, 1965.

Wilson, Clyde N. and W. Edwin Hemphill, eds. *The Papers of John C. Calhoun X, 1825–1829*. Columbia: University of South Carolina Press, 1977.

Wilson, Joan Hoff. *American Business and Foreign Policy, 1922–1933*. Lexington: University Press of Kentucky, 1971.

———. *Herbert Hoover: Forgotten Progressive*. Boston: Little, Brown, 1975.

Wilz, John Edward. "Good Neighbor Policy," *Franklin D. Roosevelt: His Life and Times*. Otis L. Graham Jr. and Meghan Robinson Wander, eds. Boston: G.K. Hall & Co., 1985.

Winham, Gilbert R. *International Trade and the Tokyo Round Negotiation*. Princeton, N.J.: Princeton University Press, 1986.

Wise, Carol, ed. *The Post-NAFTA Political Economy: Mexico and the Western Hemisphere*. University Park: Pennsylvania State University Press, 1998.

Wishart, David J. *The Fur Trade of the American West, 1807–1840*. Lincoln: University of Nebraska Press, 1979.

Wolman, Paul. *Most Favored Nation: The Republican Revisionists and U.S. Tariff Policy, 1897–1912*. Chapel Hill: University of North Carolina Press, 1992.

Womack, John Jr. *Zapata and the Mexican Revolution*. London: Thames and Hudson, 1969.

Wood, Bryce. *The Dismantling of the Good Neighbor Policy*. Austin: University of Texas Press, 1985.

Wood, Gordon S. *The Creation of the American Republic, 1776–1787*. New York: W.W. Norton, 1969.

World Trade Organization. *From GATT to the WTO: The Multilateral Trading System in the New Millennium*. Geneva: World Trade Organization, 2000.

Wright, Esmond. *Fabric of Freedom*. New York: Hill & Wang, 1961.

Wright, J. Leitch Jr. *The Only Land They Knew: The Tragic Story of the American Indians in the Old South*. New York: Free Press; London: Collier Macmillan, 1981.

Yates, W. Ross. *Joseph Wharton: Quaker Industrial Pioneer*. Bethlehem: Lehigh University Press, 1987.

Young, Robert. "Darwinism Is Social," *The Darwinian Heritage*. David Kohn, ed. Princeton, N.J.: Princeton University Press, 1990.

Zeiler, Thomas. *American Trade and Power in the 1960s*. New York: Columbia University Press, 1992.

Bibliography

Zeiler, Thomas W. *Free Trade, Free World: The Advent of GATT.* Chapel Hill: University of North Carolina Press, 1999.

Zieger, Robert H. *American Workers, American Unions, 1920–1985.* Baltimore, Md.: Johns Hopkins Press, 1994.

———. *The CIO, 1935–1955.* Chapel Hill: University of North Carolina Press, 1995.

ARTICLES

Argersinger, Peter H. "No Rights on this Floor: Third Parties and the Institutionalization of Congress." *Journal of Interdisciplinary History* 22 (spring 1992): 655–690.

Blumberg, Dorothy Rose. "Mary Elizabeth Lease, Populist Orator: A Profile." *Kansas History* 1 (spring 1978): 2–15.

Easley, Ralph. "The Work of the National Civic Federation." *Harper's Weekly Magazine* 16 (November 1904).

Gonce, R.A. "The Social Gospel, Ely and Commons' Initial Stage of Thought." *Journal of Economic Issues,* 30 (September 1996): 641–665.

Hard, William. "Nicholas Longworth." *American Review of Reviews* 71 (April 1925).

Leiter, Robert D. "Organized Labor and the Tariff." *Southern Economic Journal* 28 (1) (1961): 55–65.

Leschohier, Don. "Richard T. Ely in Retrospect." *Land Economics* 30 (November 1954): 376–377.

Nettels, Curtis P. "British Mercantilism and the Economic Development of the Thirteen Colonies." *Journal of Economic History* 12 (Spring 1952): 105–114.

Preyer, Norris W. "Southern Support of the Tariff of 1816—A Reappraisal." *Journal of Southern History* 25 (1959): 306–322.

Schrader, George D. "Constitutional History of the Income Tax." *Georgia State Bar Journal* 7 (August 1970).

Shoch, James. "Contesting Globalization: Organized Labor, NAFTA, and the 1997 and 1998 Fast-Track Fights." *Politics and Society* 28 (March 2000): 119–151.

Synder, Richard. "Commercial Policy as Reflected in Treaties from 1931 to 1939." *American Economic Review* 30 (1940).

Taylor, Flavia M. "The Political and Civic Career of Henry Baldwin, 1799–1830." *Western Pennsylvania Historical Magazine* 37 (1941).

Thompson, John A. "An Imperialist and the First World War: The Case of Albert J. Beveridge." *Journal of American Studies* (1971).

Tygiol, Jules. "Where Unionism Holds Sway: A Reappraisal of San Francisco's Union Labor Party." *California History* 62(3) (1983): 196–215.

UNPUBLISHED MATERIAL

Brannen, Ralph Neal. *John McDuffie: State Legislator, Congressman, Federal Judge, 1883–1950.* Ph.D. diss., Auburn University, 1975.

Cynn, P.P. "Philip Pendleton Barbour." *John P. Branch Historical Papers of Randolph-Macon College* 67 (1913).

Flaherty, Jane. *The Revenue Imperative.* M.A. thesis, Texas A&M University, 2000.

Hare, John S. *Allen G. Thurman: A Political Study,* Ph.D. diss., Ohio State University, 1933.

House, Albert V. *The Political Career of Samuel Jackson Randall.* Ph.D. diss., University of Wisconsin, 1935.

Parker, Ralph Halstead. *The History of the Dallas Morning News.* M.A. thesis, University of Texas, Austin, 1930.

St. Clair, Preston. *The Political Career of Charles Frederick Crisp.* Ph.D. diss., University of Georgia, 1962.

Tinkler, Robert. *"Ashes of Greatness": Politics and Reputation in the Antebellum World of James Hamilton.* Ph.D. diss.,

University of North Carolina at Chapel Hill, 1999.

Yung-Chao Chu, Power. *A History of the Hull Trade Program, 1934–1939*. Ph.D. diss., Columbia University, 1957.

NEWSPAPERS AND MAGAZINES

Amerasia, 1945–1947.

Business Week (June 18, 1930; June 25, 1930).

The Nation, 1865–present.

Time (May 12, 1930).

GOVERNMENT DOCUMENTS

Commission of Foreign Economic Policy. *Report to Congress by the Commission of Foreign Economic Policy*. Washington, D.C.: U.S. Government Printing Office, 1954.

Congressional Quarterly's Guide to Congress, 4th ed. Washington, D.C.: Congressional Quarterly, 1991.

National Archives and Records Administration. *Guide to the National Archives of the United States*. Washington, D.C.: National Archives and Records Administration, 1987.

———. *Guide to the Records of the United States House of Representatives at the National Archives 1789–1989. Bicentennial Edition*. Washington, D.C.: U.S. House of Representatives, 1989.

U.S. Army Center for Military History. *Thomas Fitzsimons*. Washington, D.C.: U.S. Army Center for Military History, 1986.

U.S. Congressional Quarterly. *National Party Conventions*. Washington, D.C.: Congressional Quarterly, Inc., 1997.

U.S. Department of State. *Foreign Relations of the United States 1964–1968*. Washington, D.C.: U.S. Government Printing Office, 1998.

U.S. Senate. *Register of Debates*. 20th Congress, 1st session, 1828.

WEBSITES

American Iron and Steel Institute. http://www.steel.org

Biographical Dictionary of the United States Congress. http://www.Bioguide.congress.gov

Economic Commission for Latin America. http://www.ecla.org/

Stokes, Bruce. "The Protectionist Myth." *Foreign Policy* (Winter 1999). Online. Accessed 1/13/01. http://www.findarticles.com/cf_l/ml181/1999_Winter/58517716/print.jhtml

United Auto Workers Union. "Reforming America's Trade Policy: Serving Workers, Saving Jobs." Online. Accessed 1/29/01. http://www.uaw.workernews/1997CAP/CAP_booklet/05.html

United States International Trade Commission. http://www.usitc.gov/

Index

Page references in **bold** type correspond with main entries in the encyclopedia.

Index

Index

Index

Index

McCulloch v. Maryland, 424
McDuffie, George, **244–245**
McDuffie, John, **245**
McDuffie-Tydings Act, **245–246**, 399, 400
McKenna, Joseph E., **246–247**
McKinley, William, xxx, 49, 114, 182, 184, 214, 218, **247–248**, 249, 328, 352
McKinley Tariff (Tariff of 1890), 8, 12, 42, 47, 48, 60, 65, 75, 93, 101, 103, 107, 108, 114, 181, 215, 222, 224, 227, 232, 247, **248–250**, 293, 302, 312, 317, 327, 352, 377, 414, 434, 435
McLane, Louis, 365
McMillin, Benton, **250**
McNary-Haugen Bill, 34
McNary-Haugenism, 101, 398
Meade, Catherine, 143
Meade, George, 143
Meany, George, 62, 221
Media. *See* Newspapers and Media
Medicaid, 338
Medicare, 338
Meiji Restoration, 209
Mellon, Andrew, 100, **251**
Mellon Institute of Industrial Research, 251
Mellon National Bank, 251
Menendez, Bob, 427
Mercantilism, xxvi, 20, 30, 31, 43, 62, 97, 119, **251–253**, 343, 392, 424
Merchants Association of New York (MANY), **253–254**, 273, 274
Metcalf, Edwin D., **254–255**
Mexican-American War, 6, 112, 196, 299, 382, 417, 425
Mexican Revolution, 256
Mexico, xxxii, 16, 55, 64, 96, 135, 166, **255–257**
Milan Decree, 239
Miles, Herbert Edwin, 254, **257–258**, 273, 275, 405, 434
Mill, James, 324
Mill, John Stuart, xxvii, 65, 121, **258–259**
Millikin, Eugene, 86
Mills, Roger Q., **259–260**
Mills, Wilbur, 191
Mills bill (Legislation), 8, 15, 60, 191, 259, **260**, 314, 319, 349, 437
Ming Dynasty, 340
Missouri Inquirer, 39
Missouri Question, 316
Mobilization on Development, Trade, Labor,

and the Environment (MODTLE), 122, **260–261**
Molasses, 148, **261**, 352
Molasses Act of 1733, 261, 330, 352
Mongrel Tariff. *See* Tariff of 1883
Monopoly, 137, 316
Monroe, James, 5, 6, 56, 104, 213, 235, **262–263**
Monroe Doctrine, 6, 263
Montesquieu, Charles-Louis de Secondat, Baron de la Brede et de, **263**
Moody, Paul, 234
Morgan, John Pierpont, 65, 75, 325, 333
Morrill, Justin S., 93, 147, 181, **264–265**, 377
Morrill Tariff, xxx, xxxi, 70, 91, 229, 264, **265–266**, 290, 351, 397, 413
Morris, Robert, 26, 175, 237, 388
Morrison, William R., 314
Most Favored Nation (MFN), 53, 76, 148, 163, 170, **266–267**, 296, 317, 326, 392, 395, 435
Motion Picture Division, 52
Mugwumps, *See* Independent Republican Party
Muir, John, 339
Mulroney, Brian, 59, **267–268**, 280
Mun, Thomas, 30, 43, 252
Murray, Philip, 221
Mysterious Stranger, 399

Nader, Ralph, **269–270**
Napoleonic Wars, xxvii, xxviii, 22, 212
Nation, 164, 269, **270–271**
National Association of Agricultural Implement and Vehicle Manufacturers (NAAIVM), 254, 257, 274
National Association of Manufacturers, 19, 117, 214, 257, **271**, 392, 423
National Civic Federation, **271–272**
National Committee on Wood Utilization, 52
National Conference for the Expansion of Foreign Trade, **272–273**
National Council of Commerce, **273**, 405
National Farmers' Alliance and Industrial Union, 351
National Foreign Trade Council, **273–274**
National Grange, 244
National Guard, 247
National Industrial Recovery Act, 86
Nationalist, 38
National Livestock Association, 18, 274

474

Index

Index

About the Editors and Contributors

CYNTHIA CLARK NORTHRUP teaches at the University of Texas at Arlington. Her field of specialization is modern U.S. history, with an emphasis on political and economic issues.

ELAINE C. PRANGE TURNEY teaches at the University of Dallas. Her field of specialization is U.S. environmental history.

MICHAEL J. ANDERSON is an associate professor and chair in the Department of History and Political Science, Clarke College.

ALBERT ATKINS is an adjunct aeronautics instructor, Embry-Riddle Aeronautical University, and adjunct business instructor, University of Phoenix.

MARRIYA BARE is a student at Gonzaga University School of Law, Spokane, Washington.

WILLIAM C. BARNHART is an assistant professor of history in the Department of History and Political Science, Caldwell College.

JOHN HERSCHEL BARNHILL, Ph.D., is an independent historian at Yukon, Oklahoma.

JOHN P. BARRINGTON is an assistant professor in the History Department, Furman University.

DANIEL K. BLEWEIT is a reference librarian at the College of DuPage, Glen Ellyn, Illinois.

ED BRADLEY is a research associate at Harpweek, Norfolk, Virginia.

DAVID S. BROWN is an assistant professor in the History Department, Elizabethtown College.

JOHN D. BUENKER is professor of history and ethnic studies in the History Department, University of Wisconsin-Parkside.

ADRIENNE CAUGHFIELD is a Ph.D. student in history at Texas Christian University.

JOHN D. COATS is an assistant professor of history, Quincy University.

PETER COLE is a professor of history, Western Illinois University.

DALLAS COTHRUM is an assistant professor of history, the University of Texas at Tyler.

ROBERT C. COTTRELL, is a professor of history and American studies, Department of History, California State University, Chico.

STEPHEN G. CRAFT is an assistant professor in the Department of Humanities/Social Sciences, Embry-Riddle Aeronautical University.

JOSEPH A. DEVINE is a professor in the History Department, Stephen F. Austin State University.

SCOTT R. DiMARCO is director of library services at Herkimer County Community College in Herkimer, New York.

CARRIE DOWDY is the community history resource manager at the Kentucky Historical Society.

LISA A. ENNIS is a librarian in the Russell Library, Georgia College & State University.

JANE FLAHERTY is a Ph.D. student in American economic history at Texas A&M University.

JOHN K. FRANKLIN is a Ph.D. student in history at Texas Christian University.

CAROLYN E. GINNO is a student at California State University, Chico.

BRUCE A. GLASRUD is dean of the School of Arts and Sciences and professor of history at Sul Ross State University, Alpine, Texas.

DANIEL C. HELLINGER is professor of political science at Webster University in St. Louis, Missouri.

CHUCK HOWLETT is an adjunct professor of history at Adelphi University and an AP history teacher for the Amityville, New York, Public Schools.

GLYNN INGRAM is an associate professor of history, Louisiana Tech University.

VIRGINIA JELATIS is an assistant professor in the History Department, Western Illinois University.

ROBERT LEESON is an associate professor in the School of Economics, Murdoch University.

DAVID E. LONG is an associate professor in the Department of History, East Carolina University, Greenville, North Carolina.

RUSSELL M. MAGNAGHI is a professor in the History Department, Northern Michigan University.

THEO EDWIN MALOY is assistant professor of public administration in the Department of History and Political Science, West Texas A&M University.

JOHN MARINO is a historian with HarpWeek, Norfolk, Virginia.

JEFFREY J. MATTHEWS is an assistant professor of cross-disciplinary studies, School of Business and Public Administration, University of Puget Sound.

MATT McCOOK is a Ph.D. student in the Department of History, Florida State University.

JAMIE MILLER is deputy director of the Bard College Program on Globalization and International Affairs, Annandale-on-Hudson, New York.

MICHAEL V. NAMORATO is a professor in the Department of History, University of Mississippi.

CARYN E. NEUMANN is a Ph.D. student in history at Ohio State University.

SHANNON DANIEL O'BRYAN is an M.A. student at the University of Central Oklahoma.

CHRISTOPHER OHAN is a Fulbright lecturer of history at the Moscow State Institute of International Relations.

LISA L. OSSIAN is an instructor in the English Department, Southwestern Community College, Creston, Iowa.

CHRISTOPHER M. PAINE is an assistant professor in the Department of History, Middle Tennessee State University.

JONATHAN V. PARRENT is the registrar at Kentucky Wesleyan College, Owensboro, Kentucky.

JAMES DAVID PERRY is a project analyst at the Strategic Assessment Center, Science Applications International Corporation, Reston, Virginia.

JOHN GRADY POWELL is an undergraduate student in economics at Furman University.

JOSH PRATT is an undergraduate student seeking dual degrees in economics and political science at the University of Oklahoma.

PETER RAINOW is a Ph.D. student from San Mateo, California.

JOHN DAVID RAUSCH JR. is an assistant professor of political science in the Department of History and Political Science, West Texas A&M University.

TY M. REESE is an assistant professor in the History Department, University of North Dakota.

MARGARET SANKEY is a Ph.D. student in the History Department at Auburn University.

SAYURI SHIMIZU is an associate professor in the Department of History, Michigan State University.

HENRY B. SIRGO is professor of political science, McNeese State University.

STEVEN E. SIRY is a professor in the Department of History, Baldwin-Wallace College.

About the Editors and Contributors

WOODRUFF D. SMITH is a professor in the Department of History, University of Massachusetts, Boston.

MARY STOCKWELL is an associate professor of history and chair of the Department of History, Political Science, and Geography at Lourdes College, Sylvania, Ohio.

ROBERT P. SUTTON is a professor in the History Department, Western Illinois University.

BRUCE TAP is an independent scholar who holds a Ph. D. from the University of Illinois at Urbana-Champaign.

H. MICHAEL TARVER is an associate professor of history, McNeese State University.

CAROL TERRY is a Ph.D. student in history at Texas Christian University.

GEORGE THADATHIL is an associate professor in the History and Political Science Department, Paul Quinn College.

ROBERT TINKLER is an assistant professor in the History Department, California State University, Chico.

KATHLEEN A. TOBIN is an assistant professor in the Department of History and Political Science, Purdue University, Calumet.

DAVID E. WALKER is a professor of communication studies in the Department of Speech and Theatre, Middle Tennessee State University.

ARTEMUS WARD is an assistant professor of political science, California State University, Chico.

TONY WARD is an associate professor in the Economics Department, Brock University.

EDMUND F. WEHRLE is an assistant professor in the Department of History, Eastern Illinois University.

DAVID J. WEILAND III is a professor of Latin American History, Cambridge University.

THOMAS E. WOODS JR. is an instructor of history in the Department of Social Sciences at Suffolk Community College, Brentwood, New York.

RALPH LEE WOODWARD JR. is a professor emeritus in the Department of History, Tulane University.

BEN WYNNE is an instructor in the History Department, University of Mississippi.

WARREN YOUNG is an associate professor in the Department of Economics at Bar Ilan University, Ramat Gan, Israel.

GUOQIANG ZHENG is an assistant professor in the Department of History, Angelo State University.